Lecture Notes in Computer Science 16682

The series Lecture Notes in Computer Science (LNCS), including its subseries Lecture Notes in Artificial Intelligence (LNAI) and Lecture Notes in Bioinformatics (LNBI), has established itself as a medium for the publication of new developments in computer science and information technology research, teaching, and education.

LNCS enjoys close cooperation with the computer science R & D community, the series counts many renowned academics among its volume editors and paper authors, and collaborates with prestigious societies. Its mission is to serve this international community by providing an invaluable service, mainly focused on the publication of conference and workshop proceedings and postproceedings. LNCS commenced publication in 1973.

Eva Darulova · Anthony W. Lin ·
Philipp Rümmer
Editors

Computer Aided Verification

38th International Conference, CAV 2026
Lisbon, Portugal, July 26–29, 2026
Proceedings, Part I

Springer

Editors
Eva Darulova
Uppsala University
Uppsala, Sweden

Anthony W. Lin
University of Kaiserslautern-Landau
Kaiserslautern, Germany

Philipp Rümmer
Uppsala University
Uppsala, Sweden

University of Regensburg
Regensburg, Germany

ISSN 0302-9743 ISSN 1611-3349 (electronic)
Lecture Notes in Computer Science
ISBN 978-3-032-32518-1 ISBN 978-3-032-32519-8 (eBook)
https://doi.org/10.1007/978-3-032-32519-8

This Springer imprint is published by the registered company Springer Nature Switzerland AG
The registered company address is: Gewerbestrasse 11, 6330 Cham, Switzerland

Preface

This volume contains papers presented at the 38th International Conference on Computer Aided Verification (CAV), held in Lisbon, Portugal, on July 26–29, 2026. CAV is an annual conference dedicated to the advancement of the theory and practice of computer-aided formal analysis methods for hardware and software systems. In particular, CAV warmly welcomes contributions that extend the frontiers of verification techniques to new domains such as security, quantum computing, and machine learning, including connections to Large Language Models (LLMs). This year, CAV was held as part of the Federated Logic Conference (FLoC), which unites premier conferences relating logic and computer science once in every four years.

CAV 2026 introduced a number of significant changes in our submission categories and reviewing procedures. In particular, maturity was now included as an evaluation criterion for short tool papers. In addition, we also introduced two additional short paper categories: (i) short application papers and (ii) industrial experience reports and case studies. In regards to reviewing procedures, we implemented for the first time a two-stage reviewing process, where each paper received two reviews in the first round and, given sufficient support, received two additional reviews in the second round; reviews were double blind.

This year's CAV received 319 submissions. We accepted a total of 81 papers, consisting of 54 regular papers, 21 short tool papers, and 6 industrial experience reports and case studies. This amounts to an acceptance rate of roughly 25.4% overall. The accepted papers cover a wide spectrum of topics, from theoretical results to applications of formal methods. These papers apply or extend formal methods to a wide range of domains such as concurrency, machine learning and neural networks, quantum systems, as well as hybrid and stochastic systems. The program featured keynote talks by Guy Katz (Hebrew University of Jerusalem, Israel) and Maria Christakis (TU Wien, Austria). In addition to the contributed and invited talks, CAV 2026 also hosted the CAV Award ceremony, and Logic Lounge, which is a series of discussions on computer science topics targeting a general audience. This year's Logic Lounge speaker was Kathleen Fisher (Advanced Research and Invention Agency, UK).

Organizing a flagship conference like CAV requires a great deal of effort from the community. The Program Committee for CAV 2026 consisted of 90 PC members, 8 area chairs, and three PC chairs. In all, the committee members wrote over 1110 reviews while investing significant effort to maintain and ensure the high quality of the conference program. We are grateful to the CAV 2026 Program Committee for their outstanding efforts in evaluating the submissions and making sure that each paper got a fair chance. Additionally, we have sought a handful of external expert reviews for a number of papers, which we felt required additional inputs. We are extremely thankful for their help.

CAV 2026 made artifact evaluation optional for all accepted papers. This year we received 68 artifact submissions, of which 67 received at least one badge. The Artifact

Evaluation Committee consisted of 75 members and two co-chairs, who put in significant effort to evaluate each artifact. The goal of this process was to provide constructive feedback to tool developers and help make the research published in CAV more reproducible. We are also very grateful to the Artifact Evaluation Committee for their hard work and dedication in evaluating the submitted artifacts.

CAV 2026 would not have been possible without the tremendous help we received from a number of individuals, and we would like to thank everyone who helped make CAV 2026 a success. First, we would like to thank our area chairs Alan Hu, Corina S. Păsăreanu, David Parker, Dirk Beyer, Georg Weissenbacher, Joost-Pieter Katoen, Marieke Huisman, and Yu-Fang Chen. Moreover, we would like to thank Magnus Myreen and Ondřej Lengál for chairing the Artifact Evaluation Committee. Additionally, we are extremely grateful to a small team from Uppsala University, in particular Andrea Gilot and Fridtjof Stoldt for their assistance during the preparation of the proceedings and Neea Rusch for taking care of the conference website. Since this year CAV was part of FLoC, the CAV 2026 local organization was taken care of by a dedicated FLoC team, spearheaded by Nuno Lopes. We are extremely thankful for their support. Last but not least, we would like to thank the members of the CAV Steering Committee (Kenneth McMillan, Aarti Gupta, Orna Grumberg, and Daniel Kroening) for helping us with several important aspects of organizing CAV 2026.

We hope that you will find the proceedings of CAV 2026 scientifically interesting and thought-provoking!

June 2026

Eva Darulova
Anthony W. Lin
Philipp Rümmer

Organization

Steering Committee

Orna Grumberg	Technion, Israel
Aarti Gupta	Princeton University, USA
Daniel Kroening	Amazon, USA
Kenneth McMillan	University of Texas at Austin, USA

Conference Co-chairs

Eva Darulova	Uppsala University, Sweden
Anthony W. Lin	University of Kaiserslautern-Landau, Germany and Max-Planck Institute for Software Systems, Germany
Philipp Rümmer	University of Regensburg, Germany and Uppsala University, Sweden

Artifact Evaluation Co-chairs

Magnus Myreen	Chalmers University of Technology, Sweden
Ondřej Lengál	Brno University of Technology, Czech Republic

Area Chairs

Alan Hu	University of British Columbia, Canada
Corina S. Păsăreanu	NASA, USA
David Parker	University of Oxford, UK
Dirk Beyer	LMU Munich, Germany
Georg Weissenbacher	TU Wien, Austria
Joost-Pieter Katoen	RWTH Aachen, Germany
Marieke Huisman	University of Twente, The Netherlands
Yu-Fang Chen	Academia Sinica, Taiwan

Website Chair

Neea Rusch	Uppsala University, Sweden

Program Committee

Aina Niemetz	Stanford University, USA
Albert Rubio	Complutense University of Madrid, Spain
Alberto Griggio	Fondazione Bruno Kessler, Italy
Alessandro Abate	University of Oxford, UK
Alessandro Cimatti	Fondazione Bruno Kessler, Italy
Alexander Nadel	Technion & NVIDIA, Israel
Alfons Laarman	Leiden University, The Netherlands
Alwen Tiu	The Australian National University, Australia
Anastasia Mavridou	KBR Inc./NASA Ames Research Center, USA
Anastasia Volkova	Inria, France
Andrea Turrini	Institute of Software, Chinese Academy of Sciences, China
Ankush Desai	Snowflake, USA
Arie Gurfinkel	University of Waterloo, Canada
Azalea Raad	Imperial College London, UK
Bai Xue	Institute of Software, Chinese Academy of Sciences, China
Benjamin Lucien Kaminski	Saarland University, Germany and University College London, UK
Borzoo Bonakdarpour	Michigan State University, USA
Burcu Kulahcioglu Ozkan	Delft University of Technology, The Netherlands
Caterina Urban	Inria & ENS/PSL, France
Cesar Sanchez	IMDEA Software Institute, Spain
Cesare Tinelli	The University of Iowa, USA
Chih-Duo Hong	National Chengchi University, Taiwan
Chih-Hong Cheng	Carl von Ossietzky University of Oldenburg, Germany
Christel Baier	TU Dresden, Germany
Christian Schilling	Aalborg University, Denmark
Constantin Enea	École Polytechnique, LIX, CNRS, France
Damien Zufferey	NVIDIA, Switzerland
Daniel Neider	TU Dortmund University, Germany
Daniel Stan	LRE EPITA, ICube, University of Strasbourg, France
David Parker	University of Oxford, UK

David Sanan	Singapore Institute of Technology, Singapore
Dung Tran	University of Florida, USA
Ekaterina Komendantskaya	University of Southampton, UK
Elaine Li	New York University, USA
Erika Abraham	RWTH Aachen University, Germany
Fu Song	Institute of Software, Chinese Academy of Science, China
Gennaro Parlato	University of Molise, Italy
Gidon Ernst	LMU Munich, Germany
Grant Passmore	Imandra Inc., USA and Clare Hall, Cambridge, UK
Hadar Frenkel	Bar-Ilan University, Israel
Haniel Barbosa	Universidade Federal de Minas Gerais, Brazil
Harald Ruess	SRI International, USA
Hongfei Fu	Shanghai Jiao Tong University, China
Hossein Hojjat	Tehran Institute for Advanced Studies, Iran
Ichiro Hasuo	National Institute of Informatics, Japan
Jan Křetínský	Masaryk University, Czech Republic and TU Munich, Germany
Javier Esparza	TU Munich, Germany
Ji Guan	Institute of Software, Chinese Academy of Sciences, China
Jianwen Li	East China Normal University, China
Jie-Hong Roland Jiang	National Taiwan University, Taiwan
Jingbo Wang	Purdue University, USA
Jorge Navas	Certora, USA
Julian Parsert	RPTU Kaiserslautern, Germany
Juneyoung Lee	Amazon Web Services, USA
Kenneth McMillan	University of Texas at Austin, USA
Krishna Shankaranarayanan	IIT Bombay, India
Loris D'Antoni	University of California, San Diego, USA
Lukas Holik	Aalborg University, Denmark and Brno University of Technology, Czech Republic
Mahesh Viswanathan	University of Illinois Urbana-Champaign, USA
Marco Eilers	ETH Zurich, Switzerland
Margus Veanes	Microsoft Research, USA
Maximilian Weininger	Ruhr University Bochum, Germany
Milan Ceska	Brno University of Technology, Czech Republic
Mingsheng Ying	University of Technology Sydney, Australia
Mingshuai Chen	Zhejiang University, China
Mirco Giacobbe	University of Birmingham, UK
Mohamed Faouzi Atig	Uppsala University, Sweden

Nikola Beneš	Masaryk University, Czech Republic
Ocan Sankur	CNRS, France
Oded Padon	Weizmann Institute of Science, Israel
Ondřej Lengál	Brno University of Technology, Czech Republic
Orna Grumberg	Technion, Israel
Orna Kupferman	The Hebrew University, Israel
Pavithra Prabhakar	University of New Mexico, USA
Pierre Ganty	IMDEA Software Institute, Spain
Qinheping Hu	Bytedance, USA
Roderick Bloem	Graz University of Technology, Austria
Rohit Chadha	University of Missouri, Columbia, USA
S. Akshay	Indian Institute of Technology Bombay, India
Sharon Shoham	Tel Aviv University, Israel
Stanley Bak	Stony Brook University, USA
Stefano Tonetta	Fondazione Bruno Kessler, Italy
Suguman Bansal	Georgia Institute of Technology, USA
Supratik Chakraborty	IIT Bombay, India
Sylvie Putot	École Polytechnique, France
Xujie Si	University of Toronto, Canada
Yakir Vizel	Technion, Israel
Yedi Zhang	National University of Singapore, Singapore
Yong Kiam Tan	Institute for Infocomm Research, A*STAR and Nanyang Technological University, Singapore
Zhilin Wu	Institute of Software, Chinese Academy of Sciences, China

Additional Reviewers

A. R. Balasubramanian
Alberto Bombardelli
Alberto Sambrotta
Alex Odzemir
Alex Potanin
Alexander Ivrii
Andoni Rodriguez
Andrew Reynolds
Anran Wang
Arend-Jan Quist
Arjun Viswanathan
Augusto Mafra
Benedikt Maderbacher
Bettina Könighofer
Bruno Andreotti
Clara Rodríguez-Núñez
Calvin Chau
Daniel Larraz
Daniela Kaufmann
Daniele Cozzo
David Chocholatý
David Perera
Deep Ganguly
Diganta Mukhopadhyay
Diptarko Roy
Dylan Trenti
Eden Frenkel
Ekaterina Zhuchko

Enrique Martin-Martin
Eric Goubault
Filip Macak
Filippo Fantinato
Florian Bruse
Francesco Fabiano
Frederik Mathiesen
Gabriel Dengler
Giacomo Bais
Gianluca Redondi
Giulia Sindoni
Guillaume Melquiond
Guy Katz
Hans-Jörg Schurr
Hassan Farimani
Hassen Saidi
Hengzhi Yu
Hou Zhe
Hrishikesh Balakrishnan
Huangying Dong
Ian Li
Ian Varatalu
Igor Walukiewicz
Jacques Cloete
Jakob Schulz
Jan Corazza
Jesús Correas
Jingyi Mei
Jinwoo Kim
João Carlos Mendes Pereira
Johannes Lehmann
Jonas Fiala
Josia Pietsch
Juhan Ernits
Juraj Síč
Justin Hsu
Kanghee Park
Karthik Nukala
Kartik Sabharwal
Kyle Thompson
Linyu Yang
Luca Geatti
Lucas Kehrer
Mahdi Nazeri
Mallku Soldevila
Manoj Acharya
Marian Lingsch-Rosenfeld
Marco Sälzer
Marta Grobelna
Masaki Waga
Mathias Preiner
Maximilian Prokop
Michael Blondin
Michael Luttenberger
Michal Hečko
Michal Šedý
Miguel Isabel
Mingqi Yang
Minjian Zhang
Miriam Garcia Soto
Mislav Stojanović
Mustafa Yalçıner
Nabarun Deka
Nery Riquelme-Granada
Nicolas Ray Klose
Nikolaus Vertovec
Ofer Strichman
Oliver Markgraf
Omer Rappoport
P. Habeeb
Pablo Gordillo
Paolo Di Biase
Pedro Saccomani
Qing Liu
R. Garcia
Ratan Lal
Raz Lotan
Robert Lorch
Roman Andriushchenko
Rupak Majumdar
Sabine Rieder
Sairam Vaidya
Samir Genaim
Sascha Klüppelholz
Sayan Mukherjee
Sergey Ichtchenko
Shaan Nagy
Shaohang Han
Shrisha Rao
Shweta Rajiv

Simon Perdrix
Srajan Goyal
Steef Hegeman
Stefan Pranger
Subrat Panda Prasad
SungWoo Choi
Tengjie Lin
Tereza Kinska
Thomas Hader
Thomas Sewell
Tim Coopmans
Timm Spork
Tobias Gürtler
Tobias Meggendorfer
Tomaz Mascarenhas
Valentin Krasotin
Virginie Debauche
Vlad Bercovici
Vojtěch Havlena
Wangyue Lu
Wei-Lin Wu
Xinyu Ge
Xuanyu Peng
Yannik Schnitzer
Yazhou Tang
Yizhak Yisrael Elboher
Yoav Ben Shimon
Yogev Shalmon
Yun Chen Tsai
Yuntao Li
Zafer Esen
Zhongyi Wang
Zilin Chen

Artifact Evaluation Committee

Abdelrahman Sayed	Université Gustave Eiffel, France
Abhimannyu Basu	IIT Bombay, India
Aditya Ranjan Jha	National University of Singapore, Singapore
Alberto Bombardelli	Fondazione Bruno Kessler, Italy
Aniruddha Joshi	University of California, Berkeley, USA
Anna Becchi	USI Lugano, Switzerland
Aurea Bílá	ETH Zurich, Switzerland
Ben Wooding	Vanderbilt University, USA
Benjamin von Berg	Graz University of Technology, Austria
Bishnu Bhusal	University of Missouri, Columbia, USA
Bruno Andreotti	Federal University of Minas Gerais, Brazil
Cas Widdershoven	Liverpool John Moores University, UK
Cole Vick	University of Texas at Austin, USA
David Chocholatý	Brno University of Technology, Czech Republic
David Shriver	Unaffiliated, USA
Dylan Trenti	Fondazione Bruno Kessler and University of Udine, Italy
Eden Frenkel	Tel Aviv University, Israel
Filip Macák	Brno University of Technology, Czech Republic
Florian Renkin	EPITA, LRE, Paris, France
Gaspard Reghem	LIX, École Polytechnique, France
Govind Rajanbabu	Institute of Mathematical Sciences, India

Han Su	National Institute of Informatics, Japan
Huan Sun	Zhejiang University, China
Jack Stodart	The Australian National University, Australia
Jan-Gustav Michnia	RWTH Aachen University, Germany
Jayaraj Jayakumar	University of California, Santa Cruz, USA
Jingyi Mei	Leiden University, The Netherlands
John Lu	University of Waterloo, Canada
Jule Schmidt	Ruhr University Bochum, Germany
Julie Cailler	University of Lorraine, CNRS, Inria, LORIA, Nancy, France
Junkil Park	Waymo, USA
Kanak Das	University of California, Riverside, USA
Kevin Zhou	National Institute of Informatics, Japan
Kittiphon Phalakarn	National Institute of Informatics, Japan
Lei Huang	University of Illinois Urbana-Champaign, USA
Maris Galesloot	Radboud University, The Netherlands
Maykel Mattar	CEA-LIST, France
Meilin Zhu	Institute of Software, Chinese Academy of Sciences, China
Michal Hečko	Brno University of Technology, Czech Republic
Michal Šedý	Aalborg University, Denmark
Milad Rabizadeh	Michigan State University, USA
Minghao Liu	University of Oxford, UK
Mingkai Miao	Hong Kong University of Science and Technology, Guangzhou, China
Mingyu Huang	Institute of Software, Chinese Academy of Sciences, China
Mohammad Afzal	TCS Research and IIT Bombay, India
N. Ege Saraç	CISPA Helmholtz Center for Information Security, Germany
Namratha Gangamreddypalli	École Polytechnique, France
Neta Elad	Tel Aviv University, Israel
Omkar Vijaykumar Tuppe	IIT Bombay, India
Paolo Di Biase	Gran Sasso Science Institute, Italy
Pedro Saccomani	Federal University of Minas Gerais, Brazil
Peng Wu	Institute of Software, Chinese Academy of Sciences, China
Ruijie Fang	University of Texas at Austin, USA
Rémi Garcia	Nantes Université, France
Sachin Gupta	eBay, USA
Samuel Grahn	Uppsala University, Sweden
Sarvin Bahmani	University of Liverpool, UK

Sayan Mukherjee	Indian Institute of Technology Bombay, India
Stephan Spengler	Uppsala University, Sweden
SungWoo Choi	University of Florida, USA
Titouan Ouillon	LIX, École Polytechnique, CNRS, France
Tomaz Mascarenhas	Federal University of Minas Gerais, Brazil
Tomáš Kocourek	Brno University of Technology, Czech Republic
Tooba Khan	University of Southern California, USA
Vipin Singh	Google, USA
Xinyu Ge	Aalborg University, Denmark
Yanju Chen	University of California, San Diego, USA
Yogev Shalmon	Technion, Israel
Yuntao Li	University of Florida, USA
Yusen Su	University of Waterloo, Canada
Zafer Esen	Uppsala University, Sweden
Zhongkui Ma	The University of Queensland, Australia
Zihao Li	Institute of Software, Chinese Academy of Sciences, China
Ziteng Wang	University of Texas at Austin, USA
Ziyi Yang	Hong Kong University of Science and Technology, Guangzhou, China

Additional Artifact Reviewers

David Kozák

Deriving Test Oracles for Verification Infrastructure (Invited Talk)

Maria Christakis

TU Wien, Vienna, Austria
maria.christakis@tuwien.ac.at

Abstract. Program analyzers are increasingly trusted as infrastructure for software correctness: they prove safety properties, find bugs, discharge verification conditions, and support automated-reasoning pipelines. Yet analyzers are themselves complex software systems, built from abstract domains, fixpoint engines, symbolic executors, solvers, frontends, encodings, and heuristics. Fully verifying modern analyzers is rarely realistic. This raises a complementary question: how can we systematically test the tools that verify our programs?

This article describes an escalation of techniques for addressing the oracle problem in analyzer testing. When mathematical contracts are available, specification-based testing can check critical analyser components directly. In the absence of such specifications, program generation can produce analyzable programs whose properties are known by construction, although typically within a restricted fragment of the input space. When ground truth is unavailable, differential testing can compare analyzers against one another. When such comparisons are unavailable, metamorphic testing can derive expected outputs by transforming inputs in ways that preserve or predictably change their semantics. Finally, interrogation testing makes metamorphic testing adaptive: instead of asking isolated questions, it cross-examines analyzers and solvers using their own previous answers to expose contradictions.

We close by discussing how these ideas extend beyond analyzers to other systems that make semantic claims, including zero-knowledge systems, secure multiparty computation compilers, and machine-learning models.

Keywords: Program analysis, Oracle problem, Interrogation testing

1 From Specifications to Interrogation

A natural response to bugs in analyzers is to ask whether the analyzers themselves should be verified. In principle, this is the cleanest solution: a verified analyzer would come with a proof that its answers are sound with respect to a formal semantics. In practice, however, modern analyzers combine frontends, intermediate representations, abstract domains, fixpoint engines, symbolic execution, solvers, memory models, optimizations, and reporting mechanisms. The implemented system is usually too large, too heterogeneous, or too rapidly evolving to be verified end-to-end.

This makes testing a necessary complement to verification. The difficulty is the oracle problem: for many interesting programs, we do not know in advance whether the analyzer should report safe, unsafe, or unknown. A proof of safety may be correct, or it may be an unsound false negative; an alarm may reveal a real bug, or it may be a loss of precision. Even auxiliary artifacts, such as invariants or counterexamples, may be inconsistent with the claimed result.

The following techniques address different oracle-construction obstacles in analyzer testing. When a component has a mathematical contract, specification-based testing can check the implementation directly, as in our work on numerical abstract domains [1]. Without such specifications, program generation can produce analyzable programs whose relevant properties are known by construction, though typically within a restricted fragment of the input space [5, 12]. When ground truth is unavailable, differential testing can compare analyzers and treat disagreement as evidence of soundness or precision issues [10].

Metamorphic testing addresses the absence of ground truth or comparable analyzers: it transforms analyzer inputs in ways that preserve or predictably change their semantics, so that the expected output for the transformed input can be derived from the original one. We used this idea for Datalog engines, first through transformations that preserve or predictably change query results, and later through dependency-aware transformations that exploit rule dependencies [11, 13]. Interrogation testing addresses limitations of such one-step transformations. It uses richer information from analyzer answers and a knowledge base of past queries to guide future ones. This makes the testing process adaptive: instead of asking isolated questions, it records previous queries and answers, uses them to generate follow-up tests, and searches for contradictions. We used this methodology to expose soundness and precision issues in program analyzers [8] and CHC solvers, a foundational layer beneath many verification tools [9].

2 Beyond Program Analyzers

The need to derive useful test oracles is not unique to program analyzers. It arises whenever a system makes a semantic claim that is hard to check directly. A zero-knowledge system claims that a proof attests to a valid computation without revealing private data. A secure multiparty computation compiler claims that the generated protocol implements the source program. A machine-learning model is often expected to satisfy semantic relations over multiple input-output pairs. In each case, the test must derive an oracle for the claim being checked.

We have derived such oracles in several ways. For zero-knowledge systems [6, 7], we used metamorphic testing and fault injection to check whether implementations accept invalid claims or reject valid ones. For secure multiparty computation compilers [14], we used differential testing against an oracle implementation of the source program. For machine-learning models [2–4], we used specifications expressing metamorphic relations between inputs and predictions. Across these domains, the common theme is to make correctness claims testable by turning the artifacts that systems expose into oracles.

References

1. Bugariu, A., Wustholz, V., Christakis, M., Muller, P.: Automatically testing implementations of numerical abstract domains. In: ASE, pp. 768–778. ACM (2018). https://doi.org/10.1145/3238147.3240464
2. Christakis, M., Eniser, H.F., Hoffmann, J., Singla, A., Wustholz, V.: Specifying and testing k-safety properties for machine-learning models. In: IJCAI, pp. 4748–4757. ijcai.org (2023). https://doi.org/10.24963/IJCAI.2023/528
3. Eniser, H.F., Gros, T.P., Wustholz, V., Hoffmann, J., Christakis, M.: Metamorphic relations via relaxations: an approach to obtain oracles for action-policy testing. In: ISSTA, pp. 52–63. ACM (2022). https://doi.org/10.1145/3533767.3534392
4. Eniser, H.F., Wustholz, V., Christakis, M.: Automatically testing functional properties of code translation models. In: AAAI, pp. 21055–21062. AAAI (2024). https://doi.org/10.1609/AAAI.V38I19.30097
5. Fleischmann, M., Kaindlstorfer, D., Isychev, A., Wustholz, V., Christakis, M.: Constraintbased test oracles for program analyzers. In: ASE, pp. 344–355. ACM (2024). https://doi.org/10.1145/3691620.3695035
6. Hochrainer, C., Isychev, A., Wustholz, V., Christakis, M.: Fuzzing processing pipelines for zero-knowledge circuits. In: CCS, pp. 783–797. ACM (2025). https://doi.org/10.1145/3719027.3744791
7. Hochrainer, C., Wustholz, V., Christakis, M.: Arguzz: testing zkVMs for soundness and completeness bugs. In: Security. USENIX (2026). to appear
8. Kaindlstorfer, D., Isychev, A., Wustholz, V., Christakis, M.: Interrogation testing of program analyzers for soundness and precision issues. In: ASE, pp. 319–330. ACM (2024). https://doi.org/10.1145/3691620.3695034
9. Kaindlstorfer, D., Isychev, A., Wustholz, V., Christakis, M.: Interrogation testing of CHC solvers. In: FSE, ACM (2026). to appear
10. Klinger, C., Christakis, M., Wustholz, V.: Differentially testing soundness and precision of program analyzers. In: ISSTA, pp. 239–250. ACM (2019). https://doi.org/10.1145/3293882.3330553
11. Mansur, M.N., Christakis, M., Wustholz, V.: Metamorphic testing of Datalog engines. In: ESEC/FSE, pp. 639–650. ACM (2021). https://doi.org/10.1145/3468264.3468573
12. Mansur, M.N., Christakis, M., Wustholz, V., Zhang, F.: Detecting critical bugs in SMT solvers using blackbox mutational fuzzing. In: ESEC/FSE, pp. 701–712. ACM (2020). https://doi.org/10.1145/3368089.3409763
13. Mansur, M.N., Wustholz, V., Christakis, M.: Dependency-aware metamorphic testing of Datalog engines. In: ISSTA, pp. 236–247. ACM (2023). https://doi.org/10.1145/3597926.3598052
14. Watzinger, S., Wustholz, V., Garg, D., Christakis, M.: Cost-effective testing of MPC compilers. In: FSE, ACM (2026). to appear

Contents

Synthesis

Hardware Verification

Invited Talk

Learning to Split: A Reinforcement-Learning-Guided Splitting Heuristic for Neural Network Verification (Invited Talk)

Maya Swisa and Guy Katz(✉)

The Hebrew University of Jerusalem, Jerusalem, Israel
{maya.swisa,g.katz}@mail.huji.ac.il

Abstract. Modern neural network verifiers often encode neural network verification as constraint satisfaction problems. When dealing with standard piecewise-linear activation functions, such as ReLUs, verifiers typically employ branching heuristics that break a complex constraint satisfaction problem into multiple, simpler problems. The verifier's performance depends heavily on the order in which this branching is performed: a poor selection may give rise to exponentially many sub-problems, hampering scalability. Here, we focus on the setting in which many related verification queries must be solved for the same neural network. The core idea is to use past experience to make good branching decisions, expediting verification. We present a reinforcement-learning-based branching heuristic that achieves this, by applying Deep Q-learning from Demonstrations (DQfD). Our experimental evaluation demonstrates a substantial reduction in average verification time and in the average number of iterations required, compared to modern splitting heuristics. These results highlight the great potential of reinforcement learning in the context of neural network verification.

1 Introduction

Deep neural networks (DNNs) have emerged as highly powerful tools, which are increasingly being integrated into complex systems in the fields of computer vision [8], natural language processing [18], and aerospace [15]. However, DNNs are also prone to mistakes: for example, they will often fail when presented with mildly perturbed ("adversarial") inputs [3,7,22]. The growing reliance on DNNs, combined with their susceptibility to error, highlights the need for formal guarantees regarding their behavior; and indeed, great strides have been made on DNN verification in the past decade to try and meet this goal.

Despite these advancements, a substantial disparity remains between the scale of DNNs amenable to current verification techniques and the complexity of those required for real-world applications [1]. This is primarily due to the fact that DNN verification with piecewise-linear activations is NP-complete [13],

E. Darulova et al. (Eds.): CAV 2026, LNCS 16682, pp. 3–15, 2026.
https://doi.org/10.1007/978-3-032-32519-8_1

indicating that the computational cost can grow exponentially with the size of the network. This intractability necessitates the further development of sophisticated and efficient verification techniques.

Many modern verifiers operate by translating the verification problem into the Satisfiability Modulo Theories (SMT) setting (alongside other techniques, such as symbolic bound propagation [1,24]). This approach provides sound and complete guarantees for a DNN's correctness, or a counterexample demonstrating the undesirable behavior. While these methods guarantee a definitive answer, they rely on *case splitting*—the translation of piecewise-linear constraints to disjunctions of linear constraints—to handle the piecewise-linear activation functions of the DNN. This process transforms a complex problem into a long sequence of simpler problems, and is known to cause scalability issues [13]. It is known that the selection of neurons on which a solver splits can have a tremendous effect on the size of the search space that is eventually explored; and so multiple splitting heuristics have been proposed with the goal of minimizing this search space (e.g., Pseudo-Impact [26], polarity [25], and BaBSR [2]).

A fundamental limitation of existing approaches is that a single, static heuristic is typically chosen and applied throughout the entire verification process. This method overlooks three key points. First, it is very difficult to know, a priori, which heuristic will be the most useful for the problem at hand; second, it may be useful to change heuristics during the verification procedure, as different parts of the search space are traversed; and third, in many applications, a verification query is actually not stand-alone, but part of a set of related queries—and in that case, it can be useful to transfer knowledge from one run of the verifier to the next, potentially reducing the overall verification time.

To address these limitations, we propose a novel approach: we use Double DQN with demonstrations (DQfD) to learn a state-conditioned, adaptive splitting policy. Rather than fixing a single heuristic a priori, we train an agent that selects the next split according to an estimated action value at the current verifier state. This enables state-dependent branching decisions, allows the preferred split to change as the search evolves, and exploits experience from related verification queries through demonstrations.

To evaluate our approach, we implemented it on top of the Marabou solver [14], and trained and evaluated the learned policy on the ACAS Xu benchmark family [13]. We considered both the standard ACAS Xu safety properties [11] and local robustness queries, requiring the predicted advisory to remain unchanged within an ℓ_∞ ball around a given input. Compared with Marabou's built-in splitting heuristics, our learned policy solved more instances and reduced average verification time, with improvements most evident on harder instances. Across the evaluated settings, the average time reduction ranged from 5.88% to 56.20%, highlighting the potential of learned branching for DNN verification.

The rest of the paper is organized as follows. Section 2 provides background on deep neural networks, their verification, and reinforcement learning. In Sect. 3, we present our methodology for learning adaptive splitting policies. Section 4 reports on implementation details and experimental evaluation on safety and robustness benchmarks, followed by Sect. 5 where we discuss related work. Finally, Sect. 6 concludes and outlines directions for future work.

2 Preliminaries

2.1 Neural Networks and their Verification

Deep neural networks (DNNs) are composed of layers of interconnected neurons. The output of neuron j in layer l is $a_j^{(l)} = \sigma(W_j^{(l)} a^{(l-1)} + b_j^{(l)})$, where σ is the activation function. We focus on the ReLU activation function, $\text{ReLU}(x) = \max(0, x)$. For each ReLU neuron n_i, we write n_i^b and n_i^a for its pre- and post-activation values, respectively, so that $n_i^a = \max(0, n_i^b)$. This notation separates the network's linear layers from its nonlinear parts.

Running Example. Consider the network in Fig. 1, with inputs $x_1 \in [-1, 1]$ and $x_2 \in [0, 1]$, two hidden ReLU units n_1, n_2 with pre-activations n_1^b, n_2^b and post-activations n_1^a, n_2^a, and a single output y. All bias values are zero.

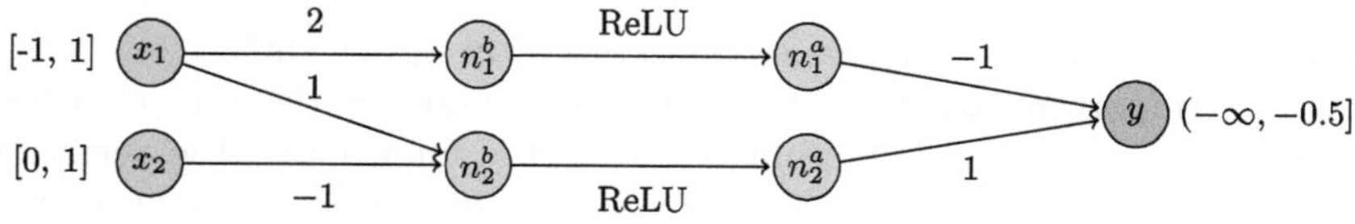

Fig. 1. A toy neural network with two inputs.

For this network, $n_1^b = 2x_1$, $n_2^b = x_1 - x_2$, $n_1^a = \text{ReLU}(n_1^b)$, $n_2^a = \text{ReLU}(n_2^b)$, and $f(x_1, x_2) = -n_1^a + n_2^a = -\text{ReLU}(2x_1) + \text{ReLU}(x_1 - x_2)$. For input $(x_1, x_2) = (0.3, 0.7)$, the neuron values are: $n_1^a = \text{ReLU}(0.6) = 0.6$, $n_2^a = \text{ReLU}(-0.4) = 0$, and $y = -0.6 \leq -0.5$.

Neural Network Verification. We formulate DNN verification as a satisfiability problem. Let $f : \mathbb{R}^n \to \mathbb{R}^m$ be a neural network, $X \subseteq \mathbb{R}^n$ an input domain, and ϕ a property over outputs that encodes an *undesirable* behavior (e.g., a violation of a safety constraint). The verification problem is to determine whether there exists $x \in X$ such that $\phi(f(x))$ holds. If so, the network exhibits the undesirable behavior, and the query is said to be satisfiable (SAT); otherwise, the network is safe with respect to ϕ, and the query is unsatisfiable (UNSAT) [4].

Example 1. Consider the network in Fig. 1, and let $X := (x_1, x_2) \in [-1, 1] \times [0, 1]$. Consider the property $\phi(f(x_1, x_2)) \equiv (f(x_1, x_2) \leq -0.5)$. The verification problem is to determine whether $\exists\, (x_1, x_2) \in [-1, 1] \times [0, 1] : f(x_1, x_2) \leq -0.5$ holds. For the specific input $(x_1, x_2) = (0.3, 0.7)$, the network evaluates to $f(0.3, 0.7) = -0.6 \leq -0.5$. Thus, $(0.3, 0.7)$ is a witness to satisfiability, and the query is SAT.

2.2 Verification via Branch-and-Bound (BaB)

DNNs with ReLU activations mix easy-to-solve, linear constraints (affine layers) with hard-to-solve non-linearities (ReLUs) [13]. An *activation pattern* is an assignment of active/inactive status to all ReLUs. Once an activation pattern is fixed, the network reduces to a single affine transformation, and checking feasibility becomes easily solvable. However, a network with N ReLUs induces up to 2^N activation patterns, rendering exhaustive enumeration infeasible.

Many verifiers adopt a branch-and-bound (BaB) search to tackle the verification problem [6]. BaB organizes the problem as a binary *splitting tree*: the root encodes the original verification problem; each node's children correspond to a case split of one ReLU into its two phases; and each leaf corresponds to an activation pattern whose satisfiability has been decided. The process terminates when a SAT sub-problem is found (the original problem is also SAT); or when all paths in the search tree are determined to end in an UNSAT node.

In order to prune the search tree, BaB-based solvers usually apply *bound tightening*: they compute sound bounds on pre-activation values of the various ReLUs, and use them to identify ReLUs that are always active or always inactive for the current sub-problem. Whenever such a ReLU is discovered, there is no need to branch on it, and this expedites verification significantly.

Another important aspect in BaB-based techniques is the *prioritization of splits*: choosing which ReLU to split on, using the information the verifier has obtained so far on the current sub-problem (e.g., the currently known bounds). Effective prioritization directs the search quickly toward proofs or counterexamples, reducing the explored portion of the tree.

Running Example. We return to the toy network from Fig. 1 and the query

$$\exists (x_1, x_2) \in [-1, 1] \times [0, 1] : f(x_1, x_2) \leq -0.5.$$

Suppose the verifier first branches on n_1, considering the case $n_1^b \leq 0$. Since $n_1^b = 2x_1$, this implies $x_1 \leq 0$. Because $x_2 \in [0, 1]$, it follows that $n_2^b = x_1 - x_2 \leq 0$, and so n_2 must also be inactive. Therefore $n_1^a = n_2^a = 0$, which yields $y = 0$. This contradicts the property $y \leq -0.5$, and thus the entire branch $n_1^b \leq 0$ is pruned without any further splitting.

Now, consider the case where the verifier first branches on n_2. In the branch $n_2^b \leq 0$, we obtain only the relation $x_1 \leq x_2$; in the branch $n_2^b \geq 0$, we obtain only $x_1 \geq x_2$. In either case, the phase of n_1 is not determined. Thus, unlike in the previous case, the verifier must continue branching. This illustrates how a good branching decision can lead to a smaller search space.

2.3 Splitting Heuristics

A good heuristic prioritizes splits that are likely either to quickly lead to UNSAT by pruning large, infeasible subtrees, or to uncover a satisfying assignment early. Modern solvers employ several such heuristics, including Sum of Infeasibilities (SoI), which prioritizes nodes whose assignments in the current, relaxed solution significantly violate the corresponding ReLU constraint [26]; the Pseudo-Impact heuristic, which tracks the historical impact of branching on each ReLU [26]; Polarity, which favors ReLUs whose pre-activation bound interval is more balanced around zero [25]; and BaBSR, which scores candidate splits by their estimated contribution to bound tightening [2].

2.4 Reinforcement Learning

Reinforcement Learning (RL) is a method for producing an autonomous agent that can make sequential decisions and interact with an environment, with the goal of maximizing a cumulative reward. The core components of an RL system are the agent, the environment, states, actions, and rewards [20]. In value-based RL, the objective is to learn an action-value function that estimates the long-term utility of taking a given action in a given state.

Double DQN [23] is a value-based method that improves training stability by decoupling action selection from action evaluation through a target network. Training typically follows an ε-greedy exploration strategy, whereby the agent selects the action with the highest estimated value with probability $1 - \varepsilon$, and explores alternative actions with probability ε.

Deep Q-learning from Demonstrations (DQfD) [9] augments Q-learning with expert trajectories. The objective combines a value-learning term with a large-margin supervised term that encourages imitation of expert actions, enabling training to start from demonstration data rather than pure exploration.

3 Methodology

3.1 Adaptive Splitting Heuristic

While existing splitting heuristics can significantly reduce the complexity of DNN verification queries, they operate under a fundamental limitation: they are static policies, in the sense that a single heuristic is typically chosen at the beginning of the verification procedure, and is then applied throughout the search process. The performance of these heuristics is highly sensitive to the specific network architecture and the property being verified. However, there is often no a-priori way of knowing which heuristic will be most effective for a given task, and a choice that works well in one scenario may fail miserably in another.

We argue that it is preferable to consider a splitting strategy that is not static, but which can instead adapt as the search progresses, choosing nodes and split variables based on the current state. Many practical settings involve repeated queries on the *same* network (often over related input regions or properties): e.g., a lane-detection model verified under different conditions [5,11,16]. Treating each query in isolation discards valuable information about the network's structure and the efficacy of past branching decisions. By learning from this cumulative data, we can tap into information that was previously unavailable. An adaptive heuristic can observe the success or failure of past splitting choices and use this feedback to inform future decisions, effectively transferring knowledge from one query to the next. To achieve these goals, we propose to leverage reinforcement learning to train an agent that implements a dynamic branching heuristic.

3.2 Formulation

MDP Formulation. We frame the ReLU splitting process within a Markov Decision Process (MDP), which allows an RL agent to learn an optimal policy for making sequential branching decisions. Intuitively, the agent's task is to learn a policy that maps the current state to the most effective action, aiming to either quickly prune an infeasible branch or find a counter-example. The MDP in our problem is defined by the tuple $(\mathcal{S}, \mathcal{A}, P, R, \gamma)$:

- **State** $\mathcal{S}$: A state $s \in \mathcal{S}$ represents a specific node in the verification search tree, together with a numerical summary of the current subproblem. The state is given by a feature vector containing both local and global information. The local features, for each candidate ReLU, include its lower and upper pre-activation bounds, phase status, and heuristic scores such as SoI, polarity, and BaBSR. The global features summarize the search, including the total number of unfixed ReLUs, the current search tree depth, and the number of splits performed so far. These features capture information commonly used by splitting-based verification algorithms.
- **Action** $\mathcal{A}$: An action $a \in \mathcal{A}$ corresponds to selecting an unfixed ReLU and choosing one of its two branching phases (*active* or *inactive*). Thus, at each search node, the agent scores candidate (ReLU, phase) pairs, and the selected action determines the next branching decision.
- **Transition Function** $P(s'|s, a)$: The transition from state s to the next state s' after taking action a is determined by the underlying verifier. This includes bound propagation, relaxation tightening, and constraint feasibility/validity checks. The next state s' is the updated subproblem.
- **Reward (penalty) function** $R(s, a)$: We empirically observed that setting a uniform -1 reward per step, which is a common choice in RL, did not guide the search towards effective splits well enough—presumably due to the large search space. We therefore use a task-aligned reward function: each split action on neuron n incurs a delayed, normalized penalty proportional to the size of the subtree that action induces. Let $k(n)$ be the number of unfixed neurons before action a splits on neuron n. The potential subtree size, $\text{full}(n) = 2^{k(n)} - 1$, upper-bounds the number of internal nodes in a full binary tree with up to $2^{k(n)}$ leaves. Let $\text{actual}(n)$ denote the number of internal splits (actions) performed within the subtree rooted at n until that subtree's search is complete (either pruned, or fully explored). We assign a single, delayed penalty when the subtree closes: $R(s, a) = -\frac{\text{actual}(n)}{\text{full}(n)}$. This normalization makes penalties comparable across neurons with different remaining depth: actions that trigger early pruning yield small (near-zero) penalties, whereas actions that force exhaustive exploration yield penalties near -1.
- **Discount Factor** $\gamma \in [0, 1]$: Controls the agent's sensitivity to future rewards. A value closer to 1 prioritizes long-term rewards, encouraging the

agent to consider each split's future impact. We empirically set $\gamma = 0.9$, utilizing this effect while avoiding the instability associated with higher discount factors.

Leveraging Expert Demonstrations. Training a DRL agent from scratch proved highly sample-inefficient: with sparse effective policies and a complex environment, purely exploratory learning from the available state features incurred prohibitively high computational cost and yielded no end-to-end gains. To mitigate this, we leveraged existing splitting heuristics as *expert demonstrations*. Although sub-optimal, these heuristics encode useful structure; using them to guide the policy via imitation pretraining followed by RL fine-tuning provides a viable path to faster, more reliable learning than uninformed exploration.

Q-Learning Integration. We solve the MDP using Double DQN with demonstrations (DQfD) [9]. Training proceeds in two phases. First, the agent is pretrained on expert transitions generated by running the verifier with the heuristics described in Sect. 2 (although additional domain- or verifier-specific heuristics could be used as well). This learning-from-demonstrations phase optimizes a combined objective consisting of a Q-learning loss and a margin-based imitation loss, allowing the agent to learn from the outcomes of expert actions and to mimic them. Second, the agent is fine-tuned by interacting with the environment, while continuing to learn from both expert- and self-generated transitions. Over time, the weight of the imitation term is gradually reduced, allowing the policy to move beyond imitation and discover improved splitting strategies. During evaluation, the trained policy is deployed directly within the solver's branching loop, where it replaces existing heuristics.

Hyperparameters and Trade-Offs. Training involves balancing learning from expert demonstrations with exploration driven by the ε-greedy strategy. Greater weight on demonstrations or the imitation loss yields a stronger initial policy, but may limit the discovery of improved splitting decisions. We use a standard ε-decay schedule, starting at 1.0 and multiplying by 0.95 each iteration until reaching a minimum of 0.05.

As in most reinforcement-learning settings, there is also a trade-off between training time and final performance; accordingly, all reported experiments use a fixed hyperparameter configuration selected in preliminary experiments and applied uniformly throughout the evaluation.

Initial Splits: Pseudo-impact. The Pseudo-Impact heuristic employs a specialized strategy for the initial splits. We found this strategy to be efficient for networks with relatively low input dimensions. We applied a common initial branching policy across all strategies to ensure a fair comparison and to isolate the contribution of our learned heuristic to the deeper, more complex portions of the search tree. For all experiments presented in this paper, we applied the Pseudo-Impact heuristic for the first three splits of the search tree (depth ≤ 3), with the respective splitting policies taking over from that point onward.

4 Results

4.1 Implementation

To implement our learned branching policy, we integrated a DQfD agent into the SMT-based verifier *Marabou* [14]. As fixed heuristic baselines, we used *Polarity*, *Pseudo-Impact*, and *BaBSR* (with the first splits always performed using Pseudo-Impact, as previously discussed). All of our code and experiments are available online [21].

We evaluated our implementation on the ACAS-Xu networks for airborne collision avoidance [11], under two verification setups:

(i) **Safety specifications.** The original specifications used in the ACAS-Xu benchmarks, denoted ϕ_1-ϕ_4, across all 45 ACAS-Xu networks [12], resulting in a total of 180 queries (4 properties $\times$ 45 networks).
(ii) **Local robustness.** ℓ_∞ local-robustness verification queries, generated for randomly selected inputs on ACAS-Xu network $N_{1,1}$. For an input x_0, a local robustness query verifies that the network's predicted advisory remains unchanged throughout the ball $\|x - x_0\|_\infty \leq \delta$ around x_0. We tested 1000 randomly selected inputs with three radius values: $\delta \in \{0.08, 0.09, 0.1\}$, producing a total of 3000 queries. The varying inputs and robustness radii produced a mix of satisfiable, unsatisfiable, and timed-out instances, allowing for a more informative comparison between strategies.

We trained a separate agent for each of the two setups. Training included a DQfD warm start followed by Double DQN and used approximately 5% of the queries available in the respective benchmark; and evaluation was then performed on the benchmark's remaining queries.

The training budget was fixed a priori to 45,000 splitting steps: 5 epochs $\times$ 1,000 steps with demonstrations (DQfD), followed by 40 epochs $\times$ 1,000 steps with self-exploration/exploitation (DDQN). Each agent required about 2 h of offline training. All experiments were conducted on single-CPU machines with 2 GB of memory, running Debian 12, and with a 1-hour timeout.

4.2 Performance

For each splitting policy, we report the number of queries where a counterexample was found (*SATs*), unsatisfiable queries (*UNSATs*), and runs that exceeded the time limit (*Timeouts*). We also report the average time per instance (*Avg Time*) and the average number of solver main-loop iterations (*Avg Iterations*). Both averages are computed over all queries. For runs that exceeded the time limit, we use the timeout threshold as the runtime.

Setup (i): ACAS Xu Safety Properties. On the original ACAS Xu properties, our learned splitting heuristic outperforms all other heuristics in the number of solved instances and average verification time. The aggregate results appear in Table 1, demonstrating the effectiveness of our method.

Table 1. ACAS-Xu runs across all networks: averages over all instances, with timeouts counted as 1 h.

Heuristic	SAT	UNSAT	Timeout	Avg. Time (ms)	Avg. Iter.
DQfD Agent	**42.00**	**105.00**	**23.00**	**692691.04**	838986.76
Polarity	40.00	103.00	27.00	771287.04	795486.79
Pseudo-Impact	23.00	84.00	63.00	1347021.98	1183586.92
BaBSR	41.00	104.00	25.00	775690.24	**779218.49**

Setup (ii): Local-Robustness Properties. Table 2 summarizes the results for setup (ii). The learned splitting heuristic achieves the best average verification time, although it requires a slightly greater number of iterations compared to the Polarity heuristic. Moreover, it solves a significantly higher number of instances compared to the baselines.

Table 2. Summary of robustness runs for common (ExampleID, Epsilon).

Heuristic	SAT	UNSAT	Timeout	Avg. Time (ms)	Avg. Iter.
DQfD Agent	**253.00**	**2595.00**	**122.00**	**328457.31**	235690.92
Polarity	252.00	2574.00	144.00	348988.84	**222903.82**
Pseudo-Impact	88.00	2319.00	563.00	749976.29	732681.33
BaBSR	244.00	2550.00	176.00	376507.73	265502.52

Figure 2 demonstrates that the learned splitting heuristic closely tracks the strongest baseline on easier instances—indicating an effective imitation of expert behavior. On harder instances, however, it surpasses the baseline, suggesting more effective splitting choices.

5 Related Work

Exact Verification via SMT and BaB. Complete solvers repeatedly perform case splitting on piecewise-linear activations and propagate bounds to prune the search space [13,14]. Recent work strengthens this paradigm through tighter

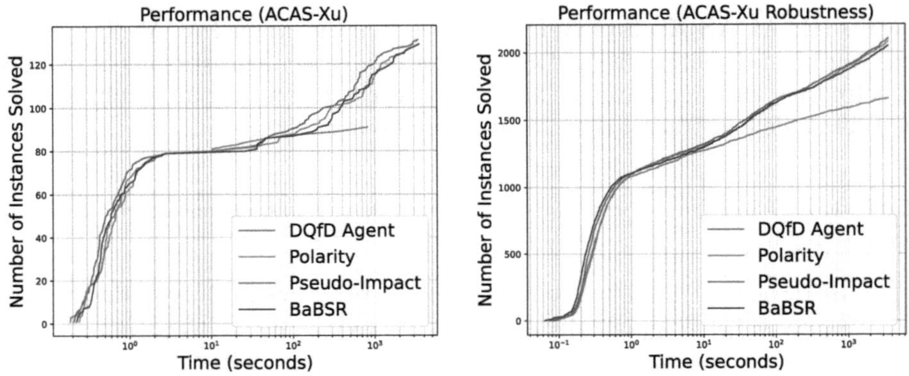

(a) Setup (i). (b) Setup (ii).

Fig. 2. Cumulative instances solved vs. time (log scale) on the two setups.

relaxations and improved branching scores [2]. Our contribution is complementary: we learn a splitting policy that can be inserted into a BaB framework or an SMT-based solver, replacing hand-crafted splitting heuristics.

Learning for Branching and Verification. Learning-guided branching has been explored in several related settings. In neural network verification, Jeong et al. [10] use a graph neural network to guide *node selection*. Our work is distinct: we use DQfD to learn the *branching rule* itself, directly affecting how subproblems are created and, consequently, the effectiveness of bound tightening and pruning. Qu et al. [19] apply reinforcement learning to branching in general MILP queries; however, DNN verification is structurally different, because branching must interact with specialized nonlinear relaxations and sound bound-tightening procedures. Liang et al. [17] propose an online adaptive branching heuristic for CDCL SAT solvers; while similarly motivated, their setting involves Boolean branching with online feedback, whereas our policy is learned offline from demonstrations and transferred across related verification queries.

6 Conclusion and Future Work

We introduced a novel reinforcement-learning-guided splitting heuristic for DNN verifiers. Our method integrates learning from demonstrations with Double DQN inside an SMT-based verifier, and improves verification performance speed.

Several directions remain for future work, aimed at making learned branching a more reusable and scalable. First, the current framework can be improved by enriching the MDP representation. Additional state features and alternative reward signals may better inform the agent's decisions and help optimize overall verification performance. Second, our evaluation focuses on ACAS Xu and feed-forward networks with ReLU activations. Assessing the broader applicability of the approach will require experiments on a wider range of benchmarks and network architectures. Finally, an important goal is to improve the portability of learned splitting policies across networks and properties. This includes studying transfer across networks with different input sizes and architectural variations. Progress in this direction could significantly reduce the cost of applying learned branching to new verification tasks.

Acknowledgments. This work was partially funded by the European Union (ERC, VeriDeL, 101112713). Views and opinions expressed are however those of the author(s) only and do not necessarily reflect those of the European Union or the European Research Council Executive Agency. Neither the European Union nor the granting authority can be held responsible for them. This research was additionally supported by a grant from the Israeli Science Foundation (grant number 558/24).

Data Availibility Statement. The code and experiments reported in this paper are available online [21].

Disclosure of Interests. The authors have no competing interests to declare that are relevant to the content of this article.

References

1. Brix, C., Bak, S., Johnson, T., Wu, H.: The Fifth International Verification of Neural Networks Competition (VNN-COMP 2024): Summary and Results. Technical report (2024). https://arxiv.org/abs/2412.19985. https://doi.org/10.48550/arXiv.2412.19985
2. Bunel, R., Lu, J., Turkaslan, I., Torr, P.H.S., Kohli, P., Kumar, M.P.: Branch and bound for piecewise linear neural network verification. J. Mach. Learn. Res. **21**(42), 1–39 (2020)
3. Carlini, N., Wagner, D.: Towards evaluating the robustness of neural networks. In: Proceedings of IEEE Symposium on Security and Privacy (S&P), pp. 39–57 (2017)
4. Casadio, M., et al.: Neural network robustness as a verification property: a principled case study. In: Proceedings of 34th International Conference on Computer Aided Verification (CAV), pp. 219–231 (2022). https://doi.org/10.1007/978-3-031-13185-1_11
5. Elboher, Y., et al.: Robustness assessment of a runway object classifier for safe aircraft taxiing. In: Proceedings of 43rd Digital Avionics Systems Conference (DASC), pp. 1–6 (2024)
6. Ferrari, C., Müller, M.N., Jovanovic, N., Vechev, M.: Complete Verification via Multi-Neuron Relaxation Guided Branch-and-Bound. Technical report (2022). https://arxiv.org/abs/2205.00263. https://doi.org/10.48550/arXiv.2205.00263
7. Goodfellow, I., Shlens, J., Szegedy, C.: Explaining and harnessing adversarial examples. In: Proceedings of International Conference on Learning Representations (ICLR) (2015)
8. He, K., Zhang, X., Ren, S., Sun, J.: Deep residual learning for image recognition. In: Proceedings of IEEE Conference on Computer Vision and Pattern Recognition (CVPR), pp. 770–778 (2016)
9. Hester, T., et al.: Deep Q-learning from demonstrations. In: Proceedings of AAAI Conference on Artificial Intelligence, vol. 32, no. 1 (2018)

10. Jaeckle, F., Lu, J., Kumar, M.P.: Neural Network Branch-and-Bound for Neural Network Verification. Technical report (2021). https://arxiv.org/abs/2107.12855. https://doi.org/10.48550/arXiv.2107.12855
11. Julian, K., Kochenderfer, M., Owen, M.: Deep neural network compression for aircraft collision avoidance systems. J. Guid. Control. Dyn. **42**(3), 598–608 (2019)
12. Katz, G., Barrett, C., Dill, D., Julian, K., Kochenderfer, M.: Reluplex: a calculus for reasoning about deep neural networks. Formal Methods Syst. Des. (FMSD) (2021). https://doi.org/10.1007/s10703-021-00363-7
13. Katz, G., Barrett, C., Dill, D.L., Julian, K., Kochenderfer, M.J.: Reluplex: an efficient SMT solver for verifying deep neural networks. In: Majumdar, R., Kunčak, V. (eds.) CAV 2017. LNCS, vol. 10426, pp. 97–117. Springer, Cham (2017). https://doi.org/10.1007/978-3-319-63387-9_5
14. Katz, G., et al.: The marabou framework for verification and analysis of deep neural networks. In: Dillig, I., Tasiran, S. (eds.) CAV 2019. LNCS, vol. 11561, pp. 443–452. Springer, Cham (2019). https://doi.org/10.1007/978-3-030-25540-4_26
15. Katz, G., Levy, N., Refaeli, I., Yerushalmi, R.: DEM: a method for certifying deep neural network classifier outputs in aerospace. In: Proceedings of 43rd Digital Avionics Systems Conference (DASC), pp. 1–8 (2024)
16. Kessler, C., et al.: Neural network verification for gliding drone control: a case study. In: Proceedings of International Symposium on AI Verification (SAIV) (2025)
17. Liang, J., Ganesh, V., Poupart, P., Czarnecki, K.: Learning rate based branching heuristic for SAT solvers. In: Proceedings of 19th International Conference on Theory and Applications of Satisfiability Testing (SAT), pp. 123–140 (2016)
18. OpenAI. ChatGPT (2022). https://chatgpt.com
19. Qu, Q., et al.: An Improved Reinforcement Learning Algorithm for Learning to Branch. Technical report (2022). https://arxiv.org/abs/2201.06213. https://doi.org/10.48550/arXiv.2201.06213
20. Sutton, R.S., Barto, A.G.: Reinforcement Learning: An Introduction. MIT Press (2018)
21. Swisa, M., Katz, G.: Learning to Split: A Reinforcement-Learning-Guided Splitting Heuristic for Neural Network Verification (Code) (2025). https://github.com/mayaswissa/LearningToSplit
22. Szegedy, C., et al.: Intriguing Properties of Neural Networks. Technical report (2013). https://arxiv.org/abs/1312.6199. https://doi.org/10.48550/arXiv.1312.6199
23. van Hasselt, H., Guez, A., Silver, D.: Deep reinforcement learning with double Q-learning. In: Proceedings of AAAI Conference on Artificial Intelligence, vol. 30, no. 1, pp. 2094–2100 (2016)
24. Wang, S., et al.: Beta-CROWN: efficient bound propagation with per-neuron split constraints for neural network robustness verification. In: Proceedings of 35th Conference on Neural Information Processing Systems (NeurIPS) (2021)
25. Wu, H., et al.: Parallelization techniques for verifying neural networks. In: Proceedings of Formal Methods in Computer-Aided Design (FMCAD), pp. 128–137 (2020). https://doi.org/10.34727/2020/isbn.978-3-85448-042-6_20
26. Wu, H., Zeljić, A., Katz, G., Barrett, C.: Efficient neural network analysis with sum-of-infeasibilities. In: TACAS 2022. LNCS, vol. 13243, pp. 143–163. Springer, Cham (2022). https://doi.org/10.1007/978-3-030-99524-9_8

Verification of Parallel, Concurrent, and Distributed Systems

On the Complexity of Checking Soundness of Natural Reductions

Constantin Enea[1], Azadeh Farzan[2], and Dominik Klumpp[1](✉)

[1] LIX – CNRS – École Polytechnique, Palaiseau, France
{cenea,klumpp}@lix.polytechnique.fr
[2] University of Toronto, Toronto, Canada
azadeh@cs.toronto.edu

Abstract. The verification of *reductions*, representative subsets of interleavings, simplifies correctness proofs of parameterized concurrent programs. We introduce an expressive class of syntactic reductions, which we call *natural reductions*. Natural reductions are specified by introducing atomic blocks and global rendezvous points in the parameterized program's thread template. We study the problem of deciding whether a given natural reduction is sound wrt. a given (semi-)commutativity relation. In the case that there is no synchronization between threads, we present a sound and complete polynomial-time algorithm. In the case where synchronization is considered, we provide a general lower bound for the problem (parametric in the synchronization mechanism), and show that the problem is coNP-hard already for a simple mechanism like locking.

1 Introduction

A *reduction* of a concurrent program is a program with a subset of the behaviors of the original that can be *soundly* verified in its place. A big body of research in program verification, in both algorithmic and deductive traditions, has argued that the use of reductions can be critical to the success of the verification task. On the algorithmic verification side, the reductions either come from an a priori fixed set [10,11] or the verification algorithm has to pay the steep cost of searching for them [13]. On the deductive verification side, proof systems like CSPEC [2], Armada [22], Anchor [14] and Civl [19] include proof tactics based on Lipton's reduction [21] for showing that a user-provided reduction is sound, which can be interleaved with other proof tactics that relate to inductive invariant reasoning, for instance. These proof systems have been used to verify real-world examples such as a concurrent garbage collector [19], an implementation of the Paxos protocol [20], or concurrent data structures [24]. Reductions play a critical role in the proofs of these examples.

In this paper, we investigate the complexity of checking whether some given reduction of a concurrent program is sound. We focus on *parameterized concurrent programs*, that is, concurrent programs in which an arbitrary number of threads can be instantiated from a single thread template. These programs

E. Darulova et al. (Eds.): CAV 2026, LNCS 16682, pp. 19–41, 2026.
https://doi.org/10.1007/978-3-032-32519-8_2

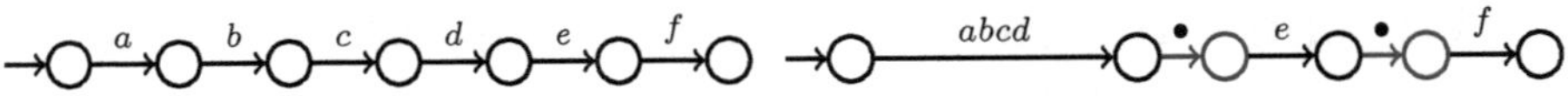

(a) Thread template (control flow graph). (b) Thread template of a natural reduction.

Fig. 1. Example of natural reductions. The symbol • synchronizes all threads.

appear everywhere in distributed and parallel computing. We consider a class of reductions that we call *natural* that can be specified syntactically with ease and make it straightforward for programmers to envision the reduced program and reason about it. Hence, *natural reductions* enable programmers to interact with verification tools by proposing reductions that may simplify verification tasks.

Natural reductions are defined through two syntactic program transformations, which both have deep connections to traditions of reasoning about concurrent programs:

- *Atomic Blocks*: The programmer can specify any number of syntactic atomic blocks in the program, which accordingly prunes the space of possible concurrent program behaviours, excluding all behaviours in which one thread's execution of the atomic block is interrupted by another thread.
- *Synchronous Reductions:* The programmer uses a unique symbol as a *global rendezvous point* among all existing threads, and as such restricts the space of program behaviours to those in which the threads meet at the rendezvous point before continuing.

The former has been broadly used as the foundation of *local reasoning* in concurrency [2,6,14,18,19,21,22], and the latter has been used to simplify reasoning about distributed protocols [3,5,7,16]. In many distributed protocols, the behavior of each process is structured as a sequence of rounds and it can be shown that processes executing rounds synchronously and in lock-step is a sound reduction of the original set of asynchronous behaviors (where processes may be executing different rounds at a point of time). The user can use a combination of both to restrict the set of concurrent program behaviours and hence *specify* a reduction.

Example. Consider a program whose thread template is given by the control flow graph in Fig. 1a, where a, b, c, d, e, f are the atomic actions of the program. A user can specify a synchronous reduction by inserting global rendezvous points between the actions d and e resp. between e and f. This eliminates all program behaviours in which the actions e and f interleave with the actions a, b, c, d resp. with each other. The behaviours of the reduced program are thus partitioned into three *rounds* or *phases*: a first phase where all threads execute a, b, c and d; a second phase where all threads execute e; and a third phase where all threads execute f. Furthermore, the user can specify that the first phase executes atomically; thereby allowing the verification to use local reasoning without interference by other threads (that also execute a, b, c, or d). The specified natural reduction is represented by the thread template in Fig. 1b. The global rendezvous points are represented by the symbol •, and the atomic execution of the first phase is represented by a single edge labeled with the concatenated actions $abcd$.

We say a (specified) reduction is *sound* if every behaviour of the original program is equivalent to a behaviour in the reduction up to an *equivalence relation* induced by a *sound commutativity relation* on their common set of actions. A sound commutativity relation is a (not necessarily symmetric[1]) relation on the set of atomic actions that includes a pair (a_1, a_2) if and only if the semantics of a_2a_1 includes all behaviours of a_1a_2. A *sound reduction* can be soundly verified in place of the original program (i.e., the reduction satisfies the same postconditions as the original program). Hence, given a *natural reduction* specified by the user, we are interested in the problem of determining whether it is sound.

Example. Let the following be a sound commutativity relation:

$$\mathrm{I} = \big(\{e\} \times \{a,b,c,d\}\big) \cup \big(\{f\} \times \{a,b,c,d,e\}\big) \cup \{a,b,c,d\}^2$$

Then the natural reduction given in Fig. 1 is sound. The first term of the union ensures e can always be commuted to the second phase of an execution, and similarly the second term ensures f can be commuted to the third phase. The third term suffices to ensure the soundness of considering only atomic executions of the first phase (though not all commutation pairs are necessary for this).

In this paper, we investigate the soundness problem of natural reductions for two different abstract models of program behaviours. First, we consider a model in which program data is entirely abstracted away, and every syntactic behaviour of the program is valid behaviour in the abstract model. In a sense, the only information remaining about program semantics is given through the *sound commutativity* relation on the set of actions. This is the model that underlies previous works on reductions in deductive verification, in particular those based on Lipton's reduction [21]. We show that under this model, any natural reduction can be checked in *polynomial time* for soundness (Theorem 4.14). Our argument is constructive. We present an algorithm that checks soundness of a reduction proposed by atomic blocks in polynomial time. We also present an algorithm that checks soundness of a synchronous reduction in polynomial time. We then argue how the algorithms compose, and hence, a natural reduction with several atomic blocks and a rendezvous point can be checked for soundness in polynomial time.

Second, we consider a model in which the original program uses locks for synchronization, and the abstraction level at which the semantics of locking is visible and respected. This adds a layer of complication to the problem because one has to argue that every behaviour of the original program, *that respects the locking semantics*, has an equivalent up-to-commutativity behaviour in the specified natural reduction. We show that checking the soundness of a natural reduction in this setup is coNP-hard, no matter how much we limit the use of constructs. In other words, it is coNP-hard even if a natural reduction is specified using a single atomic block, and it is coNP-hard even if it is specified only using a rendezvous point. Consequently, while fully respecting the locking semantics is theoretically more precise, it is typically too costly for practical application in deductive proof systems.

[1] In the non-symmetric case, the equivalence relation degenerates to a preorder.

Example. Consider the parameterized program where each thread executes the code shown in Fig. 2 (ignoring the instrumentation in purple). At the most abstract level (where all program data is abstracted away), this program is represented by the thread template shown in Fig. 1a. The statements have been replaced by action names a, b, c, d, e, f without semantic information. The commutativity relation is the only semantic information. For the specific actions a, b, c, d, e, f given in Fig. 2, we have the commutativity relation $I = \{a, b, c, d, e, f\}^2 \setminus \{(b, c), (c, b), (c, c), (d, a), (e, f)\}$. The instrumentation in Fig. 2 is a syntactic representation of the natural reduction in Fig. 1b. However, this natural reduction is *unsound* in the fully abstract model; in particular, *abcd* cannot be atomic. Consider the case that thread 1 executes b, then thread 2 executes c, and finally thread 1 executes c. As $(b, c) \notin I$ and $(c, c) \notin I$, this behaviour has no representative in the reduction (where *abcd* executes atomically).

```
atomic {
   acq(m)                          // a
   idx  :=  ctr                    // b
   ctr  :=  idx  +  1              // c
   rel(m)                          // d
}
sync()                             // •
   arr[idx]  :=  42                // e
sync()                             // •
   assume  idx  ==  0  ||
              arr[idx-1]  ==  42   // f
```

Fig. 2. Concrete source code for threads (`idx` is local; `ctr`, the array `arr` and the lock `m` are shared). The instrumentation in purple specifies a natural reduction.

However, if we consider the program at an abstraction level that respects locks, represented by the thread template in Fig. 3, it becomes clear that the described behaviour is not possible, as both threads would have to hold the lock `m`. In this model, the specified reduction is sound. Finally, note that the introduction of the two global rendezvous points is sound in either model.

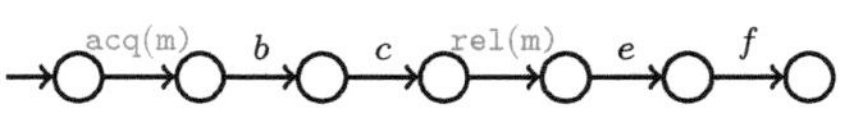

Fig. 3. Thread template model at abstraction level that respects lock synchronization.

Roadmap. Section 2 introduces our formalism for parameterized concurrent programs and (general) reductions. We define *natural* reductions in Sect. 3. Section 4 contains the key results of the paper on deciding soundness of atomic blocks (Sect. 4.1), global rendezvous points (Sect. 4.2) and their combination (Sect. 4.3). We contrast our approach with the classical technique of *Lipton reductions* in Sect. 5. Then, Sect. 6 studies the soundness problem for programs with lock synchronization. We give an overview of related work in Sect. 7 and conclude in Sect. 8.

An extended version of our paper, including proofs, is available online [8].

2 Parameterized Programs and Reductions

We use finite sequences to represent behaviours (*interleavings*) of concurrent programs. X^* denotes the set of all finite sequences σ over elements in a given set X (the free monoid generated by X). $\wp(X)$ is the powerset of X. We call a function $\mu : X \to \wp(Y^*)$ a *morphism* and extend it to a function $\mu : X^* \to \wp(Y^*)$ (with $\mu(\varepsilon) = \{\varepsilon\}$, $\mu(x\sigma) = \mu(x)\mu(\sigma)$ for $x \in X, \sigma \in X^*$) and further to a function $\mu : \wp(X^*) \to \wp(Y^*)$ (with $\mu(L) = \bigcup_{\sigma \in L} \mu(\sigma)$). By $\tau|_Z$, we denote the projection of τ to Z (the morphism with $z|_Z = \{z\}$ for $z \in X \cap Z$ and $x|_Z = \{\varepsilon\}$ for $x \in X \setminus Z$). The expression $|\sigma|$ denotes the length of σ, and $|\sigma|_x$ is the number of occurrences of x in σ. Square brackets $[x, y, z]$ denote multisets.

2.1 Parameterized Programs

A *parameterized program* is a concurrent program, where, at runtime, n threads all execute the same thread template (the number n is the *parameter*). For the purpose of this paper, we model atomic actions in the thread template abstractly as elements $a, b, c, \ldots$ of an infinite set Act.

Given a set of actions A, we write A_{idx} for $A \times \mathbb{N}$, the set of indexed actions, where an *indexed action* $\langle a : i \rangle \in A_{\mathsf{idx}}$ represents action a being executed by the i-th thread (the thread executing an action may matter, e.g. if the action accesses thread-local variables). We represent the interleavings of actions from different threads by *indexed traces* $\tau \in A^*_{\mathsf{idx}}$, and write $\langle \tau : i \rangle$ for $\tau \in A^*$ to denote the corresponding indexed trace where all actions are executed by thread i. By $\lfloor \tau \rfloor_i$, we denote the trace of all actions a where $\langle a : i \rangle$ appears in τ (the morphism with $\lfloor \langle a : i \rangle \rfloor_i = \{a\}$ and $\lfloor \langle a : j \rangle \rfloor_i = \{\varepsilon\}$ for $j \neq i$). We lift a morphism $\mu : X \to \wp(Y^*)$ to indexed actions by defining the morphism $\widehat{\mu}$ with $\widehat{\mu}(\langle a : i \rangle) = \{ \langle \tau : i \rangle \mid \tau \in \mu(a) \}$.

Though we generally abstract away from specific actions and their semantics, we need to model the semantics of certain actions for the purpose of *synchronization* between the threads, through locks, semaphores, rendez-vous etc.

Definition 2.1. *A* synchronization alphabet $(\mathbb{S}, \mathsf{sync})$ *consists of a set* $\mathbb{S}$ *of synchronization actions (disjoint from* Act*) and a predicate* sync *over traces in* $(\mathsf{Act} \cup \mathbb{S})^*_{\mathsf{idx}}$*, where* sync *is preserved by all permutations of thread indices.*

In particular, the *lock synchronization alphabet* over the infinite set M of lock variables is given by $\mathbb{S}_{\mathsf{lock}} = \{ \mathtt{acq}(m), \mathtt{rel}(m) \mid m \in M \}$ and the predicate $\mathsf{sync}_{\mathsf{lock}}$ such that for all $\tau \in (\mathsf{Act} \cup \mathbb{S}_{\mathsf{lock}})^*_{\mathsf{idx}}$, we have $\mathsf{sync}_{\mathsf{lock}}(\tau)$ if and only if

$$\forall m \in M \,.\, \tau|_{\{\mathtt{acq}(m), \mathtt{rel}(m)\}_{\mathtt{idx}}} \in \{\langle \mathtt{acq}(m)\mathtt{rel}(m) : i \rangle \mid i \in \mathbb{N}\}^* \cdot (\{\varepsilon\} \cup \{\langle \mathtt{acq}(m) : i \rangle \mid i \in \mathbb{N}\}) \quad (2.1)$$

The *trivial synchronization alphabet* is $(\emptyset, \mathsf{sync}_\top)$ where $\mathsf{sync}_\top(\tau)$ holds for all τ.

The thread template of a parameterized program is a control flow graph.

Definition 2.2. *Given a synchronization alphabet* $(\mathbb{S}, \mathsf{sync})$*, a* control flow graph $G = (\mathbb{L}, \Delta, \ell_{\mathsf{init}}, \ell_{\mathsf{exit}})$ *consists of a finite set of locations* $\mathbb{L}$*, a finite transition relation* $\Delta \subseteq \mathbb{L} \times (\mathsf{Act} \cup \mathbb{S}) \times \mathbb{L}$*, an initial location* $\ell_{\mathsf{init}} \in \mathbb{L}$ *and an exit location* $\ell_{\mathsf{exit}} \in \mathbb{L}$*, with* $\ell_{\mathsf{init}} \neq \ell_{\mathsf{exit}}$.

We assume that every location is reachable from ℓ_{init}, and ℓ_{exit} is reachable from every location. Furthermore, for each $a \in \mathsf{Act}$, there exists at most one edge in Δ labeled by a (this assumption is only for notational convenience). We denote the set of actions occurring in G by $\Sigma(G)$ (i.e., $\Sigma(G) \subseteq \mathsf{Act} \cup \mathbb{S}$). We write $\ell \xrightarrow{\tau}_{\Delta} \ell'$ for $\ell, \ell' \in \mathbb{L}$ and $\tau \in \Sigma(G)^*$ if there is a path from ℓ to ℓ' labeled by τ. $\mathcal{T}(G)$ is the language of all traces $\tau \in \Sigma(G)^*$ such that $\ell_{\mathsf{init}} \xrightarrow{\tau}_{\Delta} \ell_{\mathsf{exit}}$ holds.

Definition 2.3. *A* parameterized program $P = ((\mathbb{S}, \mathsf{sync}), G)$ *consists of a synchronization alphabet* $(\mathbb{S}, \mathsf{sync})$ *and a control flow graph G (the* thread template*).*

The interleavings of a program $P = ((\mathbb{S}, \mathsf{sync}), G)$ are given by

$$\begin{aligned}\mathcal{L}(P) = \{\tau \in \mathsf{Act}_{\mathsf{idx}}^* \mid \exists \hat{\tau} \in (\mathsf{Act} \cup \mathbb{S})_{\mathsf{idx}}^* \,.\, \tau = \hat{\tau}|_{\mathsf{Act}_{\mathsf{idx}}} \text{ and } \mathsf{sync}(\hat{\tau}) \\ \text{and } \forall i \in \mathbb{N} \,.\, \lfloor \hat{\tau} \rfloor_i \in \mathcal{T}(G) \cup \{\varepsilon\}\}\end{aligned} \quad (2.2)$$

Every interleaving τ corresponds to a trace $\hat{\tau} \in (\mathsf{Act} \cup \mathbb{S})_{\mathsf{idx}}^*$ which follows the synchronization discipline (e.g., no two threads hold the same lock at the same time), and in which every thread follows a path from the initial to the exit location (or does not run at all). In the interleaving τ itself, the synchronization actions are dropped; their only purpose is to enforce the synchronization discipline. As every thread must reach the exit location, this language of interleavings is suitable for the verification of *postconditions*.

2.2 Reductions

The central idea behind *commutativity* and *Mazurkiewicz equivalence* [23] is that certain actions (of different threads) in an interleaving can be swapped without changing its behaviour. This idea generalizes to *semi-commutativity* [4], in which some pairs of actions can be swapped in one direction (yielding a superset of behaviours) but not vice versa. As a result, Mazurkiewicz equivalence degenerates to a preorder (the relation is not necessarily symmetric).

For a program $P = ((\mathbb{S}, \mathsf{sync}), G)$, we presume a given (semi-)commutativity relation $I \subseteq (\Sigma(G) \cap \mathsf{Act})^2$, not necessarily symmetric, which defines the actions that may be swapped if performed by different threads (actions from the same thread can never be reordered). Formally, the *covering preorder* $\sqsubseteq_I$ is the smallest reflexive-transitive relation over $\mathsf{Act}_{\mathsf{idx}}^*$ with $\rho \langle a : i \rangle \langle b : j \rangle \sigma \sqsubseteq_I \rho \langle b : j \rangle \langle a : i \rangle \sigma$ for all $\rho, \sigma \in \mathsf{Act}_{\mathsf{idx}}^*$, $(a, b) \in I$ and $i \neq j \in \mathbb{N}$.

Definition 2.4. *Given* $L_1, L_2 \subseteq \mathsf{Act}_{\mathsf{idx}}^*$*,* L_1 *is a* Mazurkiewicz reduction *of* L_2 *if* $L_1 \subseteq L_2$ *holds, and for all* $\tau \in L_2$*, there exists some* $\tau' \in L_1$ *with* $\tau \sqsubseteq_I \tau'$.

Note that I is a relation over actions in Act only; we do not consider commutativity of synchronization actions in $\mathbb{S}$. The reason is that I is an abstraction of the concrete semantics of actions (which we do not model). In particular, it can be thought of as the information which actions can be swapped without affecting the semantics. By contrast, we explicitly model the semantics of synchronization actions with the predicate sync, and only consider interleavings that obey the semantics. Hence, there is no need to abstract this semantics with I.

3 Natural Reductions

This section formally defines our notion of *natural reductions* based on the syntactic introduction of *atomic blocks* and *global rendez-vous points* in a thread template. The definitions here describe the permissible syntactic changes; they do not guarantee by construction that the reduced program soundly represents the original program. Rather, our definitions specify permissible inputs for the problem of *deciding* the soundness. We discuss the corresponding decision problems (as well as concrete algorithms) in the subsequent sections.

In the following, and for the remainder of the paper, we fix a parameterized program $P = ((\mathbb{S}, \mathsf{sync}), G)$ and a commutativity relation $I \subseteq (\Sigma(G) \cap \mathsf{Act})^2$.

3.1 Atomic Blocks

The following definition captures the syntactic introduction of an atomic block in our control flow graph-based formalism:

Definition 3.1. *An* atomic fusion $\mathcal{F} = (G', (\beta_1, G_{\beta_1}), \ldots, (\beta_n, G_{\beta_n}))$ *for* P *consists of a control flow graph* G'*, distinct actions* $\beta_1, \ldots, \beta_n \in \Sigma(G')$*, and control flow graphs* $G_{\beta_1}, \ldots, G_{\beta_n}$*, where for all* $k = 1, \ldots, n$*, we have*

- $\Sigma(G_{\beta_k}) \subseteq \mathsf{Act} \setminus \{\beta_1, \ldots, \beta_n\}$*, i.e.,* G_{β_k} *contains neither synchronization actions nor any* $\beta_{k'}$*,*
- $\mathcal{T}(G_{\beta_k}) \neq \emptyset$*, i.e.,* G_{β_k} *has at least one path from the initial to the exit location,*
- $G = G'[\beta_1 \mapsto G_{\beta_1}, \ldots, \beta_n \mapsto G_{\beta_n}]$*, i.e.,* G *can be derived from* G' *by inserting each* G_{β_k} *in place of the (unique) edge labeled by the respective* β_k*.*

In the definition above, G' is a new thread template. Each *block symbol* β_k represents an (atomic) execution of an atomic block, whereas G_{β_k} describes the possible paths through the body of the atomic block. There may be multiple paths through an atomic block, due to branching and loops.

Proposition 3.2. *Let* $\mathcal{F} = (G', (\beta_1, G_{\beta_1}), ..., (\beta_n, G_{\beta_n}))$ *be an atomic fusion for* P*, and* $\mu_{\mathcal{F}} : \mathsf{Act} \cup \mathbb{S} \to \wp((\mathsf{Act} \cup \mathbb{S})^*)$ *the morphism with* $\mu_{\mathcal{F}}(\beta_k) = \mathcal{T}(G_{\beta_k})$ *for all* k*, and* $\mu_{\mathcal{F}}(a) = \{a\}$ *for all other* $a \in \mathsf{Act} \cup \mathbb{S}$*. It holds that* $\mathcal{T}(G) = \mu_{\mathcal{F}}(\mathcal{T}(G'))$*.*

We call $\mu_{\mathcal{F}}$ the *fusion morphism* and make use of it throughout the paper.

An atomic fusion induces a new program $P \lhd_{\mathsf{at}} \mathcal{F} := ((\mathbb{S}, \mathsf{sync}), G')$. The interleavings of $P \lhd_{\mathsf{at}} \mathcal{F}$ correspond to interleavings of P where the atomic block is executed without interruption by other threads (the precise path through the atomic block is abstracted by a block symbol β_k). Hence, $\widehat{\mu_{\mathcal{F}}}(\mathcal{L}(P \lhd_{\mathsf{at}} \mathcal{F}))$ always contains a subset of the interleavings in $\mathcal{L}(P)$. However, it is not a priori clear that this subset of interleavings is representative, i.e., forms a sound reduction.

Definition 3.3. *An atomic fusion $\mathcal{F}$ of P is* sound *(wrt. I) if $\widehat{\mu_{\mathcal{F}}}(\mathcal{L}(P \lhd_{\mathsf{at}} \mathcal{F}))$ is a Mazurkiewicz reduction (up to I) of $\mathcal{L}(P)$.*

Section 4.1 discusses the problem of *deciding* if an atomic fusion is sound.

3.2 Synchronous Reductions

To support synchronous reductions, that for instance align multiple *rounds* performed by threads, we introduce a notion of *global rendezvous points*, or *sync-points* for short. When a thread encounters a sync-point, it waits until all other threads also reached a sync-point. Only then, all threads can pass the sync-point together; afterwards, each thread continues with its respective computation. The only exception is that a thread that has already reached its exit location need not participate in sync-points (the still-running threads can pass their sync-points without it).

We formalize sync-points as a synchronization alphabet $(\mathbb{S}_\bullet, \mathsf{sync}_\bullet)$, with a unique *sync-point symbol* $\bullet$ (i.e., $\mathbb{S}_\bullet = \{\bullet\}$). To define the synchronization predicate, given a finite set $T = \{t_1, \ldots, t_n\} \subseteq \mathbb{N}$, we let $\langle \bullet : T \rangle$ denote the sequence $\langle \bullet : t_1 \rangle \ldots \langle \bullet : t_n \rangle$. We then define inductively, for all finite sets $T \subseteq \mathbb{N}$:

$$\mathsf{sync}_{\bullet,T}(\tau) \iff \tau = \tau_1\tau_2 \wedge \tau_1 \in ((\mathsf{Act} \times T)^* + \langle \bullet : T \rangle)^* \wedge \exists T' \subsetneq T \,.\, (\mathsf{sync}_{\bullet,T'}(\tau_2) \vee \tau_2 = \varepsilon) \tag{3.1}$$

$$\mathsf{sync}_\bullet(\tau) \iff \exists T \subseteq_{\text{fin}} \mathbb{N} \,.\, \mathsf{sync}_{\bullet,T}(\tau) \tag{3.2}$$

The definition of $\mathsf{sync}_\bullet$ states that whenever some set of threads T are running, they can only pass a sync-point $\bullet$ together (as in the sequence $\langle \bullet : T \rangle$). At any point, some threads may terminate (i.e., not perform any further actions); from thereon only the remaining threads T' need to synchronize on sync-points.

As sync-points may be added to programs that already use other synchronization actions, we note that synchronization alphabets $(\mathbb{S}_1, \mathsf{sync}_1), (\mathbb{S}_2, \mathsf{sync}_2)$, with $\mathbb{S}_1 \cap \mathbb{S}_2 = \emptyset$, combine to a synchronization alphabet $(\mathbb{S}_1, \mathsf{sync}_1) \oplus (\mathbb{S}_2, \mathsf{sync}_2) := (\mathbb{S}_1 \cup \mathbb{S}_2, \mathsf{sync}_{12})$, where $\mathsf{sync}_{12}(\tau)$ holds if and only if $\mathsf{sync}_1(\tau|_{(\mathsf{Act} \cup \mathbb{S}_1)_{\mathsf{idx}}})$ and $\mathsf{sync}_2(\tau|_{(\mathsf{Act} \cup \mathbb{S}_2)_{\mathsf{idx}}})$ hold. We define sync-point instrumentation as follows:

Definition 3.4. *A* sync-point instrumentation *of P is a control flow graph G' over $\mathsf{Act} \cup \mathbb{S} \cup \mathbb{S}_\bullet$ with $\mathcal{T}(G) = \mathcal{T}(G')|_{\mathsf{Act} \cup \mathbb{S}}$, and for all $\tau_1, \tau_2 \in \mathcal{T}(G')$, we have that $\tau_1|_{\mathsf{Act}} = \tau_2|_{\mathsf{Act}}$ implies $\tau_1 = \tau_2$.*

A sync-point instrumentation is thus a modified thread template that inserts the sync-point symbol $\bullet$ at various locations. The injectivity condition for projection means that for every $\tau \in \mathcal{T}(G)$, there is a *unique* way to insert sync-points in it and derive a trace in $\mathcal{T}(G')$. One way to ensure this injectivity syntactically is to construct G' from $G = (\mathbb{L}, \Delta, \ell_{\mathsf{init}}, \ell_{\mathsf{exit}})$ by inserting sync-points at a set of locations $M \subseteq \mathbb{L}$. I.e., we define $G' = (\mathbb{L} \uplus \{\hat{\ell} \mid \ell \in M\}, \Delta', \ell_{\mathsf{init}}, \ell_{\mathsf{exit}})$ with

$$\Delta' = \{ (\ell, a, \ell') \in \Delta \mid \ell \notin M \} \cup \{ (\ell, \bullet, \hat{\ell}) \mid \ell \in M \} \\ \cup \{ (\hat{\ell}, a, \ell') \mid \ell \in M \wedge (\ell, a, \ell') \in \Delta \} .$$

We add a copy $\hat{\ell}$ of every location $\ell \in M$, such that ℓ retains its incoming edges, ℓ and $\hat{\ell}$ are connected by a sync-point, and all outgoing edges of ℓ are moved to $\hat{\ell}$ (i.e., after the sync-point). This syntactic sync-point insertion at locations M is sufficient to specify reductions e.g. for distributed protocols based on *rounds*, as the point where a thread advances from one round to another can be identified syntactically in the code. Moreover, sync-points can faithfully implement lockstep execution for thread templates with a single loop. However, if the template contains multiple loops, the lockstep scheduler cannot be modeled precisely with sync-points, due to the injectivity condition.

Observation 3.5. *Any G' constructed as described above is a sync-point instrumentation of P.*

A given sync-point instrumentation G' induces a new program $P \lhd_{\bullet} G' := ((\mathbb{S}_{+\bullet}, \mathsf{sync}_{+\bullet}), G')$ with the combined synchronization alphabet $(\mathbb{S}_{+\bullet}, \mathsf{sync}_{+\bullet}) := (\mathbb{S}, \mathsf{sync}) \oplus (\mathbb{S}_{\bullet}, \mathsf{sync}_{\bullet})$. The additional synchronization enforced by the sync-points yields a subset of interleavings: $\mathcal{L}(P \lhd_{\bullet} G') \subseteq \mathcal{L}(P)$.

Definition 3.6. *A sync-point instrumentation G' of P is* sound *(with respect to I) if $\mathcal{L}(P \lhd_{\bullet} G')$ is a Mazurkiewicz reduction (up to I) of $\mathcal{L}(P)$.*

Section 4.2 discusses the problem of *deciding* whether a given sync-point instrumentation is sound.

3.3 Combining Atomic Blocks and Synchronous Reductions

We combine atomic blocks and synchronous reductions in a straightforward manner in order to define the class of *natural reductions.*

Definition 3.7. *A* natural reduction specification *$(\mathcal{F}, G')$ for P consists of an atomic fusion $\mathcal{F}$ of P and a sync-point instrumentation G' of $P \lhd_{\mathsf{at}} \mathcal{F}$.*

Note that by this definition, atomic blocks may not contain sync-points. There would be no point for a thread to wait on all other threads at a sync-point, while simultaneously preventing other threads from making progress and reaching sync-points (as that would interrupt the atomic block).

The notion of soundness follows directly from soundness of atomic fusions and sync-point instrumentations:

Definition 3.8. *A natural reduction specification $(\mathcal{F}, G')$ for P is* sound *(wrt. I) if $\widehat{\mu_{\mathcal{F}}}(\mathcal{L}(P \lhd_{\mathsf{at}} \mathcal{F} \lhd_{\bullet} G'))$ is a Mazurkiewicz reduction (up to I) of $\mathcal{L}(P)$.*

4 Deciding the Soundness Problem

We first consider the problems of deciding soundness for atomic fusions and sync-point instrumentations separately, in Sect. 4.1 and Sect. 4.2, respectively. Section 4.3 then proposes a combined algorithm for deciding soundness of natural reduction specifications.

4.1 Deciding Soundness of Atomic Blocks

We turn to the problem of deciding whether a given atomic fusion is sound. The complexity of this problem, like many problems over parameterized programs, depends crucially on the mechanisms allowed for synchronization between threads [9]. In fact, we link its complexity to the *coverability problem* for configurations of arbitrary width.

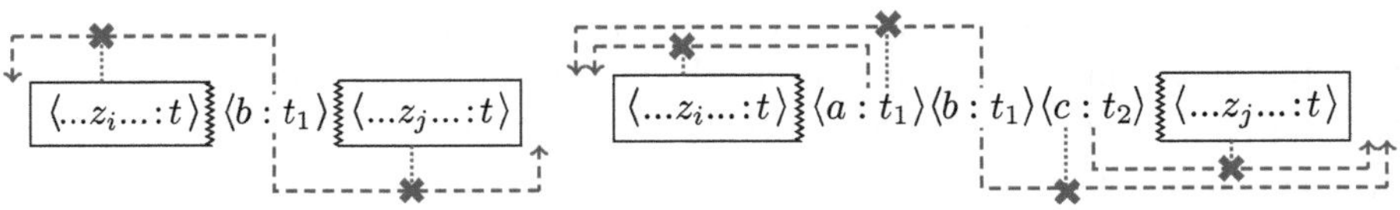

(a) $(z_i, b) \notin I, (b, z_j) \notin I$. (b) $(z_i, a) \notin I, (a, b) \in \mathsf{po}, (b, c) \notin I, (c, z_j) \notin I$

Fig. 4. Action b cannot escape to the left/right of the atomic block $z_1 \ldots z_m$.

We begin by examining the notion of a *sound* atomic fusion $\mathcal{F}$ of P more closely. In essence, it states that every interleaving of the original program P is covered by some interleaving in which the actions inside an atomic block execute without interruption by other threads. To ensure this, we must check that each action that may be interleaved inside the atomic block can be swapped either before all actions of the atomic block (it *escapes to the left*) or after all actions of the atomic block (it *escapes to the right*).[2] There can be different obstacles that prevent an action from escaping an atomic block $z_1 \ldots z_m$, thus causing the atomic fusion to be unsound. In the simplest case, illustrated in Fig. 4a, an action b does not commute to the left of some z_i nor to the right of some z_j, with $i < j$. Then, the kind of interleaving shown in Fig. 4a has no representative where $z_1 \ldots z_m$ executes atomically, and the given atomic fusion is unsound.

However, the problem can be more complex. For instance, in Fig. 4b, b commutes to the left of all $z_1, \ldots, z_m$, but a previous action a of the same thread does not commute with z_i. As we cannot swap $\langle b : t_1\rangle$ with $\langle a : t_1\rangle$, in this scenario, $\langle b : t_1\rangle$ cannot escape to the left. On the other hand, $\langle b : t_1\rangle$ cannot escape to the right either, due to the presence of an action $\langle c : t_2\rangle$ such that

[2] This is a shift from the classical perspective [21], which reasons about *moving* the actions *of the atomic block*. We discuss limitations of that perspective in Sect. 5.

$(b, c) \notin I$. In order for $\langle b : t_1 \rangle$ to escape to the right, $\langle c : t_2 \rangle$ would also have to escape *to the right*, but we have $(c, z_j) \notin I$.

As shown here, even if individual actions interleaved in an atomic block can escape, in general we have to reason about complex chains of dependencies (e.g., if $\langle a : t_1 \rangle$ can only escape to the right, then $\langle b : t_1 \rangle$ must also escape to the right, and hence the same applies to $\langle c : t_2 \rangle$). Whether such a chain of dependencies causes unsoundness however crucially depends on whether the actions $\langle a : t_1 \rangle, \langle b : t_1 \rangle, \langle c : t_2 \rangle$ can actually be interleaved inside the block in this manner, or whether synchronization prevents this. For instance, if actions b and c are protected by the same lock, the issue above could not occur (t_1 and t_2 cannot both hold the lock at the same time). The soundness of atomic fusions is thus tightly linked to the question of *coverability* under synchronization:

Definition 4.1. (Coverability). *Let $C = [\ell_1, \ldots, \ell_n]$ be a finite multiset of locations of P. The configuration C is* coverable *in P if there exist a trace $\hat{\tau} \in (\Sigma(G) \cup \mathbb{S})^*_{\mathsf{idx}}$ with $\mathsf{sync}(\hat{\tau})$, and (distinct) $t_1, \ldots, t_n \in \mathbb{N}$ with $\ell_{\mathsf{init}} \xrightarrow{\lfloor \hat{\tau} \rfloor_{t_i}}_{\Delta} \ell_i$.*

Theorem 4.2. *For every synchronization alphabet, the coverability problem over programs with this synchronization alphabet is polynomial-time reducible to the problem of deciding whether a given atomic fusion of a given program is unsound wrt. a given commutativity relation.*

Proof (sketch). Given configuration $C = [\ell_1, \ldots, \ell_n]$, we let n fresh actions $a_1, \ldots, a_n$ form a dependency chain with actions b_1, b_2 belonging to an atomic block (i.e., $(b_1, a_1) \notin I$, $(a_i, a_{i+1}) \notin I$, $(a_n, b_2) \notin I$); all other actions commute. We insert the actions a_i at the corresponding locations ℓ_i, and add the atomic block $b_1 b_2$ as a branch from the initial to the exit location. The atomic fusion is unsound if and only if a trace containing $\langle b_1 : i_0 \rangle \langle a_1 : i_1 \rangle \ldots \langle a_n : i_n \rangle \langle b_2 : i_0 \rangle$ is allowed by sync, which holds if and only if C is coverable.

In particular, the width of the configurations in the coverability problem corresponds to the size of simple cycles in the complement of I.

As a corollary of Theorem 4.2, deciding soundness of atomic fusions for programs with powerful synchronization mechanisms such as *broadcast* has non-elementary complexity [9]. Even for programs with simpler synchronization mechanisms, such as boolean variables, the problem is coNP-hard. This motivates us to consider an abstract view of the program, which ignores the semantics of such synchronization actions, and treats them like any other ordinary actions. This yields an over-approximation of the program, which contains some interleavings that would be ruled out by the synchronization mechanism. Reasoning on this abstract view of the program allows us to *certify* the soundness of atomic fusions (and later, of natural reductions generally): any atomic fusion that is sound wrt. the abstract view is also sound wrt. a more concrete view. A determination that an atomic fusion is *unsound* does not transfer to the concrete level: the perceived unsoundness may be an artifact of the abstraction. Yet, the abstract view provides for an efficient and predictable decision procedure.

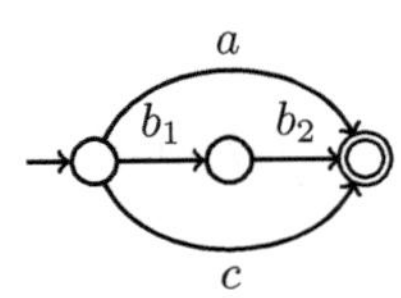

(a) Example of a thread template. The actions b_1b_2 should be fused into an atomic block.

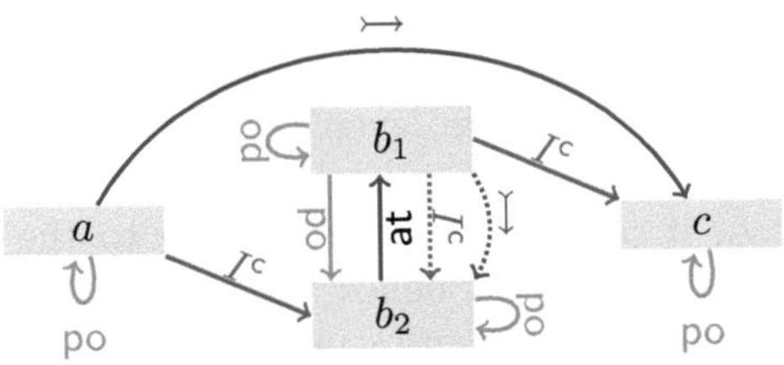

(b) Relations between the actions. Solid lines for $I_1 = \{a, b_1, b_2, c\}^2 \setminus \{(a, b_2), (b_1, c)\}$; solid and dotted lines for $I_2 = I_1 \setminus \{(b_1, b_2)\}$.

Fig. 5. Illustration of Proposition 4.3 and relevant relations between actions.

Consequently, we assume for the remainder of this section that our program P uses the trivial synchronization alphabet $(\emptyset, \mathsf{sync}_\top)$. Furthermore, let $\mathcal{F} = (G', (\beta_1, G_{\beta_1}), \ldots, (\beta_n, G_{\beta_n}))$ be an atomic fusion of P. We present an algorithm to decide whether the given atomic fusion $\mathcal{F}$ is sound wrt. I.

The algorithm is based on detecting the different kinds of "obstacles" that might prevent an action interleaved inside an atomic block from escaping, as discussed above (and illustrated in Fig. 4). For $a, b \in \Sigma(G)$, we write $(a, b) \in \mathsf{po}$ (*program order*) if there exists a trace of the form $\rho\iota\sigma \in \mathcal{T}(G)$, where ι begins with a and ends with b (possibly $a = \iota = b$). $I^c := \Sigma(G)^2 \setminus I$ denotes the complement of I. We write $(a, b) \in \mathsf{at}$ if there exists $\rho b\iota a\sigma \in \mathcal{T}(G_{\beta_k})$, for some β_k (the reverse program order within atomic sections). We define $\rightarrowtail$ as the relation $I^c \circ \big((\mathsf{po} \cup \mathsf{at}) \circ I^c\big)^+$, where $\circ$ denotes relational composition. The following result formalizes the idea that soundness of $\mathcal{F}$ corresponds to the non-existence of the kind of dependence chains $\langle z_i : t\rangle, \langle a : t_1\rangle, \langle b : t_1\rangle, \langle c : t_2\rangle, \langle z_j : t\rangle$ as in the example of Fig. 4b.

Proposition 4.3. *The atomic fusion $\mathcal{F}$ is sound if and only if there do not exist $z_1 \ldots z_m \in \mathcal{T}(G_{\beta_k})$ (for some k) and $i < j \in \{1, \ldots, m\}$ such that $z_i \rightarrowtail z_j$ holds.*

Proof (sketch). If $z_i \rightarrowtail z_j$ holds, we construct an interleaving in which $z_1 \ldots z_m$ cannot be made atomic, except possibly by breaking apart another atomic block. Conversely, under the assumption that no $z_1 \ldots z_m$ with $z_i \rightarrowtail z_j$ exists, we show that every interleaving can be transformed into one where all atomic blocks are represented by their respective block symbol β_k.

Example 4.4. Consider the thread template in Fig. 5a, and the atomic fusion that combines b_1b_2 into an atomic block. By Proposition 4.3, this atomic fusion is sound if and only if $b_1 \not\rightarrowtail b_2$ holds. As illustrated in Fig. 5b, this is the case for $I_1 = \{a, b_1, b_2, c\} \setminus \{(a, b_2), (b_1, c)\}$.

However, if b_1 and b_2 do not commute, as for $I_2 = I_1 \setminus \{(b_1, b_2)\}$, we have $(b_1, b_2) \notin I_2$, $(b_2, b_1) \in \mathsf{at}$, and $(b_1, b_2) \notin I_2$. Hence, it holds that $b_1 \rightarrowtail b_2$. The proof of Proposition 4.3 constructs the interleaving $\langle b_1 : 1\rangle\langle b_1 : 2\rangle\langle b_2 : 2\rangle\langle b_2 : 1\rangle$.

This interleaving cannot be transformed (through commutations allowed by I_2) into an interleaving where both thread 1 and thread 2 execute $b_1 b_2$ atomically.

Using Proposition 4.3, the following algorithm decides soundness of $\mathcal{F}$. As the bodies G_{β_k} of atomic blocks may contain complex control flow including loops, we cannot simply enumerate all possible $z_1 \dots z_m \in \mathcal{T}(G_{\beta_k})$. Hence, the algorithm reasons on the level of strongly connected components (SCCs) of G_{β_k}.

Algorithm 4.5. *Execute the following steps:*

(1) Compute the graph $(\Sigma(G), \rightarrowtail)$*. Perform the subsequent steps for each* β_k*.*
(2) Compute the SCCs of the edges of G_{β_k}*, along with the reachability relation* $\preceq$ *between SCCs (a partial order).*
(3) Compute $\min(a)$ *for each* $a \in \Sigma(G)$*, the set of* $\preceq$*-minimal SCCs of* G_{β_k} *containing some edge labeled by an action* $b \in \Sigma(G_{\beta_k})$ *with* $(b, a) \notin I$*.*
(4) Compute $\max(a)$ *for each* $a \in \Sigma(G)$*, the set of* $\preceq$*-maximal SCCs of* G_{β_k} *containing some edge labeled by an action* $b \in \Sigma(G_{\beta_k})$ *with* $(a, b) \notin I$*.*
(5) Check if there exist SCCs S_1, S_2 *of* G_{β_k} *such that*

- $S_1 \preceq S_2$*, and if* $S_1 = S_2$ *then* S_1 *is a non-trivial SCC*[3]*, and*
- *the graph* $(\Sigma(G), \rightarrowtail)$ *has an edge from some* a *to some* b *with* $S_1 \in \min(a)$ *and* $S_2 \in \max(b)$*.*

If such S_1, S_2 *exist (for some* β_k*), then* $\mathcal{F}$ *is unsound. Otherwise,* $\mathcal{F}$ *is sound.*

Theorem 4.6. *Algorithm 4.5 decides soundness of atomic fusions, and terminates in polynomial time.*

4.2 Deciding Soundness of Synchronous Reductions

Next, we consider the soundness problem for synchronous reductions. Hence, let $P = ((\emptyset, \mathsf{sync}_\top), G)$ once again be a program over the trivial synchronization alphabet, and let G' be a sync-point instrumentation of P. We are interested in deciding whether G' is sound, i.e., whether $\mathcal{L}(P \lhd_\bullet G')$ is a Mazurkiewicz reduction of $\mathcal{L}(P)$, up to the commutativity relation I. Recall that $\mathcal{L}(P \lhd_\bullet G')$ is given by

$$\mathcal{L}(P \lhd_\bullet G') = \{\tau \in \mathsf{Act}^*_{\mathsf{idx}} \mid \exists \hat{\tau} \in (\mathsf{Act} \cup \mathbb{S}_\bullet)^*_{\mathsf{idx}} \,.\, \tau = \hat{\tau}|_{\mathsf{Act}_{\mathsf{idx}}} \text{ and } \mathsf{sync}_\bullet(\hat{\tau}) \text{ and } \forall i \in \mathbb{N} \,.\, \lfloor \hat{\tau} \rfloor_i \in \mathcal{T}(G') \cup \{\varepsilon\}\} \tag{4.1}$$

By the definition of $\mathsf{sync}_\bullet$ (Eq. (3.1)), the underlying traces $\hat{\tau}$ with $\mathsf{sync}_\bullet(\hat{\tau})$ can be split into "phases" consisting of actions from Act, separated by occurrences of sequences $\langle \bullet : t_1 \rangle \dots \langle \bullet : t_n \rangle$, where $t_1, \dots, t_n$ are the threads that are still

[3] A non-trivial SCC must either contain at least two elements, or its single element must have a self-loop.

running. In order for the sync-point reduction to be sound, it must be possible to bring every interleaving of the original program P into such a "phase form" by swapping commuting actions and then inserting occurrences of $\langle \bullet : t_1 \rangle \dots \langle \bullet : t_n \rangle$ in the right places. Based on this idea, we define a "phase order" on actions:

Definition 4.7. *The* phase order *is the relation* $\mathsf{pho} \subseteq \Sigma(G)^2$,*with* $(a, b) \in \mathsf{pho}$ *if there exists a trace* $\hat{\tau} \in (\mathsf{Act} \cup \mathbb{S}_\bullet)^*_{\mathsf{idx}}$ *with* $\mathsf{sync}_\bullet(\hat{\tau})$ *and* $\hat{\tau}|_{\mathsf{Act}_{\mathsf{idx}}} \in \mathcal{L}(P \lhd_\bullet G')$ *such that for some* $i \neq j$*, we have* $\lfloor \hat{\tau} \rfloor_i = \tau_1 a \sigma_1$*,* $\lfloor \hat{\tau} \rfloor_j = \tau_2 b \sigma_2$*, and* $|\tau_1|_\bullet < |\tau_2|_\bullet$.

Intuitively, the phase order captures that a can occur in a strictly later phase than b, in some execution of the instrumented program. As we are considering programs without synchronization (other than the newly-introduced sync-point $\bullet$), we can break this condition down further:

Observation 4.8. *We have* $(a, b) \in \mathsf{pho}$ *if and only if there exist two traces* $\rho_1 a \sigma_1, \rho_2 b \sigma_2 \in \mathcal{T}(G')$ *with* $|\rho_1|_\bullet < |\rho_2|_\bullet$.

Given pho, it is straightforward to decide soundness of the reduction:

Proposition 4.9. *The sync-point instrumentation* G' *is sound if and only if* $\mathsf{pho} \subseteq I^{-1}$ *holds.*

Proof (sketch). If there exists a pair $(a, b) \in \mathsf{pho} \setminus I^{-1}$, we construct an interleaving (containing a and b), and use the injectivity condition in Definition 3.4 to show that no representative for this interleaving exists in $\mathcal{L}(P \lhd_{\mathsf{at}} G)$.

Conversely, if $\mathsf{pho} \subseteq I^{-1}$ holds, we show that every $\tau \in \mathcal{L}(P)$ does have a representative in $\mathcal{L}(P \lhd_{\mathsf{at}} G)$.

The fact that the above proof uses the injectivity condition of Definition 3.4 only for one direction of the equivalence implies that even for an extended class of sync-point instrumentations that do not satisfy injectivity, $\mathsf{pho} \subseteq I^{-1}$ implies soundness of the instrumentation. Our approach thus remains sound in this extended class, though not complete.

To check soundness of a sync-point instrumentation, the only remaining difficulty is to compute pho. In a program model without synchronization, this is possible in polynomial time, using the following approach:

Algorithm 4.10. *We compute* pho *as follows:*

(1) Compute $\min_\bullet(a) := \min\{\, |\tau|_\bullet \mid \exists \sigma \,.\, \tau a \sigma \in \mathcal{T}(G') \,\}$ *for each action* a*, by a shortest-path computation on* G'*, where the initial location of* G' *is the source, locations enabling* a *are the targets, and the weight of an edge is 1 if labeled by* $\bullet$ *and 0 otherwise.*

(2) Compute $\max_\bullet(a) := \max\{\, |\tau|_\bullet \mid \exists \sigma \,.\, \tau a \sigma \in \mathcal{T}(G') \,\} \in \mathbb{N} \cup \{\infty\}$ *for each action* a*.*
To do so, consider all loop-free paths from the initial location to a location enabling a*. Determine if any such path can be pumped with a loop that contains* $\bullet$ *(the loop may also include* a *itself). If so, then* $\max_\bullet(a)$ *is* ∞*. Otherwise,* $\max_\bullet(a)$ *is the maximum weight of the loop-free paths, where the weight of an edge is 1 if labeled by* $\bullet$ *and 0 otherwise.*

(3) Check for all pairs (a, b) *whether* $\min_\bullet(a) < \max_\bullet(b)$. *If so, then* $(a, b) \in \mathsf{pho}$ *holds. Otherwise, we have* $(a, b) \notin \mathsf{pho}$.

Theorem 4.11. *Soundness of sync-point instrumentations (in programs with the trivial synchronization alphabet) can be decided in polynomial time.*

4.3 Deciding Soundness of Natural Reductions

Let P be a program, and $(\mathcal{F}, G')$ be a natural reduction specification for P. When deciding whether $(\mathcal{F}, G')$ is sound, it is of course desirable to make use of the algorithms introduced in the previous subsections. And indeed, the following observation gives us some hope that soundness checking of complicated reductions can be decomposed into smaller steps.

Proposition 4.12. *Let* $L_1, L_2, L_3 \subseteq \mathsf{Act}_{\mathsf{idx}}^*$ *such that* $L_1 \subseteq L_2 \subseteq L_3$. *Then* L_1 *is a Mazurkiewicz reduction of* L_3 *if and only if* L_1 *is a Mazurkiewicz reduction of* L_2, *and* L_2 *is a Mazurkiewicz reduction of* L_3.

Recall that $(\mathcal{F}, G')$ is sound (wrt. I) if $\widehat{\mu_\mathcal{F}}(\mathcal{L}(P \lhd_{\mathsf{at}} \mathcal{F} \lhd_\bullet G'))$ is a Mazurkiewicz reduction (up to I) of $\mathcal{L}(P)$. As an instantiation of the above result, we get that $(\mathcal{F}, G')$ is sound if and only if

(1) $\widehat{\mu_\mathcal{F}}(\mathcal{L}(P \lhd_{\mathsf{at}} \mathcal{F} \lhd_\bullet G'))$ is a Mazurkiewicz reduction up to I of $\widehat{\mu_\mathcal{F}}(\mathcal{L}(P \lhd_{\mathsf{at}} \mathcal{F}))$,
(2) and $\widehat{\mu_\mathcal{F}}(\mathcal{L}(P \lhd_{\mathsf{at}} \mathcal{F}))$ is a Mazurkiewicz reduction up to I of $\mathcal{L}(P)$.

Condition (2) directly corresponds to soundness of the atomic fusion $\mathcal{F}$, and can therefore be decided using Algorithm 4.5. The situation is more complex for condition (1), as (due to the presence of $\widehat{\mu_\mathcal{F}}$) it does not correspond directly to soundness of G'. Conceptually, it is not even immediately clear what soundness of G' would mean: $\mathcal{L}(P \lhd_{\mathsf{at}} \mathcal{F})$ and $\mathcal{L}(P \lhd_{\mathsf{at}} \mathcal{F} \lhd_\bullet G')$ are not languages over $\Sigma(G)$; they contain the block symbols introduced by $\mathcal{F}$ (in addition to a subset of actions from $\Sigma(G)$). However, we can define the following commutativity relation, where $\mathcal{F} = (G'', (\beta_1, G_{\beta_1}), \ldots, (\beta_n, G_{\beta_n}))$, and a, b range over $\Sigma(G)$:

$$
\begin{aligned}
\tilde{I} := {} & I \cap \Sigma(G')^2 \\
& \cup \{ (a, \beta_k) \mid \forall b \in \Sigma(G_{\beta_k}) \,.\, (a, b) \in I \} \\
& \cup \{ (\beta_k, b) \mid \forall a \in \Sigma(G_{\beta_k}) \,.\, (a, b) \in I \} \\
& \cup \{ (\beta_{k_1}, \beta_{k_2}) \mid \forall a \in \Sigma(G_{\beta_{k_1}}) \; \forall b \in \Sigma(G_{\beta_{k_2}}) \,.\, (a, b) \in I \}
\end{aligned}
$$

For this commutativity relation, we show:

Lemma 4.13. *Condition (1) holds if and only if* $\mathcal{L}(P \lhd_{\mathsf{at}} \mathcal{F} \lhd_\bullet G')$ *is a Mazurkiewicz reduction up to* $\tilde{I}$ *of* $\mathcal{L}(P \lhd_{\mathsf{at}} \mathcal{F})$.

This lemma allows us to decide condition (1) using the approach from Sect. 4.2. We conclude:

Theorem 4.14. *The soundness of a natural reduction specification for a program without synchronization is decidable in polynomial time.*

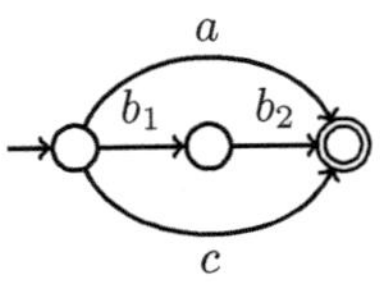

(a) The atomic fusion of $b_1 b_2$ is sound wrt. $I = \{a, b_1, b_2, c\}^2 \setminus \{(a, b_2), (b_1, c)\}$.

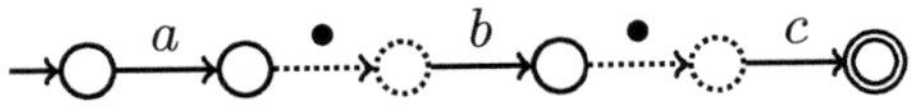

(b) The dotted sync-point instrumentation is sound wrt. $I = \{a, b, c\}^2 \setminus \{(b, b), (c, c)\}$.

Fig. 6. Examples for incompleteness of mover reasoning.

Observe that, in the case of programs with synchronization, our hardness result for atomic blocks carries over to the more general problem of soundness of natural reduction specifications.

Corollary 4.15. *For every synchronization alphabet, the coverability problem is polynomial-time reducible to the soundness of natural reduction specifications.*

Proof. Follows directly from Theorem 4.2.

5 On the Incompleteness of Mover Reasoning

There is a wealth of literature on sound reductions given by atomic blocks. This literature builds on the seminal work of Lipton [21] and the idea of *movers*. We show that, while sound, mover reasoning is incomplete (i.e., fails to admit some sound atomic fusions). Completeness requires moving from mostly local reasoning (as in Lipton's rule) to a global view (as in our algorithm). A similar observation also holds for sync-points.

We begin by introducing movers and Lipton's rule for atomic blocks, reformulated in our formal setting. As before, we assume a program $P = ((\emptyset, \mathsf{sync}_\top), G)$ and a commutativity relation $I \subseteq \Sigma(G)^2$.

Definition 5.1. ([21]). *An action $a \in \Sigma(G)$ is:*

- *a* left-mover *if $(b, a) \in I$ for all $b \in \Sigma(G)$,*
- *a* right-mover *if $(a, b) \in I$ for all $b \in \Sigma(G)$,*
- *a* both-mover *if it is both a left-mover and a right-mover,*
- *and a* non-mover *if it is neither a left-mover nor a right-mover.*

Lipton's rule is the following result:

Proposition 5.2. ([21]). *An atomic fusion $(G', (\beta_1, G_{\beta_1}), ..., (\beta_n, G_{\beta_n}))$ is sound if every $\tau \in \mathcal{T}(G_{\beta_k})$ (for every k) can be written as $\tau = \tau_r\, a\, \tau_l$, for a sequence of right-movers τ_r, some action a and a sequence of left-movers τ_l.*

While Lipton's rule is sufficient to ensure soundness, it is not a necessary condition, as demonstrated by the following example.

Example 5.3. Consider the thread template in Fig. 6a, over $\Sigma = \{a, b_1, b_2, c\}$. Assume the given commutativity relation is $I = \Sigma^2 \setminus \{(a, b_2), (b_1, c)\}$.

Then, b_1 is a left-mover (but not a right-mover), whereas b_2 is a right-mover (but not a left-mover). Hence, Lipton's rule is not sufficient to conclude that $b_1 b_2$ can be fused in an atomic block. Yet, it *is* sound to make $b_1 b_2$ atomic. In any interleaving, all occurrences of a can be commuted to the beginning, and all occurrences of c can be commuted to the end of the interleaving. The remaining interleaved occurrences of b_1, b_2 (from different threads) commute freely against each other, and can be reordered such that each $\langle b_1 b_2 : i\rangle$ executes atomically.

Going further, if we consider $I' = I \setminus \{(b_1, b_2)\}$, the mover properties of all actions remain unchanged. Yet, the atomic fusion of $b_1 b_2$ is unsound wrt. I': the interleaving $\langle b_1 : 1\rangle\langle b_1 : 2\rangle\langle b_2 : 1\rangle\langle b_2 : 2\rangle$ has no representative in which $\langle b_1 b_2 : 1\rangle$ and $\langle b_1 b_2 : 2\rangle$ execute atomically. Hence, mover properties are generally insufficient to characterize sound atomic fusions (even beyond Lipton's rule).

By contrast, our algorithm is sound and complete; but it requires a global (rather than local) view that takes e.g. control flow into account. In particular, Example 4.4 explains how our algorithm handles the above example.

As a notable aside, in the case where I is symmetric (every left- or right-mover is a both-mover), Lipton's rule is indeed complete for parameterized programs.

Proposition 5.4. *Let I be symmetric. If $\mathcal{F} = (G', (\beta_1, G_{\beta_1}), \ldots, (\beta_n, G_{\beta_n}))$ is sound wrt. I, then all $\tau \in \mathcal{T}(G_{\beta_k})$ (for every k) can be written as $\tau = \tau_r\, a\, \tau_l$, for a sequence of both-movers τ_r, some action a, and a sequence of both-movers τ_l.*

Proof (sketch). Assuming an atomic block that is not in Lipton form, we construct an interleaving of four threads (two of which execute the atomic block), such that no representative of this interleaving executes the block atomically. The construction makes use of the fact that the program is parameterized (in the number of threads) and that there is no synchronization between threads.

We conclude this section by showing that mover reasoning is similarly unable to provide a characterization of sound sync-point instrumentations.

Example 5.5. Consider the thread template and sync-point instrumentation in Fig. 6b, over actions $\Sigma = \{a, b, c\}$. This sync-point instrumentation is sound wrt. the commutativity relation $I = \Sigma^2 \setminus \{(b, b), (c, c)\}$. However, this fact cannot be justified purely with mover properties. In this example, we have that a is a both-mover, whereas b and c are non-movers. If we consider a different commutativity relation $I' = \Sigma^2 \setminus \{(b, c), (c, b)\}$, the mover properties remain unchanged, yet the sync-point instrumentation is unsound wrt. I'.

Unlike for atomic blocks, the inability of mover properties to characterize sound sync-point instrumentations thus persists even in the case of symmetric commutativity (both I and I' in the example above are symmetric).

6 Reduction Soundness in the Presence of Locks

Ignoring all synchronization between threads is a rather coarse abstraction. One may be tempted to allow for at least some light-weight synchronization mechanisms to be considered during reduction checking. For instance, locks (mutexes) are such a light-weight mechanism, compared to more powerful synchronization via e.g. (global) boolean variables, broadcast, etc. Locks are also ubiquitously used in concurrent programs. However, we show in this section that allowing locks immediately leads to coNP-hardness for the soundness problem of natural reductions, even in the simplest cases.

Atomic Blocks. As shown in Theorem 4.2, coverability over programs with a certain synchronization alphabet is polynomial-time reducible to the *un*soundness of atomic fusions (with only a single atomic block) for the same class of programs. For the case of synchronization via locks, we show:

Theorem 6.1. *The coverability problem over programs with locks is NP-hard.*

Proof (sketch). We reduce 3-SAT to reachability in a bounded-thread program with locks, and then to coverability in a parameterized program with locks. For the latter step, we construct a thread template where each thread of the bounded-thread program is a separate branch, protected by a dedicated lock to ensure this branch can only be taken by one thread instance. For the reduction from 3-SAT, we introduce one lock m_i^l for each pair of a literal l over the propositional variables and a clause i. There is one thread for each clause i, which consists of choosing one of the literals l in the clause to satisfy, acquiring the lock m_i^l, checking that no thread for some other clause j has made a contradictory choice (i.e., $m_j^{\neg l}$ must be free), and reaching some location ℓ_i. The configuration of all ℓ_i is reachable if and only if the conjunction of all clauses is satisfiable.

Corollary 6.2. *Atomic fusion soundness in programs with locks is* coNP*-hard.*

Proof. Follows directly from Theorem 4.2 and Theorem 6.1.

The corresponding upper-bound is (to our knowledge) an open question.

Furthermore, we note that previous work [12] has shown coNP-hardness for a special case of atomic fusion soundness (*conflict serializability*) in programs with a bounded number of threads (even without synchronization). Interestingly, this previous result provides for an alternative proof of Corollary 6.2: We can reduce the soundness problem in parameterized programs to the bounded case, by using dedicated locks to limit the number of running threads. Hence, while the shift from a bounded number of threads to parameterized programs significantly simplifies the soundness problem in the absence of synchronization, lock synchronization yields back the hardness.

Synchronous Reductions. For synchronous reductions (resp. sync-point instrumentations), we have not shown a general result relating coverability (for configurations of arbitrary width) and reduction checking. In fact, the algorithm in Sect. 4.2 at first suggests that only pairwise checks are needed (for the computation of the phase-order). Yet, the difficulty lies in the fact that sync-points themselves are synchronization actions, and may interfere with other synchronization mechanisms such as locks. Using this observation, we show:

Theorem 6.3. *The coverability problem of programs with locks is polynomial-time reducible to the sync-point soundness problem (of programs with locks).*

Proof (sketch). Given a program P and a configuration $C = [\ell_1, \ldots, \ell_n]$ for which to decide coverability, we modify the thread template as follows. We take fresh locks $m_1, \ldots, m_n$, add a fresh location ℓ'_{exit}, and chose ℓ'_{exit} as the new exit location. From each location $\ell_i \in C$, we add a subgraph that first acquires m_i, then branches over all $j \neq i$ and checks that m_j is still free (by acquiring and releasing it), and then finally releases m_i, reaching ℓ'_{exit}. For the sync-point instrumentation, we add a single sync-point $\bullet$ immediately before the final step (releasing m_i). We note that C is coverable (in P) if and only if it is reachable. Any interleaving τ of P reaching a sub-configuration of C is an interleaving of the modified program (all threads can reach ℓ'_{exit}). However, in an interleaving reaching exactly C, the sync-point instrumentation forces at least one of the n threads to deadlock when trying to acquire some m_j (and hence, all other threads are blocked at the sync-point). Thus, the sync-point instrumentation is sound (wrt. any I) if and only if C is not coverable.

Using Partial Information About Locks. We conclude this section with a short outlook on how soundness checking for natural reductions can nevertheless benefit from (possibly incomplete, but sound) information about locks. Suppose that we have information available about a set of locks M_ℓ that a thread *must* hold whenever it is at location ℓ. Such information could for instance be derived from a static analysis, or a thread-modular proof given to a deductive verifier by a user. Then one can soundly declare that outgoing actions a_ℓ of ℓ and $a_{\ell'}$ of ℓ' commute whenever the sets M_ℓ and $M_{\ell'}$ overlap.

More generally, any kind of *thread-modular invariants* $\varphi_\ell, \varphi_{\ell'}$ that hold whenever a thread is at location ℓ resp. ℓ' can be used to increase commutativity, by determining if actions $a_\ell, a_{\ell'}$ commute *under the assumption* $\varphi_\ell \wedge \varphi_{\ell'}$ [11]. The idea for locks described above corresponds to the special case that $\varphi_\ell \wedge \varphi_{\ell'} \equiv \bot$ (it is impossible that both threads hold the same lock), under which the actions vacuously commute. The resulting extended commutativity relation $I' \supseteq I$ can increase the power of both mover reasoning [21] as well as our algorithms.

7 Related Work

Sound reductions proposed by atomic blocks have been studied and implemented in many deductive proof systems for concurrent and distributed systems [2,6,14,18,19,21,22]. These approaches are based on Lipton's reductions [21] and are thus inherently incomplete (see Sect. 5). In principle, our sound and complete algorithm for atomic blocks may serve as a replacement for the current implementations in these proof systems. Yet, some hurdles remain. Practical tools such as CIVL [19] typically support specifications via `assert` statements, whereas our approach currently only targets verification of postconditions. While we do not expect the extension to `assert` statements to change the complexity picture significantly, it requires non-trivial conceptual adjustments, in particular when the execution of a single atomic block is not guaranteed to terminate (due to loops or recursion, see e.g. [15]).

Similarly, sound but possibly incomplete techniques for proving soundness of synchronous reductions have been studied in [16,20]. These techniques are also based on the mover types from Lipton's reduction theory.

Checking *conflict serializability* for transactions can be seen as an instance of deciding soundness of atomic blocks, where the commutativity relation is fixed: read accesses commute against one another, and (read or write) accesses to different shared variables also commute. The complexity of checking serializability has been studied in [1,12], but these results do not extend to arbitrary commutativity relations as in our paper.

On the side of algorithmic verification (and more classically, finite-state model checking), *partial order reduction* algorithms [17] are employed to automatically compute reductions that are sound by construction. The works of Farzan et al. [10,11] define an algorithmic verification framework for concurrent programs that includes computing sound reductions. The syntactic representation of these reductions is somewhat complex, which is fine in the context of a fully automated, non-interactive proof. In our paper, we look at classes of reductions which are humanly readable and use simple syntactic constructs.

8 Conclusion

We have proposed *natural reductions* of parameterized concurrent programs, an approach for users to specify a subset of interleavings that may be easier to verify. Natural reductions can be specified with ease, by adding atomic blocks and global rendez-vous points to the thread template.

We have studied the problem of deciding whether a natural reduction given by a user is indeed *sound*, and can thus be soundly verified in place of the original program. We link the complexity of this problem to the corresponding coverability problem. As a consequence, the problem becomes intractable (coNP-hard) as soon as even very light-weight synchronization between threads is allowed (in particular, locks). This motivates us to take an abstract view of the program, i.e., to abstract away from the semantics of locks and other synchronization operators. We present the first complete decision procedure for checking soundness of natural reductions in this setting, and show that it runs in polynomial time. Hence, our approach overcomes the inherent incompleteness of previous work based on *mover reasoning*, while retaining polynomial complexity.

In the future, our decision procedure could replace resp. complement mover reasoning in reduction-based deductive verifiers such as Civl [19] or Anchor [14], broadening the range of specifiable reductions and providing a guarantee of completeness. As part of such an application, a relevant question for study is the extension of our polynomial-time algorithm to other settings. In particular, it is of interest to determine whether some form of synchronization (even more light-weight than locks), such as *structured concurrent programs*, *permissions*, or specific *locking disciplines* can be accommodated. Given that in such cases, it is typically easy to determine which parts of the program may run in parallel, there is some hope that polynomial runtime can be retained.

At the same time, there also remain open questions in the cases where a precise, polynomial-time decision procedure does not exist. First, the matching upper bounds for our complexity results remains a question of theoretical interest, even if the practical impact for deductive proof systems may be limited. Second, we have shown that a precise solution requires a global view of the program, and the purely-local reasoning of Lipton movers is incomplete. This raises the question of whether there are (practically useful and feasible) intermediate points within the gap between fully-local, polynomial-time Lipton reasoning and a fully-global, super-polynomial algorithm. For the case of locks, we have sketched one such intermediate solution in Sect. 6.

Acknowledgments. Constantin Enea and Dominik Klumpp are partially supported by the French National Research Agency (projects “SCEPROOF” and “CENTEANES”).

Disclosure of Interests. The authors have no competing interests to declare that are relevant to the content of this article.

References

1. Bouajjani, A., Emmi, M., Enea, C., Hamza, J.: Verifying Concurrent Programs against Sequential Specifications. In: Felleisen, M., Gardner, P. (eds.) ESOP 2013. LNCS, vol. 7792, pp. 290–309. Springer, Heidelberg (2013). https://doi.org/10.1007/978-3-642-37036-6_17
2. Chajed, T., Kaashoek, M.F., Lampson, B.W., Zeldovich, N.: Verifying concurrent software using movers in CSPEC. In: OSDI, pp. 306–322. USENIX Association (2018)
3. Chou, C., Gafni, E.: Understanding and verifying distributed algorithms using stratified decomposition. In: PODC, pp. 44–65. ACM (1988). https://doi.org/10.1145/62546.62556
4. Clerbout, M., Latteux, M., Roos, Y.: Semi-commutations. In: The Book of Traces, pp. 487–552. World Scientific (1995). https://doi.org/10.1142/9789814261456_0012
5. Damian, A., Drăgoi, C., Militaru, A., Widder, J.: Communication-Closed Asynchronous Protocols. In: Dillig, I., Tasiran, S. (eds.) CAV 2019. LNCS, vol. 11562, pp. 344–363. Springer, Cham (2019). https://doi.org/10.1007/978-3-030-25543-5_20
6. Elmas, T., Qadeer, S., Tasiran, S.: A calculus of atomic actions. In: POPL, pp. 2–15. ACM (2009). https://doi.org/10.1145/1480881.1480885
7. Elrad, T., Francez, N.: Decomposition of distributed programs into communication-closed layers. Sci. Comput. Program. **2**(3), 155–173 (1982). https://doi.org/10.1016/0167-6423(83)90013-8
8. Enea, C., Farzan, A., Klumpp, D.: On the complexity of checking soundness of natural reductions (extended version). Tech. rep. (2026). https://doi.org/10.48550/arXiv.2605.13780

9. Esparza, J.: Keeping a crowd safe: On the complexity of parameterized verification (invited talk). In: STACS, pp. 1–10. LIPIcs, Schloss Dagstuhl - Leibniz-Zentrum für Informatik (2014). https://doi.org/10.4230/LIPICS.STACS.2014.1
10. Farzan, A., Klumpp, D., Podelski, A.: Sound sequentialization for concurrent program verification. In: PLDI, pp. 506–521. ACM (2022). https://doi.org/10.1145/3519939.3523727
11. Farzan, A., Klumpp, D., Podelski, A.: Commutativity simplifies proofs of parameterized programs. Proc. ACM Program. Lang. **8**(POPL), 2485–2513 (2024). https://doi.org/10.1145/3632925
12. Farzan, A., Madhusudan, P.: The Complexity of Predicting Atomicity Violations. In: Kowalewski, S., Philippou, A. (eds.) TACAS 2009. LNCS, vol. 5505, pp. 155–169. Springer, Heidelberg (2009). https://doi.org/10.1007/978-3-642-00768-2_14
13. Farzan, A., Vandikas, A.: Reductions for safety proofs. Proc. ACM Program. Lang. **4**(POPL), 13:1–13:28 (2020). https://doi.org/10.1145/3371081
14. Flanagan, C., Freund, S.N.: The Anchor verifier for blocking and non-blocking concurrent software. Proc. ACM Program. Lang. **4**(OOPSLA), 156:1–156:29 (2020). https://doi.org/10.1145/3428224
15. Gangamreddypalli, N., Enea, C., Qadeer, S.: Reduction for structured concurrent programs. In: ESOP (1), pp. 252–282. LNCS, Springer, Cham (2026). https://doi.org/10.1007/978-3-032-22720-1_10
16. von Gleissenthall, K., Kici, R.G., Bakst, A., Stefan, D., Jhala, R.: Pretend synchrony: synchronous verification of asynchronous distributed programs. Proc. ACM Program. Lang. **3**(POPL), 59:1–59:30 (2019). https://doi.org/10.1145/3290372
17. Godefroid, P. (ed.): Partial-Order Methods for the Verification of Concurrent Systems. LNCS, vol. 1032. Springer, Heidelberg (1996). https://doi.org/10.1007/3-540-60761-7
18. Hawblitzel, C., et al.: Ironfleet: proving practical distributed systems correct. In: SOSP, pp. 1–17. ACM (2015). https://doi.org/10.1145/2815400.2815428
19. Hawblitzel, C., Petrank, E., Qadeer, S., Tasiran, S.: Automated and Modular Refinement Reasoning for Concurrent Programs. In: Kroening, D., Păsăreanu, C.S. (eds.) CAV 2015. LNCS, vol. 9207, pp. 449–465. Springer, Cham (2015). https://doi.org/10.1007/978-3-319-21668-3_26
20. Kragl, B., Enea, C., Henzinger, T.A., Mutluergil, S.O., Qadeer, S.: Inductive sequentialization of asynchronous programs. In: PLDI, pp. 227–242. ACM (2020). https://doi.org/10.1145/3385412.3385980
21. Lipton, R.J.: Reduction: a method of proving properties of parallel programs. Commun. ACM **18**(12), 717–721 (1975). https://doi.org/10.1145/361227.361234
22. Lorch, J.R., et al.: Armada: low-effort verification of high-performance concurrent programs. In: PLDI, pp. 197–210. ACM (2020). https://doi.org/10.1145/3385412.3385971
23. Mazurkiewicz, A.: Trace theory. In: Brauer, W., Reisig, W., Rozenberg, G. (eds.) ACPN 1986. LNCS, vol. 255, pp. 278–324. Springer, Heidelberg (1987). https://doi.org/10.1007/3-540-17906-2_30
24. Mutluergil, S.O., Tasiran, S.: A mechanized refinement proof of the Chase-Lev deque using a proof system. Computing **101**(1), 59–74 (2019). https://doi.org/10.1007/S00607-018-0635-4

Deadlock Verification via Ordering-Constrained Mutex Modeling

Pei Wang[1,2], Zhilei Han[1,2], Zhihang Sun[1,2], and Fei He[1,2](✉)

[1] School of Software, BNRist, Tsinghua University, Beijing 100084, China
{wang-p23,hzl21,sunzh20}@mails.tsinghua.edu.cn, hefei@tsinghua.edu.cn

[2] Key Laboratory for Information System Security, MoE, Beijing, China

Abstract. Mutexes are fundamental synchronization primitives in concurrent programming, but their improper use can lead to deadlocks. Conventional assume-based modeling abstracts mutex semantics via assumptions, simplifying safety verification but hindering deadlock verification. Although prior efforts have aimed to address this limitation, we show that state-of-the-art methods remain inaccurate. In this paper, we propose a novel modeling approach that captures mutex semantics using ordering constraints, enabling accurate deadlock verification within partial-order-based concurrent verification frameworks. We formally prove the correctness of our method and implement it in a prototype tool, Deagle-DL. We evaluate Deagle-DL against a state-of-the-art bounded model checker ESBMC that employs the conventional modeling approach, and a state-of-the-art static analysis tool for deadlock detection. Our experiments show that Deagle-DL significantly outperforms both tools in terms of precision, while maintaining substantial efficiency.

1 Introduction

Locks [55,56,62] are fundamental synchronization mechanisms in concurrent programs, commonly used to enforce mutual exclusion when accessing critical sections. However, improper use of locks can lead to deadlocks [12,27,37–39], a class of concurrency bugs that can severely compromise system reliability. Effective techniques for modeling synchronization primitives and detecting deadlocks are thus essential for building robust concurrent software systems.

This paper focuses on mutexes [8,25,53], one of the most widely used synchronization mechanisms in concurrent programming. Verifying mutex operations poses particular challenges due to the waiting behavior associated with lock acquisition. A straightforward solution is to explicitly model the waiting behavior (e.g., using loops), but it significantly increases verification complexity. A widely adopted alternative is assume-based modeling [19,24,35,42,43,58], where lock primitives are modeled using `assume` statements. While this method

E. Darulova et al. (Eds.): CAV 2026, LNCS 16682, pp. 42–66, 2026.
https://doi.org/10.1007/978-3-032-32519-8_3

is effective for safety verification, it is unsound for deadlock verification [43], as it abstracts away the waiting behavior that is essential for identifying deadlocks.

To address this limitation, prior works [13,43] attempt to augment assume-based modeling with counters that track the number of running and blocked threads. These methods intend to provide a sound framework for deadlock detection. However, they relies heavily on accurate modeling of mutex semantics through updates to counters. Given the intricacies and the volume of subtle cases involved, maintaining precise tracking of blocked threads remains a substantial challenge. It is evidenced by the false positives we first expose in the approaches [13,43] that utilize these modeling methods, as detailed in Sect. 2.2.

In this paper, we tackle this challenge from a new perspective. The possible behavior of a lock operation is either *immediate acquisition*, *eventual acquisition*, or *indefinite waiting* (see Sect. 3.1 for details). Our key insight is that both eventual acquisition and indefinite waiting violates the `assume` statements used in assume-based modeling, yet they are semantically distinct, because only indefinite waiting constitutes a true deadlock. It reveals a core limitation of assume-based modeling, in that it is unable to differentiate between eventual acquisition and indefinite waiting, which is essential for deadlock verification.

The basic idea of our approach is that, if executions with eventual acquisitions could be excluded, a lock request in the remaining executions then results in either immediate acquisition or indefinite waiting. Therefore, by checking whether any `assume` statement in the assume-based modeling of lock operations is violated, we can precisely identify indefinitely waiting lock requests and thus recognize true deadlocks. To efficiently identify and exclude such executions, we introduce *eventual acquisition constraint* (see Sect. 4.3), an ordering constraint that precisely encodes eventual acquisition. We then incorporate this constraint into our partial-order-based concurrent program verification framework to accurately eliminate such executions. The result is an accurate model of lock primitives without explicitly modeling their waiting behaviors.

Based upon our modeling, we present a deadlock verification method (see Sect. 4.4) that reduces the deadlock verification problem to checking satisfiability of an SMT formula. We formally prove that the formula is satisfiable if and only if the program contains a deadlock.

We implemented our approach in a prototype tool, DEAGLE-DL, built atop DEAGLE [23,24]. We evaluate DEAGLE-DL against two state-of-the-art tools: a bounded model checker called ESBMC [19] that employs the conventional assume-based modeling, and a state-of-the-art static analysis tool [34] for deadlock detection. We evaluate our approach using two benchmarks suites: classical benchmarks and SV-Benchmarks. DEAGLE-DL demonstrates superior performance over the baselines across both benchmark suites. In particular, one previously *unknown* bug in a SV-Benchmarks has been detected by our approach (see Sect. 5.3), which was missed by the baselines.

The primary contributions of this paper are summarized as follows:

1. We reveal that the state-of-the-art methods that utilize assume-based modeling for deadlock detection produce false positives.

2. We devise a novel modeling method for mutex that is based on eventual acquisition constraint. It precisely captures mutex semantics without explicitly modeling its waiting behavior.
3. We propose an efficient deadlock verification approach that integrates our modeling into a partial-order-based concurrent verification framework.
4. We implement a prototype tool, and experimental results show competitive performance of our tool compared with state-of-the-art tools.

2 Existing Approaches for Modeling Mutexes

This section reviews existing modelings of mutexes and highlights their limitations. In particular, we expose a critical flaw of the prevailing assume-based modeling with counters: it can introduce false positives in deadlock detection.

We begin with an informal introduction to mutexes and deadlocks, deferring formal definitions to Sect. 4.1. A mutex m is in either a *locked* ($m = 1$) or *unlocked* ($m = 0$) state, and can only be modified by the `lock` and `unlock` operations. A `lock` operation acquires the mutex if it is unlocked; otherwise, the thread blocks and waits. A `unlock` operation unblocks one waiting thread if any exist; otherwise, it sets the mutex to unlocked. A *deadlock* is a situation in which at least one thread is blocked by a lock operation for a mutex that is never subsequently unlocked by the thread currently holding it [13,37,43].

2.1 Assume-Based Modeling

Assume-based modeling, illustrated below, is adopted in many verification techniques [19,24,35,42,43,58]. Its core idea is to use an `assume` statement to model `lock`. It avoids the main complexity of modeling the waiting behavior, i.e., when a mutex is already locked, the thread attempting to acquire it must *wait* until the mutex is released. Instead, it only admits executions where the lock is acquired immediately and discards all others, effectively ignoring waiting behavior.

$$\texttt{lock}(\&m) \stackrel{\text{def}}{=} \texttt{atomic}\{\texttt{assume}(m == 0); m = 1;\}$$
$$\texttt{unlock}(\&m) \stackrel{\text{def}}{=} \texttt{atomic}\{\texttt{assert}(m == 1); m = 0;\}$$

An execution is said to be *wait-free* if it contains no attempts to lock a mutex that is already in the locked state. The soundness of the modeling relies on the assumption that any errors appearing in a non-wait-free execution appear also in an equivalent[1] wait-free execution [43]. While this assumption holds for many safety properties, it does not extend to properties like deadlock freedom, which fundamentally depend on the interleaving and waiting semantics of mutexes. As a result, assume-based modeling is inherently *unsound* for deadlock verification.

[1] More precisely, *mutex-free-equivalent*, meaning the execution reaches the same states when the internal behavior of mutexes is disregarded.

2.2 Assume-Based Modeling with Counters

To address the limitations of assume-based modeling, an enhanced approach incorporating counters has been proposed [13,43]. The core idea is to use two global counters to track the number of running and blocked threads, respectively. By comparing counts, a deadlock is reported if the number of blocked threads equals the number of running threads. However, this approach requires precise tracking of the number of running and blocked threads throughout the program execution, which depends heavily on the scheduling behavior of the underlying operating system. Accurately modeling such behavior is highly challenging.

The modeling of this approach [13,43] is shown below, where *bcnt* and *rcnt* are two global counters that track the numbers of blocked and running threads, respectively. While the modeling of `unlock` remains unchanged, the modeling of `lock` is split into two atomic blocks. The first atomic block checks whether the target mutex is already locked. If not, it locks the mutex; otherwise, it considers the thread as blocked and increments *bcnt* by 1. The second atomic block checks whether the mutex has since been unlocked. If so, the thread is considered to have recovered from the blocked state, and *bcnt* is decremented by 1. This block also asserts that $bcnt < rcnt$. If the assertion fails, a deadlock is reported.

$$
\texttt{lock}(\&m) \stackrel{\text{def}}{=} \left\{ \begin{array}{l} \texttt{atomic}\left\{ \begin{array}{l} ul = (m == 0); \\ \texttt{if}(ul)\ m = 1; \texttt{else}\ bcnt{+}{+}; \end{array} \right\} \\ \texttt{atomic} \left\{ \begin{array}{l} \texttt{if}(m == 0)\ bcnt{-}{-}; \\ \texttt{if}(!ul) \left\{ \begin{array}{l} dlf = bcnt < rcnt; \\ \texttt{assert}(dlf); \\ \texttt{assume}(!dlf) \end{array}\right\} \end{array}\right\} \end{array} \right\}
$$

$$
\texttt{unlock}(\&m) \stackrel{\text{def}}{=} \texttt{atomic}\{\texttt{assert}(m == 1); m = 0; \}
$$

Importantly, other threads can be scheduled before the second atomic block is reached, therefore an arbitrary number of instructions may occur between the two atomic blocks. We observe that this can lead to an overestimation of the number of blocked threads. For example, if the mutex has already been released, but the blocked thread has not yet reached the second block. Such overestimation of *bcnt* can lead to *false positives* in deadlock detection.

Consider the deadlock-free example and an illustration of its false positive execution[2] under this modeling in Fig. 1. To make it easier to understand, we use `lock().fir` and `lock().sec` to represent the two atomic blocks involved in a single lock operation. Initially, *bcnt* and *rcnt* are both 0. First, thread t_1 holds mutex m (line $1-2$), and thread t_2 holds mutex n (line $3-4$). The counter *rcnt* is incremented to 2. Next, thread t_2 executes the first atomic block within `lock`($\&m$) (line 5). It attempts to lock mutex m but fails, incrementing *bcnt* to

[2] We confirm that the current implementation(v8.2) of ESBMC exhibits this false positive. Though it has evolved over the years, its underlying principles are unchanged.

1. Then, thread t_1 unlocks mutex m (line 6). Subsequently, thread t_1 executes the first atomic block within `lock`($\&n$) (line 7). It attempts to lock mutex n but fails, incrementing *bcnt* to 2. Finally, thread t_1 executes the second atomic block within `lock`($\&n$) (line 8), and finds that the assertion $bcnt < rcnt$ is violated because both *bcnt* and *rcnt* are equal to 2. As a result, the program terminates and incorrectly concludes that a deadlock has occurred. However, it is clearly a false positive, as t_2 should no longer be blocked once t_1 unlocks m.

t_1	t_2
`lock(&m);`	`lock(&n);`
`unlock(&m);`	`lock(&m);`
`lock(&n);`	`unlock(&m);`
`unlock(&n);`	`unlock(&n);`

⇒

	t_1	t_2
1	`lock(&m).fir`	
2	`lock(&m).sec`	
3		`lock(&n).fir`
4		`lock(&n).sec`
5		`lock(&m).fir`
6	`unlock(&m)`	
7	`lock(&n).fir`	
8	`lock(&n).sec`	

Fig. 1. A false positive execution (right) of a deadlock-free program (left) under assume-based modeling with counters.

3 The Challenge of Distinguishing Eventual Acquisitions

In this section, we examine the behavior of mutexes from a semantic perspective and show that the central challenge in deadlock verification is to efficiently identify lock operations whose acquisition is eventual.

3.1 Three Possible Outcomes of a Lock Operation

Let m be a mutex variable, and assume executions are fair. A lock operation `lock`($\&m$) performed by a thread t can behave in one of following ways:

- *Immediate Acquisition*: If m is currently in the unlocked state (i.e., $m = 0$), thread t immediately acquires the mutex and sets m to the locked state.
- *Eventual Acquisition*: If m is currently locked (i.e., $m = 1$) but will eventually be released, thread t waits for a while and then successfully acquires m.
- *Indefinite Waiting*: If m is locked and never released, thread t waits indefinitely, resulting in a *deadlock*.

The two threads in Fig. 2a illustrate an eventual acquisition scenario. The right thread, denoted t_2, attempts to acquire m, which is currently held by the left thread, denoted t_1. Here, *st* is used to denote an arbitrary statement. Regardless of whether t_2's `lock` occurs before, after or in between the execution of t_1's *st*, thread t_2 must wait until t_1's `unlock` completes. From the perspective of observable effects, these cases are equivalent to the immediate acquisition case shown in Fig. 2b, where t_2 performs its `lock` only after t_1 performs its `unlock`.

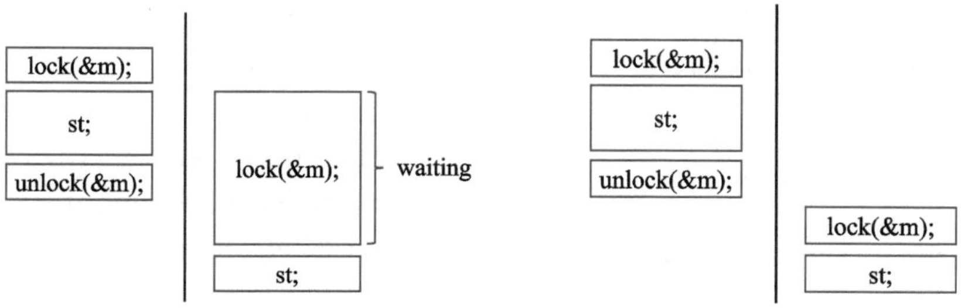

(a) Eventual acquisition (b) Immediate acquisition

Fig. 2. Eventual acquisition and the corresponding immediate acquisition.

3.2 The Central Challenge

In assume-based modeling (Sect. 2.1), the `assume` statement captures the expectation that the mutex is available at the time of acquisition. Among the three outcomes of a lock operation, only the first (immediate acquisition) satisfies the `assume` condition. The other two (eventual acquisition and indefinite waiting) both violate the assumption, but with different implications. Specifically, only the third case corresponds to a *true* deadlock, while the second involves merely a temporary waiting. Therefore, detecting a violation of the `assume` statement is insufficient for determining whether a deadlock has occurred.

We now consider the program in Fig. 2 under assume-based modeling. For clarity, we use ①, ②, and ③ to denote, respectively, the modeling of `lock`, the statement *st*, and the modeling of `unlock` in thread t_1. Similarly, ④ and ⑤ denote the modeling of `lock` and the statement *st* in thread t_2. Without loss of generality, assume that t_1's `lock` occurs before t_2's `lock`. A key advantage of assume-based modeling is that mutex operations are represented as atomic operations. This simplifies reasoning about executions: an execution becomes merely an interleaving of these atomic statements. Assuming that *st* is also atomic, all three following interleavings are valid under assume-based modeling (noting that ⑤ becomes unexecutable if the `assume` statement in ④ is violated): ①④②③, ①②④③, and ①②③④⑤. The first two correspond to the eventual acquisition scenario in Fig. 2a, while the last corresponds to the immediate acquisition case depicted in Fig. 2b. If we were to detect deadlocks with violations of the `assume` statement, the first two interleavings would be classified as deadlocks.

However, as previously discussed, an eventual acquisition does not constitute a deadlock, and therefore the deadlock is spurious. Consequently, executions with eventual acquisitions should be excluded from deadlock analysis. It is safe because an eventual acquisition is always equivalent in effect to an immediate acquisition, as shown in Fig. 2. If such executions can be effectively identified and filtered out, such as the first two interleavings discussed above, then a violation of the `assume` statement becomes a sufficient condition for deadlock detection.

The central challenge, therefore, is how to efficiently identify and exclude executions involving eventual acquisitions. This problem is highly non-trivial

Basic domains	
$a \in \boldsymbol{a}$	Local Variables
$x \in \boldsymbol{x}$	Shared Variables
$m \in \boldsymbol{m}$	Mutexes
$v \in \boldsymbol{v}$	Values
$t \in \text{TID}$	Thread IDs

Programs

$P \in \text{PROG} \triangleq \text{TID} \rightarrow \text{COM}$

Expressions and Commands

$$\text{EXPR} \ni e ::= v \mid a \mid e \ \mathbf{op}\ e$$

$$\begin{aligned}\text{COM} \ni c ::= &\ \texttt{skip} \mid c \mid x := a \mid a := e \mid a := x \\ &\mid \texttt{if}\ (e)\ \texttt{then}\ c_1\ \texttt{else}\ c_2 \mid c_1; c_2 \\ &\mid \texttt{assume}(e) \mid \texttt{assert}(e) \mid \texttt{atomic}\{c\} \\ &\mid \texttt{lock}(\&m) \mid \texttt{unlock}(\&m)\end{aligned}$$

Fig. 3. Syntax of the Language.

due to the infinite, or at least prohibitively large, execution space. Our solution is to formally encode the eventual acquisition constraint and incorporate it into the analysis, thereby systematically filtering out such executions.

4 Ordering-Constrained Mutex Modeling

In this section, we propose a novel mutex modeling approach based on ordering constraints. We then develop a deadlock verification method that integrates this modeling into a partial-order-based concurrent verification framework. Finally, we formally establish the correctness of the proposed approach.

4.1 Formal Definitions

We use the imperative language shown in Fig. 3 to illustrate our approach, where a concurrent program P is a mapping from each thread to its command. The syntax does not include loop statements, since we assume that loops in the input program have already been handled by other means, such as loop unrolling. For convenience, we assume that the local variables of all threads are disjoint.

A *data state* $s : \boldsymbol{m} \cup \boldsymbol{x} \cup \boldsymbol{a} \rightarrow \boldsymbol{v}$ is a valuation over $\boldsymbol{m} \cup \boldsymbol{x} \cup \boldsymbol{a}$. A thread $t \in \text{TID}$ is said to be *blocked* if it attempts to acquire a mutex that is currently held by some thread. Note that a single locked mutex may block multiple threads simultaneously. To record this information, we introduce the notion of a *blocking state*, which captures, for each mutex, the sequence of threads currently blocked by it. Formally, a blocking state is a mapping $b : \boldsymbol{m} \rightarrow \text{TID}^*$, where $b(m)$ is the sequence of threads blocked on mutex m. We use ϵ to denote the empty sequence and $\cdot$ denotes sequence concatenation.

An *environment* is a pair (s, b) of a data state s and a blocking state b. A thread t is *blocked* under an environment (s, b) if there exists a mutex $m \in \boldsymbol{m}$ and an index i such that the i-th element of the sequence $b(m)$ is t, i.e., $t = b(m)[i]$. We introduce the predicate $B(t)$ to indicate whether thread t is *blocked*.

A *thread-local configuration* is a pair $\langle c, (s, b)\rangle$, where $c \in \text{COM}$ is a command and (s, b) is an environment. A thread-local small-step transition $\langle c, (s, b)\rangle \xrightarrow{e} \langle c', (s', b')\rangle$ is labeled with an event e. An event label may be one of the following: $R(t, x, v)$, denoting that thread t reads value v from shared variable x; $W(t, x, v)$, denoting that thread t writes value v to shared variable x; $L(t, m)$, denoting that thread t attempts to acquire mutex m; $U(t, m)$, denoting that thread t releases mutex m; or $\epsilon(t)$, denoting that thread t performs a silent transition that does not access shared variables or mutexes. Let $tid(e)$ denote the thread from which e originates. The small-step semantics of `lock` and `unlock` is shown in Fig. 4. Other commands follow the standard operational semantics, with the sole exception that any transition in thread t requires $\neg B(t)$.

$$\text{Lock-Acquire}\ \frac{\neg B(t) \qquad s(m) = 0}{\langle \texttt{lock}(\&m), (s, b)\rangle \xrightarrow{L(t,m)} \langle \texttt{skip}, (s[m \mapsto 1], b)\rangle}$$

$$\text{Lock-Wait}\ \frac{\neg B(t) \qquad s(m) = 1}{\langle \texttt{lock}(\&m), (s, b)\rangle \xrightarrow{L(t,m)} \langle \texttt{skip}, (s, b[m \mapsto b(m) \cdot t])\rangle}$$

$$\text{Unlock-Await}\ \frac{\neg B(t) \qquad s(m) = 1 \qquad b(m) = t' \cdot \mathbb{L}}{\langle \texttt{unlock}(\&m), (s, b)\rangle \xrightarrow{U(t,m)} \langle \texttt{skip}, (s, b[m \mapsto \mathbb{L}])\rangle}$$

$$\text{Unlock-NoAwait}\ \frac{\neg B(t) \qquad s(m) = 1 \qquad b(m) = \epsilon}{\langle \texttt{unlock}(\&m), (s, b)\rangle \xrightarrow{U(t,m)} \langle \texttt{skip}, (s[m \mapsto 0], b)\rangle}$$

$$\text{Interleaving}\ \frac{P(t) = c \qquad tid(e) = t \qquad \langle c, (s, b)\rangle \xrightarrow{e} \langle c', (s', b')\rangle}{\langle P, (s, b)\rangle \xrightarrow{e} \langle P[t \mapsto c'], (s', b')\rangle}$$

Fig. 4. Semantics of lock, unlock and interleaving.

A *global configuration* is a pair $\langle P, (s, b)\rangle$, such that for each thread $t \in \text{TID}$, $\langle P(t), (s, b)\rangle$ is the thread-local configuration of t. The interleaving semantics, shown in Fig. 4, defines a transition relation over global configurations, where each step selects one thread and advances its command while updating the shared environment accordingly.

A thread-local configuration $\langle c, (s, b)\rangle$ is *stuck* if there exists no configuration $\langle c', (s', b')\rangle$ such that $\langle c, (s, b)\rangle \xrightarrow{e} \langle c', (s', b')\rangle$ is derivable by some transition rule. In other words, a stuck local configuration cannot make any progress. A global configuration is *stuck* if all of its thread-local configurations are stuck. A global configuration is *deadlocked* if it is stuck and at least one thread is blocked in that configuration.

An *execution* is a sequence of transitions over global configurations, denoted by $\langle p_0, (s_0, b_0)\rangle \xrightarrow{e_1} \langle p_1, (s_1, b_1)\rangle \xrightarrow{e_2} \cdots \xrightarrow{e_n} \langle p_n, (s_n, b_n)\rangle$, that satisfies the following conditions: (1) for all natural number $i < n$, $\langle p_i, (s_i, b_i)\rangle \xrightarrow{e_{i+1}} \langle p_{i+1}, (s_{i+1}, b_{i+1})\rangle$ is derivable by some transition rule; (2) the final configuration $\langle p_n, (s_n, b_n)\rangle$ is stuck; and (3) the transitions corresponding to commands within an atomic block occur consecutively. An execution witnesses a *deadlock* if its final configuration is deadlocked.

t_1	t_2
①: atomic { `assume`$(m_1 == 0)$; $m_2 = 1$; }	③: atomic { `assume`$(m_5 == 0)$; $m_6 = 1$; }
②: atomic { `assert`$(m_3 == 1)$; $m_4 = 0$; }	④: atomic { `assert`$(m_7 == 1)$; $m_8 = 0$; }

Fig. 5. SSA form of the two-threaded example.

4.2 Happens-Before Orders

For a program P, given an execution $\langle p_0, (s_0, b_0)\rangle \xrightarrow{e_1} \langle p_1, (s_1, b_1)\rangle \xrightarrow{e_2} \cdots$, we can induce some order relations over its events $e_1, e_2, \cdots$, which are used in ordering constraints that characterize a certain subset of executions:

- The *program order* relation $\prec_{po}$ is a total order of events from the same thread. Intuitively, $e_1 \prec_{po} e_2$ means that e_1 occurs earlier than e_2 and they are issued by the same thread.
- The *atomicity* relation $\approx$ is an equivalence relation. Intuitively, $e_1 \approx e_2$ means that e_1 and e_2 are contained in the same atomic block.
- The *write serialization* relation $\prec_{ws}$ is a total order among write events that access the same address. Intuitively, $e_1 \prec_{ws} e_2$ iff a write event e_1 occurs earlier than a write event e_2 and they access the same address.
- The *read-from* relation $\prec_{rf}$ links a write event e_1 to a read event e_2. Intuitively, $e_1 \prec_{rf} e_2$ iff e_2 reads the value written by e_1.
- The *from-read* relation $\prec_{fr}$ is derived from the $\prec_{ws}$ and $\prec_{rf}$ relations. Specifically, given a pair of write events e_1 and e_2, and a read event e_3. If $e_1 \prec_{ws} e_2$ and $e_1 \prec_{rf} e_3$, then the $\prec_{fr}$ relation ensures that e_3 happens before e_2, i.e., $e_3 \prec_{fr} e_2$, which prevents e_3 from reading from e_2.

4.3 Eventual Acquisition Constraints

Consider an example consisting of two threads, each containing a lock operation followed by an unlock operation. For clarity, we omit all non-synchronization statements and focus solely on the synchronization behavior. The static single assignment (SSA) form of this example under assume-based modeling is shown in Fig. 5, where each occurrence of a shared variable or mutex – regardless of whether it is read or written – is replaced with a fresh SSA variable.

Given an SSA variable x_i, we write $(\!|x_i|\!)$ for its corresponding access event [23]. Let $\mathbb{E}$ represent the set of all events issued by the program. If the type of event is known, we write $(\!|x_i|\!)^w$ for a write access and $(\!|x_i|\!)^r$ for a read access. Consider the example program in Fig. 5, $(\!|m_1|\!)^r, (\!|m_3|\!)^r, (\!|m_5|\!)^r$ and $(\!|m_7|\!)^r$ represent read accesses, while $(\!|m_2|\!)^w, (\!|m_4|\!)^w, (\!|m_6|\!)^w$ and $(\!|m_8|\!)^w$ represent write accesses.

Without loss of generality, assume that t_1's lock operation precedes that of t_2. Figure 6 illustrates the ordering of access events involved in the synchronization operations ①, ② and ③. Since t_1 acquires the mutex, it retains ownership until it explicitly releases it at ②. As a result, the read access m_3 must read the value written by m_2. We denote this read-from relation between m_2 and m_3 in Fig. 6 using a solid edge. The read access m_5, which appears in t_2's lock operation, may obtain its value from either m_2 or m_4. If m_5 reads from m_2, the `assume` statement in ③ fails; however, since t_1 will eventually release the mutex, this scenario corresponds to the interleaving ①③②, which is an instance of eventual acquisition (refer to previous discussion in Sect. 3.2) and should be excluded from deadlock verification. In conclusion, if t_1 has acquired the mutex and will release it in the future (i.e., m_3 reads from m_2), then t_2's lock operation must not read its value from t_1's lock operation (i.e., m_5 must not read from m_2).

Formally, given a program P, let $\mathbb{E}_L^w$ denote the set of write events on mutexes that are generated by lock operations in the program. For any write event $e \in \mathbb{E}_L^w$, let $\pi_U^r(e)$ be the set of read events that (i) originate from *unlock* operations of the *same* thread as e, and (ii) may read from e. Similarly, let $\pi_L^r(e)$ be the set of read events that (i) originate from *lock* operations of the *other* thread, and (ii) may read from e. Then we define the following constraint:

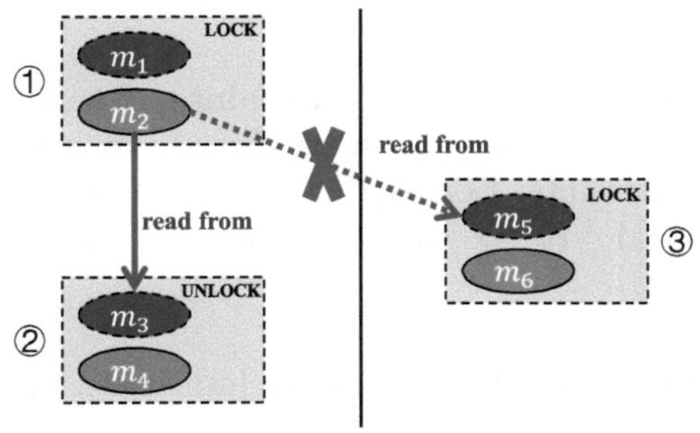

Fig. 6. The orderings of access events: blue represents read, and orange represents write. (Color figure online)

Definition 1 (Eventual Acquisition Constraint). *For any write event $e \in \mathbb{E}_L^w$, if there exists a read event $e' \in \pi_U^r(e)$ that reads from e, then for every $e'' \in \pi_L^r(e)$, it must not read from e. Formally,*

$$\bigwedge_{e \in \mathbb{E}_L^w} \left(\bigvee_{e' \in \pi_U^r(e)} e \prec_{rf} e' \rightarrow \bigwedge_{e'' \in \pi_L^r(e)} e \not\prec_{rf} e'' \right).$$

Intuitively, if a thread has acquired a mutex (i.e., its lock operation writes to the mutex) and will eventually release it (i.e., a later unlock operation reads from this write), then any lock operation of another thread must not read from that write – such interleavings represent eventual acquisition scenarios, which do not constitute deadlocks and should be excluded from deadlock analysis.

Consider the example, we have $\mathbb{E}_L^w = \{(\!|m_2|\!)^w, (\!|m_6|\!)^w\}$ and

$$\pi_U^r((\!|m_2|\!)^w) = \{(\!|m_3|\!)^r\}, \quad \pi_L^r((\!|m_2|\!)^w) = \{(\!|m_5|\!)^r\},$$
$$\pi_U^r((\!|m_6|\!)^w) = \{(\!|m_7|\!)^r\}, \quad \pi_L^r((\!|m_6|\!)^w) = \{(\!|m_1|\!)^r\}.$$

The eventual acquisition constraint is $((\!|m_2|\!)^w \prec_{rf} (\!|m_3|\!)^r \rightarrow (\!|m_2|\!)^w \not\prec_{rf} (\!|m_5|\!)^r) \wedge ((\!|m_6|\!)^w \prec_{rf} (\!|m_7|\!)^r \rightarrow (\!|m_6|\!)^w \not\prec_{rf} (\!|m_1|\!)^r)$.

4.4 Symbolic Encoding of the Verification Condition

We extend the encoding framework in [1,18,23] to support deadlock verification. The framework encodes all possible interleavings of a concurrent program as an SMT formula, thereby reducing the verification task to checking the satisfiability of the resulting formula. Let *guard*(e) be the guard condition for an event e, and $(\!|m_0|\!)^w$ be the write event corresponding to the initialization of the mutex m.

Value Assignment Encoding. Value assignments of variables in each thread can be encoded by directly interpreting the SSA statements. We use ρ_{va} to represent the encoding. The value assignment encoding of the example is $\rho_{va} := (m_0 = 0) \wedge (m_1 = 0 \rightarrow (m_2 = 1 \wedge m_4 = 0)) \wedge (m_5 = 0 \rightarrow (m_6 = 1 \wedge m_8 = 0))$.

Program Order Constraints. The program order $\prec_{po}$ is a natural order of events from the same thread. We use ρ_{po} to represent the program order constraints. Considering the example, $\rho_{po} := ((\!|m_0|\!) \prec_{po} (\!|m_1|\!)) \wedge ((\!|m_0|\!) \prec_{po} (\!|m_5|\!)) \wedge ((\!|m_1|\!) \prec_{po} (\!|m_2|\!) \prec_{po} (\!|m_3|\!) \prec_{po} (\!|m_4|\!)) \wedge ((\!|m_5|\!) \prec_{po} (\!|m_6|\!) \prec_{po} (\!|m_7|\!) \prec_{po} (\!|m_8|\!))$.

Atomicity Constraints. Intuitively, $e_1 \approx e_2$ if event e_1 and event e_2 are in the same atomic operation. We use $\rho_{\approx}$ to represent the atomicity constraints. The atomicity constraint of the exmaple is $\rho_{\approx} := ((\!|m_1|\!) \approx (\!|m_2|\!)) \wedge ((\!|m_3|\!) \approx (\!|m_4|\!)) \wedge ((\!|m_5|\!) \approx (\!|m_6|\!)) \wedge ((\!|m_7|\!) \approx (\!|m_8|\!))$.

Basic Order Constraints. Let $\omega(e)$ be the set of write events that the read event e may read from. For any read $(\!|x_i|\!)^r$ and each write $(\!|x_j|\!)^w \in \omega((\!|x_i|\!)^r)$ on the same variable $x \in \boldsymbol{x} \cup \boldsymbol{m}$, we introduce a Boolean variables $rf^x_{j,i}$, called a *RF variable*, to represent whether event $(\!|x_i|\!)^r$ reads from event $(\!|x_j|\!)^w$. Similarly, we define a Boolean variable $ws^x_{i,j}$, called a *WS variable*, for each pair of writes $(\!|x_i|\!)^w$ and $(\!|x_j|\!)^w$ on the same variable $x \in \boldsymbol{x} \cup \boldsymbol{m}$, to represent whether $(\!|x_i|\!)^w$ occurs earlier than $(\!|x_j|\!)^w$. And for each variable $x \in \boldsymbol{x} \cup \boldsymbol{m}$, we derive from-read relation from RF and WS variables. We encode these three partial-order relations following the approach of [18,23]. Let ρ_{rf} the conjunction of all read-from constraints, ρ_{ws} denote the conjunction of all write-serialization constraints, and ρ_{fr} the conjunction of all from-read constraints.

Eventual-Acquisition Constraint. For any write event $(\!|m_i|\!)^w \in \mathbb{E}^w_L$, if there is a read $(\!|m_j|\!)^r \in \pi^r_U((\!|m_i|\!)^w)$ obtaining its value from $(\!|m_i|\!)^w$, then for any read $(\!|m_k|\!)^r \in \pi^r_L((\!|m_i|\!)^w)$, it must not read from $(\!|m_i|\!)^w$. Since we have already defined the *RF variables* to represent the read-from relations, the eventual-acquisition constraint mentioned in Definition 1 can now be expressed as follows:

$$\rho_{eac} := \bigwedge_{(\!|m_i|\!)^w \in \mathbb{E}^w_L} \left(\bigvee_{(\!|m_j|\!)^r \in \pi^r_U((\!|m_i|\!)^w)} rf^m_{i,j} \rightarrow \bigwedge_{(\!|m_k|\!)^r \in \pi^r_L((\!|m_i|\!)^w)} \neg rf^m_{i,k} \right)$$

Considering the example, the corresponding eventual acquisition constraint can be expressed as: $\rho_{eac} := (rf^m_{2,3} \rightarrow \neg rf^m_{2,5}) \wedge (rf^m_{6,7} \rightarrow \neg rf^m_{6,1})$.

Potential-Deadlock Constraint. Let $\mathbb{E}^r_L$ be the set of all read events on mutex variables that are generated by lock operations in the program. An execution is flagged as potentially deadlocked if at least one `assume` statement used to model a lock operation is violated, i.e., the following constraint is satisfied:

$$\rho_{dl} := \bigvee_{(\!|m_k|\!)^r_l \in \mathbb{E}^r_L} guard((\!|m_k|\!)^r_l) \wedge (m_k = 1)$$

Consider the example program, we have $\mathbb{E}^r_L = \{(\!|m_1|\!)^r_l, (\!|m_5|\!)^r_l\}$. Since there is no control flow statements preceding $(\!|m_1|\!)^r$ and $(\!|m_5|\!)^r$, their guard conditions are both *true*. So the potential-deadlock constraint ρ_{dl} is:

$$\rho_{dl} := (m_1 = 1) \vee (m_5 = 1)$$

The Whole Encoding Formula. The whole encoding formula for a program is $\Psi := \Phi_{valid} \wedge \rho_{eac} \wedge \rho_{dl}$, where $\Phi_{valid} := \rho_{va} \wedge \rho_{po} \wedge \rho_{\approx} \wedge \rho_{ws} \wedge \rho_{rf} \wedge \rho_{fr}$.

4.5 Correctness

Given a concurrent program P, let P' denote the program obtained by replacing all mutex primitives in P with assume-based modeling. Let $[\![P]\!]$ be the set of executions of P, and $[\![P']\!]$ be the set of executions of P'. We write R_l and R_u to signify specifically the read generated by lock and unlock operations.

Definition 2 (Eventual Acquisition). *An execution $\sigma' \in [\![P']\!]$ has eventual acquisitions, if $\exists t_1, t_2 \in \mathrm{TID}, t_1 \neq t_2$, $\exists m \in \boldsymbol{m}$, σ' has a subsequence of the form:*

$$\ldots \xrightarrow{W(t_1,m,1)} \ldots \xrightarrow{R_l(t_2,m,1)} \ldots \xrightarrow{W(t_1,m,0)} \ldots$$

and there is no other write to m between $W(t_1, m, 1)$ and $W(t_1, m, 0)$.

Lemma 1. *An execution $\sigma' \in [\![P']\!]$ violates the eventual acquisition constraint if and only if it has eventual acquisitions.*

Proof. From Definition 1, the constraint is violated if and only if σ' has a write $(\!|m_i|\!)^w \in \mathbb{E}^w_L$ (i.e., $W(t_1, m, 1)$), satisfying the following conditions:

- $\exists (\!|m_j|\!)^r \in \pi^r_U((\!|m_i|\!)^w)$ such that $(\!|m_i|\!)^w \prec_{rf} (\!|m_j|\!)^r$, i.e., $R_u(t_1, m, 1)$ from an unlock operation reads from $W(t_1, m, 1)$. It means that there is no intervening write to $W(t_1, m, 1)$ and $R_u(t_1, m, 1)$. Moreover, since $R_u(t_1, m, 1)$ is immediately followed by the write $W(t_1, m, 0)$ generated by the same unlock operation, there is no other write to m between $W(t_1, m, 1)$ and $W(t_1, m, 0)$.

- $\exists (\!| m_k |\!)^r \in \pi_L^r((\!| m_i |\!)^w)$ such that $(\!| m_i |\!)^w \prec_{rf} (\!| m_k |\!)^r$, i.e., $R_l(t_2, m, 1)$ from a lock operation ($t_2 \neq t_1$) reads from $W(t_1, m, 1)$. It means that $R_l(t_2, m, 1)$ must occur between $W(t_1, m, 1)$ and $W(t_1, m, 0)$.

So σ' contains the subsequence "$\ldots \xrightarrow{W(t_1,m,1)} \ldots \xrightarrow{R_l(t_2,m,1)} \ldots \xrightarrow{W(t_1,m,0)} \ldots$" and there is no other write to m between $W(t_1, m, 1)$ and $W(t_1, m, 0)$. Therefore, it has eventual acquisitions. $\square$

By enforcing the eventual acquisition constraint, we systematically eliminate executions involving eventual acquisitions, thereby preserving the intended semantics of lock operations without explicitly modeling waiting behaviors.

Formally, an execution $\sigma' \in [\![P']\!]$ is *potentially deadlocked* if $\exists t \in \text{TID}$, $\exists m \in \boldsymbol{m}$, σ' has a subsequence of the form "$\ldots \xrightarrow{R_l(t,m,1)} \ldots$". Such an execution lead either to an eventual acquisition or to a deadlock involving indefinite waiting.

We can prove Theorem 1 to ensure the correctness of our modeling.

Theorem 1. *There is an execution $\sigma \in [\![P]\!]$ that witnesses a deadlock if and only if there is an execution $\sigma' \in [\![P']\!]$ such that σ' is flagged as potentially deadlocked and satisfies the eventual acquisition constraint.*

Proof. ($\Leftarrow$): Suppose $\sigma' \in [\![P']\!]$ is flagged as potentially deadlocked, i.e., $\exists t_1 \in \text{TID}$, $\exists m \in \boldsymbol{m}$ such that σ' has a read $R_l(t_1, m, 1)$; and σ' satisfies the eventual acquisition constraint, i.e., σ' has no eventual acquisitions by Lemma 1. Let the last write to m preceding $R_l(t_1, m, 1)$ be $W(t_2, m, 1)$. We can get an execution $\sigma \in [\![P]\!]$ by replacing each read and write to a mutex in σ' with the corresponding lock or unlock operation. Let $W(t_2, m, 1)$ in σ' corresponds to $e_j : L(t_2, m)$ in σ, and let $R_l(t_1, m, 1)$ in σ' correspond to $e_k : L(t_1, m)$ in σ, where j and k are the indices in σ. According to the semantics in Fig. 4, after executing $L(t_1, m)$, t_1 is blocked (i.e. $B(t_1)$ holds). If $t_1 = t_2$ (denoted by t), then since the only thread that can unblock t is t itself, $B(t)$ must hold in every environment (s_i, b_i) of σ for all $i > k$. If $t_1 \neq t_2$, no $W(t_2, m, 0)$ occurs after $W(t_2, m, 1)$ in σ' because σ' has no eventual acquisitions. So for all $i > k$, $e_i \neq U(t_2, m)$ in σ, and $B(t_1)$ holds in environment (s_i, b_i) of σ. Therefore, the final configuration (s_n, b_n) of σ is deadlocked, i.e., σ witnesses a deadlock.

($\Rightarrow$): Suppose $\sigma \in [\![P]\!]$ witnesses a deadlock, i.e., $B(t_1)$ holds in the final configuration (s_n, b_n) of σ. According to the semantics in Fig. 4, the only transition rule that can block a thread is Lock-Wait. Hence, there must exist a lock event $e_k : L(t_1, m)$ in σ that satisfies $s_{k-1}(m) = 1$. As shown in Fig. 2, an eventual acquisition scenario of P can be transformed into the corresponding immediate acquisition scenario by delaying the corresponding lock operation. So we assume without loss of generality that σ contains no eventual acquisitions; formally, no transition in σ is derived using the Unlock-Await rule. By substituting each lock or unlock operation in σ with the corresponding read and write to the mutex, we obtain an execution $\sigma' \in [\![P']\!]$. Clearly, σ' contains no eventual acquisitions and thus satisfies the eventual acquisition constraint by Lemma 1. Moreover, the lock event $e_k : L(t_1, m)$ in σ induces a read event $R_l(t_1, m, 1)$ in σ', which causes σ' to be flagged as potentially deadlocked. $\square$

To establish the correctness of our encoding, we rely on results from prior work [1,18,23]: *The formula Φ_{valid} characterizes all valid executions of the program.* Therefore, we derive the following theorem:

Theorem 2. *The formula Ψ is satisfiable if and only if there is an execution $\sigma \in [\![P]\!]$ that witnesses a deadlock.*

Proof. By prior work [1,18,23], $\Psi = \Phi_{valid} \wedge (\rho_{eac} \wedge \rho_{dl})$ is satisfiable iff there is an execution $\sigma' \in [\![P']\!]$ such that σ' satisfies the eventual-acquisition constraint ρ_{eac} and the potential-deadlock constraint ρ_{dl}. According to Theorem 1, it means that there is an execution $\sigma \in [\![P]\!]$ that witnesses a deadlock. □

4.6 Discussion on Extensibility

In principle, our approach can be naturally extended to synchronization primitives that rely on a waiting mechanism (e.g., semaphores, recursive locks, spinlocks, read-write locks, ...). Their behavior could be classified into either immediate success, eventual success, or indefinite waiting. And they could be modeled analogously to eliminate the eventual success case.

We take semaphores as an example to illustrate how our approach can be extended. Let S be a semaphore with N available resources, equipped with an internal counter $S.count$ that records the number of currently available resources. Initially, $S.count = N$. The semaphore provides the following two primitives:

- `sem_wait`($\&S$): if $S.count = 0$, the calling thread blocks; otherwise, it acquires one unit of the resource and decrements $S.count$;
- `sem_post`($\&S$): the calling thread releases one unit of the resource, increments $S.count$, and wakes up one blocked thread (if any).

Similar to Sect. 3.1, we can classify a `sem_wait`($\&S$) operation executed by a thread t into the following three cases:

- *Immediate Success*: If there are currently available resources (i.e., $S.count > 0$), t immediately acquires one unit of the resource and decrements $S.count$;
- *Eventual Success*: If there are currently no available resources (i.e., $S.count = 0$) but a resource will be released in the future, then t waits for a while and then acquires one unit of the resource;
- *Indefinite Waiting*: If there are currently no available resources and no resource will be released, then t waits indefinitely, resulting in a deadlock.

Similar to our discussion in Sect. 3.1, the eventual success does not need to be considered during verification, as it is equivalent to an immediate success. Therefore, it is safe to eliminate the eventual success case during verification. Assume that we model `sem_wait`($\&S$) as `atomic{assume`($S.count > 0$)$;S.count - -;$`}` and `sem_post`($\&S$) as `atomic{assert`($S.count < N$)$;S.count + +;$`}`. Then, we can eliminate all eventual success cases by introducing a constraint similar to the one in Sect. 4.3. Intuitively, it must ensure that for any `sem_wait(&S)` operation that acquires the last available resource (i.e., $S.count = 1$), if it is read by any `sem_post(&S)` operation from the same thread, then it must not be read by any `sem_wait(&S)` operation from a different thread.

In addition, our core idea (i.e., using ordering constraints to eliminate *eventual acquisition* cases during verification) remains applicable under weak memory models. The main challenge in this extension lies in accurately characterizing valid executions. In fact, the framework on which we build has already extended Φ_{valid} to TSO and PSO weak memory models [18]. Based on these updated Φ_{valid} constraints, our encoding can be transferred to the corresponding weak memory models with only minimal modifications.

5 Implementation and Evaluation

5.1 Implementation, Baseline and Setup

We implemented our approach in a prototype tool, DEAGLE-DL, built on top of DEAGLE [23,24]. DEAGLE comprises two main components: a frontend and a backend. The frontend, primarily adapted from CBMC [35], models concurrent programs using partial orders, while the backend implements an enhanced SMT solver for verifying concurrent programs. We extend DEAGLE's frontend by incorporating our proposed modeling approach for mutexes and encoding of potential-deadlock constraints, enabling DEAGLE-DL to conduct automated deadlock verification. DEAGLE-DL handles loops via unrolling. Crucially, it enforces full unrolling for loops inside critical sections. The reason is that a partially unrolled loop within a critical section may omit a subsequent `unlock` operation, causing the mutex to be spuriously left unreleased in the unrolled program, and thereby introducing false deadlocks that do not exist in the original program.

To assess the effectiveness of DEAGLE-DL, we compare it against two representative state-of-the-art tools: a bounded model checker called ESBMC [19] and a static analyzer developed by Daniel Kroening et al. [34].

- ESBMC [19] is a model checker that adopts the assume-based modeling with counters (Sect. 2.2) to support deadlock verification. It represents a state-of-the-art deadlock verifier based on traditional mutex modeling.
- The static analyzer [34] is a state-of-the-art static analysis tool for deadlock detection. It performs context- and thread-sensitive lockset analysis to construct a lock graph, followed by iterative cycle refinement.

All experiments were conducted on a server equipped with two AMD EPYC 7H12 64-core processors, running Ubuntu 20.04.6 LTS. Following the experimental settings of SV-COMP, each verification task was given a time limit of 900 s. Both DEAGLE-DL and ESBMC [19] handles loops via unrolling. There are heuristics for selecting loop unrolling depths. For example, users may set the bound based on the maximum number of loop iterations observed in typical executions or test suites. In our evaluations, we adopt a standard strategy that increments the loop unrolling bound following the Fibonacci sequence until either a counterexample is found (reported as *deadlock*) or the unrolling depth is deemed sufficient (reported as *deadlock-free*). If the time limit is reached before either condition is met, the result is reported as *bounded deadlock-free.* Note that a *bounded deadlock-free* result gives users increased confidence that the program is deadlock-free, but it does not provide a full correctness guarantee. A special case arises when the time limit is reached before the tool completes checking the first unrolling; in this case, the result is reported as *unknown.* For the static analyzer [34], *bounded deadlock-free* results do not apply. If a deadlock is detected, it reports *deadlock*; otherwise, it reports *deadlock-free.* Any unexpected interruption or error is reported as *error.*

Table 1. Results on Classical Benchmarks. The table reports the number of tasks classified as *deadlock (dl)*, *deadlock-free (dlf)*, and *bounded deadlock-free (bdf)* by each tool, where **x(y)** means the tool reported **y** results in this category, of which only **x** are correct.

Tool	Reported Results			Avg. Costs	
	dl	dlf	bdf	Time (s)	Memory (MB)
DEAGLE-DL	15	15	0	3.7	49
ESBMC	0	0	**15(30)**	900	27097
STATIC ANALYZER	**0(12)**	**3(18)**	0	<0.1	8

5.2 Evaluation on Classical Benchmarks

We conducted experiments on a suite of classical concurrent programming benchmarks [3,15,26,50]. These include the *dining philosophers*, *bank transfer*, *traffic intersection*, *tasks-printers*, and *chefs-appliances* problems. For each benchmark, we considered both deadlocking and deadlock-free variants, resulting in a total of 10 parameterized programs. The former corresponds to the implementation of the original problem, while the latter is obtained by integrating the deadlock-avoidance strategies commonly presented in tutorials into the original versions.

We instantiated these with varying numbers of threads (e.g., 3,5,7), yielding a total of 30 concrete instances. Table 1 presents the results of the tools.

Precision. DEAGLE-DL produces no incorrect results across all instances, outperforming baselines. ESBMC failed to detect any of the 15 deadlocking instances within the allotted time, and also produced only bounded deadlock-free results for the 15 deadlock-free instances. The static analyzer failed to correctly identify any deadlock among the 15 deadlocking instances, which is likely due to imprecision introduced by its overly approximate pointer analysis. For the 15 deadlock-free instances, the static analyzer produced 12 false positives and correctly identified only 3 as deadlock-free. This is largely because the deadlock-avoidance strategies in these classical problems often rely on subtle techniques.

Such non-trivial control flows are difficult to track under the approximations and abstractions adopted by the static analysis tool, often leading to false positives. In contrast, our method comprehensively captures and models these control flows, thereby ensuring accurate reasoning about deadlock.

Efficiency. DEAGLE-DL outperforms ESBMC in both runtime and memory efficiency, but remains less efficient than the static analyzer. ESBMC requires on average nearly 900 s of runtime and 26 GB of memory. In contrast, DEAGLE-DL requires on average only 3.7 s and 49 MB of memory. The advantages of DEAGLE-DL in efficiency can be theoretically explained at the modeling level. As discussed in Sect. 2.2, traditional modeling introduce counters and a large number of auxiliary statements to maintain them for deadlock verification, which leads to significant overhead in both time and space. In contrast, we directly model the effect of waiting by introducing additional eventual acquisition constraints, which allows us to bypass the intricate details involved in modeling the waiting process. Furthermore, since these constraints exclude certain unnecessary executions from the valid execution set, they reduce the total number of executions that need to be explored during verification, which in some cases can further alleviate the time and space burdens.

The static analyzer is highly efficient, requiring no more than 0.1 s and 8 MB across all examples. However, it comes at the cost of extensive approximations and abstractions of the program. As discussed above, such approximations can produce numerous imprecise results and provide comparatively weaker theoretical guarantees. This poses a challenge for complex concurrent programs, where manually inspecting potential deadlocks is far from trivial. In contrast, our method produces no false positives and ensures (bounded) completeness.

5.3 Evaluation on SV-Benchmarks

We conducted our second set of experiments using the *Concurrency* category of the SV-Benchmarks suite [6], specifically the *svcomp25-freeze* version (the frozen release prepared for SV-COMP 2025). Derived from real-world applications and research prototypes, these benchmarks are more complex and representative than classical ones and have been widely adopted in the evaluation of concurrent program verification techniques [1,6,18,23,45,54]. We excluded benchmark programs that do not use mutex primitives (e.g., `lock` and `unlock`) or that relied on other synchronization primitives, resulting in a total of 288 benchmark programs. For all experiments, we used the `.i` files provided by SV-Benchmarks, which are the preprocessed versions of the original source files. Since the SV-Benchmarks suite does not include labeled ground truth for deadlock properties, we established the ground truth through cross-referencing and manual inspection.

For each tool evaluated, Table 2 presents the reported results on the SV-Benchmarks, and Table 3 shows the average time and memory usage.

Table 2. Verification results on the SV-Benchmarks. The table lists the number of tasks reported as *deadlock (dl)*, *deadlock-free (dlf)*, *bounded deadlock-free (bdf)*, *unknown (unk)*, and *error (err)* by each tool.

Benchmark	#.	DEAGLE-DL				ESBMC				STATIC ANALYZER		
Subcategories	Tasks	dl	dlf	bdf	unk	dl	dlf	bdf	unk	dl	dlf	err
goblint-regression	190	9	110	71	0	**6(33)**	60	82	15	**9(13)**	177	0
ldv-races	19	0	17	2	0	0	12	0	7	0	11	8
pthread	19	0	6	13	0	0	0	4	15	**0(3)**	13	3
pthread-C-DAC	3	0	0	3	0	0	0	1	2	0	3	0
pthread-atomic	4	0	2	2	0	0	0	0	4	0	3	1
pthread-complex	2	0	2	0	0	0	0	2	0	0	2	0
pthread-deagle	2	0	2	0	0	0	0	0	2	0	2	0
pthread-divine	1	0	0	1	0	0	0	0	1	0	1	0
pthread-ext	20	1	0	19	0	0	0	13	7	0	**13(14)**	6
pthread-lit	2	0	0	2	0	0	0	1	1	0	2	0
pthread-nondet	2	0	0	2	0	0	0	0	2	0	2	0
pthread-race-challenges	24	0	4	20	0	0	0	13	11	0	24	0
Overall	288	10	143	135	0	**6(33)**	72	116	67	**9(16)**	**253(254)**	18

Precision. Table 2 shows that DEAGLE-DL significantly outperforms baselines in terms of the precision of deadlock detection as well as deadlock-free verification. For the 10 benchmark programs that contains deadlocks (9 from the *goblint-regression* and 1 from the *pthread-ext* subcategory), DEAGLE-DL successfully detected all of them without any false positives. For the 278 deadlock-free programs, DEAGLE-DL proved that over half are free of deadlocks, and established bounded deadlock-freedom for the rest. Notably, the deadlock detected by DEAGLE-DL in the *pthread-ext* subcategory revealed a previously *unknown* bug that could potentially influence the final SV-COMP results. This issue is caused by an `unlock` operation that was mistakenly written as a `lock` operation. We discovered this bug through deadlock detection and confirmed via code inspection that it was indeed a coding mistake. We reported this issue to the SV-Benchmarks organizers, and it was subsequently fixed. Interestingly, this bug had gone unnoticed by both ESBMC and the static analyzer.

ESBMC reported 33 deadlocks, of which only 6 were correct. Among the 27 false positives, 4 were caused by the failure to account for the program termination semantics of the return statement in the main function[3]. The remaining 23 false positives arise from the previously mentioned flaws (Sect. 2.2) of assume-based modeling with counters. In addition, ESBMC misses 4 programs with deadlocks (including the unnoticed deadlock mentioned above) because it

[3] When the main function returns, the program terminates immediately, so threads waiting for resources not released by main are not considered a deadlock in practice.

is unable to find corresponding counterexamples within the time limit. At the same time, ESBMC proved fewer deadlock-free (or bounded) results compared with DEAGLE-DL. The static analyzer reported 16 deadlocks, of which only 9 were correct. Notably, among the 254 programs that the static analyzer reported as deadlock-free, only 253 were truly deadlock-free. The missed deadlock corresponds exactly to the unnoticed mistake in SV-Benchmarks.

In addition, we evaluated two dynamic analysis tools on 10 deadlocking examples from the SV-Benchmarks suite: UNDEAD [61] (to our knowledge the most recent open-source dynamic deadlock detector for C programs) and THREADSANITIZER [49] (a widely used industrial dynamic analysis tool developed by Google). Since these tools do not recognize some verification-only functions, we manually removed or replaced them (e.g., replacing `__VERIFIER_nondet_int()` with `random()`). Within the given time limit, these tools continuously sample execution traces for analysis until a deadlock is detected. They were both able to detect deadlocks in only 3 out of the 10 programs. Notably, neither tool detected the previously unknown bug discovered by our tool.

Efficiency. Table 3 shows that DEAGLE-DL demonstrates substantial improvements in efficiency within bounded model checking, though the static analysis method remains the most efficient overall. Compared with ESBMC, DEAGLE-DL achieves on average a 1.5× improvement in runtime and reduces memory consumption significantly. In contrast, the static analysis tool [34] still outperforms both bounded model checking tools, DEAGLE-DL and ESBMC, in terms of efficiency. However, as discussed earlier, this efficiency of the static analysis approach is achieved at the cost of imprecise results and weaker theoretical guarantees, stemming from the extensive approximations and abstractions it relies on.

Table 3. Average Costs on SV-Benchmarks.

Tool	Time (s)	Mem (GB)
DEAGLE-DL	384	2.26
ESBMC	593	25.26
STATIC ANALYZER	<1	<1

6 Related Work

Static deadlock detection analyzes the source code of the program itself rather than specific executions. The key benefit lies in its potential to exhaustively examine all executions to identify potential deadlocks. There are plenty of researches focusing on static deadlock detection:

Dataflow-analyses-based techniques track relations between threads and usage of resources, building an approximation of a dependency graph. Representative tools include LOCKLINT [14], which requires user annotations; RACERX [16], which applies lockset analysis without pointer analysis; INFER [21], a compositional but context-insensitive analyzer; and PEAHEN [11], which constructs context-insensitive lock graphs and incrementally refines the deadlock cycles. Brotherston et al. [7] propose a compositional static deadlock detector with abstract interpretation for Android Java, which is designed for code-review-time and incremental analysis over large industrial codebases, prioritizing scalability. Kroening et al. [34] proposes a context- and thread-sensitive static analyzer, which speeds up pointer analysis with dependency analysis, and reduces false positives with non-concurrency graph analysis. While these approaches gain efficiency from approximation and abstraction, they tend to generate some false positives. On the other hand, our approach offers stronger theoretical guarantees.

Bounded-model-checking-based techniques have recently shown strong potential for verifying concurrent programs. Alglave et al. [1,2] propose a partial-order-based bounded verification framework. He et al. [18,23,54] have enhanced this framework by deeming some relations unnecessary and eliminating them. Other researchers have further developed and applied it, as seen in projects like YOGAR-CBMC [58–60], LAZY-CSEQ [30], DARTAGNAN [20,36], and more. TCBMC [43] first introduced the assume-based modeling of mutexes. It further proposed the incorporation of counters within assume-based modeling to determine whether deadlock occurs. ESBMC [13] refines it, considering additional scenarios and details to enhance the accuracy of counters. Our approach requires no consideration of the intricate details as in the aforementioned modeling, and achieves deadlock verification in a natural and straightforward manner, yielding not only more precise results but also significantly improved efficiency.

Dynamic deadlock detection focuses on analyzing concrete executions of a program rather than its source code. These techniques have sought to combine testing with formal reasoning to address the inherent limitations of purely testing-based approaches. For instances, the classic GoodLock algorithm [22] has inspired a series of improvements [5,9,49,61], some of which employ re-execution strategies to confirm potential deadlocks [4,31,46,47,52]. Predictive analyses infer bugs in alternate executions [28,29,33,40,41,44,48,51] and avoid false positives, which has effectively detected deadlocks [10,17,32].

7 Conclusion

In this paper, we propose a novel approach to model mutexes, which captures lock semantics while avoiding the need to explicitly model waiting behavior. Our modeling addresses issues that many complex patches in previous work could not fully resolve, by introducing a simple constraint, termed the eventual acquisition constraint. We further propose a deadlock verification method and prove its theoretical correctness. We have implemented our method in a prototype tool. It demonstrates the competitive performance compared to state-of-the-art tools.

Acknowledgments. We thank the anonymous reviewers for their insightful comments, which improved the presentation of this paper. This work was supported by the National Natural Science Foundation of China (No. 62072267 and No. 62021002).

Data Availibility Statement. The artifact contains the source code, executable binaries, scripts, benchmark data, and result-processing scripts required to reproduce the experimental results presented in our paper. It is available on Zenodo [57].

Disclosure of Interests. The authors have no competing interests to declare that are relevant to the content of this article.

References

1. Alglave, J., Kroening, D., Tautschnig, M.: Partial Orders for Efficient Bounded Model Checking of Concurrent Software. In: Sharygina, N., Veith, H. (eds.) CAV 2013. LNCS, vol. 8044, pp. 141–157. Springer, Heidelberg (2013). https://doi.org/10.1007/978-3-642-39799-8_9
2. Alglave, J., Maranget, L., Sarkar, S., Sewell, P.: Fences in Weak Memory Models. In: Touili, T., Cook, B., Jackson, P. (eds.) CAV 2010. LNCS, vol. 6174, pp. 258–272. Springer, Heidelberg (2010). https://doi.org/10.1007/978-3-642-14295-6_25
3. Andrews, G.R.: Concurrent programming: principles and practice. Benjamin-Cummings Publishing Co., Inc (1991)
4. Bensalem, S., Fernandez, J.C., Havelund, K., Mounier, L.: Confirmation of deadlock potentials detected by runtime analysis. In: Proceedings of the 2006 Workshop on Parallel and Distributed S: Testing and Debugging, pp. 41–50 (2006). https://doi.org/10.1145/1147403.1147412
5. Bensalem, S., Havelund, K.: Dynamic Deadlock Analysis of Multi-threaded Programs. In: Ur, S., Bin, E., Wolfsthal, Y. (eds.) HVC 2005. LNCS, vol. 3875, pp. 208–223. Springer, Heidelberg (2006). https://doi.org/10.1007/11678779_15
6. Beyer, D., Strejček, J.: Improvements in software verification and witness validation: SV-COMP 2025. In: International Conference on Tools and Algorithms for the Construction and Analysis of Systems, pp. 151–186. Springer, Cham (2025). https://doi.org/10.1007/978-3-031-90660-2_9
7. Brotherston, J., Brunet, P., Gorogiannis, N., Kanovich, M.: A compositional deadlock detector for android java. In: 36th IEEE/ACM International Conference on Automated Software Engineering (ASE), pp. 955–966. IEEE (2021). https://doi.org/10.1109/ASE51524.2021.9678572
8. Butenhof, D.R.: Programming with POSIX threads, Addison-Wesley Professional (1993)
9. Cai, Y., Meng, R., Palsberg, J.: Low-overhead deadlock prediction. In: Proceedings of the ACM/IEEE 42nd International Conference on Software Engineering, pp. 1298–1309 (2020). https://doi.org/10.1145/3377811.3380367
10. Cai, Y., Yun, H., Wang, J., Qiao, L., Palsberg, J.: Sound and efficient concurrency bug prediction. In: Proceedings of the 29th ACM Joint Meeting on European Software Engineering Conference and Symposium on the Foundations of Software Engineering, pp. 255–267 (2021). https://doi.org/10.1145/3468264.3468549
11. Cai, Y., Ye, C., Shi, Q., Zhang, C.: Peahen: Fast and precise static deadlock detection via context reduction. In: Proceedings of the 30th ACM Joint European Software Engineering Conference and Symposium on the Foundations of Software Engineering, pp. 784–796 (2022). https://doi.org/10.1145/3540250.3549110
12. Coffman, E.G., Elphick, M., Shoshani, A.: System deadlocks. ACM Comput. Surv. (CSUR) **3**(2), 67–78 (1971). https://doi.org/10.1145/356586.356588

13. Cordeiro, L., Fischer, B.: Verifying multi-threaded software using SMT-based context-bounded model checking. In: Proceedings of the 33rd International Conference on Software Engineering, pp. 331–340 (2011). https://doi.org/10.1145/1985793.1985839
14. Corporation, O.: Locklint overview. https://docs.oracle.com/cd/E19059-01/wrkshp50/805-4947/6j4m8jrng/index.html
15. Dijkstra, E.W.: Cooperating sequential processes. In: The origin of concurrent programming: from semaphores to remote procedure calls, pp. 65–138. Springer, Cham (2002). https://doi.org/10.1007/978-1-4757-3472-0_2
16. Engler, D., Ashcraft, K.: RacerX: Effective, static detection of race conditions and deadlocks. ACM SIGOPS Oper. Syst. Rev. **37**(5), 237–252 (2003). https://doi.org/10.1145/945445.945468
17. Eslamimehr, M., Palsberg, J.: Sherlock: scalable deadlock detection for concurrent programs. In: Proceedings of the 22nd ACM SIGSOFT International Symposium on Foundations of Software Engineering, pp. 353–365 (2014). https://doi.org/10.1145/2635868.2635918
18. Fan, H., Sun, Z., He, F.: Satisfiability modulo ordering consistency theory for SC, TSO, and PSO memory models. ACM Trans. Program. Lang. Syst. **45**(1), 1–37 (2023). https://doi.org/10.1145/3579835
19. Gadelha, M.R., Monteiro, F.R., Morse, J., Cordeiro, L.C., Fischer, B., Nicole, D.A.: ESBMC 5.0: an industrial-strength C model checker. In: Proceedings of the 33rd ACM/IEEE International Conference on Automated Software Engineering, pp. 888–891 (2018). https://doi.org/10.1145/3238147.3240481
20. Gavrilenko, N., Ponce-de-León, H., Furbach, F., Heljanko, K., Meyer, R.: BMC for Weak Memory Models: Relation Analysis for Compact SMT Encodings. In: Dillig, I., Tasiran, S. (eds.) CAV 2019. LNCS, vol. 11561, pp. 355–365. Springer, Cham (2019). https://doi.org/10.1007/978-3-030-25540-4_19
21. Harmim, D., Marcin, V., Pavela, O.: Scalable static analysis using facebook Infer. I, VI-B (2019)
22. Havelund, K.: Using Runtime Analysis to Guide Model Checking of Java Programs. In: Havelund, K., Penix, J., Visser, W. (eds.) SPIN 2000. LNCS, vol. 1885, pp. 245–264. Springer, Heidelberg (2000). https://doi.org/10.1007/10722468_15
23. He, F., Sun, Z., Fan, H.: Satisfiability modulo ordering consistency theory for multi-threaded program verification. In: Proceedings of the 42nd ACM SIGPLAN International Conference on Programming Language Design and Implementation, pp. 1264–1279 (2021). https://doi.org/10.1145/3453483.3454108
24. He, F., Sun, Z., Fan, H.: Deagle: An SMT-based verifier for multi-threaded programs (Competition contribution). In: International Conference on Tools and Algorithms for the Construction and Analysis of Systems, pp. 424–428. Springer, Cham (2022). https://doi.org/10.1007/978-3-030-99527-0_25
25. Herlihy, M., Shavit, N., Luchangco, V., Spear, M.: The art of multiprocessor programming, Newnes (2020)
26. Hoare, C.A.R.: Communicating sequential processes. Commun. ACM **21**(8), 666–677 (1978). https://doi.org/10.1145/359576.359585
27. Holt, R.C.: Some deadlock properties of computer systems. ACM Comput. Surv. (CSUR) **4**(3), 179–196 (1972). https://doi.org/10.1145/356603.356607
28. Huang, J.: UFO: predictive concurrency use-after-free detection. In: Proceedings of the 40th International Conference on Software Engineering, pp. 609–619 (2018). https://doi.org/10.1145/3180155.3180225

29. Huang, J., Meredith, P.O., Rosu, G.: Maximal sound predictive race detection with control flow abstraction. In: Proceedings of the 35th ACM SIGPLAN Conference on Programming Language Design and Implementation, pp. 337–348 (2014). https://doi.org/10.1145/2594291.2594315
30. Inverso, O., Nguyen, T.L., Fischer, B., La Torre, S., Parlato, G.: Lazy-CSeq: A context-bounded model checking tool for multi-threaded C-programs. In: 30th IEEE/ACM International Conference on Automated Software Engineering (ASE), pp. 807–812. IEEE (2015). https://doi.org/10.1109/ASE.2015.108
31. Joshi, P., Park, C.S., Sen, K., Naik, M.: A randomized dynamic program analysis technique for detecting real deadlocks. ACM Sigplan Notices **44**(6), 110–120 (2009). https://doi.org/10.1145/1542476.1542489
32. Kalhauge, C.G., Palsberg, J.: Sound deadlock prediction. Proc. ACM Program. Lang. **2**(OOPSLA), 1–29 (2018). https://doi.org/10.1145/3276516
33. Kini, D., Mathur, U., Viswanathan, M.: Dynamic race prediction in linear time. ACM SIGPLAN Notices **52**(6), 157–170 (2017). https://doi.org/10.1145/3062341.3062374
34. Kroening, D., Poetzl, D., Schrammel, P., Wachter, B.: Sound static deadlock analysis for C/Pthreads. In: Proceedings of the 31st IEEE/ACM International Conference on Automated Software Engineering, pp. 379–390 (2016). https://doi.org/10.1145/2970276.2970309
35. Kroening, D., Tautschnig, M.: CBMC – C Bounded Model Checker. In: Ábrahám, E., Havelund, K. (eds.) TACAS 2014. LNCS, vol. 8413, pp. 389–391. Springer, Heidelberg (2014). https://doi.org/10.1007/978-3-642-54862-8_26
36. Ponce-de León, H., Furbach, F., Heljanko, K., Meyer, R.: BMC with memory models as modules. In: 2018 Formal Methods in Computer Aided Design (FMCAD), pp. 1–9. IEEE (2018). https://doi.org/10.23919/FMCAD.2018.8603021
37. Love, R.: Linux kernel development, Pearson Education (2010)
38. Lu, L., Arpaci-Dusseau, A.C., Arpaci-Dusseau, R.H., Lu, S.: A study of linux file system evolution. ACM Trans. Storage (TOS) **10**(1), 1–32 (2014). https://doi.org/10.1145/2560012
39. Lu, S., Park, S., Seo, E., Zhou, Y.: Learning from mistakes: a comprehensive study on real world concurrency bug characteristics. In: Proceedings of the 13th International Conference on Architectural Support for Programming Languages and Operating Systems, pp. 329–339 (2008). https://doi.org/10.1145/1346281.1346323
40. Mathur, U., Pavlogiannis, A., Viswanathan, M.: Optimal prediction of synchronization-preserving races. Proc. ACM Program. Lang. **5**(POPL), 1–29 (2021). https://doi.org/10.1145/3434317
41. Pavlogiannis, A.: Fast, sound, and effectively complete dynamic race prediction. Proc. ACM Program. Lang. **4**(POPL), 1–29 (2019). https://doi.org/10.1145/3371085
42. Qadeer, S., Wu, D.: KISS: keep it simple and sequential. In: ACM-SIGPLAN Symposium on Programming Language Design and Implementation (2004). https://doi.org/10.1145/996841.996845
43. Rabinovitz, I., Grumberg, O.: Bounded Model Checking of Concurrent Programs. In: Etessami, K., Rajamani, S.K. (eds.) CAV 2005. LNCS, vol. 3576, pp. 82–97. Springer, Heidelberg (2005). https://doi.org/10.1007/11513988_9
44. Roemer, J., Genç, K., Bond, M.D.: SmartTrack: efficient predictive race detection. In: Proceedings of the 41st ACM SIGPLAN Conference on Programming Language Design and Implementation, pp. 747–762 (2020). https://doi.org/10.1145/3385412.3385993

45. Sales, E., Inverso, O., Tuosto, E.: Accurate static data race detection for C. In: International Symposium on Formal Methods, pp. 443–462. Springer, Cham (2024). https://doi.org/10.1007/978-3-031-71162-6_23
46. Samak, M., Ramanathan, M.K.: Multithreaded test synthesis for deadlock detection. In: Proceedings of the 2014 ACM International Conference on Object Oriented Programming Systems Languages & Applications, pp. 473–489 (2014). https://doi.org/10.1145/2660193.2660238
47. Samak, M., Ramanathan, M.K.: Trace driven dynamic deadlock detection and reproduction. ACM SIGPLAN Notices **49**(8), 29–42 (2014). https://doi.org/10.1145/2692916.2555262
48. Şerbănuţă, T.F., Chen, F., Roşu, G.: Maximal Causal Models for Sequentially Consistent Systems. In: Qadeer, S., Tasiran, S. (eds.) RV 2012. LNCS, vol. 7687, pp. 136–150. Springer, Heidelberg (2013). https://doi.org/10.1007/978-3-642-35632-2_16
49. Serebryany, K., Iskhodzhanov, T.: ThreadSanitizer: data race detection in practice. In: Proceedings of the workshop on binary instrumentation and applications, pp. 62–71 (2009). https://doi.org/10.1145/1791194.1791203
50. Silberschatz, A., Galvin, P.B., Gagne, G.: Operating system concepts essentials, Wiley Publishing (2013)
51. Smaragdakis, Y., Evans, J., Sadowski, C., Yi, J., Flanagan, C.: Sound predictive race detection in polynomial time. ACM Sigplan Notices **47**(1), 387–400 (2012). https://doi.org/10.1145/2103621.2103702
52. Sorrentino, F.: PickLock: A Deadlock Prediction Approach under Nested Locking. In: Fischer, B., Geldenhuys, J. (eds.) SPIN 2015. LNCS, vol. 9232, pp. 179–199. Springer, Cham (2015). https://doi.org/10.1007/978-3-319-23404-5_13
53. Stallings, W.: Operating Systems: Internals and Design Principles, 9/e. Pearson IT Certification (2018)
54. Sun, Z., Fan, H., He, F.: Consistency-preserving propagation for SMT solving of concurrent program verification. Proc. ACM Program. Lang. **6**(OOPSLA2), 929–956 (2022). https://doi.org/10.1145/3563321
55. Tanenbaum, A.S., Bos, H.: Modern operating systems. Pearson Education Inc., (2015)
56. Walia, E.: Operating system concepts, KHANNA PUBLISHING HOUSE (2002)
57. Wang, P., Han, Z., Sun, Z., He, F.: The artifacts of DEAGLE-DL (2026). https://doi.org/10.5281/zenodo.19696864
58. Yin, L., Dong, W., Liu, W., Li, Y., Wang, J.: YOGAR-CBMC: CBMC with Scheduling Constraint Based Abstraction Refinement. In: Beyer, D., Huisman, M. (eds.) TACAS 2018. LNCS, vol. 10806, pp. 422–426. Springer, Cham (2018). https://doi.org/10.1007/978-3-319-89963-3_25
59. Yin, L., Dong, W., Liu, W., Wang, J.: Scheduling constraint based abstraction refinement for weak memory models. In: Proceedings of the 33rd ACM/IEEE International Conference on Automated Software Engineering, pp. 645–655 (2018). https://doi.org/10.1145/3238147.3238223
60. Yin, L., Dong, W., Liu, W., Wang, J.: On scheduling constraint abstraction for multi-threaded program verification. IEEE Trans. Softw. Eng. **46**(05), 549–565 (2020). https://doi.org/10.1109/TSE.2018.2864122

61. Zhou, J., Silvestro, S., Liu, H., Cai, Y., Liu, T.: UNDEAD: Detecting and preventing deadlocks in production software. In: 2017 32nd IEEE/ACM International Conference on Automated Software Engineering (ASE), pp. 729–740. IEEE (2017). https://doi.org/10.1109/ASE.2017.8115684
62. Zou, M., Du, D., Dong, M., Chen, H.: Using dynamically layered definite releases for verifying the RefFS file system. In: 18th USENIX Symposium on Operating Systems Design and Implementation (OSDI 24), pp. 629–648 (2024). https://www.usenix.org/conference/osdi24/presentation/zou

Complete Local Reasoning About Parameterized Programs Over Topologies

Ruotong Cheng and Azadeh Farzan(✉)

University of Toronto, Toronto, Canada
azadeh@cs.toronto.edu

Abstract. This paper investigates the algorithmic safety verification problem of infinite-state parameterized concurrent programs over a rich set of communication topologies. The goal is to automatically produce a proof of correctness in the form of a *universally quantified* inductive invariant, where the quantification is over the nodes in the topology. We illustrate that under reasonable assumptions on the underlying topology, the problem can be reduced to and solved as a *compositional* scheme, that is, the verification of the parameterized family is reduced to a set of *local* proofs, in a *complete* manner. We propose a verification algorithm and demonstrate through a set of benchmarks over several different topologies that our approach is effective in proving parameterized programs safe.

1 Introduction

Verifying the safety of parameterized programs is a fundamental and well-studied problem in computer-aided verification. This paper focuses on an instance of this problem that is specified by two distinguishing features: (1) The parameterized programs are *infinite-state* and defined over *a rich class of underlying communication topologies.* (2) Safety is formulated as the reachability of an error state that relates a constant number of threads.

In verification of concurrent programs, compositional verification, often called *thread-modular reasoning*, aims to construct a proof of correctness for the entire program by composing correctness proofs for individual threads. This is, however, known to be *incomplete* for reasoning about parameterized programs. In [17], the concept of *thread modularity at many levels* is proposed as an alternative. It is proved to be *complete* w.r.t. a class of proofs in the form of universally quantified invariants, called *Ashcroft Invariants.* Rather than focusing on one thread at a time, the *local* proof can be the proof of the parallel product of k threads, for a fixed k, when an Ashcroft invariant with $k-1$ quantifiers proves the program correct. This scheme, however, is deeply tied to the assumption that the program comprises replicated threads communicating through a *bounded number* of shared global variables. What is the nature of compositional verification of parameterized programs if they are over an arbitrary communication topology?

We propose an answer to this question by using the inherent *symmetry* in such parameterized programs. Let us use an example to illustrate the core ideas.

E. Darulova et al. (Eds.): CAV 2026, LNCS 16682, pp. 67–89, 2026.
https://doi.org/10.1007/978-3-032-32519-8_4

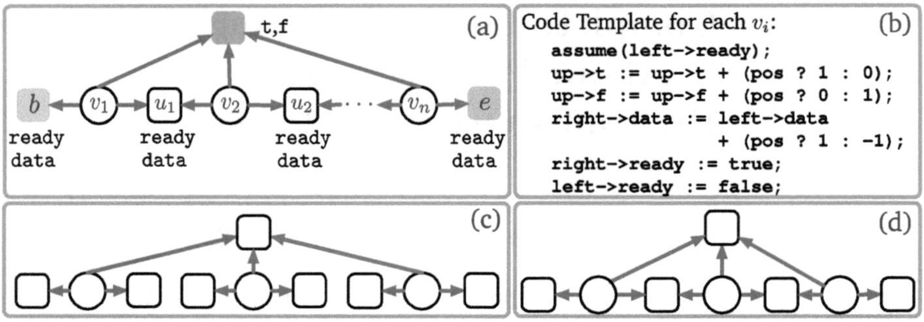

Fig. 1. Pipeline Example (a,b). Small pipeline subprograms (c,d).

Consider the parameterized program given in Fig. 1(a, b), which is a family of pipelines with n processes (depicted as circle nodes) arranged on a line in linear order, where the first and last nodes are *distinguished* from the rest. Each pair of neighbouring processes shares two variables, an integer-typed `data` and a Boolean-typed `ready`, which reside on the square nodes in between. `ready` being true indicates that `data` has been computed and is ready to be read; all instances of `ready` are initially `false`. Additionally, the green (top) square node hosts two *global* counters `t` and `f`. Each process has an uninitialized Boolean-typed variable `pos`, which serves as a nondeterministic Boolean choice. Observe that there are *unboundedly many shared variables and local variables*, which is an important point of departure from classic models such as that of [13,17].

Assume that each circle node atomically executes the given code template, where `left` and `right` refer to the corresponding square node neighbour of the process. The idea is that, depending on the nondeterministic value of `pos`, the process increments or decrements the value before passing it along. Separately, the counts of true and false values for local `pos` variables are recorded in global counters `t` and `f`. We want to prove the property below, which can be proved using a universally quantified inductive invariant:

$$e \triangleright \texttt{ready} \implies e \triangleright \texttt{data} = b \triangleright \texttt{data} + \texttt{t} - \texttt{f}.$$

How can we discover this proof compositionally? The first key observation is that the smaller proofs do correspond to small subprograms (of programs in the parameterized family), but they do not necessarily have to be a single (or several) threads. For instance, Fig. 1(c, d) illustrates two small subprograms with three processes each. In each case, the program includes processes *and* the *neighbourhoods* accessed by them. The distinction between the two programs is that in (d), the processes are strictly neighbours, but not in (c). The three-threaded programs in (c, d), however, *do not* belong in the pipeline parameterized family. It is clear why (c) is not a pipeline, and (d) does not have distinguished beginning and end nodes, and hence is not in the family.

The thesis of this paper is that the proof for the pipeline parameterized family can be composed from the proofs of such subprograms. Intuitively, to construct the proof for any arbitrarily-sized pipeline, we break it into smaller pieces. If we have proofs for sufficiently many pieces that are distinct up-to-isomorphism, then we can use these proofs to give a proof for the entire pipeline program. This is fundamentally based on a *symmetry* argument formalized through an appropriate notion of local isomorphism.

In Sect. 4, we prove a core result that if the parameterized family includes *sufficiently many such small programs*, then a generalized Ashcroft invariant proves the entire family correct *if and only if* it proves the small programs correct. Since programs in the family are instantiated from topologies in the family, this effectively puts a condition on the family of topologies. This has two orthogonal implications: (1) A candidate Ashcroft invariant can be verified using a bounded number of checks (Theorem 2), and (2) rather than searching for an Ashcroft invariant for the entire family, one can look for one for this bounded set. The former is a *cut-off* style theorem for verification. The latter is a key observation behind our compositional verification algorithm. This is inspired by the proof of relative completeness from [9], where we linked a (different) proof system for parameterized programs to a generalization of Ashcroft invariants. We use these invariants, which accommodate arbitrary topologies, use a core observation from the proof, and extend it to prove our *cut-off* theorem.

The generalized Ashcroft invariants are not exactly *local* proofs, even for the small programs. The proof of the cut-off theorem relies on the insight that, without loss of generality, isomorphic neighbourhoods can share proofs, even if they are in different parts of the topology. In Sect. 5, we rely on this insight again to argue that each Ashcroft invariant can be syntactically rearranged (i.e., *normalized*) so that proofs of isomorphic neighbourhoods are *syntactically grouped.* We refer to this transformation as *normalization*, and it streamlines the ingredients (function and predicate symbols) used in the matrix of the formula so that (1) there are distinct parts about the topology and the data manipulated by the program, and (2) using symmetry, one can enforce a bound on the size of terms in the matrix (Lemma 1). This results in a *bounded search space* for the ingredients of Ashcroft invariants, which can now be discovered through purely *local* proof searches for small programs. In other words, *normalization* produces a *complete template* for proof search. This search is then performed through the collection of *local* verification conditions as a system of constrained Horn clauses (CHC). As a consequence of (1), these local proofs become entirely oblivious to the program topology, which eliminates the need for axiomatizing the topology.

One can produce a proof for the entire parameterized family by using the procedure outlined above to collect constraints from all sufficiently many small programs of our cut-off theorem. There are, however, two obstacles to making this a pragmatic solution. First, we already mentioned that our pipeline example does not include the required small subprograms. In general, a typical user-friendly topology family (e.g. rings, lines, and grids) does not include these small subprograms. In [9], we argue that one can *close* these topologies by adding the missing small programs while preserving the safety/unsafety status of the entire family. Second, even if one liberally closes the family, there is an enormous amount of redundancy in constraints collected from all necessary small programs. In Sect. 6, we give a construction that takes a standard user-friendly topology family, like the pipelines of Fig. 1, and populates it with enough small programs to guarantee the required sufficiency conditions for compositional reasoning, and produces a CHC system with less redundancy from them. We take our treatment of redundancy further by introducing a set of *complete* optimizations in Sect. 7. These optimizations take advantage of the fact that our methodology of extracting a *complete template* for proof search from normalized Ashcroft invariants brings a degree of flexibility to this search. The normal form can change, and the set of templates for the search changes with it, but the guarantee of completeness remains.

We have implemented our methodology in a tool called MOSAIC, which takes as input a family of parameterized programs specified as a family of topologies and an assignment of nodes to a bounded number of code templates. Our experimental results show that the method is very effective in proving interesting properties of programs over a broad set of topologies. Furthermore, in Sect. 8, as a theoretical case study, we derive the algorithm of [17] as a special case of our framework to demonstrate its robustness.

2 Background

Structures and Maps Between Them. We are concerned with structures in the context of first-order logic with equality. A *vocabulary* $\mathcal{V}$ is a set of predicate symbols and function symbols, each with a certain *arity* given by a global map ar. A $\mathcal{V}$*-structure* $\mathbb{A}$ is defined as an *underlying set* with an *interpretation* of the symbols in $\mathcal{V}$. We generally use $\mathbb{A}$ to also refer to the underlying set of $\mathbb{A}$.

Let $\mathbb{A}, \mathbb{B}$ be two $\mathcal{V}$-structures. An *embedding* $f : \mathbb{A} \hookrightarrow \mathbb{B}$ is an injection that preserves and reflects the interpretation of all predicate and function symbols. An *isomorphism* is a surjective embedding. An *automorphism* is an isomorphism from a structure to itself. If there is an embedding from $\mathbb{A}$ into $\mathbb{B}$, we say $\mathbb{A}$ is an *embedded substructure* of $\mathbb{B}$; if furthermore, the underlying set of $\mathbb{A}$ is a subset of that of $\mathbb{B}$ and the inclusion map is an embedding, we say $\mathbb{A}$ is a *substructure* of $\mathbb{B}$. The *substructure generated* by a subset A of $\mathbb{A}$ is the smallest substructure containing A that is closed under applying functions from $\mathcal{V}$.

Constrained Horn Clauses. For brevity, we assume the background theory (for program data) is given by a $\mathcal{V}_{\mathsf{Data}}$-structure $\mathbb{D}$. Let $\mathcal{R}$ be a set of predicate symbols representing unknowns, disjoint from $\mathcal{V}_{\mathsf{Data}}$. A *constrained Horn clause* (CHC) is a formula in the vocabulary $\mathcal{V}_{\mathsf{Data}} \cup \mathcal{R}$ that is of the form $B_1 \wedge \cdots \wedge B_n \wedge C \Rightarrow H$, where every B_i is an application $p(x_1, \ldots, x_{\mathsf{ar}(p)})$ of an unknown predicate symbol $p \in \mathcal{R}$ to free variables $x_1, \ldots, x_{\mathsf{ar}(p)}$, C is a $\mathcal{V}_{\mathsf{Data}}$-formula, and the *head* H is either $\bot$ or an application as in B_i.

A *CHC system* $\mathcal{C}$ is a finite set of CHCs. It is *satisfiable* if there exists an interpretation for each unknown predicate symbol that makes the universal closure of each clause in $\mathcal{C}$ valid modulo $\mathbb{D}$. A (syntactic) *solution* to $\mathcal{C}$ maps every unknown p in $\mathcal{C}$ to a $\mathcal{V}_{\mathsf{Data}}$-formula with $\mathsf{ar}(p)$ free variables such that the subsets defined by these formulas constitute a satisfying interpretation.

3 Parameterized Programs and Their Proofs

In this section, we formalize concurrent programs over individual topologies and then parameterized programs over parameterized families of topologies. We formalize a class of safety proofs for such parameterized programs in the form of universally quantified inductive invariants.

3.1 Concurrent Program Over Topology

In our setup, a *topology* is a finite logical structure $\mathbb{T}$ over a vocabulary $\mathcal{V}_{\mathsf{Node}}$, whose underlying elements are called *nodes*. For a set of nodes V, we define the *neighbourhood* $N(V)$ as the substructure generated by the nodes in V. For example, Fig. 1(d) illustrates the neighbourhood of two consecutive nodes in a pipeline, and Fig. 1(c) that of two non-neighbouring nodes. We sometimes identify a tuple of nodes $\boldsymbol{v} \in \mathbb{T}^k$ with the set $\{v_1, \ldots, v_k\}$ and write $N(\boldsymbol{v})$.

We assume there is a variable on every node, which can be a structure consisting of multiple variables, standing in for variables local to a process or shared between neighbouring processes. Intuitively, a process that runs on a node only has access to the variables in its neighbourhood. For brevity, we fix a single data domain $\mathbb{D}$ over a vocabulary $\mathcal{V}_{\mathsf{Data}}$ and assume all variables have domain $\mathbb{D}$.

States and Transitions. For any node v, we say a valuation $N(v) \to \mathbb{D}$ is a *local state* of v. A valuation $\mathbb{T} \to \mathbb{D}$ is a *global state*. A *concurrent program* $\mathbf{P}$ *over a topology* $\mathbb{T}$ can be viewed as a transition system that captures the changes in the local states, which together comprise changes in the global state.

Formally, $\mathbf{P}$ is a pair $\langle \mathbb{T}, [\![-]\!] \rangle$, where $[\![-]\!]$ maps every node a to a binary relation on its local states, which induces a transition relation over the global states by declaring that variables outside the neighbourhood are unaffected: for any global states μ, μ', we have $\mu \xrightarrow{v} \mu'$ if $(\mu|_{N(v)}, \mu'|_{N(v)}) \in [\![v]\!]$ and $\mu|_{\overline{N(v)}} = \mu'|_{\overline{N(v)}}$. We say $\mu \to \mu'$ if $\mu \xrightarrow{v} \mu'$ for some $v \in \mathcal{V}_{\mathsf{Node}}$.

We consider the vocabulary $\mathcal{V}_{\mathsf{Node}}$ (resp. $\mathcal{V}_{\mathsf{Data}}$) to have a single sort Node (resp. Data). Let $\upmu$ and $\upmu'$ be two formal symbols of type $\mathsf{Node} \to \mathsf{Data}$. We define a set $\textsc{Transition}[\mathbb{T}]$ consisting of formulas of the form $\phi[\upmu(\boldsymbol{u}), \upmu'(\boldsymbol{w})]$ (the notation $\upmu(\boldsymbol{u})$ abbreviates the list $\upmu(u_1), \ldots, \upmu(u_{|\boldsymbol{u}|})$, and similarly for $\upmu'(\boldsymbol{w})$), where ϕ is a $\mathcal{V}_{\mathsf{Data}}$-formula and $\boldsymbol{u}, \boldsymbol{w}$ are tuples over $\mathbb{T}$. We assume every $[\![v]\!]$ is definable by such a formula where the nodes are from $N(v)$.

Safety Specification. We assume that the *safety* of a concurrent program is specified through a pair of functions $\langle \mathsf{init}, \mathsf{error} \rangle$, where init and error map each node $v \in \mathbb{T}$ to a set of local states of v.[1] For a global state μ, we say μ satisfies

[1] To simplify presentation, we assume error is a unary function in our formalism. It is straightforward to account for an m-ary error function, where m is no more than the width of the Ashcroft invariant to search for (see Sect. 3.3).

init if $\mu|_{N(v)} \in \mathsf{init}(v)$ for all $v \in \mathbb{T}$, and μ satisfies error if $\mu|_{N(v)} \in \mathsf{error}(v)$ for some $v \in \mathbb{T}$. A program $\mathbf{P}$ is safe w.r.t. $\langle \mathsf{init}, \mathsf{error} \rangle$ if for any global states μ, μ' such that $\mu \to \mu'$, if μ satisfies init, then μ' does not satisfy error.

The class of formulas ASSERTION[$\mathbb{T}$] is defined similarly to TRANSITION[$\mathbb{T}$], except that the symbol μ' does not appear. We assume that every $\mathsf{init}(v)$ and $\mathsf{error}(v)$ is definable by such a formula where the nodes are from $N(v)$.

We abuse notations slightly and also use $\mathsf{init}(v)$, $\mathsf{error}(v)$, and $[\![v]\!]$ to refer to the formula that defines each.

3.2 Parameterized Program Over a Family of Topologies

Parameterized programs are generally defined over a notion of *symmetry*. That is, two programs are considered to be part of the same family when they are in some sense symmetric. In other words, we want symmetric nodes to have symmetric semantics. To formalize this, we use a *local* notion of symmetry defined based on the concept of a *local isomorphism*, inspired by [9].

Symmetry Equivalence. For structures $\mathbb{T}$ and $\mathbb{T}'$ over the same vocabulary, given tuples $\boldsymbol{u} \in \mathbb{T}^d$ and $\boldsymbol{v} \in \mathbb{T}^{d'}$, we say any isomorphism $\beta : N(\boldsymbol{u}) \to N(\boldsymbol{v})$ is a *local isomorphism* (from $\boldsymbol{u}$ to $\boldsymbol{v}$) if it maps $\boldsymbol{u}$ to $\boldsymbol{v}$ (component-wise). *Local isomorphisms* induce an equivalence relation $\simeq$, called *local symmetry*, on tuples over $\mathbb{T}$ and $\mathbb{T}'$: we have $\boldsymbol{u} \simeq \boldsymbol{v}$ if there is a local isomorphism from $\boldsymbol{u}$ to $\boldsymbol{v}$. For example, in the pipeline topology of Fig. 1(a), any two circle nodes are equivalent up to symmetry, as long as they are not the distinguished begin/end circle node; those two nodes are in two other symmetry equivalence classes.

The local isomorphism $\beta : N(\boldsymbol{u}) \to N(\boldsymbol{v})$ induces a map $\beta^* : (N(\boldsymbol{v}) \to \mathbb{D}) \to (N(\boldsymbol{u}) \to \mathbb{D})$ between local states by $\mu \mapsto \mu \circ \beta$. We lift β^* to (sets of) tuples of valuations in the natural way. In other words, symmetric nodes have symmetric semantics, which means that proof arguments from one generalize to the other up to symmetry.

Parameterized Programs. Given a vocabulary $\mathcal{V}_{\mathsf{Node}}$ and a data domain $\mathbb{D}$, a *parameterized (concurrent) program* is an infinite family $\mathcal{P}$ of programs over $\mathcal{V}_{\mathsf{Node}}$-topologies such that for every pair of programs $\langle \mathbb{T}, [\![-]\!] \rangle$ and $\langle \mathbb{T}', [\![-]\!]' \rangle$ in the family, for any $v \in \mathbb{T}$ and $v' \in \mathbb{T}'$ such that $v \simeq v'$ via β (namely $v' = \beta(v)$), we have $[\![v]\!] = \beta^* [\![v']\!]$. We write $\mathcal{P}$ as an indexed set $\{\mathbf{P}_i\}_{i \in \mathcal{I}}$, where $\mathbf{P}_i = \langle \mathbb{T}_i, [\![-]\!]_i \rangle$.

Safety Specification. The safety of a parameterized program is expressed by a *parameterized specification* $\{\langle \mathsf{init}_i, \mathsf{error}_i \rangle\}_{i \in \mathcal{I}}$, where the pair $\langle \mathsf{init}_i, \mathsf{error}_i \rangle$ is a safety specification for $\mathbf{P}_i$. Naturally, we expect the specification to also be symmetric: Formally, for any $i, j \in \mathcal{I}$, $u \in \mathbb{T}_i$, and $v \in \mathbb{T}_j$ such that $u \simeq v$ via β, we have $\mathsf{init}_i(u) = \beta^* \mathsf{init}_j(v)$ and $\mathsf{error}_i(u) = \beta^* \mathsf{error}_j(v)$. We say $\mathcal{P}$ is safe if $\mathbf{P}_i$ is safe w.r.t. $\langle \mathsf{init}_i, \mathsf{error}_i \rangle$ for every $i \in \mathcal{I}$.

3.3 Generalized Ashcroft Invariants

We adapt a class of universally quantified invariants for a generic set of topologies that appear in [9] with the simplifying assumption that program counter variables are available, and the control flow can be encoded through them; this is without loss of generality. The complete formal definition is recalled in [7, Appendix A]. In short, we define QF-ASHCROFT as a fragment of first-order formulas over the vocabulary $\mathcal{V}_{\mathsf{Node}} \uplus \mathcal{V}_{\mathsf{Data}} \uplus \{\mathrm{\mu}\}$ of two sorts, Node and Data, where the special symbol $\mathrm{\mu}$ is typed Node $\rightarrow$ Data, such that no quantification is over Node and every free variable is of sort Node. A generalized Ashcroft assertion of *width* k is a sentence of the form $\forall \nu_1, \ldots, \nu_k . \varphi[\nu_1, \ldots, \nu_k]$, where $\varphi \in$ QF-ASHCROFT and $\nu_1, \ldots, \nu_k$ are Node-sorted variables.

The truth value of a (generalized) Ashcroft assertion is given by a $\mathcal{V}_{\mathsf{Node}}$-topology $\mathbb{T}$ and a global state $\mu : \mathbb{T} \rightarrow \mathbb{D}$, interpreting the symbol $\mathrm{\mu}$ (recall that we fix the data domain). For a program **P** and a safety specification $\langle \mathsf{init}, \mathsf{error} \rangle$, a *generalized Ashcroft invariant* is an Ashcroft assertion that is *inductive* w.r.t. **P** in the standard sense and *sufficient* to establish safety. $\varPhi$ is an Ashcroft invariant for a parameterized program w.r.t. a parameterized specification if it is an invariant for every member of the family.

4 A Cut-Off Theorem for Ashcroft Invariants

The key observation of this section is as follows. Under certain conditions about the underlying family of topologies, an Ashcroft assertion for *a bounded number of programs* in a parameterized family is also an Ashcroft invariant for the entire parameterized family. This is formally stated as Theorem 1 at the end of this section. This can be viewed as a *cut-off* style theorem for Ashcroft invariants over these topologies. It is intuitively clear that the conditions required for such a theorem to hold have to do with the amount of *symmetry* present in the topology family. In some sense, we want the finite set of programs to enumerate all possible different *scenarios* that one may observe in any instance of the family of any size. In [9], such a condition is defined, albeit used for a different purpose:

Definition 1 ([9]). *Let* $k \in \mathbb{N}_+$ *and* $\mathcal{T}$ *be a family of topologies over a vocabulary* $\mathcal{V}$. *A* basis of rank k *for* $\mathcal{T}$ *is a set* $\mathcal{S}$ *of* $\mathcal{V}$*-topologies where for any* $\mathbb{T} \in \mathcal{T}$ *and* $\boldsymbol{v} \in \mathbb{T}^k$, *there is some* $\mathbb{S} \in \mathcal{S}$ *and embedding* $f : \mathbb{S} \hookrightarrow \mathbb{T}$ *such that* $\boldsymbol{v} \in f(\mathbb{S})^k$.

Recall the Pipeline example of Fig. 1. Let us assume $k = 3$. If we pick three arbitrary *middle* circle nodes from the pipeline, there are three possibilities, depending on whether any pair is consecutive or not. Figure 1(c,d) illustrates two of them. A full basis of rank 3 with 15 members is listed in [7, Appendix A]. Since the *first* and *last* nodes of the pipeline are distinguished, there are other choices of three *arbitrary* nodes beyond choosing only *middle* points.

We can now state the following new theorem that relates Ashcroft invariants of a parameterized program to Ashcroft invariants of a *finite* parameterized program, specifically the one over the basis:

Theorem 1 *Let $\mathcal{P} = \{\mathbf{P}_i\}_{i\in\mathcal{I}}$ be a parameterized program over a topology family $\mathcal{T} = \{\mathbb{T}_i\}_{i\in\mathcal{I}}$. For any $k \in \mathbb{N}$, if $\mathcal{T}$ contains a basis $\{\mathbb{T}_j\}_{j\in\mathcal{J}}$ of rank $k+1$ as a subset, then for any Φ of width k and parameterized safety specification, Φ is an Ashcroft invariant for $\mathcal{P}$ if and only if it is an Ashcroft invariant for $\{\mathbf{P}_j\}_{j\in\mathcal{J}}$.*

We give a formal proof in [7, Appendix C]. To get a sense of why the theorem holds, and its connection to the *rank of the basis* for the topology family, we give an informal argument for the nontrivial direction here. Assume we have an Ashcroft invariant Φ for the basis $\{\mathbb{T}_j\}_{j\in\mathcal{J}}$, but Φ is not an Ashcroft invariant of the parameterized family. Then, it must not be an invariant of a specific member based on some topology $\mathbb{T}_i$. Assuming the problem is not with initialization or safety of the invariant, there must be a specific statement of a specific node v violating the inductivity of Φ, which must be witnessed by a concrete tuple of nodes $\boldsymbol{u}$ of length k. By the premise and Definition 1, we know that some substructure of $\mathbb{T}_i$ containing v and $\boldsymbol{u}$ can be identified with a topology in the basis, which is a contradiction, because this violation must be observed in that member of the basis against our assumptions.

Observe that Theorem 1 also indicates that checking whether a given Ashcroft assertion is indeed an invariant can be done through a bounded number of checks under the same conditions. In Sect. 5.2, we further argue (see Proposition 4) that these checks are limited to entailments in the data domain $\mathbb{D}$ and hence *independent* of the topology family. In a sense, the topology family through the high level view of Theorem 1 determines a set of such checks, but any individual check is oblivious to it.

Theorem 2 *Let $k \in \mathbb{N}$ and $\mathcal{T}$ be a topology family such that a finite basis of rank $k+1$ contained in $\mathcal{T}$ is given. For any Ashcroft assertion Φ of width k, parameterized program over $\mathcal{T}$, and parameterized safety specification, one can compute a $\mathcal{V}_{\mathsf{Data}}$-sentence that is valid modulo $\mathbb{D}$ iff Φ is an Ashcroft invariant.*

5 From Ashcroft Invariants to Local Proofs

Theorem 1 links the proofs of small programs over the *basis* of the topology to the proof of the entire parameterized family. These proofs, however, are in the form of Ashcroft invariants. In this section, we shift gears to local proofs, which are algorithmically searchable. We first introduce a normalization procedure for Ashcroft invariants, and then model the resulting *local* verification conditions as a set of Hoare triples. Finally, we state the proof search problem for a single program in the topology as a CHC system.

5.1 Normalizing Ashcroft Assertions

A free-form Ashcroft invariant of width k can have an arbitrarily sized and shaped matrix, which can mix and match terms on the topology family and the underlying data. We use the underlying symmetry of the topology family to argue that any Ashcroft invariant can be rearranged in a way that would syntactically separate the terms about the topology family and the data, and further put a bound on the size of the universe of terms that can appear in it.

We start with two related key observations: (1) Every *quantifier-free formula* represents the union of a number of *local symmetry equivalence classes*, and (2) Under appropriate conditions, every *local symmetry equivalence class* can be represented by a single *quantifier-free formula.*

There is a well-established concept of *types of quantifier rank* r in model theory (e.g., see [22, Sec. 3.4]), where a special case would be when the rank $r = 0$, and hence the focus is on quantifier-free formulas. Consider a tuple $\boldsymbol{v} \in \mathbb{T}^k$ where $\mathbb{T}$ is a $\mathcal{V}$-structure. The *quantifier-free k-type of $\boldsymbol{v}$ over $\mathbb{T}$*, denoted $\mathsf{qftype}(\mathbb{T}, \boldsymbol{v})$, is the set of quantifier-free $\mathcal{V}$-formulas ϕ such that $\mathbb{T} \models \phi(\boldsymbol{v})$. We say $(\mathbb{T}, \boldsymbol{v})$ *realizes* $\mathsf{qftype}(\mathbb{T}, \boldsymbol{v})$. Quantifier-free k-types precisely capture the quotient $\mathbb{T}^k/\simeq$ (i.e. local symmetry equivalence classes) as follows:

Proposition 1 *Let $\mathbb{T}$ and $\mathbb{T}'$ be $\mathcal{V}$-structures. For any tuples $\boldsymbol{v} \in \mathbb{T}^k$ and $\boldsymbol{u} \in \mathbb{T}'^k$, we have $\boldsymbol{v} \simeq \boldsymbol{u}$ if and only if* $\mathsf{qftype}(\mathbb{T}, \boldsymbol{v}) = \mathsf{qftype}(\mathbb{T}', \boldsymbol{u})$.

Example 1 Consider a simplification of the example in Fig. 1, where the top node and associated statements are omitted, and the beginning and ending nodes are exposed as constant symbols instead. There are 6 quantifier-free 1-types that are realized in the topology family $\{\mathbb{T}_n\}_{n \geq 3}$:

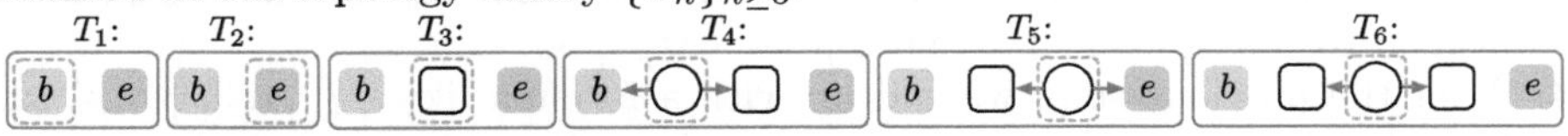

where in each case, the tuple (of size 1) realizing the 1-type is marked. □

Under certain finiteness conditions, a *single* quantifier-free formula is sufficient to determine a quantifier-free k-type. We say a family $\mathcal{T}$ of topologies is *uniformly locally finite* (see [16, Sec. 6.4]) if for any $d \in \mathbb{N}_+$, there is a number $n \in \mathbb{N}$ such that the size of any neighbourhood generated by d nodes is bounded above by n, in any member of $\mathcal{T}$. Practically, such topologies can encode networks where every process is connected to a bounded number of shared resources through bounded set of edge labels. Under the assumption of a finite vocabulary and uniform local finiteness, we can establish two important facts:

Lemma 1 *Given a topology family that is uniformly locally finite and has a finite vocabulary, we have:*

(L1) There are finitely many quantifier-free types (or equivalently local symmetry equivalence classes), and each is definable by a single quantifier-free formula. Moreover, these formulas are computable.
(L2) Every quantifier-free formula is equivalent to the disjunction of finitely many quantifier-free formulas, where each defines a distinct local symmetry equivalence class (as per the above item).

Example 2 (Continuation of Example 1) Assume every `pos` is initialized to `true`. Suppose the vocabulary $\mathcal{V}_{\mathsf{Node}}$ consists of unary function symbols `l` and `r` (for left and right), constant symbols `b` and `e`, and the unary predicate symbol `isProc` indicating a process/circle node. Then, the quantifier-free formula $\alpha_1[\nu]$ defining T_1 from Example 1 is

$$(\nu = \mathtt{l}(\nu) = \mathtt{r}(\nu) = \mathtt{b}) \wedge (\nu \neq \mathtt{e}) \wedge (\mathtt{e} = \mathtt{l}(\mathtt{e}) = \mathtt{r}(\mathtt{e})) \wedge \neg\mathtt{isProc}(\nu) \wedge \neg\mathtt{isProc}(\mathtt{e}).$$

The lemma is analogous to [22, Theorem 3.15], but the proof is slightly more involved due to the function symbols in $\mathcal{V}$. Intuitively, uniform local finiteness ensures that it suffices to consider quantifier-free formulas where the terms are of a bounded height; combined with the finiteness of the vocabulary, it follows that there are finitely many such formulas.

Given an Ashcroft assertion $\forall \boldsymbol{\nu}.\, \varphi[\boldsymbol{\nu}]$, we *normalize* as follows:

1. By pushing negations inward, $\varphi[\boldsymbol{\nu}]$ is rewritten as a positive Boolean combination of formulas of two distinct forms $\phi_{\mathsf{Node}}[\boldsymbol{\nu}]$ and $\phi_{\mathsf{Data}}[\boldsymbol{\nu}]$, where ϕ_{Node} is a quantifier-free $\mathcal{V}_{\mathsf{Node}}$-formula.
2. Using Lemma 1(L2), we replace each sub-formula of the form $\phi_{\mathsf{Node}}[\boldsymbol{\nu}]$ with a disjunction of α_r's, where $\alpha_1, \ldots, \alpha_m$ define the $\simeq$-equivalence classes in the topology family. This results in a formula $\varphi'[\boldsymbol{\nu}]$.
3. We convert $\varphi'[\boldsymbol{\nu}]$ into disjunctive normal form. Observe that, since α_r and $\alpha_{r'}$ $(r \neq r')$ define two disjoint equivalence classes, we have $\alpha_r \wedge \alpha_{r'} \equiv \bot$. Hence, each disjunct can have at most one appearance of some α_r. To ensure that each disjunct has precisely one appearance of some α_r, we do this process instead to the equivalent formula $\varphi'[\boldsymbol{\nu}] \wedge \bigvee_{r=1}^{m} \alpha_r$.
4. After the previous step, we end up with a formula like $\bigvee_{r=1}^{m} \alpha_r[\boldsymbol{\nu}] \wedge \varphi'_r[\boldsymbol{\nu}]$. But, the $\mathcal{V}_{\mathsf{Node}}$-terms that appear under φ'_r can be arbitrary. This means that the same node can be referenced in several different ways. As the last step, we put these $\mathcal{V}_{\mathsf{Node}}$-terms into normal forms so that we impose a unique way of referencing each node. Fortunately, one can argue (see Remark 1) that for every $\simeq$-equivalence class, there is a bounded set of representative terms such that every node can be referenced in a unique way. Let $t_r^{(1)}, \ldots, t_r^{(n_r)}$ be a list of representative terms. We change all references to nodes in $\psi_r[\boldsymbol{\nu}]$ to use the representative terms and get the following formula as the result of the normalization process: $\forall \boldsymbol{\nu}.\, \bigvee_{r=1}^{m} \alpha_r[\boldsymbol{\nu}] \wedge \phi_r[\mu(t_r^{(1)}[\boldsymbol{\nu}]), \ldots, \mu(t_r^{(n_r)}[\boldsymbol{\nu}])]$.

Remark 1 For any k-tuple $\boldsymbol{v}$ over $\mathbb{T} \in \mathcal{T}$, the neighbourhood $N(\boldsymbol{v})$ is of bounded size. Let the tuple $\boldsymbol{u}$ represent all nodes in $N(\boldsymbol{v})$ and for each $i = 1, \ldots |N(\boldsymbol{v})|$. A set of representative terms chooses a term for each u_i, which are by construction free of repetitions. Alternatively, equalities between different possible choices of representative terms appear as formulas in $\mathsf{qftype}(\mathbb{T}, \boldsymbol{v})$, and the choice of the representative term can be viewed as choosing one of the equivalent terms. We call $\boldsymbol{t}$ a list of *representative terms* for $\mathsf{qftype}(\mathbb{T}, \boldsymbol{v})$ where $t^{(i)}(\boldsymbol{v}) = u_i$.

Theorem 3 *Under the condition in Lemma 1, every Ashcroft assertion is equivalent over $\mathcal{T}$ to a normalized Ashcroft assertion of the same width.*

Example 3 (Continuation of Example 1) Let $\alpha_1[\nu], \ldots, \alpha_6[\nu]$ be quantifier-free formulas defining the types $T_1, \ldots, T_6$. Consider the given Ashcroft assertion

$$\forall \nu.(\mathtt{isProc}(\nu) \wedge \mathtt{l}(\nu) \neq \mathtt{b}) \rightarrow \mathtt{ready}(\mu(\mathtt{r}(\nu))) \rightarrow \mathtt{data}(\mu(\mathtt{b})) < \mathtt{data}(\mu(\mathtt{r}(\nu))).$$

After step 1, a ϕ_{Node} subformula in this can be $\neg(\mathtt{isProc}(\nu) \wedge \mathtt{l}(\nu) \neq \mathtt{b})$. It is satisfied in the topology family by a union of equivalence classes, which in this case correspond to $T_1, \ldots, T_4$, and hence this subformula is replaced in step 2 with $\bigvee_{r=1}^{4} \alpha_r[\nu]$. After step 3, the formula $\varphi_5'[\nu]$, corresponding to T_5 (from Example 1), is $\mathtt{ready}(\mu(\mathtt{r}(\nu))) \rightarrow \mathtt{data}(\mu(\mathtt{b})) < \mathtt{data}(\mu(\mathtt{r}(\nu)))$. If we choose $(\nu, \mathtt{l}(\nu), \mathtt{b}, \mathtt{e})$ as the representative terms for T_5, then in step 4 this is rewritten to $\mathtt{ready}(\mu(\mathtt{e})) \rightarrow \mathtt{data}(\mu(\mathtt{b})) < \mathtt{data}(\mu(\mathtt{e}))$. However, if we choose $(\nu, \mathtt{l}(\nu), \mathtt{b}, \mathtt{r}(\nu))$ as the representative terms, then $\varphi_5'[\nu]$ stays as it is. □

5.2 Hoare Triples From a Normalized Ashcroft Invariant

A normalized Ashcroft assertion is basically a template invariant of width k. To instantiate the template, we need to search for interpretations for its uninterpreted symbols. Given a specific program, the verification conditions for the validity of the invariant can be used as constraints in this search. Below, we define precisely what these verification conditions are in the form of Hoare triples obtained from the normalized Ashcroft invariant for a specific program.

Fix vocabularies $\mathcal{V}_{\mathsf{Node}}$ and $\mathcal{V}_{\mathsf{Data}}$. For any formula $\varphi[\nu_1, \ldots, \nu_k]$ in QF-Ashcroft, topology $\mathbb{T}$, and tuple $\boldsymbol{v}$ in $\mathbb{T}^k$, expanding the vocabulary $\mathcal{V}_{\mathsf{Node}}$ with parameters from $\mathbb{T}$, we can obtain a closed QF-Ashcroft formula $\varphi[\boldsymbol{v}]$ by substituting $\boldsymbol{v}$ for the free variables. Then, for a given topology $\mathbb{T}$, any Ashcroft assertion $\Phi := \forall \boldsymbol{\nu}.\, \varphi[\boldsymbol{\nu}]$ is equivalent to a conjunction $\bigwedge_{\boldsymbol{v} \in \mathbb{T}^k} \varphi[\boldsymbol{v}]$, and we can relate Φ to a set of Hoare triples in Fig. 2.

$\forall \boldsymbol{w} \in \mathbb{T}^k, \forall v_0, w \in \mathbb{T}$:

$$\{\bigwedge_{v \in \mathbb{T}} \mathsf{init}(v)\}\ \epsilon\ \{\varphi[\boldsymbol{w}]\} \qquad (\text{Init})$$

$$\{\bigwedge_{\boldsymbol{v} \in \mathbb{T}^k} \varphi[\boldsymbol{v}]\}\ v_0\ \{\varphi[\boldsymbol{w}]\} \qquad (\text{Cont})$$

$$\{\bigwedge_{\boldsymbol{v} \in \mathbb{T}^k} \varphi[\boldsymbol{v}]\}\ \epsilon\ \{\neg\mathsf{error}(w)\} \qquad (\text{Safe})$$

Fig. 2. Set $H_\Phi^{\mathbb{T}}$ of Hoare triples for Φ.

In [9, Proposition 6.3], valid Hoare triples are obtained from an Ashcroft invariant in the same style. We observe that the *converse* also holds.

Proposition 2 *Let* **P** *be a program over a finite topology* $\mathbb{T}$*. For any* Φ*, the Hoare triples in* $H_\Phi^{\mathbb{T}}$ *are valid if* ***and only if*** Φ *is an Ashcroft invariant for* **P**.

We say a Hoare triple is in normal form if its precondition and postcondition are Assertion[$\mathbb{T}$] formulas for some $\mathcal{V}_{\mathsf{Node}}$-structure $\mathbb{T}$.

Proposition 3 *Any Hoare triple in* $H_\Phi^{\mathbb{T}}$ *is equivalent to one in normal form.*

In particular, for a normalized Ashcroft assertion $\forall \boldsymbol{\nu}.\, \varphi[\boldsymbol{\nu}]$, we have

$$\varphi[\boldsymbol{v}] \equiv \phi_r[\mu(t_r^{(1)}(\boldsymbol{v})), \ldots, \mu(t_r^{(n_r)}(\boldsymbol{v}))] \qquad (1 \leq r \leq m)$$

where r is the unique number such that $T_r = \mathsf{qftype}(\mathbb{T}, \boldsymbol{v})$, also denoted by $r(\boldsymbol{v})$.

For every node v, let x_v be a fresh Data-sorted variable; it is fine to overlap names between different topologies. We define a substitution operation on any

$$\forall \boldsymbol{w} \in \mathbb{T}^k, \forall v_0, w \in \mathbb{T}_i: \quad \bigwedge_{v \in \mathbb{T}_i} \textsc{Subst}(\mathsf{init}_i(v)) \implies Inv_{r(\boldsymbol{w})}(\boldsymbol{x}_{U(\boldsymbol{w})}) \qquad (1)$$

$$\bigwedge_{\boldsymbol{v} \in \mathbb{T}_i^k} Inv_{r(\boldsymbol{v})}(\boldsymbol{x}_{U(\boldsymbol{v})}) \wedge \textsc{Subst}(\mathsf{Global}_{\mathbb{T}_i}[\![v_0]\!]_i) \implies Inv_{r(\boldsymbol{w})}(\boldsymbol{x}'_{U(\boldsymbol{w})}) \qquad (2)$$

$$\bigwedge_{\boldsymbol{v} \in \mathbb{T}_i^k} Inv_{r(\boldsymbol{v})}(\boldsymbol{x}_{U(\boldsymbol{v})}) \implies \textsc{Subst}(\neg\mathsf{error}_i(w)) \qquad (3)$$

Fig. 3. Constrained Horn Clauses for a single program over topology $\mathbb{T}_i$

Assertion[$\mathbb{T}$] or Transition[$\mathbb{T}$] formula φ: let $\textsc{Subst}(\varphi)$ be the $\mathcal{V}_{\mathsf{Data}}$-formula obtained from φ by substituting $\mu(v)$ with x_v and $\mu'(v)$ with x'_v for all $v \in \mathbb{T}$. In addition, we use φ' to denote the formula obtained from φ by replacing every μ with μ'. The following proposition relates the validity of a Hoare triple in normal form to an entailment in the background theory $\mathbb{D}$ for program data. We define $\mathsf{Global}_{\mathbb{T}}[\![v]\!]$ as the formula $[\![v]\!] \wedge \bigwedge_{u \in \mathbb{T} \setminus N(v)} (\mu(u) = \mu'(u))$.

Proposition 4 *Let φ and ψ be* Assertion[$\mathbb{T}$] *formulas.*

- *For any $a \in \mathbb{T}$, the Hoare triple $\{\varphi\}\ a\ \{\psi\}$ is valid if and only if $\mathbb{D} \models \textsc{Subst}(\varphi \wedge \mathsf{Global}_{\mathbb{T}}[\![a]\!] \Rightarrow \psi')$.*
- *The Hoare triple $\{\varphi\}\ \epsilon\ \{\psi\}$ is valid if and only if $\mathbb{D} \models \textsc{Subst}(\varphi \Rightarrow \psi)$.*

5.3 CHC Encoding for Normalized Ashcroft Invariants

We start by using the observations from Propositions 2 and 4 to set up a search for an Ashcroft invariant for a single program in the topology as a CHC encoding. From the normalization procedure (Theorem 3), we collect the quantifier-free k-types T_r and their corresponding representative terms $t_r^{(1)}, \ldots, t_r^{(n_r)}$, for each T_r ($1 \leq r \leq m$). Let $\mathbf{P}_i$ be a program over a topology $\mathbb{T}_i \in \mathcal{T}$. The CHC system for searching for an Ashcroft invariant of width k for $\mathbf{P}_i$ is based on unknown predicates of the form $Inv_i : \mathbb{D}^{n_i} \to \mathsf{bool}$ ($1 \leq i \leq m$).

The clauses are listed in Fig. 3. For any $\mathbb{T} \in \mathcal{T}$ and tuple $\boldsymbol{v} \in \mathbb{T}^k$, the tuple $\boldsymbol{x}_{\boldsymbol{v}}$ abbreviates $(x_{v_1}, \ldots, x_{v_k})$ and the tuple $U(\boldsymbol{v})$ lists the neighbours of $\boldsymbol{v}$ in the same order as $t_{r(\boldsymbol{v})}$, i.e., $U(\boldsymbol{v}) = (t_j^{(1)}(\boldsymbol{v}), \ldots, t_j^{(n_j)}(\boldsymbol{v}))$, where $j = r(\boldsymbol{v})$.

The clauses are based on Proposition 4 for the validity of the Hoare triples $H_{\Phi}^{\mathbb{T}_i}$ (see Fig. 2), which certify that the Ashcroft assertion Φ is an invariant for the program over $\mathbb{T}_i$.

Theorem 4 *The CHC system of Fig. 3 is (syntactically) satisfiable iff an Ashcroft invariant of width k for $\langle \mathbb{T}_i, [\![-]\!]_i \rangle$ w.r.t. $\langle \mathsf{init}_i, \mathsf{error}_i \rangle$ exists. Moreover, the invariant has the form $\forall \boldsymbol{\nu}.\ \bigvee_{r=1}^{m} \alpha_r[\boldsymbol{\nu}] \wedge Inv_r[\mu(t_r^{(1)}[\boldsymbol{\nu}]), \ldots, \mu(t_r^{(n_r)}[\boldsymbol{\nu}])]$.*

6 Compositional Proof Search for an Ashcroft Invariant

In Sect. 5, we established how to effectively search for ingredients of an Ashcroft invariant for a single program. Combining this with the observation of Theorem 1, one can immediately see how this can be extended to an entire parameterized program. Intuitively, we list all the constraints for all the programs in the basis as stated in Theorem 1.

Theorem 5 *Let $\mathcal{P} = \{\langle \mathbb{T}_i, [\![-]\!]_i \rangle\}_{i \in \mathcal{I}}$ be a parameterized program whose topologies satisfy the finiteness assumptions. Let $\mathcal{S} = \{\langle \mathsf{init}_i, \mathsf{error}_i \rangle\}_{i \in \mathcal{I}}$ be a parameterized specification. For any $k \in \mathbb{N}$, given a finite subset of $\mathcal{T}$ that constitutes a basis of rank $k+1$, one can effectively construct a CHC system that has a solution if and only if there is an Ashcroft invariant of width k for $\mathcal{P}$ w.r.t. $\mathcal{S}$.*

There are however two problems with this process as a practical algorithm: (1) Practically no user-friendly topology family has a finite basis to satisfy the conditions of Theorem 1, and (2) Even for those that do, this process may produce a CHC system with a very high amount of *redundancy*. In [9], the first problem is addressed through a procedure that augments topologies with all the missing small programs to form a finite basis. We use this idea and turn it into a reasonable algorithm that permits the user to specify the input parameterized program using a natural family of topologies (e.g. *rings*) that does not contain a finite basis, and generates the CHC encoding by efficiently deciding what small programs to add and which constraints from Fig. 3 to include.

6.1 Subprograms and Downward Closure

Given a program $\mathbf{P} = \langle \mathbb{T}, [\![-]\!] \rangle$, for any substructure $\mathbb{S}$ of $\mathbb{T}$, the *subprogram* of $\mathbf{P}$ over $\mathbb{S}$ is the program $\mathbf{P}|_{\mathbb{S}} = \langle \mathbb{S}, [\![-]\!]|_{\mathbb{S}} \rangle$. Note that a safety specification for $\mathbf{P}$ can be restricted to a safety specification for any subprogram. Adding subprograms to a parameterized program always preserves unsafety. We show that under certain conditions, it also preserves safety. Given a topology $\mathbb{T}$, we say an initial condition init is *extensible* if for any substructure $\mathbb{S}$ of $\mathbb{T}$, for any initial global state μ on $\mathbb{S}$, there is an initial global state μ' on $\mathbb{T}$ such that $\mu'|_{\mathbb{S}} = \mu$.

Theorem 6 *Let $\mathcal{P}$ and $\mathcal{P}'$ be parameterized programs such that $\mathcal{P} \subset \mathcal{P}'$ and every program of $\mathcal{P}'$ is a subprogram of some program in $\mathcal{P}$. Given any parameterized safety specification for $\mathcal{P}$, the safety of $\mathcal{P}'$ implies the safety of $\mathcal{P}$, and the converse holds if the initial condition on every topology in $\mathcal{P}$ is extensible.*

For any topology $\mathbb{T}$, define $\mathsf{sub}_k(\mathbb{T})$ as the set of substructures of $\mathbb{T}$ generated by k not necessarily distinct nodes. For any parameterized program $\mathcal{P} = \{\mathbf{P}_i\}_{i \in \mathcal{I}}$, where $\mathbf{P}_i$ is over topology $\mathbb{T}_i$, define $\mathsf{CL}(\mathcal{P}, k)$ as the parameterized program obtained from $\mathcal{P}$ by adding the subprogram $\mathbf{P}_i|_{\mathbb{S}}$ for any $i \in \mathcal{I}$ and $\mathbb{S} \in \mathsf{sub}_k(\mathbb{T}_i)$. The following proposition, which follows from [9, Proposition 6.7], presents a finite basis of rank k contained in the topologies of $\mathsf{CL}(\mathcal{P}, k)$ under the assumptions in Theorem 3.

Proposition 5 *Let $k \in \mathbb{N}_+$ and $\mathcal{T}$ be a locally uniformly finite class of topologies over a finite vocabulary. Let $\mathcal{S} := \bigcup_{\mathbb{T}\in\mathcal{T}} \mathsf{sub}_k(\mathbb{T})$. Then $\mathcal{S}$ is a basis for $\mathcal{T}$ of rank k that is finite up to isomorphism.*

6.2 CHCs for Downward Closure

If we blindly collect Hoare triples from all small programs in the basis, we end up with redundant Hoare triples with the same postcondition and command, but different preconditions, where one is subsumed by the other in a purely syntactic way. Avoiding these redundancies by constructing the full set and pruning it is clearly not a desirable solution. In Algorithm 1, we present an alternative. It takes as input a parameterized program $\mathcal{P}$, a parameterized specification $\mathcal{S}$, and a number $k \in \mathbb{N}_+$, and returns a CHC system that encodes the existence of an Ashcroft invariant for the downward closure of $\mathcal{P}$. The indexed sets $\mathcal{P}$ and $\mathcal{S}$ are given as computable functions. We assume there is an oracle QF-Types$(\mathcal{T}, k)$ that returns a list of all quantifier-free k-types in $\mathcal{T}$, where each type is represented by a k-tuple in a topology in $\mathcal{T}$. The algorithm may simplify the verification condition of one program by deferring to that of a smaller program, leveraging the fact that the *smallest* substructure containing the nodes in a command and postcondition is in the downward closure.

Algorithm 1. CHCs for a Downward Closure

Require: Program $\mathcal{P} = \{\langle \mathbb{T}_i, [\![-]\!]_i\rangle\}_{i\in\mathcal{I}}$ on topologies $\mathcal{T} = \{\mathbb{T}_i\}_{i\in\mathcal{I}}$ satisfying the finiteness assumptions, $\mathcal{S} = \{\mathbf{S}_i\}_{i\in\mathcal{I}}$ is a parameterized specification, and $k \in \mathbb{N}_+$

procedure Chcs-for-Downward-Closure$(\mathcal{P}, \mathcal{S}, k)$
  compute $\alpha_1, \ldots, \alpha_m$ and representative terms $t_r^{(j)}$ as per Theorem 3
  $\mathcal{C} \leftarrow \varnothing$
  for all $(\mathbb{T}_i, \boldsymbol{w}) \in$ QF-Types$(\mathcal{T}, k)$ **do**
    $\mathcal{C} \leftarrow \mathcal{C} \cup \left\{\bigwedge_{v\in N(\boldsymbol{w})} \textsc{Subst}(\mathsf{init}_i(v)) \Rightarrow Inv_{r(\boldsymbol{w})}(\boldsymbol{x}_{U(\boldsymbol{w})})\right\}$
  for all $(\mathbb{T}_i, v_0\,\boldsymbol{w}) \in$ QF-Types$(\mathcal{T}, k+1)$ **do**
    $\phi \leftarrow \textsc{Subst}(\mathsf{Global}_{N(v_0\boldsymbol{w})}[\![v_0]\!]_i)$
    $\mathcal{C} \leftarrow \mathcal{C} \cup \left\{\bigwedge_{\boldsymbol{v}\in N(v_0\boldsymbol{w})^k} Inv_{r(\boldsymbol{v})}(\boldsymbol{x}_{U(\boldsymbol{v})}) \wedge \phi \Rightarrow Inv_{r(\boldsymbol{w})}(\boldsymbol{x}'_{U(\boldsymbol{w})})\right\}$
  for all $(\mathbb{T}_i, w) \in$ QF-Types$(\mathcal{T}, 1)$ **do**
    $\mathcal{C} \leftarrow \mathcal{C} \cup \left\{\bigwedge_{\boldsymbol{v}\in N(w)^k} Inv_{r(\boldsymbol{v})}(\boldsymbol{x}_{U(\boldsymbol{v})}) \Rightarrow \textsc{Subst}(\neg\mathsf{error}_i(w))\right\}$
  return $\mathcal{C}$

Theorem 7 *The algorithm* Chcs-for-Downward-Closure$(\mathcal{P}, \mathcal{S}, k)$ *returns a CHC system that is (syntactically) satisfiable if and only if there is an Ashcroft invariant of width k for $\mathsf{CL}(\mathcal{P}, k+1)$ w.r.t. $\mathcal{S}$.*

There are $|$QF-Types$(\mathcal{T}, k)|$ unknown predicates produced by Algorithm 1, the same as Theorem 5, and $O(|$QF-Types$(\mathcal{T}, k+1)|)$ clauses are generated. Both are characteristics of the topology family, which reflect its complexity.

For a specific topology family $\mathcal{T}$, the procedure QF-TYPES$(\mathcal{T}, k)$ can often be implemented by enumerating node tuples of length k in small instances of $\mathcal{T}$. For instance, if $\mathcal{T}$ is the family of lines in the style of Fig. 1 (a), it suffices to enumerate node tuples in line instances with up to $2k+1$ circle nodes.

7 Complete Encoding Optimizations

A key feature of our solution is that the normalization process grants us flexibility and control in devising the *complete* template for proof search. In this section, we take advantage of this control to introduce a couple of *complete* optimizations for the encoding. We first lay the formal foundation for these optimizations through a *parametric* variance of the normalization process introduced in Sect. 5.1. Concrete optimizations are defined as instantiations of the parameter. This means that we can give a single proof of completeness for the template (Theorem 8) and the completeness of all individual optimizations presented in this section immediately follows. The soundness is trivial, as any instantiation of a restricted template can be converted into an instantiation of a full template.

7.1 Parametric Normalization of Ashcroft Invariants

Let us continue with the normalization procedure in Sect. 5.1. We claim that with further syntactic manipulations to a normalized Ashcroft assertion, the formulas ϕ_r's can be guaranteed to be *symmetric*: Let the types in the topology family be $T_1, \ldots, T_m$ and $\boldsymbol{v}_r$ be a node tuple that realizes T_r for each r. We say the formula ϕ_r is *symmetric* (w.r.t. the type T_r) if for any automorphism f on $N(\boldsymbol{v}_r)$, we have $\phi_r[x_1, \ldots, x_{n_r}] \equiv \phi_r[x_{\pi_f(1)}, \ldots, x_{\pi_f(n_r)}]$, where π_f is the permutation on indices $\{1, \ldots, n_r\}$ induced by f and the representative terms of T_r. We exploit the symmetry of these formulas in Sect. 8.

Moreover, some ϕ_r's can be assumed to be $\top$ (true). We use an *indicator* vector $\chi \in \{\top, \bot\}^m$ to *indicate* which. We say χ *selects a basis of rank* k from $\mathcal{T}$ if the collective neighbourhoods of the node tuples at the indicated indices form a basis of rank k for the topology; formally, if $\mathcal{U} := \{N(\boldsymbol{v}_r) : \chi_r \equiv \top\}$ is a basis of rank k for $\mathcal{T}$.

Theorem 8 *Assume the setting of Theorem 3. Let $\chi \in \{\top, \bot\}^m$ be any indicator vector that selects a basis of rank k from $\mathcal{T}$. Then over $\mathcal{T}$, any Ashcroft assertion is equivalent to a normalized Ashcroft assertion of the same width*

$$\forall \nu_1, \ldots, \nu_k. \bigvee_{r=1}^{m} \alpha_r[\boldsymbol{\nu}] \wedge \phi_r[\mu(t_r^{(1)}[\boldsymbol{\nu}]), \ldots, \mu(t_r^{(n_r)}[\boldsymbol{\nu}])]$$

such that for every r, ϕ_r is symmetric w.r.t. the type T_r, and $\phi_r \equiv \top$ if $\chi_r \equiv \bot$.

The proof idea is that, given a formula $p[x_1, x_2]$, the conjunction $p[x_1, x_2] \wedge p[x_2, x_1]$ is invariant under any permutation on the indices $\{1, 2\}$.

We use the symmetry of ϕ_r's in Sect. 8 and the indicator vector $\boldsymbol{\chi}$ to define optimizations in this section. Given $\boldsymbol{\chi}$, we may modify Algorithm 1 by skipping $\boldsymbol{w}$ such that $\chi_{r(\boldsymbol{w})} \equiv \bot$ in line 4 and 6 and, similarly, skipping $\boldsymbol{v}$ such that $\chi_{r(\boldsymbol{v})} \equiv \bot$ in line 8 and 10. For an input parameterized program $\mathcal{P}$ to the algorithm, this simplification is *complete* if $\boldsymbol{\chi}$ selects a basis of rank k from the topology family of $\mathsf{CL}(\mathcal{P}, k+1)$.

7.2 One Predicate per Neighbourhood

By default, our CHC encoding uses one unknown predicate per quantifier-free k-type $T_1, \dots, T_m$ in $\mathcal{T}$. Let $\mathbb{U}_r$ be the neighbourhood of an arbitrary tuple with type T_r, which is unique up to isomorphism. We define an equivalence relation on the types $T_1, \dots, T_m$ based on these neighbourhoods: we say $T_r \sim T_s$ if $\mathbb{U}_r$ is isomorphic to $\mathbb{U}_s$. Then, the $\sim$ relation provides a choice of $\boldsymbol{\chi}$ that always induces a complete optimization to Algorithm 1: for each equivalence class in $\{T_1, \dots, T_m\}/\!\sim$, χ_r chooses precisely one representative from the class. The net effect is that we use one unknown predicate per neighbourhood generated by k nodes. In Sect. 9, we refer to this optimization as `OPN`.

7.3 Distinct Process Nodes as Generators

We start by assuming that the nodes in a topology $\mathbb{T}$ are partitioned into two kinds: process nodes and resource nodes; for example, circles and squares in Fig. 1. Resource nodes do not execute code. We add a unary predicate isProc to the vocabulary $\mathcal{V}_{\mathsf{Node}}$ to indicate whether a node is a process node. We require that the neighbourhood of any resource node contains no process node, and every resource node is in the neighbourhood of some process node.

Skipping Resource Nodes. Recall that Algorithm 1 implicitly adds subprograms over the topologies $\{N(\boldsymbol{v}) \mid \boldsymbol{v} \text{ is a } (k+1)\text{-tuple over some } \mathbb{T} \in \mathcal{T}\}$ to guarantee a basis of rank $k+1$. Under the modelling assumptions mentioned above, however, it suffices to consider $\boldsymbol{v}$ consisting of process nodes. We can exclude the rest, which are theoretically unnecessary by, for each r, setting χ_r to $\bot$ if $\boldsymbol{v}_r$ (an arbitrary tuple that realizes T_r, as defined in Sect. 7.1) contains a resource node. Meanwhile, in lines 6 and 9 of Algorithm 1, we also skip any v_0 and w that are resource nodes.

Distinct Generators. We can further exclude topologies generated by fewer than k process nodes from the downward closure, by setting χ_r to $\bot$ for any r such that $\boldsymbol{v}_r$ contains repetitive nodes. Since line 9–10 of Algorithm 1 implicitly closes $\mathcal{T}$ under substructures generated by one node, we change them to the following:

for all $(\mathbb{T}, w) \in \textsc{Substructures}(\mathcal{T}, k, 1)$ **do**

$$\mathcal{C} \leftarrow \mathcal{C} \cup \left\{ \textstyle\bigwedge_{\boldsymbol{v} \in \mathbb{T}^k : \chi_{r(\boldsymbol{v})}} \mathit{Inv}_{r(\boldsymbol{v})}(\boldsymbol{x}_{U(\boldsymbol{v})}) \Rightarrow \textsc{Subst}(\neg \mathsf{error}_i(w)) \right\}$$

where SUBSTRUCTURES($\mathcal{T}, k, 1$) returns, up to isomorphism, a list of all structures $\mathbb{T}$ together with a distinguished node $w \in \mathbb{T}$ such that $\mathbb{T}$ is generated by k distinct process nodes over any topology in $\mathcal{T}$. We refer to the combined optimization in this subsection as DPG.

8 Theoretical Case Study: Deriving the Solution of [17]

To illustrate that the solution presented in this paper is robust, we look at the specific classic topology of *identical replicated threads sharing boundedly many global variables*, which is the premise of [17], and show that the solution of [17] is a special case of our solution.

$$\begin{aligned}
\mathit{Init}(x_0, x_1) \wedge \mathit{Init}(x_0, x_2) &\implies \mathit{Inv}(x_0, x_1, x_2)\\
\mathit{Inv}(x_0, x_1, x_2) \wedge \mathit{Inv}(x_0, x_2, x_1) \wedge s(x_0, x_1, x_0', x_1') &\implies \mathit{Inv}(x_0', x_1', x_2)\\
\mathit{Inv}(x_0, x_1, x_2) \wedge \mathit{Inv}(x_0, x_2, x_1) \wedge s(x_0, x_2, x_0', x_2') &\implies \mathit{Inv}(x_0', x_1, x_2')\\
\mathit{Inv}(x_0, x_1, x_2) \wedge \mathit{Inv}(x_0, x_3, x_2) \wedge \mathit{Inv}(x_0, x_1, x_3) &\\
\mathit{Inv}(x_0, x_2, x_1) \wedge \mathit{Inv}(x_0, x_2, x_3) \wedge \mathit{Inv}(x_0, x_3, x_1) \wedge s(x_0, x_3, x_0', x_3') &\implies \mathit{Inv}(x_0', x_1, x_2)\\
\mathit{Inv}(x_0, x_1, x_2) \wedge \mathit{Inv}(x_0, x_2, x_1) &\implies \neg \mathit{Error}(x_0, x_1)
\end{aligned}$$

Fig. 4. Clauses generated by Algorithm 1 for the star topology.

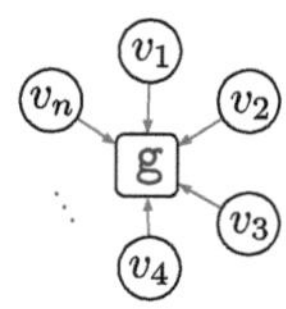

First, we model the topology as a *star*. The vocabulary $\mathcal{V}_{\mathsf{Node}}$ consists of a single constant symbol g. The $\mathcal{V}_{\mathsf{Node}}$-structure $\mathbb{T}_n$ has underlying set $\{0, 1, \ldots, n\}$, where 0 is the interpretation of g (the resource node hosting all shared variables), and the positive numbers stand for the n indistinguishable process nodes v_i's.

In [17], the safety specification is given as a pair of $\mathcal{V}_{\mathsf{Data}}$-formulas *Init* and *Error*, and the transitions are given by a $\mathcal{V}_{\mathsf{Data}}$-formula s. To simplify the presentation, we fix $k = 2$ and assume *Error* is stated for a single node. In our notation, for any $n \in \mathbb{N}_+$ and $v \neq 0$, we have $\mathsf{init}_n(v) = \mathit{Init}(\mu(0), \mu(v))$, $\mathsf{error}_n(v) = \mathit{Error}(\mu(0), \mu(v))$, and $[\![v]\!]_n = s(\mu(0), \mu(v), \mu'(0), \mu'(v))$; for $v = 0$, we have $\mathsf{init}_n(v) = \top$, $\mathsf{init}_n(v) = \bot$, and $[\![v]\!]_n = \bot$.

Let $\mathcal{P} := \{\langle \mathbb{T}_n, [\![-]\!]_n \rangle\}_{n \geq 2}$. The refined downward closure process in Sect. 7.3 does not add any new subprogram to $\mathcal{P}$, as the topology family already contains $\{\mathbb{T}_2, \mathbb{T}_3\}$, which is also a basis of rank 3.

Our normalization produces $\forall u_1, u_2.\, \alpha[u_1, u_2] \rightarrow \phi[\mu(\mathsf{g}), \mu(u_1), \mu(u_2)]$, where $\alpha[u_1, u_2] := u_1 \neq u_2 \wedge \mathsf{isProc}(u_1) \wedge \mathsf{isProc}(u_2)$, as a *complete* template for an Ashcroft assertion of width 2 for $\mathcal{P}$, which incidentally is precisely how an Ashcroft assertion is defined in [17].

Running Algorithm 1 modified with the optimization described in Sect. 7.3, with minor syntactic simplification, we obtain the clauses $\mathcal{C}$ in Fig. 4.

By the discussion in Sect. 7.1, without loss of generality, we may assume that $Inv(x_0, x_1, x_2) \equiv Inv(x_0, x_2, x_1)$ for all x_0, x_1, x_2, which prunes the clauses illustrated in gray, and results in a set of clauses $\mathcal{C}'$ that is equisatisfiable to $\mathcal{C}$. The set of clauses $\mathcal{C}'$ is exactly the CHC encoding for 2-thread-modular proofs [17, Figure 6], except that we do not treat control locations explicitly.

9 Experimental Results

Implementation. Our tool, Mosaic, takes as input a number $k \in \mathbb{N}_+$, a parameterized program over topologies $\mathcal{T} = \{\mathbb{T}_i\}_{i \in \mathcal{I}}$ over a finite vocabulary $\mathcal{V}$ (assuming the indices $\mathcal{I}$ are consecutive natural numbers), a parameterized safety specification, and a pair of numbers $i, i' \in \mathcal{I}$ with the assumption that all quantifier-free $(k+1)$-types appear in $\mathcal{T}$ already appear in $\{\mathbb{T}_j \mid i \leq j \leq i'\}$. For the parameterized safety specification, we allow a more general form of error states that can relate m nodes in a topology, where $m \leq k$. Mosaic implements Algorithm 1 with optimization options `OPN` and `DPG` (Sect. 7). The output encoding is in SMT-LIB2 format and can be passed to a variety of existing CHC solvers [6,18,21]. Here, we report the results for Z3/Spacer [10,21] except for one benchmark, which can be solved by Golem [6] but not Spacer. Details about the experiment can be found in [7, Appendix D].

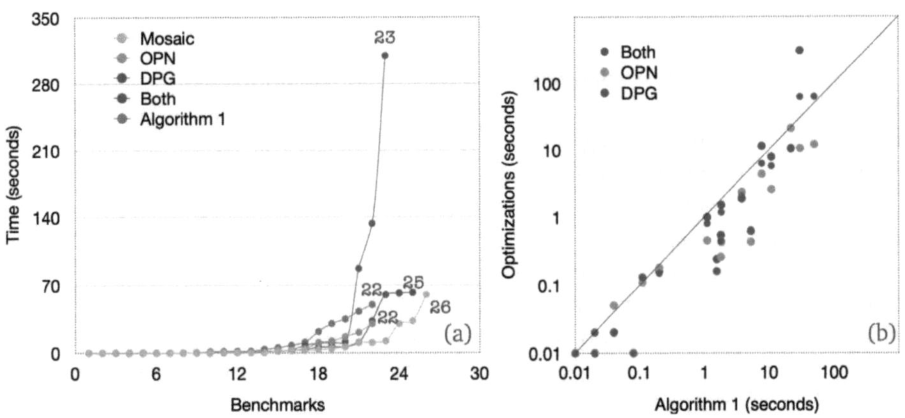

Fig. 5. (a) Quantile plot. (b) Scattered plot of optimizations vs baseline.

Evaluation Goals. The main goal of our evaluation is straightforward: Establishing whether Mosaic can prove interesting properties of parameterized programs over a rich family of topologies. As a secondary goal, we evaluate the impact of the optimizations proposed in Sects. 7.2 and 7.3.

Benchmarks. There is not a lot of diversity in the example pool in the literature when it comes to different topologies for parameterized programs. Hence, beyond including a few examples from the literature, we designed many more benchmarks over many more topologies. In particular, we have 30 programs over (1) rings, (2) lines (like example of Fig. 1), (3) grids, (4) bounded-depth trees [9], and (5) binary trees (full list in [7, Appendix D.1]). The generality and flexibility offered by logical structures are very helpful in modelling some extra requirements for specialized versions of some of these topologies. For instance, a direction predicate for the line and an orientation predicate for the ring can be added effortlessly, and our benchmark set also includes these variations.

Results. Figure 5 presents our results, where MOSAIC corresponds to the best performance of all options. The quantile plot includes the count of benchmarks solved by each option. Of the 26 benchmarks solved by MOSAIC, the winning time of 16 is by `OPN`, 8 by `DPG`, 13 by the combination, and 4 by Algorithm 1 (counting ties). The optimizations clearly have a significant impact. Remarkably, they do not consistently lead to an improved time: There are a few outliers above the middle line in Fig. 5(b), which incidentally do not include the 3 cases where Algorithm 1 times out. This is because they target the size of the encoding, but a smaller encoding is not necessarily always easier to solve for the backend solver. [7, Appendix D.2] lists the full results, including encoding sizes.

The 4 benchmarks that MOSAIC cannot solve are due to one of the following reasons: (1) non-linear reasoning required (1 tree benchmark), (2) encoding is too large (1 grid benchmark), and (3) CHC solver fails (1 line and 1 ring benchmark).

Limitations and Discussion. The key limitations are related to the unscalability and unpredictability of the backend CHC solvers. Large encodings (e.g. a grid example) cannot be handled. A minor change in Fig. 1 example can flip the status of its solvability, without much change in the encoding size.

Another bottleneck for scalability is that the basis of rank $k+1$ becomes too large as k increases, especially for a larger vocabulary $\mathcal{V}_{\mathsf{Node}}$. For instance, this happens for width-2 invariants for grid examples, since the distinctness of the four neighbours causes the basis to include 347 small programs even with optimizations, and one of two such examples times out.

Finally, we came across benchmarks (not included) that do not admit universally quantified inductive invariants as proofs, where a richer class of invariants or ghost variables are required to handle them.

10 Related Work

The problem of verification of parameterized programs is generally known to be undecidable [4]. Our focus is on the *algorithmic* verification of infinite-state parameterized programs. As such, we do not survey the rich literature on finite-state parameterized programs [1] nor deductive verification techniques [5,28].

Compositional Proofs of Parameterized Programs. Compositional proofs have been a central theme in concurrency verification. We made a thorough comparison with the work in [17] in Sect. 8, which is singled out because it is sound and complete, albeit for a fixed topology. Similar results, but for finite-state programs, have appeared in [24]. However, general cut-off results like ours and the one in [17] for the star topology were not given.

The work in [5,25–27] is noteworthy for the common themes of the use of symmetry in compositional verification. In particular, in [26], the insight of identifying *balanced* (therefore *locally symmetric*) nodes in compositional verification is used to establish *compositional cutoffs*. The programs are finite-state, and the key result is the decidability of compositional model checking in polynomial time. Specifically, the problem is formally framed as deciding, for all programs in the parameterized family, the existence of interference-free local proofs for every process, which collectively become a global universal invariant *with one quantifier*. Our work generalizes this view by permitting universal quantification of any depth and generalizing compositional cutoffs to bases of any rank. However, the starting point of [26] is local proofs, whereas we start with global invariants and look for a sound and complete reduction to local proofs.

Handling Multiple Communication Topologies. Several topologies are studied for finite-state programs with multiple communication primitives in [2], where the decision procedure for each topology requires a bespoke representation of the configurations and a pre-order on them that induces subconfigurations for abstraction. Later in [3], parameterized finite-state programs over a rich set of topologies are studied, where several uniform (across topology classes) decidability and complexity results are given. The focus for decidability is on what they call *homogeneous* topologies, and none of the topologies in our benchmark set is homogeneous. In particular, there are known undecidability results [11] about rings. For infinite-state programs, a rich class of topologies are targeted in [5] in the context of deductive verification. However, the invariant templates are predetermined by the user, and their small model property relates to checking concrete verification conditions rather than safety through Ashcroft invariants.

Parameterized Model Checking of Infinite-State Programs. For algorithmic verification of infinite-state parameterized programs, there exist techniques that automatically generate universally quantified invariants [12,15,19, 23], all for a single topology. One can view *thread-modular proofs at many levels* [13,17] as the conclusion of this line of work by proposing proof systems that form a strict hierarchy and are relatively complete w.r.t. Ashcroft invariants.

11 Conclusion and Future Work

On the conceptual side, this paper observes that under certain conditions about the families of topologies, a universally quantified invariant of an unbounded family of concurrent parameterized programs over these topologies can be verified through a bounded number of checks (Theorem 1), which are limited to entailments in the underlying data domain (Theorem 2). Hence, verification conditions do not require any axiomatization of the underlying topology family. On the algorithmic side, using the above observations, we propose a *complete* algorithm for discovering such an invariant of a given width k, if one exists.

Our implementation uses CHC encodings (and solvers) as a point of convenience. The solvers do not yet scale to the level of handling the encodings of larger programs. The paper offers two *complete* optimizations to improve the encoding, but a more practical algorithm will have to rely on a combination of abstraction and decomposition techniques to make the invariant search tractable. We hope that our conceptual contribution in separation of reasoning about data and topologies will bring new opportunities for discovery on this path.

Recall that Algorithm 1 relies on an oracle that computes the quantifier-free types for a topology family. In the implementation, these are computed through brute-force enumeration relying on upper-bounds that are manually calculated for the topology class. The technical problem of necessary/sufficient conditions that guarantee efficient computability of quantifier-free types remains open.

Universally quantified invariants are clearly not enough to capture every proof (or even every specification) of interest in these contexts. It will be interesting to investigate if similar cut-off results can be proven for richer classes of invariants with quantifier alternations (e.g., see [20]), and independently, if commutativity-based reductions can be used so that a universally quantified invariant is sufficient for proving the reduced parameterized program safe (see [14] for the star topology).

Data Availibility Statement. Proofs and experiment details can be found at [7]. Our tool MOSAIC and the benchmarks used in the evaluation (Sect. 9) can be found at [8], where version 0.1.1 was submitted for artifact evaluation and includes the first 21 benchmarks listed in [7, Appendix D.1].

Disclosure of Interests. Nothing relevant to declare.

References

1. Abdulla, P.A., Delzanno, G.: Parameterized verification. Int. J. Softw. Tools Technol. Transfer **18**(5), 469–473 (2016). https://doi.org/10.1007/s10009-016-0424-3
2. Abdulla, P.A., Haziza, F., Holík, L.: All for the price of few. In: Giacobazzi, R., Berdine, J., Mastroeni, I. (eds.) Verification, Model Checking, and Abstract Interpretation, pp. 476–495. Springer, Cham (2013). https://doi.org/10.1007/978-3-642-35873-9_28
3. Aminof, B., Kotek, T., Rubin, S., Spegni, F., Veith, H.: Parameterized model checking of rendezvous systems. Distrib. Comput. **31**(3), 187–222 (2018). https://doi.org/10.1007/s00446-017-0302-6
4. Apt, K.R., Kozen, D.C.: Limits for automatic verification of finite-state concurrent systems. Inf. Process. Lett. **22**(6), 307–309 (1986). https://doi.org/10.1016/0020-0190(86)90071-2
5. Ashmore, R., Gurfinkel, A., Trefler, R.: Local Reasoning for Parameterized First Order Protocols. In: Badger, J.M., Rozier, K.Y. (eds.) NFM 2019. LNCS, vol. 11460, pp. 36–53. Springer, Cham (2019). https://doi.org/10.1007/978-3-030-20652-9_3
6. Blicha, M., Britikov, K., Sharygina, N.: The Golem Horn Solver. In: Enea, C., Lal, A. (eds.) Computer Aided Verification, pp. 209–223. Springer, Cham (2023). https://doi.org/10.1007/978-3-031-37703-7_10

7. Cheng, R., Farzan, A.: Complete Local Reasoning About Parameterized Programs Over Topologies (2026). https://doi.org/10.48550/arXiv.2605.15143
8. Cheng, R., Farzan, A.: Mosaic: artifact for "complete local reasoning about parameterized programs over topologies". Zenodo (2026). https://doi.org/10.5281/ZENODO.19851981
9. Cheng, R., Farzan, A.: Symmetric Proofs of Parameterized Programs (2026). https://doi.org/10.48550/arXiv.2601.18745
10. de Moura, L., Bjørner, N.: Z3: An Efficient SMT Solver. In: Ramakrishnan, C.R., Rehof, J. (eds.) TACAS 2008. LNCS, vol. 4963, pp. 337–340. Springer, Heidelberg (2008). https://doi.org/10.1007/978-3-540-78800-3_24
11. Emerson, E.A., Namjoshi, K.S.: Reasoning about rings. In: Proceedings of the 22nd ACM SIGPLAN-SIGACT Symposium on Principles of Programming Languages, pp. 85–94. POPL '95, Association for Computing Machinery, New York, NY, USA (1995). https://doi.org/10.1145/199448.199468
12. Emmi, M., Majumdar, R., Manevich, R.: Parameterized verification of transactional memories. In: Proceedings of the 31st ACM SIGPLAN Conference on Programming Language Design and Implementation, pp. 134–145. PLDI '10, Association for Computing Machinery, New York, NY, USA (2010). https://doi.org/10.1145/1806596.1806613
13. Farzan, A., Kincaid, Z., Podelski, A.: Proof spaces for unbounded parallelism. In: Proceedings of the 42nd Annual ACM SIGPLAN-SIGACT Symposium on Principles of Programming Languages, pp. 407–420. ACM, Mumbai India (2015). https://doi.org/10.1145/2676726.2677012
14. Farzan, A., Klumpp, D., Podelski, A.: Commutativity Simplifies Proofs of Parameterized Programs. Proc. ACM Program. Lang. **8**(POPL), 2485–2513 (2024). https://doi.org/10.1145/3632925
15. Gurfinkel, A., Shoham, S., Meshman, Y.: SMT-based verification of parameterized systems. In: Proceedings of the 2016 24th ACM SIGSOFT International Symposium on Foundations of Software Engineering, pp. 338–348. FSE 2016, Association for Computing Machinery, New York, NY, USA (2016). https://doi.org/10.1145/2950290.2950330
16. Hodges, W.: A Shorter Model Theory. Cambridge University Press, Cambridge; New York (1997)
17. Hoenicke, J., Majumdar, R., Podelski, A.: Thread modularity at many levels: A pearl in compositional verification. In: Proceedings of the 44th ACM SIGPLAN Symposium on Principles of Programming Languages, pp. 473–485. ACM, Paris, France (2017). https://doi.org/10.1145/3009837.3009893
18. Hojjat, H., Rümmer, P.: The ELDARICA Horn Solver. Formal Methods in Computer Aided Design (FMCAD), pp. 1–7 (2018). https://doi.org/10.23919/FMCAD.2018.8603013
19. Hojjat, H., Rümmer, P., Subotic, P., Yi, W.: Horn clauses for communicating timed systems. EPTCS **169**, 39–52 (2014)
20. Koenig, J.R., Padon, O., Immerman, N., Aiken, A.: First-order quantified separators. In: Proceedings of the 41st ACM SIGPLAN Conference on Programming Language Design and Implementation, pp. 703–717. ACM Conferences, Association for Computing Machinery (2020). https://doi.org/10.1145/3385412.3386018
21. Komuravelli, A., Gurfinkel, A., Chaki, S.: SMT-based model checking for recursive programs. Formal Methods Syst. Des. **48**(3), 175–205 (2016). https://doi.org/10.1007/s10703-016-0249-4
22. Libkin, L.: Elements of Finite Model Theory. Springer Berlin Heidelberg, Berlin, Heidelberg (2004). https://doi.org/10.1007/978-3-662-07003-1

23. Monniaux, D., Gonnord, L.: Cell Morphing: From Array Programs to Array-Free Horn Clauses. In: Rival, X. (ed.) SAS 2016. LNCS, vol. 9837, pp. 361–382. Springer, Heidelberg (2016). https://doi.org/10.1007/978-3-662-53413-7_18
24. Namjoshi, K.S.: Symmetry and Completeness in the Analysis of Parameterized Systems. In: Cook, B., Podelski, A. (eds.) VMCAI 2007. LNCS, vol. 4349, pp. 299–313. Springer, Heidelberg (2007). https://doi.org/10.1007/978-3-540-69738-1_22
25. Namjoshi, K.S., Trefler, R.J.: Local Symmetry and Compositional Verification. In: Kuncak, V., Rybalchenko, A. (eds.) VMCAI 2012. LNCS, vol. 7148, pp. 348–362. Springer, Heidelberg (2012). https://doi.org/10.1007/978-3-642-27940-9_23
26. Namjoshi, K.S., Trefler, R.J.: Parameterized Compositional Model Checking. In: Chechik, M., Raskin, J.-F. (eds.) TACAS 2016. LNCS, vol. 9636, pp. 589–606. Springer, Heidelberg (2016). https://doi.org/10.1007/978-3-662-49674-9_39
27. Namjoshi, K.S., Trefler, R.J.: Symmetry Reduction for the Local Mu-Calculus. In: Beyer, D., Huisman, M. (eds.) TACAS 2018. LNCS, vol. 10806, pp. 379–395. Springer, Cham (2018). https://doi.org/10.1007/978-3-319-89963-3_22
28. Padon, O., McMillan, K.L., Panda, A., Sagiv, M., Shoham, S.: Ivy: safety verification by interactive generalization. ACM SIGPLAN Notices **51**(6), 614–630 (2016). https://doi.org/10.1145/2980983.2908118

Scalable Deductive Verification of Data-Level Parallel Programs

Lars B. van den Haak[1(✉)], Anton Wijs[1], and Marieke Huisman[2]

[1] Eindhoven University of Technology, Eindhoven, The Netherlands
{l.b.v.d.haak,a.j.wijs}@tue.nl
[2] University of Twente, Enschede, The Netherlands
m.huisman@utwente.nl

Abstract. This paper introduces several techniques that improve the scalability of the deductive verification of data-level parallel programs working on arrays and matrices. First of all, we introduce a technique to rewrite expressions with (nested) quantifiers, so suitable triggers can be generated for these expressions. We have proven this rewrite technique correct using a theorem prover. Second, we make reasoning about potentially overlapping arrays easier, by providing specification constructs to indicate and verify that two arrays are not aliases, or that they are immutable, so they can be modelled as mathematical sequences. All our techniques are implemented in the VerCors program verifier. We illustrate how the combination of our techniques improves scalability via a large number of experiments. Using our techniques on a set of typical GPU kernels, we achieve a reduction of verification time by, on average, a factor of 9, with outliers being up to 150 times faster. Additionally, applying these techniques to earlier experiments and an earlier case study of a radio telescope pipeline permitted to obtain verification results that were previously either unobtainable or only in a significantly longer verification time.

Keywords: Deductive Verification · Separation Logic · Parallel · GPU · GPGPU · Quantifiers

1 Introduction

Data (or *Data-level*) *parallel programming* is an approach to parallel programming in which multiple threads concurrently perform the same operations on different data elements [15]. Over the years, this approach to parallel programming has become increasingly popular, particularly in the form of the *Single Instruction, Multiple Threads* (SIMT) and *Single Instruction, Multiple Data* (SIMD) paradigms. Modern *Graphics Processing Units* (GPUs) provide a prominent platform for SIMT programming, and *Central Processing Units* (CPUs) support SIMD instructions. GPU computing, and therefore data parallel programming,

E. Darulova et al. (Eds.): CAV 2026, LNCS 16682, pp. 90–112, 2026.
https://doi.org/10.1007/978-3-032-32519-8_5

has had a major impact on scientific computing in fields such as computational biology (e.g., genomics) [26], statistics [19], and physics (e.g., fluid dynamics) [2]. Furthermore, GPUs effectively accelerate computations involving matrix-vector and matrix-matrix multiplications [9,27], and they made an enormous impact on Artificial Intelligence with deep learning [16].

Due to this success, these days, there is a plethora of programming languages supporting this paradigm, such as SYCL, OpenCL, CUDA and OpenMP. Typical data structures that are used in these programs are arrays and matrices.

There is a need for formal method tools to verify data parallel programs [12]. However, deductive verification of these programs, i.e., verifying that they satisfy formal contracts, often runs into scalability issues. Verification of a computation quickly takes (too) long or becomes unfeasible. Bottlenecks are in the reasoning at the SMT level: the deductive verification tool applies program logics that create SMT proof obligations. We have identified multiple causes for this:

- Generated proof obligations often contain (multiple) nested quantifier expressions, and SMT solvers have difficulty reasoning about them. SMT solvers typically allow users to specify *trigger* patterns [7], as hints on possible instantiations, but nested quantifier expressions require instantiations that are not allowed as trigger patterns.
- If a program uses multiple arrays, matrices, or higher dimensional array structures, then these could potentially be aliases of each other. This needs to be verified because it may influence correctness. However, doing so leads to many additional proof obligations.

We introduce multiple solutions to address these causes. All our solutions are implemented in the deductive program verifier VerCors [1], however, we believe they are also applicable to many other verifiers. VerCors uses permission-based separation logic as its specification language, which means that for all shared memory, the user needs to specify permission annotations that capture whether a thread has read or write access at a certain moment. Moreover, all functional properties are framed, i.e. one can only state something about that part of the memory to which one has access.

First of all, after the background has been explained in Sect. 2, we propose a rewriting procedure in Sect. 3 to flatten expressions with nested quantifiers into equivalent expressions with single quantifiers, for which triggers can be generated that make the verification process efficient. We have proven the correctness of this procedure using Lean.

Second, in Sect. 4, we propose a mechanism to indicate that arrays (and other data structures) are not aliases of each other. For this, we use *uniqueness types*. This helps to significantly reduce the reasoning about potential aliases.

Sometimes, multiple arrays may be aliases of each other, but they are never updated in the program. For this case, we propose to indicate that the arrays are immutable. By doing so, the deductive verifier can reason about them as if they are (VerCors) *sequences*,[1] which are defined as finite and immutable lists.

[1] See the VerCors tutorial: https://vercors.ewi.utwente.nl/wiki/.

Listing 1. An OpenCL GPU kernel to swap the contents of two arrays, inspired by the `Xswap` kernel from CLBlast [23].

```
/*@ ...
  context (∀ int i; 0 ≤ i ∧ i < n/get_global_size(0);
    Perm(ygm[\gtid + i*get_global_size(0)], write)) ∧
    Perm(xgm[\gtid + i*get_global_size(0)], write));
  ensures (∀ int i; 0 ≤ i ∧ i < n/get_global_size(0);
    ygm[\gtid + i*get_global_size(0)] ≡ \old(xgm[\gtid + i*get_global_size(0)]) ∧
    xgm[\gtid + i*get_global_size(0)] ≡ \old(ygm[\gtid + i*get_global_size(0)]));
@*/
// Swap the contents of two arrays in parallel.
__kernel void XswapFast(const int n, __global float* xgm, __global float* ygm) {
  /*@ loop_invariant \gtid ≤ id ∧ id < n + get_global_size(0);
      loop_invariant (∀ int i; 0 ≤ i ∧ i < n/get_global_size(0);
        Perm(ygm[\gtid + i*get_global_size(0)], write)) ∧
        Perm(xgm[\gtid + i*get_global_size(0)], write));
      loop_invariant (∀ int i; id/get_global_size(0) ≤ i ∧ i < n/get_global_size(0);
        ygm[\gtid + i*get_global_size(0)] ≡ \old(ygm[\gtid + i*get_global_size(0)]) ∧
        xgm[\gtid + i*get_global_size(0)] ≡ \old(xgm[\gtid + i*get_global_size(0)]));
      loop_invariant (∀ int i; 0 ≤ i ∧ i < id/get_global_size(0);
        ygm[\gtid + i*get_global_size(0)] ≡ \old(xgm[\gtid + i*get_global_size(0)]) ∧
        xgm[\gtid + i*get_global_size(0)] ≡ \old(ygm[\gtid + i*get_global_size(0)]));
  @*/
  for (int id = get_global_id(0); id < n; id += get_global_size(0)) {
    float temp = xgm[id];
    xgm[id] = ygm[id];
    ygm[id] = temp;
  }
}
```

Furthermore, in Sect. 5, we discuss a large number of experiments that demonstrate how the combination of these features together speeds up verification and verifies previously unverifiable cases of a Radio Telescope Pipeline case study, including an implementation of the Padre algorithm [14].

Finally, related work is discussed in Sect. 6, and conclusions are drawn in Sect. 7.

2 Background

Deductive verification tools use formal contracts, consisting of pre- and post-conditions, written as *requires* and *ensures* statements, respectively, to formally verify a program. To support concurrent programs, the VerCors [1] tool uses first-order logic, enhanced with (concurrent) separation logic concepts [5]. For each memory location (or *heap* location) `a`, one needs to specify a permission to access it: `Perm(a, p)`, with `p` a fractional number between `0` and `1`, where `p≡1` indicates that we can write to location `a` and `0<p<1` indicates read permission. A permission of `1` is often written as `write`. Correct permission annotations allow VerCors to prove memory safety. To verify a program, VerCors translates it into Viper's [8,22] intermediate verification language. In turn, Viper queries SMT solvers to solve the proof obligations.

Listing 1 presents an example of an OpenCL GPU kernel that can be used to swap the contents of two arrays `xgm` and `ygm`, both of size `n`, in parallel.

The special comments `/*@` and `@*/` indicate annotations. The contract for this function states that the array contents are indeed swapped: at lines 2–4 (l.2–4), the *context* is given that the kernel has write permission for both arrays (`context` refers to the fact that this holds both before and after executing the kernel), and at l.5–7, the postcondition is given that the array contents have been swapped, with `\old` referring to the old contents of the arrays before the kernel was launched. A number of keywords and functions are used to refer to the thread hierarchy on a GPU. Using CUDA terminology, threads are executed in *blocks* of a predefined size, and a predefined number of blocks make up a *grid*. Both blocks and grids can be one-, two-, or three-dimensional. In this example, we use only one dimension. We use the following functions, with `i` referring to a dimension ($0 \leq \texttt{i} \leq 2$):

- `get_local_size(i)` returns the size of a thread block in the `i`-dimension.
- `get_num_blocks(i)` returns the total number of blocks in the `i`-dimension.
- `get_local_id(i)` returns the (block-local) ID of the current thread in the `i`-dimension. Note that $0 \leq$ `get_local_id(i)` $<$ `get_local_size(i)`.
- `get_block_id(i)` returns the ID of the block in which the thread resides in the `i`-dimension. Note that $0 \leq$ `get_block_id(i)` $<$ `get_num_blocks(i)`.
- `get_global_id(i)` returns the *global* ID of the thread in the `i`-dimension, defined as `get_local_size(i)` $\cdot$ `get_block_id(i)` $+$ `get_local_id(i)`.
- `get_global_size(i)` returns the total number of threads in the `i`-dimension, defined as `get_num_blocks(i)` $\cdot$ `get_local_size(i)`.

Finally, `\gtid` is equal to `get_global_id(0)` for the one-dimensional case.

Note that these functions are used to divide the work among the threads: Initially, every thread accesses those elements in `xgm` and `ygm` located at index `get_global_id(0)`. As the arrays can be larger than the total number of threads, the for-loop at l.22–26 is actually a *grid-stride* loop, which is very common in GPU kernels: after accessing their initial element, every thread jumps `get_global_size(0)` positions ahead in the arrays to access the next elements, and this continues until the end of the arrays has been reached. To reason about the loop, note the *loop invariants* at l.11–21 that also use the functions mentioned above. These are essential for VerCors to prove the contract of the kernel.

VerCors encodes parallel functions, such as GPU kernels, using *parallel blocks*. To verify a GPU kernel, one needs to quantify over all thread blocks in a grid and all threads in each thread block [4], resulting in two nested parallel blocks. We have made this explicit in Listing 2, using VerCors' intermediate language PVL. For convenience, the grid-stride loop has been removed. Note that the contract for the parallel block labelled `blocks` quantifies over all threads in a block, and that the contract for the kernel in turn quantifies over all threads in the grid. Although given here explicitly, VerCors typically derives these contracts automatically from a given contract for a thread block, which is possible due to the very structured way in which GPU threads operate. For the kernel in Listing 1, VerCors would also internally generate these contracts, given the contract at l.1–8.

Listing 2. A GPU PVL kernel to swap the contents of two arrays, with the number of threads being at least as large as the number of elements.

```
/*@ ...
    ensures ∀ int i; 0 ≤ i ∧ i < n*m; xgm[i] ≡ \old(ygm[i]) ∧ ygm[i] ≡ \old(xgm[i]);
@*/
void XswapFastSmallArrays(const int n, float* xgm, float* ygm, int nb, int nt) {
  par blocks (int bid = 0 .. nb)
  {
    /*@ ...
        ensures ∀ int i; 0 ≤ i ∧ i < n; xgm[bid*nt + i] ≡ \old(ygm[bid*nt + i]);
        ensures ∀ int i; 0 ≤ i ∧ i < n; ygm[bid*nt + i] ≡ \old(xgm[bid*nt + i]); @*/
    par threads (int tid = 0 .. nt)
      /*@ ...
          ensures xgm[bid*nt + tid] ≡ \old(ygm[bid*nt + tid]);
          ensures ygm[bid*nt + tid] ≡ \old(xgm[bid*nt + tid]); @*/
    {
      float temp = xgm[bid*nt + tid];
      xgm[bid*nt + tid] = ygm[bid*nt + tid];
      ygm[bid*nt + tid] = temp;
    }
  }
}
```

Listing 3. A PVL function example to illustrate triggers. Here `f` is some uninterpreted side-effect free function.

```
1 /*@ requires x>10 ∧ y>10;
2     requires (∀ int k; 0≤k ∧ k≤x ; {: f(k, y) :} ≡ 0);
3     requires (∀ int k, int i; 0≤k ∧ k≤x ∧ 0≤i ∧ i≤y; f(k*i, z) ≡ 0); @*/
4 void bar(int x, int y, int z) {
5    assert f(x, y) ≡ 0; // this verifies, as "f(x,y)" triggers the first quantifier
6    assert f(10, z) ≡ 0; // this assertion fails, as no quantifier is triggered
7 }
```

Triggers. Contracts for deductive verification frequently involve *quantifiers*, for instance in a statement such as `∀int i; 0≤i<n; A[i]≡0`. During verification, a deductive verification tool needs to apply such a statement whenever applicable, for instance when encountering the ground term `A[1]` in the code: the quantifier must be *instantiated.* Mapping `1` to `i` is straightforward, but for more complex expressions, heuristics are typically required, although they often lead to incompleteness of the verification. Therefore, VerCors relies on pattern-based quantifier instantiation [7] (or E-matching): the user should indicate that an expression in an annotation should serve as a *trigger* (or *pattern*) for quantification, by enclosing it in `{:` and `:}`. This trigger (or possibly a set of triggers) should mention all quantified variables. Furthermore, Viper's intermediate verification language does not allow triggers to involve arithmetic expressions.

For instance, consider the code and contract in Listing 3. At l.2, `f(k,y)` is marked as a trigger. The assertion at l.5 verifies, as `f(x,y)` matches the trigger at l.2. On the other hand, the assertion at l.6 fails to verify, as in order to match `f(10,z)`, the solver needs the information of the quantifier in l.3. However, it is not allowed to specify `f(k*i,y)` as a trigger, as it contains arithmetic. Even if we introduce a helper function for `*`, such that it can be used as a trigger, the solver cannot match suitable instances for `i` and `k` when given `f(10, z)`. Instead, it would need to be written as either `f(5*2, z)`, `f(2*5, z)`, `f(1*10, z)` or `f(10*1, z)`.

3 Triggers for Nested Quantifiers

As data-level parallel programs typically involve data stored in arrays, their contracts usually contain annotations that quantify over the data elements. To reason about these, the underlying automated solver used by a deductive verification tool needs to automatically find instantiations of those quantifiers. To illustrate this, consider Listing 1 again, in particular, the postcondition given at l.5–6. We indicate that the index expression for `ygm` should be used as a trigger:

```
∀ int i; 0 ≤ i < n/get_global_size(0); {:ygm[\gtid + i*get_global_size(0)]:} ≡
  \old(xgm[\gtid + i*get_global_size(0)])
```

When trying to verify the kernel, the solver tries to find suitable instantiations of the quantified variables in the given postcondition, but it is not able to do this, as the index expression contains arithmetic operations.

The solution that we develop here is to automatically rewrite the quantifier expression in such a way that the arithmetic operations are removed from the trigger. We do this by defining a bijective mapping from a linear arithmetic expression containing quantified variables to a single quantified variable, and adding suitable conditions, such that the validity of the expression remains unchanged. For this concrete example, assuming for the moment that `\gtid` is a given value instead of one calculated using several values, this gives the following rewritten quantifier.

```
∀ int x; (abs(x-\gtid))%get_global_size(0)≡0 ∧ 0 ≤ x-\gtid < get_global_size(0)*(n/
  get_global_size(0)); ygm[x] ≡ \old(xgm[x]);
```

After the rewriting, `ygm[x]` can be used as a trigger. In this section, we explain our rewriting procedure. In general, if an index is computed injectively, then we can apply this rewriting by determining an inverse function. If we have an indexing function and its inverse, we can translate between the original and the rewritten quantifier.

Rewriting Quantifiers. In general, the quantifiers we wish to rewrite are of the following form, with `A` an array.

```
∀ int x₁, ..., xₖ; X(x₁, ..., xₖ); R(A[aₖ*xₖ + ... + a₁*x₁ + b], (x₁, ..., xₖ))
```

The predicate $\texttt{X(x}_1\texttt{, ..., x}_k\texttt{)}$ determines the *domain* of the quantifier, i.e., all values of $\texttt{(x}_1\texttt{, ..., x}_k\texttt{)}$ for which the quantifier holds. Furthermore, `R` is a predicate with free variables $\mathtt{x}_1, \ldots, \mathtt{x}_k$ that may involve conditions on the $\mathtt{x}_i$, besides the definition of their domains and the index expression. Based on the index expression in the quantifier form given above, we define a function for array indexing:

$$f(\mathtt{x}_1, \ldots, \mathtt{x}_k) = \mathsf{a}_k \cdot \mathtt{x}_k + \cdots + \mathsf{a}_1 \cdot \mathtt{x}_1 + \mathsf{b} = \sum_{i=1}^{k} \mathsf{a}_i \cdot \mathtt{x}_i + \mathsf{b}$$

To reverse this indexing, we can use a statement such as `A[x]` as a trigger, and map `x` back to the corresponding $(\mathtt{x}_1, \ \ldots, \ \mathtt{x}_k)$ that satisfies $f(\mathtt{x}_1, \ldots, \mathtt{x}_k) = \mathtt{x}$. To achieve this, we need to define the inverse function f^{-1}. For this to work, it must be that each $\mathtt{x}_i$ has an (inclusive) lower bound min_i defined in the domain X. When the domain also has an (exclusive) upper bound for an $\mathtt{x}_i$, we denote this by max_i. The upper bound max_k for $\mathtt{x}_k$ must be defined, to bound the overall quantification. With $n_k = max_k - min_k$, we refer to the size of the $\mathtt{x}_k$-dimension. All in all, this means that $\mathtt{X}(\mathtt{x}_1, \ldots, \mathtt{x}_k)$ should be defined as follows.

$$\mathtt{X}(\mathtt{x}_1, ..., \mathtt{x}_k) = \mathtt{C}(\mathtt{x}_1, ..., \mathtt{x}_k) \wedge \bigwedge_{i=1}^{k} (min_i \leq \mathtt{x}_i) \wedge \mathtt{x}_k < max_k$$

Here, $\mathtt{C}(\mathtt{x}_1, \ \ldots, \ \mathtt{x}_k)$ is a predicate expressing additional constraints on the variables, besides the constraints for the bounds. With `X` as above, we wish to rewrite the original quantifier to an equivalent quantifier with a single variable, of the following form.

```
∀ int x; Y(x); R(A[x], f⁻¹(x))
```

Here, the predicate `Y(x)` determines the domain of the new quantifier. To define f^{-1}, we first define an offset *off* and a helper function $base_i$. Intuitively, *off* is the value where we start indexing array A, which is the position related to the case where each $\mathtt{x}_i$ has its lowest possible value. The function $base_i$ maps $\mathtt{x}$ back to $\mathsf{a}_i \cdot \mathtt{x}_i$, meaning that we can retrieve $\mathtt{x}_i$ by computing $base_i(\mathtt{x})/|\mathsf{a}_i|$.

$$off = \sum_{i=1}^{k} \mathsf{a}_i \cdot min_i + \mathsf{b}$$

$$base_i(\mathtt{x}) = \begin{cases} |\mathtt{x} - off| & \text{if } i = k, \\ base_{i+1}(\mathtt{x}) \bmod \mathsf{a}_{i+1} & \text{if } 1 \leq i < k. \end{cases}$$

Next, we can define the function f^{-1} as follows.

$$f^{-1}(\mathtt{x}) = (base_1(\mathtt{x})/|\mathsf{a}_1| + min_1, \ldots, base_k(\mathtt{x})/|\mathsf{a}_k| + min_k)$$

This rewriting is correct, provided that

$$n_k > 0 \tag{1}$$

and the following conditions hold for all $\mathtt{a}_i$ $(1 \leq i \leq k)$.

$$\mathtt{a}_i \neq 0 \tag{2}$$

$$i < k \Rightarrow \mathtt{a}_i \geq 0 \iff \mathtt{a}_{i+1} \geq 0 \tag{3}$$

$$i < k \Rightarrow \forall (\mathtt{x}_1, \ldots, \mathtt{x}_k) \in X, \sum_{j=1}^{i} |\mathtt{a}_j| \cdot (\mathtt{x}_j - min_j) < |\mathtt{a}_{i+1}| \tag{4}$$

Finally, we define $\mathtt{Y}(\mathtt{x})$ as follows.

$$\mathtt{Y}(\mathtt{x}) = \mathtt{C}(f^{-1}(\mathtt{x})) \wedge base_1(\mathtt{x}) \bmod \mathtt{a}_1 = 0 \wedge$$
$$(\mathtt{a}_1 > 0 \Rightarrow 0 \leq \mathtt{x} - \mathit{off} < \mathtt{a}_k \cdot n_k) \wedge (\mathtt{a}_1 < 0 \Rightarrow \mathtt{a}_k \cdot n_k < \mathtt{x} - \mathit{off} \leq 0)$$

The following theorem states the correctness of our rewriting.

Theorem 1. *Given a quantifier of the form* $\forall$ `int` $\mathtt{x}_1$`, ...,` $\mathtt{x}_k$`; X(`$\mathtt{x}_1$`, ...,` $\mathtt{x}_k$`); R(A[`$\mathtt{a}_k$`*`$\mathtt{x}_k$`+ ... +` $\mathtt{a}_1$`*`$\mathtt{x}_1$`+ b], (`$\mathtt{x}_1$`, ...,` $\mathtt{x}_k$`))` *, with* $k > 0$*. If Eqs. 1–4 hold, then*

$$\forall (\mathtt{x}_1, \ldots, \mathtt{x}_k) \in \mathbb{Z}^k . \mathtt{X}(\mathtt{x}_1, \ldots, \mathtt{x}_k) \Rightarrow R(A[f(\mathtt{x}_1, \ldots, \mathtt{x}_k)], (\mathtt{x}_1, \ldots, \mathtt{x}_k))$$
$$=$$
$$\forall \mathtt{x} \in \mathbb{Z} . \mathtt{Y}(\mathtt{x}) \Rightarrow R(A[\mathtt{x}], f^{-1}(\mathtt{x}))$$

with f and f^{-1} as defined above.

Proof sketch. A full proof has been written in about 2500 lines of Lean 4 [20] code, and can be found in the accompanying artefact of the current paper. Here, we provide a sketch of how this proof is structured. With X and Y, we refer to the domains determined by predicates $\mathtt{X}(\mathtt{x}_1, \ldots, \mathtt{x}_k)$ and $\mathtt{Y}(\mathtt{x})$, respectively. Initially, the theorem can be proven for the case that $\mathtt{C}(\mathtt{x}_1, \ldots, \mathtt{x}_k) = true$, $min_i = 0$ for all i and $\mathtt{b} = 0$. This implies that $\mathit{off} = 0$. In this case, it can be proven that $\forall \mathtt{x} \in Y . f(f^{-1}(\mathtt{x})) = \mathtt{x}$ and that $\forall (\mathtt{x}_1, \ldots, \mathtt{x}_k) \in X . f^{-1}(f(\mathtt{x}_1, \ldots, \mathtt{x}_k)) = (\mathtt{x}_1, \ldots, \mathtt{x}_k)$. This proves that f and f^{-1} are inverses on X and Y.

Next, we prove that the image of f under X is contained in Y, and vice versa for f^{-1}. This, together with the first part of the proof, proves that f is a bijection between X and Y.

Subsequently, this is generalised to the case where $\mathtt{b}$, off and the min_i have arbitrary values. We prove that the definitions of f and f^{-1} can be constructed from the simpler ones used at the start of the proof, using function composition. Then, we prove that the function compositions are also inverses and bijections.

Then, we prove that the theorem is still correct for an arbitrary predicate $\mathtt{C}(\mathtt{x}_1, \ldots, \mathtt{x}_k)$. As this predicate introduces the same constraints for both X and Y, both domains are restricted in the same way.

Finally, we prove that f and f^{-1} being inverses and f being a bijection between X and Y implies the equality of the two quantifiers. □

Next, we revisit the example taken from Listing 1.

Example 1. Consider again the following quantifier.

```
∀ int i; 0 ≤ i < n/get_global_size(0); {:ygm[\gtid + i*get_global_size(0)]:} ≡
  \old(xgm[\gtid + i*get_global_size(0)])
```

Note that it matches the linear quantifier pattern, with $\texttt{b} = \texttt{\textbackslash gtid}$, $\texttt{x}_1 = \texttt{i}$, $\texttt{a}_1$ =`get_global_size(0)`, $min_1 = 0$ and max_1 =`n/get_global_size(0)`. Furthermore, there is no C-predicate. From this, we can derive that $\mathit{off} = \texttt{\textbackslash gtid}$ and $base_1(\texttt{x}) = |\texttt{x} - \texttt{\textbackslash gtid}|$ and n_1 =`n/get_global_size(0)`, leading to $\texttt{Y}(\texttt{x}) = |\texttt{x} - \texttt{\textbackslash gtid}| \bmod \texttt{get\_global\_size(0)} = 0 \wedge 0 \leq \texttt{x} - \texttt{\textbackslash gtid} < \texttt{get\_global\_size(0)} \cdot \texttt{(n/get\_global\_size(0))}$. As previously stated, this produces the following new quantifier.

```
∀ int x; (abs(x-\gtid))%get_global_size(0)≡0 ∧ 0 ≤ x-\gtid < get_global_size(0)*(n/
  get_global_size(0)); ygm[x] ≡ \old(xgm[x]);
```

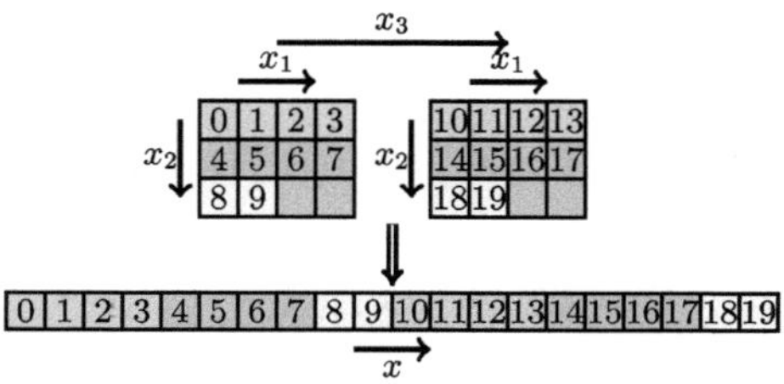

Fig. 1. An example of storing two matrices together in one array.

The second condition may be confusing, but note that with integer division, `get_global_size(0)*(n/get_global_size(0))` is not necessarily equal to `n`. Furthermore, note that `x` represents the original index expression `\gtid + i*get_global_size(0)`, hence `x - \gtid` equals `i*get_global_size(0)`. From this, we can derive that 0 ≤`i*get_global_size(0)<get_global_size (0)* (n/get_global_size(0))`, which implies 0 ≤`i` <`n/get_global_size(0)` , i.e., the condition for `i` in the original quantifier.

Besides the use of block and thread IDs for array accessing, another cause for quantifier issues is the *flattening* of multi-dimensional arrays, such as matrices. To achieve regular memory access patterns, it is generally a good strategy to store matrices in one-dimensional arrays, sometimes even multiple matrices in a single array. In the following example, we address such a situation.

Example 2. Consider Fig. 1, with two matrices stored in a single array with one dimension. A quantifier suitable for the original, non-flattened matrices is the following.

```
∀ int x1, int x2, int x3; 0≤x1<4 ∧ 0≤x2<3 ∧ 0≤x3<2 ∧ 4*x2+x1<10;
  A[10*x3+4*x2+x1]>x2;
```

Note the constraint `4*x₂+x₁<10`, which ensures that the grey cells are not accessed. It serves as the C-constraint in the definition of $X(x_1,\ldots,x_k)$. Note also that every time x_2 is incremented, we jump four elements ahead in the flattened array, corresponding to the upper-bound of x_1, and when x_3 is incremented, we jump ahead ten elements, due to the constraint $4{*}x_2{+}x_1{<}10$. To rewrite this quantifier, first note that $a_1 = 1$, $a_2 = 4$, and $a_3 = 10$. Furthermore, we have

$$\begin{aligned}
\mathit{off} &= 10 \cdot 0 + 4 \cdot 0 + 0 + 0 = 0 \\
\mathit{base}_3(\mathtt{x}) &= \mathtt{x} - 0 = \mathtt{x} \\
\mathit{base}_2(\mathtt{x}) &= \mathit{base}_3(\mathtt{x}) \bmod 10 = \mathtt{x} \bmod 10 \\
\mathit{base}_1(\mathtt{x}) &= \mathit{base}_2(\mathtt{x}) \bmod 4 = (\mathtt{x} \bmod 10) \bmod 4
\end{aligned}$$

This means that $Y(x)$ is defined as

$$\begin{aligned}
&4 \cdot ((\mathtt{x} \bmod 10)/4) + ((\mathtt{x} \bmod 10) \bmod 4)/1 < 10 \land \\
&((\mathtt{x} \bmod 10) \bmod 4) \bmod 1 = 0 \land 0 \le \mathtt{x} < 10 \cdot 2
\end{aligned}$$

Note that $((\mathtt{x} \bmod 10) \bmod 4) \bmod 1 = 0$ is always true, and so is

$$4 \cdot ((\mathtt{x} \bmod 10)/4) + ((\mathtt{x} \bmod 10) \bmod 4)/1 < 10$$

(remember that '/' refers to integer division that discards any remainder). This leads to the following new quantifier.

```
∀ int x; 0≤x<2*10; A[x]>((x%10)/4);
```

Note that if the original formula already contained nonlinear expressions, then the resulting rewritten quantifier may also still have nonlinear terms. For example, consider the following quantifier, with positive integers n_1, n_2:

```
∀ int x₁, int x₂; 0≤x₁<n₁ ∧ 0≤x₂<n₂ ∧ x₁%2≡0; A[x₁+n₁*x₂]>0
```

This is rewritten to `∀int x; 0≤x<n₁*n₂∧(x%n₁)%2≡0; A[x]>0` . This quantifier still contains subexpressions `x%n₁` and `n₁*n₂`, which are both nonlinear. It depends on the capabilities of the underlying SMT solver whether this poses a problem. One could alternatively add additional lemmas to resolve this.

Other verifiers, such as Dafny [18] and Viper [8,22], often introduce additional structure as a way to circumvent the restriction that arithmetic is not allowed in triggers. With this approach, one could define, for instance, `acc(int x, int b, int a)= x*a + b` allowing one to write `A[acc(x, b, a)]` as a trigger. One issue is that this requires to modify the code to be verified to *always* use this indexing. Furthermore, some programs will access arrays in various ways. For example, performing a reduction in a GPU kernel or applying loop-tiling will lead to different access patterns. In those cases, the quantifier will not instantiate anymore. For successful verification, one needs to add complicated verification lemmas relating the different access functions to properly trigger the quantifiers again.

However, the quantifier rewrite method of this section can be *combined* with this additional structure, which is what we have done for the GPU experiments of Sect. 5. We use the function `int acc1d(int x, int b, int n, int a)=x*a + b` to add additional structure. Therefore, an example trigger used in the complete version of Listing 1 has the following structure: `xgm[acc1d(\gtid+ i*get_global_size(0), x_offset, n, x_inc)]` . The benefit is twofold: (1) we can easily access the array in other ways since less structure is present, and (2) we can add additional nonlinear information from lemmas to the contract of the `acc1d`. This additional information helps in dealing with potential incompleteness caused by nonlinearity. Concretely, if we have `a` $>$`0` $\wedge$`n` $>$`0` $\wedge$`x` $\geq$`0` $\wedge$`x` $<$`n` as a precondition for `acc1d`, we know that `b`$\leq$`x*a+b` $\wedge$`x*a+b`$\leq$`b+(n-1)*a`. This is added as a verification lemma to the postcondition of `acc1d`, which has the effect that the SMT solver has knowledge of this nonlinear information each time `acc1d` is used.

Implementation in VerCors. The rewriting procedure described in this section has been implemented in VerCors. To check whether the conditions are met for a quantifier marked as a trigger by the user, VerCors needs to take into account the context of surrounding annotations and statements. Often, Eqs. 1–3 can be derived with basic reasoning. Equation 4, however, tends to be harder to determine. For this reason, we identified Lemma 1 that simplifies checking this condition. We added a straightforward symbolic evaluator to VerCors to verify whether all conditions are satisfied.

Internally in VerCors, we check Eq. 4 by starting at the lowest $i = 1$ and iterating up to k. Suppose that you know that up to $i - 1$ we have proven the Equation, and now we want to prove that it holds for i.

We consider two cases in which we can prove this. In both cases $\mathtt{x}_i$ should have an upper bound max_i, such that n_i is defined and $n_i > 0$. The first case is that $n_i \cdot \mathtt{a}_i = \mathtt{a}_{i+1}$ holds, the second is that $|\mathtt{a}_i| \cdot n_i \leq |\mathtt{a}_{i+1}|$ holds. In the following lemma, we prove that this is correct. If these two cases do not hold, the condition of Eq. 4 is checked directly.

Lemma 1. *Suppose that for any integers i and k, $1 \leq i < k$, and all $(\mathtt{x}_1, \ldots, \mathtt{x}_k) \in X$, it is proven that*

$$\forall i' \in \mathbb{Z}, 1 \leq i' < i \Rightarrow \sum_{j=1}^{i'} |\mathtt{a}_j| \cdot (\mathtt{x}_j - min_j) < |\mathtt{a}_{i'+1}| \tag{5}$$

holds, we have that $\mathtt{a}_i \neq 0$, $n_i > 0$, all $\mathtt{a}_i$ have the same sign, and we have either that $n_i \cdot \mathtt{a}_i = \mathtt{a}_{i+1}$ or that $|\mathtt{a}_i| \cdot n_i \leq |\mathtt{a}_{i+1}|$ holds. Then, we also have

$$\sum_{j=1}^{i} |\mathtt{a}_j| \cdot (\mathtt{x}_j - min_j) < |\mathtt{a}_{i+1}| \tag{6}$$

Proof. The proof of this lemma can be found in Appendix B of [11].

Finally, even though the rewriting procedure is described for an index expression consisting of a single linear pattern $\mathtt{a}_k\mathtt{*x}_k\mathtt{+} \ \ldots \ \mathtt{+} \ \mathtt{a}_1\mathtt{*x}_1\mathtt{+ \ b}$, our implementation contains a generalisation of this, supporting the detection of multiple linear patterns in an expression. By recursively replacing such patterns with single variables using the rewriting procedure, the complete expression is simplified such that it can be used as a trigger.

4 Unique and Immutable Types for Arrays

Data-level parallel programs tend to work with data stored in arrays, often more than one. Unfortunately, as this number of arrays increases, the verification time tends to grow quadratically [14], making programs often unverifiable. A major cause for this is that *permission quantifiers*, as used in separation logic [21], require numerous internal checks for completeness, and these quantifiers are essential for verifying parallel programs. For instance, Listing 1 uses permission quantifiers at l.2–4, to indicate that a thread executing the kernel is allowed to write to particular array cells. The internal checks are needed, since permissions could be combined in case the arrays overlap in memory, and program correctness may depend on this. Over time, the heuristics used in deductive verifiers to reason about arrays possibly overlapping, and the effects of that happening, have improved, but for complex programs, this problem has not been solved. In particular, in earlier work [14] we tried to address the problem by using predicate-based information hiding. This shows a small performance increase on a small artificial benchmark, but it does not scale to larger ones. Folding and unfolding such predicates still expands to quantified permission chunks and creates snapshots that accumulate in the internal state. Thus, the quantifiers appear hidden in the specification but not to the solver, leading to poor performance.

However, we observe that in the case of data-level parallel programs, often (1) the contents of some arrays remain constant throughout the program, and (2) different arrays typically do not overlap in memory. To exploit this, we introduce the *type qualifiers* `immutable` and `unique` to reduce the number of required verification checks.

Before discussing the type qualifiers, we address why verification times tend to grow rapidly as the number of arrays increases, at least with the symbolic execution technique for quantified permissions used by VIPER [21].

A permission quantifier is, internally in VIPER, modelled as a *quantified heap chunk*, i.e., a function that takes a memory reference `r.f`, with `r` a quantified (reference-typed) receiver and `f` a field, and returns a tuple $(v(\texttt{r}), p(\texttt{r}))$, consisting of a symbolic value $v(\texttt{r})$ and a (symbolic) permission $p(\texttt{r}) \in \langle 0, 1]$. For example, when adding the permissions of quantifier `∀int i; 0≤i<9 ⇒Perm( xs[i], write)` to the internal state (i.e., inhaling), a new chunk is produced mapping each of the first nine elements of `xs` to a symbolic field value and a `write` permission. Subsequent quantifiers for the same array(s) produce additional chunks, as opposed to updating existing ones. Whenever an assertion is processed, a *snapshot* is created, which contains the chunks that are relevant for the assertion, i.e., that contain the symbolic values referred to in the assertion [25]. For the completeness of verification, VIPER needs to periodically compare snapshots to check if they are the same. This is because a function call to a side-effect-free function is considered equal if all the arguments are the same, including heap-dependent arguments. This involves comparing all the chunks of one snapshot with all the chunks of the other snapshot, causing the quadratic execution time.

Immutable Qualifier. With the `immutable` qualifier for (a pointer to) an array, for instance in `immutable int* xs`, we propose to indicate that the pointer refers to data that does not change throughout execution of the program. For such pointers, in VerCors, the data can be encoded using an immutable *sequence*, as opposed to a mutable pointer block. Elements of a sequence are not stored on the heap.

With this new qualifier, functions can be defined with immutable pointer parameters. However, when called, the given pointer argument may not be immutable. To allow this, the mutable pointer needs to be coerced to an immutable one. Once this has happened, the pointer cannot be changed anymore. This is achieved by requiring that the mutable pointer releases a positive amount of permission for each of its elements when coerced.

Listing 4. Examples of unique type modifier used on pointers and structs.

```
1  /*@unique<1>@*/ int* xs1; // The pointer points to integers with uniqueness number 1
2  int /*@unique<1>@*/* xs2; // The same type as above
3  xs1 = xs2; // Allowed: both have the same uniqueness number for their integers
4  int /*@unique<2>@*/* xs3; // This involves integers with uniqueness number 2
5  xs1 = xs3; // Not allowed: the pointers have different uniqueness numbers
6  /*@unique<1>@*/ int a; // Uniqueness not relevant, as integers are not stored on heap
7  xs1 = &a; // Address of a is tracked as heap variable, hence uniqueness number matters
8  int* /*@unique<1>@*/ * zs; // The zs pointer has uniqueness number 1
9  xs1 = *zs; // Not allowed: *zs values do not have a uniqueness number
10 struct v { int n; int* xs; /*@unique<2>@*/ int* ys; }; // Uniqueness used in a struct
11 struct v a; // A struct stored in variable a with uniqueness numbers as defined for v
12 /*@unique_field<n,1>@*/ struct v b; // Member n has uniqueness number 1
13 /*@unique_pointer_field<xs,1>@*/ struct v c; // Type of xs member is unique<1> int *
14 a.xs = xs1; // Not allowed: a.xs* values do not have a uniqueness number
15 c.xs = xs1; // Allowed: the uniqueness numbers match
16 xs1 = &(b.n); // Allowed: the uniqueness numbers match
17 void sort(int* xs, int len){...} // A previously defined sorting function
18 int f(/*@unique<1>@*/int* xs, int n){
19   sort(xs, n);
20 }
```

Unique Type Qualifier. We propose the `unique<i>` type qualifier to distinguish non-overlapping data, allowing for a more efficient encoding in Viper. Here, `i` is a *uniqueness number*: only pointers of the same type *and* that have the same uniqueness number can potentially alias. Unique type qualifiers are applicable for all heap locations, such as arrays, pointers, members of structs, and fields of classes. In Listing 4, we show several examples of how this qualifier can be used, including some restrictions. For instance, `xs1` (l.1) and `xs3` (l.4) have the same type, but different uniqueness numbers, making the assignment at l.5 illegal. At l.7, the address of `a` is queried, resulting in the variable being stored on the heap as an integer with uniqueness number 1 (l.6).

Like `const` in C, the unique type qualifier associates to the left, and pointer markers (`*`) denote uniqueness at different levels. For example, at l.8, the content of `zs`, of integer pointer type, has uniqueness number 1. Yet, the inner pointer of `zs` has no uniqueness number, so the assignment at l.9 is not allowed.

Unique types can also be applied to struct members, see l.10. Sometimes, it may be known that different struct instances do not overlap their internal data. For this purpose, we propose the type qualifier annotations `unique_field` and `unique_pointer_field`. These features are demonstrated at l.11–16.

Heap locations in VIPER are encoded using *fields*, with all memory locations of the same type using the same field. When using the unique type qualifiers, types with different uniqueness numbers use different fields. When comparing snapshots, as mentioned earlier, only chunks that refer to the same field are compared. Therefore, by separating non-overlapping arrays into different fields, significant verification time improvements can be achieved. For more on the practical impact of this, see Sect. 5.

Finally, previously defined functions, as, for instance, provided in libraries, should be usable in combination with unique type qualifiers. For instance, consider l.19, where the integer array `xs` with uniqueness number 1 is given as parameter to a predefined sorting function (l.17), in which uniqueness numbers are not given. This will not type check, as `sort` accepts only non-unique arrays. However, such function calls should be supported regardless of the exact uniqueness number, as long as uniqueness between arrays is respected. We consider a function call *consistent* if the type signature of a call partitions the parameters in the same way as the called function. For example, a function `f (unique<0>int* x, unique<0>int* y)` can be called with both arguments of type `unique<1>int*`, but not if one has type `unique<0>int*` and the other has type `unique<1>int*`.

5 Experiments

In this section, we evaluate the effectiveness of the techniques proposed in Sects. 3 and 4 to verify data-level parallel programs. Regarding the rewrite procedure of Sect. 3, the conclusion is clear: none of the experiments we report on in this section were verifiable without the use of this procedure. Using them in combination with the type qualifiers `unique` and `immutable` further improves the verification of data-level parallel programs that contain multiple arrays.

We chose three representative sets of experiments that heavily rely on quantifiers and flattened multi-dimensional arrays. The first set contains the GPU kernels from the CLBlast library [23], consisting of OpenCL kernels that implement the Basic Linear Algebra Subprograms (BLAS). These experiments are conducted to evaluate whether our proposed techniques are applicable to typical GPU kernels. The next two sets of experiments were chosen from [13,14], among which is an implementation of the Padre algorithm, as part of the software for

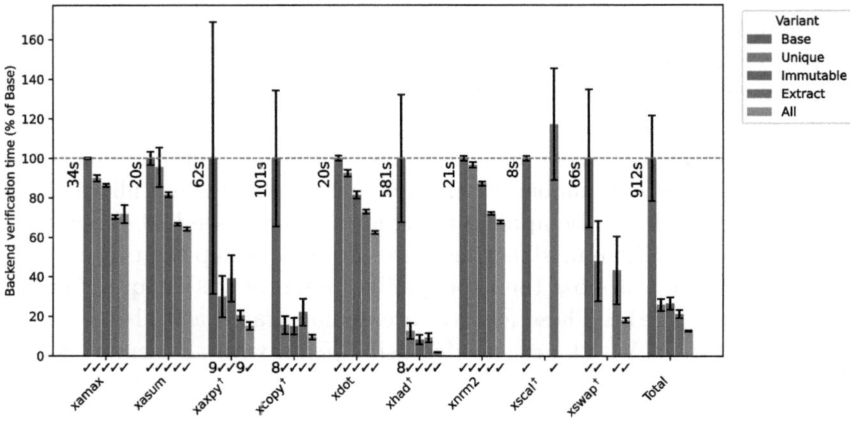

(a) Level 1

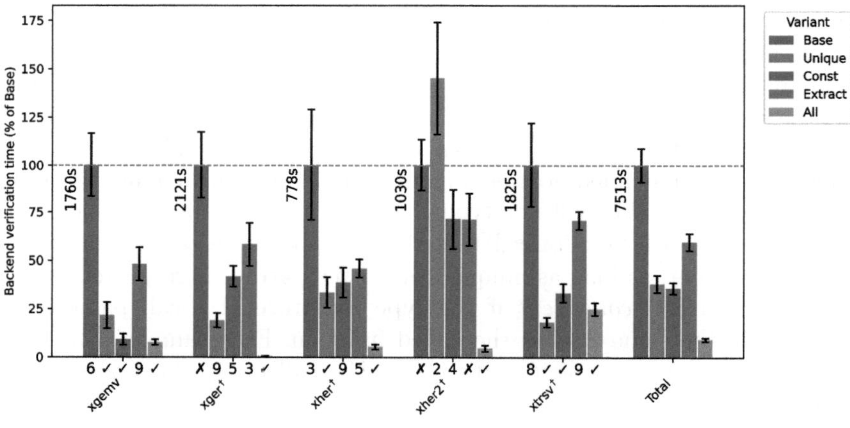

(b) Level 2

Fig. 2. Verification of CLBlast kernels, normalized so Base=100%. **Base** is compared against versions with unique type qualifiers (**Unique**), immutable arrays (**Immutable**), extracted kernel bodies (**Extract**), and **All** which enables all these features. Below the bars: number of successful runs (✓ = 10/10, ✗ 0/10). Next to base bars: average time of the 10 base runs in seconds. The † indicates we (try to) prove functional correctness in addition to memory safety.

a Radio Telescope Pipeline [14]. In these papers, we ran into limitations of the underlying verifiers due to the many arrays and quantifiers present. These works contain optimised parallel CPU programs generated from the Domain Specific Language Halide [24]. The HaliVer [13] tool adds verification annotations to these programs such that they can be verified by VerCors.

Setup. We used a machine with an 11th Gen Intel Core i7-11800H @ 2.30 GHz and 32 GB of RAM running Ubuntu 23.04. We ran each experiment ten times and reported the average of these. The VerCors version used is included in the accompanying artefact. We ran VerCors with the options `--silicon-quiet --dev-time-backend --dev-total-timeout=3600 --dev-assert-timeout 60 --target x86_64-linux-gnu`, and used the Silicon verifier of Viper, which is based on symbolic execution. Additionally, the experiments from [13,14] were also run with `--no-infer-heap-context-into-frame` as these options were also used in the original experiments.

GPU Kernel Body Extraction. Verifying monolithic functions can be more costly than verifying code that is functionally the same but is divided into several functions. The slowdown mainly occurs because the underlying SMT solver has *too much* information. Additionally, as mentioned in Sect. 4, too many program statements increase the number of quantified chunks, which harms performance. Strategies for decomposing large programs into smaller functions for verification have been previously explored in Dafny [18] and Gobra [28]. For GPU kernels, we observed major improvements when the body of an encoded kernel is *extracted* into a separate function with its own contract, and verified in isolation. Since these contracts are almost identical to standard VerCors GPU kernel contracts, we added an option to perform this extraction automatically via the `extract_body` annotation for GPU kernels. For instance, for Listing 2, which roughly corresponds to a PVL encoding of Listing 1 without a grid-strided loop, this means extracting the code at l.15–17 to be verified in isolation without its enclosing parallel blocks. We also evaluated this feature in our GPU experiments.

Results. The results are shown in Fig. 2 and Tables 1 and 2. All times are in seconds, and we set a timeout of one hour. We only report the backend verification time (T) and the standard deviation of the mean times (σ_{mean}). For the tables, we compare using `unique` and `immutable` type qualifiers (**Qualifiers**) with not using them (**Base**). In all configurations, however, the rewriting procedure was applied, as this was essential to make the experiments succeed. The verification result can be successful (✓), fail (✗), or timeout (T.O.). The one 'Error' result for `gemmm-V3` indicates that the rewrite method could not rewrite a quantifier, and VerCors reports this as a user error. With #, we indicate how many times an experiment yielded a certain result, summing up to 10 for each experiment. Speed-up is calculated by dividing T of the **Base** version by T of the specific version for all results (✓, ✗ and T.O).

Evaluation of Section 4. The CLBlast experiments (Fig. 2) cover the level 1 and level 2 subroutines of BLAS. Level 1 covers vector operations only, while level 2 covers matrix–vector operations, which are more complicated. Kernels with no immutable pointers (xswap, xscal) are not evaluated for `immutable`, and kernels

Table 1. Reverification of the experiments presented in [13].

			Base			Qualifiers			
Name	**V**	**Result**	#	**T**	σ	#	**T**	σ	**Speedup**
blur	0	✓	10	13	1	10	9	1	1.4
	1	✓	10	14	1	10	10	1	1.4
	2	✓	10	18	1	10	13	1	1.4
	3	✓	10	20	1	10	20	7	1.0
hist	0	✓	10	25	1	10	26	7	1.0
	1	✓	10	30	1	10	17	1	1.7
	2	✓	10	42	1	10	23	1	1.8
	3	✓	10	79	3	10	32	2	2.5
conv_layer	0	✓	10	153	1	10	53	1	2.9
	1	✓	10	171	1	10	72	6	2.4
	2	✓	10	246	3	10	71	1	3.5
	3	✓	10	227	2	10	68	1	3.3
gemm	0	✓	10	61	1	10	22	1	2.8
	1	✓	10	133	1	10	45	4	2.9
	2	✓	10	250	11	10	131	18	1.9
	3	Error	10			10			
auto_viz	0	✓	10	19	1	9	21	2	0.9
		✗	0			1	15	-	
	1	✓	8	63	1	10	52	1	2.1
		✗	2	290	1	0			
	2	✓	10	67	1	10	55	1	1.2
	3	✓	10	49	1	10	36	1	1.4
Total				1722	33		774	22	2.2

(a) Functional correctness & Memory safety

			Base			Qualifiers			
Name	**V**	**Result**	#	**T**	σ	#	**T**	σ	**Speedup**
blur	0	✓	10	13	1	10	10	1	1.3
	1	✓	10	13	1	10	10	1	1.3
	2	✓	10	17	1	10	14	3	1.2
	3	✓	10	14	1	10	11	1	1.4
hist	0	✓	10	22	1	10	15	1	1.5
	1	✓	10	27	1	10	20	2	1.4
	2	✓	10	36	1	10	32	10	1.1
	3	✓	10	46	1	10	29	2	1.6
conv_layer	0	✓	10	144	2	10	60	6	2.4
	1	✓	10	162	1	10	65	1	2.5
	2	✓	10	220	3	10	74	5	3.0
	3	✓	10	201	2	10	72	5	2.8
gemm	0	✓	10	56	1	10	21	1	2.6
	1	✓	10	110	1	10	35	1	3.2
	2	✓	10	152	8	10	53	6	2.9
	3	Error	10			10			
auto_viz	0	✓	10	18	1	10	21	4	0.9
	1	✓	9	34	1	10	45	10	1.3
		✗	1	266	-	0			
	2	✓	10	36	1	10	39	10	0.9
	3	✓	10	34	1	10	28	1	1.2
bilateral_grid		✓	10	48	1	10	39	1	1.2
camera_pipe		✓	10	205	7	10	122	14	1.7
depthwise_ separable_conv		✓	10	201	2	10	143	1	1.4
Total				1831	26		956	26	1.9

(b) Functional correctness & Memory safety

with only one pointer (xscal) are not evaluated for `unique`. When both cases are applicable, the **Qualifiers** version is the same as the **Base** version. We fixed the thread block sizes of these experiments to a concrete value, as otherwise verification of these kernels could run into incompleteness due to nonlinearity.

The experiments show that applying type qualifiers is always a good idea and can lead to verification times that are up to ten times faster. Similarly, extracting the body of a kernel is always a good idea and speeds up verification (for 'xscal', the difference is not statistically relevant). However, the combination of the techniques shows the most impressive results, being **up to 150 times faster** for 'xger'. Especially for the more complex level 2 kernels, this leads to the results being more reliable (all have ten out of ten successful verification runs), and being able to verify previously unverifiable cases, such as 'xger' and 'xher2'. In total, the combination of features (All) is 8.5 times faster for the total time of level 1 and 10.8 times faster for level 2.

For the experiments taken from [13] (Table 1), **V** indicates that each program has up to four different Halide *schedules* that explore different optimisations that

Table 2. Reverification of the experiments presented in [14].

		Base			Qualifiers			
Version	**Result**	#	**T**	σ	#	**T**	σ	**Speedup**
CB	✓	10	56	1	10	48	1	1.2
NCB	✓	10	56	1	10	50	1	1.1

(a) `step`

		Base			Qualifiers			
Version	**Result**	#	**T**	σ	#	**T**	σ	**Speedup**
CB	✓	10	466	9	10	142	4	3.3
NCB	✓	0			1	901	-	1.3
	✗	10	1028	58	9	780	89	

(b) `sub_direction`

		Base			Qualifiers			
Version	**Result**	#	**T**	σ	#	**T**	σ	**Speedup**
CB	✓	0			10	961	14	3.4
	✗	2	2086	1404	0			
	T.O.	8	-	-	0			
NCB	✗	9	1139	131	6	1211	468	
	T.O.	1	-	-	4	-	-	

(c) `solve_direction`

		Base			Qualifiers			
Version	**Result**	#	**T**	σ	#	**T**	σ	**Speedup**
CB	✓	0			10	2799	38	1.2
	✗	6	3146	101	0			
	T.O.	4	-	-	0			
NCB	✗	1	3589	-	0			
	T.O.	9	-	-	10	-	-	

(d) `perform_iteration`

influence parallelisation and the ordering of computations. **Qualifiers** combines the use of the `immutable` and `unique` encodings.

These experimental results demonstrate that using `immutable` and `unique` type qualifiers mostly has a positive influence. In total, the verification time is reduced by a factor of more than 1.9. Again, this is a speedup achieved after having made the benchmarks verifiable to begin with, by using the rewriting procedure.

For the experiments taken from [14] (Table 2), we make a distinction between versions with concrete bounds (CB) and non-concrete bounds (NCB). The NCB versions already contain nonlinear arithmetic, which can lead to incompleteness. In [14], we tried to address this by adding verification lemmas about nonlinear arithmetic, which only led to successful verification in some cases. In the original experiments, the complete algorithm (`perform_iteration`) was not included as it could not be verified. Now, however, we have been able to verify the CB version.

The experimental results demonstrate that when successful verification is possible, use of the encodings of Sect. 4 always speeds up the verification. In addition, more importantly, it allows three cases to be verified that cannot be verified without using the type qualifier encodings. As a way forward for successfully verifying the NCB version, we expect that extracting parts of the code, as done for the CLBlast benchmarks, will help by reducing the in-scope information during nonlinear reasoning.

Evaluation of Section 3. All experiments above rely on the rewrite method of Sect. 3. Without it, the benchmarks cannot be verified as they are. A similar quantifier rewriter, in a rudimentary form, had been implemented in VerCors before, but that approach had not been formally proven correct, nor described in the literature. However, for the experiments in [13,14], we depended on this rewriter for our results. The current paper proposes a more generally applicable rewriter, involving better symbolic checks to detect patterns in quantifiers, the first that enables complete verification of the Padre algorithm used in the software of a Radio Telescope Pipeline. In addition, this rewriting procedure is described in full detail, and refers to a LEAN correctness proof.

In principle, most quantifiers could be rewritten manually, but not those that VERCORS must introduce automatically for parallel blocks and GPU kernels, which occur in most benchmarks. Among all experiments, `gemm_3` is the only one we could not verify. The rewriting procedure currently fails because its contract uses a linear pattern with the modulo (`%`) operator, which is not yet supported.

Conclusion. In conclusion, the rewriting procedure is highly effective and allows us to automatically find triggers for most of the data-level parallel programs we considered. Additionally, the qualifiers of Sect. 4, especially when used in combination with the kernel extraction method discussed in the current section, are effective: they significantly reduce verification time and allow for the verification of otherwise unverifiable results.

6 Related Work

We divide our related work into two parts. First, we discuss some other approaches to support reasoning about quantifiers. Dafny [18] defines symbolic equivalent functions for several arithmetic operators, which can be used in trigger patterns. This increases the expressiveness of trigger patterns. However, when an array is accessed in a different way than the *precise* arithmetic form given in the trigger, it will not instantiate. To achieve successful verification in these cases, further complex reasoning about triggers is needed. Nonetheless, in the special case where arrays are always accessed in the exact same way, this is a valid alternative. Further, Dafny also supports a technique to automatically identify suitable triggers [17]. In this paper our focus is complementary, as we try to increase the chances to find a matching pattern by rewriting the quantified expressions so that they can be matched with a larger number of terms in the specifications.

Second, we look at related work that identifies special restrictions, such as non-aliasing or immutability, by using types. Charguéraud and Pottier [6] propose 'temporary read-only permissions', an extension to standard separation-logic permissions that can mark memory locations as temporarily read-only without extra verification or specification overhead. This is similar to our `immutable` type modifier, except that once an array is marked immutable, it stays that way. In SYMPLAR [3], Bierhoff introduces *symbolic permissions* as an alternative to fractional permissions. Users annotate types with `@Excl` (exclusive) or `@Imm` (immutable), and SYMPLAR checks these annotations. Our approach is similar but we integrate it with fractional permissions and still allow arrays with the same uniqueness type to alias, capturing a wider range of behaviours. Haack and

Poll [10] present a type system for object immutability in Java. Our `immutable` reference corresponds to their `RdWr` type qualifier. The idea is the same, however we work in a verification setting. They also describe 'Read-only references', where the object's state cannot be modified through this reference, analogous to `const` pointers in C. A different encoding for read-only pointers seems feasible, but would still require permission bookkeeping in a separation-logic setting.

7 Conclusions and Future Work

To improve the capabilities of deductive verifiers to verify data-level parallel programs, first of all, we introduced a rewriting procedure for nested quantifiers, which improves trigger matching, and thereby greatly contributes to more efficient verification. This rewriting technique can be used by any verifier using SMT solvers where quantified formulas over flattened arrays must be handled. More generally, functions with linear arguments are also supported: $f(5\mathrm{x}+3, g(\mathrm{y}-2, 6j+3i))$ can be rewritten to $f(\mathrm{x}', g(\mathrm{y}', ij'))$ to act as a suitable trigger, if the correct conditions are met.

We also introduced two special type qualifiers, to indicate that arrays are immutable or are not aliases of each other. The use of these qualifiers can be verified with type checking, and tend to greatly reduce verification time. The array type modifiers are useful in any separation-logic-based verifier that needs quantified permissions (or iterated separating conjunction, ISC). To the best of our knowledge, the approach of Müller et al. [21] is the only available method for having ISC, so other tools aiming for this expressiveness can also benefit.

The experimental results demonstrate the advantages of our optimisations. With these optimisations combined, we could significantly reduce verification times and verify previously unverifiable cases of a Radio Telescope Pipeline case study [14]. In addition, employing all the suggested encoding optimisations makes the verification, on average, 9 times faster for the CLBlast GPU kernels, with maximum improvements of up to 150 times faster.

For future work, we see several possibilities for further improvements. For instance, we could add our rewriting procedure directly to VIPER, allowing it to query the SMT solver immediately when Eqs. 1–4 need to be checked. This has the advantage that the program state is already modelled at that point, and it enables other VIPER front-ends to reuse our rewriting technique.

Furthermore, we see opportunities to apply the rewrite method for quantifiers to establish correctness properties of *layouts* employed in machine learning compilers, such as CuTE layouts[2] and Triton linear layouts [29]. The access pattern that we rewrite within quantifiers corresponds to the class of injective layouts. Such layouts provide alternative indexing schemes for accessing the same underlying data. The rewrite method, as presented, can be used to transform a multidimensional layout into an equivalent one-dimensional layout. If distinct

[2] See https://github.com/NVIDIA/cutlass/tree/main/media/docs/cpp/cute (visited on 13 May 2026).

layouts rewrite to an identical one-dimensional representation, it follows that they access exactly the same data.

In addition, it would be interesting to investigate whether the `unique` type qualifier can be automatically applied in a program based on the results of some static analysis. This would grant the programmer the benefits of this qualifier without burdening them with the annotation task.

Disclosure of Interests. The authors have no competing interests to declare that are relevant to the content of this article.

Data-Availability Statement. The data for the experiments (Sect. 5), the LEAN proof (Sect. 3), and the version of the VERCORS tool used in this paper can be found in an accompanying artefact at https://doi.org/10.5281/zenodo.19830296.

References

1. Armborst, L., et al.: The VerCors verifier: a progress report. In: CAV. LNCS, vol. 14682, pp. 3–18. Springer (2024). https://doi.org/10.1007/978-3-031-65630-9_1
2. Bertolli, C., Betts, A., Mudalige, G., Giles, M., Kelly, P.: Design and performance of the op2 library for unstructured mesh applications. In: Alexander, M., et al. (eds.) Euro-Par 2011. LNCS, vol. 7155, pp. 191–200. Springer, Heidelberg (2012). https://doi.org/10.1007/978-3-642-29737-3_22
3. Bierhoff, K.: Automated program verification made SYMPLAR: symbolic permissions for lightweight automated reasoning. In: Proceedings of the 10th SIGPLAN Symposium on New Ideas, New Paradigms, and Reflections on Programming and Software, pp. 19–32. ACM (2011). https://doi.org/10.1145/2048237.2048242
4. Blom, S., Huisman, M., Mihelčić, M.: Specification and verification of GPGPU programs. Sci. Comput. Program. **95**, 376–388 (2014). https://doi.org/10.1016/j.scico.2014.03.013
5. Brookes, S.: A semantics for concurrent separation logic. In: Gardner, P., Yoshida, N. (eds.) CONCUR 2004. LNCS, vol. 3170, pp. 16–34. Springer, Heidelberg (2004). https://doi.org/10.1007/978-3-540-28644-8_2
6. Charguéraud, A., Pottier, F.: Temporary read-only permissions for separation logic. In: Yang, H. (ed.) ESOP 2017. LNCS, vol. 10201, pp. 260–286. Springer, Heidelberg (2017). https://doi.org/10.1007/978-3-662-54434-1_10
7. Detlefs, D., Nelson, G., Saxe, J.B.: Simplify: a theorem prover for program checking. J. ACM **52**(3), 365–473 (2005). https://doi.org/10.1145/1066100.1066102
8. Eilers, M., Schwerhoff, M., Summers, A.J., Müller, P.: Fifteen years of viper. In: CAV, pp. 107–123. Springer-Verlag, Berlin (2025). https://doi.org/10.1007/978-3-031-98668-0_5
9. Grewe, D., Lokhmotov, A.: Automatically generating and tuning GPU code for sparse matrix-vector multiplication from a high-level representation. In: Proceedings of the 4th Workshop on General Purpose Processing on Graphics Processing Units (GPGPU). ACM (2011). https://doi.org/10.1145/1964179.1964196
10. Haack, C., Poll, E.: Type-based object immutability with flexible initialization. In: Drossopoulou, S. (ed.) ECOOP 2009. LNCS, vol. 5653, pp. 520–545. Springer, Heidelberg (2009). https://doi.org/10.1007/978-3-642-03013-0_24
11. van den Haak, L.B., Wijs, A., Huisman, M.: Scalable deductive verification of data-level parallel programs (2026). https://arxiv.org/abs/2605.13616

12. van den Haak, L.B., Wijs, A., van den Brand, M., Huisman, M.: Formal methods for GPGPU programming: is the demand met? In: Dongol, B., Troubitsyna, E. (eds.) IFM 2020. LNCS, vol. 12546, pp. 160–177. Springer, Cham (2020). https://doi.org/10.1007/978-3-030-63461-2_9
13. van den Haak, L.B., Wijs, A.J., Huisman, M., van den Brand, M.G.J.: HaliVer: deductive verification and scheduling languages join forces. In: TACAS. LNCS, vol. 14572, pp. 71–89. Springer (2024). https://doi.org/10.1007/978-3-031-57256-2_4
14. van den Haak, L.B., Wijs, A.J., Huisman, M., van den Brand, M.G.J.: Verifying a radio telescope pipeline using HaliVer: solving nonlinear and quantifier challenges. In: FMICS. LNCS, vol. 14952, pp. 152–169. Springer (2024). https://doi.org/10.1007/978-3-031-68150-9_9
15. Hillis, W.D., Steele, G.L.: Data parallel algorithms. Commun. ACM **29**(12), 1170–1183 (1986). https://doi.org/10.1145/7902.7903
16. Le, Q., Ngiam, J., Coates, A., Lahiri, A., Prochnow, B., Ng, A.: On Optimization methods for deep learning. In: Proceedings of the 28th International Conference on Machine Learning (ICML), pp. 265–272. Omnipress (2011). https://doi.org/10.5555/3104482.3104516
17. Leino, K.R.M., Pit-Claudel, C.: Trigger selection strategies to stabilize program verifiers. In: CAV. LNCS, vol. 9779, pp. 361–381. Springer (2016). https://doi.org/10.1007/978-3-319-41528-4_20
18. Leino, K.R.M.: Dafny: an automatic program verifier for functional correctness. In: Clarke, E.M., Voronkov, A. (eds.) LPAR 2010. LNCS (LNAI), vol. 6355, pp. 348–370. Springer, Heidelberg (2010). https://doi.org/10.1007/978-3-642-17511-4_20
19. Liu, X., Tan, S., Wang, H.: Parallel statistical analysis of analog circuits by GPU-accelerated graph-based approach. In: Proceedings of the 2012 Conference and Exhibition on Design, Automation & Test in Europe (DATE), pp. 852–857. IEEE (2012). https://doi.org/10.1109/DATE.2012.6176615
20. Moura, L., Ullrich, S.: The lean 4 theorem prover and programming language. In: Platzer, A., Sutcliffe, G. (eds.) CADE 2021. LNCS (LNAI), vol. 12699, pp. 625–635. Springer, Cham (2021). https://doi.org/10.1007/978-3-030-79876-5_37
21. Müller, P., Schwerhoff, M., Summers, A.J.: Automatic verification of iterated separating conjunctions using symbolic execution. In: Chaudhuri, S., Farzan, A. (eds.) CAV 2016. LNCS, vol. 9779, pp. 405–425. Springer, Cham (2016). https://doi.org/10.1007/978-3-319-41528-4_22
22. Müller, P., Schwerhoff, M., Summers, A.J.: Viper: a verification infrastructure for permission-based reasoning. In: Jobstmann, B., Leino, K.R.M. (eds.) VMCAI 2016. LNCS, vol. 9583, pp. 41–62. Springer, Heidelberg (2016). https://doi.org/10.1007/978-3-662-49122-5_2
23. Nugteren, C.: CLBlast: a tuned OpenCL BLAS library. In: Proceedings of the International Workshop on OpenCL (WOCL), pp. 1–10. ACM (2018). https://doi.org/10.1145/3204919.3204924
24. Ragan-Kelley, J., et al.: Halide: decoupling algorithms from schedules for high-performance image processing. Commun. ACM **61**(1), 106–115 (2017). https://doi.org/10.1145/3150211
25. Schwerhoff, M.H.: Advancing automated, permission-based program verification using symbolic execution. Doctoral Thesis, ETH Zurich (2016). https://doi.org/10.3929/ethz-a-010835519
26. Wienke, S., Springer, P., Terboven, C., an Mey, D.: OpenACC — first experiences with real-world applications. In: Kaklamanis, C., Papatheodorou, T., Spirakis, P.G.

(eds.) Euro-Par 2012. LNCS, vol. 7484, pp. 859–870. Springer, Heidelberg (2012). https://doi.org/10.1007/978-3-642-32820-6_85
27. Wijs, A.J., Bošnački, D.: Improving GPU sparse matrix-vector multiplication for probabilistic model checking. In: Donaldson, A., Parker, D. (eds.) SPIN 2012. LNCS, vol. 7385, pp. 98–116. Springer, Heidelberg (2012). https://doi.org/10.1007/978-3-642-31759-0_9
28. Wolf, F.A., Arquint, L., Clochard, M., Oortwijn, W., Pereira, J.C., Müller, P.: Gobra: modular specification and verification of go programs. In: Silva, A., Leino, K.R.M. (eds.) CAV 2021. LNCS, vol. 12759, pp. 367–379. Springer, Cham (2021). https://doi.org/10.1007/978-3-030-81685-8_17
29. Zhou, K., et al.: Linear layouts: robust code generation of efficient tensor computation using F_2. In: Proceedings of the 31st ACM International Conference on Architectural Support for Programming Languages and Operating Systems (ASPLOS), vol. 1. pp. 132–146. ACM (2026). https://doi.org/10.1145/3760250.3762221

On the Verification Problem of Remote Direct Memory Access Programs

Parosh Aziz Abdulla[1,2], Mohamed Faouzi Atig[1], Govind Rajanbabu[3], and Stephan Spengler[1(✉)]

[1] Uppsala University, Uppsala, Sweden
{parosh.abdulla,mohamed_faouzi.atig,stephan.spengler}@it.uu.se
[2] Mälardalen University, Västerås, Sweden
[3] The Institute of Mathematical Sciences (IMSc), Chennai, India
govind@imsc.res.in

Abstract. Remote Direct Memory Access (RDMA) is a technology that allows direct memory access from the memory of one computer into that of another without involving either one's operating system. This enables high-throughput, low-latency networking, which is especially useful in massively parallel computer clusters.

In this paper, we study the reachability and robustness problems for RDMA programs. We show that reachability is undecidable in general, even for a restricted fragment of the model. We then focus on robustness, which asks whether a program exhibits the same behaviours under the RDMA and sequential consistency (SC) semantics, and prove that this problem is decidable. Our central technical result establishes a normal form for robustness violations, showing that any non-robust program admits a violating execution of a specific form. We then leverage this normal form to obtain a decision procedure that reduces robustness to reachability in finite-state programs with counters, yielding an EXPSPACE upper bound in the general case, and a PSPACE upper bound in the absence of poll operations. Finally, we also show that both of these bounds are optimal.

Keywords: RDMA · Weak Memory Models · Robustness · Verification · Concurrent Systems

1 Introduction

Modern multiprocessor architectures implement weak memory models that relax the guarantees of sequential consistency (SC) to enable aggressive hardware and compiler optimisations. Classical models such as TSO, PSO, ARM, POWER, and RC11 permit various forms of reordering, buffering, and speculation, thereby admitting behaviours that are impossible under SC. While essential for performance, these relaxations significantly complicate reasoning about concurrent programs. This increased complexity is inherent and well-established. For

E. Darulova et al. (Eds.): CAV 2026, LNCS 16682, pp. 113–135, 2026.
https://doi.org/10.1007/978-3-032-32519-8_6

instance, reachability for finite-state concurrent programs is PSPACE-complete under SC, but becomes non-primitive recursive under TSO and undecidable under the Release-Acquire (RA) fragment of RC11. Thus, verifying safety properties under weak memory models is fundamentally harder than under SC, posing significant challenges for program analysis.

Remote Direct Memory Access (RDMA) has recently gained prominence in high-performance computing [10,11]. RDMA enables a process to directly read from or write to the memory of a remote machine, bypassing the remote CPU and operating system on the critical path. This paradigm is widely used in data centres, where it offers low latency and high throughput. However, RDMA introduces a non-trivial memory model that differs fundamentally from both shared-memory concurrency and message passing. RDMA supports one-sided operations, provides weak ordering guarantees, and allows remote memory updates to be observed asynchronously with respect to local CPU accesses. Consequently, reasoning about correctness requires explicit consideration of visibility, ordering, and synchronisation mechanisms such as fences and completion events. These characteristics distinguish RDMA from existing weak memory models, necessitating specialised verification techniques.

In this work, we first study the reachability problem for RDMA programs. We show that reachability is undecidable in general, via a reduction from Post's Correspondence Problem. Notably, this undecidability holds even for finite-state RDMA programs without *poll* operations or *fence* instructions, highlighting the inherent complexity of the model.

The difficulty of proving safety properties under weak memory has motivated the study of correctness notions that enable sound reasoning despite relaxed semantics. A fundamental question is whether a program behaves *robustly* under a given weak memory model [14]. Informally, a program is robust if every behaviour under the weak model is observationally equivalent to some behaviour under SC. Robustness is appealing for two reasons. First, if a program is robust and correct under SC, then it remains correct under the weak model. Second, verifying robustness can be simpler than verifying safety directly. For example, checking reachability under TSO is non-primitive-recursive [12,13], whereas checking robustness is PSPACE-complete [14].

Recently, Ambal et al. [11] initiated the study of robustness for RDMA programs. They established sufficient conditions for robustness, but these are restrictive and do not characterise all robust programs (see, e.g., Fig. 6(b) in [11]). Their work leaves open the decidability and complexity of robustness. In this work, we resolve these questions by showing that robustness of finite-state RDMA programs is decidable and EXPSPACE-complete. Our approach relies on a structural characterisation of robustness violations, enabling a reduction to reachability in SC programs augmented with finite control and counters.

To formalise RDMA behaviours, we build on the axiomatic semantics of Ambal et al. [10]. Their consistency check requires verifying acyclicity of two relations over execution events, which is rather complex. We revisit this semantics and introduce a simpler, equivalent characterisation of RDMA consistency.

This refined view serves as the foundation for our decidability results. To establish the ExpSpace upper bound, we introduce a novel instrumentation technique that transforms an RDMA program into an SC program. This SC program simulates all behaviours of the original while preserving observational equivalence, enabling the use of existing SC verification tools. We also identify a simpler fragment – RDMA programs without poll operations – for which robustness reduces to reachability in purely finite-state SC programs.

In summary, our main contributions are:

- We prove that reachability for RDMA programs is undecidable, even without poll operations or fences.
- We simplify the axiomatic RDMA semantics of [10], providing an equivalent but more tractable consistency check.
- We establish a normal form for robustness violations by rearranging computations around a pivotal event.
- We present a decision procedure for robustness based on an instrumentation that transforms RDMA programs into SC programs with counters, yielding an ExpSpace upper bound (PSpace without poll operations).
- We prove matching lower bounds: robustness is ExpSpace-complete in general and PSpace-complete without poll operations.

Related Work. We base our formalisation of RDMA behaviours on the RDMA semantics proposed by Ambal et al. [10,11]. In [10], the authors assume TSO processors per node, while [11] considers SC processors. Both works present axiomatic and operational semantics for RDMA and propose consistency-checking procedures. An earlier semantics by Dan et al. [19] fails to capture certain RDMA behaviours, as shown in [10].

The reachability problem has been extensively studied for various weak memory models, such as TSO [5,8,12,13], RA [1], Causal Consistency [23], PSO [7], Power [2], Intel-x86 with Persistency [3,4], Promising Semantics [6], and Localized Release-Acquire [27]. The complexity of the reachability problem varies significantly across these models, ranging from non-primitive recursive to undecidable, depending on the specific memory model and program restrictions. To the best of our knowledge, our work is the first to study the reachability problem for RDMA programs, establishing its undecidability in general.

The robustness problem has also been extensively studied for various memory models [14–17,20,21]. For RDMA, Ambal et al. [11] initiated the study of robustness, providing sufficient (but restrictive) conditions for ensuring robustness; their paper also gives robust examples not covered by these conditions (Fig. 6(b) in [11]). To the best of our knowledge, our work is the first to establish decidability and complexity results for robustness and reachability-based safety verification under RDMA semantics.

2 RDMA Program Semantics

A program consists of a finite set of threads that operate on a distributed memory system composed of multiple nodes. Each node contains its own local memory and processes, and nodes communicate with each other using Remote Direct Memory Access (RDMA) operations. We consider a finite instruction set consisting of local reads and writes, remote write operations, remote read operations, polling instructions, and a remote-fence instruction. Local instructions operate directly on the node's memory, whereas remote instructions access the memory of other nodes via their *network interface controllers* (NIC).

In the following, $x, y, z \in \mathsf{Loc}$ denote memory locations, $v_r, v_w \in \mathsf{Val}$ denote values, and $n \in \mathsf{Node} = \{1, \ldots, N\}$ denotes nodes. A bar above a location or node indicates a remote location or node, respectively. Each thread (or *process*) P in an RDMA program is defined by the following grammar:

$$\begin{aligned} \mathsf{P} ::= \quad & \texttt{skip} \mid \mathsf{P}_1;\mathsf{P}_2 \mid \mathsf{P}_1 + \mathsf{P}_2 \mid \mathsf{P}^* \\ & \mid x := v_w \mid \texttt{assume}(x = v_r) \mid \texttt{assume}(x \neq v_r) \mid x := \texttt{CAS}(z, v_r, v_w) \\ & \mid x := \bar{y} \mid \bar{y} := x \mid \texttt{rfence}(\bar{n}) \mid \texttt{poll}(\bar{n}) \end{aligned}$$

To model communication between nodes, each process P maintains a distinct buffer system (or *queue pair* in the terminology of [10]) for every remote node $\bar{n}$ whose memory it may access. Remote operations issued by process P towards node $\bar{n}$ are first placed in the buffer system, which consists of multiple FIFO buffers. Their arguments are not defined at the point when they are issued, since they may depend on local memory reads that occur after the remote operation is issued. Furthermore, they need to travel through the buffer system before they are propagated to the remote node. Therefore, the completion of remote operations is not instantaneous, and may occur out of order with respect to the program order of the issuing process. This allows the reordering of remote operations with respect to each other and with respect to local memory accesses, inducing a weak memory model.

We briefly describe the key buffers in the queue system; the full operational model involves additional buffers and is detailed in [10]. When a process issues a remote write, a symbolic entry $\bar{y} := x$ is placed in the first buffer B_1. This entry is not yet instantiated with the value of x – the local variable x may be modified by subsequent CPU operations before the entry is processed. When the entry reaches the head of B_1, the current value v of x is read from local memory, and an instantiated entry $\bar{y} := v$ is forwarded to buffer B_2. This delayed instantiation allows local writes to overtake the value read by pending remote operations. Buffer B_2 transmits the instantiated write to the remote node, where it updates the target memory location $\bar{y}$. Upon completion, an acknowledgment is placed in buffer B_3, which returns to the issuing node. Remote reads follow a similar pattern, with instantiation occurring at the remote node. Both remote read and remote write operations generate acknowledgments that can be consumed by `poll` operations.

`poll` operations provide a mechanism for synchronising with the completion of remote operations. A poll instruction $\texttt{poll}(\bar{n})$ blocks until the earliest (in program order) pending remote operation issued by the calling process towards node $\bar{n}$ has completed. `poll` operations can be used to prevent undesired reordering between remote operations and subsequent local memory accesses by ensuring that a remote operation has completed before execution proceeds. However, note that each `poll` waits for exactly one remote operation to complete, rather than for all pending operations towards the same node. A remote-fence instruction `rfence` ensures that all remote operations issued by the calling process towards a node prior to the fence are completed before any subsequent remote operations towards the same node are issued.

We will recall the full details of the axiomatic semantics in Sect. 4.

3 Undecidability of Reachability

In this section, we show that the reachability problem for RDMA programs is undecidable. Here, reachability is classical control-state reachability: given an RDMA program and a control state of one thread, we ask whether some execution from the initial configuration reaches a configuration in which that thread is in the target control state, while all other threads may be in arbitrary control states. The proof will follow from a reduction from Post's Correspondence Problem (PCP) [25], a well-known undecidable problem. An instance of PCP is given by two sequences of non-empty words over some finite alphabet Σ, say $u_1, u_2, \ldots, u_N$ and $v_1, v_2, \ldots, v_N$. The problem asks whether there exists a sequence $i_1, i_2, \ldots, i_k$ of indices such that $u_{i_1} u_{i_2} \ldots u_{i_k} = v_{i_1} v_{i_2} \ldots v_{i_k}$. We will propose an RDMA program R consisting of four processes P_1, P_2, P_3, and P_4, each on a different node, such that there is an execution of R reaching a final configuration (i.e., all four processes terminate) if and only if PCP has a solution for the aforementioned instance (Fig. 1).

The idea is that process P_1 guesses a solution of PCP, which is a sequence of indices $i_1, i_2, \ldots, i_k$, and sends the guessed indices to both P_2 and P_3. For each received index i, process P_2 (P_3) sends the letters of u_i (v_i) to process P_4. Process P_4 checks that the sequences of letters received from P_2 and P_3 are identical.

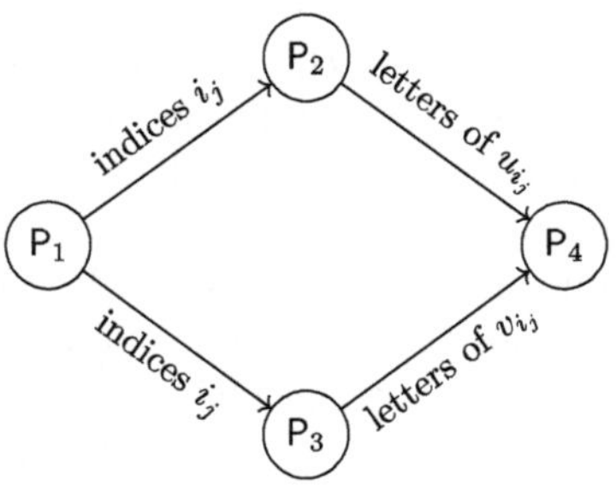

Fig. 1. The PCP program.

In order to implement this idea, we need to ensure that the sequences of letters sent by the processes are received without any losses or duplications. Since the set of letters is finite, the problem amounts to showing that we can transfer a sequence of letters over a finite alphabet from one process to another. The main challenge is that remote writes propagate through the buffer system (cf. Sect. 2), and the receiving process has no built-in mechanism to detect when a new value arrives. This can lead to missed or duplicated reads: the receiver may read before the value arrives, or read the same value multiple times. We address this using an alternating bit protocol.

Figure 2 illustrates the problem. Process P_1 wants to send a sequence of symbols from a finite alphabet $\{1, 2\}$ to process P_2. To send each symbol, process P_1 uses a dedicated register for that symbol (register a always holds 1, register

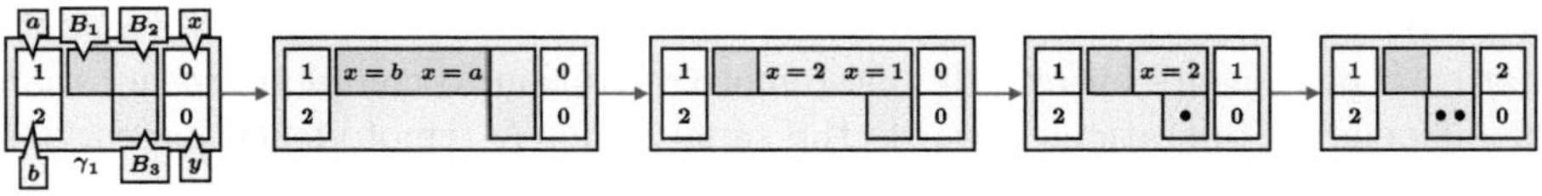

Fig. 2. Message loss due to unsynchronised reads.

b always holds 2), and performs $\bar{x} := a$ or $\bar{x} := b$ accordingly. Using constant values avoids complications from the delayed instantiation in buffer B_1 (see Sect. 2). However, process P_2 may not observe all sent symbols: in Fig. 2, process P_1 sends the sequence $1, 2$, but P_2 may read only the final value 2, missing the intermediate 1. To fix this synchronisation problem, we use an alternating bit protocol (ABP) between each pair of processes. The ABP ensures that each sent symbol is received exactly once by the receiving process. The protocol uses two extra registers f and g at the sender and receiver processes, respectively. Register f at the sender process holds the alternating bit, while register g at the receiver process observes the alternating bit. The key invariant is that each symbol is accepted only when g changes to the sender's bit, which prevents both losses and duplicate deliveries. The protocol works as follows (see Fig. 3). The initial value of f and g are $\top$ and $\bot$, respectively, while a and b hold the values from the alphabet (here 1 and 2). In Fig. 3, we assume that process P_1 wants to send a word over the alphabet $\{1, 2\}$ to process P_2, of the form $\cdots 21$, i.e., the word starts with 1 followed by 2. The process P_1 first performs $\bar{x} := a$ to send the value 1 to P_2, and then $\bar{g} := f$ to set the flag g to $\top$, indicating that a new value 1 has been sent (see configuration γ_2). When these two messages reach the head of buffer B_1, they acquire their values (1 resp. $\top$), and are forwarded to buffer B_2 (cf. configuration γ_3). When $x = 1$ is at the head of buffer B_2, the node of P_2 updates its local variable x to 1 (cf. configuration γ_4). Once process P_2 has read the value 1, we need to ensure that it can detect and read the next value. To that end, process P_2 carries out a sequence of operations, where it first performs the local write operation $\mathtt{wr}(x, \bot)$ to reset x to its initial value $\bot$. Then it checks that the receiver-side flag is still unset by performing the local read operation $\mathtt{rd}(g, \bot)$ (cf. configuration γ_5). This ensures that no additional write operations were performed in the previous steps. Next, process P_2 performs the local read operation $\mathtt{rd}(g, \top)$ to detect the next fresh delivery and ensure that the old value 1 will not be read again (cf. configuration γ_8). Finally, it resets the flag g to its initial state $\bot$.

Using this protocol, we can implement the PCP reduction as follows (details can be found in the extended version [9]). Process P_1 uses the ABP to send the guessed indices to both P_2 and P_3. For each received index i, process P_2 uses the ABP to send the letters of u_i to P_4, while P_3 sends the letters of v_i. Process P_4 checks that the two received letter sequences are identical, alternating between receiving from P_2 and P_3. The buffered communication is essential: since P_2 and P_3 may produce letters at different rates, the buffers decouple their execution, allowing the final sequences to match even when the corresponding words u_i and

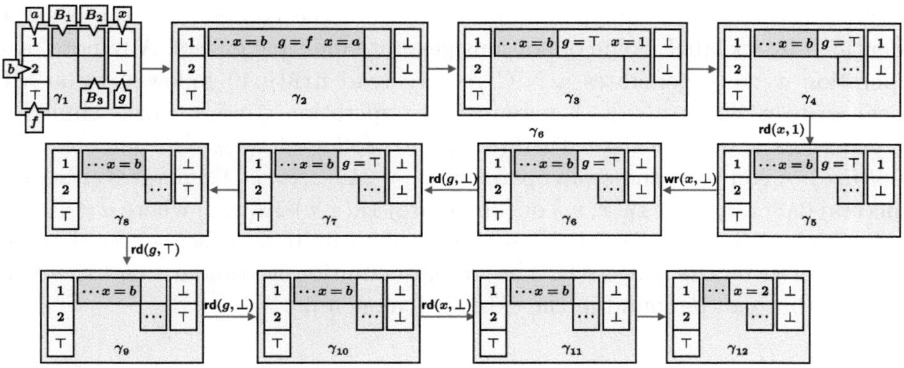

Fig. 3. The Alternating Bit Protocol.

v_i have different lengths. The program reaches a final configuration if and only if PCP has a solution. This establishes the following result.

Theorem 1. *The reachability problem for RDMA programs is undecidable.*

We note that the reduction uses only a restricted fragment of the RDMA model: it requires only local operations and remote writes, without remote reads or any synchronisation primitives such as `poll` or `rfence`. This demonstrates that reachability is undecidable even for this minimal fragment.

4 The Declarative Semantics of RDMA

We build upon the declarative semantics for RDMA developed by Ambal et al. [10,11]. The CPU part of our model and the general notion of sequential consistency follow standard definitions from the literature. The RDMA-specific aspects – NIC operations, their labels and events, pf, nfo and derived relations, and the RDMA consistency conditions – are adopted from their work.

An RDMA program R is a collection of threads $(\mathsf{P}_t)_{t\in\mathsf{Tid}}$, where $\mathsf{Tid} = \{1,\ldots,M\}$ is the set of thread identifiers. We assume a function $n : \mathsf{Loc} \longrightarrow \mathsf{Node}$ that maps variables to their node. An execution of a program generates events, which are labelled by their type. Let Lab consist of all labels of the following forms:

NIC remote read:	$\mathtt{nrR}(\bar{y}, v_r)$	CPU local read:	$\mathtt{lR}(x, v_r)$
NIC local write:	$\mathtt{nlW}(x, v_w, \bar{n})$	CPU local write:	$\mathtt{lW}(x, v_w)$
NIC local read:	$\mathtt{nlR}(x, v_r, \bar{n})$	CPU compare-and-swap:	$\mathtt{CAS}(z, v_r, v_w)$
NIC remote write:	$\mathtt{nrW}(\bar{y}, v_w)$	CPU poll:	$\mathtt{poll}(\bar{n})$
NIC fence:	$\mathtt{nF}(\bar{n})$		

An *event* is defined as a triple $e = \langle \iota, t, l\rangle$ where $\iota \in \mathbb{N}$ is the program counter, $t \in \mathsf{Tid}$ is the thread id, and $l \in \mathsf{Lab}$ is a label. We omit the program counter

ι and the thread id t when they are clear from the context, i.e. the event is identified by its label. Some operations generate multiple events. A remote read operation $x := \bar{y}$ generates a NIC remote read $\mathtt{nrR}(\bar{y}, v)$ followed by a NIC local write $\mathtt{nlW}(x, v, n(\bar{y}))$. A remote write operation $\bar{y} := x$ works similarly: it generates a NIC local read $\mathtt{nlR}(x, v, n(\bar{y}))$ followed by a NIC remote write $\mathtt{nrW}(\bar{y}, v)$. A compare-and-swap operation $x := \mathtt{CAS}(z, v_r, v_w)$ generates either (on success) $\mathtt{CAS}(z, v_r, v_w) \cdot \mathtt{lW}(x, v_r)$ or (on failure) $\mathtt{lR}(z, v) \cdot \mathtt{lW}(x, v)$ where $v \neq v_r$. We inductively define $\mathsf{Seq}(\mathsf{P}) \subseteq \mathsf{Lab}^*$ as the set of all finite label sequences that can be generated by the process P. The formal definition is standard and therefore omitted, but can be found in the extended version [9].

Notation. We use $\iota(e)$, $t(e)$, $n(e)$, $\bar{n}(e)$, $\mathsf{loc}(e)$, $v_r(e)$ and $v_w(e)$ to refer to the program counter, thread id, local node, remote node, location, read value and write value of e, whenever applicable.

Let E be a set of events. With $E.\mathtt{nrR}, E.\mathtt{nlW}, \ldots$ we refer to the subset of events of E that have label $\mathtt{nrR}, \mathtt{nlW}, \ldots$, respectively. We define:

$$\begin{aligned}
E.\mathtt{CPU} &= E.\mathtt{lR} \cup E.\mathtt{lW} \cup E.\mathtt{CAS} \cup E.\mathtt{poll} && \text{(CPU events)}\\
E.\mathtt{nW} &= E.\mathtt{nlW} \cup E.\mathtt{nrW} && \text{(NIC write events)}\\
E.\mathtt{W} &= E.\mathtt{nlW} \cup E.\mathtt{nrW} \cup E.\mathtt{lW} \cup E.\mathtt{CAS} && \text{(write events)}\\
E.\mathtt{R} &= E.\mathtt{nlR} \cup E.\mathtt{nrR} \cup E.\mathtt{lR} \cup E.\mathtt{CAS} && \text{(read events)}\\
E.\mathtt{Inst} &= E \setminus (E.\mathtt{nlW} \cup E.\mathtt{nrW}) && \text{(instantaneous events)}
\end{aligned}$$

Given a relation $\mathsf{rel} \subset E \times E$ and a subset $E' \subset E$, we use $\mathsf{rel}^{-1} = \{(e_2, e_1) \mid (e_1, e_2) \in \mathsf{rel}\}$, $[E'] = \{(e, e) \mid e \in E'\}$ and $\mathsf{rel}\,|_{E'} = \mathsf{rel} \cap E' \times E'$. We usually write $e_1 \xrightarrow{\mathsf{rel}} e_2$ if $(e_1, e_2) \in \mathsf{rel}$. If $\mathsf{rel}' \subset E \times E$ is another relation, then $\mathsf{rel}; \mathsf{rel}' = \{(e_1, e_3) \mid \exists\ e_2 \in E : (e_1, e_2) \in \mathsf{rel}, (e_2, e_3) \in \mathsf{rel}'\}$. Lastly, we define the *same-queue-pair* relation $\mathsf{sqp} = \{(e_1, e_2) \in E \times E \mid t(e_1) = t(e_2) \wedge \bar{n}(e_1) = \bar{n}(e_2)\}$.

Definition 2 (Trace). *A* trace *of an RDMA program* $\mathsf{R} = (\mathsf{P}_t)_{t \in \mathsf{Tid}}$ *is a tuple* $T = \langle E, \mathsf{po}, \mathsf{pf}, \mathsf{rf}, \mathsf{mo}, \mathsf{nfo}\rangle$ *where:*

- $E = E^0 \cup \bigcup_{t \in \mathsf{Tid}} E^t$ *is a finite set of events such that:*
  - $E^0 = \{(\_, \_, \mathtt{lW}(x, v_x)) \mid x \in \mathsf{Loc}\}$ *is the set of* initialisation events, *where* v_x *is the* initial value *of* x.
  - *For each* $t \in \mathsf{Tid}$, *there is* $s_t \in \mathsf{Seq}(\mathsf{P}_t)$ *and* $0 \leq n \leq |s_t|$ *such that* $E^t = \{\langle \iota, t, s_t[\iota]\rangle \mid 1 \leq \iota \leq n\}$ *(i.e., the events of each thread form a prefix of some path in* $\mathsf{Seq}(\mathsf{P}_t)$*).*
- $\mathsf{po} \subset \bigcup_{t \in \mathsf{Tid}}(E^t \times E^t)$ *is the* program order *relation on* E, *which is a strict total order on the events of each thread, uniquely defined such that* $(e_1, e_2) \in \mathsf{po}$ *if and only if* $\iota(e_1) < \iota(e_2)$ *and* $t(e_1) = t(e_2)$.
- $\mathsf{pf} \subset (E.\mathtt{nW} \times E.\mathtt{poll}) \cap \mathsf{po} \cap \mathsf{sqp}$ *is the* polls-from *relation on* E, *that relates NIC write events to later (w.r.t.* po*) poll events on the same queue pair. It is uniquely defined such that every poll event polls from exactly one NIC write,*

which must be the earliest (w.r.t. po*) non-polled one. That is,* $(e_1, e_2) \in \mathsf{pf}$ *if and only if* $e_1 \in E.\mathtt{nW}$, $e_2 \in E.\mathtt{poll}$, $(e_1, e_2) \in \mathsf{po} \cap \mathsf{sqp}$ *and:*

$$|\{e'_1 \in E.\mathtt{nW} \mid (e'_1, e_1) \in \mathsf{po} \cap \mathsf{sqp}\}| = |\{e'_2 \in E.\mathtt{poll} \mid (e'_2, e_2) \in \mathsf{po} \cap \mathsf{sqp}\}|$$

- $\mathsf{rf} \subset E.\mathtt{W} \times E.\mathtt{R}$ *is the* reads-from *relation on* E*, which relates write events to read events on the same variable and with the same value. That is,* $(e_1, e_2) \in \mathsf{rf}$ *only if* $\mathsf{loc}(e_1) = \mathsf{loc}(e_2)$ *and* $v_w(e_1) = v_r(e_2)$*. Furthermore, each read event reads from exactly one write event.*
- $\mathsf{mo} = \bigcup_{x \in \mathsf{Loc}} \mathsf{mo}_x \subset E.\mathtt{W} \times E.\mathtt{W}$ *is the* modification order *relation on* E*. Each* mo_x *is a strict total order on the write events on location* x*, such that* $E^0_x \times (E.\mathtt{W}_x \backslash E^0_x) \subset \mathsf{mo}_x$*, where* $E^0_x = \{(\_, \_, \mathtt{lW}(x, v_x))\} \subseteq E^0$ *and* $E.\mathtt{W}_x = \{e \in E.\mathtt{W} \mid \mathsf{loc}(e) = x\}$.
- $\mathsf{nfo} \subset \mathsf{sqp}$ *is the* NIC flush order *relation on* E*, which relates NIC events on the same queue pair in the following way: For all* $(e_1, e_2) \in \mathsf{sqp}$*, if* $e_1 \in E.\mathtt{nlR}$ *and* $e_2 \in E.\mathtt{nlW}$*, then exactly one of the pairs* (e_1, e_2) *or* (e_2, e_1) *is in* nfo*. The same holds true for* $e_1 \in E.\mathtt{nrR}$ *and* $e_2 \in E.\mathtt{nrW}$.

Definition 3 (Derived Relations). *Given a trace* $T = \langle E, \mathsf{po}, \mathsf{pf}, \mathsf{rf}, \mathsf{mo}, \mathsf{nfo}\rangle$*, we define:*

$$\begin{aligned}
&\mathsf{rb} = (\mathsf{rf}^{-1}; \mathsf{mo}) && \text{(reads-before)}\\
&\mathsf{sc} = (\mathsf{po} \cup \mathsf{rf} \cup \mathsf{rb} \cup \mathsf{mo})^+ && \text{(sequential consistency)}\\
&\mathsf{ippo} \subset \mathsf{po} \textit{ as in Figure 4} && \text{(issue-preserved program order)}\\
&\mathsf{oppo} \subset \mathsf{po} \textit{ as in Figure 4} && \text{(observation-preserved program order)}\\
&\mathsf{ib} = (\mathsf{ippo} \cup \mathsf{rf} \cup \mathsf{pf} \cup \mathsf{nfo})^+ && \text{(issued-before)}\\
&\mathsf{ob} = (\mathsf{oppo} \cup \mathsf{rf} \cup ([\mathtt{nlW}]; \mathsf{pf}) \cup \mathsf{nfo} \cup \mathsf{rb} \cup \mathsf{mo} \cup ([\mathtt{Inst}]; \mathsf{ib}))^+ && \text{(observed-before)}
\end{aligned}$$

The rb relation ensures that if $w_1 \xrightarrow{\mathsf{rf}} r$ and $w_1 \xrightarrow{\mathsf{mo}} w_2$, then r was observed before w_2. To build intuition for the remaining relations, recall that NIC writes are non-instantaneous (they may be buffered), while events in Inst are instantaneous. Hence we distinguish *issue* order from *observation* order.

The relation ippo captures po-edges that must be preserved at issue points, whereas oppo captures those that must be preserved at observation points. Thus oppo is closer to the usual notion of preserved program order. In Fig. 4, a ✓ means that po-edges between the two event types are contained in both ippo and oppo, whereas × means that po-edges are not contained in either relation. sqp means that po-edges between two events on the same queue pair are preserved in both relations and ippo: sqp means that these edges are only preserved in ippo but not oppo. For example, a NIC write followed by a fence on the same queue pair is in ippo but not necessarily in oppo: the write is issued first, but may be observed later due to buffering.

po ↱	CPU	nlR	nrW	nrR	nlW	nF
CPU	✓	✓	✓	✓	✓	✓
nlR	×	sqp	sqp	sqp	sqp	sqp
nrW	×	×	sqp	sqp	sqp	ippo: sqp
nrR	×	×	×	×	sqp	sqp
nlW	×	×	×	×	sqp	ippo: sqp
nF	×	sqp	sqp	sqp	sqp	sqp

Fig. 4. The relations ippo and oppo as subsets of po.

The relation ib collects ordering constraints at issue points (including ippo, rf, pf, and nfo), while ob is the corresponding observation-level causality relation (including oppo, rf, ($[\mathtt{nlW}]; \mathsf{pf}$), nfo, rb, mo, and ($[\mathtt{Inst}]; \mathsf{ib}$)). Intuitively, ($[\mathtt{Inst}]; \mathsf{ib}$) lifts issue-order constraints to observation order when the source event is instantaneous.

We use the notation 'T.' to refer to the various components of T, e.g. $T.E$ is the event set of T and $T.\mathsf{ib}$ is the ib-relation of T.

Definition 4 (Consistency and Robustness). *A trace T is called*

- SC-consistent *if $T.\mathsf{sc}$ is acyclic (irreflexive).*
- RDMA-consistent [11] *if both $T.\mathsf{ib}$ and $T.\mathsf{ob}$ are acyclic (irreflexive).*

A program R *is said to be* robust *if all its RDMA-consistent traces are also SC-consistent. We call a trace* violating *if it is RDMA-consistent but not SC-consistent.*

The definition of SC consistency is standard. The definition of RDMA consistency is well motivated by Ambal et al. who show that the operational and declarative semantics of RDMA are equivalent. Our first result is that the first condition of RDMA-consistency, acyclicity of the issued-before relation, is redundant:

Theorem 5. *If* ib *is cyclic, then* ob *is cyclic.*

Proof. Consider a cycle in ib, i.e. a sequence of events $e_0, e_1, \ldots, e_n = e_0$ such that $e_{i-1} \xrightarrow{\mathsf{rel}_i} e_i$ and $\mathsf{rel}_i \in \{\mathsf{ippo}, \mathsf{rf}, \mathsf{pf}, \mathsf{nfo}\}$ for all $1 \leq i \leq n$. If all edges of the cycle are in ob, we are done. So, assume that there exists at least one edge $e_{i-1} \xrightarrow{\mathsf{rel}_i} e_i$ that is not contained in ob. In particular, it holds that:

$$(e_{i-1}, e_i) \in (\mathsf{ippo} \cup \mathsf{rf} \cup \mathsf{pf} \cup \mathsf{nfo}) \setminus \mathsf{ob} \subseteq (\mathsf{ippo} \setminus \mathsf{oppo}) \cup ([\mathtt{nrW}]; \mathsf{pf})$$
$$= ([\mathtt{nrW}]; \mathsf{po}; [\mathtt{nF}]) \cup ([\mathtt{nlW}]; \mathsf{po}; [\mathtt{nF}]) \cup ([\mathtt{nrW}]; \mathsf{pf})$$

The event e_i must be a NIC fence or a poll event, which are both instantaneous. We conclude $(e_i, e_i) \in \mathsf{ib}$ and since $([\mathtt{Inst}]; \mathsf{ib}) \subseteq \mathsf{ob}$, it follows that $(e_i, e_i) \in \mathsf{ob}$, which means that ib is cyclic.

Henceforth, we only need to check acyclicity of ob when verifying RDMA-consistency.

5 Normal Form for Violating Computations

Our main result is that every non-robust RDMA program has a violating trace in a special *normal form*:

Theorem 6 (Normal Form). *If an RDMA program* R *has a violating trace, then it has a violating trace whose event set can be partitioned as $E = E_1 \cup E_2$ such that:*

1. *The events within E_1 and E_2 are in an SC-consistent order, respectively. That is, $\mathsf{sc}|_{E_1}$ and $\mathsf{sc}|_{E_2}$ are acyclic.*
2. *All* ob*-edges between E_1 and E_2 go from E_1 to E_2, that is, for all $e_1 \in E_1$ and $e_2 \in E_2$, if e_1 and e_2 are related by* ob*, then $e_1 \xrightarrow{\mathsf{ob}} e_2$.*

The key insight is that we can simplify any violating trace by identifying a *maximal event* – one that could be the last issued event – and reorganising the execution around it. This reorganisation removes unnecessary delays while preserving both RDMA-consistency and the SC-violation.

This chapter presents the construction of the normal form trace and establishes the correctness of Theorem 6. The next chapter shows how this normal form enables a practical robustness decision procedure: we can systematically search for violating traces by building up E_1 and E_2 in parallel during a single SC-simulation, non-deterministically assigning each generated event to either E_1 or E_2.

5.1 Example

Consider the program R on the right. It has two nodes with two variables each: node 1 has variables x and y, node 2 has variables z and w. We consider only a single thread on node 1, with three instructions: a remote read of w into y, a remote write of x into z, and a local write of 2 into x. This program is not robust:

$x = 1$	$z = 0$
$y = 0$	$w = 1$
1: $y := \overline{w}$	
2: $\overline{z} := x$	
3: $x := 2$	

The read on x in line 2 can be delayed after the write on x in line 3 due to the RDMA memory model, causing it to read the value 2 instead of the initial value 1. This gives rise to a trace $T = \langle E, \mathsf{po}, \mathsf{pf}, \mathsf{rf}, \mathsf{mo}, \mathsf{nfo}\rangle$ with event set

$$E = E_0 \,\cup\, \{\mathtt{nrR}(\overline{w}, 1), \mathtt{nlW}(y, 1, \overline{2}), \mathtt{nlR}(x, 2, \overline{2}), \mathtt{nrW}(\overline{z}, 2), \mathtt{lW}(x, 2)\}$$

and relations:

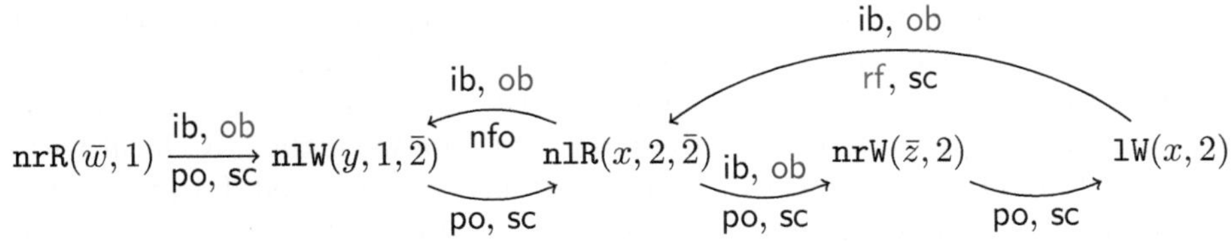

The set of initial events E_0 is not shown in the figure, but since these events have only outgoing edges, they cannot be part of any cycle. T is RDMA-consistent, since ob is acyclic, and violating, since sc is cyclic. Furthermore, it is minimal, since removing the last event (w.r.t. po) makes it non-violating. Note that we cannot remove any other event, since this would not yield a valid trace of R.

We choose the maximal event $e = \texttt{lW}(x, 2)$ and consider one possible ordering of when events happen, called a *linearisation* $\tau = \tau_1\ e\ \tau_2$:

$$\tau = \texttt{nrR}(\bar{w}, 1)\ \texttt{lW}(x, 2)\ \texttt{nlR}(x, 2, \bar{2})\ \texttt{nrW}(\bar{z}, 2)\ \texttt{nlW}(y, 1, \bar{2})$$

Removing e from τ and adjusting the values of events that depended on it yields the event sequence τ':

$$\tau' = \texttt{nrR}(\bar{w}, 1)\ \texttt{nlR}(x, 1, \bar{2})\ \texttt{nrW}(\bar{z}, 1)\ \texttt{nlW}(y, 1, \bar{2})$$

The corresponding trace T' on the event set $E' = E \backslash \{e\}$ is:

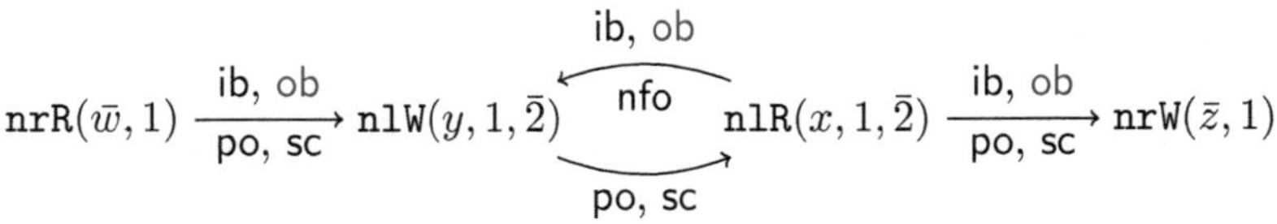

We observe that the values of the read and write events of the instruction $z := x$ have been adjusted, since they now read and write the initial value instead of the value written by the removed event. T' is both RDMA-consistent and SC-consistent, since T'.ob and T'.sc are acyclic, respectively.

Since T' is SC-consistent, we can find an ordering of its events that respects all SC constraints:

$$\sigma = \texttt{nrR}(\bar{w}, 1)\ \texttt{nlW}(y, 1, \bar{2})\ \texttt{nlR}(x, 1, \bar{2})\ \texttt{nrW}(\bar{z}, 1)$$

We now construct the normal form trace T'' by inserting the maximal event e back into this SC-consistent ordering. Specifically, we place events that happened before e in τ (only $\texttt{nrR}(\bar{w}, 1)$ in this case), then e itself, then the remaining events in their SC-consistent order:

$$\tau'' = \texttt{nrR}(\bar{w}, 1)\ \texttt{lW}(x, 2)\ \texttt{nlW}(y, 1, \bar{2})\ \texttt{nlR}(x, 2, \bar{2})\ \texttt{nrW}(\bar{z}, 2)$$

The linearisation τ'' corresponds to the trace T'':

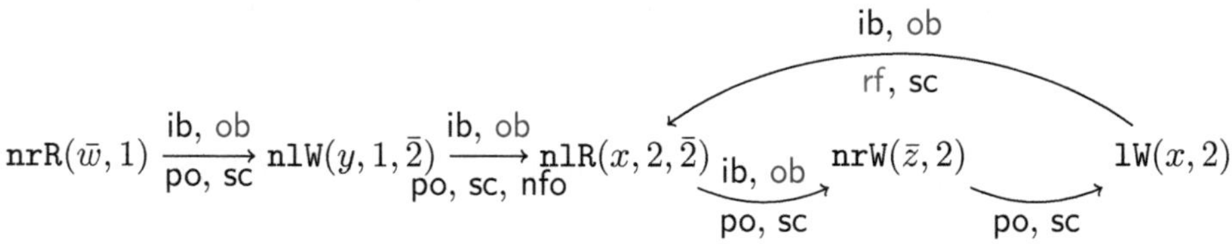

It is RDMA-consistent and uses the same set of events as T. Furthermore, it has the same SC relation as T and is therefore also violating.

Note that although T and T'' have exactly the same events, their ordering relations differ. In particular, the nfo-relation between the NIC local write $\texttt{nlW}(y, 1, \bar{2})$ and the NIC local read $\texttt{nlR}(x, 1, \bar{2})$ has been reversed. Intuitively, the normal form eliminates the unnecessary delay of $\texttt{nlW}(y, 1, \bar{2})$ after the read and write events of the later instruction $z := x$.

5.2 Definitions and Properties

Definition 7 (Linearisation of a Trace). *A* linearisation *of an RDMA-consistent trace* $T = \langle E, \mathsf{po}, \mathsf{pf}, \mathsf{rf}, \mathsf{mo}, \mathsf{nfo}\rangle$ *is a strict total order on the events* $E = \{e_1, \ldots, e_n\}$ *that is an extension (a superset) of* $T.\mathsf{ob}$*. We usually write it as a sequence* $\tau = e_1 \ \ldots \ e_n$*. Similarly, a* linearisation *of an SC-consistent trace* T *is a strict total order extending* $T.\mathsf{sc}$*.*

Given a sequence of events $\tau = e_1 \ \ldots \ e_n$, we write $e_i <_\tau e_j$ if $i < j$. Furthermore, we define $T(\tau) = \langle E, \mathsf{po}, \mathsf{pf}, \mathsf{rf}, \mathsf{mo}, \mathsf{nfo}\rangle$, where:

- $E = \{e_1, \ldots, e_n\}$
- po and pf are defined as in Definition 2 with respect to the event set E
- $e \xrightarrow{\mathsf{rf}} e'$ if and only if $e <_\tau e'$, e is a write event, e' is a read event on the same variable, and there is no other write event on the same variable between e and e' in τ
- $e \xrightarrow{\mathsf{mo}} e'$ if and only if $e <_\tau e'$ and both e and e' are write events on the same variable
- $e \xrightarrow{\mathsf{nfo}} e'$ if and only if $e <_\tau e'$, both e and e' are events belonging to the same queue pair, exactly one of them is a read event and one of them is a write event, and they are either both local or both remote NIC events

$T(\tau)$ is a (not necessarily RDMA-consistent) trace of R if and only if the event set E, the polls-from relation pf and the reads-from relation rf are *well-formed*, meaning they are in the form as required in Definition 2. In particular, there must be at least as many NIC writes as polls on each queue pair at any time, and each pair of events related by rf must have matching values. All other requirements for relations are automatically fulfilled.

Definition 8 (Maximal Event). *Given a trace* T*, an event* $e \in E$ *is* maximal *if it is* po*-maximal and there is no CPU-event* e' *such that* $e \xrightarrow{\mathsf{ib}} e'$*.*

Lemma 9. *Any RDMA-consistent trace* T *has at least one maximal event* e*.*

Proof. Assume that there is no maximal event. Construct a sequence of events $e_1, e_1', e_2, e_2', \ldots$ as follows. Let e_1 be any po-maximal event. For all $i \in \mathbb{N}$, let e_i' be a CPU-event such that $e_i \xrightarrow{\mathsf{ib}} e_i'$ and let e_{i+1} be a po-maximal event such that $e_i' \xrightarrow{\mathsf{po}^*} e_{i+1}$. Because there are only finitely many po-maximal events, this sequence must eventually repeat and form a cycle. Since po-edges from CPU-events to later events are in ippo and therefore in ib, the cycle is completely contained in ib, which contradicts that T is RDMA-consistent.

5.3 Construction

Consider an RDMA program R that is not robust. Choose a violating trace T that is minimal in the sense that any trace with fewer events is not violating. In particular, $T = \langle E, \mathsf{po}, \mathsf{pf}, \mathsf{rf}, \mathsf{mo}, \mathsf{nfo}\rangle$ is RDMA-consistent and $T.\mathsf{sc} = \langle E, \mathsf{po}, \mathsf{rf}, \mathsf{rb}, \mathsf{mo}\rangle$

is cyclic. Let e be a maximal event and let $\tau = \tau_1\ e\ \tau_2$ be a linearisation of T. We remove the maximal event e from τ to obtain τ' in the following way. For each event $\bar{e} \in E \backslash \{e\}$ in τ:

- If $\bar{e}$ is a NIC local read $\mathtt{nlR}(x, v_r, \bar{n})$ or a NIC remote read $\mathtt{nrR}(\bar{y}, v_r)$, we replace the value v_r with the value of the last write event on x or $\bar{y}$, respectively.
- If $\bar{e}$ is a NIC remote write $\mathtt{nrW}(\bar{y}, v_w)$ or a NIC local write $\mathtt{nlW}(x, v_w, \bar{n})$, we replace the value v_w with the value of the local or remote read coming immediately before $\bar{e}$ in po.
- Otherwise we keep the event $\bar{e}$ unchanged.

We claim that $T' = T(\tau')$ is an RDMA-consistent trace of R. Since T was minimal, it follows that T' is not violating and therefore $T'.\mathsf{sc}$ is acyclic. Let σ be a linearisation of $T'.\mathsf{sc}$. Define $\tau'' = \tau_1 \downarrow_\sigma\ e\ \tau_2 \downarrow_\sigma$ where $\tau_i \downarrow_\sigma$ are the events of τ_i in the order in which they appear in σ.

Theorem 10. *$T'' = T(\tau'')$ is a violating trace of* R.

The full proof can be found in the extended version [9]. It proceeds in two phases, corresponding to the two trace transformations performed on the original trace T. In the first phase, we establish that after removing the maximal event e from τ and adjusting dependent NIC read/write values, the resulting trace T' remains both well-formed and RDMA-consistent. In the second phase, we analyse the trace T'' obtained by reinserting e into T'. The key structural observation is that several fundamental relations (po, ippo, oppo, pf, rf, mo, rb) remain unchanged between T and T''. Building on this, we prove that T'' is RDMA-consistent by showing all ob''-edges follow the order given by τ'', that is, they relate events earlier in τ'' to events later in τ''. Finally, we establish that $T.\mathsf{sc} = T''.\mathsf{sc}$, completing the proof that T'' violates the same SC properties as T while being RDMA-consistent.

This establishes Theorem 6: the partition required by the theorem is given by $E_1 = \{e\} \cup \{e' \in E'' \mid e' \in \tau_1\}$ and $E_2 = \{e' \in E'' \mid e' \in \tau_2\}$. The SC-consistency within each partition follows from the construction, which orders events in τ_1 and τ_2 according to the SC-linearisation σ of T'. Note that due to maximality, e is po-later than any event in τ_1, which means it can be added to E_1 while preserving SC-consistency. The directionality of ob-edges between the two partitions is guaranteed by the proof that all ob''-edges respect the ordering of τ''.

6 An EXPSPACE-Algorithm for Robustness

6.1 Overview

The previous section established that every non-robust RDMA program has a violating trace whose event set can be partitioned as $E = E_1 \cup E_2$ where events within each partition are SC-consistent and all ob-edges between partitions go from E_1 to E_2. This chapter leverages this normal form to establish an upper bound for the computational complexity of the robustness problem.

We show that RDMA-robustness can be reduced to reachability in a finite-state program augmented with net counters ($\in \mathbb{N}$), which implies membership in EXPSPACE: This follows immediately from the fact that the state reachability problem for Vector Addition Systems with States (VASS) is in EXPSPACE [26]. For RDMA programs that do not use poll operations, the reduction yields a purely finite-state program without counters. Since state reachability for finite-state programs is in PSPACE [28], we obtain PSPACE-membership for the special case.

Theorem 11 (Upper Bounds for RDMA-Robustness).

1. *RDMA-robustness is in* EXPSPACE *in the general case.*
2. *RDMA-robustness for programs without poll operations is in* PSPACE.

The key to establishing the upper bounds is to construct an instrumented program running under SC that systematically searches for violating traces in normal form. The instrumented program builds up the two partitions E_1 and E_2 in parallel, non-deterministically assigning each generated event to either partition. To implement this effectively, we work with linearisations τ_1 and τ_2 (explicit total orderings of E_1 and E_2) rather than the partitions directly. This choice is motivated by the need to verify RDMA-consistency: maintaining explicit orderings allows us to check that all ob-edges are forward edges, which is simpler than reasoning about acyclicity in a partial order.

In the following, $\tau = \tau_1\tau_2$ denotes the violating trace in normal form that we are constructing. Events are appended to the end of either τ_1 or τ_2, preserving SC-consistency within each sequence. The instrumented program ensures that the concatenation $\tau = \tau_1\tau_2$ forms an RDMA-consistent trace with an SC-cycle, thereby witnessing non-robustness of the original RDMA program.

6.2 Key Idea

The key idea is to simulate the program R and, for each generated event, non-deterministically decide whether it belongs to τ_1 or τ_2. The instrumented program runs two simulations in parallel, building up τ_1 and τ_2 in the process: The first simulation tracks the effects of the events of τ_1 on the memory, while the second simulation does the same for the events of τ_2 on a separate copy of the memory.

Crucially, generated events are always appended to the end of either τ_1 or τ_2. This preserves SC-consistency *within* each τ_i, but not necessarily *between* τ_1 and τ_2. The instrumented program must keep track of and ensure RDMA-consistency of the resulting trace $\tau = \tau_1\tau_2$. Since we are trying to guess τ as an ob-linearisation, all ob-edges must be forward edges. If all edges are both well-formed and forward edges, then the resulting trace is RDMA-consistent.

Memory Consistency. The memory after simulating τ_1 must match the memory at the start of the simulation of τ_2. To ensure this, we non-deterministically guess the memory state after τ_1 at the start of the program and use this for the simulation of τ_2. After the instrumented program has simulated all of τ, it checks that the memory of the τ_1-simulation matches what the τ_2-simulation started with.

SC-Cycle Detection. The algorithm must also check whether there exists an SC-cycle. An SC-cycle consists of a cycle of events where each event and its successor are related by po, rf, rb, or mo. At a high level, we guess which threads participate in the cycle and in which order they are visited. During simulation, each thread may mark one entry and one exit event as its local contribution to the cycle and store the corresponding metadata (type, variable, value, and whether the event is in τ_1 or τ_2). After simulation stops, the main thread checks whether these local guesses compose into a valid global SC-cycle. The precise justification and checks are given in Sect. 6.5.

6.3 Algorithm Description

The instrumented program consists of one main thread that orchestrates the simulation plus one simulation thread for each thread in the original RDMA program. Additionally to some bookkeeping and status variables, the instrumented program stores the following:

- Three copies of each variable of the RDMA program: one copy to simulate τ_1 and τ_2 respectively, and the third to check that the value after τ_1 matches the memory at the beginning of τ_2.
- For each thread, information about the entry and exit point of the SC cycle, together with the threads's predecessor and successor in the SC cycle.
- For each queue pair, information about which type of events have already been added to τ_2.
- For each queue pair, two counters to track the number of polls that can be executed in τ_1 and τ_2, respectively.

The instrumented program works as follows:

1. The main thread guesses the value of each variable after executing τ_1. It keeps each value in two copies of the variable: one for the τ_2-simulation to work on, and one to later verify that the value matches the result after τ_1.
2. The main thread signals the other threads to start simulating.
3. Concurrently, each simulation thread of the instrumented program simulates a thread of the RDMA program as follows. For each simulated event:
   (a) Non-deterministically decide whether the event should be in τ_1 or τ_2.
   (b) Check that the event can be added to τ_1 or τ_2, respectively, without violating RDMA-consistency (see Sect. 6.4).
   (c) Execute the effect of the event on the copy of the memory corresponding to τ_1 or τ_2, respectively.

   (d) Non-deterministically decide whether the event should be the entry point of the SC-cycle in this thread. If so, save the event and check that it can form a valid connection (via rf, mo, or rb) with the corresponding exit point of its predecessor thread in the SC-cycle (see Sect. 6.5).
   (e) Do the same for the exit point.
4. Non-deterministically, the main thread decides to signal the other threads to stop the simulation. It waits for each thread to finish their current event.
5. The main thread checks that the memory after τ_1 matches the memory at the beginning of τ_2.
6. The main thread checks that there is a valid SC-cycle. If so, it enters the *target state.*

The original RDMA program is robust if and only if the instrumented SC program *cannot* reach the target state.

6.4 Ensuring RDMA-Consistency

To ensure that an event can be added to the trace in an RDMA-consistent way (step 3b), the program must check that each ob-edge is a forward edge. Additionally, it must verify that rf is well-formed, i.e., that the value of a read event matches the value of its write event.

The most challenging cases are oppo and ([Inst]; ib), which can potentially form backward edges. For oppo, we track per queue pair which event types have been added to τ_2, preventing events from being added to τ_1 if this would create a backward edge. For ([Inst]; ib), we perform additional checks based on case analysis to ensure all paths remain forward-directed. The poll-from relation ([nlW]; pf) requires counters to track unpolled NIC writes, with additional bookkeeping to force certain polls into τ_2. The remaining relations (rf, nfo, rb, mo) are always forward edges and require only basic well-formedness checks.

Details of all consistency checks can be found in the extended version [9].

6.5 Detecting SC-Cycles

To detect SC-cycles, we non-deterministically guess the entry and exit points of the SC-cycle in each thread. The entry and exit points are the po-first and po-last events of the thread on the cycle, respectively.

A key observation is that it is sufficient to consider cycles that visit each thread at most once. This is independent of the normal-form assumption (and of RDMA robustness): it holds for any cycle over po, rf, rb, and mo edges. If a cycle visits some thread more than once, let e_1 be the po-latest cycle event on that thread, and let e_2 be the next cycle event on the same thread encountered when following the cycle after e_1. Then the segment from e_2 to e_1 can be contracted to the single edge $e_2 \xrightarrow{\text{po}} e_1$, yielding a shorter cycle. Repeating this contraction removes repeated visits, so an equivalent cycle exists that visits each thread at most once.

Therefore, it is enough to check connectivity between consecutive threads in the guessed cycle order by verifying that their selected exit/entry events are related by rf, mo, or rb.

The instrumented program ensures proper ordering between exit and entry points across partition boundaries (τ_1 and τ_2) through appropriate tracking during simulation. After all threads finish, the main thread verifies that all pairs of entry and exit points form a valid cycle.

Details can be found in the extended version [9].

6.6 Complexity Analysis

The instrumented program described above establishes the upper bounds of robustness as in Theorem 11. It uses a finite amount of state to track:

- Three copies of the memory (for τ_1 and τ_2 simulations and comparison),
- Per-queue-pair tracking of event types added to τ_2 (for oppo checking),
- Information about entry and exit points of the SC-cycle,
- Additional bookkeeping for ib-consistency checks.

All of this requires space polynomial in the size of the original RDMA program.

For programs with poll operations, the instrumented program additionally uses two counters per queue pair to track unpolled NIC writes. This makes the instrumented program a finite-state program augmented with net counters, which is essentially a vector addition system with states. Since the reachability problem for VASS is decidable in ExpSpace [26], we obtain ExpSpace-membership.

For programs without poll operations, no counters are needed, yielding a purely finite-state instrumented program. Reachability for finite-state programs is in PSpace [28], thus robustness for poll-free programs is in PSpace.

To validate this construction, we have implemented a tool that translates RDMA programs to instrumented Promela programs, which can then be verified using the SPIN model checker. SPIN is not intended for unbounded VASS-style counter reachability in full generality; however, it is sufficient for our proof-of-concept experiments on small acyclic litmus tests, where the number of polls is bounded and the translation therefore requires only bounded counters. We evaluated our tool on all sequential and concurrent litmus tests created by Ambal et al. [10], all of which produced the expected results.

7 Robustness is EXPSPACE-Complete

The previous section established that RDMA-robustness is decidable in ExpSpace for the general case and in PSpace for programs without poll operations. We now show that these upper bounds are tight by establishing matching lower bounds. This demonstrates that the algorithm from the previous section is optimal.

We establish ExpSpace-hardness by reduction from the state-reachability problem for Vector Addition Systems with States (VASS) [22]. A VASS consists of a finite-state control with a finite number of counters ranging over the natural numbers $\mathbb{N}$. Each transition either increments or decrements a counter. Increment transitions are always enabled, while decrement transitions can only fire when the counter value is strictly positive. The state-reachability problem asks whether, starting from a given initial state with all counters set to zero, there exists a sequence of transitions leading to a designated accepting state (with arbitrary counter values). This problem is ExpSpace-complete [24,26].

The key insight is that RDMA programs can naturally simulate VASS executions: control states are encoded in program variables, while counter values correspond to the number of unpolled remote writes on queue pairs. We construct an RDMA program that simulates a VASS and then extend it to witness non-robustness precisely when the VASS reaches its accepting state.

7.1 Reduction from VASS

The reduction simulates a VASS execution using an RDMA program R. Given a VASS $V = (Q, d, T, q_0)$ with control states Q, d counters, transitions T, and initial state q_0, we construct an RDMA program as follows. For each counter $c \in \{1, \ldots, d\}$, we introduce an auxiliary node n_c containing a single variable x_c. A distinguished leader node n_L simulates the control state of the VASS using a local variable x.

The reduction maintains the following invariants: The leader node stores the current VASS control state in x. For each counter c, its value is represented by the number of remote writes to node n_c that have not yet been matched by a poll operation. Thus, issuing a remote write increments the counter, while a poll operation decrements it. Since each poll operation matches exactly one pending write, the number of pending acknowledgements corresponds precisely to the counter value.

1: assume($x = q$)	1: assume($x = q$)
2: $\overline{x}_c := 1$	2: poll(n_c)
3: $x := q'$	3: $x := q'$

Fig. 5. The RDMA code fragment corresponding to VASS transitions incrementing (left) and decrementing (right) a counter c.

More precisely, for each transition $t = (q, c, j, q') \in T$, the leader uses the code fragment given in Fig. 5 to simulate the transition t. It first checks that the value of x is q, then performs the RDMA operations corresponding to the value of j: an increment of counter c (i.e., $j = 1$) is simulated by issuing a remote write to x_c, while a decrement (i.e., $j = -1$) is simulated by a poll operation on n_c.

Suppose the VASS has k transitions $\{t_1, t_2, \ldots, t_k\}$. The leader repeatedly executes a non-deterministic choice among all such code fragments (one per transition), thereby simulating arbitrary VASS transition sequences. Formally, let C_i denote the code fragment corresponding to transition i. Let C_a be a code fragment that checks whether x equals the accepting state q_a. The leader node executes the following loop: $(\mathsf{C}_1 + \mathsf{C}_2 + \cdots + \mathsf{C}_k + \mathsf{C}_a)^*$. It follows that the accepting state q_a is reachable in the VASS if and only if C_a is reachable in R. The construction is polynomial in the size of the VASS. Note that R is robust: all operations execute in program order from the leader's perspective, and even though NIC writes may be delayed past subsequent polls, this is not observable since there are no competing reads or writes to the auxiliary nodes.

7.2 Extension to Robustness

To reduce to the robustness problem, we modify the RDMA program R into a new program R' such that R' is non-robust if and only if the state q_a is reachable in the VASS. We append some code fragment known to be non-robust (for example, the code from Sect. 5.1) to the end of C_a to obtain the new code C_a'. If needed, we also add additional nodes and variables to the RDMA program, as required by the non-robust code fragment. Let R' be the program $(\mathsf{C}_1+\mathsf{C}_2+\cdots+\mathsf{C}_k+\mathsf{C}_a')^*$.

If q_a is reachable in the VASS (i.e., C_a is reachable in R), then C_a' is reachable in R', causing a robustness violation. Conversely, if q_a is not reachable in the VASS, then the code fragment C_a' can never be executed, and hence there is no robustness violation. This establishes ExpSpace-hardness for the general case.

For the restricted case of RDMA programs without poll operations, we use a simpler construction. Since no counters are needed, we reduce from the reachability problem for ordinary finite-state programs instead of VASS, which is PSpace-hard [18].

Theorem 12 (Complexity of RDMA-Robustness).

1. *RDMA-robustness is* ExpSpace*-complete in the general case.*
2. *RDMA-robustness for programs without poll operations is* PSpace*-complete.*

This establishes that the algorithm presented in the previous section is optimal: the ExpSpace upper bound cannot be improved without advances in the complexity of VASS reachability, and similarly for the PSpace bound in the poll-free case. The robustness problem is thus computationally equivalent to reachability in finite-state programs with counters (general case) or without counters (poll-free case).

8 Conclusion

In this paper, we studied verification problems for RDMA programs and showed that reachability is undecidable in general, even for restricted fragments. We then proved that robustness for RDMA programs is decidable and ExpSpace-complete, based on a normal-form characterisation of robustness violations. This result yields a decision procedure that reduces robustness checking to reachability under sequential consistency, with a PSpace bound for programs without poll operations. In contrast to prior RDMA robustness work that provided restrictive sufficient criteria, our results give full decidability and complexity characterisations for robustness and for reachability-based safety verification under RDMA semantics.

We hope that our work will serve as a foundation for practical tools for automated robustness checking of RDMA programs. Our own implementation is a proof of concept, and scaling it to real-world benchmarks remains a challenge. We also plan to extend the techniques to richer RDMA features and to other baseline memory models.

Disclosure of Interests. The authors have no competing interests to declare.

Data-Availability Statement. Our prototype, along with the litmus tests used, is publicly available at https://github.com/StephanSpengler/RDMA-implementation.

References

1. Abdulla, P.A., Arora, J., Atig, M.F., Krishna, S.N.: Verification of programs under the release-acquire semantics. In: PLDI, pp. 1117–1132. ACM (2019). https://doi.org/10.1145/3314221.3314649
2. Abdulla, P.A., Atig, M.F., Bouajjani, A., Derevenetc, E., Leonardsson, C., Meyer, R.: On the state reachability problem for concurrent programs under power. In: Georgiou, C., Majumdar, R. (eds.) NETYS 2020. LNCS, vol. 12129, pp. 47–59. Springer, Cham (2021). https://doi.org/10.1007/978-3-030-67087-0_4
3. Abdulla, P.A., Atig, M.F., Bouajjani, A., Kumar, K.N., Saivasan, P.: Deciding reachability under persistent x86-tso. Proc. ACM Program. Lang. **5**(POPL), 1–32 (2021). https://doi.org/10.1145/3434337
4. Abdulla, P.A., Atig, M.F., Bouajjani, A., Kumar, K.N., Saivasan, P.: Verification under intel-x86 with persistency. Proc. ACM Program. Lang. **8**(PLDI), 1189–1212 (2024). https://doi.org/10.1145/3656425
5. Abdulla, P.A., Atig, M.F., Bouajjani, A., Ngo, T.P.: The benefits of duality in verifying concurrent programs under TSO. In: CONCUR. LIPIcs, vol. 59, pp. 5:1–5:15. Schloss Dagstuhl - Leibniz-Zentrum für Informatik (2016). https://doi.org/10.4230/LIPIcs.CONCUR.2016.5
6. Abdulla, P.A., Atig, M.F., Godbole, A., Krishna, S., Vafeiadis, V.: The decidability of verification under PS 2.0. In: ESOP. Lecture Notes in Computer Science, vol. 12648, pp. 1–29. Springer, Cham (2021). https://doi.org/10.26226/morressier.604907f41a80aac83ca25d26
7. Abdulla, P.A., Atig, M.F., Kara, A., Rezine, O.: Verification of buffered dynamic register automata. In: Bouajjani, A., Fauconnier, H. (eds.) NETYS 2015. LNCS, vol. 9466, pp. 15–31. Springer, Cham (2015). https://doi.org/10.1007/978-3-319-26850-7_2
8. Abdulla, P.A., Atig, M.F., Ngo, T.-P.: The best of both worlds: trading efficiency and optimality in fence insertion for TSO. In: Vitek, J. (ed.) ESOP 2015. LNCS, vol. 9032, pp. 308–332. Springer, Heidelberg (2015). https://doi.org/10.1007/978-3-662-46669-8_13
9. Abdulla, P.A., Atig, M.F., Rajanbabu, G., Spengler, S.: On the verification problem of remote direct memory access programs (extended version with appendix) (2026). https://arxiv.org/abs/2605.10631

10. Ambal, G., Dongol, B., Eran, H., Klimis, V., Lahav, O., Raad, A.: Semantics of remote direct memory access: operational and declarative models of RDMA on TSO architectures. Proc. ACM Program. Lang. **8**(OOPSLA2), 1982–2009 (2024). https://doi.org/10.1145/3689781
11. Ambal, G., Lahav, O., Raad, A.: Sufficient conditions for robustness of RDMA programs. In: ESOP (1). Lecture Notes in Computer Science, vol. 15694, pp. 56–87. Springer, Cham (2025). https://doi.org/10.1007/978-3-031-91118-7_3
12. Atig, M.F., Bouajjani, A., Burckhardt, S., Musuvathi, M.: On the verification problem for weak memory models. In: POPL, pp. 7–18. ACM (2010). https://doi.org/10.1145/1706299.1706303
13. Atig, M.F., Bouajjani, A., Burckhardt, S., Musuvathi, M.: What's decidable about weak memory models? In: Seidl, H. (ed.) ESOP 2012. LNCS, vol. 7211, pp. 26–46. Springer, Heidelberg (2012). https://doi.org/10.1007/978-3-642-28869-2_2
14. Bouajjani, A., Derevenetc, E., Meyer, R.: Checking and enforcing robustness against TSO. In: Felleisen, M., Gardner, P. (eds.) ESOP 2013. LNCS, vol. 7792, pp. 533–553. Springer, Heidelberg (2013). https://doi.org/10.1007/978-3-642-37036-6_29
15. Bouajjani, A., Derevenetc, E., Meyer, R.: Robustness against relaxed memory models. In: Software Engineering. LNI, vol. P-227, pp. 85–86. GI (2014). https://dl.gi.de/handle/20.500.12116/30973
16. Bouajjani, A., Meyer, R., Möhlmann, E.: Deciding robustness against total store ordering. In: Aceto, L., Henzinger, M., Sgall, J. (eds.) ICALP 2011. LNCS, vol. 6756, pp. 428–440. Springer, Heidelberg (2011). https://doi.org/10.1007/978-3-642-22012-8_34
17. Calin, G., Derevenetc, E., Majumdar, R., Meyer, R.: A theory of partitioned global address spaces. In: FSTTCS. LIPIcs, vol. 24, pp. 127–139. Schloss Dagstuhl - Leibniz-Zentrum für Informatik (2013). https://doi.org/10.4230/LIPIcs.FSTTCS.2013.127
18. Cheng, A., Esparza, J., Palsberg, J.: Complexity results for 1-safe nets. Theor. Comput. Sci. **147**(1&2), 117–136 (1995). https://doi.org/10.1016/0304-3975(94)00231-7
19. Dan, A.M., Lam, P., Hoefler, T., Vechev, M.T.: Modeling and analysis of remote memory access programming. In: OOPSLA, pp. 129–144. ACM (2016). https://doi.org/10.1145/2983990.2984033
20. Derevenetc, E.: Robustness against Relaxed Memory Models. Ph.D. thesis, University of Kaiserslautern (2015). https://nbn-resolving.org/urn:nbn:de:hbz:386-kluedo-40743
21. Derevenetc, E., Meyer, R.: Robustness against power is PSpace-complete. In: Esparza, J., Fraigniaud, P., Husfeldt, T., Koutsoupias, E. (eds.) ICALP 2014. LNCS, vol. 8573, pp. 158–170. Springer, Heidelberg (2014). https://doi.org/10.1007/978-3-662-43951-7_14
22. Hopcroft, J.E., Pansiot, J.: On the reachability problem for 5-dimensional vector addition systems. Theor. Comput. Sci. **8**, 135–159 (1979). https://doi.org/10.1016/0304-3975(79)90041-0
23. Lahav, O., Boker, U.: What's decidable about causally consistent shared memory? ACM Trans. Program. Lang. Syst. **44**(2), 8:1–8:55 (2022). https://doi.org/10.1145/3505273
24. Lipton, R.J.: The reachability problem requires exponential space. Research report (Yale University. Department of Computer Science), Department of Computer Science, Yale University (1976). https://books.google.de/books?id=7iSbGwAACAAJ

25. Post, E.L.: A variant of a recursively unsolvable problem. Bull. Am. Math. Soc. **52**(4), 264–268 (1946). https://doi.org/10.1090/S0002-9904-1946-08555-9
26. Rackoff, C.: The covering and boundedness problems for vector addition systems. Theor. Comput. Sci. **6**, 223–231 (1978). https://doi.org/10.1016/0304-3975(78)90036-1
27. Singh, A.K., Lahav, O.: Decidable verification under localized release-acquire concurrency. In: TACAS (3). Lecture Notes in Computer Science, vol. 14572, pp. 235–254. Springer, Cham (2024). https://doi.org/10.1007/978-3-031-57256-2_12
28. Sistla, A.P., Clarke, E.M.: The complexity of propositional linear temporal logics. J. ACM **32**(3), 733–749 (1985). https://doi.org/10.1145/3828.3837

Model Checking for Flexible Network Protocols

Andrew Johnson[1(✉)], Dennis Fetterly[2], Sean Song[2], and Jonathan Zolla[2]

[1] Princeton University, Princeton, NJ 08544, USA
aj3189@princeton.edu
[2] Google, Inc., Mountain View, CA 94043, USA
flexible-network-protocols-cav@google.com

Abstract. Operating a network is a daunting task. Operating one at a global scale, with stringent service objectives and requirements to be available during maintenance and failures, is even more so. At Google, we operate such a network. This paper details our experience applying formal methods to some of the networking protocols that are developed and maintained by in-house engineers. These protocols centrally route network traffic to respond to changes in demand, react to network failures, and allow for maintenance and upgrades.

We used formal methods to target a class of bugs stemming from unclear specifications, unintended system interactions, and logical errors at the specification level. We show how we modeled our protocols using an off-the-shelf model checker and a custom harness to scale the model horizontally. We were able to recreate several recent bugs and verify that the fixes implemented were correct. Finally, we present a method called state projection that we used to increase confidence in the coverage of our models, which we added to the TLC model checker for TLA+. We created 7 different TLA+ models and showed that they were effective at recreating bugs and verifying our fixes to those bugs.

1 Introduction

Google operates B4, one of the largest privately operated networks in the world [11,12], with stringent requirements for availability, bandwidth, and connectivity. It is managed with internally-developed control plane protocols for centralized traffic engineering, automatic failure recovery, and operator-initiated changes. A global scale and rapidly changing demand in response to traffic patterns or business needs stretch the network to operate in virtually every conceivable edge case. Furthermore, they are frequently updated. Engineers are able to fix bugs, add features, and rework the protocols with a release time of weeks to months; in contrast, changes to public internet protocols require coordination between many stakeholders, taking years and requiring backwards-compatibility.

Control-plane protocols for B4 work at the abstraction level of *sites*, which are composed of control *domains* that contain physical network devices. Traffic

A. Johnson—Work completed while at Google.

E. Darulova et al. (Eds.): CAV 2026, LNCS 16682, pp. 136–150, 2026.
https://doi.org/10.1007/978-3-032-32519-8_7

is grouped into *flows*, which transit the network via *tunnels* that consist of a list of sites. Traffic Engineering (TE) is a centralized system that periodically publishes a Traffic Engineering Database (TED), which is a plan for tunneling traffic in response to changing demand and network conditions. A TED entry is globally unique, and its value defines a mapping for a flow to a tunnel or a tunnel to sites. The goal of TE is to keep each domain's TED up to date with the centrally planned one. TED entries are added, removed, or modified on domains via *TE Ops*. Finally, each domain can be *OK* or *FailOpen*, determining whether or not it will accept TED changes. The global controller deals with failed domains by maintaining a global status (*Ready* or *NotReady*) for each domain. The pair of state and global status is a domain's *status*.

Figure 1a shows a sample up-to-date network with two sites, A and B, each with two domains. Figure 1b shows the corresponding global plan (TED), with flow F_1 mapped to tunnel T_1, defined as a tunnel from site A to B. Domain B_1 is in state $FailOpen$, shown with its red shading. B_1 is also globally $NotReady$, as shown by the dotted lines depicting traffic from site A to it.

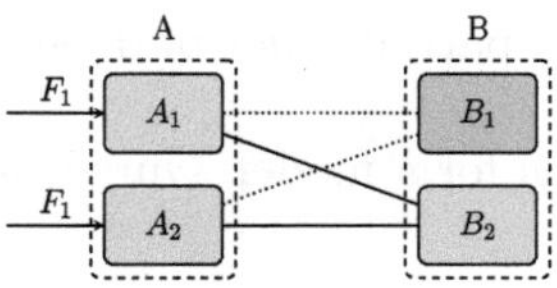

(a) Topology

Key	Value
F_1	$\rightarrow T_1$
T_1	$\rightarrow A, B$

(b) Example global TED.

Fig. 1. A sample topology and corresponding TED. (Color figure online)

We modeled the installation of a TED on individual domains using TLA+ (Temporal Logic of Actions), a formal specification language [14,25]. TLA+ can be used to test *safety* properties, e.g. "Traffic never blackholes" or *liveness* properties, e.g. "TE Ops are eventually successful." A TLA+ model has constants, variables (the program state), an initial state formula, and a transition relation. TLA+ specifications can be used as mathematically precise documentation and as input to TLC [14], which is an explicit-state model checker for TLA+ models.

TLC was not able to handle our use case immediately. Including enough detail from our protocols to reproduce simple bugs became infeasible. The tool does not scale well horizontally because it must maintain a global set of previously seen states. Instead, we developed a way to split the protocol into distinct phases and horizontally parallelize our model by input (network topology and desired TED). This allowed us to run many instances of TLC which, when combined, explore the entire state space of the protocol. It also allowed us to perform symmetry reduction on the network topology, saving redundant work [5]. Finally, our production topology is too large for any model checker. Instead, we designed abstract interpretation-based summaries of the safety-critical portions of a state called state projections which provide a coverage criterion for exploration.

2 Model Description

The scope of our model is TED installation: TE Op generation, dependency computation, and installation order, as well as domain failure and recovery. We do not model the desired TED computation [11], instead assuming an optimal TED is given as input. We also do not model *link* failure and recovery, and exclude any transient network changes.

Constants. The specifics of the network topology are constants. This includes the sets of sites and domains, as well as the relationships between them.

Variables. In TLA+, variables are the primary drivers of exploration time, as they define the criteria for a unique state. Our model includes these variables:

1. Desired TED: The current desired TED
2. Domain TEDs: Map from domains to their current TED
3. Domain Status: Map from domains to their status
4. CurrOps: Ops that have yet to be complete
5. OpDependencies: Pairs of ops indicating a partial order of dependencies

Actions. Actions define the transition relation for a model. Ours has the following:

1. *ComputeOps*: Computes CurrOps (the difference between each Domain's initial TED and the desired TED) and OpDependencies. The calculation of the OpDependencies caused many of our targeted historical bugs. Example dependencies include requiring tunnels to be installed on all domains before flows that use them, or conversely removing a flow that uses a tunnel from all domains before removing the tunnel. Dependency computation also takes into account whether domains are *FailOpen* or *NotReady*.
2. *InstallOp*: The model can install any Op from CurrOps which does not depend on an incomplete Op and for which the domain is *OK* (a failed domain would result in a failed Op). We model all possible Op interleavings.
3. *DomainStatusChange*: Domains can fail or recover at any time. Many bugs arose from dependencies on failed domains. When a domain fails, it immediately changes its status to *FailOpen*. Then, it creates an Op (and updates dependencies) to change its status to *NotReady*, since this must be communicated from the central controller to neighboring domains. Similarly, a domain returning to *OK* status creates an Op to mark it *Ready*.
4. *ComputeTED*: At the end of each round, compute a new TED to install.

Once there are no more ops, the round is complete and we non-deterministically choose a new desired TED for the next round. Figure 2 shows a sample of one round of the protocol on the topology and desired TED from Fig. 1. The current TED is depicted by which lines are drawn. The initial state, shown in Fig. 2(c), begins with the current TED being empty in A_1 and B_1, and already matching the desired TED in A_2 and B_2, as shown by A_2 having an arrow for F_1 while A_1 does not. Domains A_1, A_2, and B_2 begin with status *OK*, shown with the color green, while B_1 begins as *FailOpen*, shown with the color red. The dashed line from A_2 to B_1 indicates no traffic can flow on that link, since B_1 is *NotReady*, while the other domains are *Ready*. In Fig. 2(d), no change has occurred in the network, but the ops to install T_1 on A_1 and B_2 and F_1 on A_1 have been generated. Since F_1 uses T_1, it depends on both tunnel install ops. In Fig. 2(e), T_1 has been installed on A_1, and B_1 returns from *FailOpen* to *OK*. This creates a new op to mark it *Ready*, which depends on the tunnel install op. Figure 2(f) is the final state of the network after ops are completed.

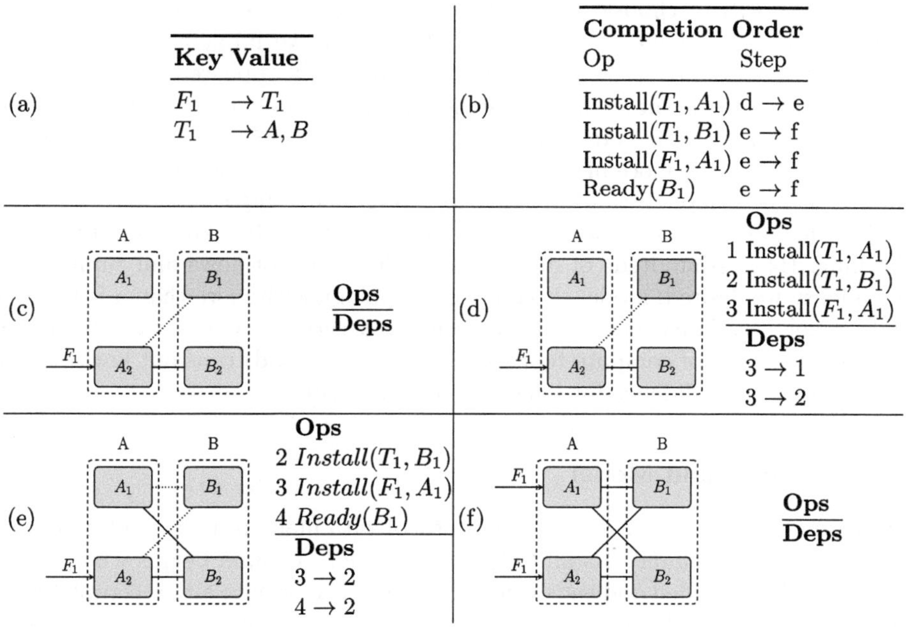

Fig. 2. This shows a sample run of our model with one domain recovering and a total of four ops. Part (a) shows the desired TED. Part (b) shows the order the ops are completed, and the steps between which they finish. Parts (c)–(f) show snapshots of the state at different points in the model run.

Invariants. We include the following definitions to explain our invariants:

Definition 1. *A tunnel t is* used *at domain d if there exists a domain d′, flow f, and tunnel t such that at d′, f maps to t and t includes the site where d is located.*

Definition 2. *A domain d is* blackholing *if there exists a tunnel t that is used at d, t is not installed at d, and d is ready. A state is* blackholing *if it contains a blackholing domain.*

The simplest invariant we check is that there are no blackholing domains (NoBlackHoles). We also wished to check the model in situations where the initial state may already contain blackholing traffic, which can be caused by factors external to the model. To do so, we utilized TLA+'s temporal faculties to specify a temporal version of the above property: Once a domain is not blackholing, it never becomes blackholing. This allows for us to start in blackholing states, but does not allow our logic to *cause* black holes.

3 Modeling Experience

Our process was to choose a past bug and create a TLA+ model that was as simple as possible while exhibiting the bug. Then, we implemented the bug's fix in the model and verified that the bug no longer appeared. We wished to model our protocols at a high enough fidelity to catch bugs and reflect the actual structure of our code. The further abstracted our models are from the implementation, the more likely mistakes become when translating any protocol changes into the model, causing spurious errors or missing edge cases.

We quickly ran into the scaling problem inherent to explicit-state model checking. B4 has hundreds of domains and thousands of flows and tunnels. At the fidelity we desired, model checking any topology with more than a few nodes and tunnels was infeasible. In this section, we describe how we built our model to take advantage of compute to scale short (single-round) runs out horizontally while giving us confidence for long (multi-round) runs.

3.1 Single-Round Model

The example from Sect. 2 describes a protocol with many rounds of TE updates, which we call the Tunnel Install (TI) Linear model. A round begins when a new desired TED is decided and ends when all of the TE Ops have either completed or failed. Once we added any more complexity, this became infeasible because it was not only testing op interleavings *within* rounds, but also all possible interleavings of *desired TEDs*. Instead, we model a single round, and then check every possible single-round run of the model, which we call the TI model. The TI and TI Linear models are equivalent in the states they explore, as we show in Sect. 5.

Instead of generating a new TED at the end of each round, the TI model changes the desired TED from a variable to a constant. We also add a new constant, which determines all the possible *starting* TEDs. This simulates all possible states the multi-round model could be in when the *ComputeTED* action ends the round. Each TED becomes a distinct starting state so that we do not miss states that would arise from rounds ending with incomplete ops.

To scale horizontally, we wrote a test harness in Python that enumerates all possible desired TEDs to use as input constants. We performed symmetry reduction on most topology elements at this stage to reduce duplicate work. For each desired TED generated after performing symmetry reduction, we run the model from every possible starting configuration of domain TEDs. The result is running every starting configuration to every (symmetry-reduced) ending configuration, which is equivalent to the multi-round model. The key advantage of this is that each desired TED can be run as a separate instance of TLC. This allows us to easily parallelize them and scale model checking horizontally.

4 Projected States

It is impossible to run our model with a topology at the size of our production network. To increase confidence that our models have enough coverage on small topologies, we compute succinct, topology-agnostic abstractions of concrete states, which we call state *projections*. Intuitively, small topologies are "big enough" because, in our protocols, tunnels and flows are independent of one another and tunnel length does not matter. We are completing an exhaustive state space exploration, so we will explore every possible state that a short tunnel can reach, and the states of a long tunnel will be variations on that theme.

TLC uses hash fingerprints to keep track of previously seen states. We modified TLC to include another fingerprint for the state projection. Projections should be topology-agnostic; that is, the set of *possible* projections should be the same no matter the topology. Formally, a TLA+ model has a (possibly infinite) *concrete* state space $\mathcal{S}$ and a finite projected state space $\mathcal{A}$. The state projection, α, has domain $\mathcal{S}$ and range $\mathcal{P}(\mathcal{A})$ (the set of subsets of $\mathcal{A}$). This is most similar to classical predicate abstraction [2,6,9]. However, each concrete state maps to a set of per-domain summaries, making projections simpler to express. In our example model from Sect. 2, we define a projection as follows:

Definition 3. *A* domain projection *of a domain d and tunnel t is a tuple containing the following:*

1. *The domain's state, either OK or $FailOpen$*
2. *The domain's global status, either $Ready$ or $NotReady$.*
3. *A boolean indicating whether or not t is used at domain d.*
4. *A boolean indicating whether or not t is installed at d.*

The projection of a concrete state s is the set of domain projections for any combination of domain and tunnel.

This projection summarizes the safety-relevant state of each domain. The domain projection is enough to tell whether a domain is blackholing: a domain must be ready and used by a tunnel that is not installed. It is topology-agnostic as it does not scale with the number of domains or tunnels (there are 16 possible projections). This projection is hand-crafted, but is relatively clear from the system design. We verify in Sect. 6 that our models visit a state with every safe domain projection, and use this as a proxy for the coverage of our models. This does not provide a proof that no additional projected states can be discovered after a plateau, called stuttering. To provide such a proof, one would need to create an abstract program that operates over sets of projected states, or find another way to rule out stuttering behavior, such as with resource-unbounded analysis [13,15,16].

Implementation. We added a new configuration keyword, `PROJECTION`, to the TLC model checker that takes the name of a definition that is used to compute the projected state set, i.e. `PROJECTION proj_state_set`. The argument can be any TLA+ enumerable, meaning it can be expressed with the built-in TLA+ language features, including formulas containing state variables. The projection is evaluated in each state and enumerated, and each element is fingerprinted in a second fingerprint set. We compare fingerprint hashes directly across single-round runs by normalizing the value and using a fixed hash seed.

5 Evaluation

In evaluating our approach, we asked the following questions:

1. Did our models scale enough to give us confidence we are not missing bugs?
2. Were we able to complete model checking in a reasonable amount of time?
3. Did our single-round optimization of the tunnel installation protocol explore all the same states as the linear one?

5.1 Setup

We created the following models for testing:

1. Tunnel Install (TI) Linear: The model described in Sect. 2.
2. TI: The model described in Sect. 3.1.
3. TI NoFail: The same as TI, but without domain failure or recovery.
4. TI Groups (TI+G): This model adds the concept of Tunnel Groups to TI. Groups spread large flows across multiple tunnels, which may take different paths. This was required to recreate a bug which allowed tunnels to be added to groups before they were fully installed.
5. TI+G NoFail: The same as TI+G, but without domain failure or recovery.
6. Domain Drain: This is the network protocol used by the control plane to "drain" a domain, meaning moving traffic away from it. It is modeled at the same abstraction level as the Tunnel Install models, and is the implementation of the step in those models that changes a domain to or from "Ready". We used a projection that tracks a domain's status, readiness status, and the status of its connected external links.
7. Local Drain: This is the protocol used to drain a single network device *within* a domain. It is modeled at the level of a single domain. We used a projection that tracks a domain's status and the status of its connected external links.

We chose 5 sample topologies that all of the models were able to finish exploring, starting from the simplest possible and increasing in complexity. For example, with the TI models, topology 1 has two nodes and one tunnel and flow, while topology 5 has six nodes with two tunnels and two flows. They are equivalent up to differences required for the different models (e.g. the addition of tunnel groups). For each model, we wrote a Python test harness to determine all possible desired TEDs and initial states for a topology, up to symmetry reduction.

We only included desired TEDs that are *consistent*, meaning non-blackholing. We generate configurations in less than a second for all our examples. In order to properly compare the TI Linear (which never enters inconsistent states) with the single-round models, we only included non-blackholing starting states. Including blackholing starting states had similar performance and caused our models to reach all projected states. Each model is a correct version of the protocol after the bug fix was implemented. These are the most time consuming as they require TLC to run to completion; models of buggy versions discovered error traces quickly.

We ran each example TED as a separate run of TLC in its own job using Google's cluster management engine Borg [24,26] with 64GB memory. Our results are recorded in Table 1. The models are listed in column 1. In column 2, the topologies are numbered 1-5 in order of size. In column 3, we report how many different desired TEDs we ran after symmetry reduction (the number of tasks). In column 4, we list the total number of states generated from all runs, which is a good measure of total effort. In column 5, we list the number of projected states encountered across all tasks. In column 6, we list the average time runs took, while column 7 contains the time of the longest-running TED.

5.2 Results

We found that our models were able to scale past when the topology is big enough to saturate the (safe) projected state space. The two projected states left unexplored by all of the TI models are unsafe. For the models without domain failure, they never explore projected states with domain statuses other than (*OK, Ready*). For ones with domain failure, they explore these early and then plateau, exploring the same projected states with much larger topologies.

We also found that with the single-round model checking approach, our models all complete in a reasonable amount of time. The largest topology with the most complex model (TI+G with failure) takes less than an hour. Most complete in less than a minute. This is fast enough to be run repeatedly while updating the model. We had outlier topologies for the single-round approach (the max time was much greater than the average) due to combinatorial explosion in the initial state space for *empty* desired TEDs. We also created a linear model with groups, but it became infeasible for all but the smallest topology, which is evidence that our approach scales better than the linear one.

Finally, to verify that our single-round optimization does not miss states, we ran the TI model with no initial symmetry reduction alongside the TI Linear model. We had TLC dump the states for both and combined all of the dumped states from the single-round runs. Then, we verified that the single-round version explored the exact same states as the linear one by comparing the values of the variables in each state (excluding the additional variables required to track state across rounds). This was true for all of the TI Linear runs.

Table 1. We present our results for each example on 5 sample topologies.

Example	Topology	TEDs	States	Proj.States	Avg.Time(s)	MaxTime(s)
TI Linear	1	1	33	3	-	3
	2	1	6847	14	-	3
	3	1	388752	14	-	10
	4	1	3019565	14	-	13
	5	1	1118743386	14	-	2499
TI	1	3	48	3	0	0
	2	3	122603	14	1	1
	3	5	2382764	14	4	6
	4	8	5699172	14	5	7
	5	51	2607175615	14	240	2183
TI NoFail	1	3	48	3	0	0
	2	3	124	3	0	1
	3	5	699	3	1	1
	4	8	11230	3	1	1
	5	51	409669	3	2	4
TI+G	1	4	74	3	1	1
	2	4	64662	14	2	2
	3	7	4793197	14	4	7
	4	21	40445111	14	9	20
	5	105	29096754964	14	1003	3450
TI+G NoFail	1	4	74	3	1	1
	2	4	408	3	1	1
	3	7	1296	3	1	1
	4	21	225238	3	2	2
	5	105	3950608	3	2	5
Drain Domain	1	4	16	4	0	0
	2	6	411	12	0	0
	3	8	1763	12	1	1
	4	18	1275	12	1	1
	5	24	54156	12	1	1
Drain Local	1	1	13	4	0	0
	2	3	291	4	0	0
	3	12	6942	4	0	0
	4	12	184332	4	1	1
	5	60	184380	4	1	1

6 Discussion

Developer Effort. We found TLA+ to have a steep but short learning curve. Once overcome, each model took a developer about one week to create while learning the specifics of the design. Developing and testing multiple iterations of the single-round versions, complete with Python harnesses and test scripts for use in Google's Borg system took about two person-months, most of which produced reusable scaffolding. The "Drain" models (6 and 7) were created for future changes rather than previous bugs, and showed success with design-time modeling, as they helped find multiple errors in early protocol proposals and forced engineers to write their protocol change and desired properties precisely. This saved significant effort when compared to implementing and testing the changes in a network simulator, which may not have caught the errors. We also experimented with liveness properties such as verifying that all ops are eventually installed under different fairness assumptions, but focused on the NoBlackHoles safety property for the evaluation because it is equivalent between all of our examples. Finally, we found the single-round model useful in development because it was easy to run quickly (with limited starting states) while changing the protocol. It also made counterexamples easier to read than tracing a long, multi-round run.

Computational Cost. The primary challenge was ensuring our models ran efficiently. There is an inherent tension with models that are not provably connected to the runtime system: on one hand, we wished to optimize the models for faster runtimes and bigger topologies. On the other hand, the further the model gets from the real system, the more "hand-waving" is required to be sure one is not fabricating bugs, or worse, missing them. We needed a high level of abstraction in order to get something different from a network simulator for testing, which is already done extensively on all B4 changes.

Extensibility. We faced unique challenges in this project that depart from one-shot academic verification projects, including the need for fast changes, a global scale, and a long list of specific problems to target. We think two main takeaways are useful for developers wishing to apply similar methods.

First, the "single-round" approach was successful because it gave a start and end to a reactive system, which was possible because the single TE process acted as a leader that defined the rounds. We believe there are many problems in networking and other areas that have layers of abstraction where one can perform the "outer loop" in parallel to increase compute efficiency. For example, BGP could treat each route announcement as a "single round." In networking specifically, control plane protocols are a good match for model checking because they are insulated by well-defined abstraction layers from concerns like individual packets and physical links. It also allowed us to perform symmetry reduction at the example level with symmetries that could not be applied at the level of a fixed model. Since there was no single state set, the number of different configurations could be very large and we were able to run dozens of jobs in parallel.

Second, pen-and-paper design documents were a useful level of abstraction for formal modeling. They are early enough in the development process to catch bugs before incurring the cost of bringing a change to a testable state. Google employs a wide variety of network testing schemes, but all require a change to be designed and at least partially implemented, whereas model-checking is able to find errors at the pseudo-code level.

Limitations. We left as out of scope errors that occur between the network devices and domain controllers, as well as a host of other concerns such as the mechanics of retransmitted messages, hardware malfunctions other than total failures, and bugs in unmodeled systems. We also do not model every piece of the protocol, instead choosing to simplify models as much as possible while still recreating real-world bugs. A monolithic model would be infeasible for model checking, so we hope to have a range of simplified models (about one per design document) to allow engineers to choose the best abstraction level.

The single-round method improves performance, but still suffers from combinatorial explosion. Techniques for sharing the fingerprint state set across parallel computations, such as those developed for DiVinE [3], could aid in reducing repeated work. We found our approach to scale better than the distributed mode of TLC, which also cannot check liveness properties. Furthermore, for very large topologies, generating (and symmetry reducing) possible configurations could also suffer, though this might be avoided with better reduction techniques [7].

Currently, temporal formulas cannot be included in state projections. While it was not required for our models, this would be an interesting avenue for future work and would allow for more complex projections. We would also like to close the Abstract Interpretation loop for projected states by developing a way to compute an abstract program from a TLA+ model. This could be especially challenging if temporal formulas were added to projections, but would give a verification procedure for topologies of any size.

7 Related Work

There is a wide range of network verification systems that have been developed, each with different tradeoffs of user effort to guarantee strength. On one end of the spectrum are systems such as IronFleet, Verdi, Ivy, I4, Minesweeper, CCAC, and TimePiece, which all focus on finding strong inductive invariants of distributed systems [1,10,17,22,27]. Because they require significant dedicated user effort, they are meant for widely-used systems such as public-internet protocols or consensus protocols. A similar large, one-time effort to formalize and verify Google's algorithms would be difficult to maintain across protocol changes. Efforts to lower this cost such as DistAI, which attempts to automatically generate invariants, and Grove, which employs separation logic to modularize proofs, still require protocol specifications in a proof language [23,28]. A model-checking approach makes the most sense for our use case, as model complexity matches the level of design documentation and changes will be similar and proportional to implementation changes.

Symmetry reduction has been used in many forms to tackle state space explosion, for example in hardware verification [19], parameterized systems [4,8], and symbolic model checking [7,20]. These approaches provide strong theoretical guarantees but would require implementation in TLC. The best available tools are TLC's refinement checker or Apalache [21], which still require the user to provide the entire abstract program in addition to the abstraction. State projections are a practical starting point for defining abstractions without symbolic execution or BDD machinery.

In contrast to proof-based systems, network *runtime* verification systems such as Aragog or Pivot Tracing are automated but incur a runtime cost and only check events that they observe directly [18,29]. Google already uses runtime verification extensively. Our approach is in the middle: it can find bugs at the level of *design documents*, is easy to set up and modify as it does not touch the production system, and does not require modeling the entirety of the network.

8 Conclusion

We presented our experience using TLA+ to model some of the control plane protocols running on Google's B4. We modeled various protocols at a high level of abstraction akin to a design document. To perform model checking on them, we present a novel technique to horizontally parallelize model checking in our specific domain. Furthermore, we added an abstraction mechanism to TLA+ to ensure we explored all abstract states of interest to developers. We evaluated our techniques on various network topologies and showed that they made the model checking problem feasible.

Acknowledgments. We thank Subhasree Mandal, Aman Shaikh, and the anonymous CAV reviewers for their comments on earlier drafts of this paper. We also thank Nathan Flath, Kal Nasser, Li Qiu, Shuanglong Zhang, and Yang Zhang for their contributions throughout the project.

Data Availability Statement. The data and artifact for this paper were not made publicly available to retain intellectual property.

Disclosure of Interests. Andrew Johnson was employed as a Student Researcher at Google, Inc. while this work was completed. The authors have no competing interests.

References

1. Alberdingk Thijm, T., Beckett, R., Gupta, A., Walker, D.: Modular control plane verification via temporal invariants. Proc. ACM Program. Lang. **7**(PLDI), 50–75 (2023). ISSN: 2475-1421. https://doi.org/10.1145/3591222
2. Ball, T., Majumdar, R., Millstein, T., Rajamani, S.K.: Automatic predicate abstraction of C programs. SIGPLAN Not. **36**(5), 203–213 (2001). ISSN: 0362-1340. https://doi.org/10.1145/381694.378846

3. Barnat, J., et al.: DiVinE 3.0 – an explicit-state model checker for multithreaded C & C++ programs. In: Sharygina, N., Veith, H. (eds.) CAV 2013. LNCS, vol. 8044, pp. 863–868. Springer, Heidelberg (2013). https://doi.org/10.1007/978-3-642-39799-8_60
4. Chou, C.-T., Mannava, P.K., Park, S.: A simple method for parameterized verification of cache coherence protocols. In: Hu, A.J., Martin, A.K. (eds.) FMCAD 2004. LNCS, vol. 3312, pp. 382–398. Springer, Heidelberg (2004). https://doi.org/10.1007/978-3-540-30494-4_27
5. Clarke, E.M., Emerson, E.A., Jha, S., Sistla, A.P.: Symmetry reductions in model checking. In: Hu, A.J., Vardi, M.Y. (eds.) CAV 1998, pp. 147–158. Springer, Heidelberg (1998). ISBN: 978-3-540-69339-0
6. Cousot, P., Cousot, R.: Abstract interpretation: a unified lattice model for static analysis of programs by construction or approximation of fixpoints. In: Proceedings of the 4th ACM SIGACT-SIGPLAN Symposium on Principles of Programming Languages, POPL 1977, Los Angeles, California, pp. 238–252. Association for Computing Machinery (1977). ISBN: 9781450373500. https://doi.org/10.1145/512950.512973
7. Emerson, E.A., Wahl, T.: Dynamic symmetry reduction. In: Halbwachs, N., Zuck, L.D. (eds.) TACAS 2005. LNCS, vol. 3440, pp. 382–396. Springer, Heidelberg (2005). https://doi.org/10.1007/978-3-540-31980-1_25
8. Fang, Y., McMillan, K.L., Pnueli, A., Zuck, L.D.: Liveness by invisible invariants. In: Najm, E., Pradat-Peyre, J.-F., Donzeau-Gouge, V.V. (eds.) FORTE 2006. LNCS, vol. 4229, pp. 356–371. Springer, Heidelberg (2006). https://doi.org/10.1007/11888116_26
9. Flanagan, C., Qadeer, S.: Predicate abstraction for software verification. SIGPLAN Not. **37**(1), 191–202 (2002). ISSN: 0362-1340. https://doi.org/10.1145/565816.503291
10. Hawblitzel, C., et al.: IronFleet: proving practical distributed systems correct. In: Proceedings of the 25th Symposium on Operating Systems Principles. SOSP 2015, Monterey, California, pp. 1–17. Association for Computing Machinery (2015). ISBN: 9781450338349. https://doi.org/10.1145/2815400.2815428
11. Hong, C.-Y., et al.: B4 and after: managing hierarchy, partitioning, and asymmetry for availability and scale in Google's software-defined WAN. In: Proceedings of the 2018 Conference of the ACM Special Interest Group on Data Communication. SIGCOMM 2018, Budapest, Hungary, pp. 74–87. Association for Computing Machinery, 2018. ISBN: 9781450355674. https://doi.org/10.1145/3230543.3230545
12. Jain, S., et al.: B4: experience with a globally-deployed software defined wan. SIGCOMM Comput. Commun. Rev. **43**(4), 3–14 (2013). ISSN: 0146-4833. https://doi.org/10.1145/2534169.2486019
13. Johnson, A., Wahl, T.: Delay-bounded scheduling without delay! In: Silva, A., Leino, K.R.M. (eds.) CAV 2021. LNCS, vol. 12759, pp. 380–402. Springer, Cham (2021). https://doi.org/10.1007/978-3-030-81685-8_18
14. Lamport, L.: Specifying Systems: The TLA+ Language and Tools for Hardware and Software Engineers. Addison-Wesley Longman Publishing Co., Inc., USA (2002). ISBN: 032114306X
15. Liu, P., Wahl, T.: CUBA: interprocedural context-unbounded analysis of concurrent programs. In: Proceedings of the 39th ACM SIGPLAN Conference on Programming Language Design and Implementation. PLDI 2018, Philadelphia, PA, USA, pp. 105–119. Association for Computing Machinery (2018). ISBN: 9781450356985. https://doi.org/10.1145/3192366.3192419

16. Liu, P., Wahl, T., Lal, A.: Verifying asynchronous event-driven programs using partial abstract transformers. In: Dillig, I., Tasiran, S. (eds.) CAV 2019. LNCS, vol. 11562, pp. 386–404. Springer, Cham (2019). https://doi.org/10.1007/978-3-030-25543-5_22
17. Ma, H., Goel, A., Jeannin, J.B., Kapritsos, M., Kasikci, B., Sakallah, K.A.: I4: incremental inference of inductive invariants for verification of distributed protocols. In: Proceedings of the 27th ACM Symposium on Operating Systems Principles. SOSP 2019, Huntsville, Ontario, Canada, pp. 370–384. Association for Computing Machinery (2019). ISBN: 9781450368735. https://doi.org/10.1145/3341301.3359651
18. Mace, J., Roelke, R., Fonseca, R.: Pivot tracing: dynamic causal monitoring for distributed systems. In: Proceedings of the 25th Symposium on Operating Systems Principles. SOSP 2015, Monterey, California, pp. 378–393. Association for Computing Machinery (2015). ISBN: 9781450338349. https://doi.org/10.1145/2815400.2815415
19. McMillan, K.L.: A methodology for hardware verification using compositional model checking. Sci. Comput. Program. **37**(1), 279–309 (2000). ISSN: 0167-6423. https://doi.org/10.1016/S0167-6423(99)00030-1
20. McMillan, K.L.: Eager abstraction for symbolic model checking. In: Chockler, H., Weissenbacher, G. (eds.) CAV 2018. LNCS, vol. 10981, pp. 191–208. Springer, Cham (2018). https://doi.org/10.1007/978-3-319-96145-3_11
21. Otoni, R., Konnov, I., Kukovec, J., Eugster, P., Sharygina, N.: Symbolic model checking for TLA+ made faster. In: Sankaranarayanan, S., Sharygina, N. (eds.) Tools and Algorithms for the Construction and Analysis of Systems, pp. 126–144. Springer, Cham (2023). ISBN: 978-3-031-30823-9. https://doi.org/10.1007/978-3-031-30823-9_7
22. Padon, O., McMillan, K. L., Panda, A., Sagiv, M., Shoham, S.: Ivy: safety verification by interactive generalization. SIGPLAN Not. **51**(6), 614–630 (2016). ISSN: 0362-1340. https://doi.org/10.1145/2980983.2908118
23. Sharma, U., Jung, R., Tassarotti, J., Kaashoek, F., Zeldovich, N.: Grove: a separation-logic library for verifying distributed systems. In: Proceedings of the 29th Symposium on Operating Systems Principles, SOSP 2023, Koblenz, Germany, pp. 113–129. Association for Computing Machinery (2023). ISBN: 9798400702297. https://doi.org/10.1145/3600006.3613172
24. Tirmazi, M., et al.: Borg: the next generation. In: Proceedings of the Fifteenth European Conference on Computer Systems. EuroSys 2020, Heraklion, Greece. Association for Computing Machinery (2020). ISBN: 9781450368827. https://doi.org/10.1145/3342195.3387517
25. tlaplus. TLA+ Model Checker and Toolbox Source Code (2025). https://github.com/tlaplus/tlaplus. GitHub repository. Accessed 8 Oct 2025
26. Verma, A., Pedrosa, L., Korupolu, M., Oppenheimer, D., Tune, E., Wilkes, J.: Large-scale cluster management at Google with Borg. In: Proceedings of the Tenth European Conference on Computer Systems. EuroSys 2015, Bordeaux, France. Association for Computing Machinery (2015). ISBN: 9781450332385. https://doi.org/10.1145/2741948.2741964
27. Wilcox, J.R., et al.: Verdi: a framework for implementing and formally verifying distributed systems. SIGPLAN Not. **50**(6), 357–368 (2015). ISSN: 0362-1340. https://doi.org/10.1145/2813885.2737958

28. Yao, J., Tao, R., Gu, R., Nieh, J., Jana, S., Ryan, G.: DistAI: data-driven automated invariant learning for distributed protocols. In: 15th USENIX Symposium on Operating Systems Design and Implementation (OSDI 2021), pp. 405–421. USENIX Association (2021). ISBN: 978-1-939133-22-9
29. Yaseen, N., Arzani, B., Beckett, R., Ciraci, S., Liu, V.: Aragog: scalable runtime verification of shardable networked systems. In: Operating systems and implementations (OSDI) (2020). https://www.microsoft.com/en-us/research/publication/aragogscalable-runtime-verification-of-shardable-networked-systems/

The TLA+ Model Checker Apalache

Rodrigo Otoni[1(✉)], Shon Feder[2], Jure Kukovec[3], Andrey Kupriyanov[3], Gabriela Moreira[4], Philip Offtermatt[5], Thomas Pani[3], Thanh-Hai Tran[6], and Igor Konnov[3]

[1] University of Groningen, Groningen, Netherlands
r.b.otoni@rug.nl
[2] Tarides, Toronto, Canada
shon@tarides.com
[3] Vienna, Austria
andrey@kuprum.xyz, thomas@thpani.net, igor@konnov.phd
[4] Informal Systems, Joinville, Brazil
gabriela@informal.systems
[5] Informal Systems, Munich, Germany
philip.offtermatt@informal.systems
[6] Université Paris-Saclay, CEA, List, Palaiseau, France
thanh-hai.tran@cea.fr

Abstract. The TLA$^+$ language has been widely used, both in academia and industry, to specify and reason about distributed systems. This paper presents Apalache, an efficient and flexible symbolic model checker for TLA$^+$. Apalache's engine is based on bounded model checking, with symbolic transitions being extracted from TLA$^+$ specifications and verification conditions suitable for satisfiability modulo theories (SMT) solvers being generated from them. Reasoning can be done in terms of safety and liveness properties, with liveness checking realised via a liveness-to-safety reduction. Apalache's flexibility lies in its three complementary functionalities: bounded exhaustive verification, for bounded guarantees, randomised symbolic execution, for prototyping and bug detection, and inductiveness checking, for unbounded guarantees. The paper describes Apalache's architecture and features, including its support for PlusCal and Quint, two languages that share the same semantic foundation as TLA$^+$. Industrial usage of Apalache is also presented, together with a case study which illustrates how Apalache can be used to verify the agreement property of a consensus protocol.

Keywords: model checking · SMT solving · distributed systems

1 Introduction

Distribution has become an integral part of a large number of computer systems, providing them with essential improvements to aspects such as performance and fault-tolerance. These improvements, however, often come with the need for

J. Kukovec, A. Kupriyanov, T. Pani and I. Konnov—Independent Researcher.

E. Darulova et al. (Eds.): CAV 2026, LNCS 16682, pp. 151–166, 2026.
https://doi.org/10.1007/978-3-032-32519-8_8

complex coordination strategies not required for sequential and concurrent systems. Due to the critical nature of many of the distributed systems underpinning our modern digital infrastructure, their correctness is of crucial importance.

One way to establish guarantees about the behaviour of distributed systems is through the writing of, and reasoning about, TLA$^+$ specifications [31], an approach that has been adopted both in academia and in industry, e.g., at Amazon Web Services [40]. TLA$^+$ is a specification language based on a variant of linear-time temporal logic called temporal logic of actions (TLA) [30], which allows for the behaviour of a system to be described in a way that abstracts implementation details that do not impact high-level properties, such as memory management. Having specified a system in TLA$^+$, model checking [9] can then be employed to ensure correctness in an automated way. In addition to its adoption by Amazon [7], TLA$^+$ has many other success stories, e.g., in the context of Microsoft's Cosmos DB [16] and of MongoDB [48].

Reasoning about distributed systems is a notoriously difficult task, due to the numerous interleavings admitted by distributed algorithms, with state spaces generally growing exponentially with the number of network nodes. With the aim of aiding in the practical verification of distributed systems, this paper presents Apalache[1], an efficient and flexible symbolic model checker for TLA$^+$. At its core, Apalache extracts symbolic transitions from TLA$^+$ specifications and generates verification conditions that are checked by satisfiability modulo theories (SMT) solvers [26]. Verification can be done in terms of both safety and liveness properties. Apalache follows a bounded model checking approach and has two quantifier-free SMT encodings, based on the combination of nonlinear integer arithmetic with the theories of uninterpreted functions [22] and arrays [44]. Notably, Apalache exploits its engine to enable not only bounded exhaustive verification, but also randomised symbolic execution and inductiveness checking. By providing three complementary functionalities, Apalache allows users to obtain the guarantees they need with the computational resources they have.

The development of Apalache started at TU Wien in 2016 and has since spanned various institutions. Many successes have been achieved over the years, with Apalache being used to verify protocols for blockchain synchronization [6] and consensus [14,21,51], and algorithms for the detection of failures [49] and termination [34], as well as to aid in test case generation [28,37]. Apalache has also been used at NVIDIA for validation of safety-critical software development tooling, in the context of the ISO 26262 standard [27]. Furthermore, Apalache usage extends to other TLA-based languages, such as PlusCal [32]. Regarding terms of use, Apalache is developed under the open source Apache 2.0 license.

The remainder of this paper presents Apalache's architecture and features, some of which have not been described in any prior academic publication, e.g., randomised symbolic execution, and is structured as follows. Section 2 introduces a running example and the basics of TLA$^+$. Section 3 provides an overview of Apalache and its capabilities. Section 4 describes a case study which showcases how Apalache can be used in practice. Section 5 discusses industrial adoption and related work. Finally, Sect. 6 presents closing remarks and future work.

---

[1] Apalache is available at https://github.com/apalache-mc/apalache.

```
──────────────────── MODULE Ben_Or ────────────────────
EXTENDS FiniteSets, Integers, typedefs
CONSTANTS N, T, F, CORRECT, FAULTY, ROUNDS
VARIABLES value, decision, round, step, msgs1, msgs2
NO_DECISION ≜ −1   alias indicating that no decision has yet been taken
Init ≜   predicate describing the set of initial states
    ∧ value ∈ [CORRECT → VALUES]   nondeterministically choose the initial values
    ∧ decision = [r ∈ CORRECT ↦ NO_DECISION]
    ∧ round = [r ∈ CORRECT ↦ 1]
    ∧ step = [r ∈ CORRECT ↦ S1]   correct participants start on S1, standing for step 1
    ∧ msgs1 = [r ∈ ROUNDS ↦ {}]
    ∧ msgs2 = [r ∈ ROUNDS ↦ {}]
Step1(id) ≜   send proposal message to all participants
    LET r ≜ round[id] IN   update msgs1 and step, with M1 defining a record
        ∧ step[id] = S1
        ∧ msgs1' = [msgs1 EXCEPT ![r] = @ ∪ {M1(id, r, value[id])}]
        ∧ step' = [step EXCEPT ![id] = S2]
        ∧ UNCHANGED ⟨value, decision, round, msgs2⟩
Step2(id) ≜ ...   receive proposals and react to them (omitted for brevity)
Step3(id) ≜ ...   consider if a decision can be made (omitted for brevity)
CorrectStep ≜   predicate describing the operation of correct participants
    ∃ id ∈ CORRECT :   correct participants execute the steps of the protocol
        Step1(id) ∨ Step2(id) ∨ Step3(id)
FaultyStep ≜   predicate describing the operation of faulty participants
    ∃ r ∈ ROUNDS :   faulty participants collectively inject messages for a single round
        ...   omitted for brevity
Next ≜   predicate describing the transition relation
    ∨ CorrectStep
    ∨ FaultyStep
Agreement ≜   predicate describing the agreement property
    ∀ id1, id2 ∈ CORRECT :   no two correct participants decide on different values
        ∨ decision[id1] = NO_DECISION
        ∨ decision[id2] = NO_DECISION
        ∨ decision[id1] = decision[id2]
───────────────────────────────────────────────────────
```

Fig. 1. Condensed specification of Ben-Or's Byzantine consensus protocol [2].

2 Running Example

To illustrate APALACHE's capabilities, we use a TLA$^+$ specification of Ben-Or's Byzantine consensus protocol [2]. The protocol's relative simplicity, combined with its use of primitives present in many state-of-the-art protocols, makes it a suitable running example. A condensed version of the specification is shown in Fig. 1, with the complete specification being available online[2]. In summary, the protocol operates by having the correct participants perform three steps per round, in which specific messages are exchanged in order, with faulty participants

[2] Detailed protocol specification at https://github.com/konnov/apalache-examples.

sending messages in an arbitrary manner; it is assumed that less than 1/5 of the participants are faulty.

TLA$^+$ specifications represent state machines, with the *Init* predicate describing the set of initial states and the *Next* predicate describing the transition relation. Predicates are also used to describe the actions possible, e.g., *CorrectStep* and *FaultyStep*, and the properties to be checked, e.g., *Agreement*. Notably, specifications are parametrised, meaning that constants dictating the total number of participants, N, the tolerated number of faulty participants, T, and the actual number of faulty participants, F, can be instantiated with different values. Further details on TLA$^+$ can be found in Lamport's book [31].

3 Overview

A description of APALACHE's main components is given in Sect. 3.1. The type system enforced is discussed in Sect. 3.2. The core of APALACHE, its SMT-based model checking engine for handling safety properties, is detailed in Sect. 3.3. Liveness checking is covered in Sect. 3.4. Lastly, APALACHE's support for other TLA-based languages is described in Sect. 3.5.

3.1 Architecture

The high-level architecture of APALACHE is given in Fig. 2. APALACHE works via a command-line interface and receives as input a TLA$^+$ specification. In TLA$^+$ the properties are traditionally written as part of the specification, with the user being able to select the property to be checked via a command-line option; deadlock absence is checked if no property is provided. The output is either a statement that no errors were found during the search, together with a trace which illustrates a valid protocol execution, or the summary of a violation, together with a concrete concrete counterexample (CEX). By default, exhaustive search is conducted for 10 unrollings of the transition relation of the specified protocol; this and other parameters can be changed via command-line options.

APALACHE uses SANY [15] for parsing the TLA$^+$ input and its own type checker, called SNOWCAT, to ensure type correctness. The preprocessor performs

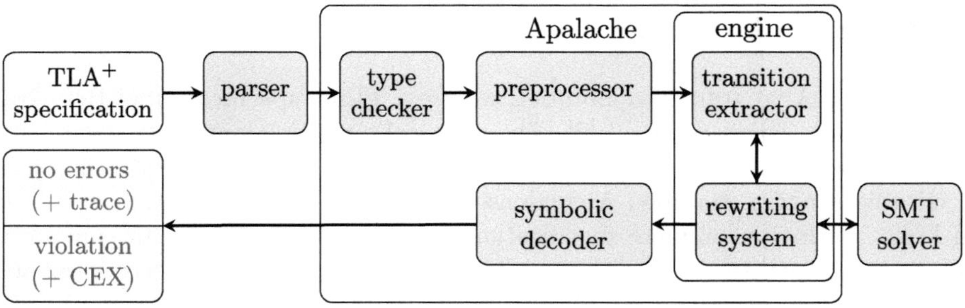

Fig. 2. Architecture of APALACHE.

$$
\begin{aligned}
\langle \mathrm{T} \rangle &::= \mathtt{Bool} \mid \mathtt{Int} \mid \mathtt{Str} \mid \langle \mathrm{T} \rangle \to \langle \mathrm{T} \rangle \mid \mathtt{Set}(\langle \mathrm{T} \rangle) \mid \mathtt{Seq}(\langle \mathrm{T} \rangle) \mid \\
&\quad \ll\langle \mathrm{T} \rangle, \ldots, \langle \mathrm{T} \rangle\gg \mid (\langle \mathrm{T} \rangle, \ldots, \langle \mathrm{T} \rangle) \Rightarrow \langle \mathrm{T} \rangle \mid \langle \mathrm{typeConst} \rangle \mid \\
&\quad \langle \mathrm{typeVar} \rangle \mid \mathtt{Variant}(\langle \mathrm{typeVar} \rangle) \mid (\langle \mathrm{T} \rangle) \mid \\
&\quad \langle \mathrm{variantOption} \rangle \mid \ldots \mid \langle \mathrm{variantOption} \rangle \mid \\
&\quad \{\langle \mathrm{field} \rangle : \langle \mathrm{T} \rangle, \ldots, \langle \mathrm{field} \rangle : \langle \mathrm{T} \rangle\} \\
\langle \mathrm{field} \rangle &::= \textit{an identifier that matches } \mathtt{[a\text{-}zA\text{-}Z\_][a\text{-}zA\text{-}Z0\text{-}9\_]}^* \\
\langle \mathrm{typeConst} \rangle &::= \textit{an identifier that matches } \mathtt{[A\text{-}Z\_][A\text{-}Z0\text{-}9\_]}^* \\
\langle \mathrm{variantOption} \rangle &::= \textit{an identifier that matches } \mathtt{[A\text{-}Z\_][A\text{-}Z0\text{-}9\_]}^* \\
\langle \mathrm{typeVar} \rangle &::= \textit{a single letter from } \mathtt{[a\text{-}z]}
\end{aligned}
$$

Fig. 3. Grammar of APALACHE's type system.

a number of simplifications to improve checking efficiency, including inlining operator calls and normalising expressions to be in negation normal form. The model checking engine consists of two modules: the transition extractor, which generates a symbolic transition system from the specification, and the rewriting system, which generates verification conditions in terms of SMT queries. An off-the-shelf solver is used to solve the SMT queries, with APALACHE currently employing Z3 [38]. The symbolic decoder produces, in case of a violation, a CEX trace that reaches a state violating the property being checked.

3.2 Type System

TLA$^+$ was not designed with automated reasoning in mind, with the language being untyped as a result. Typing, however, is very useful for verification, especially in regards to the generation of SMT queries. As a way to benefit from typing while not altering the language, APALACHE makes use of annotations to add types to TLA$^+$ specifications. These annotations, whose grammar can be seen in Fig. 3, are lightweight and automatically checked by SNOWCAT; concretely, all definitions are checked for type correctness w.r.t. the type system. Usually, the user simply has to add types to constants and variables, since APALACHE can infer the types of most operators [25]; in our experience AI tools can produce such annotations effortlessly. Annotations for the constants and variables in the running example can be seen in Fig. 4. Further details on both SNOWCAT and the type system can found in APALACHE's documentation[3].

3.3 Model Checking Engine

APALACHE's engine generates a symbolic transition system [26] and then uses its rewriting system to generate SMT formulas in the theory of quantifier-free uninterpreted functions and nonlinear integer arithmetic (QF_UFNIA) [22] or

[3] Typing details at https://apalache-mc.org/docs/tutorials/snowcat-tutorial.html.

CONSTANTS	VARIABLES
@type: *Int*;	@type: *REPLICA* → *Int*;
N, total number of participants	*value*, current value of a participant
@type: *Int*;	@type: *REPLICA* → *Int*;
T, bound on the number of faulty participants	*decision*, decision of a participant
@type: *Int*;	@type: *REPLICA* → *Int*;
F, actual number of faulty participants	*round*, round number of a participant
@type: *Set*(*REPLICA*);	@type: *REPLICA* → *STEP*;
CORRECT, set of the correct participants	*step*, participant step: *S*1, *S*2, *S*3
@type: *Set*(*REPLICA*);	@type: *Int* → *Set*($ *msgOne*);
FAULTY, set of the faulty participants	*msgs*1, type–1 messages sent, mapped by rounds
@type: *Set*(*Int*);	@type: *Int* → *Set*($ *msgTwo*);
ROUNDS set of rounds	*msgs*2 type–2 messages sent, mapped by rounds

Fig. 4. Types of the running example; $\$msgOne$ and $\$msgTwo$ are type aliases, standing for the record $\{src : REPLICA,\ r : Int,\ v : Int\}$ and for the variant $Q(\{src : REPLICA,\ r : Int\}) \mid D(\{src : REPLICA,\ r : Int,\ v : Int\})$.

quantifier-free arrays, uninterpreted functions, and nonlinear integer arithmetic (QF_AUFNIA) [44]. The use of arrays tends to be beneficial in specifications that make ample use of sets and functions, but can lead to a slowdown if mixed data structures are used, e.g., records of sets, or in case of nesting, e.g., sets of sets, since APALACHE relies on the extensionality axiom. Note that arithmetic nonlinearity is not essential, being only present if the TLA$^+$ specification has nonlinear constraints, with the solver being free to select the suitable theory.

In its default mode, the engine incrementally generates SMT formulas to check if a state violating the property can be reached in 0, 1, 2, ..., K unrollings, with K being a user-defined bound. This is illustrated on the right, with $\cdot$ representing the unrolling of the transition relation and Inv being a given property. In addition to bounding the number of unrollings, the data structures used in the specification need to be finite. APALACHE can thus check for bounded safety in a fully automated manner. The engine's default mode can also be used for unbounded verification, if the user is able to provide it with a suitable inductive invariant, as described in Sect. 4.3.

$$
\begin{array}{l}
0 : Init \wedge \neg Inv \\
1 : (Init \cdot Next) \wedge \neg Inv \\
2 : (Init \cdot Next \cdot Next) \wedge \neg Inv \\
\qquad \ldots \\
K : (Init \cdot Next \ldots Next) \wedge \neg Inv
\end{array}
$$

In addition to exhaustive search, the engine is also used to perform randomised symbolic execution, called *simulation* in APALACHE. In simulation mode the engine picks a symbolic trace, by randomly selecting enabled protocol actions at each unrolling, and then checks if the property holds on all the executions covered by this trace. A simulation of length 3

$$
\begin{array}{l}
0 : Init \wedge \neg Inv \\
1 : (Init \cdot Step1(A)) \wedge \neg Inv \\
2 : (Init \cdot Step1(A) \cdot Step1(B)) \wedge \neg Inv \\
3 : (Init \cdot Step1(A) \cdot Step1(B) \cdot Step1(C)) \wedge \neg Inv
\end{array}
$$

is illustrated on the right, in which three participants execute the first protocol step; ids A, B, and C are left for the solver to instantiate, with different simulations potentially picking different symbolic traces. Although not capable of providing correctness guarantees, due to the loss of completeness, simulation is much faster and can be used for prototyping and bug detection. Since the exploration of a single trace yields limited information by itself, APALACHE allows users to define how many simulations are desired, with hundreds normally possible in a timely manner.

3.4 Liveness Checking

For the checking of liveness properties APALACHE employs a liveness-to-safety reduction [41], inspired by the work of Biere et al. [3]. This reductions allows users to reason about liveness in both model checking and simulation modes. It works by taking a TLA$^+$ specification S and a temporal property P and generating an instrumented version of S, called S_P, with a desired invariant I_P, such that P holds in S if and only if I_P is an invariant in S_P. Importantly, liveness checking is complete only for finite-state systems currently. Both the reduction and the checking of I_P are automated by APALACHE; the user can also request APALACHE to emit the instrumented specification into a file, so that it can be provided to other tools.

3.5 Support Beyond TLA+

Besides TLA$^+$, APALACHE also provides support for two other languages whose semantics are based on TLA, namely PlusCal and Quint.

PlusCal. Positioned as an algorithm language that can be used to replace pseudocode, PlusCal was inspired by TLA$^+$ from its inception [32]. Due to this close relation, the machinery of APALACHE can easily be used to reason about PlusCal code. The only caveat is that, similar to how it is done for TLA$^+$, users are required to add type annotations to the code; further details can be found on APALACHE's documentation[4].

Quint. Envisioned as a version of TLA$^+$ more approachable to engineers, Quint is a language that provides an alternative surface syntax to TLA. APALACHE is integrated into Quint tooling[5], which makes its use seamless, and it has been employed to verify Quint specifications of the ChonkyBFT protocol for Byzantine fault-tolerant consensus [14] and the Aztec governance smart contracts [24].

---

[4] PlusCal details at https://apalache-mc.org/docs/tutorials/pluscal-tutorial.html.

[5] Quint details at https://quint.sh/docs/model-checkers#apalache.

4 Case Study

Our running example is a consensus protocol, and as the name suggests, it aims to ensure that all (correct) participants reach the same decision, e.g., all replicas of a database decide to update a given entry with the same value. A central part of consensus is the *agreement* property, which dictates that no two correct participants may decide differently. The usage of APALACHE's three functionalities is showcased in this context, as follows: bounded verification is illustrated in Sect. 4.1, symbolic execution is covered in Sect. 4.2, and inductiveness checking is detailed in Sect. 4.3. All experiments were done using APALACHE v0.52.1 on a Linux laptop with an Intel Core i7-8650U CPU and 16 GB of RAM. For an extensive evaluation of APALACHE's performance on a range of protocols the reader is referred to [22, 44], whose results are summarised in Sect. 4.4.

4.1 Bounded Exhaustive Verification

To verify that agreement holds up to a bound we use the `check` command, with APALACHE expecting a user-defined instantiation of a given protocol. The `n6t1f1.tla` file contains a protocol instance with 6 participants, `n6`, a tolerated limit of 1 faulty participant, `t1`, and 1 actual faulty participant, `f1`.

```
$ apalache-mc check --inv=Agreement --length=10 n6t1f1.tla
...
Checker reports no error up to computation length 10 It
took me 0 days 0 hours 26 min 43 sec
```

As can be seen, the guarantees provided by `check` can be costly to achieve, due to the combinatorial explosion. Clever abstractions are often needed to make effective use of the model checking engine. As shown in Fig. 1, *Next* allows faulty participants to inject messages at every protocol step, so APALACHE has to consider all possible points in which this can happen. Since the protocol is asynchronous, and thus sent messages can be received at any point, an equivalent scenario can be achieved by injecting the messages from the faulty participants in the *Init* predicate. An alternative to *Init* is shown on the left. Since the faulty messages have been introduced in advance, the transition relation can now become the predicate *CorrectStep*.

$InitWithFaults \triangleq$

*msgs*1 and *msgs*2 are nondeterministically initialised with faulty messages

$$\begin{aligned}
&\land \exists F1 \in \text{SUBSET } [src : FAULTY,\ r : ROUNDS,\ v : VALUES] : \\
&\qquad msgs1 = [r \in ROUNDS \mapsto \{m \in F1 : m.r = r\}] \\
&\land \exists F1D \in \text{SUBSET } [src : FAULTY,\ r : ROUNDS,\ v : VALUES], \\
&\qquad F1Q \in \text{SUBSET } [src : FAULTY,\ r : ROUNDS] : \\
&\qquad msgs2 = [r \in ROUNDS \mapsto \\
&\qquad\quad \{D2(mm.src,\ r,\ mm.v) : mm \in \{m \in F1D : m.r = r\}\} \\
&\qquad\qquad \cup \{Q2(mm.src,\ r) : mm \in \{m \in F1Q : m.r = r\}\}] \\
&\land \ldots
\end{aligned}$$

value, *decision*, *round*, and *step* are as per *Init*

```
$ apalache-mc check --init=InitWithFaults --next=CorrectStep
--inv=Agreement --length=10 n6t1f1.tla
...
Checker reports no error up to computation length 10 It took
me 0 days 0 hours 1 min 24 sec
```

With the improved specification, it is also possible to efficiently verify that agreement does not hold if there are more faulty participants than tolerated. Checking the `n6t1f2.tla` file, which instantiates 2 faulty participants, leads to a violation being found and a CEX returned. The CEX includes a state in which two participants decide on different values, as captured by the value of *decision*, i.e., $decision = SetAsFun(\{\ll \text{“0”}, -1 \gg, \ll \text{“1”}, -1 \gg, \ll \text{“2”}, 0 \gg, \ll \text{“3”}, 1 \gg\})$; -1 represents that no decision has yet been made.

4.2 Randomised Symbolic Execution

Exhaustive verification tends to become increasingly expensive as protocols become more intricate, and as more participants and protocol rounds are considered. For instance, while checking `n6t1f1.tla` with `--length=10` takes less than two minutes, checking it with `--length=15` requires ∼47 h. This is explained by the presence in the specification of elements such as power sets, written in TLA$^+$ as SUBSET S for a given set S, and the cardinality function, which computes the number of elements of a finite set. These can be seen in *Step*2 on the right.

```
Step2(id) ≜  receive proposals and react to them
  LET r ≜ round[id] IN
  ∧ ∃ received ∈ SUBSET msgs1[r] :
      wait until type–1 messages are received from N − T processes
      ∧ Cardinality(Senders1(received)) ≥ N − T
      ∧ LET Weights ≜ [v ∈ VALUES ↦
          Cardinality(Senders1({m ∈ received : m.v = v}))]
      IN
      ...  omitted for brevity
```

To be able to perform fast reasoning during prototyping and potentially detect vulnerabilities cheaply, we can make use of the `simulate` command; a batch of 100 independent simulations of the file `n6t1f1.tla` with `--length=15`, via option `--max-run=100`, takes ∼17 min. Note that, although relatively slow in comparison to simulators for other formalisms, Apalache's simulation mode has to handle the richness of TLA$^+$ and its exploration is done in terms of symbolic traces rather than explicit ones.

4.3 Inductiveness Checking

To ensure that agreement holds for an arbitrary number of rounds, Apalache requires the user to provide an inductive invariant that implies agreement. Designing, or rather discovering, such an invariant is a highly nontrivial task, whose details are outside the scope of this paper. As a measure of the human effort needed, it took ~15 h of work for a co-author experienced in protocol specification to discover a suitable collection of lemmas, 13 in total, for our example.

Once the inductive invariant is at hand, APALACHE can provide unbounded guarantees via three `check` calls. The first one establishes the base case, i.e., that the invariant holds in the initial states, the second one checks that the invariant implies the property, and the third one verifies the inductive case, i.e., that if the invariant holds in one state it keeps holding after one transition. Note that unboundedness is considered here only in terms of unrollings, i.e., number of rounds, with parameters such as number of nodes still being bounded.

Inductiveness checking of our example can be achieved via the calls below. The first two checks of `n6t1f1_inductive.tla`, which contains all the needed lemmas, are relatively cheap, but checking the inductive case is more expensive. The *IndInit* predicate is an extension of *IndInv* that gives shape to the variable domains, so that it can describe initial states.

```
$ apalache-mc check --init=InitWithFaults --next=CorrectStep
--inv=IndInv --length=0 n6t1f1_inductive.tla
...
Checker reports no error up to computation length 0 It took
me 0 days 0 hours 0 min 7 sec
```

```
$ apalache-mc check -init=IndInit --next=CorrectStep
--inv=Agreement --length=0 n6t1f1_inductive.tla
...
Checker reports no error up to computation length 0 It took
me 0 days 0 hours 12 min 28 sec
```

```
$ apalache-mc check --init=IndInit --next=CorrectStep
--inv=IndInv --length=1 n6t1f1_inductive.tla
...
Checker reports no error up to computation length 1 It took
me 0 days 19 hours 26 min 15 sec
```

4.4 Evaluation on Other Protocols

Detailed quantitative evaluations of APALACHE, including comparisons with the well-established explicit-state model checker TLC [52], are reported in [22,44].

In [22], ten protocols of varying complexity were considered, from the relatively simple Bakery algorithm for mutual exclusion to the much more complex Paxos and Raft consensus algorithms. Experiments were carried out for both bounded model checking and inductiveness checking, considering different properties and numbers of participants, with 40 experiment instances conducted in total. The results, obtained using APALACHE's QF_UFNIA encoding, show that APALACHE can outperform TLC in terms of runtime and memory use in many cases. Notably, APALACHE could provide results in 8 cases in which TLC could not, given the available resources. In some scenarios, however, primarily involving smaller benchmarks or those that made extensive use of nondeterminism, TLC performed better than APALACHE w.r.t. runtime, memory use, or both.

In [44], three protocols were considered, for Byzantine agreement, consensus with Byzantine faults, and non-blocking atomic commitment. Experiments were carried out for bounded model checking, considering the agreement property and different numbers of participants, with 36 individual experiments conducted in total. A four-fold comparison was conducted between APALACHE's QF_AUFNIA encoding, two variations of APALACHE's QF_UFNIA encoding, and TLC. The results obtained indicate that APALACHE scales better than TLC, particularly the QF_AUFNIA encoding, with TLC having better performance on the scenarios with smaller state spaces; in 21 cases APALACHE could provide a result with the available resources but TLC could not.

It is important to note that APALACHE and TLC complement each other, and we do not necessarily see APALACHE as a replacement of TLC. APALACHE is more suited to scenarios with large data structures. In particular, the symbolic nature of Apalache enables it to handle Byzantine fault-tolerant algorithms, such as Ben-Or's consensus, whereas TLC normally explodes when facing such algorithms. On the other hand, TLC is more performant when dealing with benchmarks with compact state spaces, since APALACHE has the initial overhead of generating a relatively large SMT formula; for large benchmarks model checking time is dominated by solving time though. Furthermore, TLC tends to perform well with specifications that rely heavily on control nondeterminism.

5 Industrial Adoption and Related Work

There are reported uses of APALACHE by researchers and engineers of many organisations, including Informal Systems [6,28,49], the Stellar Foundation [34, 51], Matter Labs [14,20], and NVIDIA [27], with interest also arising from institutions such as the Ethereum Foundation [21], Aztec Labs [24], and Commonware [10]. These examples showcase APALACHE's maturity and impact, and its ability to provide value in industrial settings.

Besides APALACHE, two other tools are prevalent in the TLA$^+$ ecosystem [23]: the explicit-state model checker TLC [52] and the interactive proof system TLAPS [8]. TLC and APALACHE have different strengths, as detailed in Sect. 4.4, and TLAPS focuses on semi-automated proofs, also being powered by SMT solving. A translator from TLA$^+$ to B is also available [18], which allows for the use of PROB [33] for TLA$^+$ verification. When it comes to inductive invariant inference, approaches have been proposed for both TLA$^+$ [11,47] and other formalisms [17,50].

In regards to TLA$^+$ itself, related formalisms include Ivy [35,36], Veil [46], Alloy [19], and P [12], each with their own strengths, weaknesses, and tooling support. Ivy operates at the level of first-order relations, a different abstraction level than TLA$^+$, and is associated with a verification tool of the same name which supports both model checking and deductive verification; Ivy's abstractions are more amenable for automated reasoning, but in our experience distributed systems engineers in industry have a harder time understanding first-order relations than the state machine representation that underpins TLA$^+$. Veil is a framework that operates on a language closely related to Ivy, supporting both automated and interactive verification, with the distinct feature of being embedded into the Lean 4 proof assistant [39]. Alloy is similar to TLA$^+$ in its focus on transition systems, but is better suited to describe data relations than state progress; bounded verification is possible via the Alloy Analyzer. P is a state machine-based programming language centred on asynchronous events, associated with a framework grounded on assume-guarantee reasoning [13]; initially restricted to systematic testing, supporting tooling is now capable of formal verification, and a security-focused variant of the language is also available [29].

6 Conclusion

This paper presented Apalache, an efficient and flexible TLA$^+$ model checker. Apalache makes use of bounded model checking and SMT solving to provide users with three complementary functionalities: bounded exhaustive verification, randomised symbolic execution, and inductiveness checking. Its symbolic engine is capable of reasoning about safety and liveness properties, and has also been employed in the context of two other TLA-based languages, PlusCal and Quint. Industrial usage of Apalache has led to many successes over the years, including the verification of state-of-the-art Byzantine fault tolerant consensus protocols powering modern blockchain platforms.

Future work is envisioned in three directions: (1) add support for unbounded model checking in a native and fully automated way, (2) lift the finite-state restriction from liveness checking, and (3) improve the tool to enable further flexibility. The first direction could consider unboundedness in terms of unrollings or data structure size. It can be pursued via a quantified SMT encoding or one based on Horn clauses, with the latter allowing for novel algorithms such as (SPLIT-)TPA [4,5] to be exploited. Furthermore, certification of solving results [42,43] could be incorporated into Apalache to enhance the strength of its guarantees. The second direction could be centred around the design of an approach based on the technique proposed by Padon et al. [45]. Lastly, the third direction could involve adding bindings for alternative solvers, such as cvc5 [1].

Acknowledgments. The authors are grateful for the institutional support received over the years from TU Wien (2016-2020), Inria Nancy and LORIA (2018-2019), and Informal Systems (2020-2024), as well as for all the past funding that was received from the Vienna Science and Technology Fund (project APALACHE ICT 15-103 in particular), Vienna Business Agency, Austrian Science Fund, Interchain Foundation, and Swiss National Science Foundation.

Data Availibility Statement. A self-contained artifact consisting of Apalache's source code (v0.52.1), built binary, and documentation, together with all files relating to our running example and instructions on how to reproduce all reported experiments, is available at https://doi.org/10.5281/zenodo.19696472.

Disclosure of Interests. The authors have no competing interests to declare that are relevant to the content of this article.

References

1. Barbosa, H., et al.: cvc5: a versatile and industrial-strength SMT solver. In: Proceedings of the 31st International Conference on Tools and Algorithms for the Construction and Analysis of Systems (TACAS 2022). LNCS, vol. 13243, pp. 415–442. Springer, Cham (2022). https://doi.org/10.1007/978-3-030-99524-9_24
2. Ben-Or, M.: Another advantage of free choice (extended abstract): completely asynchronous agreement protocols. In: Proceedings of the 2nd ACM Symposium on Principles of Distributed Computing (PODC 1983), pp. 27–30 (1983). https://doi.org/10.1145/800221.806707
3. Biere, A., Heljanko, K., Junttila, T., Latvala, T., Schuppan, V.: Linear encodings of bounded LTL model checking. Log. Methods Comput. Sci. **2**(5), 1–63 (2006). https://doi.org/10.2168/LMCS-2(5:5)2006
4. Blicha, M., Fedyukovich, G., Hyvärinen, A.E.J., Sharygina, N.: Split transition power abstraction for unbounded safety. In: Proceedings of the 22nd Conference on Formal Methods in Computer-Aided Design (FMCAD 2022), pp. 349–358 (2022). https://doi.org/10.34727/2022/isbn.978-3-85448-053-2_42
5. Blicha, M., Fedyukovich, G., Hyvärinen, A.E.J., Sharygina, N.: Transition power abstractions for deep counterexample detection. In: Proceedings of the 31st International Conference on Tools and Algorithms for the Construction and Analysis of Systems (TACAS 2022). LNCS, vol. 13243, pp. 524–542. Springer, Cham (2022). https://doi.org/10.1007/978-3-030-99524-9_29
6. Braithwaite, S., et al.: Tendermint blockchain synchronization: formal specification and model checking. In: Proceedings of the 11th International Symposium On Leveraging Applications of Formal Methods (ISoLA 2020). LNCS, vol. 12476, pp. 471–488. Springer, Cham (2020). https://doi.org/10.1007/978-3-030-61362-4_27
7. Brooker, M., Desai, A.: Systems correctness practices at amazon web services. Commun. ACM **68**(6), 38–42 (2025). https://doi.org/10.1145/3729175
8. Chaudhuri, K., Doligez, D., Lamport, L., Merz, S.: The TLA+ proof system: building a heterogeneous verification platform. In: Proceedings of the 7th International Colloquium on the Theoretical Aspects of Computing (ICTAC 2010). LNCS, vol. 6255, pp. 44–44. Springer, Heidelberg (2010). https://doi.org/10.1007/978-3-642-14808-8_3
9. Clarke, E.M., Henzinger, T.A., Veith, H., Bloem, R.: Handbook of Model Checking. Springer (2018). https://doi.org/10.1007/978-3-319-10575-8
10. Commonware Inc.: Minimmit Formal Specification (2025). https://github.com/commonwarexyz/monorepo/tree/main/pipeline/minimmit/quint
11. Dardik, I., Kang, E.: Compositional Inductive Invariant Inference via Assume-Guarantee Reasoning (2025). https://doi.org/10.48550/arXiv.2509.06250
12. Desai, A., Gupta, V., Jackson, E., Qadeer, S., Rajamani, S., Zufferey, D.: P: safe asynchronous event-driven programming. ACM SIGPLAN Not. **48**(6), 321–332 (2013). https://doi.org/10.1145/2499370.2462184
13. Desai, A., Phanishayee, A., Qadeer, S., Seshia, S.A.: Compositional programming and testing of dynamic distributed systems. Proc. ACM Program. Lang. **2**(OOPSLA), 1–30 (2018). https://doi.org/10.1145/3276529

14. França, B., Kolegov, D., Konnov, I., Prusak, G.: ChonkyBFT: Consensus Protocol of ZKsync (2025). https://doi.org/10.48550/arXiv.2503.15380
15. Grégoire, J.C., Jefferson, D., Yu, Y.: SANY Syntactic Analyzer. https://lamport.azurewebsites.net/tla/tools.html
16. Hackett, F., Rowe, J., Kuppe, M.A.: Understanding inconsistency in azure cosmos DB with TLA+. In: Proceedings of the 45th International Conference on Software Engineering: Software Engineering in Practice (ICSE-SEIP 2023), pp. 1–12 (2023). https://doi.org/10.1109/ICSE-SEIP58684.2023.00006
17. Hance, T., Heule, M., Martins, R., Parno, B.: Finding invariants of distributed systems: it's a small (enough) world after all. In: Proceedings of the 18th USENIX Symposium on Networked Systems Design and Implementation (NSDI 2021), pp. 115–131 (2021). https://www.usenix.org/conference/nsdi21/presentation/hance
18. Hansen, D., Leuschel, M.: Translating TLA+ to B for validation with ProB. In: Proceedings of the 9th International Conference on Integrated Formal Methods (IFM 2012). LNCS, vol. 7321, pp. 24–38. Springer, Heidelberg (2012). https://doi.org/10.1007/978-3-642-30729-4_3 Proceedings of the 9th International Conference on Integrated Formal Methods IFM 2012. LNCS, vol. 7321, pp. 24–38. Springer, Heidelberg (2012). https://doi.org/10.1007/978-3-642-30729-4_3
19. Jackson, D.: Alloy: a language and tool for exploring software designs. Commun. ACM **62**(9), 66–76 (2019). https://doi.org/10.1145/3338843
20. Kolegov, D., Konnov, I.: ZKsync Governance's Quint Specification (2024). https://github.com/zksync-association/zk-governance/tree/master/spec
21. Konnov, I., Kukovec, J., Pani, T., Saltini, R., Tran, T.H.: Exploring Automatic Model-Checking of the Ethereum Specification (2025). https://doi.org/10.48550/arXiv.2501.07958
22. Konnov, I., Kukovec, J., Tran, T.H.: TLA+ model checking made symbolic. Proc. ACM Program. Lang. **3**(OOPSLA), 1–30 (2019). https://doi.org/10.1145/3360549
23. Konnov, I., Kuppe, M., Merz, S.: Specification and verification with the TLA+ trifecta: TLC, Apalache, and TLAPS. In: Proceedings of the 11th International Symposium On Leveraging Applications of Formal Methods (ISoLA 2022), pp. 88–105 (2022). https://doi.org/10.1007/978-3-031-19849-6_6
24. Konnov, I., Pani, T.: Aztec Governance Formal Specification and Verification (2025). https://github.com/konnov/aztec-governance-formal-verification-2025q3
25. Kukovec, J., Konnov, I.: Type inference for TLA+ in Apalache. In: Summaries of the 2020 TLA+ Community Event (2020). https://conf.tlapl.us/2020/07-Kukovec_and_Konnov-Type_Inference_for_TLA_+_in_Apalache.pdf
26. Kukovec, J., Tran, T.H., Konnov, I.: Extracting symbolic transitions from TLA+ specifications. Sci. Comput. Program. **187**, 102361 (2020). https://doi.org/10.1016/j.scico.2019.102361
27. Kulagin, D.: Validation Test Suite for TLA+ (2025). https://github.com/tlaplus/ValidationTestSuite
28. Kupriyanov, A., Konnov, I.: Model-based testing with TLA+ and apalache. In: Summaries of the 2020 TLA+ Community Event (2020). https://conf.tlapl.us/2020/09-Kuprianov_and_Konnov-Model-based_testing_with_TLA_+_and_Apalache.pdf
29. Kushwah, S., Desai, A., Subramanyan, P., Seshia, S.A.: PSec: programming secure distributed systems using enclaves. In: Proceedings of the 16th ACM Asia Conference on Computer and Communications Security (ASIA CCS 2021), pp. 802–816 (2021). https://doi.org/10.1145/3433210.3453113
30. Lamport, L.: The temporal logic of actions. ACM Trans. Program. Lang. Syst. **16**(3), 872–923 (1994). https://doi.org/10.1145/177492.177726

31. Lamport, L.: Specifying Systems: The TLA+ Language and Tools for Hardware and Software Engineers. Addison-Wesley Professional (2002). https://lamport.azurewebsites.net/tla/book.html
32. Lamport, L.: The PlusCal algorithm language. In: Proceedings of the 6th International Colloquium on Theoretical Aspects of Computing (ICTAC 2009). LNCS, vol. 5684, pp. 36–60. Springer, Heidelberg (2009). https://doi.org/10.1007/978-3-642-03466-4_2
33. Leuschel, M., Butler, M.: ProB: a model checker for B. In: Proceedings of the 12th International Symposium of Formal Methods Europe (FME 2003). LNCS, vol. 2805, pp. 855–874. Springer, Heidelberg (2003). https://doi.org/10.1007/978-3-540-45236-2_46
34. Losa, G., Merz, S.: Distributed Termination Detection - Verified with Apalache, Isabelle/HOL, and TLAPS (2022). https://github.com/nano-o/distributed-termination-detection
35. McMillan, K.L., Padon, O.: Deductive verification in decidable fragments with ivy. In: Proceedings of the 25th International Static Analysis Symposium (SAS 2018). LNCS, vol. 11002, pp. 43–55. Springer, Cham (2018). https://doi.org/10.1007/978-3-319-99725-4_4
36. McMillan, K.L., Padon, O.: Ivy: a multi-modal verification tool for distributed algorithms. In: Proceedings of the 32nd International Conference on Computer Aided Verification (CAV 2020). LNCS, vol. 12225, pp. 190–202. Springer, Cham (2020). https://doi.org/10.1007/978-3-030-53291-8_12
37. Moreira, G., Vasconcellos, C., Kniess, J.: Fully-tested code generation from TLA+ specifications. In: Proceedings of the 7th Brazilian Symposium on Systematic and Automated Software Testing (SAST 2022), pp. 19–28 (2022). https://doi.org/10.1145/3559744.3559747
38. de Moura, L., Bjørner, N.: Z3: an efficient SMT solver. In: Proceedings of the 14th International Conference on Tools and Algorithms for the Construction and Analysis of Systems (TACAS 2008). LNCS, vol. 4963, pp. 337–340. Springer, Heidelberg (2008). https://doi.org/10.1007/978-3-540-78800-3_24 Analysis of Systems TACAS 2008. LNCS, vol. 4963, pp. 337–340. Springer, Heidelberg (2008). https://doi.org/10.1007/978-3-540-78800-3_24
39. Moura, L., Ullrich, S.: The lean 4 theorem prover and programming language. In: Proceedings of the 28th International Conference on Automated Deduction (CADE 2021). LNCS (LNAI), vol. 12699, pp. 625–635. Springer, Cham (2021). https://doi.org/10.1007/978-3-030-79876-5_37
40. Newcombe, C., Rath, T., Zhang, F., Munteanu, B., Brooker, M., Deardeuff, M.: How amazon web services uses formal methods. Commun. ACM **58**(4), 66–73 (2015). https://doi.org/10.1145/2699417
41. Offtermatt, P., Kukovec, J., Konnov, I.: Extending apalache to symbolically reason about temporal properties of TLA+. In: Summaries of the 2022 TLA+ Conference (2022). https://conf.tlapl.us/2022/sub3.pdf
42. Otoni, R., Blicha, M., Eugster, P., Sharygina, N.: Validation of CHC satisfiability with ATHENA. Formal Aspects Comput. **37**(4), 1–20 (2025). https://doi.org/10.1145/3716505
43. Otoni, R., Blicha, M., Rivera, M.B., Eugster, P., Kofroň, J., Sharygina, N.: Unsatisfiability proofs for horn solving. In: Proceedings of the 31st International Conference on Tools and Algorithms for the Construction and Analysis of Systems (TACAS 2025), pp. 67–87 (2025). https://doi.org/10.1007/978-3-031-90653-4_4

44. Otoni, R., Konnov, I., Kukovec, J., Eugster, P., Sharygina, N.: Symbolic model checking for TLA+ made faster. In: Proceedings of the 29th International Conference on Tools and Algorithms for the Construction and Analysis of Systems (TACAS 2023), pp. 126–144 (2023). https://doi.org/10.1007/978-3-031-30823-9_7
45. Padon, O., Hoenicke, J., Losa, G., Podelski, A., Sagiv, M., Shoham, S.: Reducing liveness to safety in first-order logic. Proc. ACM Program. Lang. **2**(POPL), 1–33 (2017). https://doi.org/10.1145/3158114
46. Pîrlea, G., Gladshtein, V., Kinsbruner, E., Zhao, Q., Sergey, I.: Veil: a framework for automated and interactive verification of transition systems. In: Proceedings of the 37th International Conference on Computer Aided Verification (CAV 2025), pp. 26–41 (2025). https://doi.org/10.1007/978-3-031-98682-6_2
47. Schultz, W., Dardik, I., Tripakis, S.: Plain and simple inductive invariant inference for distributed protocols in TLA+. In: Proceedings of the 22nd Conference on Formal Methods in Computer-Aided Design, pp. 273–283 (2022). https://doi.org/10.34727/2022/isbn.978-3-85448-053-2_34
48. Schultz, W., Demirbas, M.: Design and modular verification of distributed transactions in MongoDB. Proc. VLDB Endow. **18**(12), 5045–5058 (2025). https://doi.org/10.14778/3750601.3750626
49. Tran, T.-H., Konnov, I., Widder, J.: A case study on parametric verification of failure detectors. In: Proceedings of the 41st International Conference on Formal Techniques for Distributed Objects, Components, and Systems (FORTE 2021). LNCS, vol. 12719, pp. 138–156. Springer, Cham (2021). https://doi.org/10.1007/978-3-030-78089-0_8
50. Yao, J., Tao, R., Gu, R., Nieh, J.: DuoAI: fast, automated inference of inductive invariants for verifying distributed protocols. In: Proceedings of the 16th USENIX Symposium on Operating Systems Design and Implementation (OSDI 2022), pp. 485–501 (2022). https://www.usenix.org/conference/osdi22/presentation/yao
51. Yu, Q., Losa, G., Wang, X.: TetraBFT: reducing latency of unauthenticated, responsive BFT consensus. In: Proceedings of the 43rd ACM Symposium on Principles of Distributed Computing (PODC 2024), pp. 257–267 (2024). https://doi.org/10.1145/3662158.3662783
52. Yu, Y., Manolios, P., Lamport, L.: Model checking TLA+ specifications. In: Proceedings of the 43rd ACM Symposium on Principles of Distributed Computing (CHARME 1999). LNCS, vol. 1703, pp. 54–66. Springer, Heidelberg (1999). https://doi.org/10.1007/3-540-48153-2_6

PSF: A Generic and Extensible Framework for Protocol State Fuzzing

Konstantinos Sagonas[1,3] and Thanos Typaldos[2,3](✉)

[1] Uppsala University, Uppsala, Sweden
kostis@it.uu.se
[2] Yale University, New Haven, USA
[3] National Technical University of Athens, Athens, Greece
actypaldos@gmail.com

Abstract. In recent years, protocol state fuzzing has emerged as an effective technique to analyze and test network protocol implementations, uncovering numerous security vulnerabilities, bugs, and non-conformance issues in them. This paper presents PROTOCOLSTATE-FUZZER (PSF), an open source, generic, modular, and extensible framework for state machine learning and testing of network protocol implementations. We describe the distinctive features and support that PSF offers, its architecture and implementation, and briefly overview the protocol-specific state fuzzers that currently use PSF as their basis.

Keywords: Analysis and testing of network protocol implementations · Model learning · Model-based testing · Protocol state fuzzing

1 Introduction

Implementations of network and security protocols are core components of critical infrastructures of our society. Consequently, their correctness and robustness are of paramount importance. The specifications of such protocols (e.g., their RFCs) prescribe, usually in natural language, the interaction between the protocol peers, the format of data to be exchanged, and the actions that each peer needs to take at different protocol stages. In other words, specifications implicitly outline the underlying state machine of the protocol. On the other hand, a specific implementation realizes a variant of this implicit state machine, which needs to be as close to the protocol specification as possible. Any deviation between the two can lead to a harmless error at best, to interoperability and denial-of-service errors, or to an exploitable vulnerability in the worst case. The questions then become: "How can state machines of different implementations be obtained so that they can be verified against the specification? How can they be tested for non-conformance or for detecting deviant behaviors in them?"

E. Darulova et al. (Eds.): CAV 2026, LNCS 16682, pp. 167–180, 2026.
https://doi.org/10.1007/978-3-032-32519-8_9

One way to answer these questions is through *learning*. There exist (black-box) techniques that can automatically infer a close approximation of a given implementation's state machine, usually regarding its input/output behavior. In the formal methods community, these techniques have appeared under different names, such as the *Minimally Adequate Teacher framework* [1], *active automata learning* [27,36], *model learning* [38], and, in the context of testing network protocol implementations, *protocol state fuzzing* [9,31], which is the name we will use from now on in this paper. The output of these techniques is a state machine model that can be used to analyze the implementation's behavior and check whether it complies with its protocol specification, or, if not, detect bugs and non-conformance issues in it either by ocular model inspection [6,9,31], semi-automatically by detecting differences in the learned models [2,8,18], automatically by automata-based techniques [12,13], or by model checking [10,25].

There exist publicly available libraries that can be used for automata learning, such as LearnLib [15,20] or AALpy [24]. However, for a protocol state fuzzing tool, some additional components are needed: (1) a *learning component*, (2) a *mapping component*, and (3) a *system component*. The learning component drives the learning library by sending queries (sequences of abstract input messages) to and receiving answers (sequences of abstract output messages) from the mapping component. The mapping component translates abstract messages to/from concrete ones that are understood by the System Under Learning (SUL), which is managed by the system component. Alternatively, the learning component can be swapped out by (4) a *testing component*, while most of the remaining infrastructure can be used as is. In this way, a protocol state fuzzing tool can also be used for testing or fuzzing the System Under Testing (SUT).[1]

This paper presents ProtocolState-Fuzzer (PSF, for short): a generic, modular, and extensible framework that can be used both for learning and testing of network protocol implementations. It provides the four components mentioned above as well as the support which is needed for optimization or to address practical problems. The following sections give more details about the requirements and challenges of protocol state fuzzing (Sect. 2), present PSF's design and implementation (Sects. 3 and 4), and briefly mention protocol analysis and testing tools that are currently using it as their basis (Section 5). The paper ends with related work and some concluding remarks (Sects. 6 and 7).

2 Protocol State Fuzzing: Requirements and Challenges

The two main modes of using a protocol state fuzzing tool, and thus of PSF, are *learning* and *testing* a SUL/T. For reasons that we will explain soon, PSF also supports a third mode: *timing*. In this section, we present requirements for supporting these modes, and some challenges of practical nature that they involve. We start with a paragraph reviewing state machine model learning.

---

[1] We use SUL to refer to the protocol implementation whose state machine we learn, SUT when we test/fuzz it, and SUL/T to refer to it in general.

Model learning occurs through several cycles of *hypothesis construction* and *hypothesis validation*. Hypothesis construction builds a state machine consistent with prior exchanges; this state machine is called the *hypothesis* H. Hypothesis validation then checks if H indeed correctly describes the SUL, e.g., by doing model-based testing. If the answer is "yes", H is returned as the final state machine model. If it is "no", a counterexample C exposing the inconsistency is provided to hypothesis construction, which will then use this C to produce a refined hypothesis H'. The process continues until hypothesis validation answers "yes", meaning it could not find a counterexample in the last hypothesis within some specified limit (time, number of tests, etc.). A crucial assumption by many/most automata learning algorithms is that the SUL is *deterministic*; otherwise, the above process may not terminate or may produce inaccurate state machine models. For learning state machines of protocol implementations, we need a mediating component, called *mapper*, which translates between the input/output symbols that the learning component uses, and the concrete messages that the SUL understands. In order to produce correct messages, the mapper typically needs to maintain the state of the interaction, e.g., the encryption keys necessary to produce messages that the other peer can decrypt. The learned models depend on the symbol-to-message abstraction implemented in the mapper.

In practice, there are various technical problems that need to be addressed for learning and testing of protocol implementations to run smoothly. The SUL/T, which is viewed as a black-box, is an independent OS process that needs to be managed. This process might exhibit non-deterministic behavior, or even crash. Both of these behaviors are problematic for many learning algorithms, and thus should be detected and handled appropriately. Additionally, there are often other requirements, such as configuring the SUL/T in a certain way or collecting statistics about learning. Finally, various optimizations should be supported for the learning to be efficient. The following paragraphs describe all these in detail.

Process Management. The SUL/T process needs to be managed during the learning or testing procedure. For example, when the learner issues independent queries, it usually expects that the underlying state of the SUL/T is the same. This implies that a fresh SUL/T process needs to be created before each learning query and be destroyed afterwards. Often, starting and stopping these processes depend on how the implementation is set up. For example, sometimes the SUL/T process cannot be launched directly, but only through a launch server with specific commands. PSF supports all these cases.

Handling Non-Determinism. Sometimes, the SUL/T might (seem to) exhibit non-deterministic behaviors. Non-determinism is problematic for learning. If the implementation is deterministic, then the inconsistency often originates from the user specified response timeout, namely, how long the learning component needs to wait for an SUL/T's response. From the operating system's perspective, the protocol state fuzzing tool and the SUL/T are two independent processes that communicate with each other. However, the communication's speed can fluctuate due to various reasons such as resource contention, (local) network latency, and system load. Thus, the awaited responses might sometimes be delayed more than the wait period, and make the SUL/T appear to be non-deterministic. PSF needs to detect and handle cases when input queries lead to non-determinism. One possible mitigation is to offer support for repeating such queries multiple times (e.g., five or seven), and then use *majority voting* to return the most probable response to the learner [9,23]. As another possible mitigation, PSF also supports a *timing* mode that allows measuring the time it usually takes for the system to start, respond or execute specific input queries. This information can then be used to calibrate the values for the various timeouts.

Configuration and Diagnostics. In addition to support for logging, PSF provides hooks to configure various parameters of the learner, such as the learning duration, the maximum number of queries to be performed, etc. This requires a tracking mechanism that can enforce those limits and gracefully terminate the procedure. A similar mechanism can be used to gather runtime statistics for analysis. Some useful metrics are the time each of the phases of hypothesis construction and validation took, the number of queries each performed, the number of individual inputs sent, the intermediate counterexamples found, etc.

Optimizations. PSF comes with support for optimizations that can speed up learning. The first is a caching mechanism to store the input queries and the corresponding outputs. Assuming a deterministic SUL, the next time the same input query is requested, the cache answers immediately instead of waiting for the SUL. The cache can be used in both hypothesis construction and validation phases, as well as act as a building block for a non-determinism detector. Similarly, if the SUL crashes due to a message in the input query that the SUL does not (properly) handle, a mechanism that detects the crash and immediately returns a custom response can save a lot of learning time. Otherwise, learning has to wait for a timeout for each of the remaining messages in the input query. Finally, in the hypothesis validation phase, an important optimization is to check whether a counterexample is spurious by rerunning it if needed. A spurious counterexample is discarded so that a true counterexample can be found in the same phase, this way reducing the overall learning duration.

3 Design of ProtocolState-Fuzzer

PSF is a framework that simplifies the implementation of a protocol-specific learning and testing tool. It handles the integration of the learning, mapping, system, and testing components while also dealing with the requirements and challenges described in the previous section. Specifically, PSF provides not only ready-to-use learning and testing components, but also the necessary interfaces to implement the protocol-specific mapping and system components.

Each of PSF's three modes (learning, testing, and timing) is represented by a different mode component and uses the same abstract input and output messages. For example, testing takes one or more sequences of abstract input messages, and returns the corresponding sequences of abstract output messages or an indication that the SUT crashed. Testing also accepts a (learned) state machine model as a parameter to check whether the output sequences of the

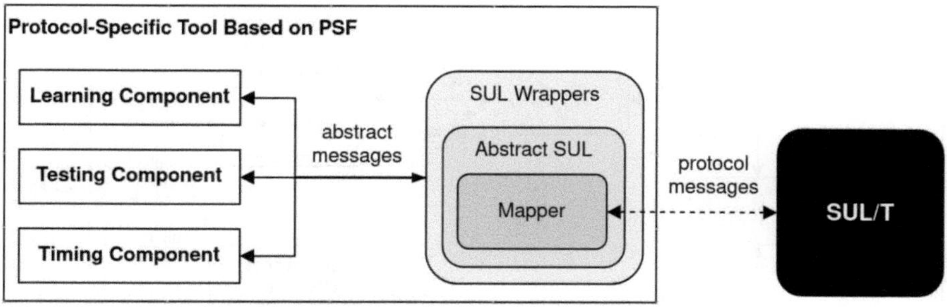

Fig. 1. The architecture of a tool for a specific network protocol based on PSF. The left part of the figure shows components corresponding to the three modes of use that PSF supports: learning, testing, and timing. The middle part shows PSF interfaces and elements that need to be implemented by the tool developer. The Mapper (orange) is protocol-specific, and is wrapped by the SUL Wrappers (yellow) and Abstract SUL (grey) of PSF's system component. The solid arrows represent same process in-memory communication, while the dashed arrow denotes inter-process network communication. (Color figure online)

model and the SUT differ. Similarly, the timing mode can be used to find the best timeout values, in a given range, that do not cause non-determinism. It can (automatically) search for the best response timeout of the SUL/T, the best startup timeout (wait time for a fresh SUL/T instance to be ready to respond), or the best additional time to wait after input messages are sent. This additional wait time is useful when specific sequences of input message (compared to the other input messages) invoke more work on the SUL/T's side and thus an extra wait is needed on top of the common response wait time.

The architecture of a protocol-specific tool based on PSF is shown in Fig. 1. The tool brings together the mode components it wants to implement, the mapping component, represented by the *Mapper*, and the system component, represented by the *Abstract SUL* wrapped in the *SUL Wrappers* that provide extra functionality. The mapping component is nested inside the system component, because both rely on the protocol to be learned/tested. PSF provides the necessary interfaces of *Abstract SUL* and *Mapper*, as well as a plethora of ready-to-use *SUL Wrappers* that help with the SUL/T communication.

Figure 2 shows the architecture of PSF's learning component. The *State Fuzzer* (blue) is responsible for coordinating learning and alternating between its two phases: *hypothesis construction* and *hypothesis validation*. The upper part, which depicts the hypothesis construction phase, contains the *Learner* (green) and its corresponding *Membership SUL Oracle* (yellow-white). The latter consists of the abstract *SUL Oracle* (white), which propagates abstract messages to the SUL through the mapping component (after the right end), and several wrapping *Helper Oracles* (yellow), which provide extra functionality. During hypothesis construction, the *Learner* performs membership queries to its *Membership SUL Oracle*, records its responses, and builds a hypothesis of the state machine

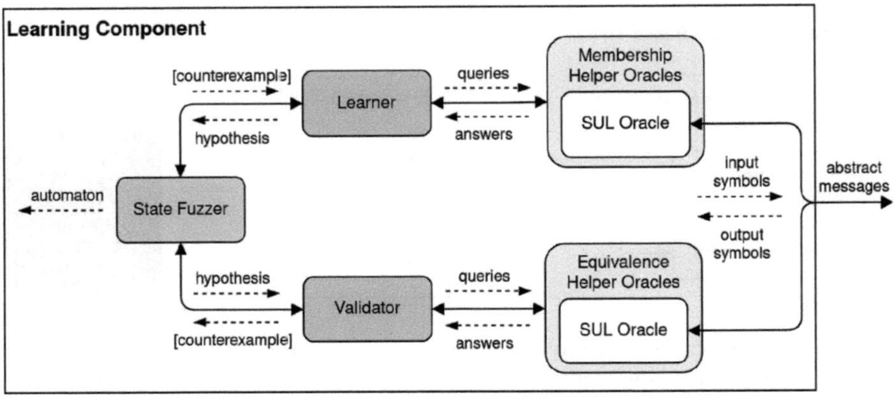

Fig. 2. The architecture of PSF's learning component with annotated data flow. The upper part represents the hypothesis construction phase, while the lower represents the hypothesis validation phase. The learning component communicates with the SUL via queries, which are sequences of input and output symbols (abstract messages). (Color figure online)

model. The lower part depicts the hypothesis validation phase. It consists of a *Validator* (red) and a corresponding *Equivalence SUL Oracle* (yellow-white). During this phase, the *Validator* uses possibly many equivalence algorithms to find a counterexample to the current hypothesis by making equivalence queries to its *Equivalence SUL Oracle*. When a counterexample C is found, the *State Fuzzer* restarts the hypothesis construction phase, and provides C to the *Learner* to refine its current hypothesis.

4 Implementation of ProtocolState-Fuzzer

In this section, we describe the most important aspects of PSF's implementation.

4.1 Learning Support

PSF is implemented in Java. For state machine learning, it currently hooks with two active automata learning (AAL) libraries. The first, LearnLib [15,20], comes with AAL algorithms that learn Finite State Machines (FSMs) models of the abstract behavior of the SUL, most notably Mealy Machines. The second library, RALib [3,7], provides algorithms for learning Register Automata (i.e. Extended FSMs), which allows learning state machine models with data parameters (e.g., sequence numbers in network packets), as opposed to input and output alphabets with plain symbols. Since PSF's learning API is already parametric on the AAL algorithm to use, using Java generics, extending the tool to support another learning library accessible from Java should not be that difficult.

All PSF modes run over abstract input and output alphabets. The input alphabet is configurable during runtime. For example, when we want some input

Table 1. Membership and equivalence algorithms available in PSF. Algorithms for learning Mealy Machines are offered by LearnLib, and for learning Register Automata by RALib. Colored in blue are custom algorithms implemented in PSF.

	Membership Algorithms	Equivalence Algorithms
Mealy Machines (FSMs)	L^* [1]	Random Walk
	TTT [19]	W Method [5]
	Rivest-Schapire [30]	WP Method [16]
	Kearns-Vazirani [21]	Random WP Method
		Sampled Tests
		WP Sampled Tests
Register Automata (EFSMs)	SL^* [3]	IO Random Walk
	SL^λ [7]	

symbols to not affect the learning procedure, these can simply be excluded from the input alphabet. In contrast, the output alphabet by default always consists of all the output symbols.

The currently supported membership and equivalence algorithms of each format are shown in Table 1; they are selectable via options. Equivalence algorithms shown in blue are custom implementations of PSF. Specifically, the Random WP Method algorithm is a variant of WP Method [16], which uses sampling, rather than enumeration, to create test queries. To accelerate the hypothesis validation phase, this algorithm comes with support for parallelization over a user-specified number of threads. The Sampled Tests algorithm allows the user to provide a list of equivalence queries that are always performed sequentially. Lastly, the WP Sampled Tests algorithm is a hybrid of the other two; it closely follows the Random WP Method, but samples from a specified list of queries a random suffix that constitutes the middle sequence of the new test query.

4.2 System Aspects

PSF tackles the practical challenges detailed in Sect. 2 using the different helper classes colored in yellow, namely the *SUL Wrappers* in Fig. 1 and the *Membership Helper Oracles* and *Equivalence Helper Oracles* in Fig. 2. All of these classes are integrated in the learning and testing procedure via implementing the necessary LearnLib interfaces. The Helper Oracles process entire sequences of inputs and outputs (sequences of abstract symbols). In contrast, the *SUL Wrappers* process only individual input and output symbols, but also expose `pre` and `post` methods to be used before and after a single query.

Process Management. PSF provides ready-to-use *SUL Wrappers* that appropriately handle the SUL/T process. The first is the `SULProcessWrapper`, which is responsible for handling the SUL/T process in one of two distinct points: either create it before and destroy it after each new query, or create it once in the beginning of the current procedure and destroy it in the end. The second wrapper is the `SULAdapterWrapper`, which can be optionally enabled when the SUL/T can only start through a launch server. The job of this wrapper is to send the necessary commands to the server in order for the SUL/T process to start or stop. Since this is protocol-specific, `SULAdapterWrapper` is based on an `SULAdapter` interface, which needs to be implemented by the tool that uses PSF.

Handling Non-Determinism. PSF handles the non-deterministic behavior of the SUL/T via two *Membership Helper Oracles*. As mentioned, these have access to the input and output queries. The first is the `MultipleRunsSULOracle`, optionally enabled, that proceeds in two phases. First, it runs every query a specified number of times and checks the outputs. If there are differing answers, this oracle optionally starts the second phase, probabilistic sanitization. This entails running the input query multiple times until an answer appears with a specified acceptable likelihood. If probabilistic sanitization is disabled or fails to find an acceptable answer, the learning stops due to detecting non-determinism, and a comprehensive error report is generated. The only problem with the `MultipleRunsSULOracle` is that it will always run the input query many times, increasing the learning duration. To overcome this, PSF also provides a `NonDeterminismRetryingSULOracle`, an extension of the previous one with an additional phase in the beginning. This phase runs the input query only once, and utilizes a shared input-output query cache to check whether the received answer differs from the cached one (if any). If they differ, it proceeds with the two phases as previously. In most cases, this oracle runs the input query once, checks the cache, and returns the cached answer immediately afterwards.

Configuration and Diagnostics. The configuration issues regarding total learning time or total number of learning queries are handled by two *SUL Wrappers* that keep track of the respective quantities. As wrappers, they handle individual input symbols, but can calculate the start and end of a new query via their `pre` and `post` methods. Similarly, diagnostics about the input queries or symbols are obtained via LearnLib's `ResetCounterSUL` and `SymbolCounterSUL`, which are incorporated as *SUL Wrappers* as well. Moreover, PSF keeps track of various other statistics regarding the learning progress, such as runtime, found counterexamples, sizes of intermediate hypotheses, etc.

Optimizations. The caching mechanism mentioned in Sect. 2 is realized in the `CachingSULOracle` that can be used either by the membership or equivalence oracles, as already mentioned in the paragraph handing non-determinism. On the other hand, PSF also supports tracking of the SUL/T's liveness status through a shared tracker. This is also used by an *SUL Wrapper* called `SULLivenessWrapper`, which answers immediately with a fixed symbol when it detects that the SUL/T process is not alive anymore. Without this immediate response, after the SUL/T has crashed, every remaining input symbol incurs a cost of at least the wait time of the response, which can be significant if the remaining symbols are many. Finally, to optimize the hypothesis validation phase, PSF provides the `CESanitizingSULOracle`, which is an extension of the

`MultipleRunsSULOracle` that tries to confirm a potential counterexample using the shared cache and rerunning it if needed.

5 Current Uses of ProtocolState-Fuzzer

The initial motivation for PSF was to facilitate the development of EDHOC-Fuzzer, an analysis and testing tool for EDHOC clients and servers. EDHOC (Ephemeral Diffie-Hellman Over COSE) is recent lightweight authenticated key exchange protocol that provides improved security with less overhead for IoT devices [35]. EDHOC-Fuzzer has been built with PSF as its basis. It has been used to analyze three different EDHOC implementations (one written in C, one in Java, and one in Rust) and has found state machine bugs in all of them [32].

The first version of PSF inherited some code from a prototype tool developed by Fiterau et al. [9] to analyze DTLS (Datagram Transfer Layer Security) servers. That prototype was later extended to also handle DTLS clients, and was released as DTLS-Fuzzer [11]. DTLS-Fuzzer has been used to analyze various different versions of the major implementations of DTLS 1.2 (GnuTLS, JSSE, MbedTLS, OpenSSL, PionDTLS, Scandium, TinyDTLS, wolfSSL, etc.), and has discovered numerous bugs and security vulnerabilities in their code bases [9,12].

Once the API of PSF became stable, DTLS-Fuzzer was adapted to use PSF as its basis, a refactoring effort that not only reduced the code size of DTLS-Fuzzer by several thousand lines of code, but also significantly eased the effort for its maintenance. Recently, DTLS-Fuzzer was extended with the ability to also analyze client and server implementations of the DTLS 1.3 protocol [4].

At the moment of this writing (January 2026), PSF's code base comprises 15 771 lines of Java code. We note that this number does not include the code sizes of LearnLib and RALib which PSF employs as libraries for active automata learning. In contrast, EDHOC-Fuzzer's code base comprises 8 596 lines of Java code, and DTLS-Fuzzer's only 3 214. Although the number of lines of code is only a rough indication of the development effort and complexity of a software tool, it should be clear that PSF allows one to offload to a library and reuse a significant portion of the code that is required to build protocol-specific analysis and testing tools. As further corroborating evidence, an M.Sc. student of our group recently built BLE-Fuzzer, an effective protocol state fuzzer for the BLE (Bluetooth Low Energy) protocol using PSF as a basis, some off-the-shelf Python libraries as a mapper, and only 475 lines of Java code [34]. Efforts to build analysis and testing tools for other network protocols (e.g., for Zigbee) using PSF as a basis are currently underway.

We refer to the publications cited in this section for more information on the quantitative aspects of tools that use PSF as a basis.

6 Related Work

Protocol state fuzzing uses model learning [27,38] to generate state machine models of network protocol implementations. In addition to DTLS and EDHOC, protocol state fuzzing has been applied to various network and IoT protocols. In the last decade, researchers have successfully used this technique to learn state machine models and test implementations of e.g., TLS [22,28,31], TCP [10], SSH [14], OpenVPN [6], MQTT [37], IPSec [17], QUIC [29], and Bluetooth devices [26], among others, and uncover a significant number of errors in them. Although all these tools are effective for their (research) purposes, a downside with them is that they are monolithic: they are protocol-specific tools that cannot be extended or reused easily for other, even similar, protocols. On the contrary, PSF is generic (i.e. protocol-agnostic) and aims to be an extensible framework that is reusable as a library.

A tool which is similar to PSF in some ways is Prognosis, a framework that offers closed-box automated learning and analysis of models of network protocol implementations [8]. Prognosis's architecture is also modular, though more involved than PSF's, requiring its users to specify more components. Prognosis also uses LearnLib for its Learner, but can learn Mealy machines using only one membership algorithm (TTT) and one equivalence algorithm (WP Method). In contrast, PSF provides a variety of membership and equivalence algorithms for Mealy Machines (cf. Table 1), including some custom ones which also come with parallelization support. Prognosis can also learn richer models that include registers (to store, e.g., packet numbers), but these richer models are derived from Mealy machines by using a *synthesis* procedure, instead of interfacing with a general library, such as RALib, and be able to use a set of algorithms that learn directly Register Automata in an efficient way. Functionality-wise, Prognosis provides learning and testing (trace running) modes for server implementations only. In contrast, PSF provides learning, testing, and timing modes for both client and server implementations of a protocol.

7 Conclusion and Future Work

This paper presented the most important aspects of the design and implementation of PSF, a generic, modular, and extensible framework that can be used as a basis for state machine learning and testing of network protocol implementations. Our experience of using PSF is that it already provides the features that are needed to overcome the most practical hurdles and build an effective protocol-specific state fuzzer tool on top of it.

Like most software libraries, PSF's functionality can be enhanced. One direction is to support additional active automata learning algorithms that exist or may become available in LearnLib, RALib, or other libraries; another is to provide support for *differential testing* of state machine models [2,18]. Currently, PSF's testing component supports (i) testing/fuzzing a SUT with a set of input queries (e.g., to find assertion violations or crash it in other ways) and (ii) testing an implementation in order to find input sequences that result in diverging outputs from a given state machine model of the system. A natural extension would be to also add the ability to take as input two (or more) state machine models of implementations of the same protocol, and produce input sequences that expose differences in their models. We are currently working towards this.

Acknowledgments. We thank Paul Fiterău for comments on a draft of this paper and for his work on DTLS-Fuzzer whose architecture and code base have provided inspiration for the first version of PSF. This research was partially funded by grant 621-2023-05363 from the Swedish Research Council (Vetenskapsrådet).

Data Availibility Statement. The latest version of the source code and additional information about PSF is at: https://github.com/protocol-fuzzing/protocol-state-fuzzer. In addition, the paper's artifact [33] can be found at: https://doi.org/10.5281/zenodo.19831626.

Disclosure of Interests. The authors have no competing interests to declare that are relevant to the content of this article.

References

1. Angluin, D.: Learning regular sets from queries and counterexamples. Inf. Comput. **75**(2), 87–106 (1987). https://doi.org/10.1016/0890-5401(87)90052-6
2. Argyros, G., Stais, I., Jana, S., Keromytis, A.D., Kiayias, A.: SFADiff: automated evasion attacks and fingerprinting using black-box differential automata learning. In: Proceedings of the 2016 ACM SIGSAC Conference on Computer and Communications Security, pp. 1690–1701. ACM (2016). https://doi.org/10.1145/2976749.2978383
3. Cassel, S., Howar, F., Jonsson, B., Steffen, B.: Learning extended finite state machines. In: Giannakopoulou, D., Salaün, G. (eds.) SEFM 2014. LNCS, vol. 8702, pp. 250–264. Springer, Cham (2014). https://doi.org/10.1007/978-3-319-10431-7_18
4. Chen, N., Fiterău-Broştean, P., Sagonas, K.: State fuzzing DTLS 1.3 implementations. In: 2025 IEEE Conference on Standards for Communications and Networking, pp. 426–432. CSCN 2025, IEEE (2025). https://doi.org/10.1109/CSCN67557.2025.11230763
5. Chow, T.S.: Testing software design modeled by finite-state machines. IEEE Trans. Softw. Eng. **SE-4**(3), 178–187 (1978). https://doi.org/10.1109/TSE.1978.231496
6. Daniel, L.A., Poll, E., de Ruiter, J.: Inferring OpenVPN state machines using protocol state fuzzing. In: IEEE European Symposium on Security and Privacy (EuroS&P) Workshops, pp. 11–19. IEEE (2018). https://doi.org/10.1109/EuroSPW.2018.00009
7. Dierl, S., Fiterau-Brostean, P., Howar, F., Jonsson, B., Sagonas, K., Tåquist, F.: Scalable tree-based register automata learning. In: Finkbeiner, B., Kovács, L. (eds.) Tools and Algorithms for the Construction and Analysis of Systems. LNCS, vol. 14571, pp. 87–108. Springer, Cham (2024). https://doi.org/10.1007/978-3-031-57249-4_5
8. Ferreira, T., Brewton, H., D'Antoni, L., Silva, A.: Prognosis: closed-box analysis of network protocol implementations. In: Proceedings of the ACM SIGCOMM 2021 Conference, pp. 762–774. SIGCOMM '21, ACM, New York, NY, USA (2021). https://doi.org/10.1145/3452296.3472938
9. Fiterau-Brostean, P., Jonsson, B., Merget, R., de Ruiter, J., Sagonas, K., Somorovsky, J.: Analysis of DTLS implementations using protocol state fuzzing. In: 29th USENIX Security Symposium, pp. 2523–2540. USENIX Security 20, USENIX Association (2020). https://www.usenix.org/conference/usenixsecurity20/presentation/fiterau-brostean

10. Fiterău-Broştean, P., Janssen, R., Vaandrager, F.: Combining model learning and model checking to analyze TCP implementations. In: Chaudhuri, S., Farzan, A. (eds.) CAV 2016. LNCS, vol. 9780, pp. 454–471. Springer, Cham (2016). https://doi.org/10.1007/978-3-319-41540-6_25
11. Fiterău-Broştean, P., Jonsson, B., Sagonas, K., Tåquist, F.: DTLS-Fuzzer: a DTLS protocol state fuzzer. In: 15th IEEE Conference on Software Testing, Verification and Validation, pp. 456–458. ICST 2022, IEEE (2022). DOIurl-https://doi.org/10.1109/ICST53961.2022.00051
12. Fiterău-Broştean, P., Jonsson, B., Sagonas, K., Tåquist, F.: Automata-based automated detection of state machine bugs in protocol implementations. In: 30th Annual Network and Distributed System Security Symposium. NDSS 2023, The Internet Society (2023). https://doi.org/10.14722/ndss.2023.23068
13. Fiterău-Broştean, P., Jonsson, B., Sagonas, K., Tåquist, F.: SMBugFinder: an automated framework for testing protocol implementations for state machine bugs. In: Proceedings of the 33rd ACM SIGSOFT International Symposium on Software Testing and Analysis, pp. 1866–1870. ISSTA 2024, ACM, New York, NY, USA (2024). https://doi.org/10.1145/3650212.3685310
14. Fiterău-Broştean, P., Lenaerts, T., de Ruiter, J., Poll, E., Vaandrager, F.W., Verleg, P.: Model learning and model checking of SSH implementations. In: Proceedings of the 24th ACM SIGSOFT International SPIN Symposium on Model Checking of Software, pp. 142–151. SPIN 2017, ACM, New York, NY, USA (2017). https://doi.org/10.1145/3092282.3092289
15. Frohme, M., Howar, F., Steffen, B.: LearnLib: 10 years later. In: Piskac, R., Rakamarić, Z. (eds.) Computer Aided Verification - 37th International Conference, CAV 2025. LNCS, vol. 15934, pp. 141–160. Springer, Cham (2025). https://doi.org/10.1007/978-3-031-98685-7_7
16. Fujiwara, S., von Bochmann, G., Khendek, F., Amalou, M., Ghedamsi, A.: Test selection based on finite state models. IEEE Trans. Softw. Eng. **17**(6), 591–603 (1991). https://doi.org/10.1109/32.87284
17. Guo, J., Gu, C., Chen, X., Wei, F.: Model learning and model checking of IPSec implementations for Internet of Things. IEEE Access **7**, 171322–171332 (2019). https://doi.org/10.1109/ACCESS.2019.2956062
18. Hussain, S.R., Karim, I., Ishtiaq, A.A., Chowdhury, O., Bertino, E.: Noncompliance as deviant behavior: an automated black-box noncompliance checker for 4G LTE cellular devices. In: Kim, Y., Kim, J., Vigna, G., Shi, E. (eds.) Proceedings of the 2021 ACM SIGSAC Conference on Computer and Communications Security. CCS 2021, pp. 1082–1099. ACM (2021). https://doi.org/10.1145/3460120.3485388
19. Isberner, M., Howar, F., Steffen, B.: The TTT algorithm: a redundancy-free approach to active automata learning. In: Bonakdarpour, B., Smolka, S.A. (eds.) RV 2014. LNCS, vol. 8734, pp. 307–322. Springer, Cham (2014). https://doi.org/10.1007/978-3-319-11164-3_26
20. Isberner, M., Howar, F., Steffen, B.: The open-source LearnLib. In: Kroening, D., Păsăreanu, C.S. (eds.) CAV 2015. LNCS, vol. 9206, pp. 487–495. Springer, Cham (2015). https://doi.org/10.1007/978-3-319-21690-4_32
21. Kearns, M.J., Vazirani, U.: An Introduction to Computational Learning Theory. The MIT Press (1994). https://doi.org/10.7551/mitpress/3897.001.0001
22. Maehren, M., Erinola, N., Merget, R., Schwenk, J., Somorovsky, J.: Towards internet-based state learning of TLS state machines. In: 34th USENIX Security Symposium. pp. 7097–7116. USENIX Security 25, Seattle, WA (2025). https://www.usenix.org/conference/usenixsecurity25/presentation/maehren

23. Moon, S.J., et al.: Alembic: automated model inference for stateful network functions. In: 16th USENIX Symposium on Networked Systems Design and Implementation (NSDI 19), pp. 699–718. USENIX Association (2019). https://www.usenix.org/conference/nsdi19/presentation/moon
24. Muškardin, E., Aichernig, B.K., Pill, I., Pferscher, A., Tappler, M.: AALpy: an active automata learning library. In: Hou, Z., Ganesh, V. (eds.) ATVA 2021. LNCS, vol. 12971, pp. 67–73. Springer, Cham (2021). https://doi.org/10.1007/978-3-030-88885-5_5
25. Peled, D.A., Vardi, M.Y., Yannakakis, M.: Black box checking. J. Autom. Lang. Comb. 7(2), 225–246 (2002). https://doi.org/10.25596/jalc-2002-225
26. Pferscher, A., Aichernig, B.K.: Fingerprinting and analysis of Bluetooth devices with automata learning. Formal Methods Syst. Des. **61**(1), 35–62 (2022). https://doi.org/10.1007/S10703-023-00425-Y
27. Raffelt, H., Merten, M., Steffen, B., Margaria, T.: Dynamic testing via automata learning. Int. J. Softw. Tools Technol. Transf. **11**(4), 307–324 (2009). https://doi.org/10.1007/s10009-009-0120-7
28. Rasoamanana, A.T., Levillain, O., Debar, H.: Towards a systematic and automatic use of state machine inference to uncover security flaws and fingerprint TLS stacks. In: 27th European Symposium on Research in Computer Security (ESORICS). LNCS, vol. 13556, pp. 637–657. Springer, Cham (2022). https://doi.org/10.1007/978-3-031-17143-7_31
29. Rasool, A., Alpár, G., de Ruiter, J.: State machine inference of quic (2019). https://doi.org/10.48550/arXiv.1903.04384
30. Rivest, R.L., Schapire, R.E.: Inference of finite automata using homing sequences. Inf. Comput. **103**(2), 299–347 (1993). https://doi.org/10.1006/inco.1993.1021
31. de Ruiter, J., Poll, E.: Protocol state fuzzing of TLS implementations. In: 24th USENIX Security Symposium, pp. 193–206. USENIX Security 15, USENIX Association, Washington, D.C. (2015). https://www.usenix.org/conference/usenixsecurity15/technical-sessions/presentation/de-ruiter
32. Sagonas, K., Typaldos, T.: EDHOC-Fuzzer: an EDHOC protocol state fuzzer. In: Proceedings of the 32nd ACM SIGSOFT International Symposium on Software Testing and Analysis, pp. 1495–1498. ISSTA 2023, ACM, New York, NY, USA (2023). https://doi.org/10.1145/3597926.3604922
33. Sagonas, K., Typaldos, T.: Artifact for CAV'2026 tool paper "PSF: a generic and extensible framework for protocol state fuzzing" (2026). https://doi.org/10.5281/zenodo.19831626
34. Schnor, H.: Using Protocol State Fuzzing to Test Bluetooth Low Energy Implementations. Master's thesis, Department of Information Technology, Uppsala University, Sweden (2025). https://urn.kb.se/resolve?urn=urn:nbn:se:uu:diva-565565
35. Selander, G., Mattsson, J.P., Palombini, F.: Ephemeral Diffie-Hellman over COSE (EDHOC). RFC 9528 (2024). https://doi.org/10.17487/RFC9528, https://www.rfc-editor.org/info/rfc9528
36. Steffen, B., Howar, F., Merten, M.: Introduction to active automata learning from a practical perspective. In: Bernardo, M., Issarny, V. (eds.) SFM 2011. LNCS, vol. 6659, pp. 256–296. Springer, Heidelberg (2011). https://doi.org/10.1007/978-3-642-21455-4_8
37. Tappler, M., Aichernig, B.K., Bloem, R.: Model-based testing IoT communication via active automata learning. In: IEEE International Conference on Software Testing, Verification and Validation, pp. 276–287. ICST 2017, IEEE (2017). https://doi.org/10.1109/ICST.2017.32

38. Vaandrager, F.: Model learning. Commun. ACM **60**(2), 86–95 (2017). https://doi.org/10.1145/2967606

Kofola 1.0: A Modular Approach to ω-Regular Complementation and Inclusion Checking

Ondrej Alexaj[1(✉)], Vojtěch Havlena[1(✉)], Lukáš Holík[1,2(✉)], Ondřej Lengál[1(✉)], Yong Li[3(✉)], and Nicolas Mazzocchi[4(✉)]

[1] Brno University of Technology, Brno, Czech Republic
xalexa09@stud.fit.vut.cz, {ihavlena,holik,lengal}@fit.vut.cz
[2] Aalborg University, Aalborg, Denmark
[3] Key Laboratory of System Software (Chinese Academy of Sciences), ISCAS, Beijing, People's Republic of China
liyong@ios.ac.cn
[4] Slovak University of Technology in Bratislava, Bratislava, Slovakia
nicolas.mazzocchi@stuba.sk

Abstract. We present KOFOLA, an efficient tool for complementation and inclusion checking of Büchi automata, two central tasks in automata-theoretic verification with applications in model checking, monitoring, and theorem proving. KOFOLA implements a state-of-the-art modular complementation framework that decomposes the input automaton into strongly connected components and applies to each component a complementation algorithm tailored to its structural properties. Building on this modular construction, KOFOLA also provides modular *inclusion checking* with new heuristics. A key ingredient is a new on-the-fly emptiness-checking algorithm for the simple generalized Rabin pair condition produced by our complementation, allowing the search to terminate as soon as the explored state space suffices. Empirical evaluation shows that KOFOLA is highly competitive with state-of-the-art complementation and inclusion-checking tools: it is the most robust tool in our evaluation and often outperforms competitors by several orders of magnitude on benchmarks from practical applications.

1 Introduction

Language inclusion checking for Büchi automata (BAs) is a cornerstone problem in automata-theoretic verification, with applications to model checking [51], monitoring [19], and theorem proving [31,42]. The problem is PSPACE-complete [35], but it remains one of the most computationally demanding tasks in verification practice. As systems and specifications continue to grow in size and complexity, the scalability of inclusion checking has become a decisive factor in the practicality of automata-based reasoning frameworks. For two ω-regular languages L_1 and L_2, deciding whether $L_1 \subseteq L_2$ reduces to checking the emptiness of $L_1 \cap \overline{L_2}$, where $\overline{L_2}$ denotes the complement of L_2. This exposes two key challenges:

E. Darulova et al. (Eds.): CAV 2026, LNCS 16682, pp. 181–197, 2026.
https://doi.org/10.1007/978-3-032-32519-8_10

(i) constructing $\overline{L_2}$ compactly, and (ii) efficiently exploring the (often enormous) state space of the product automaton for $L_1 \cap \overline{L_2}$. Addressing either of these challenges translates into performance improvements in the considered domains.

Existing tools primarily tackle these challenges by improving either the complementation of L_2 or the exploration for the product automaton. For example, tools such as BAIT [21], FORKLIFT [20], and RABIT [3,4] use Ramsey-based complementation [13,48], while improving efficiency through state-space reduction techniques—such as subsumption and simulation in RABIT or well-quasiorders in BAIT and FORKLIFT. In contrast, SPOT [22] relies on determinization-based complementation [43–45], enhanced by lightweight simulation and specialized emptiness checking procedures for EmersonLei acceptance conditions [9]. We observe that state-of-the-art inclusion checkers still largely rely on classical Ramsey- or determinization-based complementation constructions, which date back more than three decades [13,45], despite substantial recent progress in Büchi complementation. This motivates an efficient and extensible framework that brings modern complementation techniques to practical inclusion checking.

Contributions. We present KOFOLA [2], an efficient and modular tool for BA complementation and language inclusion checking, which is based on a recent decomposition-based complementation algorithm [26]. For an inclusion query $\mathcal{L}(\mathcal{A}_1) \subseteq \mathcal{L}(\mathcal{A}_2)$, KOFOLA performs a fine-grained structural analysis of the complemented automaton, namely $\mathcal{A}_2$, by classifying its maximal strongly connected components (SCCs) as: (i) non-accepting components; (ii) inherently weak accepting components (IWACs), in which all cycles accept; (iii) initial almost deterministic accepting components (IADACs) and deterministic accepting components (DACs), which have only deterministic transitions (a IADAC is a deterministic SCC reachable from initial states through deterministic SCCs only, allowing nondeterminism just on cycle-free parts between SCCs); and (iv) the remaining accepting SCCs, classified as nondeterministic accepting components (NACs). Notably, IADACs are a *newly identified component type* introduced in this paper. For each component type, KOFOLA exploits its structural properties by applying a dedicated complementation algorithm, combining the component constructions in a synchronous manner.

For inclusion checking, KOFOLA constructs an ω-automaton with a single generalized Rabin pair acceptance condition, $\mathit{Fin}(⓿) \wedge \mathit{Inf}(❶) \wedge \cdots \wedge \mathit{Inf}(\text{k-1})$, and performs *on-the-fly* emptiness checking during the modular construction. This avoids explicitly generating the full product automaton. Although SPOT can also check emptiness for generalized Rabin conditions [9], it requires the whole automaton to be constructed explicitly. To mitigate state-space explosion, KOFOLA implements a new emptiness-checking algorithm for the single generalized Rabin pair condition. The algorithm can be viewed as a variant of Couvreur's algorithm [18] extended with a *Fin* predicate. It is maximally lazy: the search terminates as soon as the explored states suffice to decide the result, helping to keep the generated part of the complement small, which is crucial since complementation is the main source of blow-up in inclusion checking.

We evaluated KOFOLA on complementation benchmarks drawn from diverse literature sources, comparing it with state-of-the-art tools SPOT, RANKER [29], and an initial implementation of decomposition-based complementation [26]. KOFOLA outperforms all competitors both in the number of solved instances and in the size of the resulting complement automata. We further evaluated KOFOLA on BA inclusion benchmarks arising from program termination checking, verification of concurrent systems, model checking of hyperproperties, and theorem proving. The results show that KOFOLA outperforms the state-of-the-art inclusion checkers BAIT, FORKLIFT, RABIT, and SPOT, in many cases by several orders of magnitude, and KOFOLA solves the most instances. These results establish KOFOLA as an efficient, extensible, and highly competitive tool for BA complementation and inclusion checking. More details are given in [6].

Related Work. BA complementation algorithms can be broadly grouped into several families. *Ramsey-based* [12,13,37,48], *rank-based* [15,25,28–30,33,36,46], and *slice-based* [7,32,50] procedures encode information about word acceptance using different data structures. *Determinization-based* constructions first determinize the automaton and then complement its acceptance condition, typically producing automata with acceptance conditions that are more complex than Büchi [38,40,43–45]. *Learning-based* approaches [39] infer a BA for the complement through membership queries. More recent *decomposition-based* constructions [26,38] partition the automaton according to structural properties and apply specialized complementation procedures to each block. KOFOLA builds on this decomposition-based approach, introduces the new IADAC component type, and, as our experiments show, improves over previous implementations [26,38] as well as rank- and determinization-based tools such as RANKER and SPOT.

Several works also optimize BA language-inclusion testing, mostly within Ramsey-based frameworks. RABIT [3,4] uses simulation and subsumption, both within and across automata, to prune the searched state space. Well-quasiorder-based approaches [20,21] are more symbolic: to decide $\mathcal{L}(\mathcal{A}_1) \subseteq \mathcal{L}(\mathcal{A}_2)$, they perform a breadth-first fixpoint search over ultimately periodic words of $\mathcal{L}(\mathcal{A}_1)$, using a well-quasiorder to discard words subsumed by already processed ones.

2 Tool Architecture

KOFOLA is implemented in C++ and available at [2] under the GNU GPL 3.0 license. Its architecture is shown in Fig. 1. The *Frontend* uses SPOT [22] to read input automata $\mathcal{A}_1$`.hoa` and, for inclusion checking only, $\mathcal{A}_2$`.hoa`, both in the `HOA` [8] format. Next, the automata enter *Preprocessing and setup*, where (i) SPOT reduces them using either `Low` or `High` reduction level, depending on their features and (ii) KOFOLA then analyzes their structure and chooses partial complementation algorithms to be used. Then, the automaton/automata are passed to top-level pro-

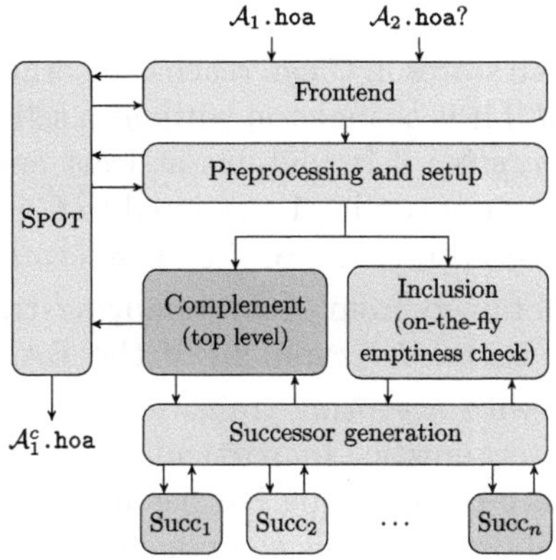

Fig. 1. Architecture of KOFOLA

cedures for *Complement* (see Sect. 4.1) or *Inclusion*, which orchestrate the chosen partial complementation algorithms (see Sect. 4.2); for inclusion checking, this includes a top-level on-the-fly emptiness checking algorithm (see Sect. 5). The main workhorse of the procedures is *Successor generation* used in generating reachable states of the complement automaton, which calls the successor functions $Succ_1, \ldots, Succ_n$ of the partial complementation algorithm and combines results. For complementation, the resulting automaton is postprocessed by SPOT(reduction level `Low`) and output as $\mathcal{A}_1^c$`.hoa`.

3 Preliminaries

We assume familiarity with standard notions on ω-automata; see, e.g., [24]. We only introduce definitions specific to this paper. Fix a finite non-empty alphabet Σ, and let ω be the first infinite ordinal. An (infinite) word is a sequence $w = w_0 w_1 \ldots$ over Σ; the set of all infinite words over Σ is denoted by Σ^ω.

A (nondeterministic transition-based) *simple generalized Rabin automaton* (SGRA) over Σ is a quintuple $\mathcal{A} = (Q, \delta, I, \Gamma, \mathsf{p})$ where Q is a finite set of *states*, $\delta \subseteq Q \times \Sigma \times Q$ is a set of *transitions* (denoted as $q \xrightarrow{a} r$), $I \subseteq Q$ is the set of *initial* states, $\Gamma = \{⓿, \ldots, \boxed{k\text{-}1}\}$ is a set of k *colours*, and $\mathsf{p}\colon \delta \to 2^\Gamma$ is a colouring function on transitions. For a set of states $C \subseteq Q$, we write $\delta|_C$ to denote the set of transitions $\{q \xrightarrow{a} r \in \delta \mid q, r \in C\}$. We call $\mathcal{A}$ *deterministic* if $|I| = 1$ and for every $a \in \Sigma$ and $q \in Q$ it holds that $|\{p \mid\in (q, a, p) \in \delta\}| \leq 1$. When ⓿ has no occurrence in p, $\mathcal{A}$ is a *generalized Büchi automaton* (GBA). When a GBA has $\Gamma = \{⓿, ❶\}$, it is a *Büchi automaton* (BA). We denote a BA as $\mathcal{A} = (Q, \delta, I, \delta_{Acc})$ where $\delta_{Acc} = \{\tau \in \delta \mid \mathsf{p}(\tau) = \{❶\}\}$. A *run* of $\mathcal{A}$ from $q \in Q$ on $w \in \Sigma^\omega$ is an infinite sequence $\rho\colon \omega \to Q$ that $\rho_0 = q$ and $\rho_i \xrightarrow{w_i} \rho_{i+1} \in \delta$ for all $i \geq 0$. Let $\mathit{inf}(\rho)$ denote the transitions occurring in ρ infinitely often. The run ρ is called *accepting* iff $\bigcup\{\mathsf{p}(\tau) \mid \tau \in \mathit{inf}(\rho)\} = \Gamma \setminus \{⓿\}$. Equivalently, in the Emerson–Lei formalism [8,23], SGRAs have acceptance condition $\mathit{Fin}(⓿) \wedge \mathit{Inf}(❶) \wedge \ldots \wedge \mathit{Inf}(\boxed{k\text{-}1})$. A word w is accepted by $\mathcal{A}$ from a state q if there exists an accepting run of $\mathcal{A}$ from q on w. We write $\mathcal{L}(\mathcal{A})$ for the language accepted from the initial states I. A state q is *useless* if no word is accepted from q.

For a BA $\mathcal{A}$, a non-empty set $C \subseteq Q$ is a *strongly connected component* (SCC) if all states in C can reach each other and C is a maximal such set. An SCC is *trivial* if it is a singleton without a self-loop, and *non-trivial* otherwise. An SCC C is *accepting* if it contains at least one ❶-transition and *inherently weak* iff either (i) every run in $\mathcal{A}$ restricted to C is accepting, or (ii) no run in $\mathcal{A}$ restricted to C is accepting. An SCC C is *deterministic* iff the BA $(C, \delta|_C, \{q\}, \emptyset)$ for any $q \in C$ (obtained from $\mathcal{A}$ by removing transitions outside C) is deterministic, and it is *initial deterministic* if the BA obtained from the BA $(Q, \delta, I, \delta_{Acc}|_C)$ (i.e., $\mathcal{A}$ with accepting transitions outside C removed) by removing useless states is deterministic. In particular, a non-accepting SCC is not initial deterministic since the resulting BA has no initial states. We also generalize the notion of initial deterministic components to *initial almost deterministic components*, which are components C such that in the BA obtained from the BA $(Q, \delta, I, \delta_{Acc}|_C)$

by removing useless states, it holds that for any two transitions from the same state over the same symbol $q \xrightarrow{a} p$ and $q \xrightarrow{a} r$, either $p = r$ or the states p and r are not in the same SCC as the state q. Hence, such components are reachable from initial states on a path going through deterministic components with nondeterminism allowed only outside non-trivial SCCs. We use the following categorization of accepting SCCs of a BA: (i) **IADACs** are initial almost deterministic accepting SCCs, (ii) **IWACs** are inherently weak accepting SCCs that are not IADACs, (iii) **DACs** are deterministic accepting SCCs not covered by the above, and (iv) **NACs** are the remaining (nondeterministic) accepting SCCs. A BA $\mathcal{A}$ is called an *elevator automaton* [30] if it contains no NAC. We assume that for all transitions $\tau = q \xrightarrow{a} r \in \delta$ not within a single SCC, we have $\mathsf{p}(\tau) = \emptyset$ (this is without loss of generality since no run can loop over such transitions). A *partition block* $P \subseteq Q$ of $\mathcal{A}$ is a nonempty union of $\mathcal{A}$'s accepting SCCs, and a *partitioning* of $\mathcal{A}$ is a sequence $P_1, \ldots, P_n$ of pairwise disjoint partition blocks of $\mathcal{A}$ that contains all accepting SCCs of $\mathcal{A}$.

4 Decomposition-Based Büchi Complementation

We fix a BA $\mathcal{A} = (Q, \delta, I, \delta_{Acc})$ for the rest of this section. We first give a brief overview of the complementation framework proposed in [26] and then present our choices of partial complementation algorithms for each type of partition blocks. We also extend the framework of [26] with a new partial complementation algorithm for IADACs.

4.1 Top-Level Modular Complementation Algorithm

Inspired by [38], a modular methodology was proposed in [26] for complementing BAs. In a nutshell, the modular complementation algorithm developed in [26] first classifies the SCCs in $\mathcal{A}$ into several partition blocks according to their structural properties, then performs complementation for each of the partition blocks independently, while synchronizing the complementation algorithms for all partition blocks in each step. The intuition for complementing SCCs separately is that every run of $\mathcal{A}$ eventually gets trapped in one SCC, so we only need to consider the runs staying in the given SCC. For those runs that exit the given SCC at some point, we handle them as discontinued runs since they must eventually stay in another SCC. The complement automaton $\mathcal{A}^c$ accepts a word over which all runs of $\mathcal{A}$ are rejecting, so we only need to make sure that all runs in *accepting* SCCs over the word do not visit accepting transitions infinitely often. That is, we check only the runs in IADACs, IWACs, DACs, and NACs. Runs in rejecting SCCs do not require checking acceptance, so we just track them using traditional subset construction. We choose to decompose $\mathcal{A}$ into partition blocks where one partition block contains all IADACs, one contains all IWACs, one contains all DACs, and each NAC has a separate partition block. However, thanks to the modularity of the complementation framework, we can decompose $\mathcal{A}$ in other ways and even use different partial complementation algorithms for partition blocks of the same type. The modular complementation algorithm uses a partial algorithm $\texttt{Alg}^P$ for each partition block P. Each partial algorithm $\texttt{Alg}^P$ specifies the following: (i) the type of macrostates produced by the algorithm, (ii) the set of initial macrostates, (iii) a function $\texttt{Succ}$ returning the successors of a macrostate, possibly together with a transition color, and (iv) the acceptance condition for the partial algorithm.

The input of the top-level algorithm are, except the automaton itself, also partitions $P_1, \ldots, P_k$ of the input automaton and the partial algorithms $\texttt{Alg}^{P_1}, \ldots, \texttt{Alg}^{P_k}$. The macrostates of the top-level algoritm are then of the form $(S, M_1, \ldots, M_k)$, where S is the set of reachable states and $M_1, \ldots, M_k$ are macrostates of the partial algorithms. The successors of a macrostate are built from the results of partial algorithms' successor functions (and colors from partial successor functions are gathered on the transition) as shown in Fig. 2. The acceptance condition of $\mathcal{A}^c$ is given as a conjunction of acceptance conditions of the partial algorithms.

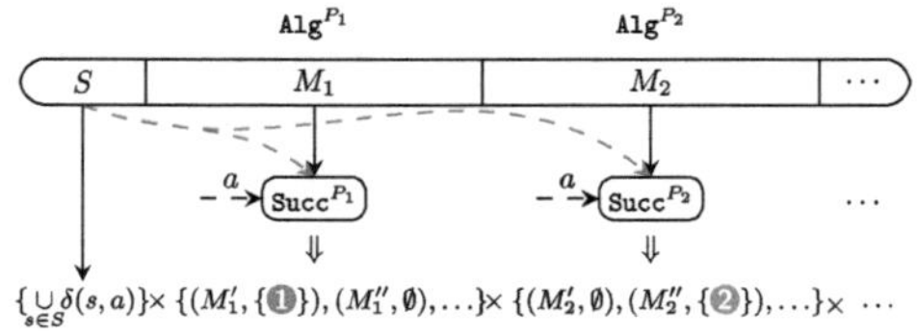

Fig. 2. Visualization of macrostate's successor computation over symbol a.

4.2 Partial Complementation Algorithms

Next, we briefly describe partial algorithms to complement partition blocks with IWACs, DACs, and NACs. Details and formal definitions can be found in [26]. Finally, we also present a new partial complementation algorithm for partition blocks with IADACs only. The sole source of the *Fin*(⓿) acceptance condition comes from IADACs, making the resulting automaton an SGRA.

IWACs. The algorithm for the partition block $\mathcal{W}$ that contains all IWACs exploits the classical *Miyano-Hayashi* construction [41], generating the acceptance condition *Inf*(❶).

DACs. For the partition block with DACs, we use a modification of the NCSB algorithm [11,16,29], which generates the acceptance condition *Inf*(❷).

NACs. For partition blocks containing a NAC $\mathcal{N}$, KOFOLA supports two algorithms: (i) determinization-based (based on the Safra-Piterman's [43,45] algorithm, specifically its version from [38]), which translates $\mathcal{N}$ into a deterministic parity automaton, and (ii) a slice-based approach from [7] (this approach generates for a given NAC the acceptance condition *Inf*(ⓚ) with $k > 2$; we note that ⓿, ❶, and ❷ are reserved for the procedures for IADACs, IWACs, and DACs respectively). Each of the algorithms is used in a different setting. The determinization-based algorithm is used in *complementation*, since it usually produces smaller results. On the other hand, the slice-based algorithm is used in *inclusion checking*, since it is more suitable for on-the-fly product emptiness test.

IADACs. Let us now generalize the partial algorithm for complementing initial deterministic components (IDCs) from [26] to IADACs. We show the construction on a BA consisting of IADACs only. Putting the construction into the formal framework of [26] is straightforward. Given a BA $\mathcal{A} = (Q, \delta, I, \delta_{Acc})$ consisting of IADACs only, the complement SGRA with the acceptance condition $Fin(⓿)$ is given as $\mathcal{B} = (2^Q, \Delta, \{I\}, \{⓿\}, \mathsf{p})$ where $\Delta = \{R \xrightarrow{a} S \mid \bigcup_{r \in R} \delta(r, a) = S\}$ and for a transition $t = R \xrightarrow{a} S$ the coloring function p is given as $\mathsf{p}(t) = \{⓿\}$ if $\bigcup_{r \in R} \delta_{Acc}(r, a) \neq \emptyset$ otherwise $\mathsf{p}(t) = \emptyset$.

Intuitively, the algorithm determinizes the IADACs using a subset construction and emits a rejecting (due to the *Fin* condition) mark ⓿ whenever some tracked run sees an accepting transition. The key argument for correctness is that the number of runs in IADACs is bounded (the directed acyclic graph representing the run—called the *run DAG*—has a finite number of branches), due to IADACs having non-deterministic branching only outside of (non-trivial) SCCs. (On the other hand, observe that a DAC having non-deterministic branching between another DAC and itself would generate unboundedly many runs.)

Theorem 1. $\mathcal{L}(\mathcal{A}) = \Sigma^\omega \setminus \mathcal{L}(\mathcal{B})$.

Proof (Sketch). Since all IADAC runs are deterministic, deciding whether w is accepted amounts to checking whether the runs on w visit δ_{Acc}-transitions only finitely often. By construction, w is not accepted in the IADAC iff every run of $\mathcal{A}$ over w emits only finitely many ⓿'s; equivalently, the corresponding run in $\mathcal{B}$ emits ⓿ only finitely often, as captured by the acceptance condition $Fin(⓿)$. □

5 Efficient Büchi Inclusion Checking

On the top level, our algorithm for testing the inclusion $\mathcal{L}(\mathcal{A}_1) \subseteq \mathcal{L}(\mathcal{A}_2)$ for BAs $\mathcal{A}_1$ and $\mathcal{A}_2$ checks emptiness of the SGRA $\mathcal{A}$ constructed as the intersection of $\mathcal{A}_1$ and the SGRA $\mathcal{A}_2^\complement$ for the complement of $\mathcal{A}_2$. Note that $\mathcal{A}$ can be explored by performing the product construction of $\mathcal{A}_1$ with $\mathcal{A}_2^\complement$ on the fly, extending the colours of $\mathcal{A}_2^\complement$ with one more colour that represents the acceptance of $\mathcal{A}_1$. Since the biggest asymptotic state space explosion comes from generating the complement $\mathcal{A}_2^\complement$, our goal is to have an emptiness checking algorithm that is maximally lazy in the sense that it stops generating new states of $\mathcal{A}_2^\complement$ as soon as the already generated states are sufficient for establishing the emptiness of $\mathcal{A}$. This precludes the use of algorithms such as [9], which require the whole automaton to identify its SCCs. To achieve this goal, below, we describe a new language emptiness algorithm for SGRAs that satisfies the laziness condition.

Algorithm 1 performs on-the-fly emptiness test for SGRAs. It uses the notation $\texttt{src}(t)/\texttt{tgt}(t)$ for the source/target state of a transition t, respectively, $\texttt{outgoing}(q)$ to denote the outgoing transitions of a state q, and lifts the colouring function p to sets in the usual manner. The algorithm is an augmentation of the on-the-fly emptiness check for GBAs by Couvreur [18], which may also be

Algorithm 1: On-the-fly emptiness test for SGRAs

Input: an SGRA $\mathcal{A} = (Q, \delta, I, \Gamma = \{$⓿, ❶, …, [k-1]$\}, \mathtt{p})$
Output: *true* iff $\mathcal{L}(\mathcal{A}) = \emptyset$, *false* otherwise
Data: sets of transitions *Entry*, *Explored*, a stack S of sets of transitions

1 $\mathit{Entry} \leftarrow$ `outgoing`(I); $\mathit{Explored} \leftarrow \emptyset$; $S \leftarrow ()$;
2 **while** $\exists t \in \mathit{Entry} \setminus \mathit{Explored}$ **do** `Explore`(t) ;
3 **return** *true*;

4 **Procedure** `Explore`(t):
5     $\mathit{Explored} \leftarrow \mathit{Explored} \cup \{t\}$;
6   **if** ⓿ $\in \mathtt{p}(t)$ **then** $\mathit{Entry} \leftarrow \mathit{Entry} \cup \{$`outgoing(tgt(`$t$`))`$\}$;
7   **else**
8   S.`push`$(\{t\})$;
9   Merge the stack S from the lowest occurrence of `tgt`(t) up to top;
10   **if** $\{$❶, …, [k-1]$\} \subseteq \mathtt{p}(S.\mathtt{top})$ **then exit program and return** *false* ;
11   **while** $\exists t' \in$ `outgoing(tgt(`S`.top))`$\setminus \mathit{Explored}$ **do** `Explore`(t') ;
12   S.`pop`();

seen as a variation of Tarjan's algorithm [49] for exploring SCCs. To avoid technicalities, Algorithm 1 is based on its high-level presentation. We emphasize that although this algorithm does not immediately resemble Tarjan's algorithm, the merged sets of transitions might efficiently be implemented similarly as Tarjan's SCCs, using a technique resembling Tarjan's stack with its low-links.

The algorithm explores the automaton in a depth-first manner from I. The stack S stores the currently explored path. When a back-edge transition t (a transition to a state already on the stack) is detected, the top part of the stack from the element including the target of t is merged and the united set of transitions is placed on the top of the stack. The set represents a (non-maximal) SCC. The stack thus becomes a sequence of sets of transitions. Line 9 specifically transforms the stack S, a sequence of sets of transitions $T_1, \ldots, T_n$ (the top being the rightmost element), into $T_1, \ldots, T_{\ell-1}, \bigcup_{i=\ell}^{n} T_i$ where ℓ is the lowest index such that T_ℓ contains a transition t' with $\mathtt{src}(t') = \mathtt{tgt}(t)$, or it can be also $\mathtt{tgt}(t') = \mathtt{tgt}(t)$ if T_ℓ has a cycle. Next, Couvreur's algorithm concludes non-emptiness when it detects a GBA cycle, i.e., a merged set of transitions on top of the stack that contains all colours. Algorithm 1, on the other hand, needs to find a *simple generalized Rabin accepting cycle*, i.e., one that satisfies the GBA acceptance and does not contain ⓿. In other words, it is a GBA accepting cycle with respect to the set $\{$❶, …, [k-1]$\}$ in the automaton $\mathcal{A}\setminus$⓿ (the automaton $\mathcal{A}$ with ⓿-transitions removed) that is still reachable from I in $\mathcal{A}$. To detect such cycles, we run a variant of Couvreur's algorithm as a sub-procedure, each time in a part of $\mathcal{A}\setminus$⓿ discovered to be reachable in $\mathcal{A}$. Each run of Couvreur's algorithm is used (i) to detect SGRA accepting cycles in a part of $\mathcal{A}\setminus$⓿ rooted at some transition t; and (ii) to discover new parts of $\mathcal{A}\setminus$⓿ reached from the explored part by ⓿-transitions. This is iterated until a GBA accepting cycle is found or there are no more unexplored reachable parts of $\mathcal{A}\setminus$⓿.

Algorithm 1 uses the set *Entry* of *entry transitions* as a data structure initialized by the outgoing transitions of I (Line 1), and applies Couvreur's algorithm to explore parts of $\mathcal{A}\backslash$⓿ from all transitions of *Entry*, while the iterations of the Couvreur's algorithm also keep adding transitions to *Entry* (due to the **while** loop on Line 2). We modify the internals of Couvreur's algorithm, presented essentially as the procedure `Explore` on Line 4, in one point: When exploring a ⓿-transition, the normal depth-first exploration (the **else** branch on Line 7) is bypassed, the transition is only marked as explored (Line 5), and the transitions continuing from its target are put to *Entry* as the entry transitions of newly discovered parts of $\mathcal{A}\backslash$⓿ (Line 6).

Theorem 2. *Algorithm 1 terminates and returns false iff* $\mathcal{L}(\mathcal{A}) \neq \emptyset$.

Proof (Sketch). Algorithm 1 terminates since each visited transition is stored in *Explored* and never revisited, and $\mathcal{A}$ has finitely many transitions. The proof follows the proof of Couvreur's algorithm. We show that $\mathcal{A}$ has an accepting run iff Algorithm 1 returns *false*. First, $\mathcal{L}(\mathcal{A}) \neq \emptyset$ iff $\mathcal{A}\backslash$⓿ contains a reachable cycle visiting all colours ❶, ..., (k-1). Whenever a transition t has colour ⓿, the algorithm stops the current DFS branch and schedules $\texttt{tgt}(t)$ as a new entry point (Line 6). Since all explored transitions are reachable from an initial state, every state in *Entry* is reachable; so the search effectively explores $\mathcal{A}\backslash$⓿. Each newly visited transition is pushed onto S (Line 8). If it closes a cycle, namely if $\texttt{tgt}(t)$ equals $\texttt{src}(t')$ or $\texttt{tgt}(t')$ for some explored t' on S, the colours on that cycle are collected and stored in $S.\texttt{top}$ (Line 9). If the algorithm returns *false*, then $S.\texttt{top}$ holds all colours ❶, ..., (k-1) (Line 10). So a reachable cycle in $\mathcal{A}\backslash$⓿ visiting all non-⓿ colours has been found, satisfying the accepting condition; therefore $\mathcal{A}$ has an accepting run. Conversely, if $\mathcal{A}$ has an accepting run, then $\mathcal{A}\backslash$⓿ contains a reachable cycle visiting all non-⓿ colours. Once the search reaches the cycle, it coincides with Couvreur's algorithm on $\mathcal{A}\backslash$⓿ and must discover it. So Line 10 is eventually triggered, and Algorithm 1 returns *false*. □

6 Experimental Evaluation

We have experimentally evaluated the complementation and inclusion checking capabilities of KOFOLA and compared it with state-of-the-art tools. All experiments were run on an Ubuntu GNU/Linux 24.04 virtual machine with 64 GiB RAM running on an AMD EPYC 9124 CPU. The timeout was set to 120 s. Correctness of answers was evaluated by cross-comparison between the tools.

6.1 Complementation

Used Tools. For complementation, the default setting of KOFOLA uses the determinization-based approach (see Sect. 4.2) for complementing NACs. We use KOFOLASLICE to denote the version that complements NACs using the slice-based construction. Before outputting a result, we reduce it using SPOT's post-processor with level set to `Low` (this performs removal of useless states and one

Table 1. Statistics for complementation. The column × has numbers of automata (out of 31,273) for which the tool ran out of resources (time or memory), **avg** contains the average number of states of the output, **time** the total time in seconds, and **unsup** the number of input automata with unsupported acceptance condition.

tool	×	avg	time	unsup
KOFOLA	0	79.24	1,069	0
SPOT	2	115.38	199	0
KOFOLASLICE	4	166.03	1,376	0
KOFOLAOLD	44	42.74	2,471	0
OWL	104	37.39	1,240	507
RANKER	443	45.80	22,817	1,336

Table 2. Statistics for inclusion checking. Column **unsolved** has numbers of inclusion problems (out of 1,014) for which the tool ran out of resources (time/memory), **time** contains the total time (in seconds) for the solved problems, **wins/losses** contains the number of problems where KOFOLA strictly won/lost over the tool, and **missing** contains for how many problems we could not convert the inputs into `.ba` files.

tool	unsolved	time	wins	losses	missing
KOFOLA	2	141			0
SPOT(DET)	28	122	263	56	0
FORKLIFT	35	1,273	997	9	8
SPOT(FORQ)	54	1,134	307	89	0
RABIT	57	4,300	996	8	8
BAIT	64	1,981	1,000	5	8

run of the simulation-based reduction [14]). We compared KOFOLA against state-of-the-art tools for Büchi complementation: SPOT (version 2.14.2) [22] (using the command line tool `autfilt --complement`), RANKER [29], OWL [34] (we ran its determinization into a parity automaton, where complementation is trivial), and the original version of KOFOLA from [26], named KOFOLAOLD hereafter. KOFOLAOLD uses the same post-processing as KOFOLA and RANKER uses a custom post-processing, which is not exactly the same, but similar to the one in SPOT.

Benchmarks. We collected as many BAs as we could, obtaining, in total, 31,273 automata [1]. These come from various sources: (i) 915 BAs from checking program termination by ULTIMATE AUTOMIZER [16] ($\text{AUTOMIZER}_{\mathcal{C}}$), (ii) 6,301 automata from solving the first-order logic of Sturmian words by PECAN [31,42] ($\text{PECAN}_{\mathcal{C}}$: these are not only BAs, but also, e.g.,. co-Büchi and parity automata), (iii) 72 BAs from model checking of HyperLTL properties using AUTOHYPER [10] ($\text{AUTOHYPER}_{\mathcal{C}}$), (iv) 370 BAs from deciding S1S formulae [27] (S1S), (v) 18 BAs from LTL to limit-deterministic BA translation [47] (LDBA4LTL), (vi) 1,721 BAs from translation from real-world and random LTL formulae [11] (SEMINATOR), and (vii) 21,876 randomly generated BAs [50] (SOBC).

Results. We compared the sizes of the complement automata that the tools generated. We let the tools output automata with any acceptance condition (KOFOLA and SPOT could exploit this to obtain smaller automata, whereas RANKER always generates automata with the Büchi condition). Statistics of the experiment are in Table 1 and interesting scatter plots are in Fig. 3 (the scatter plot for OWL looks similar as the one for SPOT with more unsolved cases). We do not include the median, which was 2 for all tools, in the table. We can see that KOFOLA was the only tool that could complement all input automata.

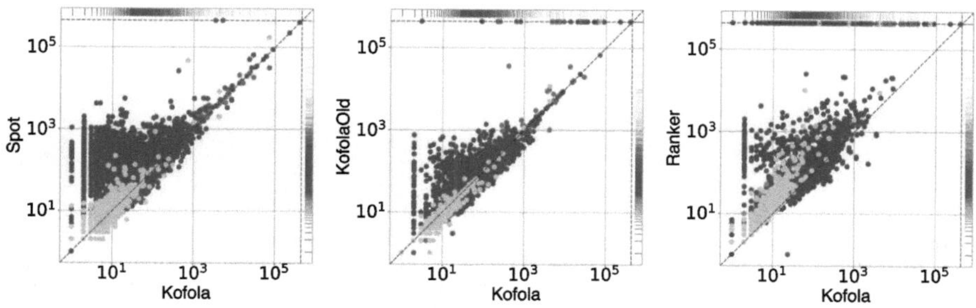

Fig. 3. Comparison of state counts of complement automata generated by KOFOLA and other tools; axes are logarithmic. Dashed lines are out-of-resources limit and rug plots on margins show distribution of data points. Colour indicates benchmark source: SOBC •, SEMINATOR •, AUTOMIZER$_C$ •, LDBA4LTL •, AUTOHYPER$_C$ •, PECAN$_C$ •, S1S •.

The second tool, SPOT, could complement all but two automata (it ran out of memory for those), however the average size of the output is much bigger. We can see this also in the plot comparing the two tools, where KOFOLA can get much smaller complements for many SOBC automata. For complementation, KOFOLASLICE gives worse average results than KOFOLA. There are, however, cases where KOFOLASLICE outputs a smaller result. The improvement of KOFOLA over KOFOLAOLD can be seen mainly in the number of solved cases. While the average size is better for KOFOLAOLD, this should be considered in the context that KOFOLA can solve the 44 benchmarks that KOFOLAOLD could not, often with a large output, which skews the average. From the plot, we can see that KOFOLAOLD could in many cases output a slightly smaller automaton than KOFOLA. This is due to the settings of the algorithms, which we optimized in KOFOLA to maximize the number of solved cases; as a consequence, sometimes the algorithms perform slightly worse. The dominance of KOFOLA over RANKER and OWL is clear from the number of solved cases and the scatter plot (RANKER has a lower average since it cannot solve harder benchmarks). 1,336 (for RANKER) and 507 (for OWL) input automata (all from PECAN) used an unsupported acceptance condition.

Our procedure for complementing IADACs helped in 225 cases, reducing the number of states of the output by an average of 5 (among the cases where it had effect). The most significant improvement was observed on one automaton from the SEMINATOR benchmark, where the number of states decreased by 236.

6.2 Inclusion Checking

Used Tools. For inclusion, KOFOLA uses the slice-based approach (Sect. 4.2) for complementing NACs, which is more suitable for on-the-fly exploration. We evaluated KOFOLA against state-of-the-art inclusion checkers BAIT [21], FORKLIFT [20], RABIT [17] v2.5.1 with argument `-fast`, and SPOT 2.14.2 [22] (using `autfilt --included-in`). For SPOT, we tried two versions: determinization-based [43–45] (SPOT(DET)) and well-quasiorder-based [20] (SPOT(FORQ)).

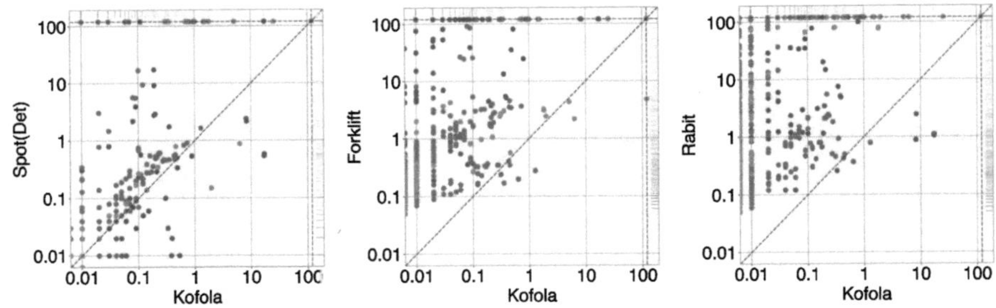

Fig. 4. Comparison of runtime of inclusion checking for Kofola and other tools. Times are in seconds, axes are logarithmic. Dashed lines represent out-of-resources limit and rug plots on margins show distribution of data points. The colour of a point indicates the source of the benchmark: AutoHyper$_\mathcal{I}$ •, Concur •, Pecan$_\mathcal{I}$ •, Automizer$_\mathcal{I}$ •.

Benchmarks. We used inclusion problems involving BAs given in the `HOA` format [8] from all available sources we are aware of that are practically motivated (the number of automata pairs is given in parentheses): (i) inclusion problems emerging from model checking of hyperproperties using the tool AutoHyper [10], denoted as AutoHyper$_\mathcal{I}$ (36; max. 66,051, avg. 2,059 states), (ii) instances occurring in program termination checking using Ultimate Automizer [16], denoted as Automizer$_\mathcal{I}$ (404; max. 88,304, avg. 904 states), (iii) inclusion problems coming from verification of concurrent systems [4] (13 instances denoted as Concur, omitting one benchmark from the source due to a missing counterpart automaton; max. 1,532, avg. 589 states), and (iv) logical implication tasks in word combinatorics from Pecan [31,42], denoted as Pecan$_\mathcal{I}$ (54 instances where it was clear how to pair them; max. 712,184, avg. 7,729 states). Without performing any pre-selection on the existing benchmarks of the literature, 98% of the 507 BAs appearing on the right-hand side of the inclusion (i.e., those that are being complemented) are elevator automata. This emphasizes the importance of exploiting automata structure in inclusion checking. From the automata on the left-hand side, 76% were elevator automata (in total, 87% of the involved BAs were elevator). To get more interesting examples for inclusion checking, we also swapped the sides of the benchmarks for a total of 1,014 inclusion problems (the vast majority of these benchmarks were non-trivial, often harder than the original problems). For tools not supporting the `HOA` format (Bait, Forklift, and Rabit), we employed Spot to convert the input automata into the `.ba` format. For four of the original inclusion problems (eight benchmarks in total), this was not possible (the translation took too many resources). Overall, inclusion holds in 12% of the benchmarks.

Results. We give statistics for inclusion checking in Table 2 and interesting scatter plots in Fig. 4. Kofola won by far on the number of solved instances and the total time. The second tool was Spot(Det), whose time is slightly lower, but solved 26 less instances. The scatter plot shows that it can sometimes beat Kofola. Ramsey-based tools follow with run times being an order of magnitude worse. The best of them is FORKLIFT (surprisingly to us, it solves more problems than SPOT(FORQ)) with SPOT(FORQ), RABIT, and BAIT trailing. From the scatter plots (we omit BAIT, which mostly behaves worse than FORKLIFT and SPOT(FORQ)), the tool most complementary to KOFOLA is SPOT.

Acknowledgments. We thank the anonymous reviewers for their constructive feedback. This work was supported in part by the National Natural Science Foundation of China (Grant No. 62102407), the CAS Project for Young Scientists in Basic Research (Grant No. YSBR-040), the Czech Science Foundation projects 26-22640S and 25-17934S, and the FIT BUT internal project FIT-S-26-9011.

Data Availibility Statement. An environment with the tools and data used for the experimental evaluation in the current study is available at [5].

Disclosure of Interests. The authors have no competing interests.

References

1. Automata-benchmarks (2025). https://github.com/ondrik/automata-benchmarks/tree/master/omega/
2. KOFOLA (2025). https://github.com/VeriFIT/kofola
3. Abdulla, P.A., et al.: Simulation subsumption in Ramsey-based Büchi automata universality and inclusion testing. In: Touili, T., Cook, B., Jackson, P. (eds.) CAV 2010. LNCS, vol. 6174, pp. 132–147. Springer, Heidelberg (2010). https://doi.org/10.1007/978-3-642-14295-6_14
4. Abdulla, P.A., et al.: Advanced Ramsey-based Büchi automata inclusion testing. In: Katoen, J.-P., König, B. (eds.) CONCUR 2011. LNCS, vol. 6901, pp. 187–202. Springer, Heidelberg (2011). https://doi.org/10.1007/978-3-642-23217-6_13
5. Alexaj, O., Havlena, V., Holík, L., Lengál, O., Li, Y., Mazzocchi, N.: Artifact: KOFOLA 1.0: a modular approach to ω-regular complementation and inclusion checking (2025). https://doi.org/10.5281/zenodo.17478623
6. Alexaj, O., Havlena, V., Holík, L., Lengál, O., Li, Y., Mazzocchi, N.: Kofola 1.0: a modular approach to ω-regular complementation and inclusion checking (technical report). CoRR **abs/2605.15390** (2026). http://arxiv.org/abs/2605.15390
7. Allred, J.D., Ultes-Nitsche, U.: A simple and optimal complementation algorithm for Büchi automata. In: Dawar, A., Grädel, E. (eds.) Proceedings of the 33rd Annual ACM/IEEE Symposium on Logic in Computer Science, LICS 2018, Oxford, UK, July 09-12, 2018, pp. 46–55. ACM (2018). https://doi.org/10.1145/3209108.3209138
8. Babiak, T., et al.: The hanoi omega-automata format. In: Kroening, D., Păsăreanu, C.S. (eds.) CAV 2015. LNCS, vol. 9206, pp. 479–486. Springer, Cham (2015). https://doi.org/10.1007/978-3-319-21690-4_31
9. Baier, C., Blahoudek, F., Duret-Lutz, A., Klein, J., Müller, D., Strejček, J.: Generic emptiness check for fun and profit. In: Chen, Y.-F., Cheng, C.-H., Esparza, J. (eds.) ATVA 2019. LNCS, vol. 11781, pp. 445–461. Springer, Cham (2019). https://doi.org/10.1007/978-3-030-31784-3_26
10. Beutner, R., Finkbeiner, B.: AutoHyper: explicit-state model checking for HyperLTL. In: Sankaranarayanan, S., Sharygina, N. (eds.) Tools and Algorithms for the

Construction and Analysis of Systems - 29th International Conference, TACAS 2023, Held as Part of the European Joint Conferences on Theory and Practice of Software, ETAPS 2022, Paris, France, April 22-27, 2023, Proceedings, Part I. LNCS, vol. 13993, pp. 145–163. Springer, Cham (2023). https://doi.org/10.1007/978-3-031-30823-9_8
11. Blahoudek, F., Duret-Lutz, A., Strejček, J.: Seminator 2 can complement generalized Büchi automata via improved semi-determinization. In: Lahiri, S.K., Wang, C. (eds.) CAV 2020. LNCS, vol. 12225, pp. 15–27. Springer, Cham (2020). https://doi.org/10.1007/978-3-030-53291-8_2
12. Breuers, S., Löding, C., Olschewski, J.: Improved Ramsey-based Büchi complementation. In: Birkedal, L. (ed.) FoSSaCS 2012. LNCS, vol. 7213, pp. 150–164. Springer, Heidelberg (2012). https://doi.org/10.1007/978-3-642-28729-9_10
13. Büchi, J.R.: On a decision method in restricted second order arithmetic, logic, methodology and philosophy of science (proc. 1960 internat. congr.) (1962)
14. Bustan, D., Grumberg, O.: Simulation based minimization. In: McAllester, D. (ed.) CADE 2000. LNCS (LNAI), vol. 1831, pp. 255–270. Springer, Heidelberg (2000). https://doi.org/10.1007/10721959_20
15. Chen, Y.-F., Havlena, V., Lengál, O.: Simulations in rank-based Büchi automata complementation. In: Lin, A.W. (ed.) APLAS 2019. LNCS, vol. 11893, pp. 447–467. Springer, Cham (2019). https://doi.org/10.1007/978-3-030-34175-6_23
16. Chen, Y., et al.: Advanced automata-based algorithms for program termination checking. In: Foster, J.S., Grossman, D. (eds.) Proceedings of the 39th ACM SIGPLAN Conference on Programming Language Design and Implementation, PLDI 2018, Philadelphia, PA, USA, June 18-22, 2018, pp. 135–150. ACM (2018). https://doi.org/10.1145/3192366.3192405
17. Clemente, L., Mayr, R.: Efficient reduction of nondeterministic automata with application to language inclusion testing. Log. Methods Comput. Sci. **15**(1) (2019). https://doi.org/10.23638/LMCS-15(1:12)2019
18. Couvreur, J.-M.: On-the-fly verification of linear temporal logic. In: Wing, J.M., Woodcock, J., Davies, J. (eds.) FM 1999. LNCS, vol. 1708, pp. 253–271. Springer, Heidelberg (1999). https://doi.org/10.1007/3-540-48119-2_16
19. Diekert, V., Muscholl, A., Walukiewicz, I.: A note on monitors and Büchi automata. In: Leucker, M., Rueda, C., Valencia, F.D. (eds.) ICTAC 2015. LNCS, vol. 9399, pp. 39–57. Springer, Cham (2015). https://doi.org/10.1007/978-3-319-25150-9_3
20. Doveri, K., Ganty, P., Mazzocchi, N.: FORQ-based language inclusion formal testing. In: Shoham, S., Vizel, Y. (eds.) Computer Aided Verification - 34th International Conference, CAV 2022, Haifa, Israel, August 7-10, 2022, Proceedings, Part II. Lecture Notes in Computer Science, vol. 13372, pp. 109–129. Springer, Cham (2022). https://doi.org/10.1007/978-3-031-13188-2_6
21. Doveri, K., Ganty, P., Ranzato, F.: Inclusion testing of Büchi automata based on well-quasiorders. In: Haddad, S., Varacca, D. (eds.) 32nd International Conference on Concurrency Theory, CONCUR 2021, August 24-27, 2021, Virtual Conference. LIPIcs, vol. 203, pp. 3:1–3:22. Schloss Dagstuhl - Leibniz-Zentrum für Informatik (2021). https://doi.org/10.4230/LIPICS.CONCUR.2021.3
22. Duret-Lutz, A., et al.: From Spot 2.0 to Spot 2.10: what's new? In: Shoham, S., Vizel, Y. (eds.) Computer Aided Verification - 34th International Conference, CAV 2022, Haifa, Israel, August 7-10, 2022, Proceedings, Part II. LNCS, vol. 13372, pp. 174–187. Springer, Cham (2022). https://doi.org/10.1007/978-3-031-13188-2_9
23. Emerson, E.A., Lei, C.: Modalities for model checking: branching time logic strikes back. Sci. Comput. Program. **8**(3), 275–306 (1987). https://doi.org/10.1016/0167-6423(87)90036-0

24. Esparza, J., Blondin, M.: Automata Theory: An Algorithmic Approach, MIT Press (2023)
25. Friedgut, E., Kupferman, O., Vardi, M.Y.: Büchi complementation made tighter. Int. J. Found. Comput. Sci. **17**(4), 851–868 (2006). https://doi.org/10.1142/S0129054106004145
26. Havlena, V., Lengál, O., Li, Y., Šmahlíková, B., Turrini, A.: Modular mix-and-match complementation of Büchi automata. In: Sankaranarayanan, S., Sharygina, N. (eds.) Tools and Algorithms for the Construction and Analysis of Systems, pp. 249–270. Springer, Cham (2023). https://doi.org/10.1007/978-3-031-30823-9_13
27. Havlena, V., Lengál, O., Šmahlíková, B.: Deciding S1S: down the rabbit hole and through the looking glass. In: Echihabi, K., Meyer, R. (eds.) NETYS 2021. LNCS, vol. 12754, pp. 215–222. Springer, Cham (2021). https://doi.org/10.1007/978-3-030-91014-3_15
28. Havlena, V., Lengál, O.: Reducing (to) the ranks: efficient rank-based Büchi automata complementation. In: Haddad, S., Varacca, D. (eds.) 32nd International Conference on Concurrency Theory, CONCUR 2021, August 24-27, 2021, Virtual Conference. LIPIcs, vol. 203, pp. 2:1–2:19. Schloss Dagstuhl - Leibniz-Zentrum für Informatik (2021). https://doi.org/10.4230/LIPIcs.CONCUR.2021.2
29. Havlena, V., Lengál, O., Šmahlíková, B.: Complementing Büchi automata with ranker. In: Shoham, S., Vizel, Y. (eds.) Computer Aided Verification - 34th International Conference, CAV 2022, Haifa, Israel, August 7-10, 2022, Proceedings, Part II. LNCS, vol. 13372, pp. 188–201. Springer, Cham (2022). https://doi.org/10.1007/978-3-031-13188-2_10
30. Havlena, V., Lengál, O., Šmahlíková, B.: Sky is not the limit. In: Fisman, D., Rosu, G. (eds.) TACAS 2022. LNCS, vol. 13244, pp. 118–136. Springer, Cham (2022). https://doi.org/10.1007/978-3-030-99527-0_7
31. Hieronymi, P., Ma, D., Oei, R., Schaeffer, L., Schulz, C., Shallit, J.O.: Decidability for Sturmian words. Log. Methods Comput. Sci. **20**(3) (2024). https://doi.org/10.46298/LMCS-20(3:12)2024
32. Kähler, D., Wilke, T.: Complementation, disambiguation, and determinization of Büchi automata unified. In: Aceto, L., Damgård, I., Goldberg, L.A., Halldórsson, M.M., Ingólfsdóttir, A., Walukiewicz, I. (eds.) ICALP 2008. LNCS, vol. 5125, pp. 724–735. Springer, Heidelberg (2008). https://doi.org/10.1007/978-3-540-70575-8_59
33. Karmarkar, H., Chakraborty, S.: On minimal odd rankings for Büchi complementation. In: Liu, Z., Ravn, A.P. (eds.) ATVA 2009. LNCS, vol. 5799, pp. 228–243. Springer, Heidelberg (2009). https://doi.org/10.1007/978-3-642-04761-9_18
34. Křetínský, J., Meggendorfer, T., Sickert, S.: Owl: a library for ω-words, automata, and LTL. In: Lahiri, S.K., Wang, C. (eds.) ATVA 2018. LNCS, vol. 11138, pp. 543–550. Springer, Cham (2018). https://doi.org/10.1007/978-3-030-01090-4_34
35. Kupferman, O., Vardi, M.Y.: Verification of fair transition systems. In: Alur, R., Henzinger, T.A. (eds.) CAV 1996. LNCS, vol. 1102, pp. 372–382. Springer, Heidelberg (1996). https://doi.org/10.1007/3-540-61474-5_84
36. Kupferman, O., Vardi, M.Y.: Weak alternating automata are not that weak. ACM Trans. Comput. Log. **2**(3), 408–429 (2001). https://doi.org/10.1145/377978.377993
37. Li, Y., Tsay, Y.-K., Turrini, A., Vardi, M.Y., Zhang, L.: Congruence relations for Büchi automata. In: Huisman, M., Păsăreanu, C., Zhan, N. (eds.) FM 2021. LNCS, vol. 13047, pp. 465–482. Springer, Cham (2021). https://doi.org/10.1007/978-3-030-90870-6_25

38. Li, Y., Turrini, A., Feng, W., Vardi, M.Y., Zhang, L.: Divide-and-conquer determinization of Büchi automata based on SCC decomposition. In: Shoham, S., Vizel, Y. (eds.) Computer Aided Verification - 34th International Conference, CAV 2022, Haifa, Israel, August 7-10, 2022, Proceedings, Part II. Lecture Notes in Computer Science, vol. 13372, pp. 152–173. Springer, Cham (2022). https://doi.org/10.1007/978-3-031-13188-2_8
39. Li, Y., Turrini, A., Zhang, L., Schewe, S.: Learning to complement Büchi automata. In: VMCAI 2018. LNCS, vol. 10747, pp. 313–335. Springer, Cham (2018). https://doi.org/10.1007/978-3-319-73721-8_15
40. Löding, C., Pirogov, A.: New optimizations and heuristics for determinization of Büchi automata. In: Chen, Y.-F., Cheng, C.-H., Esparza, J. (eds.) ATVA 2019. LNCS, vol. 11781, pp. 317–333. Springer, Cham (2019). https://doi.org/10.1007/978-3-030-31784-3_18
41. Miyano, S., Hayashi, T.: Alternating finite automata on ω-words. Theoret. Comput. Sci. **32**(3), 321–330 (1984). https://doi.org/10.1016/0304-3975(84)90049-5
42. Oei, R., Ma, D., Schulz, C., Hieronymi, P.: Pecan: an automated theorem prover for automatic sequences using Büchi automata. CoRR **abs/2102.01727** (2021). https://arxiv.org/abs/2102.01727
43. Piterman, N.: From nondeterministic Büchi and Streett automata to deterministic parity automata. Log. Methods Comput. Sci. **3**(3) (2007). https://doi.org/10.2168/LMCS-3(3:5)2007
44. Redziejowski, R.R.: An improved construction of deterministic omega-automaton using derivatives. Fundam. Informaticae **119**(3–4), 393–406 (2012). https://doi.org/10.3233/FI-2012-744
45. Safra, S.: On the complexity of omega-automata. In: 29th Annual Symposium on Foundations of Computer Science, White Plains, New York, USA, 24-26 October 1988, pp. 319–327. IEEE Computer Society (1988). https://doi.org/10.1109/SFCS.1988.21948
46. Schewe, S.: Büchi complementation made tight. In: Albers, S., Marion, J. (eds.) 26th International Symposium on Theoretical Aspects of Computer Science, STACS 2009, February 26-28, 2009, Freiburg, Germany, Proceedings. LIPIcs, vol. 3, pp. 661–672. Schloss Dagstuhl - Leibniz-Zentrum für Informatik, Germany (2009). https://doi.org/10.4230/LIPIcs.STACS.2009.1854
47. Sickert, S., Esparza, J., Jaax, S., Křetínský, J.: Limit-deterministic Büchi automata for linear temporal logic. In: Chaudhuri, S., Farzan, A. (eds.) CAV 2016. LNCS, vol. 9780, pp. 312–332. Springer, Cham (2016). https://doi.org/10.1007/978-3-319-41540-6_17
48. Sistla, A.P., Vardi, M.Y., Wolper, P.: The complementation problem for Büchi automata with applications to temporal logic. Theor. Comput. Sci. **49**, 217–237 (1987). https://doi.org/10.1016/0304-3975(87)90008-9
49. Tarjan, R.: Depth-first search and linear graph algorithms. In: 12th Annual Symposium on Switching and Automata Theory (swat 1971), pp. 114–121 (1971). https://doi.org/10.1109/SWAT.1971.10

50. Tsai, M., Fogarty, S., Vardi, M.Y., Tsay, Y.: State of Büchi complementation. Log. Methods Comput. Sci. **10**(4) (2014). https://doi.org/10.2168/LMCS-10(4:13)2014
51. Vardi, M.Y.: Automata-theoretic model checking revisited. In: Chockler, H., Hu, A.J. (eds.) HVC 2008. LNCS, vol. 5394, pp. 2–2. Springer, Heidelberg (2009). https://doi.org/10.1007/978-3-642-01702-5_2

Octopus: Practical Equivalence Checking of P4 Packet Parsers

Jort van Leenen(✉) and Tobias Kappé

LIACS, Leiden University, Leiden, The Netherlands
j.p.van.leenen@umail.leidenuniv.nl,
t.w.j.kappe@liacs.leidenuniv.nl

Abstract. P4 is a domain-specific language for programming protocol-independent packet processors, where packet parsers describe how incoming bit-streams are structured into headers and fields. Building on work by Doenges et al. (2022), we present OCTOPUS, a tool that translates P4 packet parsers into automata and then attempts to (symbolically) check their equivalence. OCTOPUS produces evidence, either in the form of a bisimulation demonstrating equivalence, or a counterexample bit-stream witnessing a behavioral difference between the two parsers. In contrast with earlier work, our tool can check equivalence between non-trivial parsers within minutes, on consumer hardware. We report on the tool's implementation and evaluate its usability in networking contexts.

1 Introduction

Hosts in a packet-switched network, such as the Internet, communicate by sending packets. *Switches* (and routers) forward packets to their destinations, indicated in the header field(s). As an example, consider the illustration of a UDP packet with its header and payload components in Fig. 1. A packet switch receives a packet in the form of a stream of bits on an incoming link. It then has to decide whether the packet is valid, and, if so, where to forward it. To make this decision, the stream of bits must be parsed into the packet's components and respective fields, which is done by a *packet parser*.

Given the central role of packet parsers, their compliance with functional specifications is critical. Nonetheless, implementation bugs do occur, and these can lead to incorrect behavior or security vulnerabilities [14, Sec. 4.5]. Examples include a set of vulnerabilities called *Ripple20* (*e.g.*, `CVE-2020-11896`), discovered in the IP stack implementation of many embedded systems, with consequences ranging from remote code execution to denial of service. This underlines the importance of applying formal methods to ensure parser correctness [22].

P4 [3] is a domain-specific programming language for *programming protocol-independent packet processors*, including the behavior of their packet parsers. Because P4 is domain-specific, its programs do not have the memory management pitfalls of a general-purpose language like C. Nevertheless, a P4 program may still contain bugs, either initially, or as a result of modifications aimed at optimizing or refactoring its code. To address this, we are interested in automatically comparing different versions of the same parser.

E. Darulova et al. (Eds.): CAV 2026, LNCS 16682, pp. 198–211, 2026.
https://doi.org/10.1007/978-3-032-32519-8_11

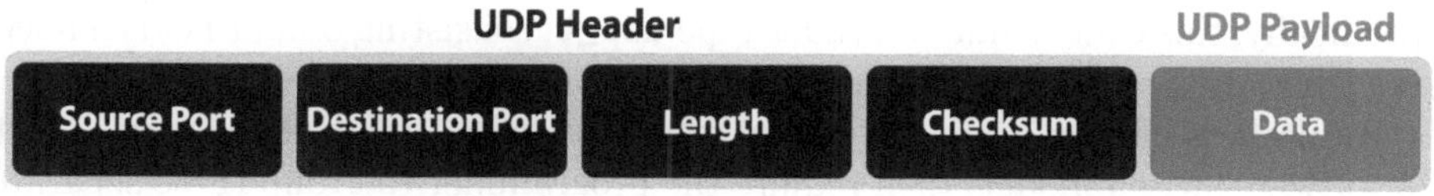

Fig. 1. An illustration of the structured information contained in a UDP packet. The left-most four blocks represent the fields comprising the packet's header. The right-most block represents the packet's payload.

Leapfrog [8] is an equivalence checker for P4 packet parsers, implemented in the Rocq proof assistant [26]. It accepts a deeply embedded representation of a subset of P4 parsers, which it attempts to prove equivalent by constructing a symbolic bisimulation [21] between their automata representations. Because this latter step is implemented in L_{tac}, Rocq's tactic language, it constructs a proof object in the Calculus of Inductive Constructions, which requires a substantial amount of resources. For example, one particularly large benchmark required more than 400 GiB of memory and had a runtime of nearly a day.

To alleviate this situation, we present Octopus, a tool that can verify equivalence for the same subset of P4 parsers as Leapfrog—but being implemented in Python, it does so without the foundational guarantees offered by Rocq. However, Octopus can run the hardest equivalence query performed by Leapfrog in under a few minutes, on consumer hardware. To still engender trust in its verdicts, Octopus generates certificates: a bisimulation in the case of equivalence, and a bit-stream witnessing the difference between the parsers otherwise. Furthermore, Octopus builds its symbolic bisimulation in a forward manner (using strongest postconditions) rather than working backwards (through weakest preconditions), obviating one of Leapfrog's preprocessing steps [8, Sec. 5.1]. Finally, Octopus accepts P4 parsers as input by hooking into P4C [25], the reference compiler of P4, which means that manual translation to Leapfrog's embedding of parsers is no longer necessary. These differences entail that Octopus enables *practical* equivalence checking of P4 packet parsers today.

Octopus is available as an open-source project under the MIT license;[1] an artifact accompanying this paper is archived permanently on Zenodo.[2]

2 Parsers in P4

A packet parser assigns meaning to different parts of its input bit-stream by moving the bits into named *fields*, while building up other metadata during its execution. These fields are typically organized by protocol into *headers*. For instance, a UDP packet header (Fig. 1) can be rendered in P4 as follows.

```
header udp_t { bit<16> src_port;  bit<16> dst_port;
               bit<16> length;    bit<16> checksum; }
```

[1] https://github.com/jortvanleenen/Octopus.
[2] https://doi.org/10.5281/zenodo.19832336.

Specifically, this code defines a header type `udp_t`, consisting of four fields named `src_port`, `dst_port`, `length`, and `checksum`, each 16 bits wide.

As packets can be nested, a parser typically defines multiple headers. Most P4 software switch models then require the programmer to group these separate header containers into a `struct`, which ultimately holds all headers that the parser might expect to see. For example, we could combine our UDP header implementation with (simplified versions of) the IP and TCP headers:

```
header ip_t       { bit<64> data; }
header tcp_t      { bit<64> data; }
struct headers_t { ip_t ip; udp_t udp; tcp_t tcp; }
```

A P4 parser is a state machine that moves input data to a header structure and decides whether the packet is accepted for further processing. It begins in a state called `start`; two additional states, `accept` and `reject`, represent the eponymous (final) parsing outcomes. The parser moves between these and user-defined states based on data ingested thus far. Returning to our example, a basic parser of IP packets containing UDP or TCP payloads may look as follows.

```
6  parser Parser(packet_in pkt, out headers_t hdr) {
7      state start {
8          pkt.extract(hdr.ip);
9          transition select(hdr.ip.data[23:20]) {
10             0: parse_tcp;
11             1: parse_udp;
12             _: reject;
13         }
14     }
15     state parse_udp {
16         pkt.extract(hdr.udp);
17         hdr.udp.length =
18             hdr.udp.length[7:0] ++ hdr.udp.length[15:8];
19         transition accept;
20     }
21     state parse_tcp {
22         pkt.extract(hdr.tcp);
23         transition accept;
24     }
25 }
```

The `pkt` variable represents the input, and `hdr` is the variable into which the bit-stream is parsed, also referred to as the *store*. Each user-defined state starts with an *operation block*, which makes modifications to the store by reading bits. Roughly speaking, operation blocks contain two kinds of statements:

1. Calls to `extract`, which move n bits from the input bit-stream to a field or header of (total) size n. In the above, this occurs on lines 8, 16, and 22.
2. Assignments, which assign the result of some calculation to a field. An example of this occurs on lines 17–18. These lines can be interpreted as changing the endianness of the length field, swapping its two bytes.

A user-defined state ends with a *transition block*, which decides where to go next. This can be unconditional (*cf*. lines 19 and 23), but more commonly the decision depends on the store; for instance, on lines 9–12, the parser decides to advance to `parse_tcp`, `parse_udp`, or `reject` based on bits 20–23 of the `ip` header. Here, `_` represents a catch-all case. Besides transition blocks, P4 parsers do not have any primitives for control flow, *i.e.*, there is no `if-then-else` or `while-do` construct.

Scope of Support. Like LEAPFROG, OCTOPUS is currently limited to parsers where (1) each state consumes at least one bit of input, (2) no lookahead is used, and (3) no header stacks appear. Assumptions (1) and (2) are primarily implementation restrictions and could likely be relaxed with further engineering effort. However, assumption (1) is already reasonable in practice, as the P4 specification permits compilers to reject parser cycles that do not advance the cursor [24]. Assumption (3) is more fundamental: unbounded header stacks can encode pushdown automata, rendering equivalence undecidable. Fixed-size header stacks, however, can be encoded using already supported primitives.

3 Automata Model

Having seen the components that make up a P4 parser, we now outline how they translate to automata. Abstracting away the nested structure of headers, we represent the defined header fields as a finite set H of *header identifiers*, with each $h \in H$ having a size $|h| \in \mathbb{N}^+$. When we write $|bv|$ for the length of a bit-vector $bv \in \{0,1\}^*$, we can define a *store* as a member of St, given by:

$$St := \{s : H \to \{0,1\}^* \mid \forall h \in H,\ |s(h)| = |h|\}.$$

The states are modeled as a set Q, where each $q \in Q$ other than `accept` and `reject` has an *operation block* $\mathsf{op}(q)$ and a *transition block* $\mathsf{tz}(q)$. We will refer to the number of bits read by an operation block as its size, denoted by $|\mathsf{op}(q)|$. As an example, in the P4 parser above, all operation blocks are 64 bits in size.

A *configuration* is a triple $\langle q, s, w\rangle$, which represents a parser in state $q \in Q$, with a store defined by $s \in St$, and the buffer holding the bits $w \in \{0,1\}^*$, with $|w| < |\mathsf{op}(q)|$. This makes C, the set of all configurations, finite.

The *transition function* maps a configuration $\langle q, s, w\rangle$ and a bit b to a next configuration, by either growing the buffer when $|wb| < |\mathsf{op}(q)|$, or executing the operation block $\mathsf{op}(q)$ and transitioning according to $\mathsf{tz}(q)$, clearing the buffer:

$$\delta(\langle q, s, w\rangle, b) = \begin{cases} \langle \mathtt{reject}, s, \epsilon\rangle & q \in \{\mathtt{accept}, \mathtt{reject}\}, \\ \langle q, s, wb\rangle & |wb| < |\mathsf{op}(q)|, \\ \langle [\![\mathsf{tz}(q)]\!](s'),\ s',\ \epsilon\rangle & |wb| = |\mathsf{op}(q)|,\ s' = [\![\mathsf{op}(q)]\!](s, wb). \end{cases}$$

In the above, $[\![\mathsf{op}(q)]\!]$ represents the semantics of the operation block attached to q as a function that takes a store s and a buffer wb of size $|\mathsf{op}(q)|$, and returns an updated store s'. By the same token, $[\![\mathsf{tz}(q)]\!]$ is a function that determines the next state, which it does based on the newly updated store s'.

Putting these parts together, we can represent a P4 parser as a deterministic finite automaton $\langle C, \delta, F\rangle$, which operates on configurations from C, has transition function δ, and accepting configurations $F = \{\langle \texttt{accept}, s, \epsilon\rangle \mid s \in St\}$. We do not select an initial configuration, as the semantics of P4 stipulate that store values need not be initialized [24]. Accepted packets are thus bit-streams accepted by any state of the form $\langle \texttt{start}, s, \epsilon\rangle$ in the traditional sense.

4 Equivalence Checking

We now present the symbolic equivalence-checking algorithm implemented in OCTOPUS, which attempts to decide whether two P4 packet parsers are behaviorally equivalent by constructing a symbolic bisimulation over their automata representations. Recall that two states in a deterministic automaton have the same language if and only if they are related by a *bisimulation.*

Definition 4.1 (Bisimulation). *Let $\langle C_i, \delta_i, F_i\rangle$ be an automaton, with $i \in \{1,2\}$. A relation $R \subseteq C_1 \times C_2$ is a* bisimulation *if, for all c_1 R c_2, we have $c_1 \in F_1$ iff $c_2 \in F_2$, and $\delta_1(c_1, b)$ R $\delta_2(c_2, b)$ for $b \in \{0,1\}$.*

Thus, equivalence checking reduces to constructing a bisimulation. Naively, one can do this by starting from an initial pair (c_1, c_2), and repeatedly adding pairs reachable by point-wise transitions. If we add a pair (c_1', c_2') where $c_1' \in F_1$ but $c_2' \notin F_2$ (or vice versa), a bisimulation cannot exist; if the process terminates without such a violation, a bisimulation has been constructed. However, automata constructed from P4 parsers are prohibitively large: even the toy parser from the previous section has roughly $3 \times 2^{63} \times 2^{3\times 64}$ possible configurations.

The key insight to a workable algorithm is that we can represent large sets of concrete pairs of configurations symbolically. While this methodology is well known, the specific symbolic representation we use stems from LEAPFROG [8].

Definition 4.2 (Template-guarded Formula (TGF)). *A* template-guarded formula *(TGF) is a 5-tuple $\gamma = \langle q_\gamma^<, q_\gamma^>, n_\gamma^<, n_\gamma^>, \varphi_\gamma\rangle$, where $q_\gamma^<$ (resp. $q_\gamma^>$) indicates the state of the left (resp. right) parser, and $n_\gamma^<$ (resp. $n_\gamma^>$) is the number of bits in the left (resp. right) parser's buffer. We refer to the first four components together as a* template, *denoted by $\tau_\gamma = \langle q_\gamma^<, q_\gamma^>, n_\gamma^<, n_\gamma^>\rangle$.*

The final component, φ_γ, is a first-order formula over variables $buf^<$, representing the buffer (of size $n^<$) in the left configuration, and $st^<$, representing the store of the left configuration (resp. $buf^>$ and $st^>$ in the right configuration).

Informally, a TGF $\langle q_\gamma^<, q_\gamma^>, n_\gamma^<, n_\gamma^>, \varphi_\gamma\rangle$ denotes pairs of configurations where (1) the configuration on the left has $q_\gamma^<$ as its state and a buffer with $n_\gamma^<$ bits (and similarly on the right), and (2) those buffers and stores together satisfy ϕ_γ.

Bisimulation Checking. Algorithm 1 builds a symbolic bisimulation, starting with the TGF $\langle \texttt{start}, \texttt{start}, 0, 0, \top\rangle$, which represents all possible pairs of initial configurations for both parsers. Here, the trivial formula $\top$ does not restrict header fields because P4 defines header fields to be uninitialized [24].

1 $\mathcal{W} \leftarrow \{\langle \texttt{start}, \texttt{start}, 0, 0, \top \rangle\}$
2 $\mathcal{K} \leftarrow \emptyset$
3 **while** $\mathcal{W} \neq \emptyset$ **do**
4 $\quad \gamma = \langle q^{<}_{\gamma}, q^{>}_{\gamma}, n^{<}_{\gamma}, n^{>}_{\gamma}, \varphi_{\gamma} \rangle \leftarrow \mathcal{W}.pop()$
5 $\quad$ **if** $\varphi_{\gamma} \models \bigvee\{\phi_{\gamma'} \mid \gamma' \in \mathcal{K} \cup \mathcal{W},\ \tau_{\gamma'} = \tau_{\gamma}\}$ **then**
6 $\quad\quad$ **continue** `// no new information`
7 $\quad$ **if not** $(q^{<}_{\gamma} = \textit{accept} \iff q^{>}_{\gamma} = \textit{accept})$ **then**
8 $\quad\quad$ **return** counterexample
9 $\quad \ell \leftarrow \min(|\mathsf{op}(q^{<}_{\gamma})| - n^{<}_{\gamma},\ |\mathsf{op}(q^{>}_{\gamma})| - n^{>}_{\gamma})$ `// read until buffer full`
10 $\quad \varphi' \leftarrow \mathsf{Extend}(\varphi_{\gamma}, \ell)$ `// read` ℓ `bits, extend buffers`
11 $\quad$ **if** $n^{<}_{\gamma} + \ell = |\mathsf{op}(q^{<}_{\gamma})|$ **then**
12 $\quad\quad \varphi' \leftarrow \mathsf{SP}^{<}(\mathsf{op}(q^{<}_{\gamma}), \varphi');\ n^{<} \leftarrow 0;\ L \leftarrow \mathsf{ST}^{<}(\mathsf{tz}(q^{<}_{\gamma}))$ `// left step`
13 $\quad$ **else** $n^{<} \leftarrow n^{<}_{\gamma} + \ell;\ L \leftarrow \{(\top, q^{<}_{\gamma})\}$
14 $\quad$ **if** $n^{>}_{\gamma} + \ell = |\mathsf{op}(q^{>}_{\gamma})|$ **then**
15 $\quad\quad \varphi' \leftarrow \mathsf{SP}^{>}(\mathsf{op}(q^{>}_{\gamma}), \varphi');\ n^{>} \leftarrow 0;\ R \leftarrow \mathsf{ST}^{>}(\mathsf{tz}(q^{>}_{\gamma}))$ `// right step`
16 $\quad$ **else** $n^{>} \leftarrow n^{>}_{\gamma} + \ell;\ R \leftarrow \{(\top, q^{>}_{\gamma})\}$
17 $\quad$ **foreach** $(c^{<}, q'^{<}) \in L$ **and** $(c^{>}, q'^{>}) \in R$ **do**
18 $\quad\quad \mathcal{W} \leftarrow \mathcal{W} \cup \{\langle q'^{<}, q'^{>}, n^{<}, n^{>}, \varphi' \wedge c^{<} \wedge c^{>} \rangle\}$
19 $\quad \mathcal{K} \leftarrow \mathcal{K} \cup \{\gamma\}$
20 **return** $\mathcal{K}$

Algorithm 1: Symbolic bisimulation checking over TGFs.

The algorithm then proceeds like the naive approach. To describe pairs of symbolic configurations, we iteratively compute successor TGFs and disjunctively add those to our candidate symbolic bisimulation. This process continues until no new TGFs arise (Line 5, implemented using an SMT solver), in which case a symbolic bisimulation has been obtained, and the parsers are deemed equivalent. Otherwise, if a TGF is reached where exactly one state in the template is accepting (Line 7), then we conclude that the parsers are not equivalent.

Calculating successor TGFs is a two-phase process. First, if a parser lacks sufficient buffered bits to execute the next operation block, the symbolic step consumes input. It extends the buffer by introducing a fresh buffer variable constrained to be the concatenation of the previous buffer and the newly read bits (Extend). Second, if enough bits are available, the operation block is executed symbolically; its effect on the formula is captured by taking the strongest postcondition, updating the symbolic relationships between both parsers' stores and buffers. Figure 2 contains a more formal description of this process.

After computing the strongest postcondition ($\mathsf{SP}^{\lessgtr}$), we must symbolically determine the next state. Updating the template to record this new state is straightforward, but it is equally necessary to record the constraints under which this branch was feasible into the formula. To correctly encode the semantics of the case structure, we conjoin to the relational formula not only the condition for the selected case, but also the negation of the conditions of all earlier cases that were not taken. The subroutine to compute these constraints and next states given a transition block is denoted $\mathsf{ST}^{\lessgtr}$, where, as in $\mathsf{SP}^{\lessgtr}$, $\lessgtr$ is $<$ or $>$

$$\mathsf{SP}^{\lessgtr}(\varphi, \mathbf{prog})$$

$$\mathsf{SP}^{\lessgtr}(\varphi, \text{extract}(hdr)) := \exists y \in \{0,1\}^{|hdr|} \quad \varphi\left[\frac{y}{\text{st}^{\lessgtr}.hdr}, \frac{\text{st}^{\lessgtr}.hdr \mathbin{+\!\!+} \text{buf}^{\lessgtr}}{\text{buf}^{\lessgtr}}\right],$$

$$\mathsf{SP}^{\lessgtr}(\varphi, \text{hdr}.x = e) := \exists y \in \{0,1\}^{|x|} \quad \varphi\left[\frac{y}{\text{st}^{\lessgtr}.hdr.x}\right] \wedge \text{st}^{\lessgtr}.hdr.x = e\left[\frac{y}{\text{st}^{\lessgtr}.hdr.x}\right],$$

$$\mathsf{SP}^{\lessgtr}(\varphi, \text{prog}_1; \text{prog}_2) := \mathsf{SP}^{\lessgtr}\big(\mathsf{SP}^{\lessgtr}(\varphi, \text{prog}_1), \text{prog}_2\big).$$

Fig. 2. The strongest postcondition ($\mathsf{SP}^{\lessgtr}$) of an operation block, with the symbol $\lessgtr \in \{<, >\}$ depending on which parser the operation block belongs to.

depending on where the transition block belongs. If no transition is executed, the symbolic transition leaves the state unchanged under the trivial constraint.

On the whole, the algorithm must terminate, simply because each iteration of the loop either grows the number of configurations (of which there are finitely many) modelled by the TGFs in $\mathcal{K}$, or keeps this quantity constant while shrinking $\mathcal{W}$. If the algorithm determines that the two given parsers are not equivalent, it will use the SMT solver to generate a model for the last TGF. The existentially quantified buffer variables contained in this model can then be used to extract a counterexample in the form of a packet accepted by one parser, but rejected by the other; we omit the details of this procedure for brevity. Otherwise, when the main loop terminates, the disjunction of the TGFs in $\mathcal{K}$ represents a symbolic bisimulation on the underlying automaton.

As an optimization, our algorithm adopts the "leaps" technique from [8] to improve upon bit-by-bit buffer building by allowing both parsers to advance in one large step until either executes an operation (and thus transition) block. In Algorithm 1, this is implemented by calculating the number of steps to advance on Line 8, before extending the buffers on Line 9. For a correctness proof of the leaps optimization, please consult [9, Lemma 5.6].

Certificate Validation. Once a certificate (a set of TGFs) is built, it can be validated by checking whether three conditions hold: (1) it contains the initial TGF $\langle \texttt{start}, \texttt{start}, 0, 0, \top \rangle$; (2) the states in every TGF agree on acceptance; and (3) the pure formula in each successor TGF is covered—where by "covered" we mean "implies the disjunction of TGFs in the certificate with the same template".

In principle, these checks could be implemented by an external checker, separate from our bisimulation-construction algorithm; in practice, these routines also comprise different parts of our codebase. Conceptually, however, certificate validation is closely related to certificate building, to the point where the same algorithm applies; indeed, Algorithm 1 can check whether a given set of TGFs constitutes a symbolic bisimulation, simply by initiating the work queue $\mathcal{W}$ to that set—in this case, running the algorithm will effectively check conditions (2) and (3) from above. This is no surprise, as the main loop of Algorithm 1 actually checks whether $\mathcal{W}$ is *contained* in a symbolic bisimulation, so instantiating $\mathcal{W}$ to $\{\langle \texttt{start}, \texttt{start}, 0, 0, \top \rangle\}$ checks whether a bisimulation satisfying (1) exists.

5 Evaluation

OCTOPUS is implemented as a command-line tool in Python. It accepts either two P4 programs, in which case P4C [25] is invoked internally to generate their compiler intermediate representation (IR) JSON, or two IR JSON inputs directly. This IR is then parsed and interpreted via the automata model described in Sect. 3, on which Algorithm 1 is executed. If successful, OCTOPUS returns a certificate of equivalence in the form of a symbolic bisimulation, represented as a disjunction of TGFs. Otherwise, it returns a counterexample bit-stream accepted by only one parser, as well as the paths taken by both parsers on this input. The counterexample is derived from the TGFs at the point of failure, and enables mechanical reproduction, while the paths support manual debugging.

By default, OCTOPUS uses Z3 [6] as its SMT solver. Profiling shows that solver performance is dominant, with about 80–85% of execution time spent in SMT calls. Although OCTOPUS supports solver portfolios via PYSMT [11], we observed no performance benefit in our experiments; instead, portfolio management introduced overhead that degraded runtime. We also evaluated using CVC5 [1] as solver: on public benchmarks (435 small parser comparisons), performance is similar, likely due to small queries and non-SMT overhead, whereas on larger benchmarks (*e.g.*, *variable-length format 3*) differences become more pronounced, and CVC5 can be up to 50% faster. We nevertheless use Z3, as CVC5 triggers a crash in the PYSMT library for some benchmarks.

Comparison with LEAPFROG. We compare OCTOPUS against LEAPFROG, first on its own benchmark suite [8], and then in terms of their trusted base.

LEAPFROG's benchmarks can be divided into two broad categories. The first consists of representative case studies that capture common parser transformations and design idioms. The second comprises larger parsers drawn from realistic networking scenarios, as well as a translation-validation benchmark.

We first reproduced LEAPFROG's benchmarks; next, we translated the deeply embedded Rocq representation of the parsers to P4 and ran the same comparisons using OCTOPUS. All experiments ran on an Intel Xeon E5-2630v3 with 1.4 TiB of memory to accommodate LEAPFROG's memory footprint, and to ensure comparability. The results for OCTOPUS are averaged over three runs.

Table 1 summarizes the results. We implemented certificate validation to run after generation, allowing us to report the validation and generation wall clock times separately. To fairly compare with LEAPFROG, their sum can be considered the total wall clock running time of OCTOPUS. Across all benchmarks where LEAPFROG terminates, OCTOPUS outperforms it by several orders of magnitude in both runtime and memory usage. In particular, the *variable-length format 3* benchmark, which exceeded the machine's memory limits with LEAPFROG, is successfully handled by OCTOPUS within half an hour. These results highlight the practical benefits of not constructing a proof object using elaborate $\mathrm{L_{tac}}$ scripting. Another interesting observation is that generation is often faster than validation. We believe that this is the result of the successor checks being performed over larger formulas.

Table 1. Resource usage for each case study in LEAPFROG's benchmark suite under both LEAPFROG and OCTOPUS. Runtime (Run.) refers to the wall-clock time (in minutes) required for equivalence checking. For OCTOPUS, runtime is divided into certificate generation (Gen.) and validation (Val.), both in minutes. Memory (Mem.) indicates the peak resident memory, in GiB, over the course of the experiment.

Name	Leapfrog		Octopus		
	Run. (m)	Mem. (GiB)	Gen. (m)	Val. (m)	Mem. (GiB)
State rearrangement	1.13	1.07	0.002	0.002	0.047
Variable-length format 2	3825.70	391.91	0.268	0.340	0.056
Variable-length format 3	–	–	12.149	10.885	0.252
Header initialization	21.56	13.48	0.004	0.003	0.048
Speculative extraction	5.45	3.26	0.003	0.003	0.047
Relational verification	1.59	1.65	0.003	0.003	0.048
External filtering	2.37	2.03	0.003	0.002	0.047
Edge	730.12	243.35	0.075	0.081	0.049
Service provider	7167.03	823.70	0.040	0.041	0.049
Datacenter	1975.92	382.17	1.176	1.949	0.062
Enterprise	817.12	66.35	0.887	1.272	0.058
Translation validation	1035.38	349.15	0.120	0.131	0.055

In the *relational verification* and *external filtering* benchmarks, the parsers are not strictly equivalent—specifically, one accepts a strict subset of the packets accepted by the other. The intention is that, for the more lenient parser, invalid packets are discarded at a later stage. OCTOPUS, like LEAPFROG, allows refining the coherence check on Line 7 of Algorithm 1 to disregard such "accepted" packets that will be rejected later. As a result, OCTOPUS can establish behavioral equivalence of the two parsers modulo this predicate.

In terms of trusted base, OCTOPUS does not produce a proof in the Calculus of Inductive Constructions, where LEAPFROG does. While our code is fairly simple, and a pen-and-paper proof of correctness for Algorithm 1 is relatively straightforward, we have not formally verified the implementation. In addition, correctness of OCTOPUS relies on that of the underlying SMT solver, as well as correctness of the translation to SMT queries handled by PYSMT. While LEAPFROG does formally verify the translation to a logic that can more-or-less be pretty-printed to an SMT query, the correspondence between the semantics of this logic and SMT queries is trusted. Finally, LEAPFROG's trusted base also includes the underlying SMT solver, as the query response is not translated into a proof (*à la* SMTCOQ [10] or COQHAMMER [4]) by their custom plugin.

Synthetic Benchmarks. We now evaluate scalability using WHIPPERSNAPPER [5], a synthetic parser generator. We consider three classes of parsers. `parse-field`, varying number of fields in a single header; `parse-header`, varying the number

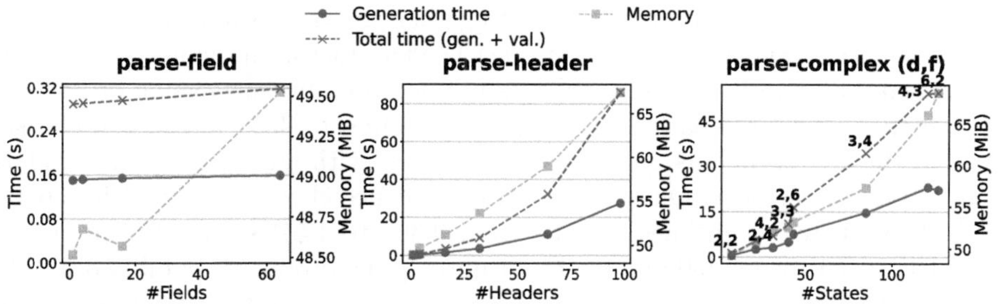

Fig. 3. The total wall-clock time (left vertical axis, in seconds) and peak resident memory (right vertical axis, in MiB) required by OCTOPUS running on synthetic benchmarks generated through WHIPPERSNAPPER.

of headers while keeping their size constant; and `parse-complex`, varying parser depth and fan-out. In all classes, a single header is parsed by a single state. Each generated parser is compared against itself, where the expected outcome is equivalence—although OCTOPUS may decide negatively when different packets can be accepted depending on the (uninitialized) values in the store. Experiments were run on the same server as the benchmarks in Table 1. Runtimes are again averaged over three runs.

Results are shown in Fig. 3. Increasing the number of fields has little impact on runtime, as it does not introduce new control-flow paths and can be handled efficiently using leaps. By contrast, increasing the number of headers or the size of the parser tree substantially increases the number of execution paths, leading to corresponding growth in both runtime and memory consumption. With an increasing number of execution paths, the respective formulas also grow in size. Per the same reasoning as before, it thus makes sense that validation time grows faster than generation time. For `parse-complex`, the number of states grows as $\frac{f^{d+1}-1}{f-1}$, where d is the depth and f the fan-out, which is reflected in the observed scalability trends. We consider these trends encouraging, as the largest parsers here already exceed the real-world parsers that we found publicly in terms of size and structural complexity.

We also verified several non-trivial equivalences between parsers drawn from the `parse-field`, `parse-header`, and `parse-complex` classes. These checks succeeded within seconds, like earlier experiments. For example, we showed an equivalence between a parser from `parse-header` with n single-field headers and one with a single header of n fields from `parse-field`, as well as between a `parse-complex` parser with a depth of n and a fan-out of 1, and a `parse-header` parser with n headers. This again demonstrates OCTOPUS's ability to reason about semantic, behavioral properties, rather than syntactic equivalence.

Public Code. Finally, we investigate the performance of OCTOPUS on code "in the wild", by examining a collection of publicly available P4 programs [12]. This dataset consists of 34 programs from research projects, tutorials, and protocol implementations. Among these, 30 fall within the scope of OCTOPUS and can be read by P4C, potentially after porting their syntax to modern P4. Of the remainder, two (`hyper4`, `axon`) contained header stacks, one more (`calc`) used lookahead, and another (`hashpipe`) was not accepted by our version of `P4C`.

We then compared each pair of parsers, leading to 435 equivalence checks. We ran these experiments on a consumer laptop, with an Intel Core i5-12500H and 24 GiB of memory. On average, an equivalence check completed in 0.659 s (std: 0.261 s), with runtimes ranging from 0.300 to 1.570 s and 50% of checks completing between 0.430 and 0.790 s. Runtime measurements exhibited a mild right skew, with a few larger parser pairs accounting for the upper tail. Peak resident memory usage averaged 51.72 MiB (std: 4.34 MiB), ranging from 46.40 to 68.21 MiB. Memory usage was more tightly concentrated around the median of 50.86 MiB, with 50% of runs falling between 49.96 and 51.86 MiB, again with a modest right tail corresponding to larger explored state spaces.

Our experiments identify two non-trivial equivalence classes: the first contains 4 parsers that do not decode further than an IPv4 header wrapped inside an Ethernet header; the second contains 6 parsers that go one step further, and may also decode a TCP header within this IPv4 header. In both cases, the parsers in question are encoded in slightly different ways. The remaining parsers are pairwise inequivalent, because they support different sets of protocols.

These measurements lead us to conclude that OCTOPUS can handle parsers from various sources (as long as they are written in modern P4), and can furthermore successfully distinguish between heterogeneous parsers.

6 Related Work

While OCTOPUS is most closely related to LEAPFROG (discussed in Sect. 1), it fits into a broader body of work applying formal methods to P4 programs.

To support developers in verifying functional correctness, several push-button verifiers have been proposed; examples include P4V [16], ASSERT-P4 [17], and AQUILA [27]. These tools verify P4 programs against user-annotated functional properties by translating them into intermediate representations, which are then analyzed using formal verification techniques. A complementary approach is taken by VERA [23], which can detect a wide range of practical bugs in P4 programs, without user annotations. In contrast with all of these, OCTOPUS does not reason about the (functional) correctness of a parser on its own. Instead, it performs *relational* verification by comparing the behaviors of two parsers. Finally, a related line of work outside the P4 ecosystem is EVERPARSE [19], which targets low-level binary message formats rather than programmable dataplane parsers. Its goal is to synthesize parsers that are correct-by-construction, memory-safe, and non-malleable with respect to a given format specification.

A distinct class of tools targets the verification of translations to concrete network configurations, commonly referred to as *tool stack verification*. An example is P4PKTGEN [18], which can generate a wide range of test cases to evaluate the correctness of a parser. Such tools' goals are different from our own, which focus specifically on parser *equivalence* rather than end-to-end correctness.

Most existing tools rely either on ad hoc semantic models or on existing implementations, such as P4C [25], the reference compiler for P4. Efforts have also been made to provide formal semantics, such as P4K [13], which formalizes the $P4_{14}$ language specification in the K framework [20], and PETR4 [7], which defines formal semantics for a subset of $P4_{16}$.

7 Conclusion and Future Work

We presented OCTOPUS, a tool that can verify equivalence of P4 parsers by symbolically checking bisimilarity of their automata, inspired by LEAPFROG [8]. OCTOPUS outperformed all test cases reported for LEAPFROG, and managed an additional test case that was previously infeasible. Using the WHIPPERSNAPPER synthetic benchmark suite, we obtained a clear picture of OCTOPUS's scalability, and using the public code experiment, its applicability. Together, these results indicate that OCTOPUS is well-suited for real-world parser applications.

While OCTOPUS exhibits practical runtime performance, there remains potential for further improvement. As observed in Sect. 5, certificate validation approximately doubles execution time. One direction for future work is to embed certificates for generated SMT queries and validate those, instead of re-running the SMT solver. This could substantially reduce overall execution time.

We are also interested in extending the scope of OCTOPUS. Some extensions appear to require straightforward engineering effort, while others, such as supporting lookahead together with termination detection, likely require additional theoretical development. We are currently exploring a preliminary implementation of the latter. Such extensions could enable support for a broader range of real-world parsers, including the P4 fabric used by ONOS [2].

Acknowledgements. This work is based on the first author's bachelor's thesis [15]. The authors would like to thank Jan Martens for his comments on that version, and Emily Yu for her helpful comments on a later draft of this manuscript. We also wish to thank the anonymous reviewers for their helpful comments and suggestions.

This work was partially supported by the Dutch Research Council (NWO) under grant no. VI.Veni.232.286 (ChEOpS).

Data Availibility Statement. The data and artifact supporting the results of this study are publicly available via Zenodo at https://doi.org/10.5281/zenodo.19832336. The artifact is provided as a Docker image and enables reproduction of all reported results, except for the runtime measurements of LEAPFROG in Table 1, which are excluded due to their computational cost. The artifact and the tool's source code are released under the MIT License.

Disclosure of Interests. The authors have no competing interests to declare that are relevant to the content of this article.

References

1. Barbosa, H., et al.: cvc5: a versatile and industrial-strength SMT solver. In: TACAS 2022. LNCS, vol. 13243, pp. 415–442 (2022). https://doi.org/10.1007/978-3-030-99524-9_24
2. Berde, P., et al.: ONOS: towards an open, distributed SDN OS. In: HotSDN, pp. 1–6 (2014). https://doi.org/10.1145/2620728.2620744
3. Bosshart, P., et al.: P4: programming protocol-independent packet processors. Comput. Commun. Rev. **44**(3), 87–95 (2014). https://doi.org/10.1145/2656877.2656890
4. Czajka, L., Kaliszyk, C.: Hammer for Coq: automation for dependent type theory. J. Autom. Reason. **61**(1–4), 423–453 (2018). https://doi.org/10.1007/S10817-018-9458-4
5. Dang, H.T., et al.: Whippersnapper: a P4 language benchmark suite. In: SOSR, pp. 95–101 (2017). https://doi.org/10.1145/3050220.3050231
6. de Moura, L., Bjørner, N.: Z3: an efficient SMT solver. In: TACAS 2008. LNCS, vol. 4963, pp. 337–340 (2008). https://doi.org/10.1007/978-3-540-78800-3_24
7. Doenges, R., et al.: Petr4: formal foundations for P4 data planes. In: POPL, pp. 1–32 (2021). https://doi.org/10.1145/3434322
8. Doenges, R., Kappé, T., Sarracino, J., Foster, N., Morrisett, G.: Leapfrog: certified equivalence for protocol parsers. In: PLDI, pp. 950–965 (2022). https://doi.org/10.1145/3519939.3523715
9. Doenges, R., Kappé, T., Sarracino, J., Foster, N., Morrisett, G.: Leapfrog: certified equivalence for protocol parsers (2022). https://doi.org/10.48550/arXiv.2205.08762. Full version including proofs
10. Ekici, B., et al.: SMTCoq: a plug-in for integrating SMT solvers into Coq. In: CAV 2017. LNCS, vol. 10427, pp. 126–133 (2017). https://doi.org/10.1007/978-3-319-63390-9_7
11. Gario, M., Micheli, A.: PySMT: a solver-agnostic library for fast prototyping of SMT-based algorithms. In: SMT workshop (2015)
12. He, M., Blenk, A., Kellerer, W., Schmid, S.: Toward consistent state management of adaptive programmable networks based on P4. In: NEAT@SIGCOMM, pp. 29–35 (2019). https://doi.org/10.1145/3341558.3342202
13. Kheradmand, A., Rosu, G.: P4K: a formal semantics of P4 and applications (2018). https://doi.org/10.48550/arXiv.1804.01468
14. Kurose, J.F., Ross, K.W.: Computer Networking: A Top-Down Approach, 8th edn. Pearson Education Limited, Harlow (2022)
15. van Leenen, J.: Practical equivalence checking of P4 packet parsers. Thesis Bachelor Informatica, LIACS, Leiden University (2025). https://theses.liacs.nl/3410
16. Liu, J., et al.: P4V: practical verification for programmable data planes. In: SIGCOMM, pp. 490–503 (2018). https://doi.org/10.1145/3230543.3230582
17. Neves, M., Freire, L., Schaeffer-Filho, A., Barcellos, M.: Verification of P4 programs in feasible time using assertions. In: CoNEXT, pp. 73–85 (2018). https://doi.org/10.1145/3281411.3281421
18. Nötzli, A., Khan, J., Fingerhut, A., Barrett, C., Athanas, P.: p4pktgen: automated test case generation for P4 programs. In: SOSR, pp. 1–7 (2018). https://doi.org/10.1145/3185467.3185497
19. Ramananandro, T., et al.: EverParse: verified secure zero-copy parsers for authenticated message formats. In: USENIX Security, pp. 1465–1482 (2019). https://doi.org/10.5555/3361338.3361440

20. Rosu, G., Serbanuta, T.: An overview of the K semantic framework. J. Log. Algebraic Methods Program. **79**(6), 397–434 (2010). https://doi.org/10.1016/J.JLAP.2010.03.012
21. Sangiorgi, D.: Introduction to Bisimulation and Coinduction. Cambridge University Press (2011). https://doi.org/10.1017/CBO9780511777110
22. Sassaman, L., Patterson, M.L., Bratus, S., Locasto, M.E.: Security applications of formal language theory. IEEE Syst. J. **7**(3), 489–500 (2013). https://doi.org/10.1109/JSYST.2012.2222000
23. Stoenescu, R., Dumitrescu, D., Popovici, M., Negreanu, L., Raiciu, C.: Debugging P4 programs with vera. In: SIGCOMM, pp. 518–532 (2018). https://doi.org/10.1145/3230543.3230548
24. The P4 language consortium: $P4_{16}$ language specification - version 1.2.5 (2024). https://p4.org/wp-content/uploads/2024/10/P4-16-spec-v1.2.5.html
25. The P4 Language Consortium: P4C—the $P4_{16}$ reference compiler (2026). https://github.com/p4lang/p4c
26. The Rocq development team: The Rocq Prover (2026). https://rocq-prover.org/
27. Tian, B., et al.: Aquila: a practically usable verification system for production-scale programmable data planes. In: SIGCOMM, pp. 17–32 (2021). https://doi.org/10.1145/3452296.3472937

Synthesis

Randomise Alone, Reach as a Team

Léonard Brice[1], Thomas A. Henzinger[1], Alipasha Montaseri[1], Ali Shafiee[1], and K. S. Thejaswini[2(✉)]

[1] Institute of Science and Technology Austria, Klosterneuburg, Austria
{leonard.brice,tah,alipasha.montaseri, ali.shafiee}@ista.ac.at
[2] Université libre de Bruxelles, Bruxelles, Belgium
thejaswini.raghavan@ulb.be

Abstract. We study concurrent graph games where n players cooperate against an opponent to reach a set of target states. Unlike traditional settings, we study distributed randomisation: team players do not share a source of randomness, and their private random sources are hidden from the opponent and from each other.

We show that memoryless strategies are sufficient for the threshold problem (deciding whether there is a strategy for the team that ensures winning with probability that exceeds a threshold), a result that not only places the problem in the Existential Theory of the Reals ($\exists\mathbb{R}$) but also enables the construction of value iteration algorithms. We additionally show that the threshold problem is NP-hard. For the almost-sure reachability problem, we prove NP-completeness.

We introduce Individually Randomised Alternating-time Temporal Logic (IRATL). This logic extends the standard ATL framework to reason about probability thresholds, with semantics explicitly designed for coalitions that lack a shared source of randomness. On the practical side, we implement and evaluate a solver for the threshold and almost-sure problem based on the algorithms that we develop.

1 Introduction

Multi-agent systems provide a robust mathematical framework for modelling complex interactions across a diverse array of domains. From the formal verification of reactive systems [4,19] and cyber-physical architectures [32,37] to the study of epidemic processes [30] and distributed probabilistic programs [1], the interplay between autonomous entities is central to ensuring system correctness. In these models, such entities are typically represented as *players*, repeatedly and concurrently choosing among some set of *actions*. While classical verification often considers a single controller against an adversarial environment, there are plenty of applications that demand multi-agent models with access to varying degrees of cooperation and information.

A traditional tool to capture what coalitions of players can achieve in such settings is Alternating Temporal Logic (ATL) [2]. ATL captures specifications of

E. Darulova et al. (Eds.): CAV 2026, LNCS 16682, pp. 215–236, 2026.
https://doi.org/10.1007/978-3-032-32519-8_12

the following form: "Can a coalition achieve a given temporal objective against all strategies of the other players?" In such a setting, one need only consider deterministic strategies, since randomising among several actions does not bring any additional power. Important extensions, however, are Randomised ATL (RATL) [17] and Probabilistic ATL (PATL) [16], both of which capture notions such as almost-sure and limit-sure winning—and the latter considers threshold winning, that is, guaranteeing that the probability of winning exceeds a given threshold t. For those types of specifications, randomised strategies are strictly more powerful than deterministic ones. Nevertheless, the semantics of RATL and PATL allow coalitions to randomise their actions jointly, implicitly assuming that they can resort to shared sources of randomness, or equivalently, that they can communicate about their random choices privately. Such a hypothesis simplifies significantly the setting, since the coalition can then be seen as a single player; but it is not realistic in many real-life distributed and multi-agent systems, where challenges often lie, precisely, in the inability of the agents to communicate. This paper aims at bridging this gap.

An Example. Picture an object that needs to be moved to the other side of a sliding door. Two robots, named R2D2 and C3PO, can choose at each step to move the object either to the left or to the right, while an adversarial environment moves the sliding door, such that one among the left and the right side is open at each time step. If both R2D2 and C3PO choose the same direction as the environment, then the object moves to the other side and they win. If R2D2 and C3PO choose the same side, but the environment opens the other side then the object remains stationary, and they have to try again. If they choose different sides, the object breaks due to the opposing forces. This situation is illustrated in Fig. 1. With what probability can R2D2 and C3PO ensure reaching s_{goal}?

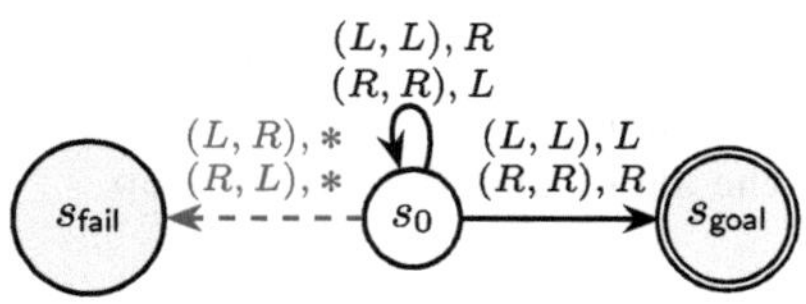

Fig. 1. The two agents choose among actions $\{L, R\}$ and the environment chooses among actions $\{L, R\}$.

Consider first the setting where R2D2 and C3PO have access to a shared source of randomness, which can't be observed by the adversary. Such games can be viewed as standard two-player concurrent games, where the team acts as a single meta-player. By playing the joint actions (L, L) or (R, R) with probability $\frac{1}{2}$ each, R2D2 and C3PO ensure that for any environmental choice, the probability of advancing is $\frac{1}{2}$, and the probability of reaching the failure state is 0. By repeating this, it is almost sure that the target will eventually be reached.

However, when R2D2 and C3PO do not share a source of randomness nor a private communication channel, they have to randomise their actions independently. One can show that against any such strategy profile, the environment can respond in such a way that the probability of eventually reaching the target does not exceed $\frac{1}{3}$. Observe here that the severity of this result relies on the order of the quantifiers: we assume that the team fixes a collective strategy first, and that the environment responds to it, hence the value $\frac{1}{3}$ is what is called in the literature the *max-min value*. If, instead, the environment must commit to a strategy first, then R2D2 and C3PO can respond deterministically and reach the target state almost surely (with probability 1), which is called the *min-max value*. It is because the team can always coordinate on a single deterministic action (e.g., both constantly playing L or R) that the environment plays with positive probability. By this, they can avoid the failure state and ensure they eventually progress. We assume the burden of pessimism and focus on the max-min value.

Our Results. We first start with the following problem for team games.

Threshold Problem: Given a game, given a rational threshold $t \in [0, 1]$, does there exist a *collective* strategy for the team that ensures the target is reached with probability strictly greater than t?

Our first main result establishes that when there exists such a collective strategy, there exists a memoryless one (Theorem 1). This implies that these games can be fully characterised by local, state-dependent strategies. Therefore, given an instance of the threshold problem, we can construct a formula in the Existential Theory of the Reals (ETR) that is satisfiable if and only if we have a positive instance. This proves that the threshold problem lies in the complexity class $\exists\mathbb{R}$ (itself contained in PSPACE [11,36]). We also prove that the problem is NP-hard using a reduction from k-clique problem. This is unlike the situation for two-player concurrent games, where no such hardness results are known. In fact, for two-player concurrent games (or for games where the team can share randomness, which reduces to the latter) the best known lower bound for the threshold problem is SQRTSUM-hardness [18] and P-hardness derived from turn-based reachability games [24] and the best known upper bound is the complexity class $\exists\mathbb{R}$ [12]. While our encoding into ETR provides an algorithm, such large logical sentences are notoriously difficult for existing solvers to solve. To provide a more computationally accessible approach, we also develop a Value Iteration (VI) algorithm that converges to the optimal max-min value—even though it might never reach it.

Secondly, we prove NP-completeness of almost-sure reachability.

Almost-sure Problem: Given a game, does there exist a collective strategy for the team that ensures that the target is reached with probability 1?

While this problem lies in P in a two-player setting, we show that it is NP-hard even with three players. Membership in NP is obtained by proving that memoryless strategies also suffice in this setting—but the proof requires techniques different from that of the threshold problem.

Thirdly, we implement solvers for the threshold and almost-sure problems, and evaluate them on existing benchmarks that we modify to fit our setting. For the threshold problem, we first encode the entire game as a single formula in $\exists\mathbb{R}$ and use SMT solvers; while this offers strong theoretical guarantees, the formula's complexity often leads to timeouts. In contrast, we employ VI algorithms using various termination criteria and heuristics. These heuristics provide *sound under-approximations*, and terminate with results close to the actual max-min values in our benchmarks. Because VI methods query the $\exists\mathbb{R}$ solver using smaller formulas, they terminate significantly faster than solving the whole encoding. For the almost-sure case, given its NP-completeness, we utilise SAT solvers on the succinct SAT encodings that we construct. We use state-of-the-art PRISM-games to solve the threshold and the almost-sure version of the strict subcase of the games with shared randomness as a baseline. Despite solving a computationally harder game, our solvers achieve runtimes comparable to PRISM-games [27].

Finally, we propose a new logic called *Individually Randomised ATL (IRATL)* to capture the inability of a coalition to randomise collectively. The syntax of IRATL extends ATL with operators capturing the fact that a coalition can enforce an objective without using any shared randomness. For example, considering our robot team, we would write the formula $\langle\langle \mathsf{R2D2}, \mathsf{C3PO} \rangle\rangle^{\mathsf{sh}}_{\mathsf{almost}}(\Diamond\{s_{\mathsf{goal}}\})$ to check if the team can reach s_{goal} almost-surely using *shared* (sh) randomness. In contrast, to query if the team can reach the target with a probability strictly greater than 0.3 using *independent* (ind) sources of randomness, we write $\langle\langle \mathsf{R2D2}, \mathsf{C3PO} \rangle\rangle^{\mathsf{ind}}_{>0.3}(\Diamond\{s_{\mathsf{goal}}\})$. As established previously, both sentences hold true in their respective settings. We effectively solve the model-checking problem for a key fragment of this logic.

Related Work

Logics for Stochastic Team Games. Alternating-time Temporal Logic (ATL) was first presented in the work of Alur et al. [2], and has inspired a rich ecosystem of extensions. While the ATL semantics considers only deterministic moves, several of those extensions introduce randomness into the picture, such as Randomised ATL (RATL) [17], PATL [16], PAMC [38], rPATL [15], and SGL [5]. SGL and rPATL are defined only on turn-based games, where the distinction between shared and individual randomisation is not relevant. RATL, PATL, and PAMC assume that players in a coalition can resort to shared randomisation, making it possible to reduce the setting to a standard two-player zero-sum game.[1]

[1] PATL and PAMC were actually defined without this hypothesis, but a careful reading of the proofs in the cited papers shows that it is then implicitly introduced, perhaps inadvertently. This ambiguity has been propagated across the subsequent literature: all results seem to assume shared randomisation, but the definitions are sometimes consistent with that hypothesis [15] and sometimes not [41]. Let us also note that the work introducing PATL [16] claims that model-checking for PATL is in NP ∩ coNP by invoking a reduction from LTL objectives to parity ones; however, such a reduction is not polynomial-time.

Strategy logic [13] is another well-known extension of ATL, that considers only deterministic strategies. Its extension Probabilistic Strategy Logic (PSL) [3] is very expressive, and since strategies are represented as variables, individual randomisation is implicitly implied. But this expressivity comes at the cost of undecidability in the general case, and very high complexities even when the players are restricted to memoryless strategies: the easiest known fragment that subsumes our setting is only known to be in EXPSPACE.

Finally, probabilistic Resource-Bounded ATL (pRB-ATL, [34]) is another logic that subsumes our setting, with a broader semantics including limited resources for the agents. No complexity upper bound is known for pRB-ATL model-checking.

Other Multiplayer Game Settings. Several works including those on population games [6], concurrent parameterised games [7], and synthesis of coalition strategies [8], work on settings with an unknown number of players as opposed to the fixed number of players in our case. Fixing the number of players enables us to obtain value-iteration-like algorithms, more amenable to implementation. A recent work on one-shot games with partially shared randomness (various sources of randomness, each of them being accessible to a given subset of players) shows that the threshold problem with a non-strict inequality (instead of strict, as in our setting) is $\exists\mathbb{R}$-complete [10] for one-shot games. However, neither the hardness nor the easiness results extend to our setting.

Fixed Environments and Multi-agent Learning. As a side observation, we consider settings where the environment is memoryless (modelling fixed but unknown stochastic process). This setting reduces to multi-agent reinforcement learning, where agents must learn to coordinate in a stochastic environment [20,25,42].

Tools. The landscape of automated verification for multi-agent systems is rich with tools, yet, to the best of our knowledge, none natively support the independent randomisation constraint central to our work. The most prominent tool, PRISM-games [14,27], extends probabilistic model checking to the two-player version. While PRISM-games can verify properties for a coalition of players (e.g., using the logic rPATL), it treats it as a single "meta-player" capable of correlated strategies. Tools such as MCMAS [31] and EVE [21] enable strategic reasoning via ATL and Nash equilibrium synthesis. However, MCMAS focuses primarily on qualitative (Boolean) verification and epistemic properties, while EVE and related Nash solvers (e.g., PRISM-Nash) target non-zero-sum equilibria.

2 Preliminaries

2.1 Probabilities

Given a finite set S, a *probability distribution* over S is a mapping $d : S \to [0,1]$ that satisfies the equality $\sum_{x \in S} d(x) = 1$. The set of probability distributions over S is denoted by $\mathsf{Dist}S$.

2.2 Games

We use the word *game* for team concurrent stochastic reachability games.

Definition 1 (Game Structure, Game). *A* game structure *is a tuple* $G = (\Sigma, S, (A_p)_{p\in\Sigma}, (\mathsf{Av}_p)_{p\in\Sigma}, \delta)$*, consisting of:*

- *a set* Σ *of* players*;*
- *a set* S *of* states*;*
- *for each player* p*, a set* A_p *of* actions*;*
- *for each player* p *and state* s*, a set* $\mathsf{Av}_p(s) \subseteq A_p$ *of actions available at state* s *(always assumed to be nonempty);*
- *a* transition function $\delta : S \times \prod_{p\in\Sigma} A_p \to \mathsf{Dist}(S)$ *that maps each tuple* $(s, (a_p)_p)$ *with* $a_p \in \mathsf{Av}_p(s)$ *for each* p *to a probability distribution over* S*.*

A game *is a tuple* $\mathcal{G} = (G, \Pi, T, s_0)$*, that consists of a game structure equipped with a* team $\Pi \subseteq \Sigma$*, a set* $T \subseteq S$ *of* target states*, and an* initial state $s_0 \in S$*.*

When referring to a game $\mathcal{G}$ or a game structure G, we often use the notations S, δ, etc., without recalling them. Given a set $P \subseteq \Sigma$ and a vertex s, we often write $\mathsf{Av}_P(s)$ (or $\mathsf{Av}(s)$ if $P = \Sigma$) to denote the product $\mathsf{Av}_P(s) = \prod_{p\in P} \mathsf{Av}_p(s)$. For technical reasons, we assume that the target set T is *absorbing*, i.e. that for every state $t \in T$ and action profile $\bar{a}$ we have $\delta(t, \bar{a})(t) = 1$.

We call *play* (resp. *history*) in the game structure G an infinite (resp. finite) word over the alphabet S. We sometimes say that the team *wins* the play π if that play contains a target state $s \in T$, and *loses* it otherwise.

2.3 Strategies, and Strategy Profiles

A *strategy* for player $p \in \Sigma$ is a mapping σ_p that maps each history hs to a probability distribution $\sigma_p(hs) \in \mathsf{Dist}\,\mathsf{Av}_p(s)$. A *strategy profile* for the set $P \subseteq \Sigma$ is a tuple $\bar{\sigma}_P = (\sigma_p)_{p\in P}$, where each σ_p is a strategy for player p. A *collective strategy* is a strategy profile $\bar{\sigma}_\Pi$ for the team. A *complete* strategy profile is a strategy profile $\bar{\sigma}_\Sigma$ for Σ, often written $\bar{\sigma}$, without subscript. Given two strategy profiles $\bar{\sigma}_P$ and $\bar{\tau}_Q$ with $P \cap Q = \emptyset$, we write $(\bar{\sigma}_P, \bar{\tau}_Q)$ for the strategy profile $\bar{\eta}_{P\cup Q}$, where $\eta_p = \sigma_p$ if $p \in P$, and τ_p if $p \in Q$. Given two strategy profiles denoted by $\bar{\sigma}_P$ and $\bar{\sigma}_{\Sigma\setminus P}$, we simply write $\bar{\sigma}$ for the complete strategy profile $(\bar{\sigma}_P, \bar{\sigma}_{\Sigma\setminus P})$. Given a strategy profile $\bar{\sigma}_P$ and a history h, we write $\bar{\sigma}(h)$ for the induced distribution over joint actions, i.e., for the distribution $\bar{\sigma}(h) : \bar{a}_P \mapsto \prod_{p\in P} \sigma_p(h)(a_p)$.

A complete strategy profile $\bar{\sigma}$ defines a probability distribution $\mathbb{P}_{\bar{\sigma}}$ over plays, where for each history hs and state t, we have:

$$\mathbb{P}_{\bar{\sigma}}(hstS^\omega) = \sum_{\bar{a}\in\mathsf{Av}(s)} \bar{\sigma}(hs)(\bar{a}) \cdot \delta(s, \bar{a})(t).$$

A strategy σ_p is *deterministic* if for every history h, there exists an action a such that $\sigma_p(h)(a) = 1$. It is *memoryless* if for every state s and every history h, we have $\sigma_p(hs) = \sigma_p(s)$.

2.4 Problems

Throughout this paper, our goal is to design collective strategies for teams that guarantee a certain property against every strategy of the other players. We always assume that the team players fix their strategies first, and the other players (the *opponents*) respond to it. From the opponents' perspective, responding to a collective strategy amounts to finding optimal strategies in a Markov decision process. It is a well-known result that deterministic strategies are sufficient in such a setting. Consequently, contrary to the team players, the fact that the opponents do not share a common source of randomness is not a restriction, and the opponents can be considered as a single player. For convenience, we will therefore always assume that the set $\Sigma \setminus \Pi$ is a singleton $\{\mathsf{O}\}$, where player O is called *opponent*. In such a setting, a natural question is to ask whether the team players can win the game with a probability greater than a given threshold.

Problem 1 (Threshold Problem). Given a game $\mathcal{G}$ and a threshold $t \in \mathbb{Q} \cap [0, 1]$, does there exist a collective strategy $\bar{\sigma}_\Pi$ such that for every strategy σ_O, the set T is reached with probability strictly greater than t?

A less ambitious question is to ask whether they can win with probability 1.

Problem 2 (Almost-sure Problem). Given a game $\mathcal{G}$, does there exist a collective strategy $\bar{\sigma}_\Pi$ such that for every strategy profile $\bar{\sigma}_\mathsf{O}$, the set T is reached with probability 1?

In the two next sections, we design algorithms for those two problems.

3 The Threshold Problem

In this section, we analyse the structure of the team's strategies and establish the theoretical foundations for solving Problem 1. The main result of this section is Theorem 1, which establishes that memoryless strategies are sufficient.

Building on this result, we provide a decision procedure by encoding the threshold problem as an ETR formula. Finally, we end the section with a result on NP-hardness for the threshold problem, which adds to the SQRTSUM-hardness result that is already known from the two-player case [18].

3.1 Optimality of Memoryless Strategies

In this subsection, we prove that memoryless strategies suffice to exceed a given threshold. The structure of the proof is similar to that of the same result in standard two-player zero-sum concurrent games [12]. However, the latter heavily relies on the equality of the max-min and min-max values, which no longer holds in our setting. Our proof requires therefore more technical effort.

Value Iteration. As a step toward our result, and as an algorithmic tool, we define a value iteration sequence. A *valuation* is a mapping $v : S \to [0,1]$. We define the *predecessor operator* based on this intuition: for a fixed valuation v and a state s, we consider a *local one-shot game* played in s. In this local game, the team players choose a joint distribution over their available actions, and the opponent responds with an action as well. If t is the subsequent state, then the team gets *payoff* $v(t)$. The team players want to maximise the expected payoff, while the opponent wants to minimise it. To avoid confusion, strategies in this one-shot game are *selectors*. The predecessor operator is defined in three steps: given fixed strategies for both the team and the opponent, given a fixed team strategy against an optimal opponent, and finally, the optimal one-step value.

First, given a valuation v, a collective selector $\bar{\xi}_\Pi$, and an opponent selector ξ_O, we define the expected payoff at state s as:

$$\mathsf{Pre}_{\bar{\xi}}(v)(s) = \sum_{\bar{a} \in \mathsf{Av}_\Pi(s)} \sum_{b \in \mathsf{Av}_\mathsf{O}(s)} \sum_{t \in S} \bar{\xi}_\Pi(s)(\bar{a}) \cdot \xi_\mathsf{O}(s)(b) \cdot \delta(s, \bar{a}, b)(t) \cdot v(t).$$

We now define the value guaranteed by a fixed collective selector $\bar{\xi}_\Pi$:

$$\mathsf{Pre}_{\bar{\xi}_\Pi}(v)(s) = \inf_{\xi_\mathsf{O} \in \Lambda_\mathsf{O}(s)} \mathsf{Pre}_{\bar{\xi}}(v)(s)$$

where $\Lambda_\mathsf{O}(s) = \mathsf{Dist}(\mathsf{Av}_\mathsf{O})$ is the set of selectors for the opponent in state s.

Finally, we define the *predecessor operator* Pre, which represents the maximum value the team can guarantee in one step against the opponent:

$$\mathsf{Pre}(v)(s) = \sup_{\bar{\xi}_\Pi \in \Lambda_\Pi(s)} \inf_{\xi_\mathsf{O} \in \Lambda_\mathsf{O}(s)} \mathsf{Pre}_{\bar{\xi}}(v)(s)$$

where $\Lambda_\Pi(s)$ is the set of collective selectors for the team in state s.

We can then define a sequence $(v_n)_n$ of valuations as follows: the valuation v_0 maps each target state to the value 1 and each other state to the value 0, and for each n, we have $v_{n+1} = \mathsf{Pre}(v_n)$. We then have the following result.

Lemma 1. *For every vertex s, the sequence $(v_n(s))_n$ converges to the max-min value of the game, when initialised in s.*

As we will show in Sect. 5, this value iteration sequence also entails a sound under-approximation algorithm. For now, let us use this tool to prove our result.

Memoryless Strategies Are Sufficient.

Theorem 1. *Let $\mathcal{G}$ be a game and let t be a threshold. If there is a collective strategy $\bar{\sigma}_\Pi$ that guarantees victory with probability strictly greater than t against every opponent's strategy, then there is a memoryless one.*

Proof (Sketch). Using Lemma 1, there exists an index n such that the nth valuation, on s_0, takes a value that is greater than t. We assign a "rank" to each state corresponding to the iteration index where its value was determined. The memoryless strategy is then constructed to ensure that at each step, the next state has either a higher valuation or a lower rank, which guarantees convergence to the states with valuation 1 and with rank 0: the target states. □

A Variant: Playing Against a Memoryless Opponent. Before proceeding to the study of the threshold problem, we make a remark about a variant of our problem: the case where the opponent is restricted to memoryless strategies. This modelling choice is well-motivated by the physical reality of autonomous systems, whose environments are often fixed (but unknown) stochastic processes rather than strategic adversaries. We show here that Theorem 1 does not extend to this setting: surprisingly, restricting the opponent to memoryless strategies can force the team players to use memory to play optimally. The following example illustrates that solving this variant would require significantly different techniques from the field of multi-agent learning.

Theorem 2. *There exists a game $\mathcal{G}$ such that against an opponent restricted to memoryless strategies, the team can achieve a strictly higher probability of reaching the target using a strategy with memory than with any memoryless collective strategy.*

Proof (Sketch). We give an example in the game in Fig. 2. Intuitively, the team players can agree to wait arbitrarily long to *learn* the probability distribution during the waiting stage and then play the appropriate action to maximise the probability of reaching the target state. □

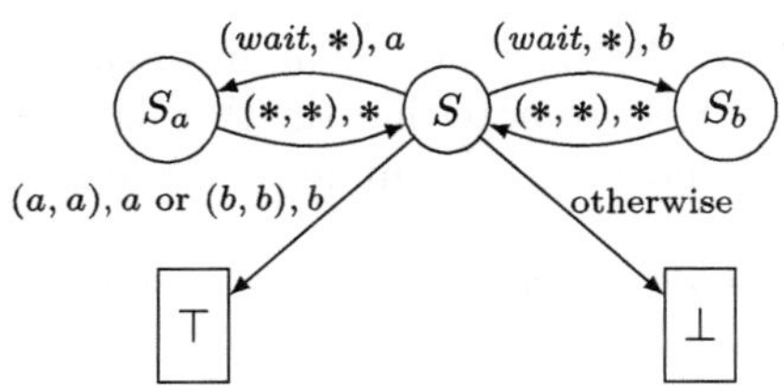

Fig. 2. An example game for opponent with no memory.

3.2 Complexity Bounds

After a short detour, we return to the setting where the opponent has (potentially) unbounded memory. We establish complexity bounds.

Membership in the Class $\exists\mathbb{R}$. We first show that the problem is in $\exists\mathbb{R}$ by constructing an equivalent ETR formula. Our construction relies on Theorem 1.

Theorem 3. *The threshold problem lies in the class $\exists\mathbb{R}$.*

Proof (Sketch). To help our reduction, we introduce λ-discounted games. These games share the same structure as concurrent games but employ a discounted payoff function parameterised by a *discount factor* $\lambda \in (0, 1)$. These games are *quantitative*: if the team reaches the target set T after k steps, the team gets the payoff λ^k (instead of 1). We construct a polynomial-size ETR formula $\Psi(\lambda)$ which is satisfiable if and only if there exists a collective strategy such that the λ-discounted value exceeds t. Since this only captures the discounted version of the problem, we then show that it is equivalent to its qualitative counterpart, in the sense that there exists λ such that the formula $\Psi(\lambda)$ is satisfiable if and only if we have a positive instance of the threshold problem.

This intermediary reduction to the λ-discounted setting is necessary. A direct encoding of the reachability problem faces a hurdle: the Bellman optimality equations for reachability generally admit multiple fixed points. Consider, for example, a simple loop $s \to s$ with no path to the target. The true reachability probability is 0. However, the assignment $v(s) = 1$ trivially satisfies the Bellman equations one would write, making it a valid but spurious fixed point. One standard solution is to impose the restriction that it is the least fixed point. However, enforcing a "least fixed point" constraint would require the min operator, which is not permitted in the standard $\exists\mathbb{R}$ framework. Alternatively, identifying the non-zero support set requires guessing (if there exists a subset of vertices from which the target can be reached with nonzero probability), which puts the problem in a larger complexity class $\mathsf{NP}^{\exists\mathbb{R}}$. This makes our intermediary detour via λ-discounted settings necessary. □

NP-hardness. We finally end with a proof of NP-hardness for this problem. Note that it is also SQRTSUM-hard, following from the two-player case [18]. For the sake of completeness, we also note that the threshold problem with non-strict inequalities was recently shown to be complete for the class $\exists\mathbb{R}$ [10, Lemma 5.7].

Theorem 4. *The threshold problem is* NP*-hard, even with three states and three players.*

Proof (Sketch). We establish NP-hardness via a reduction from the *clique problem.* Given a graph G and an integer k, we construct a game with two team players and three states: an initial state, a target state, and a trap state. The team players select actions consisting of a tuple $(u, i) \in V \times \{1, \ldots, k\}$, claiming that they have a clique whose i-th vertex is u. Simultaneously, the opponent selects a pair of indices (i, j) to verify. Transitions from s_0 are defined as follows: the play reaches the target if the team plays $((u, i), (v, j))$ and the opponent selects (i, j) such that the selection is consistent with a clique ($u = v$ if $i = j$, and $(u, v) \in E$ if $i \neq j$). The game transitions to the trap state if the team matches the opponent's indices (i, j) but fails the clique consistency check ($u \neq v$ when $i = j$, or $(u, v) \notin E$ when $i \neq j$). If the team's chosen indices do not match the opponent's query, the game loops back to repeating the round. We show that if G contains a clique of size k, the team can reach the target state with probability 1. Otherwise, the maximum probability of reaching the target is bounded by $\frac{3}{4}$. The threshold problem is therefore NP-hard, even with threshold $\frac{3}{4}$. □

4 The Almost-Sure Problem

In this section, we focus on Problem 2: deciding whether the team can win almost surely. We show that this problem is NP-complete. First, in Sect. 4.1, we show that memoryless strategies are also optimal for this problem. Second, in Sect. 4.2, we prove the upper and the lower bound.

4.1 Optimality of Memoryless Strategies

In this subsection, we show that if the team can guarantee reaching the target almost-surely, it can do so using a memoryless collective strategy. Formally, we show the correctness of the following theorem. Note that it is not a consequence of Theorem 1, since the threshold problem is defined with strict inequalities.

Theorem 5. *Let $\mathcal{G}$ be a game. If there is a collective strategy $\bar{\sigma}_\Pi$ that guarantees victory with probability* 1 *against every opponent's strategy, then there is a memoryless one.*

Proof (Sketch). We assign a rank (a value from $\mathbb{N} \cup \{\infty\}$) to each vertex, that captures "distance" from the target: the target set T has rank 0, and the states that have rank $k+1$ are exactly those where the team can force a transition to states with rank k with positive probability, without visiting a vertex of infinite rank. We construct a memoryless collective strategy as follows. At every state, the team plays to guarantee a positive probability of moving to a lower rank, while staying within the winning set (the states with finite rank). Since the probability of reducing the rank is always strictly positive, the game is forced to eventually progress and reach rank 0 (the target) with probability 1.

4.2 Complexity Bounds

SAT Encoding for NP Membership. We show the following theorem.

Theorem 6. *The almost-sure problem is in* NP.

Proof (Sketch). Based on the results of Sect. 4.1, we know that if an almost-sure winning collective strategy exists, there exists a memoryless one. We then give an explicit SAT formula Φ that is satisfiable if and only if there exists a memoryless strategy that guarantee almost-sure reachability. The construction of Φ relies on the fact that almost-sure reachability is a qualitative property: it depends only on the *support* of the strategies, not on the precise probability values. The formula Φ encodes the search for a winning set W and the set of support of strategy for each player. The constraints enforce the existence of the ranking function as defined in the proof of Theorem 5. We also apply some optimisations to reduce the number of variables, like using a binary encoding of the rank. □

We end this section with a hardness result. The following theorem is an immediate consequence of the construction presented in the proof of Theorem 4.

Corollary 1 (of Theorem 4). *The almost-sure problem is* NP-*hard.*

5 Experimental Results

We implement two algorithms to compute the max-min value and one for the almost-sure case. The algorithm for the value problem is a global reduction that maps the game to a single ETR formula. The second algorithm uses a value iteration (VI) scheme to compute the value. For the almost-sure case, we implement one algorithm based on its SAT encoding. To establish a baseline and contextualise our runtime, we also compare our approach with the state-of-the-art PRISM-games [27], which solves the two-player version of concurrent games. PRISM-games is particularly relevant as it handles both the quantitative (max-min value) and qualitative (almost-sure) versions of this problem, but where the team players have access to shared randomness. PRISM-games, therefore, solves a strict and computationally easier subcase of our setting. The source code is available at https://github.com/alipashamontaseri/Team-Concurrent-Game.

5.1 Algorithms

We evaluate three algorithms for the max-min value. The first is a global reduction. The second is a value iteration framework, for which we provide three distinct implementations. Each implementation provides a *sound under-approximation* of the value. The third is a baseline based on PRISM-games [27].

Algorithm 1: ETR-Direct. This method implements the reduction from Sect. 3.2. It translates the entire game into a single ETR formula. It then computes the game value using binary search combined with SMT solvers.

Algorithm 2: Value iteration (VI). ETR-Direct scales poorly on games with many states. Therefore, we use the value iteration scheme from Sect. 3.1. This method updates values iteratively by solving local one-shot games. In these local games, we calculate the highest probability the team can guarantee to gain in a single step, based on the current value estimates of the states. Based on this, we update the estimates of state values. The value iteration algorithm is a lower bound for the max-min value of the game, and improves it every step. Therefore, the values act as a sound under-approximation. We propose three implementations for solving these local instances:

1. **VI-ETR:** This implementation uses an SMT solver to compute each local instance reliably. This guarantees precision but may take longer on computationally difficult instances.
2. **VI-OPT:** This implementation treats each one-shot game as a non-linear optimisation problem to be faster. We use Sequential Least Squares Programming (SLSQP) [26] to solve them. Because the constraints are smooth (in C^∞), the solver uses analytical gradients. This method yields an under-approximation of the value because the solver may converge to a local optimum rather than the global one. However, our experiments show that the computed value remains close to the true value.

3. **VI-Hybrid:** This implementation combines SLSQP optimisation with exact solving. For each local game, we first generate a candidate value v^* using SLSQP. We then query the SMT solver to verify if a value $v \geq v^* + \varepsilon$ is feasible. If the query is unsatisfiable, we accept v^* as the global optimum. If satisfiable (indicating v^* is a local optimum), we solve the instance with binary search using v^* as a lower bound. Thus, this reliably computes the value of the game.

Algorithm 3: Quantitative PRISM (Baseline). We include the state-of-the-art algorithm from PRISM-games [27]. It assumes that team players share randomness (whereas our setting assumes that team players do not share randomness). Our setting is more general, as shared randomness can be modelled by a single player.

The optimisation strategy used in VI-OPT and VI-Hybrid (SLSQP) is explained in detail in the full version of the paper [9].

For the almost-sure reachability problem, we evaluate two algorithms:

Algorithm 4: SAT-Direct. This method implements the encoding described in Sect. 4.2. It translates the almost-sure problem into a SAT. We then use a SAT solver to determine if an almost-surely winning collective strategy exists. This algorithm always gives a verification guarantee.

Algorithm 5: Qualitative PRISM (Baseline). We use the qualitative verification engine of PRISM-games [27] as a baseline. Similar to Algorithm 3, this tool solves the almost-sure problem under the assumption of shared randomness, which is only a comparison point for our general setting.

Implementation. We implemented a prototype solver in Python 3.11.14 to evaluate these algorithms. We conducted all experiments on a machine running Ubuntu 24.04 LTS, equipped with an Intel Core Ultra 5 225U processor and 16 GB of RAM. We set a timeout of 600 s for each algorithm on each instance. For the max-min problem, we perform binary search until we achieve a precision of $\varepsilon = 10^{-4}$.

1. **SMT solver:** We use the Z3 SMT solver [33] for all ETR queries. This handles Algorithm 1, and the verification steps in the value iteration variants.
2. **SLSQP optimiser:** We use the SLSQP algorithm provided by SciPy [40]. This optimiser solves the local games in VI-OPT and generates the candidate values for VI-Hybrid.
3. **Stopping criteria:** We terminate the value iteration when the values stabilise. We stop the process when the maximum change across all states drops below $\varepsilon' = 10^{-4}$ and report the final values.
4. **SAT solver:** For the almost-sure reachability problem (Algorithm 4), we use the `minisat22` SAT solver [39] provided by the PySAT library.

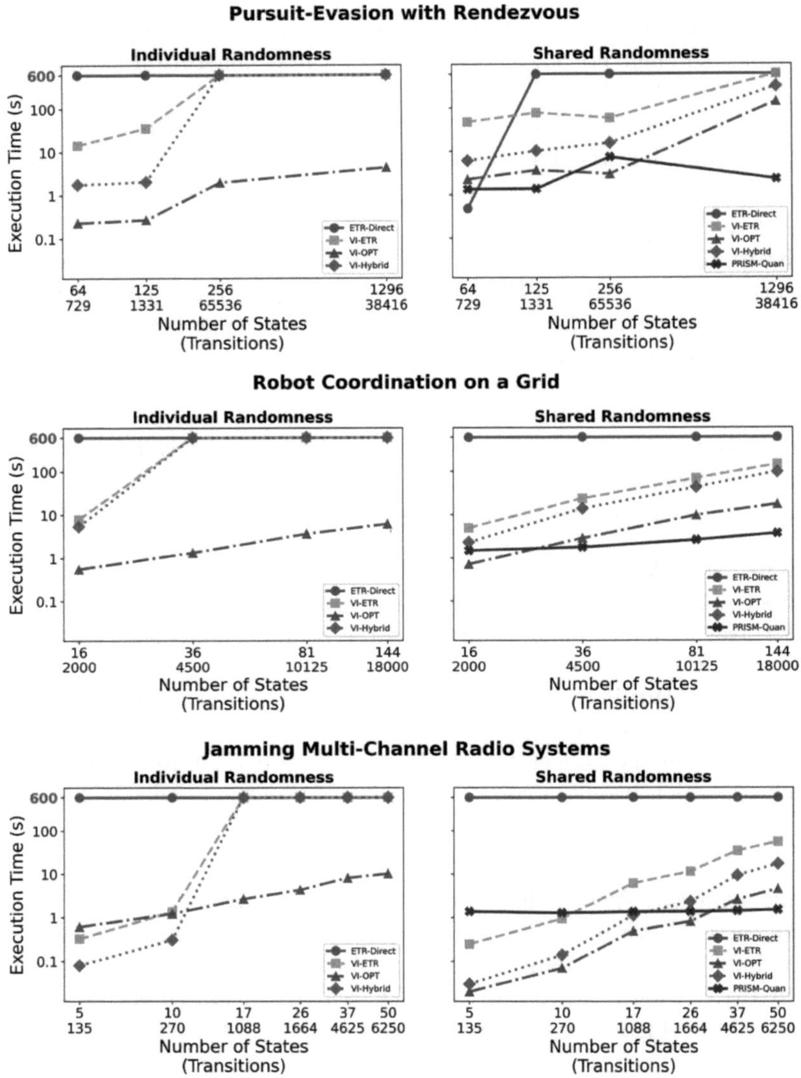

Fig. 3. Execution time of the algorithms across three benchmarks. The plots report execution time in seconds vs. the state space size: both in log scale.

5.2 Benchmarks

We evaluate our algorithms on three distinct benchmarks. The first is Pursuit-Evasion with Rendezvous, a variant of the game from [35]. In this setting, a cooperative team of agents must meet at *one vertex* in a directed graph while avoiding a pursuer. The second is Robot Coordination, adapted from PRISM-games [28], where a team of robots navigates a grid against adversarial wind conditions to reach a target configuration. The third is Jamming Multi-Channel

Radio Systems, also adapted from PRISM-games [28], which models sensors transmitting packets over frequency channels subject to adversarial jamming and collisions. We provide formal definitions, dynamics, and objective functions for all three benchmarks in the full version.

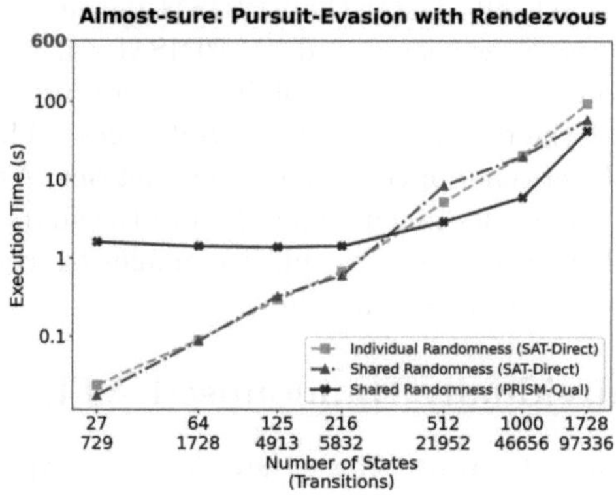

Fig. 4. The plot compares the execution time (in seconds, logarithmic scale) of SAT-Direct under individual and shared randomness constraints against the baseline qualitative solver (which assumes shared randomness).

5.3 Results

We evaluate our algorithms in two settings. The first is the general case of *individual randomness*. The second is the special case of *shared randomness*. In the latter, we model the team as a single "meta-player" with joint actions, which allows us to compare our results against PRISM-games. Detailed numerical data is provided in the full version [9].

Max-Min Problem. Across both settings, **ETR-Direct** fails to solve even small instances within the timeout. In the case of individual randomness (Fig. 3, left), the exact and hybrid VI approaches **VI-ETR**, **VI-Hybrid** solve small instances, but their execution time increases drastically as the state space grows. Conversely, the optimisation-based variant **VI-OPT** scales effectively, solving the largest instances across all benchmarks within the time limit.

In terms of precision, **VI-OPT** yields tight under-approximations in both settings, consistently converging to values very close to the exact solutions. While PRISM outperforms our general-purpose solvers in the special case of shared randomness (Fig. 3, right), **VI-OPT** stays competitive.

Almost-Sure Problem. We analyse the Pursuit-Evasion benchmark. We selected this instance because it is the only one where the team has non-trivial strategies to win with probability 1. Figure 4 presents the results.

First, we look at the case of *shared randomness*. Here, our **SAT-Direct** algorithm performs well compared to PRISM-games. On smaller instances (Scenarios 1 to 4), our method is actually faster than PRISM because it has less overhead. In the largest instances (Scenarios 6 and 7), PRISM scales slightly better, but our solver remains competitive, despite solving a more difficult problem.

Second, we look at the case of *individual randomness*. This problem is much harder because the players cannot coordinate their actions. As expected, the time needed to find a solution grows much faster than in the shared case. Despite this added difficulty, **SAT-Direct** is successful. It manages to solve large games with over 97,000 transitions within the time limit.

6 Towards Individually Randomised ATL

We conclude this paper by proposing a new logic to capture our concept of individual randomisation. A classical tool to define specifications over reactive systems is the *Alternating Temporal Logic* (ATL) [2], in which one can encode the fact that a coalition of players can guarantee surely an objective that is expressible in Linear Temporal Logic (LTL). Since only sure guarantees are considered here, the semantics of ATL need not consider randomised strategies. This changed with the introduction of *Randomised ATL* (RATL) [17] (and PATL [16]). There, sure guarantees are extended with almost-sure and limit-sure ones, and the semantics allows players to use randomness. For example, the formula $\langle\!\langle C \rangle\!\rangle_{\mathsf{almost}} \Box q$ means that the coalition C has a "collective strategy" to ensure that every state in the play satisfies q with probability 1. However, the RATL semantics defines a collective strategy for the coalition C as a mapping from histories to distributions over the whole set of tuples of actions available for the players in C, implicitly assuming that those players can randomise based on a secret common source of randomness—which can then be reduced to a 2-player setting. Our notion of collective strategy, where players in a coalition can design their strategy together but randomisation is an individual process, cannot be captured by this logic. In this section, we introduce *Individually Randomised ATL* (or IRATL), whose semantics bridge this gap.

Syntax. Our logic is defined to extend the logic RATL.

Definition 2 (IRATL Formula). *Let Q be a set of atoms. Let Σ be a set of players. An* IRATL formula *is either:*

- *a proposition $q \in Q$;*
- *or a formula $\neg\varphi$ or $\varphi \vee \psi$, where φ and ψ are IRATL formulas;*
- *or a formula $\langle\!\langle C \rangle\!\rangle_w^r \circ \varphi$, $\langle\!\langle C \rangle\!\rangle_w^r \Box \varphi$, or $\langle\!\langle C \rangle\!\rangle_w^r \varphi \mathsf{U} \psi$, where $C \subseteq \Sigma$ is a coalition of players, where $r \in \{\mathsf{sh}, \mathsf{ind}\}$ is a* randomisation type, *and where $w \in \{\mathsf{sure}, \mathsf{almost}, \mathsf{limit}\} \cup \{> t, \geq t \mid t \in [0,1)\}$ is a* winning condition, *and where φ and ψ are IRATL formulas.*

The operators $\langle\langle\rangle\rangle_w^r$ are called *path quantifiers*, the operators O, $\Box$, and U are called *temporal operators*, and subformulas of the form $\mathsf{O}\varphi$, $\Box\varphi$ or $\varphi\mathsf{U}\psi$ are called *path formulas*.

Semantics. Given a game structure G, a set of atomic propositions Q, and a labelling function $L : S \mapsto 2^Q$, we define the semantics of IRATL by cross-induction as follows. Given a state $s \in S$, we define:

- $s \models q$ if we have $q \in L(s)$;
- $s \models \neg\varphi$ if we do not have $s \models \varphi$, and $s \models \varphi \vee \psi$ if we have $s \models \varphi$ or $s \models \psi$;
- $s \models \langle\langle C\rangle\rangle_{\mathsf{sure}}^{\mathsf{ind}}\theta$ if in the game structure G, from the state s, there exists a strategy profile $\bar{\sigma}_C$ such that for every strategy profile $\bar{\sigma}_{\Sigma\setminus C}$ and every play π compatible with the strategy profile $\bar{\sigma}$, we have $\pi \models \theta$;
- $s \models \langle\langle C\rangle\rangle_{\mathsf{almost}}^{\mathsf{ind}}\theta$ if in the game structure G, from the state s, there exists a strategy profile $\bar{\sigma}_C$ such that for every strategy profile $\bar{\sigma}_{\Sigma\setminus C}$, we have $\mathbb{P}_{\bar{\sigma}}\{\pi \in S^\omega \mid \pi \models \theta\} = 1$;
- $s \models \langle\langle C\rangle\rangle_{\mathsf{limit}}^{\mathsf{ind}}\theta$ if in the game structure G, from the state s, for every $\varepsilon > 0$, there exists a strategy profile $\bar{\sigma}_C$ such that for every strategy profile $\bar{\sigma}_{\Sigma\setminus C}$, we have $\mathbb{P}_{\bar{\sigma}}\{\pi \in S^\omega \mid \pi \models \theta\} > 1 - \varepsilon$;
- $s \models \langle\langle C\rangle\rangle_{>t}^{\mathsf{ind}}\theta$ (resp. $\langle\langle C\rangle\rangle_{\geq t}^{\mathsf{ind}}\theta$) if in the game structure G, from the state s, there exists a strategy profile $\bar{\sigma}_C$ such that for every strategy profile $\bar{\sigma}_{\Sigma\setminus C}$, we have $\mathbb{P}_{\bar{\sigma}}\{\pi \in S^\omega \mid \pi \models \theta\} > t$ (resp. $\geq t$);
- $s \models \langle\langle C\rangle\rangle_w^{\mathsf{sh}}\theta$ is defined analogously, but in the game structure G_C, in which all C players have been merged into one player who can pick an action profile at each state.

On the other hand, given a play $\pi = \pi_0\pi_1\ldots$, we define:

- $\pi \models \mathsf{O}\varphi$ if we have $\pi_1\pi_2\ldots \models \varphi$;
- $\pi \models \Box\varphi$ if for every $n \in \mathbb{N}$, we have $\pi_n \models \varphi$;
- $\pi \models \varphi\mathsf{U}\psi$ if there exists $n \in \mathbb{N}$ such that we have $\pi_n \models \psi$, and $\pi_k \models \varphi$ for every $k < n$.

Other classical symbols can be derived: for example, the formula $\top$ is short for $q \vee \neg q$ for some q, and the formula $\Diamond\varphi$ for $\top\mathsf{U}\varphi$.

Model-Checking. The algorithms presented in the previous sections enable us to define a decidable fragment of IRATL.

Theorem 7. *Given a game structure G, a state s and a formula φ that does not contain the symbols $\langle\langle C\rangle\rangle_{\mathsf{limit}}^{\mathsf{ind}}$, $\langle\langle C\rangle\rangle_{\geq t}^{\mathsf{ind}}$, or $\langle\langle C\rangle\rangle_{>t}^{\mathsf{ind}}\Box$, deciding whether in the game G we have $s \models \varphi$ can be done in* PSPACE, *and in polynomial time if the size of the game structure is fixed.*

Proof. As a preliminary remark, let us remind that when a coalition C seeks to achieve an objective θ against all strategies of the other players, those can be modelled by a single opponent, as they do not need any form of randomisation to respond to the coalition's strategy. We can then apply the following recursive algorithm. Given an IRATL formula φ:

- if $\varphi = q, \neg\psi$, or $\psi \vee \chi$, treat it recursively as expected.
- If $\varphi = \langle\langle C \rangle\rangle^{\mathsf{sh}}_{w}\theta$, then apply the same recursive operations as for RATL [17] and PATL [16].
- If $\varphi = \langle\langle C \rangle\rangle^{\mathsf{ind}}_{\mathsf{sure}}\theta$: since the coalition must surely reach the target, randomising is useless, and the coalition can then be seen as a single player. We can therefore apply the algorithms cited at the previous point.
- If $\varphi = \langle\langle C \rangle\rangle^{\mathsf{ind}}_{\mathsf{almost}}\Box\psi$: this formula is semantically equivalent to $\langle\langle C \rangle\rangle^{\mathsf{ind}}_{\mathsf{sure}}\Box\psi$. We can therefore apply the previous point.
- If $\varphi = \langle\langle C \rangle\rangle^{\mathsf{ind}}_{\mathsf{almost}}\bigcirc\psi$ (resp. $\langle\langle C \rangle\rangle^{\mathsf{ind}}_{>t}\bigcirc\psi$), first compute the set T of states that satisfy the formula ψ. Then, consider the game in which the team C wants to reach the set T, and all states except s are made absorbing. Then, decide whether the team can guarantee reaching the set T almost surely (resp. with probability greater than t), using Theorem 3 (resp. Theorem6).
- If $\varphi = \langle\langle C \rangle\rangle^{\mathsf{ind}}_{\mathsf{almost}}\psi \mathsf{U} \chi$ (resp. $\langle\langle C \rangle\rangle^{\mathsf{ind}}_{>t}\psi \mathsf{U} \chi$), first compute the sets U and T of states that satisfy the formulas ψ and χ, respectively. Consider the game in which all states $s' \in S \setminus U$ are made absorbing. Then, decide whether in this game, the team C can guarantee reaching the set T almost surely (resp. with probability greater than t), using Theorem 3 (resp. Theorem 6).

The size of the recursion stack is bounded by the size of the formula, and each recursion consists in a polynomial-space algorithm, hence the conclusion. □

The decidability of the full logic IRATL will be obtained if one can handle the two following problems, which we leave as open questions.

Problem 3 (Limit-sure Problem). Given a game $\mathcal{G}$, does it hold that for every $\varepsilon > 0$, there exists a collective strategy $\bar{\sigma}_{\Pi}$ such that for any strategy $\sigma_{\mathbb{O}}$, the probability of reaching the set T under the strategy profile $\bar{\sigma}$ is greater than $1-\varepsilon$?

Problem 4 (Safety Problems). Given a game $\mathcal{G}$, can the team guarantee (with probability greater than a given threshold, or limit-surely) that the set T is *not* eventually reached?

The reader may already be convinced that the limit-sure problem requires new techniques, but believe that the safety threshold problem can be treated in a way analogous to the reachability threshold problem. This is not the case, because Theorem 1 does not extend to safety games: as shown in the work of de Alfaro et al. [17, Theorem 8]. Even in a two-player setting, infinite memory may be required to guarantee that a safety objective is satisfied with positive probability. However, in that setting, this problem can be decided by taking the perspective of the opponent—by asking whether the opponent has a strategy to make the player lose with probability at least $1 - t$. Such arguments no longer work in our setting, since the max-min value does not equal the min-max value. Hence, the safety threshold problem seems to be more challenging than its reachability counterpart.

7 Discussion

We introduced the logic IRATL, that extends the well-studied ATL to support cases where players randomise independently without a common coin. We showed that this distinction is not just semantic but requires new algorithms.

IRATL describes games where players form teams, but must randomise individually. The exact complexity of solving these games is left as an open problem. We show $\exists\mathbb{R}$-easiness and NP-hardness for the threshold problem, which is also SQRTSUM-hard, following from the two-player case [18]. It would be interesting to know the exact complexity of this problem.

Second, from a practical perspective, our current value iteration method relies on asymptotic convergence without a certified stopping criterion. Even in the simpler two-player concurrent setting, it is known that a double-exponential number of iterations might be required to approximate the value to within an ε-approximate value [22]. A promising avenue for future work is to extend recent results on stopping criteria for concurrent games [29]. By developing techniques to approximate the value from both above and below, we could rigorously guarantee ε-optimality upon termination. We leave as future work the integration into established model checkers such as PRISM-games [27] or STORM [23] enabling model checking tools that accurately model decentralised systems.

Acknowledgments. This work is a part of project VAMOS that has received funding from the European Research Council (ERC), grant agreement No 101020093. Part of this work was realised when the first author was an FNRS aspirant at Université libre de Bruxelles.

Data Availibility Statement. The artifact can be accessed at the link: https://doi.org/10.5281/zenodo.19680359.

The source code is available at: https://github.com/alipashamontaseri/Team-Concurrent-Game.

Disclosure of Interests. The authors have no competing interests to declare that are relevant to the content of this article.

References

1. de Alfaro, L., Henzinger, T.A., Jhala, R.: Compositional methods for probabilistic systems. In: CONCUR 2001 – Concurrency Theory, pp. 351–365. Springer, Berlin Heidelberg, Berlin, Heidelberg (2001). https://doi.org/10.1007/3-540-44685-0_24
2. Alur, R., Henzinger, T.A., Kupferman, O.: Alternating-time temporal logic. J. ACM **49**(5), 672–713 (2002). https://doi.org/10.1145/585265.585270
3. Aminof, B., Kwiatkowska, M., Maubert, B., Murano, A., Rubin, S.: Probabilistic strategy logic, pp. 32–38 (2019). https://doi.org/10.24963/ijcai.2019/5
4. Attoui, A.: Multi-agent based method for reactive systems formal specification and validation. IFAC Proc. Vol. **29**(2), 1–6 (1996). https://doi.org/10.1016/S1474-6670(17)43768-2. 5th IFAC/IFIP/GI/GMA Workshop on Experience With the Management of Software Projects 1995 (MSP '95)

5. Baier, C., Brázdil, T., Größer, M., Kučera, A.: Stochastic game logic. Acta Inf. **49**(4), 203–224 (2012). https://doi.org/10.1007/s00236-012-0156-0
6. Bertrand, N., Bouyer, P., Lapointe, L., Mascle, C.: Reach together: how populations win repeated games. CoRR abs/2510.02984 (2025). https://doi.org/10.48550/ARXIV.2510.02984
7. Bertrand, N., Bouyer, P., Majumdar, A.: Concurrent parameterized games. In: FSTTCS 2019. LIPIcs, vol. 150, pp. 31:1–31:15. Schloss Dagstuhl - Leibniz-Zentrum für Informatik (2019). https://doi.org/10.4230/LIPICS.FSTTCS.2019.31
8. Bertrand, N., Bouyer, P., Majumdar, A.: Synthesizing safe coalition strategies. In: FSTTCS 2020. LIPIcs, vol. 182, pp. 39:1–39:17. Schloss Dagstuhl - Leibniz-Zentrum für Informatik (2020). https://doi.org/10.4230/LIPICS.FSTTCS.2020.39
9. Brice, L., Henzinger, T.A., Montaseri, A., Shafiee, A., Thejaswini, K.S.: Randomise alone, reach as a team. CoRR abs/2603.07094 (2026). https://doi.org/10.48550/ARXIV.2603.07094
10. Brice, L., Henzinger, T.A., Thejaswini, K.S.: Dicey games: shared sources of randomness in distributed systems (2026). https://doi.org/10.48550/arXiv.2601.18303
11. Canny, J.: Some algebraic and geometric computations in PSPACE. In: Proceedings of the Twentieth Annual ACM Symposium on Theory of Computing STOC, pp. 460–467. STOC '88, Association for Computing Machinery (1988). https://doi.org/10.1145/62212.62257
12. Chatterjee, K., de Alfaro, L., Henzinger, T.A.: Strategy improvement for concurrent reachability and safety games. CoRR abs/1201.2834 (2012). https://doi.org/10.1016/j.jcss.2012.12.001, https://arxiv.org/abs/1201.2834. preprint version of the combined QEST/SODA results
13. Chatterjee, K., Henzinger, T.A., Piterman, N.: Strategy logic. Inf. Comput. **208**(6), 677–693 (2010). https://doi.org/10.1016/j.ic.2009.07.004. https://www.sciencedirect.com/science/article/pii/S0890540110000192. special Issue: 18th International Conference on Concurrency Theory (CONCUR 2007)
14. Chen, T., Forejt, V., Kwiatkowska, M.Z., Parker, D., Simaitis, A.: Prism-games: a model checker for stochastic multi-player games. In: TACAS 2013. Lecture Notes in Computer Science, vol. 7795, pp. 185–191. Springer (2013). https://doi.org/10.1007/978-3-642-36742-7_13
15. Chen, T., Forejt, V., Kwiatkowska, M., Parker, D., Simaitis, A.: Automatic verification of competitive stochastic systems. In: Flanagan, C., König, B. (eds.) TACAS 2012. LNCS, vol. 7214, pp. 315–330. Springer, Heidelberg (2012). https://doi.org/10.1007/978-3-642-28756-5_22
16. Chen, T., Lu, J.: Probabilistic alternating-time temporal logic and model checking algorithm. In: Lei, J. (ed.) FSKD 2007, pp. 35–39. IEEE Computer Society (2007). https://doi.org/10.1109/FSKD.2007.458
17. de Alfaro, L., Henzinger, T.A., Kupferman, O.: Concurrent reachability games. Theoret. Comput. Sci. **386**(3), 188–217 (2007). https://doi.org/10.1016/j.tcs.2007.07.008. expressiveness in Concurrency
18. Etessami, K., Yannakakis, M.: Recursive markov decision processes and recursive stochastic games. J. ACM **62**(2) (2015). https://doi.org/10.1145/2699431
19. Forejt, V., Kwiatkowska, M., Norman, G., Parker, D.: Automated verification techniques for probabilistic systems, pp. 53–113. Springer, Berlin, Heidelberg (2011). https://doi.org/10.1007/978-3-642-21455-4_3
20. Guestrin, C., Koller, D., Parr, R.: Multiagent planning with factored MDPs. In: Advances in Neural Information Processing Systems (NIPS). vol. 14, pp. 1523–1530. MIT Press (2002). https://doi.org/10.5555/2980539.2980737

21. Gutierrez, J., Najib, M., Perelli, G., Wooldridge, M.J.: EVE: a tool for temporal equilibrium analysis. In: Lahiri, S.K., Wang, C. (eds.) Automated Technology for Verification and Analysis - 16th International Symposium, ATVA 2018, Los Angeles, CA, USA, 7–10 October 2018, Proceedings. Lecture Notes in Computer Science, vol. 11138, pp. 551–557. Springer (2018). https://doi.org/10.1007/978-3-030-01090-4_35
22. Hansen, K.A., Ibsen-Jensen, R., Miltersen, P.B.: The complexity of solving reachability games using value and strategy iteration. In: Computer Science - Theory and Applications. Springer (2011). https://doi.org/10.1007/978-3-642-20712-9_7
23. Hensel, C., Junges, S., Katoen, J.P., Quatmann, T., Volk, M.: The probabilistic model checker storm. Int. J. Softw. Tools Technol. Transf. **24**(4), 589–610 (2022). https://doi.org/10.1007/s10009-021-00633-z
24. Immerman, N.: Number of quantifiers is better than number of tape cells. J. Comput. Syst. Sci. **22**, 384–406 (1981). https://doi.org/10.1016/0022-0000(81)90039-8, https://api.semanticscholar.org/CorpusID:40753086
25. Kok, J.R., Vlassis, N.: Collaborative multiagent reinforcement learning by payoff propagation. J. Mach. Learn. Res. (JMLR) **7**(65), 1789–1828 (2006). https://jmlr.org/papers/v7/kok06a.html
26. Kraft, D.: A software package for sequential quadratic programming. Tech. Rep. Forschungsbericht FB 88–28, Deutsche Forschungs- und Versuchsanstalt für Luft- und Raumfahrt (DFVLR), Köln, Germany (1988). https://degenerateconic.com/uploads/2018/03/DFVLR_FB_88_28.pdf
27. Kwiatkowska, M., Norman, G., Parker, D., Santos, G.: Prism-games 3.0: stochastic game verification with concurrency, equilibria and time. In: Computer Aided Verification - 32nd International Conference, CAV 2020, Los Angeles, CA, USA, 21–24 July 2020, Proceedings, Part II. Lecture Notes in Computer Science, vol. 12225, pp. 475–487. Springer (2020). https://doi.org/10.1007/978-3-030-53291-8_25
28. Kwiatkowska, M., Norman, G., Parker, D., Santos, G.: Automatic verification of concurrent stochastic systems. Formal Methods Syst. Design, 188–250 (2021). https://doi.org/10.1007/s10703-020-00356-y
29. Křetínský, J., Meggendorfer, T., Weininger, M.: Stopping criteria for value iteration on stochastic games with quantitative objectives. In: 2023 38th Annual ACM/IEEE Symposium on Logic in Computer Science (LICS), pp. 1–14 (2023). https://doi.org/10.1109/LICS56636.2023.10175771
30. Lefèvre, C.: Optimal control of a birth and death epidemic process. Oper. Res. **29**(5), 971–982 (1981). https://doi.org/10.1287/opre.29.5.971, http://www.jstor.org/stable/170234
31. Lomuscio, A., Qu, H., Raimondi, F.: MCMAS: an open-source model checker for the verification of multi-agent systems. Int. J. Softw. Tools Technol. Transf. **19**(1), 9–30 (2017). https://doi.org/10.1007/S10009-015-0378-X
32. Lyu, G., Fazlirad, A., Brennan, R.W.: Multi-agent modeling of cyber-physical systems for IEC 61499 based distributed automation. Procedia Manufact. **51**, 1200–1206 (2020). https://doi.org/10.1016/j.promfg.2020.10.168. 30th International Conference on Flexible Automation and Intelligent Manufacturing (FAIM2021)
33. de Moura, L., Bjørner, N.: Z3: an efficient SMT solver. In: Ramakrishnan, C.R., Rehof, J. (eds.) TACAS 2008. LNCS, vol. 4963, pp. 337–340. Springer, Heidelberg (2008). https://doi.org/10.1007/978-3-540-78800-3_24
34. Nguyen, H., Rakib, A.: A probabilistic logic for resource-bounded multi-agent systems, pp. 521–527 (2019). https://doi.org/10.24963/ijcai.2019/74

35. Parsons, T.D.: Pursuit-evasion in a graph. In: Theory and Applications of Graphs: Proceedings, Michigan 11–15 May 1976, pp. 426–441. Springer (2006). https://doi.org/10.1007/BFb0070400
36. Schaefer, M., Cardinal, J., Miltzow, T.: The existential theory of the reals as a complexity class: a compendium. CoRR abs/2407.18006 (2024). https://doi.org/10.48550/ARXIV.2407.18006
37. Shi, D., Elliott, R.J., Chen, T.: On finite-state stochastic modeling and secure estimation of cyber-physical systems. IEEE Trans. Autom. Control **62**(1), 65–80 (2016). https://doi.org/10.1109/TAC.2016.2541919
38. Song, F., Chen, T., Tang, Y., Xu, Z.: Probabilistic alternating-time μ-calculus. In: Proceedings of the AAAI Conference on Artificial Intelligence vol. 33, pp. 6179–6186 (2019). https://doi.org/10.1609/aaai.v33i01.33016179
39. Sorensson, N.: Minisat 2.2 and minisat++ 1.1. http://baldur.iti.uka.de/sat-race-2010/descriptions/solver_25+26.pdf (2010). https://www.semanticscholar.org/paper/MINISAT-2.2-and-MINISAT%2B%2B-1.1-S%C3%B6rensson/e46a90899c7ca924c30983cf4cede5804df7ab7f
40. Virtanen, P., et al.: SciPy 1.0 Contributors: SciPy 1.0: Fundamental algorithms for scientific computing in python. Nat. Methods **17**, 261–272 (2020). https://doi.org/10.1038/s41592-019-0686-2
41. Zhang, C., Pang, J.: On probabilistic alternating simulations. In: Calude, C.S., Sassone, V. (eds.) TCS 2010. IAICT, vol. 323, pp. 71–85. Springer, Heidelberg (2010). https://doi.org/10.1007/978-3-642-15240-5_6
42. Zhang, K., Yang, Z., Başar, T.: Multi-agent reinforcement learning: a selective overview of theories and algorithms. In: Handbook of Reinforcement Learning and Control, pp. 321–384 (2021). https://doi.org/10.1007/978-3-030-60990-0_12

Decoupled Planning for Multiple Omega-Regular Objectives

Guy Avni[1], Thomas A. Henzinger[2], Kaushik Mallik[3], Suman Sadhukhan[4], and K. S. Thejaswini[5(✉)]

[1] University of Haifa, Haifa, Israel
gavni@cs.haifa.ac.il
[2] Institute of Science and Technology Austria, Klosterneuburg, Austria
tah@ista.ac.at
[3] IMDEA Software Institute, Pozuelo de Alarcón, Spain
kaushik.mallik@imdea.org
[4] Clausthal University of Technology, Clausthal-Zellerfeld, Germany
suman.sadhukhan@tu-clausthal.de
[5] Université Libre de Bruxelles, Brussels, Belgium
thejaswini.raghavan@ulb.be

Abstract. We study the problem of generating paths on a graph that satisfy a collection of ω-regular objectives. We propose a decoupled framework in which each objective is assigned to an independent agent that selects a *local* policy, while a scheduler—oblivious to the graph and objective—dynamically composes these policies into a single path. We ask when such a composition satisfies all objectives, assuming their conjunction is realizable. The framework enables modular policy design but raises fundamental compositional challenges. We show that even extremely fair deterministic schedulers do not ensure correctness, and that *stochastic* schedulers, while necessary, are insufficient without coordination. For safety objectives, we demonstrate that fully decentralized implementations are impossible, and we introduce a protocol for synchronizing on maximal safe actions. For non-safety objectives, we introduce *conventions*—simple, a priori restrictions agreed upon before the graph or objectives are revealed—that guarantee satisfaction of all objectives when followed by all agents. We characterize minimally restrictive conventions for major subclasses of ω-regular objectives. In particular, Büchi objectives admit universal composition of finite-memory policies without scheduler communication; co-Büchi objectives require only knowledge of whether the agent was scheduled; and parity objectives additionally require knowledge of which agent was scheduled.

Keywords: ω-regular · Modular Synthesis · Runtime Composition

1 Introduction

The graph traversal problem takes as input a finite directed graph and a temporal specification over sequences of vertices, and the goal is to compute a traversal

E. Darulova et al. (Eds.): CAV 2026, LNCS 16682, pp. 237–257, 2026.
https://doi.org/10.1007/978-3-032-32519-8_13

policy for selecting the next vertex based on the history of the past vertices, such that the resulting infinite path fulfills the given specification. A primary application of graph traversal is robotic path planning [15], and other applications include parsing natural languages using stochastic grammars [19], and informational search with online learning [18]. Often, the specification requires simultaneous fulfillment of multiple, competing objectives; for example, a robot may need to simultaneously patrol a given location *and* visit the charging station intermittently. The traditional approach to solve such problems is to compute a single, monolithic policy for the conjunction of all objectives.

In this paper, we introduce a *decoupled* framework for graph traversals. Consider a collection of objectives $\varphi_1, \ldots, \varphi_N$ that a path needs to satisfy. We describe the framework as an interaction among N agents. For $1 \leq i \leq N$, Agent i is only responsible for satisfying objective φ_i and does so by selecting a *policy* that achieves φ_i. At runtime, a fixed *scheduler* composes the policies by scheduling one of the agents to choose the next vertex at each step. Our goal is to ensure that the path generated by the composition satisfies all objectives (either deterministically or *almost surely*) while achieving maximal decoupling by keeping the agents' choices and scheduler as independent as possible. Before we make these goals more concrete and discuss the features that they lead to, we first illustrate the framework and its challenges.

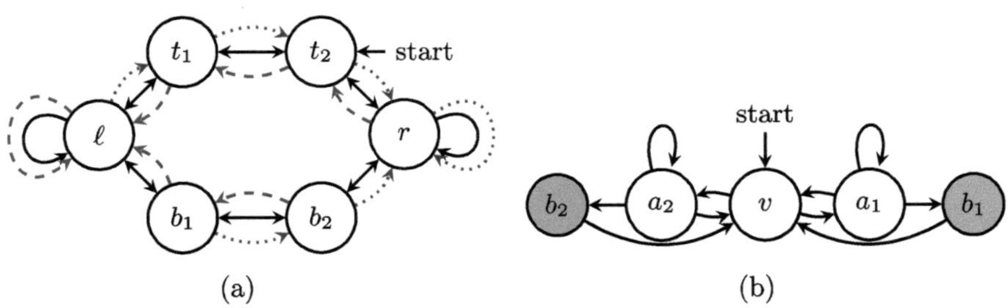

Fig. 1. (a) Reachability objectives given by $T_1 = \{\ell\}$ and $T_2 = \{r\}$, and policies π_1 dashed red and π_2 dotted blue. (b) A graph with two Büchi objectives given by accepting vertices $T_1 = \{b_1\}$ and $T_2 = \{b_2\}$.

Example 1. Consider a coffee-serving robot in an office modeled as in Fig. 1(a). The objective φ_1 requires "reach and serve coffee at ℓ" and the objective φ_2 requires "reach r". Suppose Agent 1 and Agent 2 choose policies π_1 and π_2 that always take the shortest paths towards their respective goal states. Clearly, if the robot follows only π_1 or only π_2, respectively, φ_1 and φ_2 are satisfied. We describe two schedulers for composing the policies at runtime.

First, consider a *deterministic* scheduler σ_{d} that alternates between π_1 and π_2: at odd time steps, the robot follows π_1, and at even time steps, it follows π_2. The composition does not satisfy either objective. For example, the path starting from t_2 forever alternates between t_1 and t_2. Notably, σ_{d} fulfills the *extreme fairness* property [24], because each agent is given control infinitely often. The example shows that in order to guarantee that all objectives are satisfied, our framework requires schedulers with an even stronger form of fairness.

Now consider a *stochastic* scheduler σ_s that, at each point in time, chooses which policy to follow uniformly at random. This scheduler fulfills a stronger notion of fairness, called *probabilistic fairness* [11] (also related to α-*fairness* [25]). The composition of π_1 and π_2 using σ_s now generates a random path that almost surely visits each of ℓ, t_1, t_2, and r infinitely often, thus both objectives are satisfied almost surely. □

We postpone the justification of our design choices of schedulers and policies until the end of the introduction.

The advantages of our new framework stem from its modularity; it enables a separation of concerns in designing policies and allows changing, deleting, or adding any number of policies without any extra computational overhead, offering a lightweight, plug-and-play composition operation. We point out specific advantages over the monolithic approach: (i) *parallel design*: each policy is designed independently, which enables, for example, designed on separate CPUs to increase scalability, or by different vendors increasing flexible design; (ii) *robustness*: when an objective changes, only the relevant module needs to change and the other modules can stay fixed; (iii) *iterative design*: a realistic design procedure often requires addition of objectives to the original objectives, which can be simply added as a new module; (iv) *dynamic changes*: our framework allows deleting or adding objectives to a system that has already been deployed (a "patch").

The first step of our decoupled synthesis addresses the safety components of the individual objectives. Given a graph G and an objective φ, we can use standard procedure to decompose φ into safety and liveness components, writing $\varphi = \varphi^{\mathsf{safe}} \cap \varphi^{\mathsf{live}}$, where φ^{safe} requires some unsafe vertices to be avoided at all time, and φ^{live} requires some good event to eventually occur. We show that φ^{safe} cannot, in general, be guaranteed under stochastic scheduling without additional communication. To this end, we propose a protocol in which agents communicate their sets of safe actions at each step, and the scheduled agent is required to select an action from the intersection of these sets. Under mild assumptions, we prove that this protocol suffices to ensure satisfaction of each safety objective at all times. Once safety is enforced, we remove all unsafe edges from the graph and exclusively focus on the liveness objectives in the resulting subgraph. For clarity of exposition, we assume this graph is strongly connected, although this assumption is not essential and will be relaxed later.

We first study the existence of a stochastic scheduler that composes *any* collection of policies in a way that the composition almost-surely satisfies all liveness objectives. Somewhat surprisingly, we show that, already for Büchi objectives in strongly-connected graphs, such "universal" schedulers does not exist. We sketch the intuition in the following example, and details can be found in Theorem 3.

Example 2. Consider the graph depicted in Fig. 1(b). We describe two policies π_1 and π_2 respectively for the Büchi objectives φ_1 and φ_2 given by target vertices

$\{b_1\}$ and $\{b_2\}$. Consider an exponentially increasing sequence, e.g., $n_0 = 1$ and $n_j = 2 \cdot n_{j-1}$, for $j \geq 1$. Define π_1 as follows, and π_2 is dual. When not at a_1, proceed towards b_2, and when at a_1 at time t, if $t = n_j$, for $j \geq 0$, proceed to b_1, otherwise stay at a_1. That is, π_1 spends exponentially increasing time at a_1; visits to b_1 become exponentially rare. Clearly, if π_i operates alone, it satisfies φ_i, for $i \in \{1, 2\}$. Consider a scheduler that at each point in time, chooses which policy acts uniformly at random. Intuitively, the probability that a random walk visits a_i, for $i \in \{1, 2\}$, precisely at a time n_j, for some $j \geq 1$, is exponentially decreasing, which implies that the probability of visiting b_i infinitely often tends to a constant, thus $\varphi_1 \wedge \varphi_2$ is *not* satisfied almost surely. In Theorem 3, we generalize the construction to any stochastic scheduler. □

Example 2 shows that if the agents are allowed to choose any unrestricted policies, there exist situations when the composition will violate the individual objectives. We submit that if all the agents are made to choose policies according to some suitable *convention*, the composition will be guaranteed to satisfy all objectives, almost surely. For example, for Büchi objectives, we show that the convention of choosing only finite-memory policies guarantee the fulfillment of all individual objectives. We formalize conventions as mappings from classes of objectives (Büchi, co-Büchi, etc.) to restrictions on policies (finite-memory, etc.). Importantly, the restrictions need to be finalized *before* seeing the specific graph and objectives at hand, setting our framework apart from the joint design of coordinated policies. This way, the modularity requirement is achieved: agents can independently design their policies based on the respective conventions, and addition, modification, or removal of policies do not affect the rest of the policies.

Conventions can be intuitively explained using a simple metaphor, whose inspiration comes from the work of Lewis [22]. Suppose two friends want to meet, but they are unable to talk to each other and arrange the location. Convention dictates that each of them should go to the place where they most often meet, and if both parties follow the same convention, they will successfully meet. In essence, convention is a way of inducing coordination when direct communication is not possible. Coming back to our framework, conventions help agents achieve their objectives without directly synchronizing their policies with each other.

Our goal is to establish minimally restrictive conventions for different classes of ω-regular objectives.

While the convention for Büchi objectives was merely to use finite-memory policies, the same does not suffice anymore for co-Büchi objectives, as we illustrate using the following example.

Example 3. Consider the graph that is depicted in Fig. 1(a) and two co-Büchi objectives: $\mathsf{FG}\,\ell$, requiring eventually staying in ℓ, and $\mathsf{FG}\,(\ell \vee r)$, requiring eventually staying in either ℓ or r. Observe that for $i \in \{1, 2\}$, following the finite-memory policy π_i (depicted also in Fig. 1(a) in dashed red and dotted blue) results in a path that satisfies the respective objective, but a random composition of the two visits both t_1 and t_2 infinitely often, almost surely, and thus violates both objectives. □

The challenge behind co-Büchi convention is that in order to satisfy a conjunction of co-Büchi objectives, all policies—that are oblivious to each other's target vertices—must eventually converge into a common cycle that is good for everyone. We describe a convention for co-Büchi objectives in strongly-connected graphs. Given a co-Büchi objective φ_i, Agent i chooses a policy π_i that operates as follows. (1) Randomly choose a lasso-shaped path $\rho^i = \rho_i \cdot C_i^\omega$, where C_i is a cycle that satisfies φ_i. This is Agent i's guess of the common path everyone is trying to follow. (2) If scheduled at vertex v: choose the successor v' of v on ρ^i. (3) If not scheduled: observe the next vertex u, and if $u \neq v'$, a conflict is observed: return to Step (1) and sample a new path.

Example 4. Consider again the objectives over the graph depicted in Fig. 1(a) $\varphi_1 = \mathrm{FG}\,\ell$ and $\varphi_2 = \mathrm{FG}\,(\ell \vee r)$, the initial position is t_1, and let the choice of lasso paths be $\rho^1 = t_1\ell^\omega$ and $\rho^2 = t_1t_2r^\omega$. Observe that ρ^i satisfies φ_i for each i. Suppose that π_1 is scheduled and proceeds to ℓ. Thus, π_2 observes a conflict (it expects the next vertex to be t_2), and randomly chooses an alternative lasso path that satisfies φ_2. Correctness follows from a measure-theoretic argument: If there exists a common path that satisfies all co-Büchi objectives, then there also exists a lasso-shaped path that does the same. Random scheduling implies that eventually and almost surely the policies will stabilize in a lasso-shaped path where no policies will change their guesses anymore. □

We develop sufficient conventions for major classes of ω-regular objectives, including safety, Büchi, co-Büchi, and parity, and consider path planning problems on both strongly connected and general graphs. As the objectives become more complex, the conventions become more demanding, as expected. Although our conventions are simple to describe, their correctness proofs involve intricate measure-theoretic arguments. With this, we create the foundation of a first-of-its-kind modular design framework for ω-regular decision-making.

Design Choices. We discuss the design choices of our framework. *(i) Independent policy choice.* In all our conventions, an agent chooses a policy without knowing the objectives of the other agents. This enables robustness: when objective φ_j changes, Agent i does not need to change their policy. *(ii) Minimal runtime coordination.* For Büchi objectives, conventions choose traditional policies (later called *path-aware policies*) that use no runtime coordination (see π_1 and π_2 in Example 1). This means that agents can apply off-the-shelf tools to design policies, and different agents can even apply different techniques, e.g., reinforcement learning or formal techniques. For co-Büchi objectives, policies know which time steps they are scheduled in. Importantly, such policies are *not* aware of the number of agents, meaning that additional objectives can be added (offline or at runtime) without changing the policy. *(iii) Graph-independent schedulers.* To motivate this, we return to Example 1. Intuitively, composition using the deterministic scheduler σ_d failed because none of the agents were getting enough time to reach their target. A naïve fix simply schedules each policy *three* times in a row. While this does solve the problem at hand, it is an ad hoc solution that will break if either graph or objectives change. Alternatively, one could consider a *nondeterministic* scheduler and construct policies that fulfill their objectives no matter how the nondeterminism is resolved. Unfortunately, this is too restrictive from the policy design standpoint: in Example 1, given the policies π_1 and π_2, a nondeterministic scheduler can act like an adversary and find an interleaving of the policies (like the one of σ_{d}) such that the path keeps cycling between t_1 and t_2 and never visits the targets. Defeating such an adversarial scheduler is possible, but would require the policies to take joint actions (like π_1 and π_2 making a clockwise traversal of the graph in Example 1), which would preclude the key aspect of modular design. *(iv) Simple schedulers.* We see it as a feature of our framework that our schedulers are simple and can thus run on devices with limited processing capabilities like robots or drones.

Related Work

Computing policies for multi-objective decision-making problems is a well-studied problem, both for probabilistic [6,7,10] and non-probabilistic [26] systems. Almost all works produce a single, monolithic policy that fulfills all objectives.

Decoupling has been considered in other fields with the same motivation as us; a framework that is modular, robust, and separates design concerns. For example, decoupling exploration from exploitation has been studied in RL [27], *behavioral programming* is a decoupled approach to programming [16], decoupling has been applied in control [14], and game theory [17].

We compare with two approaches for decoupled design that are closest to our work. The first kind "over-approximates" the local policies using the so-called *strategy templates* [2], which abstractly represent sets of policies that would fulfil the objectives.[1] When these local strategy templates are composed, we obtain a strategy template for the conjunction of all objectives, from which a concrete policy for the overall problem can be extracted. Unfortunately, the composition of strategy templates is computationally intensive, which creates substantial computational overhead and can impact the runtime performance of the composed policy.

The second kind of modular design uses auctions as a scheduler, and is called *auction-based scheduling* (ABS) [5]: Each policy starts with a budget, and at each step, an auction is held, where the policies use their available budgets to bid for the privilege of selecting the next action. *Bidding policies* for ABS are found by independently solving a two-player zero-sum *bidding game* [3,21]. We point to two key advantages of our approach over ABS. First, our approach allows an arbitrary number of objectives whereas ABS for multiple objectives is currently not possible due to the dependency on multi-player bidding games, which, to best of our knowledge, have not yet been studied. Second, ABS is a sound but incomplete method: it is possible that there is a path that satisfies both objectives, but there is no decoupled solution for ABS. In fact, most instances

[1] Strategy templates are originally developed on turn-based game graphs, which are generalizations of the plain graphs that we use in this work.

with a pair of co-Büchi objectives cannot be decoupled using ABS. On the other hand, our framework is guaranteed to successfully decouple any collection of parity objectives on strongly-connected graphs, assuming, of course, that they have an intersection.

In several graph games, "mixed" or *randomised policies* are used either out of necessity for winning against the opponent [12] or to reduce the memory requirements of the policies [9]. Our randomised scheduling of local policies can be viewed as randomised policies, where the randomisation over actions is facilitated by the scheduler. However, there is an important difference: usually, randomised policies are designed centrally for the entire objective, whereas our goal is to design isolated local policies independently from the scheduler.

The classical distributed view of reactive synthesis [13,20,23] uses a fundamentally different model. It is assumed that the actions chosen by each local policy affect a separate set of variables, so that all local policies can be deployed in parallel. In other words, classical distribution synthesis does not require scheduling of policies, and asks how to design local policies whose parallel composition fulfills all objectives.

All missing proofs can be found in the extended version of the paper [4].

2 Preliminaries

We use $\mathbb{N}$ to denote the set of natural numbers $\{0, 1, 2, \dots\}$. For two natural numbers i, j with $i < j$, we use $[i; j]$ to denote the set $\{i, i+1, \dots, j\}$ consisting of natural numbers that are at least i and at most j. Sometimes, for a natural number i, we use $[i]$ to denote the set $[1; i]$.

Graphs, and Paths. A graph is an ordered triple $\mathcal{G} = (V, E, v_{\mathsf{init}})$, where V is a finite set of vertices, $E \subseteq V \times V$ is a set of directed edges, and $v_{\mathsf{init}} \in V$ is the initial vertex. A path in $\mathcal{G}$ is a (finite or infinite) sequence of vertices $v_0 v_1 \dots$ such that $v_0 = v_{\mathsf{init}}$ and $(v_i, v_{i+1}) \in E$ for every valid index i. We write $Paths_{\mathsf{fin}}(\mathcal{G})$ and $Paths_{\mathsf{inf}}(\mathcal{G})$ for the sets of finite and infinite paths of $\mathcal{G}$, respectively. By convention, $Paths_{\mathsf{fin}}(\mathcal{G})$ includes the path of length 0.

Objectives. An *objective* φ in $\mathcal{G}$ is a set of infinite paths in $\mathcal{G}$. We represent objectives defined using predicates over the vertices of the given graph. We consider the following *families* of objectives.

Reachability is specified by a set of *target* vertices $T \subseteq V$, and is the set of every path that eventually visits at least one vertex in T.

Safety is specified by a set of *safe* vertices $S \subseteq V$, and is the set of every path always remaining within the vertices in S.

Parity is specified by a *colouring* function $\kappa : V \mapsto \mathbb{N}$, which associates each vertex a natural number called its *colour*. An infinite path is in the parity objective iff the largest colour that appears infinitely often is even.

Büchi is a special case of parity in which vertices are only coloured by 1 and 2, where the latter are called *Büchi* vertices. A path is in the Büchi objective iff Büchi vertices are visited infinitely often.

Co-Büchi is a special case of parity in which vertices are only coloured by 0 and 1, where the latter are called *co-Büchi* vertices or "bad" vertices. A path is in the co-Büchi objective iff it visits co-Büchi vertices only finitely often.

We will divide objectives into two complementary families, namely safety and liveness, defined below. While safety can be defined using safe vertices as above, the following definition uses an alternate, semantic variant.

Definition 1 (Safety versus liveness objectives). *Let $\mathcal{G}$ be a given graph. A given objective φ in $\mathcal{G}$ is called* liveness *if every finite path in $\mathcal{G}$ can be extended into an infinite path in φ. Dually, a given objective φ in $\mathcal{G}$ is called* safety *if every infinite path $v_0v_1 \ldots \notin \varphi$ has a finite prefix $\rho = v_0 \ldots v_i$ such that for every $j \geq i$, all infinite extensions of the path $v_0 \ldots v_j$ is not in φ.*

Almost-Sure Satisfaction. Let $\mathcal{D}(V)$ denote the set of all probability distributions over V, and given $d \in \mathcal{D}(V)$, we will write $\mathsf{Supp}(d)$ to denote the support of d. Consider a function $f : \mathit{Paths}_{\mathsf{fin}}(\mathcal{G}) \to \mathcal{D}(V)$ that, given a finite path ρ ending at a vertex v, assigns a probability distribution whose support is contained in the set of successors of v. We extend f to infinite paths as follows. For a finite path $\rho = v_0 \ldots v_k$, the cylinder set spanned by ρ, denoted $\mathrm{Cyl}(\rho)$, is the set of all infinite paths whose prefix is ρ. Define the probability distribution over cylinder sets based on f as $\Pr^f(\mathrm{Cyl}(\rho)) = \prod_{i=0}^{k-1} f(v_0 \ldots v_i)(v_{i+1})$. The function $\Pr^f$ is a pre-measure over the set $\mathit{Paths}_{\mathsf{inf}}(\mathcal{G})$, which extends to a *unique* probability measure over $\mathit{Paths}_{\mathsf{inf}}(\mathcal{G})$ by applying the Carathéodory's extension theorem [8]. For simplicity, we use the notation $\Pr^f$ to also represent the probability measure. We say that f *almost surely* satisfies an objective φ if $\Pr^f(\varphi) = 1$.

3 The Decoupled Planning Framework

We develop a decoupled framework for generating a path that satisfies a collection $\varphi_1, \ldots, \varphi_N$ of objectives. The framework has two main ingredients, N individual *agents* and *a scheduler*. Each Agent i, for $i \in [1; N]$, is solely interested in fulfilling the objective φ_i. To this end, the Agent i chooses a policy π_i, and the policies of all agents are composed at runtime by the scheduler.

This section is devoted to formalizing this framework. We start with schedulers.

Definition 2 (Schedulers: general, fair, deterministic). *A* scheduler *over $[N]$ is a function $\sigma : [N]^* \to \mathcal{D}([N])$. The scheduler σ is called* fair *if there exists $\epsilon > 0$ such that for every $u \in [N]^*$ and for every $n \in [N]$, $\Pr(n = \sigma(u)) > \epsilon$. A scheduler is called* deterministic *if it always chooses Dirac distributions.*

We reiterate the advantages of stochastic schedulers mentioned in the introduction. First, they are completely agnostic of the underlying graph and the objectives, while not obstructing policies to fulfill their objectives. Moreover, stochastic schedulers are lightweight and easy to implement. In fact such schedulers are often used in concurrent programs, where multiple programs (analogous to our policies) that are competing for a resource (being scheduled, analogous to our policies being able to execute their actions) are allocated the resource randomly. Henceforth, schedulers will by default be stochastic.

Semantics of Schedulers. Every sequence from $[N]^* \cup [N]^\omega$ is called a *schedule* which is either finite or infinite. Every scheduler σ induces a probability measure over the infinite schedules as follows. Given a finite sequence $\theta = p_0 \dots p_k \in [N]^*$, we define $\Pr^\sigma(\mathrm{Cyl}(\theta)) = \prod_{i=0}^{k-1} \sigma(p_0 \dots p_{k-1})$, which is a pre-measure that extends to a unique measure—also denoted as $\Pr^\sigma$—over the set $[N]^\omega$ by applying Carathéodory's extension theorem [8]. □

We formalize the second ingredient of our framework, the policies that the agents choose, where we define policy types with increasing knowledge of scheduling choices. We introduce some notation first. Given two alphabets A and B, and a pair of finite words of equal length $w_A = a_0 \dots a_k \in A^*$ and $w_B = b_0 \dots b_k \in B^*$, we define their element-wise cross-product as: $w_A \otimes w_B := (a_0, b_0) \dots (a_k, b_k) \in (A \times B)^*$. Furthermore, we lift this cross-product to sets of sequences: given $W_A \subseteq A^*$ and $W_B \subseteq B^*$, define $W_A \otimes W_B := \{w_A \otimes w_B \mid w_A \in W_A, w_B \in W_B\}$.

Definition 3 (Policies augmented with scheduling information). *Let σ be a scheduler over $[N]$.*

Path-aware *policies coincide with the traditional definition of policies and have no scheduling knowledge, they are of the form $\pi\colon \mathit{Paths}_{\mathsf{fin}}(\mathcal{G}) \to \mathcal{D}(V)$. We denote the set of path-aware policies by Π^{Path}.*

Scheduled-aware *policies keep track of which past time points they have been scheduled, and all choices made by it in the past. A scheduled-aware policy is a* partial *function of the form $\pi\colon \mathit{Paths}_{\mathsf{fin}}(\mathcal{G}) \otimes \{\top, \bot\}^* \otimes V^* \to \mathcal{D}(V)$, mapping the path $\rho = v_0 \dots v_k \in \mathit{Paths}_{\mathsf{fin}}(\mathcal{G})$, the history $\theta = q_0 \dots q_{k-1} \in \{\top, \bot\}^*$ of time points in which it was scheduled, where "$\top$" means "scheduled" and "$\bot$" means not scheduled, and the history of choices $\gamma = w_1 \dots w_k \in V^*$ made by it, to the distribution $\pi(\rho, \theta, \gamma)$. The distribution $\pi(\rho, \theta, \gamma)$ is defined iff ρ, θ, and γ are consistent, i.e., for every $i \in [k]$ with $q_{i-1} = \top$, $v_i = w_i$. The set of all full scheduled-aware policies will be denoted as Π^{S}.*

Full history-aware *policies enrich scheduled-aware policies by additionally including the indices of scheduled agents during times it was unscheduled (instead of just keeping track of "$\bot$" as scheduled-aware policies do). Without loss of generality, assume that the indices of the other policies are $[2; N]$. A full history-aware policy is a* partial *functions of the form $\pi\colon \mathit{Paths}_{\mathsf{fin}}(\mathcal{G}) \otimes \{\top, 2, \dots, N\}^* \otimes V^* \to \mathcal{D}(V)$, mapping the path $\rho \in \mathit{Paths}_{\mathsf{fin}}(\mathcal{G})$, the history of scheduling decisions $\theta \in \{\top, 2, \dots, N\}^*$, and the history of choices $\gamma \in V^*$ made by π, to the distribution $\pi(\rho, \theta, \gamma)$. The distribution $\pi(\rho, \theta, \gamma)$ is defined under the same conditions as for scheduled-aware policies. The set of all full history-aware policies with N agents will be denoted as Π_N^{FH}.*

For each policy, regardless of its type, for every given path $\rho v \in \mathit{Paths}_{\mathsf{fin}}(\mathcal{G})$, the support of the output distribution over vertices must be a subset of $\mathsf{Supp}(v)$.

Remark 1 (Why keep track of past choices?). One may naïvely think that it is redundant that policies in Π^{S} and Π_N^{FH} keep track of their own past choices, alongside the whole path history, because the old histories could be used to simulate the old choices on demand. This will not work since the policies are stochastic, and executing them on the same history will generate different outcomes on different instances with positive probability.

Remark 2 (Comparing decoupling strength). Decoupling is stronger when using a family of policies with weaker scheduling information. Since path-aware policies coincide with the traditional definition of policies, an agent can use any off-the-shelf tool to construct a policy for their objective. This is no longer the case with scheduled-aware and full history-aware policies. Yet, an appealing feature of scheduled-aware policies is their independence of how many policies are interacting. This enables, for example, "patching" a deployed system by removing or adding an objective at runtime. Indeed, even when N changes, no update is needed to an individual policy. This is no longer the case with full history-aware policies. We point out that decoupling with full history-aware policies still provides modularity: as long as the number of objectives is fixed, changes to objectives at runtime is possible by changing only the relevant policies.

We define the *composition* of a scheduler and a collection of full history-aware policies. This generates a probability distribution over the infinite paths generated by a random interleaving of the individual local policies.

Definition 4 (Composition). *Suppose we are given a graph $\mathcal{G}$, a scheduler σ for a set of N agents, and a set of policies $\pi_1, \ldots, \pi_N$ where for every $i \in [N]$, $\pi_i \in \Pi_N^{\mathrm{FH}} \cup \Pi^{\mathrm{S}} \cup \Pi^{\mathrm{Path}}$. The composition is the tuple $\mathcal{I} = (\mathcal{G}, \pi_i, \ldots, \pi_N, \sigma)$.*

Each composition defines a probability distribution over the paths generated, which we computed step-by-step below. Such a distribution depends on the type of scheduler, hence we define it carefully below.

Semantics of Composition. At each time point i, when the current path is $v_0 \ldots v_i \in \mathit{Paths}_{\mathsf{fin}}(\mathcal{G})$, each Agent j randomly selects the next vertex w_{i+1}^j using its policy, giving us a tuple $(w_{i+1}^1, \ldots, w_{i+1}^N)$ of selections. Out of this tuple, the choice of the scheduled agent p_i is used to extend the current path to $v_0 \ldots v_{i+1}$, where $v_{i+1} = w_{i+1}^{p_i}$, and the process continues. For a given fixed schedule $p_0 \ldots p_{k-1} \in [N]^*$, we define the probability of the sequence of selections being $(w_1^1, \ldots, w_1^N) \ldots (w_k^1, \ldots, w_k^N)$ given as:

$$\Pr^{\mathcal{I}}\left((w_1^1, \ldots, w_1^N) \ldots (w_k^1, \ldots, w_k^N) \mid (p_0, \ldots p_{k-1})\right) := \prod_{j=1}^{N} \prod_{i=0}^{k-1} D(w_{i+1}^j), \quad (1)$$

where $D(w_{i+1}^j)$ represents the probability that at time $i+1$, the policy π_j selected the vertex w_{i+1}^j, whose value is defined based on the policy type as below. In the above, the path generated by the schedule $p_0, \ldots p_{k-1}$ from the sequence

$(w_1^1, \ldots, w_1^N) \ldots (w_k^1, \ldots, w_k^N)$ is $v_0 v_1 \ldots v_k$ where $v_0 = v_{\mathsf{init}}$ and for each $i \in [k]$, $v_i = w_i^{p_{i-1}}$. The set of all policies are $\{\pi_j\}_{j\in[N]}$. Then,

$$D(w_{i+1}^j) =$$
$$\begin{cases} \pi_j\,(v_0, \ldots v_i) & \pi_j \in \Pi^{\mathrm{Path}}, \\ \pi_j\left((v_0 \ldots v_i), (q_0 \ldots q_{i-1}), (w_1^j \ldots w_i^j)\right),\ \forall t \,.\, q_t = \top \Leftrightarrow p_t = j & \pi_j \in \Pi^{\mathrm{S}}, \\ \pi_j\left((v_0 \ldots v_i), (p_0 \ldots p_{i-1}), (w_1^j \ldots w_i^j)\right) & \pi_j \in \Pi_N^{\mathrm{FH}}. \end{cases}$$

Suppose we are given a finite path $\rho = v_0 \ldots v_k \in \mathit{Paths}_{\mathsf{fin}}(\mathcal{G})$ and a schedule $\theta = p_0 \ldots p_{k-1} \in [N]^*$. We introduce the set $\Sigma_{v_0,\rho,\theta} \subseteq V^{N\times k}$ representing the set of all sequences of vertices generated by all agents such that the schedule θ would produce the path ρ starting at the initial vertex v_0. Formally, $\Sigma_{v_0,\rho,\theta} := \{(v_1^1, \ldots, v_1^N) \ldots (v_k^1, \ldots, v_k^N) \mid \forall i \in [k] \,.\, v_i = v_i^{p_{i-1}}\}$. Now we combine $\Pr^{\mathcal{I}}(\rho \mid \cdot)$ with the probability measure $\Pr^{\sigma}$ over sequences of policy indices, and write $\Pr^{\mathcal{I}}(\mathrm{Cyl}(\rho))$ as

$$\sum_{\substack{\theta\in[N]^{k-1} \\ (v_1^1,\ldots,v_1^N)\ldots(v_k^1,\ldots,v_k^N)\in\Sigma_{v_0,\rho,\theta}}} \Pr^{\mathcal{I}}((v_1^1, \ldots, v_1^N) \ldots (v_k^1, \ldots, v_k^N) \mid \theta) \cdot \Pr^{\sigma}(\theta), \quad (2)$$

which is a pre-measure and leads to a unique measure—also written $\Pr^{\mathcal{I}}$—over the set of all infinite paths by applying the Carathéodory's extension theorem [8]. We will write $\mathcal{I} \models_{\mathsf{a.s.}} \varphi$ iff $\Pr^{\mathcal{I}}(\varphi) = 1$. □

Following is the decoupling problem that we undertake.

Problem statement (informal): decoupled planning

Fix a fair, stochastic scheduler σ. Suppose $\mathcal{G}$ is a given graph and $\varphi_1, \ldots, \varphi_N$ are the objectives. Independently design the policies $\pi_1, \ldots, \pi_N$ in a way that $\mathcal{I}(\mathcal{G}, \pi_1, \ldots, \pi_N, \sigma) \models_{\mathsf{a.s.}} \varphi_1 \wedge \ldots \wedge \varphi_N$.

Towards this goal, we start by stating why a fair *deterministic* scheduler would not suffice in achieving the desired decoupling, which formalizes the informal description in Example 1.

Theorem 1 (No deterministic scheduler can be universal). *For every deterministic scheduler σ, there exist a graph $\mathcal{G}$ and reachability objectives φ_1 and φ_2 with $(\varphi_1 \cap \varphi_2) \neq \emptyset$ and deterministic policies π_1^{σ} and π_2^{σ} that respectively satisfy φ_1 and φ_2, but $(\mathcal{G}, \pi_1^{\sigma}, \pi_2^{\sigma}, \sigma) \not\models \varphi_1 \wedge \varphi_2$.*

The high level idea (slightly over-simplified) of the proof appears in Example 1, and a rigorous proof can be found in the full version of the paper. This limitation of (extremely) fair deterministic schedulers inspired us to use stochastic schedulers with the stronger probabilistic fairness [11] properties.

4 Building Support for Safety Components of ω-Regular Objectives

We start by demonstrating the challenge of incorporating safety.

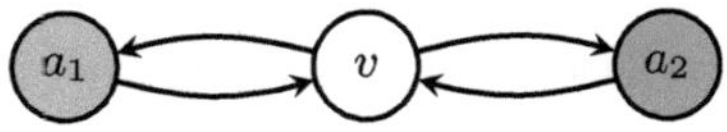

Fig. 2. A graph with a safety objective $G(\neg a_1)$ and a Büchi objective GFa_2. (Color figure online)

Example 5. Consider the graph depicted in Fig. 2, and two objectives, the safety objective φ_1 requires "avoid the Red vertex a_1" and a Büchi objective φ_2 requires "visit the Blue vertex a_2 infinitely often". Suppose that Agent 2 chooses the policy π_2 that alternates between selecting a_1 and a_2 at v. Note that if π_2 is always scheduled, then φ_2 is satisfied. Observe that no matter which policy Agent 1 chooses, any stochastic scheduler that schedules π_2 at v with probability at least $\epsilon > 0$ leads to a random walk that visits a_1 almost surely and thus violates φ_1. Finally, note that the path $(v, a_1)^\omega$ satisfies $\varphi_1 \wedge \varphi_2$. □

As demonstrated in Examples 1 and 4, liveness objectives allow for flexible decoupling. Safety, however, is rigid. Indeed, it is well known that almost-sure and sure satisfaction coincide for safety [12]. That is, in order to satisfy safety, a composition needs to satisfy it deterministically on *every* path. This requires communication, which we establish by augmenting the policies with a safety-preserving component defined as follows.

Maximally Permissive Policies. A *maximally permissive policy* for a safety specification φ is $\chi : V \to 2^V$. Intuitively, for a vertex v, the set $\chi(v)$ represents safe continuations from v. More formally, a path $\rho = v_0, v_1, \ldots$ such that $v_{i+1} \in \chi(v_i)$ satisfies φ. Maximality of χ means that for every v and every $u \notin \chi(v)$, there is a continuation from u that violates φ. In order to construct χ, we compute the set of vertices from which φ_i can be fulfilled, which we call the *winning region* and denote it by W. Then, for every $v \in W$, we define $\chi(v) = \{u : E(v, u) \wedge u \in W\}$. Observe that χ is maximal; proceeding to $u \notin \chi(v)$ violates φ.

Shielded Composition. We augment the composition defined in Definition 4 with maximally-permissive policies. Consider policies $\pi_1, \ldots, \pi_N$ and maximally-permissive policies $\chi_1, \ldots, \chi_N$. Whenever Agent $i \in [N]$ is scheduled at vertex v, every other Agent $j \neq i$ sends $\chi_j(v)$ to Agent i. Agent i selects a vertex $\pi_i(v) \in \bigcap_{1 \le j \le N} \chi_j(v)$ that is safe for all. We will prove that, under mild conditions on the graph and objectives, there is always such a safe vertex to choose.

Decomposition of ω-Regular Specifications. Consider an ω-regular objective φ_i for Agent i. It is possible to decompose φ_i into a safety and a liveness component

$\varphi_i^{\mathsf{safe}}$ and $\varphi_i^{\mathsf{live}}$, such that $\varphi_i = \varphi_i^{\mathsf{safe}} \cap \varphi_i^{\mathsf{live}}$ [1]. Let W_i be the maximal winning region, W_i^c the complement of W_i, and $\mathit{Reach}(W_i^c)$ the objective that contains all paths eventually reaching W_i^c. Define $\varphi_i^{\mathsf{live}} := \varphi_i \cup \mathit{Reach}(W_i^c)$. Observe that $\varphi_i^{\mathsf{live}}$ is a liveness objective, since no matter what prefix we have seen, we can either stay in W_i and fulfil φ_i, or reach W_i^c. Clearly $\varphi_i = \varphi_i^{\mathsf{safe}} \cap \varphi_i^{\mathsf{live}}$, and moreover, $\varphi_i^{\mathsf{live}}$ can be expressed as a parity objective (possibly with additional colours).

We describe how the agents act. Let π_i be a policy for Agent i and let χ_i be a maximally permissive policy. As before, when Agent i is scheduled following path ρ that ends at v, every other Agent j sends $\chi_j(v)$ and Agent i selects $\pi_i(\rho) \in \bigcap_j \chi_j(v)$. We call this a *shielded* composition, and denote it by $(\mathcal{G}, \pi_1, \ldots, \pi_n, \sigma)^{\mathsf{shld}}$. We omit the maximally permissive policies for brevity.

Mutual Safety Closed. Consider an objective $\varphi \subseteq V^\omega$, we define $\mathit{Pref}(\varphi) := \{u \in V^\star \mid \exists v \in V^\omega \, . \, uv \in \varphi\}$ to be the set of all finite prefixes of φ. We call a pair of objectives φ_1 and φ_2 *mutually safety-closed*, if every path ρ in $\mathcal{G}$ fulfilling $\rho \in \mathit{Pref}(\varphi_1) \cap \mathit{Pref}(\varphi_2)$ also fulfils $\rho \in \mathit{Pref}(\varphi_1 \cap \varphi_2)$. By transitivity, we can generalize mutual safety-closure to arbitrary number of objectives.

The mutually safety closed assumption guarantees that every prefix of a path has an extension that satisfies each objective. This ensures that a path that makes a "wrong step" can always recover.

Assumption 1. *The objectives $\{\varphi_1, \ldots, \varphi_N\}$ are mutually safety-closed.*

Let W_i be the maximal set of vertices in $\mathcal{G}$ from which the agent i has a policy to fulfil φ_i. In other words, $\varphi_i^{\mathsf{safe}} = \mathit{Safe}(W_i)$. Define $W := \cap_{i \in [N]} W_i$. By assumption, W is nonempty, since $v_{\mathsf{init}} \in W_i$ for all i. Let $\mathcal{G}[W]$ be the subgraph obtained by removing all the vertices $V \backslash W$ from $\mathcal{G}$, and by removing all the edges that involve these vertices. If Assumption 1 holds, then it can be shown that the subgraph $\mathcal{G}[W]$ is deadlock-free, and therefore every path can be extended into an infinite path.

We are now ready to present the main theorem of this section, which suggests the following decoupling framework for ω-regular objectives. The shielded composition that is described above keeps the path in the *strongly-connected* region $G[W]$ that is safe for all agents. This leaves us with liveness, which the policies $\pi_1, \ldots, \pi_N$ take care of. Constructing $\pi_1, \ldots, \pi_N$ is not trivial. In subsequent sections, we develop such constructions while assuming that the graph is strongly connected and all objectives are liveness objectives.

Theorem 2 (Compositional enforcement of the safety components). *Suppose Assumption 1 holds true. Then for every fair scheduler σ and every set of local policies $\pi_1, \ldots, \pi_N$ the following holds:*

$$\left[(\mathcal{G}[W], \pi_1, \ldots, \pi_N, \sigma) \models_{\mathsf{a.s.}} \bigcap_{i=1}^{N} \varphi_i^{\mathsf{live}}\right] \implies \left[(\mathcal{G}, \pi_1, \ldots, \pi_N, \sigma)^{\mathsf{shld}} \models_{\mathsf{a.s.}} \bigcap_{i=1}^{N} \varphi_i\right].$$

5 Decoupling Liveness Objectives via *Conventions*

Unlike safety objectives, we show that liveness objectives *can* be decomposed without any direct communications among agents. However, this does not rule out the need for coordination. In fact, already for Büchi objectives on strongly connected graphs, without coordination the agents may not be able to fulfill their objectives. This is somewhat surprising, and the intuition was sketched in Example 2. We formally state this result in the following theorem.

Theorem 3 (No stochastic scheduler for uncoordinated Büchi policies). *There is a graph $\mathcal{G}$ such that for any stochastic scheduler σ, there are Büchi objectives φ_1 and φ_2 with $(\varphi_1 \cap \varphi_2) \neq \emptyset$ and deterministic policies π_1^σ and π_2^σ that respectively satisfy φ_1 and φ_2, but the composition $(\mathcal{G}, \pi_1^\sigma, \pi_2^\sigma, \sigma) \not\models_{\text{a.s.}} \varphi_1 \cap \varphi_2$.*

We remark that the proof above also shows that even for a reachability objective, despite using Büchi strategies that ensure that every prefix satisfies the Büchi objective, the probability of reaching an accepting state can be bounded by 1/2 (union bound).

Corollary 1 (No stochastic scheduler for uncoordinated reachability objectives). *There exists a graph $\mathcal{G}$ such that for every scheduler σ, there exists reachability objectives φ_1 and φ_2 with $(\varphi_1 \cap \varphi_2) \neq \emptyset$ and deterministic policies π_1^σ and π_2^σ that respectively satisfy φ_1 and φ_2, but $(\mathcal{G}, \pi_1^\sigma, \pi_2^\sigma, \sigma) \not\models_{\text{a.s.}} \varphi_1 \cap \varphi_2$.*

These results motivate us to seek mechanisms that would induce the required coordination among agents, without them requiring to establish direct communication during the design and deployment of their policies. To this end, we formalize *conventions*, which are rules that agents should follow while selecting their policies, and it is guaranteed if every agent follow these conventions, the composition will fulfill all objectives. Figure 3 illustrates how conventions are used.

Definition 5 (Conventions). *Consider a family of objectives α, where we focus on $\alpha \in \{$Büchi, co-Büchi, parity$\}$. A convention $Conv_\alpha$ for the family α is a mapping that takes a graph $\mathcal{G}$, a scheduler σ, and an objective φ, and outputs a collection of policies of type β that the agent can choose from. We focus on $\beta \in \left\{\widetilde{\Pi}_N^{\text{FH}}, \widetilde{\Pi}^{\text{S}}, \widetilde{\Pi}^{\text{Path}}\right\}$ and design a convention $Conv_\alpha$ such that for every $\mathcal{G}, \sigma$, and $\varphi \in \alpha$, we have $Conv_\alpha(\mathcal{G}, \sigma, \varphi) \subseteq \beta$.*

- *Soundness: A convention $Conv_\alpha$ is sound for classes of graphs and schedules, if for every graph $\mathcal{G}$ and schedule σ from the respective class, and collection of objectives $\varphi_1, \ldots, \varphi_N \in \alpha$, if for every $i \in \{1, \ldots, N\}$ and $\pi_i \in Conv_\alpha(\mathcal{G}, \sigma, \varphi_i)$, we have $(\mathcal{G}, \pi_i, \ldots, \pi_N, \sigma) \models_{\text{a.s.}} \varphi$.*
- *A partial order on conventions: Consider two conventions $Conv_\alpha$ and $Conv'_\alpha$. We define $Conv_\alpha \preceq Conv'_\alpha$ if $Conv_\alpha$ uses policies with weaker scheduling information or if $Conv_\alpha$ is less restrictive than $Conv'_\alpha$, that is for every $\mathcal{G}, \sigma, \varphi$, we have $Conv'_\alpha(\mathcal{G}, \sigma, \varphi) \subseteq Conv_\alpha(\mathcal{G}, \sigma, \varphi)$.*

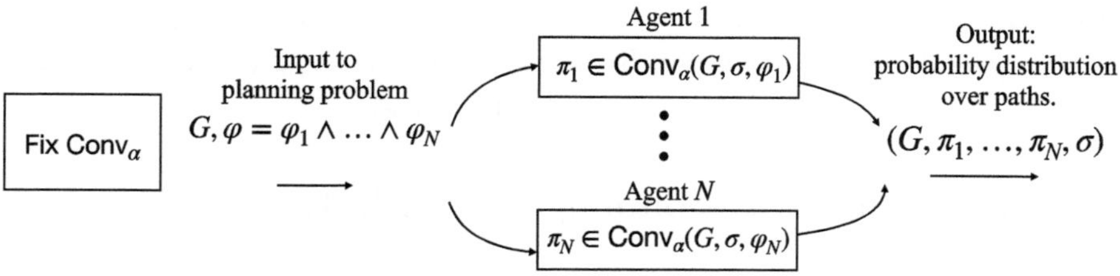

Fig. 3. Decoupling planning using a convention Conv_α. Observe that Conv_α is independent of the graph, scheduler, or specific objectives. Agent i independently chooses $\pi_i \in \mathrm{Conv}_\alpha(\mathcal{G}, \sigma, \varphi_i)$ that agrees with the convention. Soundness of Conv_α implies that the output almost-surely satisfies φ.

We now present the problem that we will study.

Problem statement: decoupled planning of liveness objectives

We focus on strongly-connected graphs and fair stochastic schedulers. For a family of objectives $\alpha \in \{\text{Büchi}, \text{co-Büchi}, \text{parity}\}$. Find a sound and minimal convention Conv_α.

Our focus is on finding sound conventions and we do not show optimality, i.e., provide lower bounds to show inexistence of better conventions. We argue that finding conventions that suffice for decoupling is a nontrivial and challenging problem since conventions are fixed before the graph, scheduler, and objectives are known. Moreover, developing conventions has practical applications whereas showing their inexistence does not.

6 Convention for Decoupling Büchi Objectives

We show that decoupling is possible for Büchi objectives with mildly restricted path-aware policies; that is, Büchi admits a strong form of decoupling.

Definition 6 (Policies with uniform bounded hitting-time). *Let $\mathcal{G} = (V, E, v_0)$ be a graph and let $\pi \in \Pi^P$ be a stochastic policy on $\mathcal{G}$. Fix a subset $B \subseteq V$ and a finite path $\alpha = v_0 v_1 \ldots v_k \in Paths_{\mathsf{fin}}(\mathcal{G})$. The* hitting time random variable *of B under π from α is defined by*

$$\tau_\pi(\alpha)(\rho) \; := \; \min\{\, t \geq 1 \mid v_{k+t} \in B \text{ in the extension } \rho \in \mathrm{Ext}_\pi(\alpha) \,\},$$

with the convention $\tau_\pi(\alpha)(\rho) = \infty$ if no such t exists. The expected hitting time *of B from α under π is then $\mathbb{E}_\pi[\tau_\pi(\alpha)] \; = \; \int_{\mathrm{Ext}_\pi(\alpha)} \tau_\pi(\alpha)(\rho) \, d\mathrm{Pr}^\pi(\rho)$. We say that π has* uniformly bounded expected hitting time *for B if there exists a finite constant L such that $\sup_{\alpha \in Paths_{\mathsf{fin}}(\mathcal{G})} \mathbb{E}_\pi[\tau_\pi(\alpha)] \; \leq \; L$.*

The following theorem proves implementation of any such policies with a stochastic scheduler is good for all. The proof can be found in the full version.

Theorem 4. *Consider a strongly connected graph $\mathcal{G}$, policies $\pi_1, \ldots, \pi_N$ with uniform bounded hitting-time for Büchi objectives $\varphi_1, \ldots, \varphi_N$, and a stochastic scheduler σ. Then, $(\mathcal{G}, \pi_1, \ldots, \pi_N, \sigma) \models_{\text{a.s.}} \bigcap_{1 \le i \le N} \varphi_i$.*

7 Convention for Decoupling Co-Büchi Objectives

We start by showing that restricting to dense path aware policies does not suffice for co-Büchi objectives.

Theorem 5. *There is a graph, two co-Büchi objectives φ_1 and φ_2 with $(\varphi_1 \cap \varphi_2) \neq \emptyset$ and deterministic memoryless policies π_1^g and π_2^g that respectively satisfy φ_1 and φ_2, but for any scheduler σ, we have $(\mathcal{G}, \pi_1^g, \pi_2^g, \sigma) \not\models_{\text{a.s.}} \varphi_1 \cap \varphi_2$.*

Proof (sketch). Consider the graph $\mathcal{G}$ depicted in Fig. 4. For $i \in \{1, 2\}$, the "bad" co-Büchi vertex for objective φ_i is v_{1i}. Note that $(\varphi_1 \cap \varphi_2) \neq \emptyset$ since v_0^ω satisfies both objectives. We define $\pi_i(v_1) = v_{1,i}$, otherwise the policies are identical. Observe that π_i satisfies φ_i. However, for any stochastic scheduler, all vertices will be almost-surely visited, which violates both objectives.

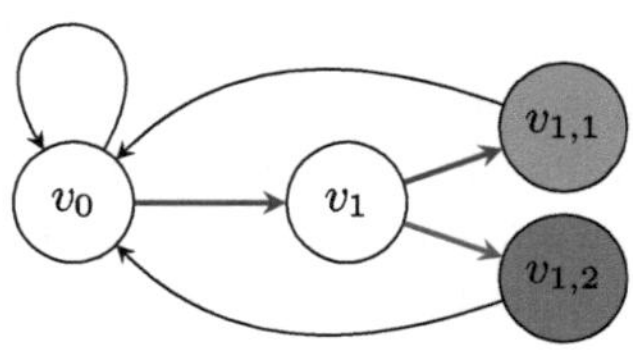

Fig. 4. A graph with two co-Büchi objectives given by bad states $v_{1,1}$ (Red) and $v_{1,2}$ (Blue). Red edges are chosen by π_1 and Blue edges by π_2. (Color figure online)

7.1 A Convention for Co-Büchi Objectives

Consider a strongly-connected graph $\mathcal{G}$, a stochastic scheduler σ, and a co-Büchi objective φ given by a set of "bad" states B. Let $\mathfrak{C}_B$ denote the set of "good" simple cycles in $\mathcal{G}$ that are disjoint from B. A policy $\pi \in \text{Conv}_{\text{co-Büchi}}(\mathcal{G}, \sigma, \varphi)$ proceeds as follows. It randomly chooses a lasso path $\rho \cdot C^\omega$, where ρ is a simple path and $C \in \mathfrak{C}_B$. If π is scheduled in a turn, if C has not yet been reached, it chooses the next vertex on ρ, and otherwise advances on C. Suppose that π is not scheduled, and let π' be the scheduled policy. Let v be the vertex that π would have chosen if it was scheduled and let v' be the vertex that π' chooses. If $v = v'$, we proceed to the next turn. If $v \neq v'$, then π' realizes it is in *conflict* with π: the lasso that π chose differs from the choice of π'. Then, π' randomly chooses a different lasso path $\rho' \cdot C'^\omega$ with $C' \in \mathfrak{C}_B$. Correctness will be derived from the property of co-Büchi objectives that if there is a path that satisfies all objectives, then there is a lasso $\rho \cdot C^\omega$ with $C \in \mathfrak{C}_B$ that is good for all. The idea is that almost surely, all policies will eventually choose the same lasso path leading to the generated path "stabilizing" on a cycle that is good for all.

We describe π formally. The memory states of π are $M = Paths_{\mathsf{fin}}(\mathcal{G}) \times \mathfrak{C}_B$, where a state $\langle \rho, C \rangle \in M$ means that π chooses cycle C and the path ρ leading to it. The interaction with a scheduler and the other policies generates a random sequence, and π's *local* view of the sequence is $\langle m_0, v_0 \rangle, \langle m_1, v_1 \rangle, \ldots$, where for $i \geq 0$, each $m_i = \langle \eta_i, C_i \rangle \in M$ is a memory state and $v_i \in V$ is a location on $\mathcal{G}$. The policy maintains the invariant that the location in $\mathcal{G}$ matches the first vertex of η, namely $\eta_i[0] = v_i$. We use $\top$ and $\bot$ to respectively denote that π is and is not scheduled. The definition of $\langle m_{i+1}, v_{i+1} \rangle = \pi(m_i, v_i, \top)$ is deterministic and depends on whether the cycle has been reached: (1) C_i has not been reached: then we define $v_{i+1} = \eta[1]$ and $m_{i+1} = \langle \eta[1:], C_i \rangle$, and (2) C_i has been reached: then $\eta_i = \epsilon$ and we define $m_{i+1} = m_i$ and v_{i+1} is the successor of v_i on C. We proceed to define $\pi(m_i, v_i, \bot)$. Let $\langle m, v \rangle = \pi(m_i, v_i, \top)$ be π's choice if it was scheduled, and let v_{i+1} be the vertex chosen by some other policy. If $v = v_{i+1}$, then the update is as above, $m_{i+1} = m$. If $v_{i+1} \neq v$, then π randomly selects $C_{i+1} \in \mathfrak{C}_B$ and a simple path η_{i+1} from v_{i+1} to C_{i+1}.

To prove the following theorem, we construct a Markov chain that simulates the global state of the policies and show that its Bottom Strongly Connected Components (BSCCs) are states in which the policies are in consensus regarding the choice of a lasso path that is good for all. The proof then follows from the property of Markov chains that a random walk reaches a BSCC almost surely.

Theorem 6. *Let $B_1, \ldots, B_N$ be a collection of co-Büchi objectives on a graph $\mathcal{G}$. For every choice of policies that satisfies the co-Büchi condition $\pi_i \in \chi_{B_i}$, for $i \in [N]$, and a fair scheduler σ, we have $(\mathcal{G}, \pi_1, \ldots, \pi_N, \sigma) \models_{\mathsf{a.s.}} \bigwedge_{1 \leq i \leq N} \varphi_i$.*

8 Convention for Decoupling Parity Objectives

We generalize the ideas for decoupling co-Büchi objectives to parity objectives. The construction requires full-history aware policies when $N > 2$. Fix a graph $\mathcal{G}$ and stochastic scheduler σ.

The co-Büchi convention relies on the property that if there is a path that satisfies all objectives, there is such a lasso path. This is no longer the case for parity objectives. For example, consider the graph depicted in Fig. 1(a) and objectives $\varphi_1 = (GF\ell) \wedge (G\neg b_1)$ and $\varphi_2 = (GFr) \wedge (G\neg b_1)$, then a path that satisfies both must cycle between r and ℓ via t_1 and t_2. This is not a simple cycle since both outgoing edges of t_1 and t_2 are traversed infinitely often. We overcome this using the following lemma whose proof can be found in the full version of the paper.

Lemma 1. *Consider parity objectives $\kappa_1, \ldots, \kappa_N : V \to \mathbb{N}$ with $\bigwedge_{i \in [1;N]} \kappa_i \neq \emptyset$. Then, there are memoryless policies $\langle \theta_1, \ldots, \theta_N \rangle : V \to V$ such that $(\mathcal{G}, \theta_1, \ldots, \theta_N, \sigma) \models_{\mathsf{a.s.}} \bigwedge_{i \in [1;N]} \kappa_i$*

For example, Fig. 1(a) depicts two memoryless policies π_1 and π_2 for which we have $(\mathcal{G}, \pi_1, \pi_2, \sigma) \models_{\text{a.s.}} \varphi_1 \wedge \varphi_2$ since the generated random walk almost surely visits each of the vertices ℓ, t_1, t_2, r infinitely often.

Parity Convention. Consider a parity objective given by a colouring function $\kappa_i : V \to \mathbb{N}$. A policy $\pi_i \in \text{Conv}_{\text{Parity}}(\mathcal{G}, \sigma, \kappa)$ randomly chooses an N-tuple of *internal* memoryless policies $\theta_1, \ldots \theta_N$ such that $(\mathcal{G}, \theta_1, \ldots \theta_N, \sigma) \models_{\text{a.s.}} \kappa_i$. Intuitively, when scheduled, π_i follows θ_i, and θ_j, for $j \neq i$, constitutes a guess of the internal policy that π_j follows. At vertex v, if π_i is scheduled, it proceed to $\theta_i(v)$ and if π_j is scheduled and chooses $u \neq \theta_i(v)$, then π_i observes a conflict and randomly chooses a new N-tuple of internal memoryless policies. In order to observe a conflict, π_i requires knowledge of who is scheduled and their choice, thus it is a full-history aware policy.

We describe π_i formally. Its memory states are $M = (V^V)^N$. The interaction with a scheduler and the other policies generates a random sequence, and π_i's *local* view of the sequence is $\langle m_0, v_0 \rangle, \langle m_1, v_1 \rangle, \ldots$, where at time $j \geq 0$, the location in $\mathcal{G}$ is $v_j \in V$ and the memory state is $m_j = \langle \theta_{j,1}, \ldots \theta_{j,N} \rangle \in M$. If π_i is scheduled at time j, we define $v_{j+1} = \theta_{j,i}(v_j)$ and the memory state is unchanged, namely $m_{j+1} = m_j$. Suppose that $\pi_{i'}$ is scheduled and chooses u, then we define $u = v_{j+1}$. If $u = \theta_{j,i}(v_j)$, then there is no conflict and $m_{j+1} = m_j$. Otherwise, $u \neq \theta_{j,i}(v_j)$, policy π_i realizes a conflict and randomly chooses $m_{j+1} = \langle \theta_{j+1,1}, \ldots \theta_{j+1,N} \rangle \in M$.

The following theorem is obtained by reasoning about the Markov chain that simulates the global state of the policies, carefully identifying consensus global states that are trivially good for all, and showing that they form the BSSCs of the Markov chain. The proof is available in Appendix ??.

Theorem 7. *Consider a strongly-connected graph $\mathcal{G}$, a stochastic scheduler σ, and a collection of N parity objectives $\kappa_1, \ldots, \kappa_N$ having $\bigcap_{1 \leq i \leq N} \kappa_i \neq \emptyset$. For every collection of policies $\pi_1, \ldots, \pi_N$ that satisfy the convention, i.e., $\pi_i \in Conv_{parity}(\mathcal{G}, \sigma, \kappa_i)$, for $i \in \{1, \ldots, N\}$, we have*

$$(\mathcal{G}, \pi_1, \ldots, \pi_N, \sigma) \models_{\text{a.s.}} \bigwedge_{1 \leq i \leq N} \kappa_i.$$

9 Discussion

We established sufficient conditions under which local policies for different ω-regular objectives can be composed under a common scheduler to almost-surely satisfy all objectives, showing that Büchi, co-Büchi, and parity objectives require progressively richer scheduler awareness.

Although our focus is on multi-parity objectives, the framework and the existence results for universal local policies naturally extend to any class of specifications implementable via finite-memory strategies, provided the memory bound is common knowledge among all modules. In this setting, each module may guess a finite-memory strategy per agent (rather than a memoryless one) whose bounded memory size is shared across modules.

Interestingly, while our analysis in Sect. 8 shows that full-history awareness is necessary in general, there are special cases that require less information. For instance, when there are only two agents with parity objectives, each can infer the scheduler's choice from the observed transition: if the transition corresponds to its own proposed action, the agent was scheduled; otherwise, the other agent was. Hence, no explicit communication from the scheduler is needed in this case.

For parity objectives, the memory size of each agent typically scales with the number of agents, as each agent must maintain a guess of a cycle for every other agent (including itself). However, if an agent has additional knowledge—e.g., that some others have Büchi or co-Büchi objectives—this requirement can be reduced. When a parity objective is combined with a (co-)Büchi objective, satisfiability can be achieved via a single simple cycle, eliminating the need for additional memory components.

Although we establish the existence of such universal schedulers, our work does not address their convergence properties. In particular, the expected convergence time of the presented protocol is likely to be exponential in the size of the underlying system. Improving this convergence time remains is not discussed in this paper. We conjecture that techniques from reinforcement learning or stochastic approximation could be adapted to accelerate convergence while preserving correctness guarantees, and is left for future work.

Acknowledgements. This work is funded by the following grants: European Research Council under Grant No.: ERC-2020-AdG 101020093, ISF grant no. 1679/21, grant RYC2024-049116, MICIU/AEI/10.13039/501100011033, the ESF+, and Volkswagen Foundation within its Momentum framework under project no. 9C283.

Disclosure of Interests. The authors have no competing interests to declare that are relevant to the content of this article.

References

1. Alpern, B., Schneider, F.B.: Recognizing safety and liveness. Distrib. Comput. **2**(3), 117–126 (1987). https://doi.org/10.1007/BF01782772
2. Anand, A., Nayak, S.P., Schmuck, A.K.: Synthesizing permissive winning strategy templates for parity games. In: Enea, C., Lal, A. (eds.) CAV 2023. LNCS, vol. 13964, pp. 436–458. Springer, Cham (2023). https://doi.org/10.1007/978-3-031-37706-8_22
3. Avni, G., Henzinger, T.A., Chonev, V.: Infinite-duration bidding games. J. ACM **66**(4), 31:1–31:29 (2019). https://doi.org/10.1145/3340295
4. Avni, G., Henzinger, T.A., Mallik, K., Sadhukhan, S., Thejaswini, K.S.: Decoupled planning for multiple omega-regular objectives. CoRR arXiv:2605.13185 (2026). https://doi.org/10.48550/arXiv.2605.13185
5. Avni, G., Mallik, K., Sadhukhan, S.: Auction-based scheduling. In: Finkbeiner, B., Kovács, L. (eds.) TACAS 2024. LNCS, vol. 14572, pp. 153–172. Springer, Cham (2024). https://doi.org/10.1007/978-3-031-57256-2_8
6. Basset, N., Kwiatkowska, M., Topcu, U., Wiltsche, C.: Strategy synthesis for stochastic games with multiple long-run objectives. In: Baier, C., Tinelli, C. (eds.)

TACAS 2015. LNCS, vol. 9035, pp. 256–271. Springer, Heidelberg (2015). https://doi.org/10.1007/978-3-662-46681-0_22

7. Basset, N., Kwiatkowska, M., Wiltsche, C.: Compositional strategy synthesis for stochastic games with multiple objectives. Inf. Comput. **261**, 536–587 (2018). https://doi.org/10.1016/j.ic.2017.09.010
8. Billingsley, P.: Probability and Measure, 3rd edn. Wiley, New York (1995). https://doi.org/10.1017/S0013091500004521
9. Chatterjee, K., De Alfaro, L., Henzinger, T.A.: Trading memory for randomness. In: 2004 Proceedings of the First International Conference on the Quantitative Evaluation of Systems, QEST 2004, pp. 206–217. IEEE (2004). https://doi.org/10.1109/QEST.2004.1348035
10. Chatterjee, K., Piterman, N.: Combinations of qualitative winning for stochastic parity games. In: 30th International Conference on Concurrency Theory, CONCUR, pp. 6:1–6:17. LIPIcs, Schloss Dagstuhl - Leibniz-Zentrum für Informatik (2019). https://doi.org/10.4230/LIPICS.CONCUR.2019.6
11. De Alfaro, L.: Formal verification of probabilistic systems. Stanford university (1998)
12. De Alfaro, L., Henzinger, T.A.: Concurrent omega-regular games. In: Proceedings Fifteenth Annual IEEE Symposium on Logic in Computer Science (Cat. No. 99CB36332), pp. 141–154. IEEE (2000). https://doi.org/10.1109/LICS.2000.855763
13. Finkbeiner, B., Schewe, S.: Uniform distributed synthesis. In: 20th Annual IEEE Symposium on Logic in Computer Science (LICS 2005), pp. 321–330. IEEE (2005). https://doi.org/10.1109/LICS.2005.53
14. Guenov, M., Barker, S.: Application of axiomatic design and design structure matrix to the decomposition of engineering systems. Syst. Eng. **8**, 29–40 (2005). https://doi.org/10.1002/sys.20015
15. Guruji, A.K., Agarwal, H., Parsediya, D.: Time-efficient A* algorithm for robot path planning. Procedia Technol. **23**, 144–149 (2016). https://doi.org/10.1016/J.PROTCY.2016.03.010
16. Harel, D., Marron, A., Weiss, G.: Behavioral programming. Commun. ACM **55**(7), 90–100 (2012). https://doi.org/10.1145/2209249.2209270
17. Hart, S., Mas-Colell, A.: Uncoupled dynamics do not lead to Nash equilibrium. Am. Econ. Rev. **93**(5), 1830–1836 (2003). https://doi.org/10.1257/000282803322655581
18. Kagan, E., Ben-Gal, I.: A group testing algorithm with online informational learning. IIE Trans. **46**(2), 164–184 (2014). https://doi.org/10.1080/0740817X.2013.803639
19. Klein, D., Manning, C.D.: A* parsing: fast exact viterbi parse selection. In: Proceedings of the 2003 Human Language Technology Conference of the North American Chapter of the Association for Computational Linguistics, pp. 119–126 (2003). https://doi.org/10.3115/1073445.1073461
20. Kupermann, O., Varfi, M.: Synthesizing distributed systems. In: Proceedings 16th Annual IEEE Symposium on Logic in Computer Science, pp. 389–398. IEEE (2001). https://doi.org/10.1109/LICS.2001.932514
21. Lazarus, A.J., Loeb, D.E., Propp, J.G., Stromquist, W.R., Ullman, D.H.: Combinatorial games under auction play. Games Econom. Behav. **27**(2), 229–264 (1999). https://doi.org/10.1006/game.1998.0676
22. Lewis, D.: Convention: A Philosophical Study. Wiley (2008). https://doi.org/10.1002/9780470693711

23. Pneuli, A., Rosner, R.: Distributed reactive systems are hard to synthesize. In: Proceedings [1990] 31st Annual Symposium on Foundations of Computer Science, pp. 746–757. IEEE (1990). https://doi.org/10.1109/FSCS.1990.89597
24. Pnueli, A.: On the extremely fair treatment of probabilistic algorithms. In: Proceedings of the Fifteenth Annual ACM Symposium on Theory of Computing, pp. 278–290 (1983). https://doi.org/10.1145/800061.808757
25. Pnueli, A., Zuck, L.D.: Probabilistic verification. Inf. Comput. **103**(1), 1–29 (1993). https://doi.org/10.1006/inco.1993.1012
26. Roijers, D.M., Vamplew, P., Whiteson, S., Dazeley, R.: A survey of multi-objective sequential decision-making. J. Artif. Intell. Res. **48**, 67–113 (2013). https://doi.org/10.1613/jair.3987
27. Schäfer, L., Christianos, F., Hanna, J.P., Albrecht, S.V.: Decoupled reinforcement learning to stabilise intrinsically-motivated exploration. In: Proceedings of the 21st AAMAS, pp. 1146–1154. IFAAMAS (2022). https://doi.org/10.65109/EYJJ1710

Repairing Regex-Dependent String-Manipulation Programs

Nariyoshi Chida[1(✉)] and Tachio Terauchi[2]

[1] NTT Social Informatics Laboratories, Tokyo, Japan
nariyoshichidamm@gmail.com
[2] Waseda University, Tokyo, Japan
terauchi@waseda.jp

Abstract. We present a new Programming-by-Examples (PBE) approach to repairing regex-dependent string-manipulation programs. Our approach has the following key features: (1) the support for a *wide range of functions* including regex-dependent functions such as `replaceAll`, `match`, `split`, list manipulation functions such as `map`, `reduce`, `filter`, and numerical functions such as `max`, `min`, `pow`, (2) the support for *real-world regexes* with non-standard semantics such as greedy/lazy Kleene star and extensions such as lookarounds and backreferences, (3) the focus on a *method-chaining style* that starts the chain of calls with a regex-dependent function, reflecting a code style used in the real-world, and (4) novel *origin-enriched* examples that allow users to communicate *intensional* behavior of programs in addition to the standard extension behavior communicated via ordinary input-output examples, and a novel *origin-tracking* semantics that formally defines when a program conforms to the behavior stipulated by such examples. We have implemented our approach as a tool named R3-S3 and evaluated it on real-world benchmarks collected from GitHub and StackOverflow. The results show that R3-S3 finds high-quality repairs efficiently.

Keywords: Regular Expression · String Transformation

1 Introduction

String manipulation plays a vital role in various software development situations. For example, it is widely employed in input sanitization [41,65], data wrangling [42,48], and parsing unstructured text [34]. Many modern programming languages provide a variety of functions to implement string manipulation, including regular expression (regex)-dependent functions such as `match` and `replaceAll`, which take a regex as a parameter, and regex-independent functions such as `reduce` and `concat`, which do not take a regex as a parameter and manipulate strings that may be returned by regex-dependent functions. Despite, writing string-manipulation programs is notoriously difficult and can cause security issues [23,29,41]. In response, researchers have proposed various

E. Darulova et al. (Eds.): CAV 2026, LNCS 16682, pp. 258–283, 2026.
https://doi.org/10.1007/978-3-032-32519-8_14

techniques to synthesize and repair string-manipulation programs *automatically* based on Programming-by-Example (PBE) methods [3–6,13,17–19,24,25,27,36–39,42,44,52,55,56]. Despite major steps forward, there still exists a gap between string-manipulation programs addressed in the prior work and those used in the real world. Namely, despite string-manipulation programs in the real world often consisting of *both* real-world regexes (i.e., regexes with non-standard semantics of operators such as greedy/lazy Kleene star [15,18,19] and extensions such as lookarounds and backreferences) [17–19] and a wide variety of functions, no existing approaches support both features.

To bridge the gap, we introduce a new class of string-manipulation programs called *regex-dependent method-chaining-style string-manipulation* (RMS) programs and an algorithm for repairing them. A key feature of RMS programs is the support of *both* real-world regexes and a wide variety of functions (e.g., regex-dependent functions such as `replaceAll`, `match`, `split`, list manipulating functions such as `map`, `reduce`, `filter`, and numerical functions such as `max`, `min`, `pow`), capturing a frequently occurring class of string manipulations. A challenge in repairing such programs is the large search space due to the rich support of real-world regexes and the variety of functions. To this end, RMS restricts the programs to the *method-chaining style* that starts the chain of calls with a regex-dependent function. The design reflects the popular code style used in real-world string-manipulation programs. We present a PBE-based repair for RMS programs. A key idea, inspired by prior work on finite-state transducers [7], regex-dependent string function repair [19], and repair of regexes for extraction [18], is a new class of examples, called *origin-enriched examples*, that are input-output strings with *origins* stipulating which substrings of the output originate from which substrings of the input. Our design allows the users to specify not only the desired extensional input-output behavior but also some *intensional* behavior of programs, allowing the users to better communicate their intention and help reduce the search space at the same time. We formally define the correctness with respect to origins by a novel *origin-tracking semantics*.

Our repair algorithm uses the origins to divide the repair problem into two subproblems: the repair of the regex and that of the rest of the program, which we call *regex-repair subproblem* and *post-regex-repair subproblem*, respectively. As for the former repair, we adopt the algorithm introduced in a prior work on repairing regexes to our setting [19]. As for the latter repair, we adopt an enumerative search algorithm, which is a widely used technique to synthesize/repair real-world programs [17–19,27,43,51,62,67]. That is, at a high level, our post-regex-repair algorithm enumerates partial programs called *templates*, which are programs with placeholders called *holes*, to change the structure of programs. We introduce novel pruning techniques called *origin-* and *value*-based prunings to reduce the search space, and a new SMT constraint generation technique called *alphabet-reduction* to instantiate a template into a solution by replacing holes with concrete values. We have implemented our algorithm as a tool named R3-S3 (Repairer for Regex-dependent and Regex-independent method-chaining-Style String-manipulation programS). Since different programming languages have different semantics of regex-dependent and regex-independent functions, we pick JavaScript for concreteness. However, our core ideas are applicable to other programming languages. We evaluated R3-S3 on real-world benchmarks collected from GitHub and StackOverflow. Results show that R3-S3 can find high-quality repairs efficiently. In summary, our contributions are as follows.

- A new class of string-manipulation programs called *regex-dependent method-chaining-style string-manipulation (RMS) programs*, capturing the features of real-world string-manipulation programs (Sect. 3).
- A novel class of *origin-enriched* examples to be used for a PBE repair of RMS programs, and a novel *origin-tracking* semantics that stipulates the correctness of the repaired programs with respect to these examples (Sect. 3.1).
- An algorithm for solving the PBE-repair problem (Sect. 4).
- An implementation of the algorithm R3-S3, and an evaluation on real-world benchmarks collected from GitHub and StackOverflow (Sect. 5).

Notations. We write $\mathbb{Z}$ for the set of integers, $\mathbb{N}$ for the set of natural numbers, $\mathbb{N}_{\geq 1}$ for $\mathbb{N}\backslash\{0\}$, $[i..j]$ for $\{i, i+1, \cdots, j\}$ where $i \leq j$, and $[i]$ for $[1..i]$. For a sequence l, we write $|l|$ for its length, $l[i]$ (resp. $l[i..j]$) for the ith element (resp. the subsequence from i to j) where $i \leq j < |l|$, $l[i..j)$ for $l[i..j-1]$ where $i \leq j-1 < |l|$, and $l[i..]$ for $l[i..|l|)$. We write ϵ for the empty sequence, and let $l[i..j) = \epsilon$ when $i > j-1$. We write $l_1 \cdot l_2$ for the concatenation of l_1 and l_2, and omit $\cdot$ when clear. We fix the finite alphabet Σ. We use _ to omit unimportant elements. The expression $\texttt{ite}(b, A, B)$ denotes A if b is *true*, and B if b is *false*. For a function f, $f[a \mapsto b]$ denotes the function $\lambda x.\texttt{ite}(x = a, b, f(x))$.

2 Overview

We illustrate how R3-S3 works using an example. Consider the following problem inspired by actual StackOverflow posts [57,58]: *Output the sum of grams enclosed within XML tags in the given input string.* For example, a programmer wants to convert the string $w_1 =$ "`<h1>5</h1>g, 51g, <h1>39</h1>g, 96g`" to "`44g`" because the sum of the grams enclosed within XML tags (i.e., h1 tags in this case) is 5g + 39g = 44g. Likewise, he wants to convert the string $w_2 =$ "`<h2>9</h2>g, <em>8</em>g, <em>3</em>`" to "`17g`" because 9g + 8g = 17g. Suppose that the programmer thought that he could do this by using a regex to extract all integers that are enclosed with XML tags and are followed by the unit "g" from the input string, and then, compute and output their sum concatenated with "g". Suppose the programmer managed to write the following code for extracting the integers using a regex: `match`((?<=<($_1$.*)$_1$>).*(?=<[/]\1>g)), where `match` is a regex-dependent function that takes a string as input and returns the list of the substrings matching the regex given as the parameter. The regex uses the positive lookbehind (?<=<($_1$.*)$_1$>) and the positive lookahead (?=<[/]\1>g) to find the opening and closing tags followed by "g", respectively, and extracts the text in between using the regex .*, which matches any string. However, the programmer now faces two problems. First, the regex is incorrect. Indeed, for the first string w_1, the string "5</h1>g, 51g, <h1>39" is extracted rather than "5" and "39", and for the second string w_2 the extracted string is just "9" rather than "9" and "8", due to the non-standard semantics of regexes. Second, the programmer has not written the rest of the program that transforms the extracted strings to the output string as described above (e.g., because the programmer lacks expertise in advanced functions such as `reduce`).

R3-S3 can be used to repair the program. To use R3-S3, the user provides the program to be repaired and a set of *examples*.[1] An example is a pair of input and output strings annotated with *origins* that describe which substrings of the output originate from which substrings of the input. Origins are denoted by $\llparenthesis_T w \rrparenthesis_T$ where w is a substring and T is a set of origin identifiers. In the running example, for the case that the input is w_1 (resp. w_2), the substring "44" (resp. "17") of the output should originate from "5" and "39" (resp. "9" and "8") of the input. Therefore, the programmer may prepare the examples "<h1>$\llparenthesis_1$5$\rrparenthesis_1$</h1>g, 51g, <h1>$\llparenthesis_2$39$\rrparenthesis_2$</h1>g, 96g $\Rightarrow$ $\llparenthesis_{1,2}$44$\rrparenthesis_{1,2}$g" and "<h2>$\llparenthesis_1$9$\rrparenthesis_1$</h2>g, <em>$\llparenthesis_2$8$\rrparenthesis_2$</em>g, <em>3</em> $\Rightarrow$ $\llparenthesis_{1,2}$17$\rrparenthesis_{1,2}$g". Here, $\llparenthesis_{1,2}$44$\rrparenthesis_{1,2}$ (resp. $\llparenthesis_{1,2}$17$\rrparenthesis_{1,2}$) stipulates that the substring "44" (resp. "17") originates from the substrings specified by the origins of the input whose identifiers are 1 and 2, i.e., $\llparenthesis_1$5$\rrparenthesis_1$ and $\llparenthesis_2$39$\rrparenthesis_2$ (resp. $\llparenthesis_1$9$\rrparenthesis_1$ and $\llparenthesis_2$8$\rrparenthesis_2$). Note that the number of examples should be small for usability in PBE. Given the program and examples, R3-S3 automatically finds a repair which satisfies all the examples and is of the smallest edit distance to the given initial program. Roughly, we say that a program *satisfies* an example if the program conforms to the input-ouput behavior stipulated by the example (i.e., returns the output string given the input string), and *additionally* respects the origins (i.e., the substrings of the output originate from the corresponding substrings of the input as stipulated by the origins). Formally, we define the satisfaction relation by a novel *origin-tracking* semantics which specifies how the origins in the input propagate to those in the output (cf. Sect. 3.1).

Next, we overview how R3-S3 finds such a repair. R3-S3 first divides the repair problem into the *regex-repair subproblem* and the remaining *post-regex-repair subproblem* by using the origins in the examples. The former subproblem takes the given regex and the origin-enriched input strings of the examples, and its goal is to return a regex that matches the substrings specified by the origins and is of the smallest edit distance from the given regex. For the running example, the given regex to be repaired is $(?<=<(_1.^*)_1>).^*(?=<[/]\backslash 1>g)$, the input strings are "<h1>$\llparenthesis_1$5$\rrparenthesis_1$</h1>g, 51g, <h1>$\llparenthesis_2$39$\rrparenthesis_2$</h1>g, 96g" and "<h2>$\llparenthesis_1$9$\rrparenthesis_1$</h2>g, <em>$\llparenthesis_2$8$\rrparenthesis_2$</em>g, <em>3</em>", and the goal is to return a repaired regex that matches "5" and "39" (resp. "9" and "8") for the first (resp. second) string and is of the smallest edit distance to the given regex. The post-regex-repair subproblem takes the part of the given program after the regex-dependent function call (called the *post-regex program*) and the examples but with the parts of the input strings irrelevant to the post-regex program reducted

[1] R3-S3 can also optionally take a set of integer constants (cf. Sect. 4).

(see below for details), and returns a repaired post-regex program part that respects the extensional and intensional behavior stipulated by the examples and is of the smallest edit distance from the pre-repair post-regex program. For the running example, the original post-regex program is empty and the examples are the two pairs of origin-annotated strings described before, but with certain information of the input strings reducted as described next. The key observation that lets us divide the repair problem into the two subproblems is the fact that the outputs of regex-dependent functions depend only on the information about which substrings are to be matched by the regex and the fact that such information is given in the examples as origins.[2] For the running example, the origins stipulate that the output of the `match` function for the first (resp. second) input must be the list $[(\!|_1\texttt{5}|\!)_1,\ (\!|_2\texttt{39}|\!)_2]$ (resp. $[(\!|_1\texttt{9}|\!)_1,\ (\!|_2\texttt{8}|\!)_2]$), and therefore the post-regex-repair subproblem can assume that the post-regex program takes these lists as its inputs independent of the regex to be returned by R3-S3 for the regex-repair subproblem. Thus, the input part of the examples can be reduced to these substrings in the post-regex repair.

To solve the regex-repair subproblem, R3-S3 adopts the algorithm for repairing a regex-dependent function introduced in the prior work [19]. In this case, the algorithm finds a repaired regex $r = (?<=\texttt{<}(_1[\texttt{0-9a-z}]^*)_1\texttt{>})[\texttt{0-9}]^*(?=\texttt{<}[/]\backslash\texttt{1>g})$. For the post-regex-repair problem, R3-S3 adopts an enumerative search with SMT solving [17,19,43,51], but extended with a new SMT constraint generation technique called *alphabet-reduction* and new pruning techniques. In this case, it returns $p = \texttt{reduce}(\lambda x.\lambda y.\texttt{toString}(\texttt{parseInt}(x)+\texttt{parseInt}(y))).\texttt{concat}(\texttt{g})$ as the repaired post-regex program. We refer to Sect. 4 for details.

Finally, R3-S3 combines the repaired regex and post-regex program with the regex-dependent function, and returns the obtained program as the solution. For the running example, R3-S3 returns the program $\texttt{match}(r).p$ where r and p are the repaired regex and post-regex program shown above. It satisfies all examples and is of the smallest edit distance to the given initial program. Note that no existing approaches can synthesize the program because it needs both the non-standard semantics of regexes with real-world extensions such as lookbehinds and advanced functions such as `reduce`.

3 RMS Programs and Origin-Tracking Semantics

Figure 1 presents the syntax of *RMS programs* (or simply *programs*). A program, *prog*, is in a *method-chaining style* [49] that starts the chain of calls with a regex-dependent function, *rdf*. The language supports three types of regex-dependent functions: `replaceAll`, `match`, and `split`. The `replaceAll` function takes two parameters: a regex to find substrings to be replaced and a *replacement* to specify how the substrings matched by the regex will be replaced. A replacement is a function that takes the substrings matched by the capturing groups in the regex as parameters and returns a string. Given an input string, `replaceAll` returns a

[2] For `replaceAll`, we additionally require that the examples contain origin annotations that specify the substrings to be captured. See Sect. 3.1 for details.

$$
\begin{aligned}
prog &::= rdf.chain \quad chain ::= \texttt{id} \mid rif.chain\\
rdf &::= \texttt{match}(reg) \mid \texttt{split}(reg) \mid \texttt{replaceAll}(reg, \lambda x_1.\cdots\lambda x_n.es.chain)\\
rif &::= sop \mid \texttt{toUpperCase}() \mid \texttt{toLowerCase}() \mid \texttt{trimStart}() \mid \texttt{trimEnd}() \mid \texttt{trim}()\\
&\mid \texttt{split}(es) \mid \texttt{join}(es) \mid \texttt{reverse}() \mid \texttt{map}(\lambda x.es) \mid \texttt{filter}(\lambda x.eb) \mid \texttt{reduce}(\lambda x.\lambda y.es)\\
es &::= w \mid x \mid x??w \mid \texttt{toString}(ei) \mid es.sop\\
ei &::= i \mid \texttt{parseInt}(es) \mid es.\texttt{length} \mid \texttt{iop}(ei, ei)\\
eb &::= es.\texttt{startsWith}(es) \mid es.\texttt{endsWith}(es) \mid es.\texttt{includes}(es) \mid es.\texttt{equals}(es)\\
sop &::= \texttt{at}(i) \mid \texttt{concat}(es) \mid \texttt{replaceAll}(w, w) \mid \texttt{repeat}(ei) \mid \texttt{slice}(i, i)
\end{aligned}
$$

Fig. 1. The syntax of RMS programs.

new string obtained by replacing the substrings matched by the regex with the strings obtained from the replacement. The `match` function takes a string and returns the list of the substrings matched by the regex. The `split` function takes a string and returns the list of the substrings obtained by splitting the string on the substrings matched by the regex. Then, the program is followed by a chain of function calls, *chain*, for manipulating the output of the regex-dependent function. The chaining operation $e_1.e_2$ first executes e_1, and then executes e_2 with the output of e_1 as the input. The function `id` is the *identity function* that returns its input. To avoid clutter, we omit `id` when clear, i.e., we write *rif* for *rif*.`id`. For manipulating values, the program supports a variety of functions that are commonly supported by modern programming languages such as JavaScript, Java, Python, .NET, and PHP. We refer to Sect. 3.1 for the formal semantics of the language. We note that Sect. 3.1 presents an *origin-tracking* semantics that, in addition to the extentional input-output behavior, stipulates the intentional behavior represented by origins. Our semantics follows the ECMAScript® 2023 Language Specification [28]. We assume that the programs are typed under a standard type system that ensures type safety. For instance, in `match`(reg).e, the type system ensures that e takes a list of strings as input.

3.1 Origins

We formally define when a substring of the output *originate from* a substring of the input. For a string w, an *origin atom* (or just *atom*) is a triple (l, r, T), where l and r are indexes of w (i.e., $l, r \in [0..|w|]$) satisfying $l \leq r$, and $T \subseteq IDs$. *IDs* is the denumerable set of *origin identifiers* (or *identifiers* when clear) used to identify origins, and is a disjoint union of the set of capturing-group indexes (ranged over by c_i for some $i \in \mathbb{N}$) and the set of other (i.e., non-capturing-group-index) identifiers. A *level-0 origin* is an atom whose set of identifiers only contains capturing group indexes. A *level-0 origin list* is a list of level-0 origins. A *level-1 origin* is a pair (a, ξ^0) where a is an atom whose set of identifiers only contains non-capturing group indexes and ξ^0 is a level-0 origin list. A *level-1 origin list* is a list of level-1 origins. The reason for this (one-)nesting structure of origin lists is explained later.

We use ξ (resp. ξ^0) to denote a level-1 (resp. level-0) origin list. We also use ξ^0 to refer to a level-1 origin list ξ when $\xi[i] = (\_, \epsilon)$ for all $i \in [|\xi|]$, i.e., when ξ only nests empty level-0 origin lists. We assert $r \leq l'$ for $i < i'$ if $(l, r, \_) \in \xi^0[i]$ and $(l', r', \_) \in \xi^0[i']$ or if $((l, r, \_), \_) \in \xi[i]$ and $((l', r', \_), \_) \in \xi[i']$, i.e., atoms are ordered in non-decreasing sequences of their indexes in origin lists. Additionally, we assert $l' \leq l \leq r \leq r'$ when $(l, r, \_) \in \xi^0$ and $((l', r', \_), \xi^0) \in \xi$, i.e., nested atoms have nested indexes. We refer to the elements of origin lists as *origins*. For brevity, we abbreviate a level-1 origin $((l, r, T), \epsilon)$ as (l, r, T). A *string with origins* is a pair (w, ξ) where ξ is a level-1 origin list of w. We write $\llparenthesis_T w[l..r) \rrparenthesis_T$ for the atom (l, r, T) of a string w. For example, we write $\llparenthesis_1 \mathtt{a} \rrparenthesis_1 \llparenthesis_2 \mathtt{b} \llparenthesis_{c_1} \mathtt{c} \rrparenthesis_{c_1} \rrparenthesis_2$ for the string with origins $(\mathtt{abc}, [(0, 1, \{1\}), (1, 3, \{2\}, \xi^0)])$ with $\xi^0 = [(2, 3, \{c_1\})]$.

3.2 Origin-Tracking Semantics

We define a formal semantics of RMS programs that we call *origin-tracking semantics*. It builds on the ECMAScript® semantics with extensions to track origins. Formally, we define the big-step judgement $\Delta \vdash \langle p, v \rangle \Downarrow v'$, which says that "under the *environment* Δ, the program term p produces the output *value* v' for the input *value* v". An environment is a mapping from a variable to a string with origins and values are classified into four types, depending on their type information: a string with origins, a list of strings with origins, an *integer with origins*, and a boolean value. An integer with origins (i, T) is a pair of an integer i and a set T of identifiers. We introduce some notations used in the rules. We use (w, T) as an abbreviation for a string with origins $(w, [(0, |w|, T)])$, i.e., the origin is attached to the whole string. We write $(\xi^0)^\natural$ for the mapping $\{c \mapsto (l, r) \mid (l, r, \{c\}) \in \xi^0\}$. Given two strings with origins (w_1, ξ_1) and (w_2, ξ_2), $(w_1, \xi_1) \triangleleft (w_2, \xi_2)$ denotes the *concatenation* of them defined by $(w_1, \xi_1) \triangleleft (w_2, \xi_2) = (w_1 \cdot w_2, \xi_1 \cdot \xi_2')$, where ξ_2' is a list obtained from ξ_2 by replacing all atoms (l, r, T) in ξ_2 with $(l + |w_1|, r + |w_1|, T)$, e.g., $\llparenthesis_1 a \rrparenthesis_1 \triangleleft \llparenthesis_2 b \llparenthesis_{c_1} c \rrparenthesis_{c_1} \rrparenthesis_2 = \llparenthesis_1 a \rrparenthesis_1 \llparenthesis_2 b \llparenthesis_{c_1} c \rrparenthesis_{c_1} \rrparenthesis_2$. The operator $\triangleleft$ is right-associative, i.e., $a \triangleleft b \triangleleft c = a \triangleleft (b \triangleleft c)$. We use the formal semantics of regexes introduced in a prior work [19] that is consistent with the ECMAScript® semantics. It is defined as the relation $(\mathit{reg}, w) \hookrightarrow [(l_1, r_1, \Gamma_1), \cdots, (l_n, r_n, \Gamma_n)]$, which states that, for each $i \in [n]$, the regex *reg* matches the substring $w[l_i..r_i)$ where Γ_i is a mapping describing the substrings extracted by the capturing groups in *reg*.

$$\frac{\xi = [(l_1, r_1, T_1), \cdots, (l_n, r_n, T_n)] \quad 1 \leq n \qquad (\mathit{reg}, w) \hookrightarrow [(l_1, r_1, \_), \cdots, (l_n, r_n, \_)] \quad \forall i \in [n]. v_i = (w[l_i..r_i), T_i)}{\Delta \vdash \langle \mathtt{match}(\mathit{reg}), (w, \xi) \rangle \Downarrow [v_1, v_2, \cdots, v_n]}$$

We discuss selected rules. We refer to the appendix for the full set of rules. The rule for `match` checks whether the regex *reg* matches the substrings specified by the origins ξ (i.e., the substrings $w[l_i..r_i)$ for each $(l_i, r_i, \_) \in \xi$), and if so returns the list of the matched substrings with their corresponding identifiers. For example, $\emptyset \vdash \langle \mathtt{match}(\mathtt{a}^+), \llparenthesis_1 \mathtt{a} \rrparenthesis_1 \mathtt{b} \llparenthesis_2 \mathtt{aa} \rrparenthesis_2 \rangle \Downarrow [\llparenthesis_1 \mathtt{a} \rrparenthesis_1, \llparenthesis_2 \mathtt{aa} \rrparenthesis_2]$ because $(\mathtt{a}^+, \mathtt{abaa}) \hookrightarrow [(0, 1, \emptyset), (2, 4, \emptyset)]$. Note that the rule propagates origins attached to the matched substrings to the output. This follows the propagation of origins used in prior work on repairing regex-dependent functions [19].

$$\frac{\xi = [((l_1, r_1, T_1), \xi_1^0), \cdots, ((l_m, r_m, T_m), \xi_m^0)] \qquad 1 \leq m \quad (reg, w) \hookrightarrow [(l_1, r_1, \Gamma_1), \cdots, (l_m, r_m, \Gamma_m)] \;\; \forall i \in [m].\; (\Gamma_i = (\xi_i^0)^\natural \wedge \Theta(i))}{\Delta \vdash \langle \mathtt{replaceAll}(reg, \lambda x_1. \cdots \lambda x_n.e), (w, \xi)\rangle \Downarrow (w'_m \cdot w[r_m..], \xi'_m)}$$

The rule for `replaceAll` illustrates the reason for allowing (one-)nested origins. For example, `replaceAll` works as follows. For $reg = ({}_{c_1}\mathtt{a})_{c_1}({}_{c_2}\mathtt{b})_{c_2}$, $\emptyset \vdash \langle \mathtt{replaceAll}(reg, \lambda c_1.\lambda c_2.c_2.\mathtt{concat}(c_1)), \llparenthesis_1 \llparenthesis_{c_1} \mathtt{a} \rrparenthesis_{c_1} \llparenthesis_{c_2} \mathtt{b} \rrparenthesis_{c_2} \rrparenthesis_1 \rangle \Downarrow \llparenthesis_1 \llparenthesis_{c_2} \mathtt{b} \rrparenthesis_{c_2} \llparenthesis_{c_1} \mathtt{a} \rrparenthesis_{c_1} \rrparenthesis_1$ because $(reg, \mathtt{ab}) \hookrightarrow [(0, 2, \{c_1 \mapsto (0,1), c_2 \mapsto (1,2)\})]$ and $\{c_1 \mapsto \llparenthesis_{c_1} \mathtt{a} \rrparenthesis_{c_1}, c_2 \mapsto \llparenthesis_{c_2} \mathtt{b} \rrparenthesis_{c_2}\} \vdash \langle c_2.\mathtt{concat}(c_1), \bot\rangle \Downarrow \llparenthesis_{c_2} \mathtt{b} \rrparenthesis_{c_2} \llparenthesis_{c_1} \mathtt{a} \rrparenthesis_{c_1}$. In the rule, $\Theta(i) = ① \wedge ②$, where $① = \Delta \cup \{x_j \mapsto (w[l'..r'), \{x_j\}) \mid \exists j \in [n].(l', r', \{x_j\}) \in \xi_i^0\} \vdash \langle e, \bot\rangle \Downarrow (w_i^{rep}, \xi_i^{0'})$ and $② = ((w'_i, \xi'_i) = (w'_{i-1}, \xi'_{i-1}) \triangleleft (w[r_{i-1}..l_i), \epsilon) \triangleleft (w_i^{rep}, [((0, |w_i^{rep}|, T_i), \xi_i^{0'})]) \wedge r_0 = 0 \wedge (w'_0, \xi'_0) = (\epsilon, \epsilon))$. As with the `match` rule, it checks that the regex *reg* matches the substrings specified by the origins (including those extracted by the capturing groups), and propagates the origins attached to the matched substrings to the output. *In addition*, it propagates the origins attached to the substrings extracted by the capturing groups to the replacement e by binding them to its parameters $x_1, \ldots, x_n$ as seen in ① of $\Theta(i)$. Note that these are substrings of each substring matched by *reg*, and they are specified by the level-0 origins nested inside the corresponding level-1 origin matching *reg*. This propagation is based on an idea introduced in prior work on repair of regexes for extraction [18]. In the last judgement of the above example, `concat` concatenates two strings with origins while preserving their origins. This naturally extends the origin-tracking semantics proposed for finite-state transducers (FSTs) [7] from just using individual characters as origins to allowing arbitrary substrings to be used as origins. We defer more detailed comparison to the origin-tracking semantics of FSTs to Sect. 6 and the appendix.

The rule for `join` evaluates the term e to (w, ξ) and inserts it between the elements of l to construct a single string with origins. Here, $\bot$ indicates a dummy input.

$$\frac{2 \leq |l| \quad \Delta \vdash \langle e, \bot\rangle \Downarrow (w, \xi) \quad \Delta \vdash \langle \mathtt{join}(e), l[1..]\rangle \Downarrow (w', \xi') \quad (w'', \xi'') = l[0] \triangleleft (w, \xi) \triangleleft (w', \xi')}{\Delta \vdash \langle \mathtt{join}(e), l\rangle \Downarrow (w'', \xi'')}$$

$$\frac{\Gamma \vdash \langle e_1, v\rangle \Downarrow v' \quad \Gamma \vdash \langle e_2, v'\rangle \Downarrow v''}{\Delta \vdash \langle e_1.e_2, v\rangle \Downarrow v''}$$

For example, $\emptyset \vdash \langle \mathtt{join}(\#), [\llparenthesis_1 \mathtt{a} \rrparenthesis_1, \llparenthesis_2 \mathtt{aa} \rrparenthesis_2]\rangle \Downarrow \llparenthesis_1 \mathtt{a} \rrparenthesis_1 \# \llparenthesis_2 \mathtt{aa} \rrparenthesis_2$. Finally, we show the self-explanatory rule for the chaining operation. For example, $\emptyset \vdash \langle \mathtt{match}(\mathtt{a}^+).\mathtt{join}(\#), \llparenthesis_1 \mathtt{a} \rrparenthesis_1 \mathtt{b} \llparenthesis_2 \mathtt{aa} \rrparenthesis_2\rangle \Downarrow \llparenthesis_1 \mathtt{a} \rrparenthesis_1 \# \llparenthesis_2 \mathtt{aa} \rrparenthesis_2$.

4 The Repair Algorithm

We present our PBE-based algorithm for repairing an RMS program. We first formally define the repair problem and give an overview of the top-level algorithm. We then describe the algorithm's key components in Sect. 4.1 and 4.2. An *example* is a pair $(w, \xi) \Rightarrow (w', \xi')$ of strings with origins satisfying the following conditions, where $\{T_1, \cdots, T_n\}$ and $\{T'_1, \cdots, T'_m\}$ are the sets of all sets of identifiers in ξ and ξ', respectively. (1) T_i is a singleton set for all $i \in [n]$, and $\bigcup_{i\in[m]} T'_i \subseteq \bigcup_{i\in[n]} T_i$. (2) All identifiers in ξ are unique, i.e., $T_i \neq T_j$ for all $i \neq j$. We say that a program p *satisfies* an example $(w, \xi) \Rightarrow (w', \xi')$ if $\emptyset \vdash \langle p, (w, \xi)\rangle \Downarrow (w', \xi')$. Also, for a set $\mathcal{E}$ of examples, we say that p satisfies $\mathcal{E}$ iff p satisfies all examples in $\mathcal{E}$.

Next, we describe a metric for measuring the quality of a repair. Our metric is based on the *edit distance* used in the prior works for regex and regex-dependent function repair [17–19,51]. That is, a program is considered to be of high quality if the edit distance between the program and the pre-repair program is small. This reflects the assumption that, although the user-provided program may be incorrect, it is likely to be syntactically close to the intended one [51]. Our metric assigns no cost to rewriting a string using associativity of concatenation (i.e., rewriting $(a \cdot b) \cdot c$ as $a \cdot (b \cdot c)$) and to inserting or deleting type-conversion functions `toString` and `parseInt`. We also adopt the *capture-insertion relation* introduced in [19] and allow insertion of capturing groups to regexes at no cost. Specifically, given a set of integers I, the capture-insertion relation $\Rightarrow_I$ over regexes is defined by: $r \Rightarrow_I r'$ iff r can be rewritten to r' using associativity of the binary operators of regexes and inserting capturing groups $(_i\cdot)_i$ where $i \notin I$. We also apply this relation to strings by interpreting a string as a regex consisting of characters and concatenations, e.g., $(\mathtt{a} \cdot \mathtt{b}) \cdot \mathtt{c} \Rightarrow_\emptyset \mathtt{a} \cdot (\mathtt{b} \cdot \mathtt{c})$.

Definition 1 (Edit Distance). For subtrees $q_1, \cdots, q_n$ of a program p, the *edit* $[q'_1/q_1, \cdots, q'_n/q_n]$ replaces each q_i with q'_i where $i \in [n]$. The *cost* of the edit is $\Sigma_{i\in[n]}, |q'_i| + |q_i|$, where, for a term q with immediate subtrees $q_1, \ldots, q_n$, $|q| = \Sigma_{i\in[n]}|q_i| + c$ such that $c = 1$ if q is neither `toString` nor `parseInt`, and $c = 0$ otherwise. Given two programs p and p', the *distance* between p and p', denoted by $D(p, p')$, is the minimum cost of an edit that rewrites p to some p'' such that p'' is obtained by replacing the regex $r_{p'}$ (resp. strings $w_{p'}$) of p' with a regex $r_{p''}$ (resp. $w_{p''}$) satisfying $r_{p''} \Rightarrow_I r_{p'}$ (resp. $w_{p''} \Rightarrow_\emptyset w_{p'}$) where I is the set of indexes of capturing groups and backreferences in $r_{p''}$.

Following a prior work [62], we assume that the integers the user intends to use are provided in advance. As remarked in [62], this benefits both the user and the synthesis algorithm, i.e., it allows the user to express their intent more precisely, while enabling the synthesis algorithm to reduce the search space. Below, we classify integers into *positions* and *non-positions*. An integer i is a non-position iff i is derived from *ei* shown in Fig. 1, i.e., only integers appearing in `at` and `slice` are positions and others are non-positions.

Definition 2 (The Repair Problem). Given a program p, a set $\mathcal{E}$ of examples, and a set C of integers, the *RMS-repair problem* is the problem of synthesizing a program p' such that (1) p' satisfies $\mathcal{E}$, (2) all non-positions newly added in p' are elements of C, and (3) the distance between p and p' is minimal, i.e., $D(p, p') \leq D(p, p'')$ for any program p'' that satisfies (1) and (2). We assume that no two examples have the same input string.

1: $reg \leftarrow$ `getReg`(p) ; $p' \leftarrow$ `getPost`(p)
2: $\mathcal{E}_{in} =$ `initExam`$_{reg}(\mathcal{E})$; $\mathcal{E}' =$ `initExam`$_{post}(\mathcal{E})$
3: $reg' =$ `repReg`$(reg, \mathcal{E}_{in})$ $||$ $p'' =$ `repPost`$(p', \mathcal{E}', C)$
4: **return** `combine`(reg', p'')

The figure on the right shows the top-level procedure. It outputs a program satisfying (1)-(3) of Definition 2 or raises an exception when no solution exists. The procedure is simple: it divides the problem into the *regex-repair subproblem* and the *post-regex-repair subproblem* (lines 1-3), and combines the solutions of the subproblems (line 4). As mentioned in Sect. 2, the division is possible thanks to the origin-enriched examples.

The regex-repair subproblem takes the regex reg of p and the set $\mathcal{E}_{in}$ of origin-enriched strings defined below, and the output is a regex reg' that matches the substrings specified by the origins and is of the smallest edit distance from reg. $\mathcal{E}_{in} = \{(w, \xi) \mid (w, \xi) \Rightarrow \_ \in \mathcal{E}\}$ if the regex-dependent function of p is either `match` or `replaceAll`. If it is `split`, we take the complement of the ranges of the level-1 origins, i.e., $\mathcal{E}_{in} = \{(w, \xi') \mid (w, \xi) \Rightarrow \_ \in \mathcal{E}\}$, where $\xi = [(l_1, r_1, \_), \cdots, (l_n, r_n, \_)]$ and $\xi' = [(r_1, l_2, \emptyset), \cdots, (r_{n-1}, l_n, \emptyset)]$. For example, suppose $p =$ `match([0-9]).join(,)` and $\mathcal{E} = \{\llparenthesis_1 \texttt{12} \rrparenthesis_1 \texttt{,} \llparenthesis_2 \texttt{3} \rrparenthesis_2 \Rightarrow \llparenthesis_1 \texttt{12} \rrparenthesis_1 \texttt{\#} \llparenthesis_2 \texttt{3} \rrparenthesis_2\}$. Then, $reg =$ [0-9] and $\mathcal{E}_{in} = \{\llparenthesis_1 \texttt{12} \rrparenthesis_1 \texttt{,} \llparenthesis_2 \texttt{3} \rrparenthesis_2\}$.

The post-regex-repair problem takes the *post-regex program* p' of p, the set $\mathcal{E}'$, and the set C of integers, and the output is a post-regex program p'' that *satisfies* $\mathcal{E}'$ and is of the smallest edit distance from p'.[3] A post-regex program is the part of an RMS program after the regex-dependent function call, i.e., the program terms derived from *chain* in Fig. 1. Also, $\mathcal{E}' = \{[v_1, \cdots, v_{|\xi|}] \Rightarrow (w', \xi') \mid (w, \xi) \Rightarrow (w', \xi') \in \mathcal{E}\}$, where $v_i = (w[l..r), T)$ and $\xi[i-1] = (l, r, T)$ for all $i \in [|\xi|]$. For example, in the above example, the post-regex program is `join(,)` and $\mathcal{E}' = \{[\llparenthesis_1 \texttt{12} \rrparenthesis_1, \llparenthesis_2 \texttt{3} \rrparenthesis_2] \Rightarrow \llparenthesis_1 \texttt{12} \rrparenthesis_1 \texttt{\#} \llparenthesis_2 \texttt{3} \rrparenthesis_2\}$. We say that a post-regex program p satisfies $\mathcal{E}'$ iff $\emptyset \vdash \langle p, [v_1, \cdots, v_n] \rangle \Downarrow v$ for all $[v_1, \cdots, v_n] \Rightarrow v \in \mathcal{E}'$. By abuse, we call the elements of $\mathcal{E}'$ *examples* when no confusion arises.

The algorithm solves the subproblems in parallel using `repPost` for the post-regex-repair subproblem (cf. Sect. 4.2) and `repReg` for the regex-repair subproblem (cf. Sect. 4.1). Once both repairs are complete, the algorithm combines the repaired regex reg' and the repaired post-regex program p'' with the regex-dependent function of the initial program p and returns it as a solution. If either repair fails, the algorithm aborts by raising an exception. For example, in the above example, the outputs of `repReg` and `repPost` are $\texttt{[0-9]}^+$ and `join(#)`, respectively. Therefore, the algorithm constructs the program `match(`$\texttt{[0-9]}^+$`).join(#)` and returns it as a solution.

Theorem 1 (Soundness and Relative Completeness). *The repair algorithm only returns a solution to the given instance. Additionally, the algorithm will find a solution given a problem instance that has a solution.*

[3] For simplicity, we assume that the regex-dependent function is not `replaceAll`, and that repairs do not change the regex-dependent function. We refer to the appendix for how these restrictions can be lifted.

Algorithm 1. The algorithm `repPost`

```
Q ← { p }
while Q is not empty do
    t ← Q.pop()
    if ¬pruneByOrig(t, ℰ) ∧ ¬pruneByVal(t, ℰ) then
        if t is instantiable ∧ ptestByOrig(t, ℰ) ∧ ptestByVal(t, ℰ) then
            if genConst(t, ℰ, C) is satisfiable then return ρ(t)
        Q.push(expandHole(t))
    Q.push(addOrReduceHole(t))
throw NoSolutionFound
```

Proof Sketch. Soundness follows from that of [19] and the fact that the SMT constraint precisely captures our origin-tracking semantics. Relative completeness follows from the completeness of [19] and the same reasoning in prior work [17–19,51], i.e., our algorithm enumerates and explores all templates in ascending order with respect to the edit distance using a priority queue, expandHole, and addOrReduceHole. □

4.1 Regex-Repair Algorithm

Thanks to the origins, the regex-repair problem can be solved by almost directly adopting the algorithm from a prior work [19] that repairs a regex for regex-dependent functions. Namely, their algorithm can be used to, given a set of strings with origins that only nest empty level-0 origin lists, find a regex of the smallest edit distance from the given regex that matches the substrings identified by the origins for each string in the set. This directly solves the problem when the regex-dependent function is `split` or `match`, in which cases an input string with origins only nests empty level-0 origin lists.

The only tricky case is when it is `replaceAll`. Let r be a regex to be repaired. In this case, an input string with origins may nest non-empty level-0 origin lists that specify the sub-substrings to be matched by the capturing groups in r. For example, for the input string with origins $\mathtt{b}(\!|_1\,\mathtt{a}(\!|_{c_1}\,\mathtt{a}|\!)_{c_1}\,\mathtt{b}|\!)_1$, we want to find r with one capturing group that matches the substring `aab` and its capturing group extracts the second `a` in the substring. The algorithm of [19] can be adopted to find r that satisfies the substring matching requirement and *almost* satisfies the sub-substring extraction requirement in that the returned r matches `aab` and extracts `a` of it but does not guarantee *which* `a` (i.e., it could extract the first `a` instead), e.g., it may find $(_{c_1}\mathtt{a})_{c_1}\mathtt{ab}$ as r. To this end, we employ a simple counterexample-guided-refinement approach that uses the algorithm to obtain a regex that satisfies the substring matching requirement and almost satisfies the sub-substring extraction requirement, checks if it actually satisfies the sub-substring extraction requirement, and if not repeats the process by strengthening the SMT constraints used in the algorithm to rule out the previously found regexes, such as $(_{c_1}\mathtt{a})_{c_1}\mathtt{ab}$ in our example, until one that satisfies both requirements is found, e.g., this may then lead to finding $\mathtt{a}(_{c_1}\mathtt{a})_{c_1}\mathtt{b}$ next which satisfies both requirements. The procedure `repReg` implements this approach to return a repaired regex or raises an exception when no solution exists.

4.2 Post-Regex-Program-Repair Algorithm

Algorithm 1 shows the post-regex-program-repair algorithm. It enumerates partial programs called *templates*, and checks whether the templates can be instantiated into a solution using SMT constraint solving. During the enumeration process, it checks the feasibility of templates using novel pruning techniques and discards infeasible templates to reduce the search space. It iterates the process until it finds a solution or confirms that no solution exists.

A template is a post-regex program with *holes*, represented by $\square$. A hole is a placeholder to be replaced with a concrete expression. Intuitively, holes in a template indicate subexpressions that are currently under repair. Formally, the syntax of templates is that of *chain* from Fig. 1 but with the production rule of each non-terminal n extended as $n ::= \cdots \mid \square$. The algorithm maintains a priority queue Q that stores templates sorted in ascending order of their distance from the given post-regex program p. Initially, it stores just p (line 1). Then, it retrieves a top template of Q at line 3 and checks the feasibility in three stages. First, it applies novel pruning techniques `pruneByOrig` and `pruneByVal` at line 4. They check whether we can obtain a solution from the template by replacing holes with *arbitrary expressions*. We describe the details of the pruning techniques in **Pruning Templates** below.

If the template remains unpruned, the algorithm then checks whether the template is *instantiable* at line 5. A template is instantiable iff it is instantiated into a *valid* post-regex program, i.e., it is well-typed, takes a list of a string with origins, and returns a string with origins, by replacing holes in the template with one of the following *constants*: a position, a character, or an integer. For the example from Sect. 4, the template `join(□)` is instantiable because we can obtain a valid program by replacing $\square$ with a character, whereas `replaceAll(a□, b).at(□)` is not because it does not take a list of strings as input. If t is instantiable, it checks the feasibility using the pruning techniques `ptestByOrig` and `ptestByVal` that conservatively check whether the template can be instantiated into a solution by replacing holes with arbitrary constants (i.e., positions, characters, or non-positions). For space, we defer the details of these checks to the appendix.

If these checks pass, then the algorithm checks whether the template can be instantiated into a solution by replacing holes with constants at line 6. To do this, it generates an SMT constraint ϕ using `genConst`, which we describe in **SMT Solving** below. The constraint ϕ consists of variables of the form v_i^a, denoting that the ith hole is replaced with the constant a iff $v_i^a = true$. If ϕ is satisfiable, then the algorithm constructs a solution $\rho(t)$ from the assignment ρ obtained by replacing each ith hole with the constant a where $\rho(v_i^a) = true$, and returns it as a solution. If ϕ is unsatisfiable, the algorithm continues the search by enumerating more templates by adopting the approach in prior work [17–19,51]. It uses two functions `expandHole` and `addOrReduceHole`, where `expandHole`(t) returns templates obtained by replacing a hole in t with an expression whose parameters are holes or a string variable, and `addOrReduceHole`(t) returns templates obtained by replacing a leaf of the abstract syntax tree (AST) representation of t with a hole and replacing an expression whose all intermediate subexpressions are holes with a hole. If line 9 is reached, it means that there is no solution, and the exception `NoSolutionFound` is raised to stop the algorithm.

SMT Solving. The figure on the right shows the `genConst`$(t, \mathcal{E}, C)$ procedure. It returns a constraint that is satisfiable iff there is a post-regex program instantiated from t that satisfies $\mathcal{E}$.

1: $\Sigma_{fin} \leftarrow \mathtt{buildAlphabet}(t, \mathcal{E})$; $\phi \leftarrow \mathit{true}$
2: **foreach** $v_{in} \Rightarrow v_{out} \in \mathcal{E}$ **then**
3: $\quad \emptyset; C; \Sigma_{fin} \vdash (t, v_{in}) \rightsquigarrow \Phi$; $\phi \leftarrow \phi \wedge \Phi(v_{out})$
4: **return** $\phi \wedge \bigwedge_{i \in holes(t)} ((\Sigma_{b \in \mathcal{B}_i} b) = 1)$

It first constructs an alphabet subset that is sufficient for the given repair problem (see Definition 3 and Lemma 1 for details), then it constructs the formula $\Phi(v_{out})$ for each example and takes the conjunction of them. Finally, it returns the conjunction of the constraint with a constraint that restricts each hole to be assigned to exactly one constant. Here, $holes(t)$ is the set of holes in t and $\mathcal{B}_i$ is the set of boolean variables in ϕ that correspond to the ith hole but interpreted as integers by $\mathit{true} = 1$ and $\mathit{false} = 0$.

We use the judgement $\Delta; C; \Sigma \vdash (t, v) \rightsquigarrow \Phi$ to generate an SMT constraint for each example. Here, Φ is a mapping from a value to an SMT constraint. The judgement means that there is a post-regex program obtained from t by replacing each hole with either a position, a character in Σ, or a non-position in C under the environment Δ, such that for each $(v', \phi) \in \Phi$, it outputs v' for the input v if ϕ is satisfiable. The rules are based on those of the origin-tracking semantics, but they may produce multiple output values to simulate multiple programs instantiated from t.

We describe some selected rules. The full rules are given in the appendix. The rule for `join` first enumerates all possible strings obtained by evaluating terms that can be instantiated from t. Then, for each string with origins (w, ξ) in Φ, it simulates the `join` function using the origin-tracking semantics.

$$\frac{\begin{array}{c}\Delta; C; \Sigma \vdash (t, \bot) \rightsquigarrow \Phi \\ \Phi' = \{((w', \xi'), \phi) \mid ((w, \xi), \phi) \in \Phi, \\ \Delta \cup \{(x, (w, \xi))\} \vdash \langle \mathtt{join}(x), l \rangle \Downarrow (w', \xi')\}\end{array}}{\Delta; C; \Sigma \vdash (\mathtt{join}(t), l) \rightsquigarrow \Phi'}$$

The rules for holes attempt to replace the holes with constants of their types, e.g., the rule for `Char`-typed holes simulates all possible characters in Σ.

As an example, consider the template $\mathtt{join}(\square_1)$ and the example $[\llparenthesis_1 \mathtt{a} \rrparenthesis_1, \llparenthesis_2 \mathtt{b} \rrparenthesis_2] \Rightarrow \llparenthesis_1 \mathtt{a} \rrparenthesis_1 \$ \llparenthesis_2 \mathtt{b} \rrparenthesis_2$. In this case, the SMT constraint $\Phi(\llparenthesis_1 \mathtt{a} \rrparenthesis_1 \$ \llparenthesis_2 \mathtt{b} \rrparenthesis_2)$ generated by the relation $\rightsquigarrow$ at line 3 is $v_1^{\$}$. Therefore, the final SMT constraint constructed at line 4 is $v_1^{\$} \wedge (\Sigma_{b \in \mathcal{B}_{v_1^{\$},1}} b = 1)$, where $\mathcal{B}_{v_1^{\$},1} = \{v_1^{\$}\}$. This is satisfiable and the assignment is $\{(v_1^{\$}, \mathit{true})\}$. According to the assignment, we can construct the solution `join($)` by replacing $\square_1$ with the character `$`.

As described above, our constraint contains conditions stipulating if a hole can be replaced with a constant, for each possible constant of the hole's type. For `Char`-typed holes, it would be prohibitively expensive to consider all (say, Unicode) character constants. Prior related work [17–19,51] use an alphabet consisting of only characters that appear in examples. Unfortunately, it does not work in our setting because there exist cases that need characters not in the examples. (See the appendix for an example.) To this end, we propose a novel alphabet-reduction method formalized by Definition 3 and Lemma 1 below. We defer the proof of the lemma to the appendix.

Definition 3. Given a template t and a set $\mathcal{E}$ of examples, the alphabet $\Sigma_{\mathit{fin}}^{t,\mathcal{E}}$ is the set consisting of the following elements: (1) the characters that appear in t and $\mathcal{E}$, (2) the lowercase (resp. uppercase) counterparts of the uppercase (resp. lowercase) letters appearing in some $e \in \mathcal{E}$ if t contains `toUpperCase` (resp. `toLowerCase`), (3) a whitespace character if t contains `trim`, `trimStart`, or `trimEnd`, (4) digits if t contains arithmetic operations, and (5) fresh characters $\alpha_1, \cdots, \alpha_n$ where n is the number of holes in t.

Lemma 1 (Alphabet Reduction). *Given a template t and a set $\mathcal{E}$ of examples, if there is a post-regex program p such that p satisfies $\mathcal{E}$ and p is instantiated from t by replacing each hole with a constant, there is a post-regex program p' such that p' satisfies $\mathcal{E}$ and p' is instantiated from t by replacing each hole with a constant where a character constant replacing a hole is from $\Sigma_{\mathit{fin}}^{t,\mathcal{E}}$.*

Pruning Templates. The origin-based pruning `pruneByOrig` checks the feasibility of a template from the perspective of *origin structure*. The origin structure is an abstraction [21] of origin-enriched values, obtained by excluding the non-origin aspects of the values. Specifically, the origin structure is defined by the syntax $o ::= o_s \mid o_{ls} \mid o_i$, where o_s, o_{ls}, and o_i represent the origin structures of a string with origins, a list of strings with origins, and an integer with origins, respectively. The origin structure o_s of a string with origins is defined by the following syntax: $o_s ::= \overline{o_{o1}}$, $o_{o1} ::= (T, \overline{o_{s0}})$, $o_{s0} ::= \overline{o_{o0}}$, and $o_{o0} ::= T$, where T is a set of identifiers. Roughly, o_{o1}, o_{s0}, and o_{o0} represent the origin structures for a level-1 origin, a level-0 origin list, and a level-0 origin, respectively. We use overlines to denote sequences. We use T for a level-1-origin origin structure (T, ϵ) when clear from the context. The origin structure o_{ls} (resp. o_i) of a list of strings with origins (resp. an integer with origins) is defined by the syntax $o_{ls} ::= \overline{o_s}$ (resp. $o_i ::= T$).

We define an abstraction function α that maps an origin-enriched value into an origin structure. For an atom (and level-0 origin), $\alpha((l, r, T)) = T$. For a level-0 origin list, $\alpha([a_1, \cdots, a_n]) = \alpha(a_1) \cdots \alpha(a_n)$. For a level-1 origin, $\alpha((a, \xi^0)) = (\alpha(a), \alpha(\xi^0))$. For a level-1 origin list, $\alpha([o_1, \cdots, o_n]) = \alpha(o_1) \cdots \alpha(o_n)$. For a string with origins, $\alpha((w, \xi)) = \alpha(\xi)$. For example, $\alpha(\llparenthesis_1 \mathtt{a} \rrparenthesis_1 \llparenthesis_{2,3} \mathtt{b} \rrparenthesis_{2,3}) = \{1\} \cdot \{2, 3\}$ and $\alpha(\llparenthesis_1 \llparenthesis_{c_1} \mathtt{a} \rrparenthesis_{c_1} \mathtt{b} \llparenthesis_{c_2,c_3} \mathtt{c} \rrparenthesis_{c_2,c_3} \rrparenthesis_1) = (\{1\}, \{c_1\} \cdot \{c_2, c_3\})$. For a list of strings with origins, $\alpha([(w_1, \xi_1), \cdots, (w_n, \xi_n)]) = [\alpha((w_1, \xi_1)), \cdots, \alpha((w_n, \xi_n))]$. For example, $\alpha([\llparenthesis_1 \mathtt{a} \rrparenthesis_1, \llparenthesis_2 \mathtt{b} \rrparenthesis_2]) = [\{1\}, \{2\}]$. For an integer with origins, $\alpha((i, T)) = T$. For example, $\alpha(5, \{1\}) = \{1\}$. The origin-structure abstraction abstracts origin-enriched examples in the following sense.

Definition 4. Given a template t and an example $v_{in} \Rightarrow v_{out}$, t *can produce* $\alpha(v_{out})$ from $\alpha(v_{in})$ if there exist p and $v'_{in} \Rightarrow v'_{out}$ such that (1) t is instantiable to p, (2) $\alpha(v'_{in}) = \alpha(v_{in})$, (3) $\alpha(v'_{out}) = \alpha(v_{out})$, and (4) $\emptyset \vdash \langle p, v'_{in}\rangle \Downarrow v'_{out}$.

Therefore, if t *cannot* produce $\alpha(v_{out})$ from $\alpha(v_{in})$ for some example $v_{in} \Rightarrow v_{out} \in \mathcal{E}$, we can safely skip `expandHole` at line 7 because programs instantiated from t do not satisfy the example with respect to origins, and so t and all templates obtained by expanding its holes can be pruned.

To check the above, we define an abstract semantics $\Downarrow^\sharp$ that abstracts the origin-tracking semantics to operate only over origin structures. For a set of origin structures $\mathcal{O}$, the judgement $\Delta^\sharp \vdash \langle t, o\rangle \Downarrow^\sharp \mathcal{O}$ says that under the *abstract environment* $\Delta^\sharp$ that maps variables to origin structures, t can produce some $o' \in \mathcal{O}$ from o, i.e., $\mathcal{O}$ is a (possibly over-approximate) set of origin structures that t can produce. Then, we let `pruneByOrig`$(t, \mathcal{E})$ return *true* if for all $v_{in} \Rightarrow v_{out} \in \mathcal{E}$, $\alpha(v_{out}) \in \mathcal{O}$ where $\emptyset \vdash \langle t, \alpha(v_{in})\rangle \Downarrow^\sharp \mathcal{O}$, and otherwise return *false*.

We present a rule of $\Downarrow^\sharp$. We refer to the appendix for the full set of rules. The rule for `join` first evaluates t to obtain the origin structures o of the possible outputs of programs instantiated from t, and then combines the elements of the input list into an origin structure of a string with origins by inserting o between them. With this, we give an example of the pruning.

$$\frac{2 \leq n \qquad \Delta^\sharp \vdash \langle t, \bot\rangle \Downarrow^\sharp \mathcal{O} \qquad \mathcal{O}' = \{o_1 \cdot o \cdots o_{n-1} \cdot o \cdot o_n \mid o \in \mathcal{O}\}}{\Delta^\sharp \vdash \langle \mathtt{join}(t), [o_1, \cdots, o_n]\rangle \Downarrow^\sharp \mathcal{O}'}$$

Let $t = \mathtt{join}(\square)$ and $\mathcal{E} = \{[\llparenthesis_1 \mathtt{5} \rrparenthesis_1, \llparenthesis_2 \mathtt{6} \rrparenthesis_2] \Rightarrow \llparenthesis_1 \mathtt{5} \rrparenthesis_1 \mathtt{\$} \llparenthesis_{1,2} \mathtt{30} \rrparenthesis_{1,2} \mathtt{\$} \llparenthesis_2 \mathtt{6} \rrparenthesis_2\}$. Then, $\emptyset \vdash \langle t, \alpha([\llparenthesis_1 \mathtt{5} \rrparenthesis_1, \llparenthesis_2 \mathtt{6} \rrparenthesis_2])\rangle \Downarrow^\sharp \{\{1\} \cdot \{2\}\}$ because $\alpha([\llparenthesis_1 \mathtt{5} \rrparenthesis_1, \llparenthesis_2 \mathtt{6} \rrparenthesis_2]) = [\{1\}, \{2\}]$ and $\emptyset \vdash \langle \square, \bot\rangle \Downarrow^\sharp \{\epsilon\}$. Because $\alpha(\llparenthesis_1 \mathtt{5} \rrparenthesis_1 \mathtt{\$} \llparenthesis_{1,2} \mathtt{30} \rrparenthesis_{1,2} \mathtt{\$} \llparenthesis_2 \mathtt{6} \rrparenthesis_2) = \{1\} \cdot \{1,2\} \cdot \{2\} \notin \{\{1\} \cdot \{2\}\}$, we determine that t and its derivatives can be pruned. It is worth noting that t *cannot be pruned* if we do not consider origins because `join($30$)` satisfies the example. However, the repair overfits the example and may be undesirable, namely, it disregards the user's intent that `30` should be derived from `5` and `6`.

As with origin-based pruning, the value-based pruning `pruneByVal` estimates the possible outputs of programs instantiated from a template on a given input. However, it considers only strings. Specifically, `pruneByVal` is similar to `pruneByOrig`, except that the abstract domain consists of a set of (non-origin-enriched) values, the abstraction function maps origin-enriched values to values, and the abstract semantics returns a set of values. For space, we defer the details to the appendix.

5 Evaluation

To evaluate our approach, we implemented the repair algorithm as a tool named R3-S3. We designed our empirical evaluation to answer the following questions: **(RQ1)** Can R3-S3 find solutions for real-world tasks from a small number of examples? Are our novel pruning techniques effective in finding solutions? **(RQ2)** Can R3-S3 find high-quality repairs? All experiments were performed on Intel(R) Xeon(R) Platinum 8360Y CUP @ 2.40 GHz. Our novel origin-based and value-based pruning techniques (cf. Sect. 4.2) are implemented by reducing the problem to regex matching. For example, the rule for `repeat` $\Delta^\sharp \vdash \langle \texttt{repeat}(t), o\rangle \Downarrow^\sharp \{o\}^*$ is interpreted as $\Delta^\sharp \vdash \langle \texttt{repeat}(t), r\rangle \Downarrow^\sharp r^*$ using the Kleene star. For space, we defer the details to the appendix.

Benchmark. There is no standard benchmark for program repair that addresses both real-world regexes and a wide variety of functions. Therefore, we prepared a benchmark collected from GitHub commits and StackOverflow posts. We prepared the examples by using the ones provided in the commits and posts when they are available, and adding new ones manually by ourselves as needed (e.g., when none was provided). For each example, we annotated origins manually. That is, for the StackOverflow posts, we read the posts and annotated origins for the input-output examples based on the intended string transformations. For the GitHub commits, we inferred the intended behavior from the fixed implementations and annotated origins accordingly.[4] As a result, for each instance, we prepared at least 10 examples. From these, we used at most 5 examples for synthesis. However, many instances (39 in total) consist of only one or two examples. The remaining examples are used as *left-out* example sets to measure the quality of the repairs.

To find the commits and posts, we first looked at all commits in the lists provided by [29] that studied string-related bugs in a wide variety of GitHub projects written in JavaScript. Next, we searched on StackOverflow with keywords such as "string" and "bug" with the tags "[javascript]" and "[regex]". Then, among these, we selected ones that are in the RMS-style (i.e., in the method-chaining style that starts with a regex-dependent function). In total, we collected 50 benchmark tasks (4 from [29] and 46 from StackOverflow). Among them, 16 instances require a non-empty set C of integers. The minimum and maximum sizes of C are 1 and 3, respectively. The size of C affects the performance of SMT constraint generation because the procedure tries all assignments of elements in C to integer-typed holes. However, in our evaluation, we observed that the size of C is generally small, which limits its impact in practice. Also, when the user provides a (strict) subset of the needed integers, some information necessary for constructing the desired program may be missing and can lead to overfitting or in the absence of any valid solution. Nevertheless, users are often able to provide the (few) necessary integer constants [67]. The average and maximum sizes of the programs, measured as the number of AST nodes, are 11.42 and 95, respectively. The benchmarks are provided as supplementary material.

[4] We believe that providing origin annotations does not impose fundamentally new burden compared to constructing standard extensional input-output examples. Origin annotations make explicit the transformation intent that is already implicit when designing such examples. As such, they can be added as part of the existing example construction process rather than requiring separate effort.

	instances	running time (seconds)		
	Solved (50)	**min**	**med**	**max**
full	40 (80%)	0.2	2.4	1191.2
wo/o	36 (72%)	0.2	1.6	807.2
wo/v	38 (76%)	0.2	2.2	1088.6
wo/o,v	34 (68%)	0.2	3.8	1482.3

To answer **RQ1**, we measured the minimum, median, and maximum running times, with a timeout of 30 min. The table on the right shows the results. In the table, **full** (resp. **wo/o**, **wo/v**, **wo/o,v**) refers to R3-S3 (resp. without origin-based pruning, without value-based pruning, without both of them). As shown in the table, R3-S3 could solve 80% of instances within the timeout, with a median running time of 2.4 s for the solved instances. R3-S3 could not solve 10 instances within the timeout. Additionally, among the 40 solved instances, regex repair (resp. SMT constraint generation and template enumeration) dominates the running time in 28 (resp. 10 and 2) cases. We inspected these instances and observed that, as in the prior work on regex repair [17–19,51], R3-S3 struggled with the repairs that required a large change from the original. For example, R3-S3 could not solve an instance whose initial program is empty (i.e., unprovided) but whose solution is $\texttt{replaceAll}((_1\backslash d^+)_1\texttt{px}(_2[\hat{}\backslash d]^*)_2(_3\backslash d^+)_3\texttt{px}, \lambda c_1.\lambda c_2.\lambda c_3.\texttt{toString}(\texttt{parseInt}(c_1) * 2 + 5).\texttt{concat}(\%).\cdots$, which requires a large change from the initial program. However, such large changes are relatively rare in practice [29]. In summary, R3-S3 *can repair real-world regex-dependent string manipulation programs efficiently.*

As for the impact of the pruning techniques, 5 additional instances could not be solved within the timeout when the origin-based pruning technique was disabled, while 1 instance that was previously unsolved could be solved. We inspected the solved instance and found that R3-S3 was able to reach the edit distance (from the original input program) at which a solution exists. However, it timed out before finding a solution. This observation suggests that pruning affects the order in which templates are retrieved from the priority queue, and perhaps the issue can be resolved by ordering the templates of the same edit distance in some way. We leave further investigation for future work. Additionally, when the value-based pruning technique was disabled, 2 additional instances could not be solved, and when both pruning techniques were disabled, 6 additional instances could not be solved compared to the case where both techniques were enabled, and among the latter, 1 instance could be solved if either pruning technique was enabled. In summary, *the new pruning techniques are impactful to the performance of the algorithm.*

Additionally, we measured how R3-S3 scales as the size of the programs increases, by comparing the running times of R3-S3 over the sizes. Figure 2 shows the plot. The points on the border colored in blue indicate the instances that R3-S3 could not find a repair within the timeout. As the figure shows, R3-S3 can solve instances of large sizes and

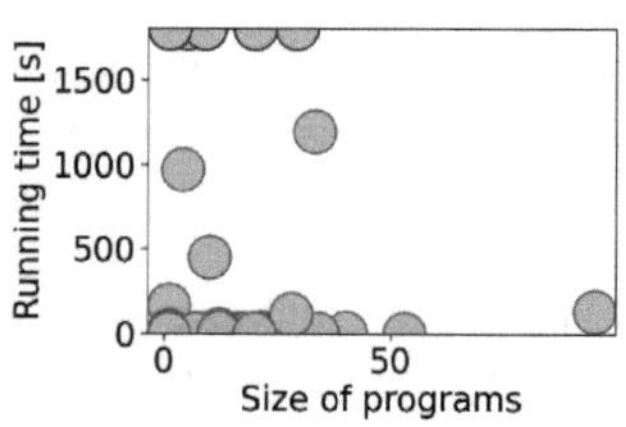

Fig. 2. Scalability.

the running times appear uncorrelated with the instance sizes. In summary, *the performance of* R3-S3 *scales with respect to the size of programs.*

To answer **RQ2**, we measured the quality of the repairs with respect to left-out example sets following the approach used in [18,19,51]. That is, we measured F1 scores using the left-out examples. The F1 score is calculated as $F1 = \frac{2 \times P \times R}{P+R}$, where P is the *precision* and R is the *recall*. The precision P is calculated as $P = \frac{TP}{TP+FP}$, where TP (resp. FP) is the number of *positive* (resp. *negative*) examples that are (resp. not) satisfied by the programs. Here, positive and negative examples are examples, but a negative example $(w, \xi) \Rightarrow (w', \xi')$ means that a program should *not* output (w', ξ') for (w, ξ). An F1 score is between 0 and 1, and scores close to 1 imply that the corresponding repairs are of high quality. Figure 3 shows the result. In 75% of instances, R3-S3 could find a repair with an F1 score of 1. Also, the median and average of the F1 scores are 1 and 0.86, respectively. We inspected the repairs with low F1 scores and observed that R3-S3 could not find a high-quality repair when the repairs required a large change from the original. For example, the user provided $\texttt{replaceAll}(({}_1\texttt{*ABC})^*_1({}_2\texttt{*DEF})_2, \lambda c_0.\epsilon)$ as the initial program and a desired program was $\texttt{replaceAll}([\texttt{0-9}](?{=}\texttt{e}), e)$, $e = \lambda c_0.\texttt{toString}(\texttt{parseInt}(c_0) * 2)$. For this instance, R3-S3 outputs $\texttt{replaceAll}(({}_1\texttt{*ABC})^*_1([128]\backslash 2\backslash 1[\quad \texttt{!\#0-9}]^*), e)$, where e is the function shown above. Unfortunately, this overfits the examples, resulting in a low F1 score of 0. Perhaps the issue can be resolved by using more examples, or by enhancing the origin-enriching idea to allow users to more accurately communicate their intentions through few examples. We leave further investigation to future work. In summary, R3-S3 *could find high-quality repairs that generalize well to left-out example sets, and therefore of high-quality.*

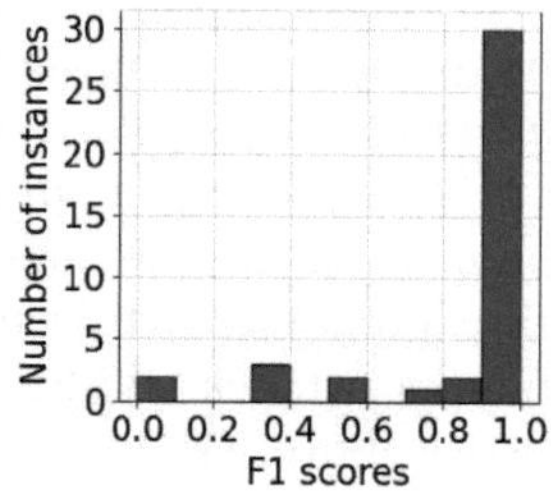

Fig. 3. Quality.

Finally, we present a comparison with large language models (LLMs), which have recently been widely used for code generation and repair. To compare with LLMs, we provided the same instances used in our evaluation to the LLMs and verified the correctness of their outputs using R3-S3.[5] In addition to the instances, we provide as prompt the supplementary information necessary to understand the repair problem, such as descriptions of RMS programs, origins, and edit distances. Additionally, we provide three in-context example instances together with their solutions. The full prompt is given in the appendix. We used the state-of-the-art GPT-5 model (GPT-5.4) [50] via the official API. As a result, GPT-5 generated programs that satisfy (both intensional and extensional aspects of) the examples for 17 instances (34%). Among these, we confirmed that 10 programs also satisfy the minimality of changes (i.e., they are actually valid solutions). For 2 of the 17 instances, since they were not solved by R3-S3, we could not verify whether the edit distance is minimal, and therefore were unable to determine whether they are valid solutions at this time. Additionally,

[5] Note that programs generated by LLMs are not guaranteed to be valid solutions.

for 6 instances, GPT-5 generated programs that satisfy the extensional input-output requirement but violate the intensional requirement. Therefore, there are 23 instances (46%) for which GPT-5 generated programs that satisfy at least the extensional input-output requirement. In summary, *GPT-5 could solve 10 instances (20%) with 2 additional instances being inconclusive.*

By inspecting the programs generated by GPT-5 and comparing them with those of R3-S3, we make the following observations. First, GPT-5 can generate programs within a few seconds even for instances requiring substantial changes, whereas R3-S3 tends to time out on such instances. Secondly, as discussed above, GPT-5 often generates invalid programs that do not satisfy the examples, whereas R3-S3 is guaranteed to only generate valid programs. In particular, we observed that GPT-5 can generate overfitting programs by failing to satisfy the intensional behavior specified by origins. We refer to the appendix for a concrete case. Finally, GPT-5 sometimes performs unnecessary changes (both introducing redundant fragments and removing necessary ones), whereas R3-S3 does not, as our approach guarantees the minimality of changes. These observations suggest that the strengths of LLMs (i.e., their ability to flexibly make substantial changes) and R3-S3 (i.e., its formal guarantees of consistency with examples and minimality of changes) are complementary. Therefore, integrating the two approaches could be an interesting direction for future work.

6 Related Work

As mentioned in the introduction, string-manipulation programs are ubiquitous, playing vital roles in various software. Therefore, many approaches for repairing or synthesizing string-manipulation programs have been proposed [3,13,25,27, 36–39,55,56]. However, the prior works focus on synthesizing a program that consists of regex-independent functions and either do not support regexes at all or do not support real-world regexes. There are also much prior work on repairing or synthesizing regexes from examples [2,5,6,9–12,14,17–19,24,30,31, 40,43,46,51,54,59,66], some [17–19] supporting real-world regexes, but all of them focus only on a regex or a single regex-dependent function and do not consider programs containing regex-independent functions.

Origin tracking was introduced in [60] in the context of term rewriting. In this context, origins are relations between subterms and used for tasks such as identifying error locations and visualizing program executions. Also, the idea of origins is widely used in the field of formal languages and automata theory [7, 8,32,33]. In this context, origins are functions that map positions of the output string to those of the input string. Our origin-enriched examples and origin-tracking semantics are inspired mainly by the latter line of work and can be seen as an extention of them from just individual positions to *pairs of positions* (so that *substrings*, instead of just individual characters, can be used as origins), and with futher extensions to support lists, arithmetic, and boolean operations which are commonly used in string-manipulation programs.

Recently, in the context of program repair, [19] used origins to specify which substrings should be matched by the regex of a regex-dependent function. However, their work considers repairing only a single regex-dependent function. We note that [19] cannot solve any of our benchmark instances, because our benchmark does not include instances that fall within the subset [19] can handle. Another closely related idea to our origin tracking is taint tracking [20,64], a widely used technique in the security field. Taint tracking attaches a taint to values and tracks its propagation to detect vulnerabilities such as SQL injection and cross-site scripting [22,26,35,41,45,47,53,63]. However, their purpose is to find a vulnerability and they do not consider using the information for program synthesis or repair. Also, prior work [1,61] have introduced streaming-string and symbolic finite-state transducers as models for string transformation, but they do not consider origins.

Finally, we mention that our origin-based and value-based prunings are inspired by abstract interpretation [21]. Namely, they are obtained by abstracting the origin-enriched values and the origin-tracking semantics to contain only the information about origins or only that about values.

7 Conclusion

This paper introduced a new class of string-manipulation programs called *RMS programs*, which support *both* real-world regexes and a wide variety of functions, and an algorithm for repairing them. Although the combination frequently occurs in real-world string manipulation programs, no prior work supports both. A main challenge in repairing the programs of this class is the large search space due to the rich support of real-world regexes and the variety of functions. To address the challenge, RMS restricts the programs to the method-chaining style that starts the chain of calls with a regex-dependent function, which reflects the code style used in real-world string-manipulation programs. We presented a PBE-based repair for RMS programs. A key idea is a new class of examples called *origin-enriched examples*, which is inspired by prior work on finite-state transducers [7], regex-dependent string function repair [19], and repair of regexes for extraction [18]. We formally defined the correctness of the programs with respect to the origins by a novel *origin-tracking semantics*. Our algorithm uses origins to divide the repair problem into two subproblems: the repair of the regex and the post-regex programs. As for the former repair, we adopted the algorithm introduced in a prior work on repairing regexes to our setting [19]. As for the latter repair, we adopted an enumerative search algorithm with a new SMT constraint generation technique called *alphabet-reduction* and novel pruning techniques called *origin-* and *value*-based prunings to reduce the search space. We implemented our algorithm as a tool named R3-S3 and evaluated it on real-world benchmarks collected from GitHub and StackOverflow. The results showed that R3-S3 finds high-quality repairs efficiently.

As future work, we plan to extend our approach to handle programs that do not follow the RMS style, e.g., those not starting with a regex-dependent function or containing multiple such functions. We also plan to explore broader applications of our origin-based idea beyond program synthesis and repair, such as program verification and type systems.

Acknowledgments. We thank the anonymous reviewers for their suggestions. This work was supported by JSPS KAKENHI Grant Number JP23K24826.

Disclosure of Interests. The authors have no competing interests to declare that are relevant to the content of this article.

Data-Availability Statement. The artifact of this paper is available at [16].

References

1. Alur, R., Černý, P.: Streaming transducers for algorithmic verification of single-pass list-processing programs. In: Proceedings of the 38th Annual ACM SIGPLAN-SIGACT Symposium on Principles of Programming Languages, POPL '11, pp. 599–610. Association for Computing Machinery, New York (2011). https://doi.org/10.1145/1926385.1926454
2. Angluin, D.: On the complexity of minimum inference of regular sets. Inf. Control **39**(3), 337–350 (1978). https://doi.org/10.1016/S0019-9958(78)90683-6
3. Arasu, A., Chaudhuri, S., Kaushik, R.: Learning string transformations from examples. Proc. VLDB Endow. **2**(1), 514–525 (2009). https://doi.org/10.14778/1687627.1687686
4. Barke, S., Peleg, H., Polikarpova, N.: Just-in-time learning for bottom-up enumerative synthesis. Proc. ACM Program. Lang. **4**(OOPSLA) (2020). https://doi.org/10.1145/3428295
5. Bartoli, A., De Lorenzo, A., Medvet, E., Tarlao, F.: Playing regex golf with genetic programming. In: Proceedings of the 2014 Annual Conference on Genetic and Evolutionary Computation, GECCO '14, pp. 1063–1070. Association for Computing Machinery, New York (2014). https://doi.org/10.1145/2576768.2598333
6. Bartoli, A., De Lorenzo, A., Medvet, E., Tarlao, F.: Automatic search-and-replace from examples with coevolutionary genetic programming. IEEE Trans. Cybern. **51**(5), 2612–2624 (2021). https://doi.org/10.1109/TCYB.2019.2918337
7. Bojańczyk, M.: Transducers with origin information. In: Esparza, J., Fraigniaud, P., Husfeldt, T., Koutsoupias, E. (eds.) ICALP 2014. LNCS, vol. 8573, pp. 26–37. Springer, Heidelberg (2014). https://doi.org/10.1007/978-3-662-43951-7_3
8. Bose, S., Muscholl, A., Penelle, V., Puppis, G.: Origin-equivalence of two-way word transducers is in PSPACE. In: Ganguly, S., Pandya, P. (eds.) 38th IARCS Annual Conference on Foundations of Software Technology and Theoretical Computer Science (FSTTCS 2018). Leibniz International Proceedings in Informatics (LIPIcs), vol. 122, pp. 22:1–22:18. Schloss Dagstuhl – Leibniz-Zentrum für Informatik, Dagstuhl (2018). https://doi.org/10.4230/LIPIcs.FSTTCS.2018.22
9. Brādzma, A.: Efficient identification of regular expressions from representative examples. In: Proceedings of the Sixth Annual Conference on Computational Learning Theory, COLT '93, pp. 236–242. Association for Computing Machinery, New York (1993). https://doi.org/10.1145/168304.168340
10. Brāzma, A.: Learning of regular expressions by pattern matching. In: Vitányi, P. (ed.) EuroCOLT 1995. LNCS, vol. 904, pp. 392–403. Springer, Heidelberg (1995). https://doi.org/10.1007/3-540-59119-2_194

11. Brāzma, A., Čerāns, K.: Efficient learning of regular expressions from good examples. In: Arikawa, S., Jantke, K.P. (eds.) AII/ALT -1994. LNCS, vol. 872, pp. 76–90. Springer, Heidelberg (1994). https://doi.org/10.1007/3-540-58520-6_55
12. Brāzma, A., Čerāns, K.: Noise-tolerant efficient inductive synthesis of regular expressions from good examples. New Gen. Comput. **15**(1), 105–140 (1997). https://doi.org/10.1007/BF03037562
13. Cambronero, J., et al.: Flashfill++: scaling programming by example by cutting to the chase. Proc. ACM Program. Lang. **7**(POPL) (2023). https://doi.org/10.1145/3571226
14. Chen, Q., Wang, X., Ye, X., Durrett, G., Dillig, I.: Multi-modal synthesis of regular expressions. In: Proceedings of the 41st ACM SIGPLAN Conference on Programming Language Design and Implementation, PLDI 2020, pp. 487–502. Association for Computing Machinery, New York (2020). https://doi.org/10.1145/3385412.3385988
15. Chen, T., et al.: Solving string constraints with regex-dependent functions through transducers with priorities and variables. Proc. ACM Program. Lang. **6**(POPL) (2022). https://doi.org/10.1145/3498707
16. Chida, N.: R3-s3 (2026). https://github.com/NariyoshiChida/CAV2026. Accessed 3 May 2026
17. Chida, N., Terauchi, T.: Repairing dos vulnerability of real-world regexes. In: 2022 IEEE Symposium on Security and Privacy (SP), pp. 2060–2077 (2022). https://doi.org/10.1109/SP46214.2022.9833597
18. Chida, N., Terauchi, T.: Repairing regular expressions for extraction. Proc. ACM Program. Lang. **7**(PLDI) (2023). https://doi.org/10.1145/3591287
19. Chida, N., Terauchi, T.: Repairing regex-dependent string functions. In: Proceedings of the 39th IEEE/ACM International Conference on Automated Software Engineering, ASE '24, pp. 294–305. Association for Computing Machinery, New York (2024). https://doi.org/10.1145/3691620.3695005
20. Clause, J., Li, W., Orso, A.: Dytan: a generic dynamic taint analysis framework. In: Proceedings of the 2007 International Symposium on Software Testing and Analysis, ISSTA '07, pp. 196–206. Association for Computing Machinery, New York (2007). https://doi.org/10.1145/1273463.1273490
21. Cousot, P., Cousot, R.: Abstract interpretation: a unified lattice model for static analysis of programs by construction or approximation of fixpoints. In: Graham, R.M., Harrison, M.A., Sethi, R. (eds.) Conference Record of the Fourth ACM Symposium on Principles of Programming Languages, Los Angeles, California, USA, January 1977, pp. 238–252. ACM (1977). https://doi.org/10.1145/512950.512973
22. Dalton, M., Kannan, H., Kozyrakis, C.: Raksha: a flexible information flow architecture for software security. In: Proceedings of the 34th Annual International Symposium on Computer Architecture., ISCA '07, pp. 482–493. Association for Computing Machinery, New York (2007). https://doi.org/10.1145/1250662.1250722
23. Davis, J.C., Coghlan, C.A., Servant, F., Lee, D.: The impact of regular expression denial of service (redos) in practice: an empirical study at the ecosystem scale. In: Proceedings of the 2018 26th ACM Joint Meeting on European Software Engineering Conference and Symposium on the Foundations of Software Engineering, ESEC/FSE 2018, pp. 246–256. Association for Computing Machinery, New York (2018). https://doi.org/10.1145/3236024.3236027
24. De Lorenzo, A., Medvet, E., Bartoli, A.: Automatic string replace by examples. In: Proceedings of the 15th Annual Conference on Genetic and Evolutionary Compu-

tation, GECCO '13, pp. 1253–1260. Association for Computing Machinery, New York (2013). https://doi.org/10.1145/2463372.2463532
25. Deng, D., et al.: Unsupervised string transformation learning for entity consolidation. In: 2019 IEEE 35th International Conference on Data Engineering (ICDE), pp. 196–207 (2019). https://doi.org/10.1109/ICDE.2019.00026
26. Denning, D.E.: A lattice model of secure information flow. Commun. ACM **19**(5), 236–243 (1976). https://doi.org/10.1145/360051.360056
27. Ding, Y., Qiu, X.: A concurrent approach to string transformation synthesis. Proc. ACM Program. Lang. **9**(PLDI) (2025). https://doi.org/10.1145/3729336
28. ECMA International: Ecmascript® 2023 language specification (2022). https://tc39.es/ecma262/2023/. Accessed 28 Jan 2026]
29. Eghbali, A., Pradel, M.: No strings attached: an empirical study of string-related software bugs. In: Proceedings of the 35th IEEE/ACM International Conference on Automated Software Engineering, ASE '20, pp. 956–967. Association for Computing Machinery, New York (2021). https://doi.org/10.1145/3324884.3416576
30. Fernau, H.: Algorithms for learning regular expressions from positive data. Inf. Comput. **207**(4), 521–541 (2009). https://doi.org/10.1016/j.ic.2008.12.008
31. Ferreira, M., Terra-Neves, M., Ventura, M., Lynce, I., Martins, R.: FOREST: an interactive multi-tree synthesizer for regular expressions. In: TACAS 2021. LNCS, vol. 12651, pp. 152–169. Springer, Cham (2021). https://doi.org/10.1007/978-3-030-72016-2_9
32. Filiot, E., Jecker, I., Löding, C., Winter, S.: A regular and complete notion of delay for streaming string transducers. In: Berenbrink, P., Bouyer, P., Dawar, A., Kanté, M.M. (eds.) 40th International Symposium on Theoretical Aspects of Computer Science (STACS 2023). Leibniz International Proceedings in Informatics (LIPIcs), vol. 254, pp. 32:1–32:16. Schloss Dagstuhl – Leibniz-Zentrum für Informatik, Dagstuhl (2023). https://doi.org/10.4230/LIPIcs.STACS.2023.32
33. Filiot, E., Maneth, S., Reynier, P.A., Talbot, J.M.: Decision problems of tree transducers with origin. Inf. Comput. **261**, 311–335 (2018). https://doi.org/10.1016/j.ic.2018.02.011
34. Fisher, K., Walker, D., Zhu, K.Q.: Learnpads: automatic tool generation from ad hoc data. In: Proceedings of the 2008 ACM SIGMOD International Conference on Management of Data, SIGMOD '08, pp. 1299–1302. Association for Computing Machinery, New York (2008). https://doi.org/10.1145/1376616.1376759
35. Guarnieri, S.: Automatically Hardening Web Applications Using Precise Tainting. USENIX Association, Baltimore (2005)
36. Gulwani, S.: Automating string processing in spreadsheets using input-output examples. SIGPLAN Not. **46**(1), 317–330 (2011). https://doi.org/10.1145/1925844.1926423
37. He, Y., et al.: Transform-data-by-example (tde): extensible data transformation in excel. In: Proceedings of the 2018 International Conference on Management of Data, SIGMOD '18, pp. 1785–1788. Association for Computing Machinery, New York (2018). https://doi.org/10.1145/3183713.3193539
38. Jin, Z., Anderson, M.R., Cafarella, M., Jagadish, H.V.: Foofah: transforming data by example. In: Proceedings of the 2017 ACM International Conference on Management of Data, SIGMOD '17, pp. 683–698. Association for Computing Machinery, New York (2017). https://doi.org/10.1145/3035918.3064034
39. Kandel, S., Paepcke, A., Hellerstein, J., Heer, J.: Wrangler: interactive visual specification of data transformation scripts. In: Proceedings of the SIGCHI Conference on Human Factors in Computing Systems, CHI '11, pp. 3363–3372. Association

for Computing Machinery, New York (2011). https://doi.org/10.1145/1978942.1979444
40. Kinber, E.: Learning regular expressions from representative examples and membership queries. In: Sempere, J.M., García, P. (eds.) ICGI 2010. LNCS (LNAI), vol. 6339, pp. 94–108. Springer, Heidelberg (2010). https://doi.org/10.1007/978-3-642-15488-1_9
41. Klein, D., Barber, T., Bensalim, S., Stock, B., Johns, M.: Hand sanitizers in the wild: a large-scale study of custom javascript sanitizer functions. In: 2022 IEEE 7th European Symposium on Security and Privacy (EuroS&P), pp. 236–250. IEEE Computer Society, Los Alamitos (2022). https://doi.org/10.1109/EuroSP53844.2022.00023
42. Le, V., Gulwani, S.: Flashextract: a framework for data extraction by examples. In: Proceedings of the 35th ACM SIGPLAN Conference on Programming Language Design and Implementation, PLDI '14, pp. 542–553. Association for Computing Machinery, New York (2014). https://doi.org/10.1145/2594291.2594333
43. Lee, M., So, S., Oh, H.: Synthesizing regular expressions from examples for introductory automata assignments. SIGPLAN Not. **52**(3), 70–80 (2016). https://doi.org/10.1145/3093335.2993244
44. Lee, W.: Combining the top-down propagation and bottom-up enumeration for inductive program synthesis. Proc. ACM Program. Lang. **5**(POPL) (2021). https://doi.org/10.1145/3434335
45. Lekies, S., Stock, B., Johns, M.: 25 million flows later: large-scale detection of dom-based xss. In: Proceedings of the 2013 ACM SIGSAC Conference on Computer & Communications Security, CCS '13, pp. 1193–1204. Association for Computing Machinery, New York (2013). https://doi.org/10.1145/2508859.2516703
46. Li, Y., et al.: Transregex: multi-modal regular expression synthesis by generate-and-repair. In: Proceedings of the 43rd International Conference on Software Engineering, ICSE '21, pp. 1210–1222. IEEE Press (2021). https://doi.org/10.1109/ICSE43902.2021.00111
47. Melicher, W., Das, A., Sharif, M., Bauer, L., Jia, L.: Riding out domsday: towards detecting and preventing dom cross-site scripting. In: Network and Distributed System Security Symposium (2018). https://api.semanticscholar.org/CorpusID:3389782
48. Miltner, A., Fisher, K., Pierce, B.C., Walker, D., Zdancewic, S.: Synthesizing bijective lenses. Proc. ACM Program. Lang. **2**(POPL) (2017). https://doi.org/10.1145/3158089
49. Nakamaru, T., Matsunaga, T., Yamazaki, T., Akiyama, S., Chiba, S.: An empirical study of method chaining in java. In: Proceedings of the 17th International Conference on Mining Software Repositories, MSR '20, pp. 93–102. Association for Computing Machinery, New York (2020). https://doi.org/10.1145/3379597.3387441
50. OpenAI: Openai gpt-5 system card (2025). arXiv preprint arXiv:2601.03267
51. Pan, R., Hu, Q., Xu, G., D'Antoni, L.: Automatic repair of regular expressions. Proc. ACM Program. Lang. **3**(OOPSLA) (2019). https://doi.org/10.1145/3360565
52. Polozov, O., Gulwani, S.: Flashmeta: a framework for inductive program synthesis. In: Proceedings of the 2015 ACM SIGPLAN International Conference on Object-Oriented Programming, Systems, Languages, and Applications, OOPSLA 2015, pp. 107–126. Association for Computing Machinery, New York (2015). https://doi.org/10.1145/2814270.2814310
53. Ray, D., Ligatti, J.: Defining code-injection attacks. SIGPLAN Not. **47**(1), 179–190 (2012). https://doi.org/10.1145/2103621.2103678

54. Rebele, T., Tzompanaki, K., Suchanek, F.M.: Adding missing words to regular expressions. In: Phung, D., Tseng, V.S., Webb, G.I., Ho, B., Ganji, M., Rashidi, L. (eds.) PAKDD 2018. LNCS (LNAI), vol. 10938, pp. 67–79. Springer, Cham (2018). https://doi.org/10.1007/978-3-319-93037-4_6
55. Singh, R.: Blinkfill: semi-supervised programming by example for syntactic string transformations. Proc. VLDB Endow. **9**(10), 816–827 (2016). https://doi.org/10.14778/2977797.2977807
56. Singh, R., Gulwani, S.: Learning semantic string transformations from examples. Proc. VLDB Endow. **5**(8), 740–751 (2012). https://doi.org/10.14778/2212351.2212356
57. StackOverflow: Find and replace numbers in string with regex (2012). https://stackoverflow.com/questions/12432237/find-and-replace-numbers-in-string-with-regex. Accessed 28 Jan 2026
58. StackOverflow: Count the numbers inside the brackets in a string (2017). https://stackoverflow.com/questions/41660778/count-the-numbers-inside-the-brackets-in-a-string. Accessed 28 Jan 2026
59. Valizadeh, M., Berger, M.: Search-based regular expression inference on a gpu. Proc. ACM Program. Lang. **7**(PLDI) (2023). https://doi.org/10.1145/3591274
60. van Deursen, A., Klint, P., Tip, F.: Origin tracking. J. Symb. Comput. **15**(5), 523–545 (1993). https://doi.org/10.1016/S0747-7171(06)80004-0
61. Veanes, M., Hooimeijer, P., Livshits, B., Molnar, D., Bjorner, N.: Symbolic finite state transducers: algorithms and applications. In: Proceedings of the 39th Annual ACM SIGPLAN-SIGACT Symposium on Principles of Programming Languages, POPL '12, pp. 137–150. Association for Computing Machinery, New York (2012). https://doi.org/10.1145/2103656.2103674
62. Wang, C., Cheung, A., Bodik, R.: Synthesizing highly expressive SQL queries from input-output examples. SIGPLAN Not. **52**(6), 452–466 (2017). https://doi.org/10.1145/3140587.3062365
63. Wassermann, G., Su, Z.: Sound and precise analysis of web applications for injection vulnerabilities. SIGPLAN Not. **42**(6), 32–41 (2007). https://doi.org/10.1145/1273442.1250739
64. Yip, A., Wang, X., Zeldovich, N., Kaashoek, M.F.: Improving application security with data flow assertions. In: Proceedings of the ACM SIGOPS 22nd Symposium on Operating Systems Principles, SOSP '09, pp. 291–304. Association for Computing Machinery, New York (2009). https://doi.org/10.1145/1629575.1629604
65. Yu, F., Alkhalaf, M., Bultan, T.: Patching vulnerabilities with sanitization synthesis. In: Proceedings of the 33rd International Conference on Software Engineering, ICSE '11, pp. 251–260. Association for Computing Machinery, New York (2011). https://doi.org/10.1145/1985793.1985828
66. Zhang, T., Lowmanstone, L., Wang, X., Glassman, E.L.: Interactive program synthesis by augmented examples. In: Proceedings of the 33rd Annual ACM Symposium on User Interface Software and Technology, UIST '20, pp. 627–648. Association for Computing Machinery, New York (2020). https://doi.org/10.1145/3379337.3415900
67. Zhou, X., Bodik, R., Cheung, A., Wang, C.: Synthesizing analytical SQL queries from computation demonstration. In: Proceedings of the 43rd ACM SIGPLAN International Conference on Programming Language Design and Implementation, PLDI 2022, pp. 168–182. Association for Computing Machinery, New York (2022). https://doi.org/10.1145/3519939.3523712

Liquid Tree Automata

Ashish Mishra[1](✉) and Suresh Jagannathan[2]

[1] IIT Hyderbad, Hyderbad, India
mishraashish@cse.iith.ac.in
[2] Purdue University, West Lafayette, USA
suresh@cs.purdue.edu

Abstract. Component-based synthesis (CBS) aims to generate loop-free programs from a set of libraries whose methods are annotated with specifications and whose output must satisfy a set of logical constraints, expressed as a query. The effectiveness of a CBS algorithm critically depends on the severity of the constraints imposed by the query. The more exact these constraints are, the sparser the space of feasible solutions. This maxim also applies when we enrich the expressivity of the specifications affixed to library methods. In both cases, search must now contend with constraints that may only hold over a small number of the possible execution paths that can be enumerated by a CBS procedure.

In this paper, we address this challenge by equipping CBS search with the ability to reason about *logical similarities* among the paths it explores. Our setting considers library methods equipped with refinement-type specifications that enrich ordinary base types with a set of rich logical qualifiers to constrain the set of values accepted by that type.

For efficient representation and enumeration of this space, we introduce a novel tree automata variant called *Liquid Tree Automata* (LTA) whose construction is driven by the typing rules of a refinement type system. This allows us to leverage subtyping constraints over the refinement types associated with enumerated terms to enable reasoning about similarity among candidate solutions as search proceeds, using this notion of similarity to eagerly merge LTA states. By doing so, we avoid exploration of semantically similar paths, leading to a significantly improved search procedure. We present an implementation of this idea in a tool called Hegel and provide a comprehensive evaluation that demonstrates Hegel's ability to synthesize solutions to complex CBS queries that go well-beyond the capabilities of the existing state-of-the-art.

1 Introduction

Component-based synthesis (CBS) aims to generate loop-free programs from a library of components, typically defined as methods provided by an API. At the heart of any CBS implementation is a search problem over a hypothesis space of programs that "glue" components together using basic control primitives, such as

E. Darulova et al. (Eds.): CAV 2026, LNCS 16682, pp. 284–307, 2026.
https://doi.org/10.1007/978-3-032-32519-8_15

```
(a) A part of the library
(*take : (x : nat) → [a] → {v : [a] | len (v) ≤ x ∨ len (v) = 0}*)
val take : int → [a] → [a]

(*splitAt : (x : nat) → (xs : [a]) → {v : (f : [a], s : [a])
| len (f) ≤ x ∧ (len (s) ≤ len (xs) - x)}*)
splitAt : int → [a] → ([a],[a])

(*decr : (x : nat) →  {v:int | x = x - 1}*)
val decr : int → int

(*fst : (x : ([a], [a])) →  {v : [a] | v = fst (x)}*)
val fst : ([a], [a]) → [a]

(*snd : (x : ([a], [a])) →  {v : [a] | v = snd (x)}*)
val snd : ([a], [a]) → [a]

(*drop : (x : nat) →  (xs : [a]) → {v : [a] | len (v) ≤ len (xs) - x}}*)
val drop : int -> [a] → [a]

(b) A functional query type
(* goal : (x:nat) →  (y : nat) →  (z : [a]) →  { v : (f : [a], s : [a])
          | len (f) ≤ x ∧ (len (s) ≤ len (z) - y} *)
goal : int → int → [a] → ([a], [a])

(c) A few correct solutions.
uncommented (black): unrefined, commented (green): refined.
(* fun x y z →  ((take x (fst (splitAt y z))), snd (splitAt y z) ) *)
fun x y z → splitAt y (drop x z)
fun x y z → splitAt x (take y z)
...
```

Fig. 1. Motivating Synthesis Problem

conditionals and function applications. If the attributes defining the behavior of components are not overly constrained, or when queries are reasonably general, the search for a feasible solution can be tractable. However, as specifications become more precise, the set of feasible programs becomes a small fraction of the overall search space, making synthesis significantly more challenging. Intuitively, we can define CBS search as a reachability analysis over a graph that relates candidate methods based on their type or other similar defining attributes. For example, a node in this graph associated with a method that has a particular result type can be connected to any node corresponding to a method that accepts an argument of this type. Such connections can be used by the synthesizer to produce a candidate solution that connect inputs to outputs through sequences of component applications. Prior work [10,14,21] has considered the construction of such graphs using simple type-based specifications. In this paper, we propose to allow richer query specifications in the form of refinement types [19] that both decorate library methods and serve as the basis for synthesis queries.

Recent advances in automated theorem proving and formal verification have made it increasingly common to have libraries be equipped with such rich specifications [4,32], motivating synthesis techniques that can effectively exploit and tame such information. While expressive specifications using refinement types have been used previously to guide synthesis [26,29], these approaches did not address the unique challenges that arise in a component-based synthesis setting, where naïve enumerative synthesis techniques are ineffective.

The synthesis query in Fig. 1 illustrates this challenge. The synthesizer is given two inputs, the first is a library of components, each specified by a type signature enriched with refinement pre/postconditions, as comments. Figure 1(a) shows a representative fragment of such a library; in practice, libraries may contain hundreds of components spanning standard data structures and operations. The second input is a synthesis query (called goal), also expressed as a refinement type, specifying both the desired input–output base types and semantic constraints on the result (Fig. 1(b)). The synthesis task is to construct a composition of library components that satisfies the query's refinement specification. Figure 1(c) shows solutions for the simple (unrefined) goal in uncommented black, and for the refined query, commented in green. A natural approach to handling such refined queries is to synthesize programs using only the unrefined base types of the query and library components [10,14,21], and to subsequently apply a verification check to discard candidates that violate refinement constraints. Although simple, this strategy is unlikely to be effective at scale; not only is the solution space now very sparse, thus making simple path exploration inefficient, but the (base) type specifications of library methods are too weak to meaningfully guide the synthesizer toward a correct solution.

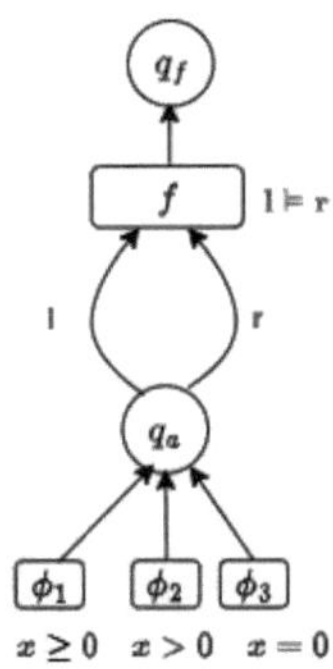

Fig. 2. An Example LTA

To illustrate, we evaluated this synthesis problem (the commented goal, plus a mid-sized component library of around 300 functions) on two state-of-the-art systems that support such refined specifications. Synquid [29] performs refinement type-driven synthesis by enumerating well typed programs from the library, while Hoogle+ [17] encodes refinements using input-output examples, and does post-facto filtering. Both tools failed to synthesize a solution for this query (e.g., the commented green definition in Fig. 1(c)) within a timeout of three minutes. The central challenge here is the ability to compactly represent the space of well typed programs and to search this space efficiently. Existing component based synthesis techniques struggle on both fronts. In contrast, because our synthesis procedure, Hegel, constructs a compact representation of the well-typed search space to enable efficient exploration, it was able to synthesize the solution in 15 s.

1.1 Solution: *Liquid Tree Automata*

Several data structures could in principle be used to represent large spaces of candidate programs, including Version Space Algebras [22], e-graphs [2] and Finite Tree Automata (FTA) [5]. In particular, FTA have been shown to be effective in representing the space of untyped programs, satisfying a set of input-output examples [11], as well as simply-typed programs [5,21]. However, these representations are insufficient for synthesis under refined library and query specifications, where correctness depends on enforcing logical implication and semantic relationships between subterms.[1]

To address these limitations, we introduce a new data structure, *Liquid Tree Automata* (LTA), that allows us to capture such logical constraints. An LTA supports a richer alphabet than other FTA variants by incorporating logical qualifiers from decidable first-order theory fragments. While it also allows constraints on its transitions similar to other constrained tree automata [5,21,24], it additionally supports semantic constraints (e.g., logical entailment), rather than being limited to syntactic equality or dis-equality constraints [5,21].

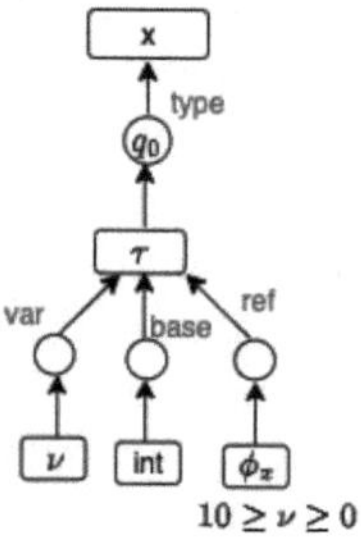

Fig. 3. A simple LTA for binding (x : { ν : int | $10 \geq \nu \geq 0$ })

For instance, Fig. 2 presents an LTA that captures the space of terms represented by the following sentence

$$\{f(t_1, t_2) \mid t_1, t_2 \in \{\phi_1, \phi_2, \phi_3\} \wedge t_1 \implies t_2\}$$

where both sub-trees are constrained using a *logical entailment* constraint (defined later) on the transition (l $\models$r). States are depicted as circles and transitions as rectangles. Each transition may have zero or more incoming states, and each incoming edge is annotated with a position label, shown in red in the figure. Here, l and r are variables that capture a specific position in the automaton and the constraint restricts which choice of t_1 and t_2 are acceptable. The automaton accepts terms $f(\phi_2, \phi_1)$ and $f(\phi_3, \phi_1)$ since, in both cases, the constraint $\phi_i \implies \phi_j$ holds; however, it rejects other syntactically valid terms like $f(\phi_1, \phi_2)$ and $f(\phi_1, \phi_3)$ where the constraint does not hold.

Representing Refinement Types using LTA. The above characteristics make LTAs effective at providing a compact embedding for rich type structures. Figure 3 illustrates this, showing a transition in a trivial LTA representing a variable x with refinement type { ν : int | $10 \geq \nu \geq 0$ }. The automaton rooted at state q_0 corresponds to the refinement type { ν : int | $10 \geq \nu \geq 0$ }, while the overall LTA represents a binding x : { ν : int | $10 \geq \nu \geq 0$ }.

[1] A detailed elaboration of these points can be found in the accompanying technical report [27].

Typing Semantics as LTA Transition Constraints. For component-based synthesis, an LTA must accept only well-refinement-typed programs. LTA construction therefore mirrors typing derivations, ensuring that ill-typed programs are excluded by construction via LTA transition constraints.

Figure 4 shows a portion of the LTA for the example library, embedding the semantics for function application. Transition app corresponds to a function application expression in a standard refinement-typed calculus. Incoming state q_f models the set of all single-argument library functions and their types. We have grayed out functions other than decr for clarity. The type edge for function decr, has two children, one for its input *argument* type and another for its *return* type, with location labels in and out respectively. State q_a models the set of all scalar arguments (showing only x). The argument's type is represented in the usual way for a base refinement type as shown in Fig. 3. The application typing semantics requires that the type of an actual argument be a subtype of the corresponding formal argument type. This requirement is captured by constraints ⓐ and ⓑ. Constraint ⓑ enforces equality of the underlying base types, while constraint ⓐ ensures logical implication between the corresponding refinement formulas. Additionally, a typing semantics often establishes logical entailment constraints between formulas under a substitution. A good example is the inferred type for an app term and the function's return type. LTAs model this using the constraints ⓒ, that equates base types, and ⓓ, that captures the logical entailment (fun.out.ref ⊨ type.ref) under the usual mapping of the actual argument to the formal for each possible choice of the function and the argument, modeled using a compact substitution relation over variables using a substitution over positions, shown as [arg/fun.in].

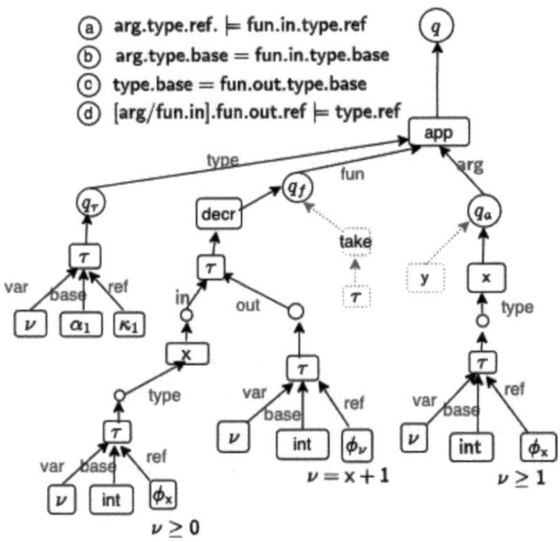

Fig. 4. An LTA fragment embedding a refinement typing semantics for function application.

Efficient Pruning and Enumeration. We exploit LTA structure to develop a CBS algorithm that combines two complementary reduction strategies. First, we prune automaton states that cannot participate in any well-typed program. Second, we identify semantic similarity between program fragments using refinement subtyping, enabling eager pruning of logically similar paths during search through merging of logically equivalent subautomata. Our key insight is that the intersection operation on tree automata generalizes naturally to a notion of *semantic* intersection over LTAs, which enables efficient enumeration even when feasible solutions are sparse. This allows the synthesizer to prune large regions of the search space that differ syntactically but are equivalent or subsumed semantically.

We implement this approach in a tool called Hegel. Our evaluation shows that Hegel can synthesize programs for complex, highly constrained CBS queries that are beyond the reach of existing systems, while maintaining soundness and completeness. This paper makes the following contributions:

- We address scalability and expressivity limitations in existing CBS frameworks, especially in the presence of queries with rich refinement-type specifications.
- We introduce *Liquid Tree Automata* (LTA), a tree automata variant that allows direct embedding of refinement-type specifications.
- We develop a novel synthesis procedure over LTAs, incorporating pruning and similarity-based reductions, and prove the procedure sound and complete.
- We implement our approach in Hegel, a CBS tool for OCaml programs; our evaluation results demonstrate significant scalability improvements over existing systems.

2 Liquid Tree Automata

$$
\begin{array}{lll}
\epsilon, p, p_i & & \in \mathit{Position} \\
\psi_a \in \mathit{Atoms} ::= & & \textsf{true} \mid \textsf{false} \\
\quad \mid p = p & & (\mathit{Syntactic}) \\
\quad \mid p \models p & & (\mathit{Semantic}) \\
\theta \ \in \mathit{Subs} := & & \overline{[p/p]} \\
\psi \ \in \Psi =:: & & \\
\quad \psi_a \mid \neg\, \psi & & \\
\quad \mid \psi \wedge \psi \mid \psi \vee \psi & & \\
\quad \mid \theta.\psi & & \\
\sigma \ \in \mathit{Schema} ::= & & \star = \star \mid \star \models \star
\end{array}
$$

Fig. 5. LTA Constraints

The target language of our synthesizer (λ_{lta}) is a standard A-normalized [13] call-by-value refinement-typed λ-calculus [33] with constructors, constants and variables, conditional expressions, and function abstraction and application. To simplify the presentation, we assume all variables have a single unique binding-site. λ_{lta} types include standard base types like int, bool etc., along with algebraic types like lists and trees over these base types and type variables α_1, α_2, etc. Refinement types τ, include *base refinements* and *arrow refinements*. A base refinement $\{\ \nu : \mathsf{t} \mid \phi\ \}$ qualifies a term of base type t with a refinement qualifier $\phi \in \Phi$. An arrow refinement refines a function type, where the argument x can occur free in the qualifier. The set of qualifiers (Φ) consist of first-order predicate logic formulae over base-typed variables along with method predicates (Q), which are user-defined, uninterpreted function symbols such as len and ord over lists used in our motivating example. A type context Γ records term variables and library functions g with their types. It also records a set of propositions relevant to a specific context.

Definition 1 (Positions in a term). *A position p in a term t is of the form i.j.k....n, a sequence of positive integers describing a path from the root of t to a sub-term. This describes what symbols are present at each position, relative to the root.*

For easier comprehension, we give human-readable labels to each number in a position. For example, consider Fig. 4 - the sequences used in the constraints like arg.type.base = fun.type.in.base are positions. type.ref is a synonym for position 1.3, fun.in.type.base for 2.1.1.2, etc.

Constraints in *Liquid Tree Automata*. An LTA constraint ψ is a predicate on terms in λ_{lta}. It is defined inductively over positions and Boolean connectives, as shown in Fig. 5. A valid *atomic constraint* ψ_a includes Boolean constants like true and false, as well as *syntactic equality* between positions, given by $p = p$ and *semantic entailment* over positions, given by $p \models p$. A *constraint* ψ is either a ψ_a or a constraint generated using Boolean connectives over other constraints. In several cases, these constraints require variable substitution at one position with another; this is captured using a list of substitutions *Subs* (θ), and a constraint $\theta.\psi$. Consequently, we can also classify *atomic constraints* into *kinds* using two constraint schemas, $\star = \star$ and $\star \models \star$, respectively.

Definition 2 (Liquid Tree Automata). *A Liquid Tree Automata, $\mathcal{A}$ defined over a finite ranked alphabet $\mathcal{F}$ derived from λ_{lta}, is a tuple $(Q, \mathcal{F}, Q_f, \Delta)$, where:*

- *Q is a finite set of states.*
- *$Q_f \subseteq Q$ is a set of final states.*
- *$\Delta \subseteq Q^n \times \mathcal{F} \times \Psi \mapsto Q$, is a set of constrained* transitions. *Each transition rule is of the form $f(q_1, q_2, ...q_n) \xhookrightarrow{\psi} q$, where $f \in \mathcal{F}$ with arity n, and a set of states $q_1, q_2, \ldots q_n \in Q$ and $\psi \in \Psi$ is a valid constraint. Here q is the target state.*

$$[\![q]\!] \quad ::= \bigcup_i ([\![\delta_i]\!]) \text{ where } \delta_i = (f(q_{i1}, q_{i2}, \ldots, q_{in}) \xhookrightarrow{\psi} q)$$

$$[\![\delta]\!] \quad ::= \{\, f\ \overline{t_i} \mid t_i \in [\![q_i]\!], f\ \overline{t_i} \models \psi, i \in [1 \ldots n] \,\}, \text{ where } \delta = (f(q_1, q_2, \ldots, q_n) \xhookrightarrow{\psi} q)$$

$$[\![\delta_\perp]\!] \quad := \varnothing$$

$$[\![\mathcal{A}]\!] ::= \bigcup_i \{[\![q_i]\!] \mid q_i \in Q_f\}$$

Fig. 6. LTA denotations.

Language of a *Liquid Tree Automaton* $[\![\mathcal{A}]\!]$. The language accepted by a LTA $\mathcal{A}$, is the set of all terms in λ_{lta} with some successful run of $\mathcal{A}$. This is, in fact, the set of all well-typed λ_{lta} terms, constructed using the methods found in a library. Formally, we define the language accepted by $\mathcal{A}$ using its denotation $[\![\mathcal{A}]\!]$ (see Fig. 6). The denotation of a state q, $[\![q]\!]$ is the set union of the denotations of each of the transitions δ_i, $[\![\delta_i]\!]$, for which q is a target state. The denotation of a transition δ builds a set of all terms, using the symbol at the current transition (f) and terms in the denotation of states incoming in

δ, filtering all terms that do not satisfy the transition constraint ψ. Symbols $f \in \mathcal{F}$ include all λ_{lta}terms including variables (x), constants (c), conditional expressions (if b then e else e), function abstractions and applications, and types (τ).

Intuitively, the satisfaction of a constraint by a term $t \vDash \psi$ maps syntactic equality constraints to equality of symbols and semantic entailment between qualifiers to logical entailment of FOL formulas. We also have a special bottom transition $\delta_{\bot}$, whose denotation is an empty set. Since an LTA can have multiple final states given by the set Q_f, the language it accepts is the union of the denotation for all its final states.

3 Synthesis Using Liquid Tree Automata

We formalize synthesis using LTAs by defining a consistency relation between a typing environment Γ and a LTA $\mathcal{A}$.

Definition 3 (Consistency between LTAs and Type Environments). *A type environment Γ is consistent with an LTA $\mathcal{A} = (Q, \mathcal{F}, Q_f, \Delta)$ iff $\forall e, \Gamma(e) = \tau \iff \exists \mathcal{A}'$ such that $\mathcal{A}'$ is a sub-automaton[2] of $\mathcal{A}$ and $e \in [\![\mathcal{A}']\!]$.*

Definition 4 (Synthesis Problem with LTAs). *Given a type environment Γ that relates library functions $f_i = \lambda(\overline{x_{i,j}}).e_{f_i}$ with their refinement types $f_i : \overline{(x_{i,j} : \tau_{i,j})} \rightarrow \{\nu : t_i \mid \phi_i\} \in \Gamma$, and a synthesis query $\varphi = \overline{(y_i : \tau_i)} \rightarrow \{\nu : t \mid \phi\}$, a solution to a CBS problem is a LTA $\mathcal{A}$, such that forall all $e \in [\![\mathcal{A}]\!]$, $\Gamma \vdash e : \varphi$ and Γ is consistent with $\mathcal{A}$.*

3.1 Synthesis Algorithm

The main synthesis algorithm, LTASynthesize is shown in Algorithm 1. It takes as input an alphabet $\mathcal{F}$, which includes symbols from $\lambda_{\mathsf{lta}}$and an annotated library of functions, a synthesis query specification φ, and a bound on the size of the terms k to synthesize.

The algorithm works in two phases: (1) an *exploration* phase adds states and transitions, expanding the automata. The resulting LTA is then pruned/reduced by (2) a reduction phase. The algorithm also keeps track of *similar* but not yet reduced transitions through an equivalence set $\mathcal{E}$. The output of the algorithm is a pair consisting of (i) an LTA, $\mathcal{A}_{\mathsf{min}}$ for the synthesis query based on $\mathcal{F}$ and the typing semantics of λ_{lta}, and (ii) a set of solution terms in λ_{lta}, possibly using $\mathcal{F}$ that satisfies the query specification. The algorithm returns a failure value ($\bot$) if it cannot find a solution within the given max-depth k.

The algorithm begins (line 1) by initializing the similarity set $\mathcal{E}$ to $\varnothing$ and constructing an initial LTA $\mathcal{A}_0$ using the well-formedness procedure WF. Given the library $\mathcal{F}$ and an empty automaton $\mathcal{A}_{\bot}$, WF deterministically constructs

[2] A sub-automaton is defined using a subset definition over states and transitions.

an LTA that represents all well-formed terms of size one consistent with the typing rules in Fig. 7, including the query specification φ. In particular, initialization introduces states and transitions corresponding to query arguments, library functions, base refinement types, and a distinguished final transition encoding the top-level constraint of φ.

At line 2, the algorithm checks whether the language of $\mathcal{A}_0$ is non-empty using procedure NEmpty (lines 14–15), which identifies final states whose denotation is non-empty. If such states exist, the algorithm extracts the set of solution terms using the LTA denotation $[\![\cdot]\!]$ (Fig. 6) and returns $(\mathcal{A}_0, [\![\mathcal{A}_0]\!])$ (line 3). Otherwise, the algorithm invokes procedure Enumerate (lines 5–13), which performs iterative exploration and reduction of the search space. If Enumerate is invoked at depth k, it returns $\perp$, indicating synthesis failure.

When the depth of $\mathcal{A}$ is less than the bound k, Enumerate first enters an exploration phase by extending $\mathcal{A}$ with new transitions using procedure Transition (line 6). This step applies the typing rules in Fig. 7 to construct larger well-typed terms.

The algorithm then enters a reduction phase. It first applies Prune (line 7) to eliminate unreachable or ill-typed portions of the automaton. Next, similarity relations between transitions are identified using Similarity (line 8), producing an updated equivalence set $\mathcal{E}$. Finally, Minimize (line 9) applies the minimization rules (M-Trans) and (M-LTA) from Fig. 9 to merge semantically redundant states and transitions, yielding a reduced automaton $\mathcal{A}_{\mathsf{min}}$.

At line 10, the algorithm again checks whether the language of $\mathcal{A}_{\mathsf{min}}$ is non-empty. If so, it returns $(\mathcal{A}_{\mathsf{min}}, [\![\mathcal{A}_{\mathsf{min}}]\!])$ (line 11). Otherwise, the algorithm recurses on $\mathcal{A}_{\mathsf{min}}$, continuing the explore–reduce–check loop until a solution is found or the depth bound is exceeded.

LTASynthesize($\langle \mathcal{F}, \varphi = \overline{(\mathsf{x_i} : \tau_i)} \rightarrow \{\mathsf{v} : \mathsf{t}|\phi\}, k\rangle$)
  `// Initialize`
(1) $\mathcal{A}_0 \leftarrow$ WF $(\mathcal{F}, \mathcal{A}_\perp)$; $\mathcal{E} \leftarrow \varnothing$
  `// Check solution in Initial` $\mathcal{A}_0$
(2) **if** $\hat{Q} =$ NEmpty *($\mathcal{A}_0$)* **then**
(3)   **return** $(\mathcal{A}_0, \bigcup_{q \in \hat{Q}} [\![\mathcal{A}_q]\!])$
  `// Iteratively explore-reduce-check`
(4) **return** Enumerate $(\mathcal{A}_0, \varphi, k)$

Enumerate($\langle \mathcal{F}, \mathcal{A}, \varphi = \overline{(\mathsf{x_i} : \tau_i)} \rightarrow \{\mathsf{v} : \mathsf{t}|\phi\}, k\rangle$)
(5) **if** *depth ($\mathcal{A}$)* $< k$ **then**
(6) $\mathcal{A} \leftarrow$ Transition $(\mathcal{F}, \mathcal{A})$;
(7) $\mathcal{A} \leftarrow$ Prune $(\mathcal{A})$;
(8) $\mathcal{E} \leftarrow$ Similarity $(\mathcal{A}, \mathcal{E})$;
(9) $(\mathcal{A}_{\mathsf{min}}, \mathcal{E}) \leftarrow$ Minimize $(\mathcal{A}, \mathcal{E})$;
(10)   **if** $\hat{Q} =$ NEmpty *($\mathcal{A}_{\mathsf{min}}$)* **then**
(11)   **return** $(\mathcal{A}_{\mathsf{min}}, \bigcup_{q \in \hat{Q}} [\![\mathcal{A}_q]\!])$
(12)   Enumerate $(\mathcal{A}_{\mathsf{min}}, \varphi, k)$
  else
(13)   **return** $\perp$

NEmpty($\langle \mathcal{A} \rangle$)
(14) $\hat{Q} \leftarrow \{q_f \mid q_f \in Q_f, [\![q_f]\!] \neq \varnothing \}$
(15) **return** $\hat{Q}$

Algorithm 1: Synthesis Algorithm.

3.2 LTA Construction

The transitions Δ for a LTA $\mathcal{A}$ are constructed using the **Well-formedness** and **Transitions** judgments given in Fig. 7.

Well-formedness $\boxed{\mathcal{F}, \mathcal{A} \vdash^{\mathsf{wf}} f \in \mathcal{F}(\overline{q_i}) \overset{\psi}{\hookrightarrow} q}$

$$\text{WF-PRIM}\ \frac{\mathsf{t} \in \mathsf{T}_{\mathcal{F}} \qquad q_{\mathsf{t}} \notin Q}{\mathcal{F}, \mathcal{A} \vdash^{\mathsf{wf}} \mathsf{t}() \hookrightarrow q_{\mathsf{t}}} \qquad \text{WF-PRED}\ \frac{\phi \in \Phi_{\mathcal{F}} \qquad q_\phi \notin Q}{\mathcal{F}, \mathcal{A} \vdash^{\mathsf{wf}} \phi \hookrightarrow q_\phi}$$

$$\text{WF-VAR}\ \frac{x \in \mathsf{Vars}_{\mathcal{F}} \qquad q_x \notin Q}{\mathcal{F}, \mathcal{A} \vdash^{\mathsf{wf}} x \hookrightarrow q_x} \qquad \text{WF-BASE}\ \frac{(\tau \equiv \{x : t \mid \phi\}) \in \tau_{\mathcal{F}} \qquad q_\tau \notin Q}{\mathcal{F}, \mathcal{A} \vdash^{\mathsf{wf}} \tau(q_x, q_t, q_\phi) \hookrightarrow q_\tau}$$

$$\text{WF-ARROW}\ \frac{(\tau_\rightarrow \equiv \tau_i \rightarrow \tau_j) \in \tau_{\mathcal{F}} \quad \tau_i, \tau_j \in \tau_{\mathcal{F}} \quad q_{\tau_\rightarrow} \notin Q}{\mathcal{F}, \mathcal{A} \vdash^{\mathsf{wf}} \tau_{\tau_\rightarrow}(q_{\tau_i}, q_{\tau_j}) \hookrightarrow q_{\tau_\rightarrow}} \qquad \text{Q-GOAL}\ \frac{\varphi = \overline{(\mathsf{x_i} : \tau_i)} \rightarrow \tau \quad q_{\mathsf{term}_k}, q_\tau \in Q \quad q_{\mathsf{goal}} \in Q_f \quad \psi = \textsc{SubType}(q_{\mathsf{term}_k} \blacktriangleright \mathsf{type}, q_{\mathsf{goal}} \blacktriangleright \mathsf{type})}{\mathcal{F}, \mathcal{A} \vdash^{\mathsf{wf}} \mathsf{goal}(q_\tau, q_{\mathsf{term}_k}) \overset{\psi}{\hookrightarrow} q_{\mathsf{goal}}}$$

Transitions $\boxed{\mathcal{F}, \mathcal{A} \vdash f \in \mathcal{F}(\overline{q_i}) \overset{\psi}{\hookrightarrow} q}$

$$\text{E-APP}\ \frac{q_f, q_a \in Q \quad \tau(\overline{q_i}) \hookrightarrow q_\tau \in \Delta \quad \theta = [q_{\mathsf{a}} \blacktriangleright \epsilon / q_f \blacktriangleright \mathsf{in}] \quad \psi = \textsc{SubType}(q_{\mathsf{a}} \blacktriangleright \mathsf{type}, q_f \blacktriangleright \mathsf{in}) \wedge \theta.(\textsc{SubType}(q_f \blacktriangleright \mathsf{out}, q_{\mathsf{app}} \blacktriangleright \mathsf{type}))}{\mathcal{F}, \mathcal{A} \vdash \mathsf{app}\ (q_\tau, q_f, q_a) \overset{\psi}{\hookrightarrow} q_{\mathsf{app}}} \qquad \text{E-VAR}\ \frac{x : \tau \in \mathcal{F} \qquad q_x \notin Q}{\mathcal{F}, \mathcal{A} \vdash x(q_\tau) \hookrightarrow q_x}$$

$$\text{E-CONST}\ \frac{\vdash c : \tau \in \mathcal{F} \quad q_c \notin Q}{\mathcal{F}, \mathcal{A} \vdash c(q_\tau) \hookrightarrow q_c} \qquad \text{E-IF}\ \frac{q_b, q_t, q_f \in Q \quad \tau(\overline{q_i}) \hookrightarrow q_\tau \in \Delta \quad \psi = ((q_b \blacktriangleright \mathsf{ref}) \wedge \textsc{SubType}(q_t \blacktriangleright \mathsf{type}, q_{\mathsf{if}} \blacktriangleright \mathsf{type})) \wedge (\neg(q_b \blacktriangleright \mathsf{ref}) \wedge \textsc{SubType}(q_f \blacktriangleright \mathsf{type}, q_{\mathsf{if}} \blacktriangleright \mathsf{type}))}{\mathcal{F}, \mathcal{A} \vdash \mathsf{if}\ (q_\tau, q_b, q_t, q_f) \overset{\psi}{\hookrightarrow} q_{\mathsf{if}}}$$

$$\underbrace{\textsc{SubType}}_{\text{ST}}(\delta_i, \delta_j) = \begin{cases} (\tau_i(\overline{q_i}) \overset{\psi_i}{\hookrightarrow} q_{\tau_i}, \tau_j(\overline{q_j}) \overset{\psi_j}{\hookrightarrow} q_{\tau_j}) & \mathsf{i.type.t} = \mathsf{j.type.t} \\ & \wedge\ \mathsf{i.type.ref} \models \mathsf{j.type.ref} \\ (\tau_{\rightarrow_i}(\overline{q_i}) \overset{\psi_i}{\hookrightarrow} q_{\tau_{\rightarrow_i}}, \tau_{\rightarrow_j}(\overline{q_j}) \overset{\psi_j}{\hookrightarrow} q_{\tau_{\rightarrow_j}}) & \mathrm{ST}(\delta_j \blacktriangleright \mathsf{in}, \delta_i \blacktriangleright \mathsf{in}) \\ & \wedge\ \mathrm{ST}(\delta_i \blacktriangleright \mathsf{out}, \delta_j \blacktriangleright \mathsf{out}) \\ (\_, \_) & \mathsf{true} \end{cases} \tag{1}$$

Fig. 7. Selected rules for constructing transitions Δ, basis for WF and TRANSITION.

The latter judgment holds if, given library $\mathcal{F}$ and automata $\mathcal{A}$, a new n-ary transition can be added to $\mathcal{A}$ corresponding to an n-ary symbol $f \in \mathcal{F}$, with $q_1, q_2, ..., q_n$ being the incoming states in the transition and q being the target state, such that ψ captures the typing constraints for the valid terms in the language of the transition $[\![.]\!]$ [3] We begin by generalizing the definition of *term at a position* (Definition 1) to LTAs. Given a state q (or transition δ), and a position p, we define *LTA states at a position* (equivalently, LTA transitions at a position) p from q (or δ), denoted as $q \blacktriangleright p$ (or $\delta \blacktriangleright p$):

Definition 5 (Transitions at a position, $q \blacktriangleright p$). *For each* $\delta_i = (f(q_{i1}, q_{i2}, \ldots, q_{in}) \overset{\varphi}{\hookrightarrow} q)$. $q \blacktriangleright \epsilon = \{q\}$ *and* $q \blacktriangleright j.p = \bigcup_i(\delta_i \blacktriangleright j.p)$*, where* $\delta \blacktriangleright j.p = q_j \blacktriangleright p$ *if* $j \leq n$ *(arity of* δ_i*) and* $\varnothing$ *otherwise.*

Well-Formedness Rules. Given an alphabet $\mathcal{F}$ (library and query), a current LTA $\mathcal{A}$, and the well-formedness typing semantics of λ_{lta}, we construct LTAs using judgments of the form $\mathcal{F}, \mathcal{A} \vdash^{\mathsf{wf}} f \in \mathcal{F}(\overline{q_i}) \overset{\psi}{\hookrightarrow} q$, which determine when a transition may be added to $\mathcal{A}$. These rules characterize when leaf and composite transitions may be added for base types, predicates, variables, refinement types, arrow types, and polymorphic types, and directly mirror the well-formedness typing rules of λ_{lta}.

To illustrate the behavior of these rules, Fig. 8 shows the application of the well-formedness and transition rules from Fig. 7 over a small example library of terms given below:

$$\mathcal{F} = \{\mathsf{f} : (\mathsf{n} : \mathsf{int}) \to (\mathsf{l} : \{\mathsf{v} : [\mathsf{a}] \mid \mathsf{len}(\mathsf{v}) > 0\}) \to \{\mathsf{v} : [\mathsf{a}] \mid \mathsf{len}(\mathsf{v}) > 0\},$$
$$\mathsf{xs} : \{\mathsf{v} : [\mathsf{int}] \mid \mathsf{len}(\mathsf{v}) > 0\}; \mathsf{ys} : [\mathsf{bool}]\}\}$$

Assume that our query φ is given by the refinement type:

$$(\mathsf{xs} : \{\mathrm{v} : [\mathrm{int}] \mid \mathrm{len}\ (\mathrm{v}) > 0\}) \to \{\nu : [\mathrm{int}] \mid \mathrm{len}\ (\nu) > \mathrm{len}\ (\mathrm{xs})\}$$

and the value of k, the term size is 2.

Rule WF-PRIM (the corresponding LTA construction is shown using the box labeled with ③ in Fig. 8) introduces a state q_{t} and a nullary transition labeled t for each primitive type t, like char, int, etc., in the language. Rule WF-PRED similarly adds leaf transitions for refinement formula ϕ in some annotation in $\mathcal{F}$ or in the query. Rule WF-BASE (shown with ②) introduces a state q_τ for each well-formed base refinement type $\tau = \{x : t \mid \phi\}$ and adds a ternary transition with incoming states q_x, q_t, and q_ϕ corresponding to the bound variable, base type, and refinement formula, respectively. These states are provided by earlier applications of WF-VAR, WF-PRIM, and WF-PRED.

Rule WF-ARROW(①) generates similar transitions for each arrow refinement type, with a symbol $\tau_\to$ and two incoming states for the argument-type and the result-type for the arrow. Rule Q-GOAL introduces a distinguished final state q_{goal} and a goal transition connecting sub-automata rooted at q_{term_k}, representing candidate terms of size k. The associated constraint ψ enforces that the

[3] For perspicuity, we have elided several details about polymorphic transition construction and type inference; these mostly concern proper scope management within an LTA. The complete set of rules can be found in the technical report [27].

synthesized term's return type is a subtype of the query's annotated return type, as generated by SUBTYPE.

Our extended λ_{lta} and typing semantics also include *type* and *refinement* abstractions, allowing parametric polymorphism in the refinement types setting [20,33]. Consequently, the above rules also extend naturally to these abstractions and their corresponding type and refinement applications.

Expression Transition Rules. Transition judgments are similar in structure to the well-formedness judgments, but simulate the refinement type judgments for the expressions and types in the λ_{lta}. These rules specify how to add transitions corresponding to λ_{lta} expressions and types. Each n-ary expression transition has n+1 incoming states, with the state at the position zero capturing the sub-automata for the possible types of the expression.

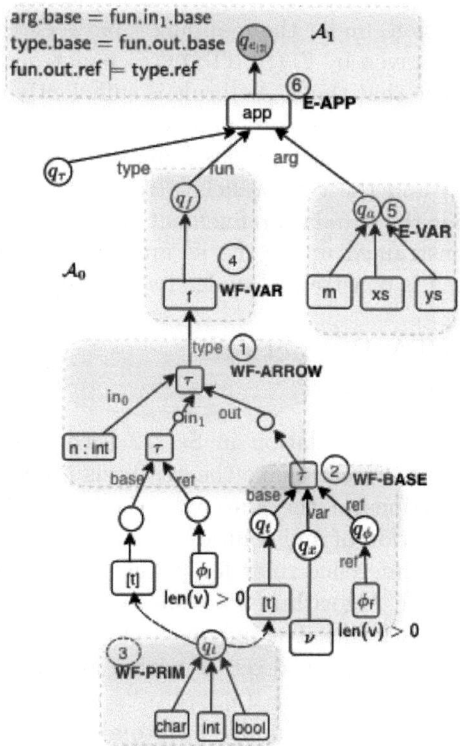

Fig. 8. Application of WELL-FORMEDNESS and TRANSITION rules to construct initial LTA $\mathcal{A}_0$ and $\mathcal{A}_1$ for the example library.

Rules E-VAR(construction shown in Fig. 8, ⑤) and E-CONST introduce transitions for variables and constants together with their types. Rule E-VAR (⑤) applies to both scalar variables and variables bound to functions; accordingly, the associated type τ is represented either as a base refinement (via WF-BASE) or as an arrow refinement (via WF-ARROW).

Rule E-APP (Fig. 8, ⑥) introduces transitions corresponding to function application expressions. It assumes the states q_f and q_a are already present for the function f and argument a. It first constructs a transition for the application's result type τ using the well-formedness judgments, with q_τ as the target state.

The inferred transition uses app as its symbol and has three incoming states, corresponding to the result type (q_τ), the function (q_f), and the argument (q_a). The key aspect of this rule is the set of constraints ψ associated with the transition. These constraints relate the three subautomata rooted at q_τ, q_f, and q_a, and encode the standard refinement-typing semantics of function application [33]. These constraints first apply the standard substitution of the possible formal arguments in the function with the actual arguments. This is done via creating a substitution θ between positions given formally as $[q_{\mathsf{a}} \blacktriangleright \epsilon / q_f \blacktriangleright \mathsf{in}]$. Second, the rule uses an auxiliary function SUBTYPE (Eq. 1), which given two transitions, returns constraints sufficient to capture the subtype relation between their types. For example, ψ in E-APP captures two main relations. The first is a subtyping constraint between a function's formal argument and the actual expression passed as the argument (SUBTYPE $(q_{\mathsf{a}} \blacktriangleright \mathsf{type}, q_f \blacktriangleright \mathsf{in})$). The second subtype relation is between the function's result type and the type of the app expression, under the mapping θ between the formal and the actual arguments. This is given by θ. (SUBTYPE$(q_f \blacktriangleright \mathsf{out}, q_{\mathsf{app}} \blacktriangleright \mathsf{type})$).

Note that the E-APP rule is sufficiently general to allow synthesis to support *partial* (i.e., higher-order) function applications. Rule E-IF introduces transitions for conditional expressions using subautomata for the Boolean condition (rooted at q_b) and the two branches (rooted at q_t and q_f). The associated constraints encode the standard refinement typing semantics of conditionals: the true branch is constrained under the assumption that the condition holds, while the false branch is constrained under its negation.

4 LTA Reductions

4.1 PRUNE

The LTA formulation in Sect. 2 accepts only well-typed terms from the λ_{lta}. However, we can make the synthesis procedure more efficient by eagerly reducing portions of the automata (i.e. sub-automata) which are irrelevant to the construction of any solution.

The inference rules for pruning irrelevant code, which underlie the PRUNE routine in Algorithm 1, are shown in Fig. 9. These rules are expressed using two judgment forms. The judgment $\mathcal{A} \vdash \Delta \rightsquigarrow \Delta'$ defines how a set of transitions Δ is reduced to a pruned set Δ' within an LTA $\mathcal{A}$. This reduction relies on a second judgment form, $\mathcal{A} \vdash (\delta_i, \delta_j) \rightsquigarrow^{\psi_a} \delta'$, which specifies how a pair of transitions δ_i, δ_j are reduced under an atomic constraint ψ_a using syntactic or semantic intersection operation, yielding a possibly simplified transition δ'.

The P-TRANS rule applies these atomic reductions to transition sets. Given a transition δ with constraint ψ, assumed to be a conjunction of atomic constraints ψ_j relating transitions at positions p_1 and p_2, the rule updates the set of transitions at position p_1 (denoted $\delta \blacktriangleright p_1$). Each such transition is replaced by its reduced form, producing an updated transition set Δ_r computed using the atomic reduction rules described below.

Rule P-SYN-EQ handles syntactic equality constraints over positions p_1 and p_2. It performs a syntactic intersection [5,21] over the two set of transitions at these position. Syntactic intersection ($\sqcap_{\mathsf{Syntax}}$) is a standard tree intersection operation. Intuitively, it compares the two transitions for syntactic equality of transition symbols while recursively intersecting each incoming state in the transition. The rule updates each transition in $\delta \blacktriangleright p_1$, with its syntactic intersection with some transition in $\delta \blacktriangleright p_2$.

Pruning $\boxed{\mathcal{A} \vdash \Delta \rightsquigarrow \Delta' \quad | \quad \mathcal{A} \vdash (\delta_i, \delta_j) \rightsquigarrow^{\psi_a} \delta'}$

$$\textsc{P-TRANS}\ \frac{\begin{array}{c} \delta \equiv f(\ldots) \xhookrightarrow{\psi_j \wedge \ldots} q \\ \psi_j \equiv p_1 (=\mid\models) p_2 \\ \delta_i \in \delta \blacktriangleright p_1 \\ \delta_j \in \delta \blacktriangleright p_2 \\ \Delta_r = \{\delta_{i,r} \mid \mathcal{A} \vdash (\delta_i, \delta_j) \rightsquigarrow^{\psi_j} \delta_{i,r}\} \end{array}}{\mathcal{A} \vdash \Delta \rightsquigarrow \Delta[\delta \blacktriangleright p_1 / \Delta_r]} \qquad \frac{\begin{array}{c} \delta \equiv f(\ldots) \xhookrightarrow{\psi_j \wedge \ldots} q \\ \psi_j \equiv p_1 = p_2 \\ \delta_1 \in \delta \blacktriangleright p_1 \\ \delta_2 \in \delta \blacktriangleright p_2 \\ \delta_{\mathsf{r}} = \sqcap_{\mathsf{Syntax}}(\delta_1, \delta_2) \end{array}}{\mathcal{A} \vdash (\delta_1, \delta_2) \rightsquigarrow^{\psi_j} \delta_{\mathsf{r}}}\ \textsc{P-SYN-EQ}$$

$$\frac{\begin{array}{c} \delta \equiv f(\ldots) \xhookrightarrow{\psi_j \wedge \ldots} q \qquad \psi_j \equiv \theta.p_1 \models p_2 \\ \delta_1 \in \delta \blacktriangleright p_1 \qquad \delta_2 \in \delta \blacktriangleright p_2 \qquad \delta_{\mathsf{r}} = \sqcap^{\psi_j}{}_{\mathsf{Semantics}}(\delta_1, \delta_2) \end{array}}{\mathcal{A} \vdash (\delta_1, \delta_2) \rightsquigarrow^{\psi_j} \delta_{\mathsf{r}}}\ \textsc{P-SEM-ENT}$$

Similarity $\boxed{\mathcal{A} \vdash^{\mathbf{sim}} \delta_i \lesssim \delta_j \quad | \quad \mathcal{A} \vdash \mathcal{E} \rightsquigarrow \mathcal{E}'}$

$$\textsc{S-TRANS}\ \frac{\begin{array}{c} \psi_{<:} = \textsc{SubType}(\delta_i \blacktriangleright \mathsf{type}, \delta_j \blacktriangleright \mathsf{type}) \\ \delta_\perp \notin \sqcap^{\psi_{<:}}{}_{\mathsf{Semantics}}(\delta_i \blacktriangleright \mathsf{type}, \delta_j \blacktriangleright \mathsf{type}) \end{array}}{\mathcal{A} \vdash^{\mathbf{sim}} \delta_i \lesssim \delta_j} \qquad \frac{\begin{array}{c} (\delta_i, \delta_j) \notin \mathcal{E} \\ \mathcal{A} \vdash^{\mathbf{sim}} \delta_i \lesssim \delta_j \end{array}}{\mathcal{A} \vdash \mathcal{E} \rightsquigarrow \mathcal{E} \cup \{(\delta_i, \delta_j)\}}\ \textsc{S-EQ}$$

Minimization $\boxed{(\mathcal{A}, \mathcal{E}) \vdash \Delta \rightsquigarrow \Delta' \quad | \quad \vdash (\mathcal{A}, \mathcal{E}) \rightsquigarrow (\mathcal{A}', \mathcal{E}')}$

$$\textsc{M-TRANS}\ \frac{\begin{array}{c} \delta_i, \delta_j \in \Delta \qquad (\delta_i, \delta_j) \in \mathcal{E} \\ \delta_i \equiv f(q_1, q_2, \ldots q_j \ldots q_n) \xhookrightarrow{\psi_i} q_i \\ \delta_j \equiv f'(q'_1, q'_2, \ldots q'_m) \xhookrightarrow{\psi_j} q_j \\ \Delta' = \bigcup_k \{\delta_k[q_j/q_i] \\ \mid \delta_k = \hat{f}(\hat{q_1}, \mathbf{q_j}, \ldots \hat{q_m}) \hookrightarrow \hat{q_k}\} \end{array}}{(\mathcal{A}, \mathcal{E}) \vdash \Delta \rightsquigarrow (\Delta \cup \Delta') \setminus \{\delta_j\}} \qquad \frac{\begin{array}{c} \mathcal{A} \equiv (Q, \mathcal{F}, Q_f, \Delta) \\ (\mathcal{A}, \mathcal{E}) \vdash \Delta \rightsquigarrow^{\star} \Delta' \end{array}}{\vdash (\mathcal{A}, \mathcal{E}) \rightsquigarrow ((Q, \mathcal{F}, Q_f, \Delta'), \varnothing)}\ \textsc{M-LTA}$$

$$\sqcap^{\psi}{}_{\mathsf{Semantics}}(\delta_i, \delta_j) = \begin{cases} \delta_i & \sigma(\psi_j) = \theta.\star \models \star, \mathsf{Symbol}(\delta_i) = \phi_i, \mathsf{Symbol}(\delta_j) = \phi_j, \\ & \text{Given the automaton } \mathcal{A},\ s.t.\ \mathcal{R}(\Gamma, \mathcal{A}) \\ & [\![\Gamma]\!] \wedge [\![\theta]\!].[\![\phi_i]\!] \implies [\![\phi_j]\!] \\ \delta_\perp & \text{otherwise} \end{cases} \tag{2}$$

Fig. 9. Selective rules for similarity inference and LTA Minimization.

Rule P-SYM-ENT handles semantic entailment constraints, where ψ_j has the form $\theta.\,p_i \vDash p_j$. In this case, syntactic intersection is insufficient, since the formulas associated with positions p_1 and p_2 cannot be compared by syntactic equality alone. We therefore introduce a semantic intersection operation, denoted $\sqcap^{\psi}{}_{\mathsf{Semantics}}$ shown in Eq. 2, which applies to transitions carrying refinement qualifiers.

Given two such transitions, the operation checks whether the refinement formula at position p_1 (extracted using an auxiliary function Symbol over the transition) logically entails the formula at position p_2 under the substitution θ and the interpretation of the environment Γ, shown as $([\![\Gamma]\!] \wedge [\![\theta]\!].[\![\phi_i]\!] \implies [\![\phi_j]\!])$. If the entailment holds, the intersection yields the transition at the more specific position p_1, otherwise, it returns a bottom transition $\delta_{\perp}$. All bottom transitions are subsequently eliminated by normalization. Intuitively, this operation compares transitions modeling refinement formulas in two types, and keeps the sub-type transition[4]. The intersection operations form the basis of PRUNE procedure in LTASYNTHESIZE.

4.2 Similarity and Minimize

The similarity inference rules are defined by the SIMILARITY judgments in Fig. 9. The S-TRANS rule characterizes when two transitions are considered *similar*, based on the relationship between their associated type sub-automata.

Similarity is determined by the constraint $\psi_{<:} = \text{SUBTYPE}(\delta_i \blacktriangleright \mathsf{type}, \delta_j \blacktriangleright \mathsf{type})$, which checks whether the types associated with the two transitions are related by the standard subtyping relation induced by the typing semantics of λ_{lta}. Rule S-EQ enumerates pairs of transitions from $\mathcal{A}$ that are not yet recorded in the similarity set, and adds to $\mathcal{E}$ whenever the similarity constraint holds.

Similarity Reduction. The similarity relation gives us a principled minimization strategy for LTAs, in which transitions that are similar up to subtyping are merged, retaining only the most specific representative. The minimization rules in Fig. 9 formalize this process.

The first judgment form, $(\mathcal{A}, \mathcal{E}) \vdash \Delta \rightsquigarrow \Delta'$, defines how the transition set of an LTA is reduced using the similarity relation $\mathcal{E}$. As specified by Rule M-TRANS, when two similar transitions are identified, the transition corresponding to the supertype is removed, while the transition corresponding to the subtype is retained. All incoming edges that previously targeted the removed transition are redirected to the retained one, preserving reachability within the automaton. The second judgment, formalized by Rule M-LTA, lifts transition minimization to the level of entire LTAs. It computes a minimized transition set Δ' by applying a transitive closure of the transition update rules. The alphabet $\mathcal{F}$ of the automaton remains unchanged during this process. After minimization, the similarity set $\mathcal{E}$ is reset, since all similar transitions have either been merged or eliminated.

[4] A detailed example can be found in the accompanying technical report [27].

Note that equivalence of terms (and of their corresponding sub-automata) is strictly stronger than similarity. As a result, similarity-based reduction also subsumes equivalence-based pruning, eliminating both semantically equivalent and strictly less-specific sub-automata. This unified treatment enables aggressive reduction of redundant terms, leading to efficient enumeration over a substantially reduced search space.

5 Handling Cycles

Although our LTA definition is general and allows cycles, our treatment thus far has deliberately excluded cycles for ease of elucidation. However, the underlying refinement-typed language λ_{lta} often contain terms whose specifications require both general parametric polymorphism (types depending on other (non-refined types)), as well as abstract refinements [34], i.e., refinement types parameterized with refinement predicates. Precisely capturing these specifications will require cyclic edges in the LTA.

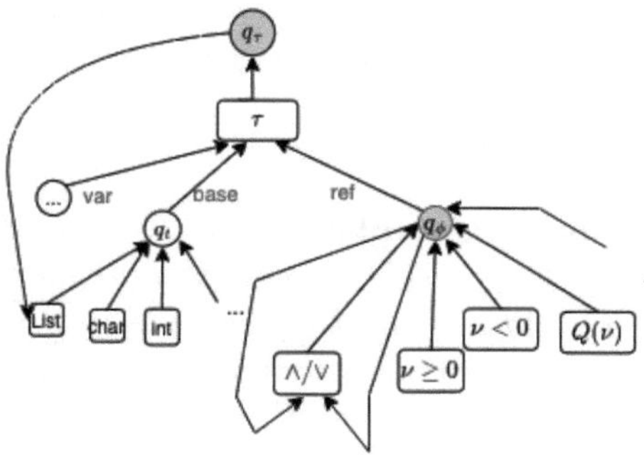

Fig. 10. Cycles in LTA for polymorphic types and abstract refinements. States in cycles are colored.

For instance, cycles allow us to model the space where a type variable α can be instantiated with any type (both base and refined), and a refinement variable ϕ to any well-formed refinement formula. This is shown graphically in Fig. 10. The state q_t captures all valid base-refinement types, where a polymorphic list constructor List can be instantiated with any possible type (the cyclic edge back to q_t). The refinement formula in τ in turn can be instantiated with all valid refinement predicates captured by another state q_ϕ, with standard predicates like $\{\ \nu \geq 0, \nu < 0, \text{etc.,}\}$, Method predicates ($Q(\nu)$), as well as conjunction and disjunction of other predicates (cyclic edges from q_ϕ).

Such cycles effectively represent an unbounded sequence of refinements and types characterized by position constraints. Thus, any transition constraint referring to a state/transition that is part of a cycle would result in a logical formula that duplicates and accumulates predicates for every potential iteration, making the formula unwieldy for the solvers. To maintain tractability, we impose a structural restriction, conceptually similar to earlier works [21], on the LTA: the position constraints associated with any transition are prohibited from referring to a state that participates in a cycle. We formally define this using a *Dependency Graph* for an LTA, and when are LTA constraints *Well-formed*:

The acyclic constraint restriction enables us to prevent the infinite unrolling of logical obligations, ensuring that the resulting SMT queries are well-behaved, while still supporting the polymorphic types and abstract refinements in specifications. Additionally, the above structural restriction on constraints allows us to directly extend our semantic intersection and pruning strategies to cyclic forms[5].

6 Soundness and Completeness

For a given upper bound k on the size of programs being synthesized, the LTA-Synthesize algorithm is both sound and complete assuming the validity of each library function against their specifications.[6]

Theorem 1 (Soundness). *Given a type environment Γ that relates library functions $f_i = \lambda(\overline{x_{i,j}}).e_{f_i}$ with their refinement types $f_i : \overline{(x_{i,j} : \tau_{i,j})} \rightarrow \{\nu : t_i \mid \phi_i\} \in \Gamma$, and a synthesis query $\varphi = \overline{(y_i : \tau_i)} \rightarrow \{\nu : t \mid \phi\}$, if* LTASynthesize *$(\Gamma, \varphi, \mathsf{k}) = (\mathcal{A}_{\mathsf{min}}, \mathsf{Terms} = \{e \mid e \in [\![\mathcal{A}_{\mathsf{min}}]\!]\})$, then $\forall e \in \mathsf{Terms}, \Gamma \vdash e : \varphi$, where Γ is consistent with $\mathcal{A}_{\mathsf{min}}$.*

Theorem 2 (Completeness). *Given a type environment Γ that relates library functions $f_i = \lambda(\overline{x_{i,j}}).e_{f_i}$ with their refinement types $f_i : \overline{(x_{i,j} : \tau_{i,j})} \rightarrow \{\nu : t_i \mid \phi_i\} \in \Gamma$, and a synthesis query $\varphi = \overline{(y_i : \tau_i)} \rightarrow \{\nu : t \mid \phi\}$, if* LTASynthesize *$(\Gamma, \varphi, \mathsf{k}) = \bot$, then $\nexists$ a term $e \in [\![\mathcal{A}_{\mathsf{complete}}]\!]$ containing fewer than $k+1$ library function calls, such that $\Gamma \vdash e : \varphi$ and Γ is consistent with $\mathcal{A}_{\mathsf{complete}}$. Where $\mathcal{A}_{\mathsf{complete}}$ is the complete LTA of size k, for the given Γ, generated without any reduction.*

7 Evaluation

Our evaluation considers the following three research questions:

- **RQ1 Effectiveness of Hegel**: How effectively does Hegel(shown as He) synthesize programs satisfying complex refinement-type specifications, compared to other specification-guided, component-based synthesis tools?
- **RQ2 Scalability with query complexity**: As synthesis queries increase in size and control-flow complexity, how well does Hegel scale in terms of success rate and synthesis time?
- **RQ3 Impact of LTA reduction strategies**: What is the impact of pruning and similarity-based reductions on LTA size, search-space reduction, and overall synthesis efficiency?

[5] Additional details about the Cyclic LTA can be found in an accompanying technical report [27].

[6] Proofs can be found can be found in the accompanying technical report [27].

7.1 RQ1: Effectiveness and Comparison with Other Tools

Benchmarks. To address RQ1, We evaluate Hegel on 14 benchmark queries drawn from Hoogle+ [17] and Hectare [21], re-implemented in OCaml and classified into first order, higher order, and polymorphic categories. Each query is refined using three distinct refinement specifications, yielding 42 total benchmarks[7]. We evaluate Hegel against Hoogle+ and Synquid [29], a deductive synthesis tool based on refinement types. A detailed description of the benchmark set is provided in the supplemental material.

Results. Figure 11 summarizes synthesis time and LTA minimization statistics for select benchmarks (20/42) where at least one other tool succeeded. Hegel successfully synthesizes solutions for all 42 benchmarks, with a maximum runtime of 11 s and an average runtime of 7.6 s. In contrast, Hoogle+ solves only 6 benchmarks and is approximately 6x slower on those instances. Synquid solves 20 benchmarks and is on average 4.5x slower than Hegel on commonly solved queries. Hectare is omitted as it does not support refinement based specifications.

22.5% of the total synthesis time on the RQ1 benchmarks was spent on solving SMT queries. Note that Hegel improves overall SMT query cost by reducing the number of such queries needed for synthesis compared to enumerative techniques, leading to substantial improvement in synthesis times.

Across benchmarks, LTA minimization substantially reduces the automaton size, with an average reduction of 73%, directly contributing to improved synthesis performance. All experiments were conducted with a timeout of 3 min and a maximum synthesis bound of five library function calls,

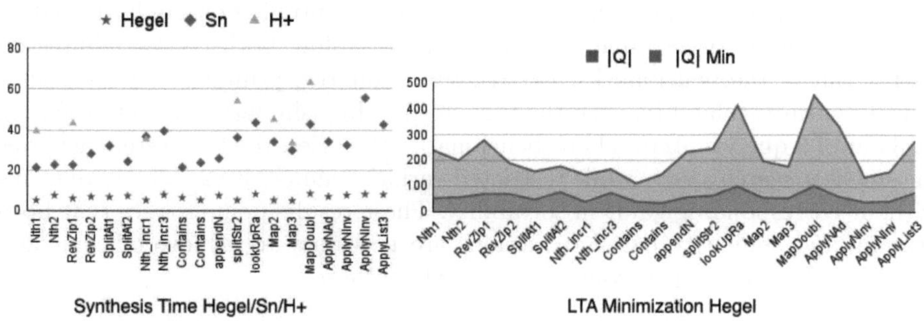

Fig. 11. Synthesis Results for selected RQ1 Benchmarks where at least one of the baselines tools succeeded. Synthesis time in seconds (Left) and LTA Minimization, showing # states without LTA reductions (|Q|) vs with LTA reductions (|Q| Min) (Right).

[7] A detailed description of our benchmark set and evaluation results can be found in the accompanying technical report [27].

7.2 RQ2, Scaling Hegel to Larger and Complex Queries

Benchmarks. To evaluate scalability, we consider eight synthesis queries adapted from verification benchmarks involving stateful database applications [16]. These benchmarks require longer call sequences, explicit state threading, and nontrivial control flow. All benchmarks are expressed using monadic state passing to enable compositional synthesis.

Results. Hegel successfully synthesizes solutions for all RQ2 benchmarks, with synthesis times ranging from 22.7 s to slightly over one minute. *The average size of for these solutions is around 19 function calls (maximum being 33) with around 4 control flow branches on average.* Synquid solves only the smallest benchmarks, requiring over two minutes in those cases, and times out on all larger instances. Hoogle+ fails to solve any benchmark within the timeout of 6 min. Across these benchmarks, the average number of LTA states constructed is approximately 1200. Pruning and minimization reduce the state space by roughly 70 percent, enabling Hegel to scale to substantially more complex synthesis tasks than existing tools.

7.3 RQ3: Impact of Irrelevant Code Pruning and Similarity Reduction

To evaluate the impact of LTA reductions, we conduct ablation experiments using three restricted variants of Hegel: one disabling pruning, one disabling similarity reduction, and a baseline disabling both. We compare variants in terms of total synthesis time and the number of enumerated program terms, relative to the baseline. For RQ1 benchmarks, disabling either pruning or similarity reduction increases synthesis time by 2–3x, while disabling both causes failures on nearly half of the benchmarks. For RQ2 benchmarks, pruning alone is insufficient to ensure scalability, with the variant disabling similarity reduction failing on 3 out of 9 queries. Across both benchmark categories, the full system achieves the smallest search space, while restricted variants enumerate 2–4.5x more terms without corresponding gains in solvability. These results demonstrate that both pruning and similarity based reductions are necessary to achieve efficient and scalable refinement typed component based synthesis.

8 Related Work

Component-Based Synthesis. There is a long line of work on the use of CBS in the context of domain-specific languages [9, 18] as well as general-purpose programming domains [8, 10, 14, 15, 26, 30, 35]. Unlike us, most prior CBS approaches rely on base types [10, 14] or limited effect information [15]. Our contributions in this paper extend prior work by enabling CBS to be applied when specifications and queries are equipped with logical refinements, substantially increasing the complexity of the search process.

Using Similarity/Equality Information for Search. E-graphs [38] allows efficient reduction of an enumeration space similar to the motivation underlying our approach. Equality saturation has been applied to enable efficient abstraction learning [3] inductive synthesis [2] and program analysis [39]. These approaches rely on syntactic equivalence and do not directly support semantic similarity notions based on refinement subtyping or logical entailment.

User provided logical equivalences have also been proposed [31] to accelerate synthesis, but do not scale to large component libraries. Our idea of similarity reduction is also related to the notion of *observational equivalence* found in programming-by-example synthesis aproaches [1,11,23]. These techniques compare synthesized programs on a given set of inputs and prune the search-space in a bottom-up, inductive synthesis setting. Its inherent unsoundness makes this mechanism infeasible for specification-guided synthesis.

Tree Automata for Program Synthesis. Tree automata have been used to compactly represent large spaces of programs [7,12,21,37] in synthesis and verification as discussed in earlier sections. However, these representations cannot express semantic relationships induced by refinement typing rules.

Blaze [36] introduces *abstract finite tree automata* (AFTA), whose states like those of LTAs, are defined by a type and an associated predicate. However, the two models differ fundamentally. First, LTA state annotations are strictly more expressive. AFTA predicates are quantifier-free formulas over an abstract domain [28], whereas LTAs admit quantified formulas over program variables, enabling a direct encoding of refinement typing semantics and the use of refinement subtyping to guide search and reduction. Second, unlike AFTA, LTAs support function types, higher-order programs, and let-bindings, leading to substantially different synthesis algorithms. CTA [24] extends tree automata with logical transition guards from decidable theories, analogous to symbolic finite automata(SFA) [6]. While this enables relational acceptance checking, CTA guards (true for SFA in general) cannot relate sub-automata as in LTA or ECTA, limiting their ability to capture typing and subtyping semantics. LTAs are strictly more general than ECTA since any ECTA can be represented as an LTA that only uses equality constraints. This can be done by replacing ternary transitions like τ (var, base, ref) (see Fig. 3) with a unary one τ (base). The operation is similar to a standard type *erasure* operation [33].

Refinement Types and Conflict-Driven Learning for Synthesis. Refinement types have been used previously to guide program synthesis [21,26,29], most notably in deductive synthesis systems such as Synquid [29]. These approaches focus on deriving programs that satisfy refinement specifications, but do not address scalability in component based synthesis with large libraries as compared extensively in our evaluations. Other synthesis techniques based on conflict driven learning [10,26] avoid re-exploring failing programs, but do not identify semantic equivalences among non failing candidates. Our approach complements refinement based synthesis by introducing a compact representation and similarity based reduction mechanism that scales to complex component based queries.

9 Conclusions

This paper presents a new component-based synthesis algorithm and tool, Hegel, for libraries and queries equipped with refinement-type specifications. Such specifications induce sparse solution spaces, rendering naive enumerative synthesis ineffective. We address this challenge using a novel tree automata variant, Liquid Tree Automata (LTA), which compactly represents the space of well-typed programs, supports efficient construction, and enables semantics-driven pruning via refinement-based similarity. Our evaluation shows that Hegel scales to complex refinement-typed queries beyond the reach of existing synthesis techniques.

Disclosure of Interests. The authors have no competing interests to declare that are relevant to the content of this article.

Data Availability Statement. The Hegel tool and the artifact used in the paper is available in [25].

References

1. Albarghouthi, A., Gulwani, S., Kincaid, Z.: Recursive program synthesis. In: Sharygina, N., Veith, H. (eds.) CAV 2013. LNCS, vol. 8044, pp. 934–950. Springer, Heidelberg (2013). https://doi.org/10.1007/978-3-642-39799-8_67
2. Bowers, M., et al.: Top-down synthesis for library learning. Proc. ACM Program. Lang. **7**(POPL), 1182–1213 (2023)
3. Cao, D., Kunkel, R., Nandi, C., Willsey, M., Tatlock, Z., Polikarpova, N.: babble: Learning better abstractions with e-graphs and anti-unification. Proc. ACM Program. Lang. **7**(POPL), 396–424 (2023)
4. Charguéraud, A., Filliâtre, J.C., Pereira, M., Pottier, F.: VOCAL – a verified OCaml library. In: ML Family Workshop (2017)
5. Comon, H.: Tree Automata Techniques and Applications (1997)
6. D'antoni, L., Veanes, M.: Extended symbolic finite automata and transducers. Form. Methods Syst. Des. **47**(1), 93–119 (2015)
7. Dauchet, M., Caron, A.-C., Coquidé, J.-L.: Automata for reduction properties solving. J. Symb. Comput. **20**(2), 215–233 (1995)
8. Feng, Y., Martins, R., Bastani, O., Dillig, I.: Program synthesis using conflict-driven learning. In: Proceedings of the 39th ACM SIGPLAN Conference on Programming Language Design and Implementation, PLDI 2018, pp. 420–435. Association for Computing Machinery, New York (2018)
9. Feng, Y., Martins, R., Van Geffen, J., Dillig, I., Chaudhuri, S.: Component-based synthesis of table consolidation and transformation tasks from examples. In: Proceedings of the 38th ACM SIGPLAN Conference on Programming Language Design and Implementation, PLDI 2017, pp. 422–436. Association for Computing Machinery, New York (2017)

10. Feng, Y., Martins, R., Wang, Y., Dillig, I., Reps, T.W.: Component-based synthesis for complex APIs. In: Proceedings of the 44th ACM SIGPLAN Symposium on Principles of Programming Languages, POPL 2017, pp. 599–612. Association for Computing Machinery, New York (2017)
11. Feser, J., Dillig, I., Solar-Lezama, A.: Inductive program synthesis guided by observational program similarity. Proc. ACM Program. Lang. **7**(OOPSLA2), 912–940 (2023)
12. Finkbeiner, B., Klein, F., Piskac, R., Santolucito, M.: Synthesizing functional reactive programs. In: Proceedings of the 12th ACM SIGPLAN International Symposium on Haskell, Haskell 2019, pp. 162–175. Association for Computing Machinery, New York (2019)
13. Flanagan, C., Sabry, A., Duba, B.F., Felleisen, M.: The essence of compiling with continuations. In: Proceedings of the ACM SIGPLAN 1993 Conference on Programming Language Design and Implementation, PLDI '93, pp. 237–247. Association for Computing Machinery, New York (1993)
14. Guo, Z., et al.: Program synthesis by type-guided abstraction refinement. Proc. ACM Program. Lang. **4**(POPL), 1–28 (2019)
15. Guria, S.N., Foster, J.S., Van Horn, D.: RbSyn: type- and effect-guided program synthesis. In: Proceedings of the 42nd ACM SIGPLAN International Conference on Programming Language Design and Implementation, PLDI 2021, pp. 344–358. Association for Computing Machinery, New York (2021)
16. Itzhaky, S., et al.: On the automated verification of web applications with embedded SQL. In: Benedikt, M., Orsi, G. (eds.) 20th International Conference on Database Theory, ICDT 2017, Venice, Italy, 21–24 March 2017, vol. 68 of LIPIcs, pp. 16:1–16:18. Schloss Dagstuhl - Leibniz-Zentrum für Informatik (2017)
17. James, M.B., et al.: Digging for fold: synthesis-aided API discovery for haskell. Proc. ACM Program. Lang. **4**(OOPSLA), 1–27 (2020)
18. Jha, S., Gulwani, S., Seshia, S.A., Tiwari, A.: Oracle-guided component-based program synthesis. In: Proceedings of the 32nd ACM/IEEE International Conference on Software Engineering, vol. 1, ICSE '10, pp. 215–224. Association for Computing Machinery, New York (2010)
19. Jhala, R., Vazou, N.: Refinement types: a tutorial. Found. Trends Program. Lang. **6**(3–4), 159–317 (2021)
20. Kaki, G., Jagannathan, S.: A relational framework for higher-order shape analysis. In: Proceedings of the 19th ACM SIGPLAN International Conference on Functional Programming, ICFP '14, pp. 311–324. Association for Computing Machinery, New York (2014)
21. Koppel, J., Guo, Z., de Vries, E., Solar-Lezama, A., Polikarpova, N.: Searching entangled program spaces. Proc. ACM Program. Lang. **6**(ICFP), 23–51 (2022)
22. Lau, T.A., Domingos, P., Weld, D.S.: Version space algebra and its application to programming by demonstration. In: Proceedings of the Seventeenth International Conference on Machine Learning, ICML '00, pp. 527–534. Morgan Kaufmann Publishers Inc., San Francisco (2000)
23. Miltner, A., Nuñez, A.T., Brendel, A., Chaudhuri, S., Dilig, I.: Bottom-up synthesis of recursive functional programs using angelic execution. Proc. ACM Program. Lang. **6**, 1–29 (2022)
24. Miltner, A., Wang, Z., Chaudhuri, S., Dillig, I.: Relational synthesis of recursive programs via constraint annotated tree automata. In: Computer Aided Verification: 36th International Conference, CAV 2024, Montreal, QC, Canada, 24–27 July 2024, Proceedings, Part III, pp. 41–63. Springer-Verlag, Heidelberg (2024). https://doi.org/10.1007/978-3-031-65633-0_3

25. Mishra, A., Jaganathan, S.: Artifact for the CAV 2026 Paper: Liquid Tree Automata. Zenodo (2026). https://doi.org/10.5281/zenodo.19821156
26. Mishra, A., Jagannathan, S.: Specification-guided component-based synthesis from effectful libraries. Proc. ACM Program. Lang. **6**(OOPSLA2), 616–645 (2022)
27. Mishra, A., Jagannathan, S.: Liquid Tree Automata (2026). https://arxiv.org/abs/2605.13456
28. Nielson, F., Nielson, H.R., Hankin, C.: Abstract Interpretation, pp. 211–282. Springer, Heidelberg (1999)
29. Polikarpova, N., Kuraj, I., Solar-Lezama, A.: Program synthesis from polymorphic refinement types. In: Proceedings of the 37th ACM SIGPLAN Conference on Programming Language Design and Implementation, PLDI '16, pp. 522–538. Association for Computing Machinery, New York (2016)
30. Shi, K., Steinhardt, J., Liang, P.: FrAngel: component-based synthesis with control structures. Proc. ACM Program. Lang. **3**(POPL), 1–29 (2019)
31. Smith, C., Albarghouthi, A.: Program synthesis with equivalence reduction. In: Enea, C., Piskac, R. (eds.) VMCAI 2019. LNCS, vol. 11388, pp. 24–47. Springer, Cham (2019). https://doi.org/10.1007/978-3-030-11245-5_2
32. Swamy, N., Weinberger, J., Schlesinger, C., Chen, J., Livshits, B.: Verifying higher-order programs with the Dijkstra monad. In: Proceedings of the 34th ACM SIGPLAN Conference on Programming Language Design and Implementation, PLDI '13, pp. 387–398. Association for Computing Machinery, New York (2013)
33. Vazou, N., Bakst, A., Jhala, R.: Bounded refinement types. In: Proceedings of the 20th ACM SIGPLAN International Conference on Functional Programming, ICFP 2015, pp. 48–61. Association for Computing Machinery, New York (2015)
34. Vazou, N., Rondon, P.M., Jhala, R.: Abstract refinement types. In: Felleisen, M., Gardner, P. (eds.) ESOP 2013. LNCS, vol. 7792, pp. 209–228. Springer, Heidelberg (2013). https://doi.org/10.1007/978-3-642-37036-6_13
35. Wang, C., Feng, Y., Bodik, R., Cheung, A.,Dillig, I : Visualization by example. Proc. ACM Program. Lang. **4**(POPL) (2019)
36. Wang, X., Dillig, I., Singh, R.: Program synthesis using abstraction refinement. Proc. ACM Program. Lang. **2**(POPL) (2017)
37. Wang, X., Dillig, I., Singh, R.: Synthesis of data completion scripts using finite tree automata. Proc. ACM Program. Lang. **1**(OOPSLA) (2017)
38. Willsey, M., Nandi, C., Wang, Y.R., Flatt, O., Tatlock, Z., Panchekha, P.: Egg: fast and extensible equality saturation. Proc. ACM Program. Lang. **5**(POPL) (2021)
39. Zhang, Y., et al.: Better together: unifying datalog and equality saturation. Proc. ACM Program. Lang. **7**(PLDI) (2023)

SemML 2.0: Synthesizing Controllers for LTL

Jan Křetínský[1,2], Tobias Meggendorfer[3], and Maximilian Prokop[1,2(✉)]

[1] Masaryk University, Brno, Czech Republic
prokopm@in.tum.de
[2] Technical University of Munich, Munich, Germany
[3] Lancaster University Leipzig, Leipzig, Germany

Abstract. Synthesizing a reactive system from specifications given in linear temporal logic (LTL) is a classical problem, finding its applications in safety-critical systems design. These systems are typically represented using either Mealy machines or AIGER circuits. We present the second version of SemML, which outperforms all state-of-the-art tools for finding either solution. Aside from implementing the classical automata-theoretic approach, our tool utilizes partial exploration and machine-learning guidance for obtaining solutions efficiently, and numerous heuristics and improvements of classic algorithms for extracting small representations of these solutions. We evaluate our tool against the existing state-of-the-art tools (in particular Strix, LtlSynt, and the previous version of SemML) on the dataset of the synthesis competition SYNTCOMP. We show that we solve significantly more instances and do so much faster than other tools, while maintaining state-of-the-art solution quality.

1 Introduction

Linear-Temporal-Logic (LTL) [21] reactive synthesis [22] is a prominent cornerstone in the long-standing quest of creating reliable software and hardware. Intuitively, the task is to create a reactive system that adheres to a specification given in LTL, and thus is "correct by construction". Additionally, LTL synthesis is a basic building block for synthesis problems in more complex domains. For instance, LTL-modulo-theories synthesis [25,26] or synthesis over infinite arenas [3] have recently emerged as extensions with practical motivation. As LTL synthesis forms a subroutine in their counterexample-refinement loops, the demand for efficient and scalable LTL synthesis tools becomes even more prominent.

On the one hand, LTL synthesis is 2-EXPTIME-complete, and thus has long remained out of reach for practical applications. On the other hand, recent advances in translating LTL formulae to small deterministic automata, e.g. [8], reignited practical interest in synthesis through the classical automata-theoretic approach [29]. Indeed, the LTL tracks of the synthesis competition SYNTCOMP [12] have been won by tools based on these advances since 2018, e.g. Strix [19].

E. Darulova et al. (Eds.): CAV 2026, LNCS 16682, pp. 308–321, 2026.
https://doi.org/10.1007/978-3-032-32519-8_16

Furthermore, in contrast to the determinization of Safra [27] and others [20,28], these translations additionally provide LTL "labels" for each automaton state, which intuitively describe its *semantics* (i.e. what remains to be satisfied from here onward). Exploiting this *semantic labelling* through various means, including machine learning (ML), is the foundational idea of our tool SemML. In its previous version [14], SemML demonstrated how partial exploration of the automaton guided by ML evaluation of this labelling further increases the scalability of this approach. In particular, SemML won the *realizability* track of SYNTCOMP, i.e. determining whether a given specification is satisfiable or not. However, additionally constructing a concrete system that does satisfy the specification (i.e. a witness to realizability) is highly relevant for most practical applications (and thus constitutes the *synthesis* track). Here, SemML only implemented "textbook" approaches, without practical optimizations, locking away its significant potential for these use cases.

On the one hand, SYNTCOMP only considers solutions in the form of AIGER circuits [4] (for fair comparison of different approaches), and only evaluates solutions for instances that are realizable in the first place (i.e. where a satisfying system exists). Hence, many of the participating tools only focus on this specific application. On the other hand, providing a reason why a given instance is not satisfiable (i.e. a counterexample) often is equally interesting, e.g. for the counter-example guided refinement loops in [3,25,26]. Further, constructing the system (or counterexample) in the form of an explicit finite state machine (Mealy machine [17]) is often desired or even required for several applications. In particular, this new functionality of our tool has already been successfully applied to several of the mentioned refinement approaches (e.g. `sweap` [2,3]). Altogether, aside from providing competitive circuits for realizable solutions, there is a need for more general forms of solution extraction.

Our Contributions. We address numerous practical shortcomings in the previous version of our tool, vastly improving the efficiency and quality of computed solutions. To this end, we

- implement efficient extraction of both Mealy machines and AIGER circuits, both as witnesses and counterexamples,
- implement heuristical and SAT-based Mealy machine minimizations ...
- ... including a non-trivial extension of the `MeMin` algorithm [1],
- add various approaches towards circuit minimization, including several non-trivial extensions to our BDD library,
- significantly re-work the ML-guided exploration for further speed-ups, and
- add numerous engineering improvements to all stages of the pipeline.

We thoroughly evaluate the efficiency of our improvements on the entire benchmark set of SYNTCOMP 2025, comparing to our previous version and other state-of-the-art tools LTLSYNT and Strix (the previous winners of SYNTCOMP). We solve significantly more samples, and do so much faster, while providing solutions of comparable or even significantly better quality. In particular, the Mealy machines produced by our tool are significantly smaller.

2 Tool Description

We provide an overview of our new version of SemML by first formally stating the problem, describing how to use the tool, and explaining its high-level approach.

LTL Synthesis. The problem of LTL reactive synthesis is defined as follows. We are given an LTL [21] formula ϕ over a set of atomic propositions AP together with a partition of AP into *environment* and *system* propositions $\mathsf{AP} = \mathsf{AP}_{\mathsf{ENV}} \cup \mathsf{AP}_{\mathsf{SYS}}$. The environment and system generate an infinite word by repeatedly choosing which of "their" atomic propositions to enable in each step (with the environment typically choosing first). The system wins this "game" if the obtained word satisfies ϕ. The central question is whether the system has a *winning strategy*, i.e. a way to choose which propositions to enable so that the combined word always satisfies the given formula. In that case, the instance is called *realizable* and *unrealizable* otherwise (this decision problem is called *LTL realizability*). For example, the formula $\phi = \mathbf{G}(r \Leftrightarrow \mathbf{X}g)$ with $\mathsf{AP}_{\mathsf{SYS}} = \{r\}$ and $\mathsf{AP}_{\mathsf{ENV}} = \{g\}$ prescribes that whenever the environment sends a *r*equest, the system should in the next step *g*rant the request, and only then. This formula is realizable, and a winning strategy is to remember whether the environment sent a request in the previous step. The problem of *LTL synthesis* asks for a concise representation of this winning strategy, typically as *Mealy machine* [17] or *AIGER circuit* [4], or report that no such strategy exists.

Tool Usage. SemML supports explicit input via an LTL formula and a partition of the propositions or, equivalently, a TLSF file [11] as used by SYNTCOMP. It can solve both realizability and synthesis problems, where both output as Mealy machines or AIGER circuits is supported. Further, SemML additionally supports counterexamples in both formats (i.e. a winning strategy of the environment for unrealizable formulae). An example invocation looks like this:

```
semml.py -f 'G(r <-> X g)' --ins=r --outs=g
```

For compatibility and simplicity, we provide SemML in a Docker container paired with a Python wrapper script, directly including the third-party dependencies `syfco` [11] (TLSF conversion), `abc` [9] (AIGER circuit simplifier), and `kissat` [5] (efficient SAT solver). To validate our implementation, we also implemented our own model checker for Mealy machines and circuits on top of numerous assertions.

High-Level Architecture. SemML solves LTL Synthesis via the *automaton-theoretic* approach [29]. Here, the formula is first translated into an equivalent automaton (typically a parity automaton, DPA). This automaton serves as an arena for a graph game where the winning condition for the system is the automaton's acceptance. Thus, a winning strategy in this game means the system can

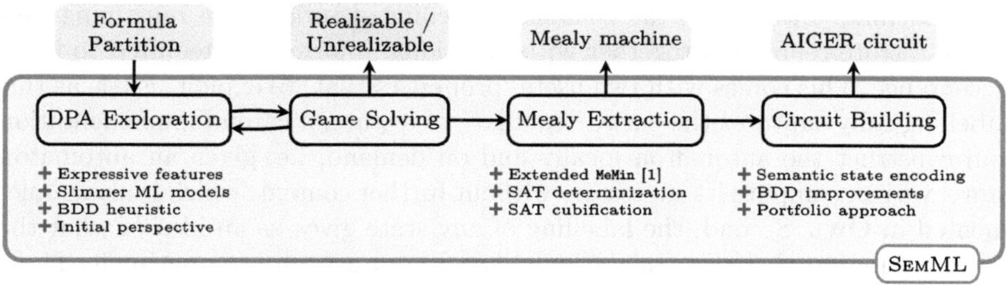

Fig. 1. Structural overview of SEMML's high-level architecture. All items marked by + are novel or significant improvements over our prior version. Additionally, several minor engineering improvements have been added to all stages.

force an accepting word in the automaton and thus satisfy the original formula. While in theory, these steps happen sequentially, in practice, SEMML interleaves automata construction and game solving, and employs ML heuristics to guide the construction (see [14] for full details).

For synthesis, SEMML then encodes the winning strategy as a Mealy machine or an AIGER circuit. Mealy machines naturally arise from the automata-theoretic approach, as they directly correspond to the reachable part of the automaton. We employ several minimization heuristics and extend the `MeMin` approach to more general Mealy machines. AIGER circuits are then obtained by applying the *Huffman* procedure for converting the Mealy machine to a circuit [10]. Here, we again employ several heuristics and minimization procedures. An overview of this architecture and the improvements over the previous version is given in Fig. 1.

3 Controller Synthesis with *SEMML*

As outlined in Fig. 1, this version of SEMML comes with several advancements compared to its predecessor. Due to space constraints, we provide an intuitive walk-through of the entire pipeline and highlight significant improvements with an intuitive explanation. Technical descriptions can be found in [16, App. B].

3.1 The Reactive Synthesis Pipeline of SemML

Semantic LTL-to-Automaton Translation. As its predecessor, SEMML uses OWL [15] to convert the LTL formula into an equivalent automaton. Internally, OWL uses *binary decision diagrams* (BDDs) [6], whose performance notoriously depends on their *variable ordering*. SEMML employs an intuitive heuristic to obtain a practically performant variable ordering (see [16, App. B.1] for details).

Furthermore, the translations of OWL are "semantic". This means that states are identified by a structured collection of LTL formulae (so-called *semantic labelling*, example in [16, App. A.2]) and successors are purely derived from this labelling. Intuitively, the semantic labelling describes the remaining language a state represents together with additional information required to track acceptance. This comes with two useful properties that we exploit. First, as this labelling fully captures the entire "context" of a state, a careful implementation can construct the automaton locally and on demand, i.e. given an automaton state, we can compute its successors without further context, which is also implemented in OWL. Second, the labelling of any state gives us an idea of what the automaton after that state might look like without actually computing it. These two properties enable a *guided partial exploration* approach, which is the core idea of our tool.

We provide full details of our construction and the resulting semantic labelling in [16, App. A.2], including so far unpublished optimizations already used in the prior version of SEMML as well as STRIX.

Guiding Partial Exploration. The (parity) automaton can be of double exponential size. However, when solving the game, in practice, often only a small part of the arena is actually reachable and thus necessary for deciding the winner. Thus, SEMML uses a partial exploration approach where it alternates between constructing the automaton and probing whether the currently constructed part already suffices to find a solution. Ideally, this approach explores the "relevant" parts (i.e. the ones that will be reachable under a winning strategy) of the automaton first. Therefore, SEMML uses machine learning based on the semantic labelling (i.e. feature-embeddings thereof) to heuristically identify winning choices and guide the exploration. For a detailed discussion of the exploration algorithm and the interplay with the game solver, we refer to our previous version [14].

Clearly, the practical gain of this approach heavily depends both on (i) how well these models predict winning choices, and (ii) how much overhead computing the guidance introduces. In this work, we improve both points. First, we introduce new, expressive features of the semantic labelling, allowing for better guidance (see [16, App. B.2]). Second, enabled by our new features, we simplify our model architecture to reduce inference time (see [16, App. B.3]). Moreover, as exploration happens from one player's perspective at a time, we introduce a new ML model to heuristically identify which player should explore first (see [16, App. B.4]).

Extracting Solutions. After finding a winning strategy, we need to encode it into the desired format (Mealy machines or AIGER circuits). While both steps are simple theoretically, numerous heuristics are required to obtain practically competitive results. In its previous version, SEMML only implemented the "textbook" method, without any sophisticated heuristics. We fully reworked the approach, implementing improvements at all stages. This allows us to solve much larger instances and obtain highly competitive controllers.

Mealy Extraction. Our game solver provides us with *non-deterministic* strategies, meaning that instead of fixing a single choice in each state, it can allow for a set of choices where any choice is correct. As such, it represents a set of strategies, i.e. a set of Mealy machines. Our goal is to find a small Mealy machine within that set, which we achieve through several heuristics. Our primary, SAT-based route works as follows: We first search for a small (successor-deterministic) Mealy machine in this set. Through a non-trivial extension of MeMin [1], we then reduce this Mealy machine (i.e. without a determinization of the outputs that MeMin requires, see Sect. 3.2). Only after the minimization, we further determinize the machine (see [16, App. B.5]), which intuitively allows the minimization to consider a larger amount of different behaviors to find matching states or edges. Since each of these steps involves numerous SAT queries, we added an efficient DIMACS interface to communicate with `kissat` [5]. Moreover, we employ several bounding heuristics and, in case the heuristical bound is too large, we switch to a faster but less efficient approach based on bisimulation reduction [24].

Circuit Extraction. Obtaining circuits from Mealy machines then follows the Huffman procedure [10]. First, the states of the mealy machine are encoded as bit strings (known as the *state encoding*), i.e. being in a particular state is represented by a particular combination of latches. Then, the behaviour of every latch and output signal is translated to a circuit.

While any state encoding gives a correct circuit, finding an encoding that e.g. exploits certain symmetries in the Mealy machine can drastically reduce the size of the circuit. Here, we provide an approach extending the (unpublished) *structured* approach of STRIX, which is based on the semantic labelling of the Mealy machine (see [16, App. B.6]). (This also means that the semantic labelling needs to be preserved during the minimization step.) To derive the circuit formulae, we follow the common approach to use binary decision diagrams (BDDs), as they naturally identify shared sub-formulae. We implemented support for complement edges and "reduced-universe-simplification" in BDD library `JBDD` [18] for additional reductions (see [16, App. B.7]). Intuitively, a BDD with complement edges can represent $a \wedge b$ and $\neg(a \wedge b)$ using the same node (once complemented), whereas a classical BDD requires different nodes. Further, when constructing the BDD nodes, we only need to ensure equivalence on actually reachable assignments. This yields additional degrees of freedom that can be used to achieve smaller simplified formulae which are only equivalent on the "reduced universe" of reachable assignments, which can be achieved efficiently on BDDs. (Formally, we can compute $g = \texttt{RESTRICT}(f, h)$, such that $g(x) = f(x)$ on all assignments x where $h(x)$ is true, but g potentially is much smaller than f, see e.g. [13, Exercise 92].) As a last step, we employ the generic circuit reduction tool `abc` [9] to compress the final circuit even further. As this pipeline contains many (partially optional) steps with complex interactions and it is often not clear which combination will yield the best results, we employ a portfolio of different configurations and return the smallest result (see [16, App. B.8] for details), similar to STRIX.

3.2 Extended Mealy Minimization

Here, we provide insights into our approach towards minimizing non-deterministic Mealy machines in more detail, as it comprises a novel extension of the `MeMin` [1] algorithm, and can be used independently of our pipeline. Recall that the game solver provides us with a non-deterministic strategy.

Successor Determinism. A Mealy machine is *successor deterministic* if for every state-input letter combination, the successor state of the machine is fixed (non-determinism in the output however is allowed). To apply the `MeMin` approach, we first need to extract such a machine from the non-deterministic parity game solution. Moreover, this machine should be as small as possible. To this end, we first heuristically determine an upper bound (using a simple graph search). If that upper bound is reasonably small, we then encode reachability and determinacy constraints into a SAT query and then search for a minimal model using counting constraints to reduce the strategy further.

MeMin with Non-deterministic Outputs. Starting from such a (successor-deterministic) Mealy machine, the `MeMin` [1] approach essentially tries to find sets of states ("classes") where all states of a class should for the same input be able to produce the same output and transition to (states of) the same successor class. Then, a (potentially smaller) *covering* Mealy machine is given by using the classes as new states, i.e. the new Mealy machine is consistent with the larger, non-deterministic one. (Note that one state can belong to multiple classes.)

For a fixed number of classes, the relevant constraints can be cast into a SAT query using a clever encoding. This allows us to search for the minimal required number of classes to obtain a covering machine. Paired with several heuristics, this approach can achieve significant reductions. However, to apply it to Mealy machines arising in our context, several adaptations are required (some of which are described in the original paper).

For example, instead of considering all 2^{AP_S} different output symbols, we can derive "meta-symbols" representing sets of outputs. In [1], an approach for Mealy machines with *cubes* as outputs is given. (A cube effectively is given by a conjunction of (potentially negated) variables, e.g. $a \wedge b \wedge \neg c$.) Essentially, one derives a partitioning of 2^{AP_S} such that every occurring output cube is a union of elements of this partition, and every such partition element becomes a meta-symbol. While [1] assumes that machines have cube outputs (likely due to the used input file format), this is not the case for us. To apply their approach, we thus would first need to "cubify" our output sets heuristically, eliminating potential for identifying shared outputs in the minimization. While Strix and LTLSYNT implement this approach, we adapt the core algorithm of `MeMin` to use arbitrary output sets. This requires deep modifications, since the SAT encoding of `MeMin` is built around the assumption that if a set of states is pairwise compatible (i.e. each pair shares an output) then they are compatible as a whole (i.e. the entire set shares an output). While this is implied by cube outputs, it no longer holds when we allow for arbitrary outputs. We solve this by introducing additional constraints that ensure this consistency. (Intuitively, we require that if state x belongs to class y, then one of state x's output partitions needs to be available in class y.) At the same time, we aim to preserve the performance of the original approach and only introduce these constraints where necessary.

In terms of heuristics, [1] identifies an initial lower bound on the number of classes by heuristically identifying an as-large-as-possible set of pairwise incompatible states. This problem effectively is a maximum clique search in the incompatibility graph. As suggested in their paper, we also added a SAT-based maximization to further refine the heuristical lower bound.

4 Empirical Evaluation

In this section, we aim to empirically answer the following research questions:

RQ1 How efficient is SEMML at solving LTL synthesis tasks?
RQ2 How big is the impact of the improvements presented in this work?
RQ3 Do speed gains come at the cost of lower quality (i.e. larger) solutions?

To answer these questions, we evaluate our tool (and competitors) on the full SYNTCOMP [12] dataset (2025 iteration), comparing the number of solves, time required, and solution quality as defined in SYNTCOMP. We first describe the experimental setup, including benchmarks, metrics evaluated, and competing tools, before discussing the results for each question separately.

4.1 Description

Tools. We compare $\text{SEMML}_{2.0}$ against the prior version [14] (written $\text{SEMML}_{1.0}$ here), which won the Realizability track of SYNTCOMP 2024 and came in second in 2025. Further, we compare to STRIX [19] and LTLSYNT [23]. STRIX also follows a partial exploration approach and provides state-of-the-art solution quality, winning the LTL tracks in all iterations of SYNTCOMP since its publication until stopping participation in 2023. LTLSYNT, part of SPOT, instead relies on highly optimized automata constructions and practical optimizations such as checks for immediately obvious strategies. Further, LTLSYNT won the LTL tracks of SYNTCOMP 2025.[1]

Data. We use the SYNTCOMP 2025 benchmark set, comprising 1585 LTL synthesis benchmarks. Note that these are of widely varying difficulty: 924 instances are solved by *all* tools in under 10 s, and 128 are solved by none in 30 min. In other words, the set of "interesting" benchmarks is only a few hundred large, and being able to solve a few dozen more is significant.

We note that our ML models were trained on purely synthetic data, i.e. they have never "seen" SYNTCOMP data.

[1] Personal communication with the authors of LTLSYNT confirmed that it was not updated since 2024. Rather, new benchmarks of SYNTCOMP 2025 triggered a trivial-to-fix crash in SemML.

Setup. We perform 3 separate runs with different targets over the entire benchmark set, namely (i) deciding realizability (Real), (ii) synthesizing a Mealy machine (Mealy), and (iii) synthesizing an AIGER circuit (Aiger). We ran each tool using the best-performing flags and options according to the last SYNTCOMP they participated in. Our experiments were run on a server with 40 cores of an Intel E5-2630 v4 CPU and 252 GB of RAM. As in SYNTCOMP, we employ a timeout of 30 min per benchmark.

Table 1. Summary of our main experimental results. For every track, we report the number of solved instances and average solution quality where applicable (measured by the SYNTCOMP sore, higher is better). Finally, we report the average speed-up of SemML compared to other tools when constructing AIGER circuits (considering only non-trivial samples, where at least one tool required over 30 s, including timeouts).

	Real	Mealy		Aiger		Avg Speedup
Tool	Solves	Solves	Quality	Solves	Quality	(> 30s)
SemML$_{2.0}$	**1412**	**1391**	1.92	**1375**	1.82	
SemML$_{1.0}$	1361	–	–	1273	1.38	5.59
Strix	1346	1314	1.70	1330	1.85	2.56
ltlsynt	1319	1204	1.68	1213	1.28	3.85

Metrics. We use the metrics of SYNTCOMP. Primarily, we are interested in the total number of instances solved within the timelimit. Furthermore, on realizable formulae, solution quality is measured by a score, defined as follows. Each solution receives $2 - \log((s+1)/(r+1))$ points, where s and r are the size of the tool's solution and the size of the best known solution (i.e. the best of the 4 tools), respectively. In other words, the best solution gets 2 points, a solution that is one order of magnitude larger gets 1 point. This score then is averaged over all benchmarks a tool solved. For Mealy machines, size is defined as the number of states and edges, and for AIGER circuits the number of latches and gates. Note that the quality score is not directly penalized for timeouts, and thus should not be considered in isolation.

To compare runtimes, we compute the (geometric) mean of the ratios between SemML's and other tools' runtimes per sample. To avoid this ratio being blurred by constant time overhead (e.g. JVM startup and loading of ML model parameters), we consider only non-trivial instances, i.e. where at least one tool required more than 30 s. When a tool ran into the 30-min timeout, we use that timeout value for the runtime ratio (benefiting tools with more timeouts).

4.2 Results and Discussion

Our results are presented in Table 1. Based on these, we discuss each research question separately. We provide an extensive analysis of our experiments, including detailed pairwise tool comparisons across all metrics, in the appendix.

RQ1. We observe that SemML$_{2.0}$ solves the most LTL synthesis benchmarks of SYNTCOMP across all three tracks. In particular, on Mealy and Aiger, our tool solves significantly more instances (77 and 45, respectively) than the prior state-of-the-art tool Strix. Recall that due to the small set of "challenging but feasible" instances in SYNTCOMP, this marks a major advancement. For runtime, we observe that SemML$_{2.0}$ offers an average speed-up of at least 2.5x compared to other tools. Interestingly, we can observe that both Strix and ltlsynt solve more Aiger than Mealy cases. This is especially surprising for Strix, which also employs the automaton-theoretic approach and constructs an intermediate Mealy machine. However, its Aiger-pipeline contains optimizations and heuristics which are not enabled when constructing Mealy machines. Further data and analysis can be found in [16, App. C].

RQ2. To assess the impact our presented improvements, we compare to the previous version SemML$_{1.0}$. For realizability, we observe 51 additional solves, which we attribute to our improved exploration guidance and engineering improvements in the exploration phase. More importantly, prior to this work, SemML$_{1.0}$ only implemented an unoptimized "textbook" approach to extracting circuits, and did not support Mealy machine output. Our new pipeline managed 102 additional solves on Aiger. Notably, only with these improvements, SemML managed to surpass the prior state-of-the-art Strix.

RQ3. Comparing our average quality score with other tools, in particular Strix, shows that our performance improvements do not come at the cost of solution quality (recall that quality is only computed on instances where a tool does not time out and should not be compared in isolation). To further investigate the performance-quality trade-off, we also implemented a "fast mode", which does not employ SAT-based reductions but only heuristics and the bisimulation-based reduction. Here, we manage even more solves (1392 on the Aiger track), however now with a steep quality reduction (down to 1.59). Further, note that while the average score is very similar to Strix, there is quite a bit of variance among benchmarks. In particular, there are samples where we produce much smaller circuits than Strix and vice versa, hinting at great potential for a solver portfolio like NeuroSynt [7]. For further details, see [16, App. C].

For Mealy machines, our solution quality even significantly exceeds that of Strix, scoring a near-perfect 1.9. We conjecture two main reasons. First, our extension of MeMin finds machines using fewer states. This is due to more matching behaviors still being available, as we did not eliminate them through any upfront cubification. Second, both Strix and ltlsynt seem to assume that the inputs of any edge are given as cubes, whereas we support edges with arbitrary Boolean expressions, heavily reducing the total number of edges required. Again, for a more detailed analysis of this, we refer to [16, App. C].

Summary. SemML$_{2.0}$ solves the most benchmarks across all three tracks and requires the least time to do so. This is achieved without a notable decrease in the quality of AIGER circuits and furthermore accompanied by a notable increase in the quality of Mealy-machines (which in several cases are more relevant than AIGER circuits). Altogether, based on our observations, $\text{SemML}_{2.0}$ is the best tool available for any LTL synthesis queries.

5 Conclusion and Future Work

With the implemented improvements at all stages and now the controller construction (synthesis in the narrower sense), SemML becomes the state-of-the-art tool for *all* standard LTL synthesis tasks, namely realizability, Mealy machine synthesis, and AIGER circuit synthesis. Methodologically, SemML illustrates that machine learning can aid in safety-critical contexts without sacrificing correctness guarantees. Practically, as SemML constructs counterexamples efficiently, it becomes useful for counterexample-guided refinement approaches.

For future work, we identify several avenues. First, it might be desirable to design an incremental variant of this synthesis pipeline. Indeed, since queries in the CEGAR applications are often only slight derivations from each other, a lot of intermediate results can often be reused instead of recomputing them every time from scratch. Second, we believe that even the successor determinization can be integrated into the `MeMin` process, further increasing the potential for reductions. Thirdly, we conjecture that there is still a lot of potential in reducing circuit size by finding appropriate state encodings, especially by further exploiting the semantic labelling. Finally, another advantage to be explored is that controllers generated by SemML are semantically labelled, which could provide e.g. runtime explanations or insight into counterexamples.

Acknowledgments. This research has received funding from the European Union under Grant Agreement No. 101171844, ERC project Intelligence-Oriented Verification&Controller Synthesis (InOVationCS). Views and opinions expressed are, however, those of the authors only and do not necessarily reflect those of the European Union or European Research Executive Agency. Neither the European Union nor the granting authority can be held responsible for them. This research has also received funding from the MUNI Award in Science and Humanities MUNI/I/1757/2021 of the Grant Agency of Masaryk University.

Data Availibility Statement. SemML is further developed at https://gitlab.com/live-lab/software/semml. The artefact containing all tools, benchmarks, and scripts to reproduce our results is available at https://doi.org/10.5281/zenodo.19763387.

Disclosure of Interests. The authors have no competing interests to declare that are relevant to the content of this article.

References

1. Abel, A., Reineke, J.: Memin: sat-based exact minimization of incompletely specified mealy machines. In: Proceedings of the IEEE/ACM International Conference on Computer-Aided Design, ICCAD 2015, Austin, TX, USA, 2–6 November 2015, pp. 94–101 (2015). https://doi.org/10.1109/ICCAD.2015.7372555
2. Azzopardi, S., Stefano, L.D., Piterman, N.: sweap: reactive synthesis for infinite-state integer problems. In: CAV (2026)
3. Azzopardi, S., Stefano, L.D., Piterman, N., Schneider, G.: Full LTL synthesis over infinite-state arenas. In: Piskac, R., Rakamaric, Z. (eds.) Computer Aided Verification - 37th International Conference, CAV 2025, Zagreb, Croatia, 23–25 July 2025, Proceedings, Part IV. Lecture Notes in Computer Science, vol. 15934, pp. 274–297. Springer (2025). https://doi.org/10.1007/978-3-031-98685-7_13
4. Biere, A.: The AIGER And-Inverter Graph (AIG) format version 20071012. Technical report 07/1, Institute for Formal Models and Verification, Johannes Kepler University, Altenbergerstr. 69, 4040 Linz, Austria (2007)
5. Biere, A., Faller, T., Fazekas, K., Fleury, M., Froleyks, N., Pollitt, F.: CaDiCaL, Gimsatul, IsaSAT and Kissat entering the SAT competition 2024. In: Heule, M., Iser, M., Järvisalo, M., Suda, M. (eds.) Proceedings of SAT Competition 2024 – Solver, Benchmark and Proof Checker Descriptions. Department of Computer Science Report Series B, vol. B-2024-1, pp. 8–10. University of Helsinki (2024)
6. Bryant, R.E.: Graph-based algorithms for boolean function manipulation. IEEE Trans. Comput. **35**(8), 677–691 (1986). https://doi.org/10.1109/TC.1986.1676819
7. Cosler, M., Hahn, C., Omar, A., Schmitt, F.: Neurosynt: a neuro-symbolic portfolio solver for reactive synthesis. In: Finkbeiner, B., Kovács, L. (eds.) Tools and Algorithms for the Construction and Analysis of Systems - 30th International Conference, TACAS 2024, Held as Part of the European Joint Conferences on Theory and Practice of Software, ETAPS 2024, Luxembourg City, Luxembourg, April 6-11, 2024, Proceedings, Part III. Lecture Notes in Computer Science, vol. 14572, pp. 45–67. Springer (2024). https://doi.org/10.1007/978-3-031-57256-2_3
8. Esparza, J., Kretínský, J., Sickert, S.: A unified translation of linear temporal logic to ω-automata. J. ACM **67**(6), 33:1–33:61 (2020). https://doi.org/10.1145/3417995
9. Fan, L., Wu, C.: FPGA technology mapping with adaptive gate decomposition. In: Ienne, P., Zhang, Z. (eds.) Proceedings of the 2023 ACM/SIGDA International Symposium on Field Programmable Gate Arrays, FPGA 2023, Monterey, CA, USA, 12–14 February 2023, pp. 135–140. ACM (2023). https://doi.org/10.1145/3543622.3573048
10. Huffman, D.: The synthesis of sequential switching circuits. J. Franklin Inst. **257**(3), 161–190 (1954). https://doi.org/10.1016/0016-0032(54)90574-8
11. Jacobs, S., Klein, F., Schirmer, S.: A high-level LTL synthesis format: TLSF v1.1. In: Piskac, R., Dimitrova, R. (eds.) Proceedings Fifth Workshop on Synthesis, SYNT@CAV 2016, Toronto, Canada, 17–18 July 2016. EPTCS, vol. 229, pp. 112–132 (2016). https://doi.org/10.4204/EPTCS.229.10
12. Jacobs, S., et al.: The reactive synthesis competition (SYNTCOMP): 2018–2021. Int. J. Softw. Tools Technol. Transf. **26**(5), 551–567 (2024). https://doi.org/10.1007/S10009-024-00754-1
13. Knuth, D.: The Art of Computer Programming: Combinatorial algorithms, Part 1. Volume 4a. Addison-Wesley (2011). https://books.google.de/books?id=jT-30QEACAAJ

14. Kretínský, J., Meggendorfer, T., Prokop, M., Zarkhah, A.: Semml: enhancing automata-theoretic LTL synthesis with machine learning. In: Gurfinkel, A., Heule, M. (eds.) Tools and Algorithms for the Construction and Analysis of Systems - 31st International Conference, TACAS 2025, Held as Part of the International Joint Conferences on Theory and Practice of Software, ETAPS 2025, Hamilton, ON, Canada, 3–8 May 2025, Proceedings, Part I. Lecture Notes in Computer Science, vol. 15696, pp. 233–253. Springer (2025). https://doi.org/10.1007/978-3-031-90643-5_12
15. Křetínský, J., Meggendorfer, T., Sickert, S.: Owl: a library for ω-words, automata, and LTL. In: Lahiri, S.K., Wang, C. (eds.) ATVA 2018. LNCS, vol. 11138, pp. 543–550. Springer, Cham (2018). https://doi.org/10.1007/978-3-030-01090-4_34
16. Křetínský, J., Meggendorfer, T., Prokop, M.: Semml 2.0: synthesizing controllers for LTL (2026). https://arxiv.org/abs/2604.24102
17. Mealy, G.H.: A method for synthesizing sequential circuits. Bell Syst. Tech. J. **34**(5), 1045–1079 (1955). https://doi.org/10.1002/j.1538-7305.1955.tb03788.x
18. Meggendorfer, T.: JBDD: a java BDD library (2017). https://github.com/incaseoftrouble/jbdd
19. Meyer, P.J., Sickert, S., Luttenberger, M.: Strix: explicit reactive synthesis strikes back! In: Chockler, H., Weissenbacher, G. (eds.) CAV 2018. LNCS, vol. 10981, pp. 578–586. Springer, Cham (2018). https://doi.org/10.1007/978-3-319-96145-3_31
20. Piterman, N.: From nondeterministic buchi and streett automata to deterministic parity automata. In: 21th IEEE Symposium on Logic in Computer Science (LICS 2006), 12–15 August 2006, Seattle, WA, USA, Proceedings, pp. 255–264. IEEE Computer Society (2006). https://doi.org/10.1109/LICS.2006.28
21. Pnueli, A.: The temporal logic of programs. In: 18th Annual Symposium on Foundations of Computer Science, Providence, Rhode Island, USA, 31 October–1 November 1977, pp. 46–57. IEEE Computer Society (1977). https://doi.org/10.1109/SFCS.1977.32
22. Pnueli, A., Rosner, R.: On the synthesis of an asynchronous reactive module. In: Ausiello, G., Dezani-Ciancaglini, M., Della Rocca, S.R. (eds.) ICALP 1989. LNCS, vol. 372, pp. 652–671. Springer, Heidelberg (1989). https://doi.org/10.1007/BFb0035790
23. Renkin, F., Schlehuber-Caissier, P., Duret-Lutz, A., Pommellet, A.: Dissecting ltlsynt. Formal Methods Syst. Des. **61**(2), 248–289 (2022). https://doi.org/10.1007/S10703-022-00407-6
24. Renkin, F., Schlehuber-Caissier, P., Duret-Lutz, A., Pommellet, A.: Effective reductions of mealy machines. In: Mousavi, M.R., Philippou, A. (eds.) Formal Techniques for Distributed Objects, Components, and Systems 42nd IFIP WG 6.1 International Conference, FORTE 2022, Held as Part of the 17th International Federated Conference on Distributed Computing Techniques, DisCoTec 2022, Lucca, Italy, 13–17 June 2022, Proceedings. Lecture Notes in Computer Science, vol. 13273, pp. 114–130. Springer (2022). https://doi.org/10.1007/978-3-031-08679-3_8
25. Rodríguez, A., Gorostiaga, F., Sánchez, C.: Counter example guided reactive synthesis for LTL modulo theories. In: Piskac, R., Rakamaric, Z. (eds.) Computer Aided Verification - 37th International Conference, CAV 2025, Zagreb, Croatia, 23–25 July 2025, Proceedings, Part IV. Lecture Notes in Computer Science, vol. 15934, pp. 224–248. Springer (2025). https://doi.org/10.1007/978-3-031-98685-7_11
26. Rodríguez, A., Sánchez, C.: Boolean abstractions for realizability modulo theories. In: Enea, C., Lal, A. (eds.) Computer Aided Verification - 35th International Conference, CAV 2023, Paris, France, 17–22 July 2023, Proceedings, Part III, pp.

305–328. Lecture Notes in Computer Science. Springer (2023). https://doi.org/10.1007/978-3-031-37709-9_15
27. Safra, S.: On the complexity of omega-automata. In: 29th Annual Symposium on Foundations of Computer Science, White Plains, New York, USA, 24–26 October 1988, pp. 319–327. IEEE Computer Society (1988). https://doi.org/10.1109/SFCS.1988.21948
28. Schewe, S.: Tighter bounds for the determinisation of büchi automata. In: de Alfaro, L. (ed.) Foundations of Software Science and Computational Structures, 12th International Conference, FOSSACS 2009, Held as Part of the Joint European Conferences on Theory and Practice of Software, ETAPS 2009, York, UK, 22–29 March 2009. Proceedings. Lecture Notes in Computer Science, vol. 5504, pp. 167–181. Springer (2009). https://doi.org/10.1007/978-3-642-00596-1_13
29. Vardi, M.Y., Wolper, P.: An automata-theoretic approach to automatic program verification. In: 1st Symposium in Logic in Computer Science (LICS). IEEE Computer Society (1986)

Fast Obligation Translation and Synthesis

Alexandre Duret-Lutz[1](✉), Giuseppe De Giacomo[2], Marcin Jurdzinski[3], Nir Piterman[4], Moshe Y. Vardi[5], and Shufang Zhu[6]

[1] LRE, EPITA, Le Kremlin-Bicêtre, France
adl@lre.epita.fr
[2] University of Oxford, Oxford, UK
[3] DIMAP, University of Warwick, Coventry, UK
[4] University of Gothenburg and Chalmers University of Technology, Gothenburg, Sweden
[5] Rice University, Houston, TX, USA
[6] University of Liverpool, Liverpool, UK

Abstract. Syntactic obligations are a fragment of LTL formulas that translate to deterministic weak ω-automata (DWA). We show that syntactic obligations can be very efficiently converted to minimal DWA represented using multi-terminal binary decision diagrams (MTBDDs), and that synthesis of such specifications can be solved directly on the MTBDD representation on the fly. Our implementation in Spot shows substantial runtime improvements in translation and synthesis.

1 Introduction

Deterministic ω-automata are a key ingredient to many formal methods [69]. They also play a key role in *reactive synthesis*, which takes temporal specifications, typically in Linear Temporal Logic (LTL) [60], and converts them to strategies that ensure their satisfaction [61]. However, the computational complexity and the complex algorithms that are involved in synthesis and, as a consequence, the capacity of tools that support synthesis techniques in their full generality, have proven to be a barrier for implementation [30,43]. Two major successes in this field have been the syntactic fragment of LTL called GR[1] [59], and LTL$_\text{f}$ [17], which is a semantic variant of LTL that considers finite rather than infinite computations. In both cases, it is possible to use efficient techniques for handling sets of states, leading to increased capacity. Furthermore, algorithmic techniques for analysis of state spaces and translation of specifications to deterministic automata are simpler [7,18]. In particular, in the context of LTL$_\text{f}$ synthesis, tools leverage the algorithmic simplicity of deterministic finite automata (DFA), in contrast to ω-automata [4,16,45,70].

Obligation properties [51], which can be expressed as a boolean combination of *safety* and *guarantee* properties, are good candidates for a fragment of LTL where we could hope to achieve efficient translation and synthesis, exploiting the simplicity of deterministic automata. Although limited in their expressivity, obli-

E. Darulova et al. (Eds.): CAV 2026, LNCS 16682, pp. 322–339, 2026.
https://doi.org/10.1007/978-3-032-32519-8_17

gation properties are very important in practice. Specifications that are used in model checking or synthesis are often simple (safety, guarantee, and obligation).

For instance, the 55 patterns of Dwyer et al. [26] contain 40 obligations. Similarly, Somenzi & Bloem's compilation of 25 LTL formulas "found in the literature" [67, Table 1] contains 16 obligations. Out of the 959 unique LTL specifications collected by the Synthesis Competition [38] at the time of writing, at least 262 specifications are obligations, so more than 27%. Efficient handling of obligation properties also benefits all cases where an obligation property appears as part of a Boolean combination with other temporal properties [65]. Obligation properties are theoretically important, forming the second level in the safety-progress hierarchy of temporal properties [51–54]. Recently, the safety-progress hierarchy has attracted renewed interest thanks to a normalization procedure that reduces the nesting depth of strong and weak operators [28].

Safety and guarantee properties can be mapped to very simple *deterministic* ω-automata [10]: a deterministic ω-automaton for a safety property only rejects runs that can reach a rejecting sink, and a deterministic ω-automaton for a guarantee only accepts runs that can reach an accepting sink. Boolean combinations of safety and guarantee can be mapped to *deterministic weak automata* (DWA) [46,47], in which each *strongly connected component* (SCC) contains only rejecting cycles or only accepting cycles. The simple nature of DWAs makes them very easy to use: they are closed under Boolean operations using algorithms similar to those of DFAs, and, after a preprocessing stage with linear-cost [47], they can also be minimized like DFAs.

Unfortunately, testing whether an LTL formula is an obligation property is nontrivial in general [15]. There are, however, well-known syntactic fragments of LTL that capture safety and guarantee properties. By considering their Boolean combinations, we get a syntactic fragment of LTL which we shall refer to as *syntactic obligation* [10,11]. Importantly, every LTL formula representing an obligation property has an equivalent syntactic-obligation formula [11]. Furthermore, many of the previously mentioned examples are syntactic-obligation formulas.

In this work, we use, on the one hand, the simple syntactic structure of syntactic obligations to easily identify obligation properties and, on the other hand, the DFA-like nature of DWAs to improve the translations and synthesis procedures for them. We generalize our recent work on a compact automaton representation of DFAs using Multi-Terminal Binary Decision Diagrams (MTBDDs), that enabled more efficient $\mathrm{LTL_f}$ translation and synthesis [25]. We show that syntactic obligations can be translated efficiently into DWAs represented using MTBDDs, and that the synthesis problem for syntactic obligations can be solved by interpreting the structure of the MTBDDs as a *weak Büchi game* that can be constructed on-the-fly.

We implemented this approach in Spot, a C++ library for LTL and ω-automata algorithms [24]. Our empirical evaluation shows that it significantly improves the generation of deterministic automata for syntactic-obligation properties as well as the synthesis performance for this class of properties. It is worth noting that by implementing efficient obligation translation and synthesis in Spot, we improve the performance of *all* tools building upon Spot whenever they deal with syntactic obligations.

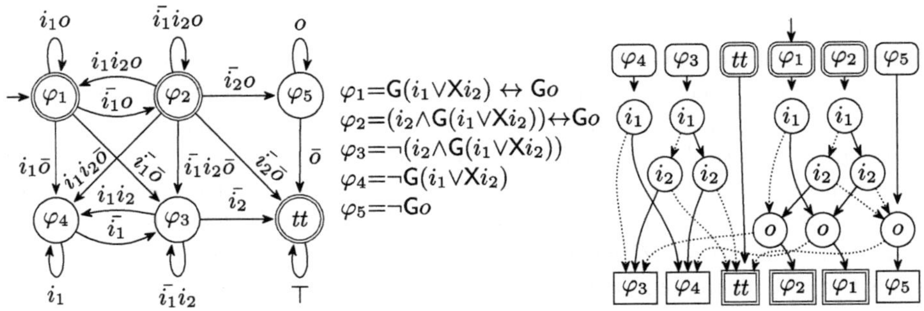

Fig. 1. A DBA for $\varphi_1 = \mathsf{G}(i_1 \vee \mathsf{X} i_2) \leftrightarrow \mathsf{G}o$, and its MTBDD representation.

2 Succinct Representation of Deterministic Büchi Automata

In this section, we introduce a representation of deterministic Büchi automata (DBA) based on multi-terminal binary decision diagrams (MTBDDs).

The left-hand side of Fig. 1 shows a deterministic Büchi automaton over the set of atomic propositions $\mathcal{P} = \{i_1, i_2, o\}$. The *letters* read by the automaton are assignments of all propositions, so there are $2^{|\mathcal{P}|}$ of them, but to simplify the notations, we label the edges of the automaton by Boolean formulas (in this example, implicit conjunctions) that are satisfied by all the assignments that would normally label the edge. In Spot, this explicit representation of automata uses edges labeled by BDDs. In this example, we have also named the states of the automaton using LTL formulas, but this is merely decorative. This DBA has four strongly-connected components: $\{\varphi_1, \varphi_2\}$, $\{\varphi_3, \varphi_4\}$, $\{\varphi_5\}$, and $\{tt\}$. The automaton is *weak* because each SCC contains only accepting states, or only rejecting states. We abbreviate *weak DBA* as *DWA*.

The right-hand side of Fig. 1 shows a semi-symbolic representation of the same DBA, where the outgoing transitions of each state are represented using MTBDDs. The representation is inspired from the representation of DFAs in Mona [36,39], and previous work [25]. The reader familiar with binary decision diagrams (BDDs) [8] will recognize the classical structure of a forest of BDDs: $(x) \overset{\ell}{\underset{h}{\rightrightarrows}}$ should be interpreted as "if x then h else ℓ", atomic propositions appear in the same order on all paths, and identical subtrees are shared. Contrary to BDDs where leaves (or terminals) are restricted to the values true or false, MTBDDs [32,39,48,55] support arbitrary values: in our case, we encode the name of destination states in the leaves. Each root represents a function from Boolean assignments of atomic propositions to destination states, corresponding to transitions of the automaton. A set of "root pointers" represented by nodes of the form $\boxed{s}\!\rightarrow$ point to an MTBDD representing the outgoing transitions of state s.

Writing $\mathsf{MTBDD}(\mathcal{P}, \mathcal{S})$ to denote an MTBDD with variables in $\mathcal{P}$ and terminals of type $\mathcal{S}$, let us define the MTBDD-based representation of a DBA (MTDBA for short).

Definition 1 (MTDBA, MTDWA). *An MTDBA is a tuple* $\mathcal{A} = \langle \mathcal{Q}, \mathcal{P}, \iota, \Delta, \lambda \rangle$*, where* $\mathcal{Q}$ *is a finite set of* states*,* $\mathcal{P}$ *is a finite (and ordered) set of* variables*,* $\iota \in \mathcal{Q}$ *is the initial state,* $\Delta : \mathcal{Q} \to \mathsf{MTBDD}(\mathcal{P}, \mathcal{Q})$ *represents the outgoing edges of each state, and* $\lambda : \mathcal{Q} \to \mathbb{B}$ *represents the acceptance status of each state. If the MTDBA is weak, we may call it MTDWA.*

Each path from a root pointer to a terminal in the MTDBA representation on the right-hand side of Fig. 1 corresponds to an edge in the explicit DBA represented on the left-hand side. The MTDBA representation is more compact because it can share common subtrees. For instance, if two states have exactly the same outgoing transitions, but differ only by their acceptance, their root pointers will designate the same MTBDD.

MTBDDs support unary and binary operations using algorithms similar to those of BDDs. For instance, given two $x, y \in \mathsf{MTBDD}(\mathcal{P}, \mathcal{S})$, and a binary operation $\odot : \mathcal{S} \times \mathcal{S} \to \mathcal{S}$ over the terminals, one can compute $z \in \mathsf{MTBDD}(\mathcal{P}, \mathcal{S})$, such that for all assignments v of all variables in $\mathcal{P}$, the terminal $z(v)$ reached in z by following v is equal to $x(v) \odot y(v)$. We can therefore lift the $\odot$ operation to the MTBDDs and write $z = x \odot y$.

3 From Syntactic Obligations to MTDWA

This section shows how to build an MTDWA for a syntactic obligation. Our construction is relatively straightforward, yet we could not find any prior work for that fragment.

3.1 Syntactic Sub-Classes of LTL

We assume that the reader is familiar with LTL [60]. The following grammar (where parentheses have been omitted, and $p \in \mathcal{P}$) defines four syntactic fragments [10,11]:

$$\begin{aligned}
\varphi_B &::= \mathit{ff} \mid \mathit{tt} \mid p \mid \neg\varphi_B \mid \varphi_B{\wedge}\varphi_B \mid \varphi_B{\vee}\varphi_B \mid \varphi_B{\leftrightarrow}\varphi_B \mid \varphi_B{\oplus}\varphi_B \mid \varphi_B{\rightarrow}\varphi_B \mid \mathsf{X}\varphi_B\\
\varphi_G &::= \varphi_B \mid \neg\varphi_S \mid \varphi_G{\wedge}\varphi_G \mid \varphi_G{\vee}\varphi_G \mid \varphi_S{\rightarrow}\varphi_G \mid \mathsf{X}\varphi_G \mid \mathsf{F}\varphi_G \mid \varphi_G \mathbin{\mathsf{U}} \varphi_G \mid \varphi_G \mathbin{\mathsf{M}} \varphi_G\\
\varphi_S &::= \varphi_B \mid \neg\varphi_G \mid \varphi_S{\wedge}\varphi_S \mid \varphi_S{\vee}\varphi_S \mid \varphi_G{\rightarrow}\varphi_S \mid \mathsf{X}\varphi_S \mid \mathsf{G}\varphi_S \mid \varphi_S \mathbin{\mathsf{R}} \varphi_S \mid \varphi_S \mathbin{\mathsf{W}} \varphi_S\\
\varphi_O &::= \varphi_G \mid \varphi_S \mid \neg\varphi_O \mid \varphi_O{\wedge}\varphi_O \mid \varphi_O{\vee}\varphi_O \mid \varphi_O{\leftrightarrow}\varphi_O \mid \varphi_O{\oplus}\varphi_O \mid \varphi_O{\rightarrow}\varphi_O \mid \mathsf{X}\varphi_O\\
&\quad\mid \varphi_O \mathbin{\mathsf{U}} \varphi_G \mid \varphi_O \mathbin{\mathsf{R}} \varphi_S \mid \varphi_S \mathbin{\mathsf{W}} \varphi_O \mid \varphi_G \mathbin{\mathsf{M}} \varphi_O
\end{aligned}$$

Formulas built using the rule for φ_S (resp. φ_G) are syntactic safety (resp. syntactic guarantee) and also correspond to the class Σ_1 (resp. Π_1) defined by Esparza et al. [28]. The “bottom” class, built using the φ_B rule, is the intersection of these two syntactic classes; it differs from Esparza's Δ_0 class in that it allows X operators. If we ignore the last four options in φ_O, the φ_O rule represents Boolean combinations of syntactic safety and syntactic guarantee, and differs from Esparza's Δ_1 class in that it is also closed under the X operator. The last four options in φ_O allow to capture more obligations syntactically [10,11].

Note that we never require formulas to be in *negative normal form* (NNF). Translations that require NNF suffer a blowup from the removal of operators $\leftrightarrow$ and $\oplus$. Instead, since DWA are closed under Boolean operations, we support these operators naturally.

In what follows, let $\mathsf{LTL}_O(\mathcal{P})$ designate the set of syntactic obligations that can be built over atomic propositions $\mathcal{P}$ and similarly for $\mathsf{LTL}_B(\mathcal{P})$, $\mathsf{LTL}_G(\mathcal{P})$, and $\mathsf{LTL}_S(\mathcal{P})$.

3.2 Translation to MTDWA

We are going to build an MTDWA $\langle \mathcal{Q}, \mathcal{P}, \iota, \Delta, \lambda \rangle$, where states $\mathcal{Q} \subseteq \mathsf{LTL}_O(\mathcal{P})$ are identified by syntactic obligations, and $\iota \in \mathsf{LTL}_O(\mathcal{P})$ is the formula to translate.

Computing Successors Using MTBDDs. Assuming $\boxed{\alpha}$ represents a terminal labeled by $\alpha \in \mathsf{LTL}_O(\mathcal{P})$, the MTBDD representation of the successors of a state, i.e., the function $\mathsf{tr} : \mathsf{LTL}_O(\mathcal{P}) \to \mathsf{MTBDD}(\mathcal{P}, \mathsf{LTL}_O(\mathcal{P}))$, is defined as follows:

$$\mathsf{tr}(tt) = \boxed{tt} \qquad \mathsf{tr}(f\!f) = \boxed{f\!f} \qquad \mathsf{tr}(a) = \text{(see diagram)} \quad \text{for any } a \in \mathcal{P}$$

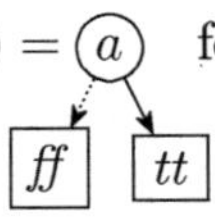

$$\mathsf{tr}(\mathsf{X}\varphi) = \boxed{\varphi} \qquad \mathsf{tr}(\neg\varphi) = \neg\mathsf{tr}(\varphi)$$

$$\mathsf{tr}(\alpha \odot \beta) = \mathsf{tr}(\alpha) \odot \mathsf{tr}(\beta) \quad \text{for any Boolean operator } \odot \in \{\wedge, \vee, \rightarrow, \leftrightarrow, \oplus, ...\}$$

$$\mathsf{tr}(\alpha\,\mathsf{U}\,\beta) = \mathsf{tr}(\beta) \vee (\mathsf{tr}(\alpha) \wedge \boxed{\alpha\,\mathsf{U}\,\beta}) \qquad \mathsf{tr}(\alpha\,\mathsf{M}\,\beta) = \mathsf{tr}(\beta) \wedge (\mathsf{tr}(\alpha) \vee \boxed{\alpha\,\mathsf{M}\,\beta})$$

$$\mathsf{tr}(\alpha\,\mathsf{W}\,\beta) = \mathsf{tr}(\beta) \vee (\mathsf{tr}(\alpha) \wedge \boxed{\alpha\,\mathsf{W}\,\beta}) \qquad \mathsf{tr}(\alpha\,\mathsf{R}\,\beta) = \mathsf{tr}(\beta) \wedge (\mathsf{tr}(\alpha) \vee \boxed{\alpha\,\mathsf{R}\,\beta})$$

$$\mathsf{tr}(\mathsf{F}\varphi) = \mathsf{tr}(\varphi) \vee \boxed{\mathsf{F}\varphi} \qquad \mathsf{tr}(\mathsf{G}\varphi) = \mathsf{tr}(\varphi) \wedge \boxed{\mathsf{G}\varphi}$$

Deciding Acceptance of States. In this simple LTL fragment, the acceptance of a state $\varphi \in \mathsf{LTL}_O(\mathcal{P})$ can be defined by simply considering the Boolean combination of safety and guarantee formulas that φ represents. This can be done using the function $\lambda(\varphi)$ defined below, which checks the top-level operator of each maximal temporal subformula of φ (strong operators F, U, M are rejecting; weak operators G, W, R are accepting) and builds their Boolean combinations.

$$\lambda(f\!f) = \lambda(\alpha\,\mathsf{U}\,\beta) = \lambda(\alpha\,\mathsf{M}\,\beta) = \lambda(\mathsf{F}\varphi) = \bot$$
$$\lambda(tt) = \lambda(\alpha\,\mathsf{W}\,\beta) = \lambda(\alpha\,\mathsf{R}\,\beta) = \lambda(\mathsf{G}\varphi) = \top$$
$$\lambda(\alpha \odot \beta) = \lambda(\alpha) \odot \lambda(\beta) \quad \text{for any Boolean operator } \odot \in \{\wedge, \vee, \leftarrow, \leftrightarrow, \oplus, ...\}$$
$$\lambda(\neg\varphi) = \neg\lambda(\varphi) \qquad \lambda(\mathsf{X}\varphi) = \lambda(\varphi) \qquad \lambda(a) = * \text{ for any } a \in \mathcal{P}$$

The special value $*$ should be ignored during Boolean operations, as shown below:

$$\begin{array}{lllll}
\top \wedge * = \top & \bot \wedge * = \bot & * \wedge * = * & \top \oplus * = \top & \bot \oplus * = \top \\
\top \vee * = \top & \bot \vee * = \bot & * \vee * = * & * \oplus * = * & \neg * = * \\
\top \rightarrow * = \bot & \bot \rightarrow * = \top & * \rightarrow * = * & * \rightarrow \top = \top & * \rightarrow \bot = \bot \\
\top \leftrightarrow * = \top & \bot \leftrightarrow * = \top & * \leftrightarrow * = * & &
\end{array}$$

A state φ such that $\lambda(\varphi) = *$ is a Boolean combination of atomic propositions, possibly with X operators. It cannot be part of a cycle, so its acceptance can be arbitrary.

In our implementation *tt* and *ff* never occur as arguments of Boolean operators or of X: such formulas are automatically simplified (e.g., trying to construct $\mathsf{X}(tt) \wedge a$ will return a). Therefore, $\lambda(tt)$ and $\lambda(ff)$ are never called recursively.

Ensuring Termination with Propositional Equivalence. It is tempting to define our automaton $\langle \mathcal{Q}, \mathcal{P}, \iota, \Delta, \lambda \rangle$ by letting $\Delta = \mathsf{tr}$, and by setting $\mathcal{Q}$ to be equal to all the formulas that can be reached transitively from ι by applying tr. This does not work because the set $\mathcal{Q}$ constructed this way is not necessarily finite. The classical solution, which we reuse, is to use propositional equivalence [25, 27].

In previous work on $\mathrm{LTL_f}$ translation [25], we used propositional equivalence to simplify formulas created at every step of the computation of $\mathsf{tr}(\cdot)$. In the current implementation we found that it was faster to do it as a separate pass: first compute the MTBDD $m = \mathsf{tr}(\varphi)$, then replace all the leaves of m by a representative of their propositional-equivalence class. This way, we avoid computing propositional equivalence for the intermediate computations of $\mathsf{tr}(\cdot)$.

Additionally, as part of propositional equivalence we consider the distribution of the X operators through Boolean operators. E.g., we interpret $\mathsf{X}(\alpha \wedge \beta) \vee \mathsf{X}(\beta)$ as $(\mathsf{X}(\alpha) \wedge \mathsf{X}(\beta)) \vee \mathsf{X}(\beta)$, so it can be found to be equivalent to $\mathsf{X}(\beta)$.

From now on, we assume that tr includes propositional-equivalence, so that $\mathcal{Q}$, the set of formulas reachable transitively from ι by applying tr, is guaranteed to be finite.

Correctness of the Construction. While propositional equivalence ensures that our construction terminates, its correctness is established by the following lemma and theorem.

Lemma 1. *For any $\iota \in \mathsf{LTL}_O(\mathcal{P})$ let $D_\iota = \langle \mathcal{Q}, \mathcal{P}, \iota, \mathsf{tr}, \lambda \rangle$ be the automaton constructed as described above, keeping $\lambda : \mathcal{Q} \to \mathbb{B} \cup \{*\}$ (unlike in Definition 1). The following statements hold:*

1. *Any state $\varphi \in \mathcal{Q}$ such that $\lambda(\varphi) = *$ belongs to a trivial SCC of D_ι.*
2. *For any bottom formula $\iota \in \mathsf{LTL}_B(\mathcal{P})$, the only possible non-trivial SCCs of D_ι are the states tt and ff (at least one of these has to exist).*
3. *For any guarantee formula $\iota \in \mathsf{LTL}_G(\mathcal{P})$, all states $\varphi \in \mathcal{Q} \setminus \{tt\}$ that belong to non-trivial SCCs of D_ι have $\lambda(\varphi) = \bot$.*
4. *For any safety formula $\iota \in \mathsf{LTL}_S(\mathcal{P})$, all states $\varphi \in \mathcal{Q} \setminus \{ff\}$ that belong to non-trivial SCCs of D_ι have $\lambda(\varphi) = \top$.*
5. *For any obligation formula $\iota \in \mathsf{LTL}_O(\mathcal{P})$, all the states of any non-trivial SCC of D_ι get assigned the same value by λ, and this value is either $\top$ or $\bot$.*

Proofs and supplementary material can be found in the extended version of this article, available on arXiv [23].

Since the states φ for which $\lambda(\varphi) = *$ cannot be part of a cycle, their acceptance can be chosen arbitrarily. In Sect. 3.3, we show that this choice is constrained if we want to minimize the automaton. For now, in order to formalize this definition, we declare those states as rejecting using the function $\lambda' : \mathcal{Q} \to \mathbb{B}$ defined as follows:

$$\lambda'(\varphi) = \begin{cases} \top & \text{if } \lambda(\varphi) = \top \\ \bot & \text{if } \lambda(\varphi) \in \{\bot, *\} \end{cases}$$

Theorem 1. *For every $\iota \in \mathsf{LTL}_O(\mathcal{P})$ the automaton $D_\iota = \langle \mathcal{Q}, \mathcal{P}, \iota, \mathsf{tr}, \lambda' \rangle$ constructed above is an MTDWA, and it satisfies $\mathscr{L}(\iota) = \mathscr{L}(D_\iota)$.*

Proof. The fact that D_ι is weak is a corollary that follows directly from Lemma 1. $\mathscr{L}(D_\iota)$ being equivalent to $\mathscr{L}(\iota)$ follows by noticing that tr implements the local truth of LTL formulas and by induction on the structure of formulas. □

3.3 Minimizing MTDWA

Contrary to DBAs [66], DWAs can be minimized in polynomial time [47]. In fact, after a very cheap preprocessing to decide for each transient state (i.e., a state that cannot be part of a loop) whether it should be accepting or rejecting, a DWA can be minimized as if it were a DFA. Löding's preprocessing [47] is based on a simple ranking function over the strongly connected components (SCC) of the DWA, such that the parity of the rank indicates the acceptance of the SCC. We can perform an SCC decomposition over the MTDWA directly, by simply interpreting the forest of MTBDDs (which is normally acyclic) as a graph where a leaf $\boxed{\alpha}$ is connected to the root of $\Delta(\alpha)$.

The minimization itself is easily done over MTBDDs by using a variant of Moore's partition-refinement algorithm [56] similar to what is implemented in Mona [36]. Assuming that each state labeled by α of the MTDWA is assigned to block $B(\alpha) \in \mathbb{N}$ in the partition of the current iteration, the next partition can be found by creating for each state s a temporary $\Delta'(s) \in \mathsf{MTBDD}(\mathcal{P}, \mathbb{N})$ in which all leaves $\boxed{\alpha}$ of $\Delta(s)$ are replaced by $\boxed{B(\alpha)}$, and partitioning the set of states according to the different MTBDDs in Δ'.

An optimization not mentioned in Löding's paper is that the only states that can be merged during minimization are those that share the same rank. Consequently, Löding's ranking function can be used to define the initial partition of the minimization.

4 LTL_O Reactive Synthesis

A reactive controller can be thought of as an electronic circuit that produces output signals based on a history of input signals. LTL Reactive Synthesis is the problem of building such a controller (usually as a Mealy machine) such that the combined histories of input and output signals satisfy some given LTL specification.

We implement synthesis to AIGER circuits [6,65], but for lack of space we only discuss the "realizability" problem, defined as follows.

Definition 2 ([30,43]). *Given two disjoint sets of variables $\mathcal{I}$ (inputs) and $\mathcal{O}$ (outputs), a controller is a function $\rho : (\mathbb{B}^{\mathcal{I}})^* \to \mathbb{B}^{\mathcal{O}}$ that, given a history of assignments of input variables, produces an assignment of output variables.*

Given a word of input assignments $\sigma \in (\mathbb{B}^{\mathcal{I}})^\omega$, the controller can be used to generate a word of output assignments $\sigma_\rho \in (\mathbb{B}^{\mathcal{O}})^\omega$. The definition of σ_ρ may use two semantics depending on whether we want the controller to have access to the current input assignment to decide the output assignment:

Mealy semantics: $\sigma_\rho(i) = \rho(\sigma(..i))$ *for all* $i \geq 0$.
Moore semantics: $\sigma_\rho(i) = \rho(\sigma(..i-1))$ *for all* $i \geq 0$.

A formula $\varphi \in \mathsf{LTL}(\mathcal{I} \cup \mathcal{O})$ is said to be Mealy-realizable, *or* Moore-realizable, *if there exists a controller ρ such that for every word $\sigma \in (\mathbb{B}^{\mathcal{I}})^\omega$, it holds that $(\sigma \sqcup \sigma_\rho) \in \mathscr{L}(\varphi)$ using the desired semantics.*

Formula φ_1 (from Fig. 1) is both Mealy-realizable and Moore-realizable.

For general LTL, synthesis or realizability can be reduced to the translation of the specification into a deterministic parity automaton, which is then interpreted and solved as a two-player game with parity acceptance: one player plays the input signals, the second player plays the output signals. The specification is realizable if the output player has a strategy to ensure that the parity acceptance is satisfied.

For syntactic obligations, realizability and synthesis are a lot easier: any $\mathsf{LTL}_\mathcal{O}$ formula can be converted to a DWA, which can also be interpreted as a two-player game with weak acceptance. Such games are known to be solvable in linear time [1, Section 6.1]. They can also be reduced to the emptiness check of 1-letter weak alternating automata [44, Theorem 4.7], or seen as a special case of weak parity games [12]. These three algorithms work similarly. Since the automaton is weak, we know that the cycles in one SCC are either all accepting (winning for the output player) or all rejecting (winning for the input player), but except for SCCs without successors, it might be possible for players to escape an SCC that is losing for them. The game is therefore solved by enumerating the SCCs and processing them bottom-up: terminal SCCs can be determined as winning for one player or the other according to their acceptance. Then the attractor of these states is grown by backpropagation. Moving up in the SCCs, undetermined states can be determined according to the acceptance of the SCC.

This algorithm can be implemented directly on the MTDWA structure, by interpreting it as a game where the input (resp., output) player makes the decision for the input (resp., output) variables, and where a play that reaches $\boxed{\alpha}$ continues from the root node associated with α. For Mealy semantics, input variables should be ordered to appear before output variables; for Moore semantics, it should be the opposite.

We implement this game solving over MTDWA on-the-fly, together with the automaton construction of Sect. 3.

The setup is very similar to our previous solution for $\mathrm{LTL_f}$ synthesis [25] where we had to construct a DFA represented using MTBDDs, and interpret it as a reachability game to be solved on-the-fly. In a reachability game, the exploration order is not important: this previous work used a BFS just because we found it marginally better than DFS. Here, for obligation synthesis, we have to explore the states in a topological order of their SCCs. Enumerating SCCs during the on-the-fly construction of an automaton is a well studied topic, and is typically used by on-the-fly explicit LTL model checkers [33,35,63]. These algorithms are all based on a DFS exploration of the automaton. Our implementation uses Dijkstra's SCC algorithm [19,20], and we construct the MTDWA as the DFS progresses. The implementation reuses the linear backpropagation over incomplete graphs from previous work [25, Algorithm 1].

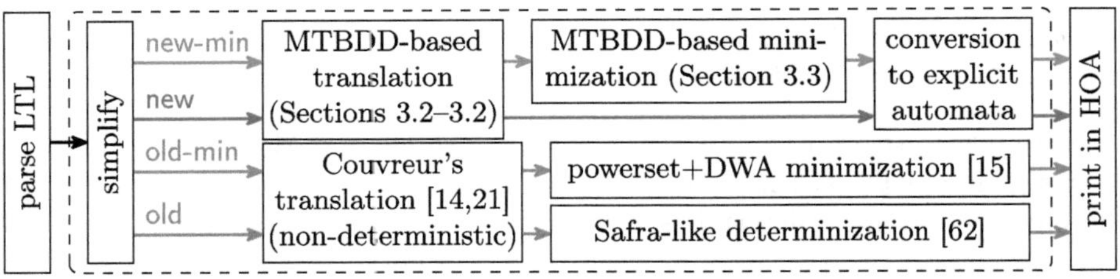

Fig. 2. Four pipelines usable by `ltl2tgba` to translate a syntactic obligation: new-min, new, old-min, and old. The `spot::translator` class implements the dashed box.

5 Implementation and Evaluation

The new constructions for translation, minimization, and game solving have been implemented [22] in Spot [24] and released as version 2.15. Many graphical examples of these constructions can be found at https://spot.lre.epita.fr/ipynb/mtdswa.html Below, we evaluate how the translation and synthesis improved compared to the previous version. We also include a comparison to a few third-party tools for reference.

5.1 Translation

The new translation procedure is used by Spot's `translator` class whenever the input formula is a syntactic obligation and the user requests a deterministic output. For evaluation purposes, we use Spot's `ltl2tgba` command-line tool, which converts LTL into various kinds of automata and outputs them in the HOA format [2].

Figure 2 shows four translation pipelines that `ltl2tgba` can use to translate syntactic obligations into DWAs. The dashed rectangle corresponds to the aforementioned `translator` class: it translates an LTL formula into an explicit ω-automaton, but it can be configured to use different approaches. The path old-min corresponds to the default behavior of Spot 2.14: after some simple syntactic simplifications, the formula is converted into a non-deterministic Büchi automaton using Couvreur's translation algorithm [14,21], to obtain a weak NBA; the result is then determinized by powerset construction and minimized as described by Dax et al. [15], and finally the resulting automaton is output in HOA. The old pipeline is used when the DWA-minimization is explicitly disabled or not applicable: this path works for any input formula, not just obligations. In that case, since the output of the translation is non-deterministic, but the goal is to have a deterministic automaton, the automaton is determinized using a Safra-based construction [62].

In both old-min and old, automata are represented as explicit graphs with edges labeled by Boolean formulas over propositions (represented as BDDs) [21, 24], as on the left-hand side of Fig. 1. In the new pipelines, called new-min and new, the MTBDD-based translation described in Sect. 3 produces an MTDWA as on the right-hand side of Fig. 1, and that can optionally be minimized using the same data structure. In order to output an MTDWA in the HOA format, we first convert this MTBDD-based representation into an explicit representation. This conversion has a significant cost because it has to enumerate all paths in the MTBDDs. Nonetheless, we will see that these new pipelines are still competitive, despite the costly conversion.

As far as we know, Spot is the only tool that can translate syntactic obligations into DWA that are guaranteed to be minimal (via the old-min or new-min pipelines). We can, however, compare to tools that produce deterministic ω-automata even if they do not guarantee minimality. We consider ltl3tela 2.1.1 [50] and ltl2dela from Owl 21.0 [41]. (The latter is an evolution of Delag [57], which we did not run.)

For a fair comparison, we set up all tools to read an LTL formula and produce an equivalent deterministic ω-automaton (with any acceptance condition) in the HOA format. We request complete automata from all tools except ltl3tela (which lacks this option). We measure the entire execution of each tool using `ltlcross` with a timeout of 60 s. The experiment was run one task at a time on a dedicated Core i7-3770 with *Turbo Boost* disabled, and the frequency scaled down to 1.6 GHz to prevent CPU throttling.

We evaluated the translation pipelines on 494 syntactic obligations:

- 310 formulas representing instances of 17 scalable patterns [13,34,42,68];
- 76 formulas collected from various works [26,29,37,58,67];
- 108 unique formulas from the synthesis competition [38]: all the instances that are syntactic obligations, except for two formulas syntactically equivalent to *tt* or *ff*.

Figure 3, where the time axis is logarithmic, clearly shows how Spot's translation has improved over this set of formulas. Note that new and new-min are barely distinguishable, suggesting that the guarantee to build minimal automata comes at no extra cost.

Keep in mind, however, that we measured the runtime of a complete translation process, including the conversion to explicit automata (for new and new-min) and HOA output (for all tools). We now turn to the evaluation of how the MTBDD-based representation of DWA improves synthesis: in this case, we do not need to convert automata to an explicit representation, saving a lot of time.

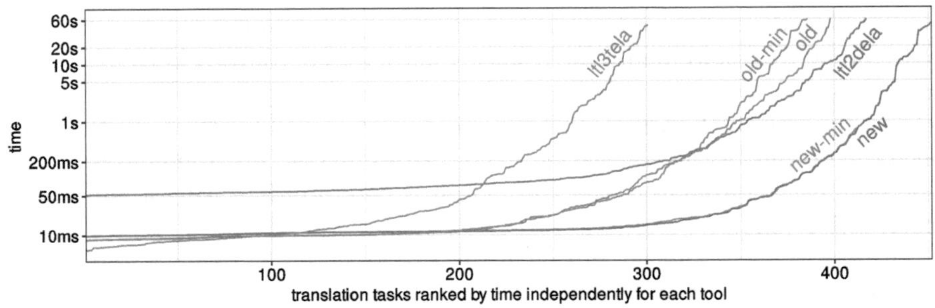

Fig. 3. Comparison of translation tools on 494 syntactic obligations from the literature.

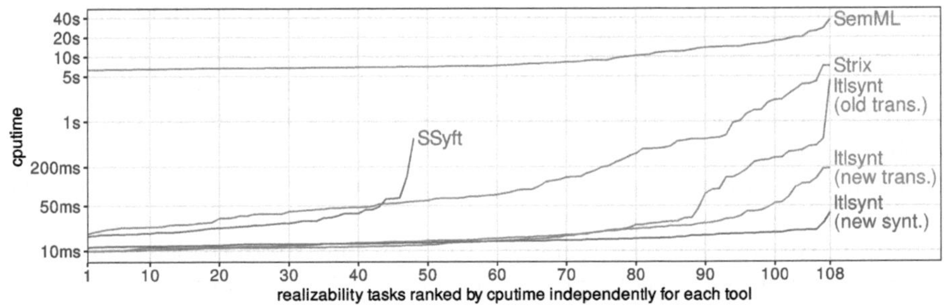

Fig. 4. Comparison of the three configurations of `ltlsynt` over the 108 specifications from SyntComp that are syntactic obligations. Third-party tools Strix, SemML, and SSyft are included for reference.

5.2 Synthesis

Previous versions of Spot's `ltlsynt` converted an LTL specification by translating it to a deterministic parity automaton (DPA), turning this DPA into a two-player game, and solving the game [65]. In the case of syntactic obligations, the DPA was obtained by the old-min translation pipeline in Fig. 2. This default behavior of `ltlsynt` 2.14 is what is called (old trans.) in this section.

The improvements described in this paper allow us to define two better configurations of `ltlsynt`. (new trans.) designates a configuration where the `spot::translator` class, used to produce the DPA, is changed to use the new-min translation pipeline in Fig. 2, where the automaton is still converted to an explicit representation, to be solved as a game. The (new synt.) configuration corresponds to the new default of `ltlsynt`, where syntactic obligations are converted into an MTBDD-based representation, and the game is solved directly on that representation as described in this paper.

Figure 4 shows the improved runtimes as a cactus plot. For this experiment, we used BenchExec 3.22 [5] to track time and memory usage. We include Strix 21.0 [49] (the winner of SyntComp'23) and SemML [40] (the winner of SyntComp'24) for comparison. (The winner of SyntComp'25 was `ltlsynt` due to a technical defect in SemML.) Moreover, SSyft [3], patched to use the Mealy semantics, is included as an example of a tool that is dedicated to syntactic-safety formulas: there are 48 of those in this benchmark. All tools were configured to check the specification for realizability: this way we do not include any time spent generating and outputting controllers.

Additional details and discussion can be found in the extended version of this article, available on arXiv [23].

6 Conclusion

We have shown that the MTBDD-based translation has made `ltl2tgba` faster at converting syntactic obligations to (weak) DBAs. This holds even when we switch back to an explicit representation. In the case of synthesis, the latter switch back is not required and the weak game can be solved directly on the MTBDD-based representation, providing an even greater speedup.

The techniques described target syntactic obligations, so we focused our experiments on those. We expect, however, that those improvements will impact other types of specifications as well. Firstly, when a specification can be seen as a conjunction of output-disjoint sub-specifications, `ltlsynt` solves each sub-specification independently [31,65]. Therefore, even if the full specification is not a syntactic obligation, it could contain a sub-specification that is a syntactic obligation, and that will be solved using the improved MTBDD-based technique. Secondly, a possible way to obtain a DPA is to first translate the specification into a deterministic Emerson-Lei automaton (DELA), which can then be converted into a DPA [9,64]. To obtain a DELA, Spot generalizes the compositional translation used by the `Delag` tool [57]: the formula to translate is broken into top-level Boolean operators, subformulas are translated to deterministic automata according to their nature, and those automata are then recombined. In this approach, subformulas that are syntactic obligations will now be translated much more efficiently.

Obvious future work would be to generalize the MTBDD-based translation, so that all LTL formulas can be turned into MTBDD-based DELA, probably using Δ_2-normalization [28], converting top-level temporal formulas to deterministic Büchi and co-Büchi automata, and using Boolean combinations for the final automaton.

Acknowledgments. NP is supported by Swedish Research Council (VR) project (No. 2020-04963) and the Wallenberg AI, Autonomous Systems and Software Program (WASP) funded by the Knut and Alice Wallenberg Foundation. GDG is partially supported by the EPSRC grant EP/Y028872/1, Mathematical Foundations of Intelligence: An Erlangen Programme for AI.

Data Availibility Statement. The source code for Spot 2.15.1, its documentation, benchmark data and scripts, some illustrative notebooks, and a Docker image containing an installation of Spot and all third-party tools measured in our benchmark, are archived on Zenodo [22].

Disclosure of Interests. The authors have no competing interests to declare that are relevant to the content of this article.

References

1. Amram, G., Bansal, S., Fried, D., Tabajara, L.M., Vardi, M.Y., Weiss, G.: Adapting behaviors via reactive synthesis. In: Silva, A., Leino, K.R.M. (eds.) CAV 2021. LNCS, vol. 12759, pp. 870–893. Springer, Cham (2021). https://doi.org/10.1007/978-3-030-81685-8_41
2. Babiak, T., et al.: The Hanoi omega-automata format. In: Kroening, D., Păsăreanu, C.S. (eds.) CAV 2015. LNCS, vol. 9206, pp. 479–486. Springer, Cham (2015). https://doi.org/10.1007/978-3-319-21690-4_31
3. Bansal, S., De Giacomo, G., Di Stasio, A., Li, Y., Vardi, M.Y., Zhu, S.: Compositional safety LTL synthesis. In: Lal, A., Tonetta, S. (eds.) Proceedings of the 14th International Conference on Verified Software, Theories, Tools and Experiments (VSTTE 2022), pp. 1–19. Springer (2023). https://doi.org/10.1007/978-3-031-25803-9_1
4. Bansal, S., Li, Y., Tabajara, L.M., Vardi, M.Y.: Hybrid compositional reasoning for reactive synthesis from finite-horizon specifications. In: Proceedings of the 34th National Conference on Artificial Intelligence (AAAI 2020), pp. 9766–9774. AAAI Press (2020). https://doi.org/10.1609/AAAI.V34I06.6528
5. Beyer, D., Löwe, S., Wendler, P.: Reliable benchmarking: requirements and solutions. Int. J. Softw. Tools Technol. Transfer **21**, 1–29 (2019). https://doi.org/10.1007/s10009-017-0469-y
6. Biere, A., Heljanko, K., Wieringa, S.: AIGER 1.9 and beyond. Technical report 11/2, Institute for Formal Models and Verification, Johannes Kepler University, Altenbergerstr. 69, 4040 Linz, Austria (2011). https://fmv.jku.at/aiger/
7. Bloem, R., Jobstmann, B., Piterman, N., Pnueli, A., Sa'ar, Y.: Synthesis of reactive(1) designs. J. Comput. Syst. Sci. **78**(3), 911–938 (2012). https://doi.org/10.1016/J.JCSS.2011.08.007
8. Bryant, R.E.: Graph-based algorithms for boolean function manipulation. IEEE Trans. Comput. **35**(8), 677–691 (1986). https://doi.org/10.1109/TC.1986.1676819
9. Casares, A., Duret-Lutz, A., Meyer, K.J., Renkin, F., Sickert, S.: Practical applications of the alternating cycle decomposition. In: TACAS 2022. LNCS, vol. 13244, pp. 99–117. Springer, Cham (2022). https://doi.org/10.1007/978-3-030-99527-0_6
10. Černá, I., Pelánek, R.: Relating hierarchy of temporal properties to model checking. In: Rovan, B., Vojtáš, P. (eds.) MFCS 2003. LNCS, vol. 2747, pp. 318–327. Springer, Heidelberg (2003). https://doi.org/10.1007/978-3-540-45138-9_26
11. Chang, E., Manna, Z., Pnueli, A.: Characterization of temporal property classes. In: Kuich, W. (ed.) ICALP 1992. LNCS, vol. 623, pp. 474–486. Springer, Heidelberg (1992). https://doi.org/10.1007/3-540-55719-9_97
12. Chatterjee, K.: Linear time algorithm for weak parity games. Technical Report UCB/EECS-2006-153, Electrical Engineering and Computer Sciences, University of California at Berkeley (2008). https://www2.eecs.berkeley.edu/Pubs/TechRpts/2006/EECS-2006-153.html
13. Cichoń, J., Czubak, A., Jasiński, A.: Minimal Büchi automata for certain classes of LTL formulas. In: Proceedings of the Fourth International Conference on Dependability of Computer Systems (DepCoS 2009), pp. 17–24. IEEE Computer Society (2009). https://doi.org/10.1109/DepCoS-RELCOMEX.2009.31

14. Couvreur, J.-M.: On-the-fly verification of linear temporal logic. In: Wing, J.M., Woodcock, J., Davies, J. (eds.) FM 1999. LNCS, vol. 1708, pp. 253–271. Springer, Heidelberg (1999). https://doi.org/10.1007/3-540-48119-2_16
15. Dax, C., Eisinger, J., Klaedtke, F.: Mechanizing the powerset construction for restricted classes of ω-automata. In: Namjoshi, K.S., Yoneda, T., Higashino, T., Okamura, Y. (eds.) ATVA 2007. LNCS, vol. 4762, pp. 223–236. Springer, Heidelberg (2007). https://doi.org/10.1007/978-3-540-75596-8_17
16. De Giacomo, G., Favorito, M.: Compositional approach to translate $\mathrm{LTL}_f/\mathrm{LDL}_f$ into deterministic finite automata. In: Proceedings of the 31st International Conference on Automated Planning and Scheduling (ICAPS 2021), pp. 122–130 (2021). https://doi.org/10.1609/icaps.v31i1.15954
17. De Giacomo, G., Vardi, M.Y.: Linear temporal logic and linear dynamic logic on finite traces. In: Proceedings of the 23rd International Joint Conference on Artificial Intelligence (IJCAI 2013), pp. 854–860. AAAI Press (2013). https://doi.org/10.5555/2540128.2540252
18. De Giacomo, G., Vardi, M.Y.: Synthesis for LTL and LDL on finite traces. In: Proceedings of the 24th International Joint Conference on Artificial Intelligence (IJCAI 2015), pp. 1558–1564. AAAI Press (2015). https://doi.org/10.5555/2832415.2832466
19. Dijkstra, E.W.: EWD 376: Finding the maximum strong components in a directed graph (1973). http://www.cs.utexas.edu/users/EWD/ewd03xx/EWD376.PDF
20. Dijkstra, E.W.: Finding the maximal strong components in a directed graph. In: A Discipline of Programming, chap. 25, pp. 192–200. Prentice-Hall (1976)
21. Duret-Lutz, A.: LTL translation improvements in Spot 1.0. Int. J. Crit. Comput.-Based Syst. **5**(1/2), 31–54 (2014). https://doi.org/10.1504/IJCCBS.2014.059594
22. Duret-Lutz, A.: Supporting material for "Fast Obligation Translation and Synthesis" (2026). https://doi.org/10.5281/zenodo.19812382
23. Duret-Lutz, A., De Giacomo, G., Jurdzinski, M., Piterman, N., Vardi, M.Y., Zhu, S.: Fast obligation translation and synthesis. arXiv (2026). https://doi.org/10.48550/arXiv.2605.12372, extended version of this article, inluding proofs and additional discussions in appendices
24. Duret-Lutz, A., et al.: From spot 2.0 to spot 2.10: what's new? In: Proceedings of the 34th International Conference on Computer Aided Verification (CAV'22). Lecture Notes in Computer Science, vol. 13372, pp. 174–187. Springer (2022). https://doi.org/10.1007/978-3-031-13188-2_9
25. Duret-Lutz, A., Zhu, S., Piterman, N., De Giacomo, G., Vardi, M.Y.: Engineering an LTLf synthesis tool. In: Proceedings of the 29th International Conference on Implementation and Applications of Automata (CIAA 2025). Lecture Notes in Computer Science, vol. 15981, pp. 129–147. Springer (2025). https://doi.org/10.1007/978-3-032-02602-6_10
26. Dwyer, M.B., Avrunin, G.S., Corbett, J.C.: Property specification patterns for finite-state verification. In: Ardis, M. (ed.) Proceedings of the 2nd Workshop on Formal Methods in Software Practice (FMSP 1998), pp. 7–15. ACM Press (1998). https://doi.org/10.1145/298595.298598
27. Esparza, J., Křetínský, J., Sickert, S.: One theorem to rule them all: a unified translation of LTL into ω-automata. In: Dawar, A., Grädel, E. (eds.) Proceedings of the 33rd Annual ACM/IEEE Symposium on Logic in Computer Science (LICS 2018), pp. 384–393. ACM (2018). https://doi.org/10.1145/3209108.3209161
28. Esparza, J., Rubio, R., Sickert, S.: Efficient normalization of linear temporal logic. J. ACM **71**(2) (2024). https://doi.org/10.1145/3651152

29. Etessami, K., Holzmann, G.J.: Optimizing Büchi automata. In: Palamidessi, C. (ed.) CONCUR 2000. LNCS, vol. 1877, pp. 153–168. Springer, Heidelberg (2000). https://doi.org/10.1007/3-540-44618-4_13
30. Finkbeiner, B.: Synthesis of reactive systems. In: Javier Esparza, Orna Grumberg, S.S. (ed.) Dependable Software Systems Engineering, NATO Science for Peace and Security Series — D: Information and Communication Security, vol. 45, pp. 72–98. IOS Press (2016). https://doi.org/10.3233/978-1-61499-627-9-72
31. Finkbeiner, B., Geier, G., Passing, N.: Specification decomposition for reactive synthesis. In: Dutle, A., Moscato, M.M., Titolo, L., Muñoz, C.A., Perez, I. (eds.) NFM 2021. LNCS, vol. 12673, pp. 113–130. Springer, Cham (2021). https://doi.org/10.1007/978-3-030-76384-8_8
32. Fujita, M., McGeer, P.C., Yang, J.C.: Multi-terminal binary decision diagrams: an efficient data structure for matrix representation. Formal Methods Syst. Des. **10**(2/3), 149–169 (1997). https://doi.org/10.1023/A:1008647823331
33. Gaiser, A., Schwoon, S.: Comparison of algorithms for checking emptiness on Büchi automata. In: Hlinený, P., Matyás, V., Vojnar, T. (eds.) Proceedings of Annual Doctoral Workshop on Mathematical and Engineering Methods in Computer Science (MEMICS'09). OASICS, vol. 13. Schloss Dagstuhl, Leibniz-Zentrum fuer Informatik, Germany (2009). https://doi.org/10.4230/DROPS.MEMICS.2009.2349
34. Geldenhuys, J., Hansen, H.: Larger automata and less work for LTL model checking. In: Valmari, A. (ed.) SPIN 2006. LNCS, vol. 3925, pp. 53–70. Springer, Heidelberg (2006). https://doi.org/10.1007/11691617_4
35. Geldenhuys, J., Valmari, A.: More efficient on-the-fly LTL verification with Tarjan's algorithm. Theor. Comput. Sci. **345**(1), 60–82 (2005). https://doi.org/10.1016/j.tcs.2005.07.004
36. Henriksen, J.G., et al.: Mona: monadic second-order logic in practice. In: Brinksma, E., Cleaveland, W.R., Larsen, K.G., Margaria, T., Steffen, B. (eds.) TACAS 1995. LNCS, vol. 1019, pp. 89–110. Springer, Heidelberg (1995). https://doi.org/10.1007/3-540-60630-0_5
37. Holeček, J., Kratochvíla, T., Řehák, V., Šafránek, D., Šimeček, P.: Verification results in Liberouter project. Technical Report 03, CESNET (2004). http://archiv.cesnet.cz/doc/techzpravy/2004/verificationresults/
38. Jacobs, S., et al.: The reactive synthesis competition (SYNTCOMP): 2018–2021. arXiV (2022). https://doi.org/10.48550/ARXIV.2206.00251
39. Klarlund, N., Møller, A.: MONA version 1.4, user manual. Technical report, BRICS (2001). https://www.brics.dk/mona/mona14.pdf
40. Křetínský, J., Meggendorfer, T., Prokop, M., Zarkhah, A.: SemML: enhancing automata-theoretic LTL synthesis with machine learning. In: Gurfinkel, A., Heule, M. (eds.) Proceedings of the 31st International Conference on Tools and Algorithms for the Construction and Analysis of Systems (TACAS 2025), pp. 233–253. Springer (2025). https://doi.org/10.1007/978-3-031-90643-5_12
41. Křetínský, J., Meggendorfer, T., Sickert, S.: Owl: a library for ω-words, automata, and LTL. In: Lahiri, S.K., Wang, C. (eds.) ATVA 2018. LNCS, vol. 11138, pp. 543–550. Springer, Cham (2018). https://doi.org/10.1007/978-3-030-01090-4_34
42. Kupferman, O., Rosenberg, A.: The blow-up in translating LTL to deterministic automata. In: van der Meyden, R., Smaus, J.-G. (eds.) MoChArt 2010. LNCS (LNAI), vol. 6572, pp. 85–94. Springer, Heidelberg (2011). https://doi.org/10.1007/978-3-642-20674-0_6

43. Kupferman, O., Vardi, M.Y.: Safraless decision procedures. In: Proceedings of the 46th Annual IEEE Symposium on Foundations of Computer Science (FOCS 2005), pp. 531–542 (2005). https://doi.org/10.1109/SFCS.2005.66
44. Kupferman, O., Vardi, M.Y., Wolper, P.: An automata-theoretic approach to branching-time model checking. J. ACM **47**(2), 312–360 (2000). https://doi.org/10.1145/333979.333987
45. Li, Y., Xiao, S., Zhu, S., Li, J., Pu, G.: A compositional framework for on-the-fly LTL_f synthesis. In: Proceedings of the 28th European Conference on Artificial Intelligence (ECAI 2025), pp. 1711–1718. Frontiers in Artificial Intelligence and Applications (2025). https://doi.org/10.3233/FAIA250999
46. Löding, C.: Methods for the transformation of ω-automata: complexity and connection to second order logic. Diploma thesis, Institute of Computer Science and Applied Mathematics Christian-Albrechts-University of Kiel (1998). https://www.lics.rwth-aachen.de/global/show_document.asp?id=aaaaaaaaabcqdty
47. Löding, C.: Efficient minimization of deterministic weak ω-automata. Inf. Process. Lett. **79**(3), 105–109 (2001). https://doi.org/10.1016/S0020-0190(00)00183-6
48. Long, D.: BDD library. https://www.cs.cmu.edu/~modelcheck/bdd.html
49. Luttenberger, M., Meyer, P.J., Sickert, S.: Practical synthesis of reactive systems from LTL specifications via parity games. Acta Informatica **57**(1–2), 3–36 (2020). https://doi.org/10.1007/S00236-019-00349-3
50. Major, J., Blahoudek, F., Strejček, J., Sasaráková, M., Zbončáková, T.: `ltl3tela`: LTL to small deterministic or nondeterministic Emerson-lei automata. In: Chen, Y.-F., Cheng, C.-H., Esparza, J. (eds.) ATVA 2019. LNCS, vol. 11781, pp. 357–365. Springer, Cham (2019). https://doi.org/10.1007/978-3-030-31784-3_21
51. Manna, Z., Pnueli, A.: A hierarchy of temporal properties. In: Proceedings of the Sixth Annual ACM Symposium on Principles of Distributed Computing (PODC 1990), pp. 377–410. ACM, New York, NY, USA (1990). https://doi.org/10.1145/93385.93442
52. Manna, Z., Pnueli, A.: The Temporal Logic of Reactive and Concurrent Systems: Specification. Springer (1992). https://doi.org/10.1007/978-1-4612-0931-7
53. Manna, Z., Pnueli, A.: Temporal Verification of Reactive Systems: Safety. Springer (1995). https://doi.org/10.1007/978-1-4612-4222-2
54. Manna, Z., Pnueli, A.: Temporal verification of reactive systems: response. In: Manna, Z., Peled, D.A. (eds.) Time for Verification. LNCS, vol. 6200, pp. 279–361. Springer, Heidelberg (2010). https://doi.org/10.1007/978-3-642-13754-9_13
55. Minato, S.I.: Representation of Multi-Valued Functions, pp. 39–47. Springer, Boston (1996). https://doi.org/10.1007/978-1-4613-1303-8_4
56. Moore, E.F.: Gedanken-experiments on sequential machines. In: Automata Studies. Annals of Mathematical Studies, no. 34, pp. 129–153. Princeton University Press (1956)
57. Müller, D., Sickert, S.: LTL to deterministic Emerson-Lei automata. In: Proceedings of the 8th International Symposium on Games, Automata, Logics and Formal Verification (GandALF'17). Electronic Proceedings in Theoretical Computer Science, vol. 256, pp. 180–194. Open Publishing Association (2017). https://doi.org/10.4204/EPTCS.256.13
58. Pelánek, R.: BEEM: benchmarks for explicit model checkers. In: Bošnački, D., Edelkamp, S. (eds.) SPIN 2007. LNCS, vol. 4595, pp. 263–267. Springer, Heidelberg (2007). https://doi.org/10.1007/978-3-540-73370-6_17
59. Piterman, N., Pnueli, A., Sa'ar, Y.: Synthesis of reactive(1) designs. In: Emerson, E.A., Namjoshi, K.S. (eds.) VMCAI 2006. LNCS, vol. 3855, pp. 364–380. Springer, Heidelberg (2005). https://doi.org/10.1007/11609773_24

60. Pnueli, A.: The temporal logic of programs. In: Proceedings of the 18th Annual Symposium on Foundations of Computer Science (FOCS 1977), pp. 46–57 (1977). https://doi.org/10.1109/SFCS.1977.32
61. Pnueli, A., Rosner, R.: On the synthesis of a reactive module. In: Proceedings of the 16th ACM SIGPLAN-SIGACT Symposium on Principles of Programming Languages (POPL 1989). Association for Computing Machinery (1989). https://doi.org/10.1145/75277.75293
62. Redziejowski, R.: An improved construction of deterministic omega-automaton using derivatives. Fund. Inform. **119**(3–4), 393–406 (2012). https://doi.org/10.3233/FI-2012-744
63. Renault, E., Duret-Lutz, A., Kordon, F., Poitrenaud, D.: Three SCC-based emptiness checks for generalized Büchi automata. In: McMillan, K., Middeldorp, A., Voronkov, A. (eds.) LPAR 2013. LNCS, vol. 8312, pp. 668–682. Springer, Heidelberg (2013). https://doi.org/10.1007/978-3-642-45221-5_44
64. Renkin, F., Duret-Lutz, A., Pommellet, A.: Practical "paritizing" of Emerson-lei automata. In: Hung, D.V., Sokolsky, O. (eds.) ATVA 2020. LNCS, vol. 12302, pp. 127–143. Springer, Cham (2020). https://doi.org/10.1007/978-3-030-59152-6_7
65. Renkin, F., Schlehuber-Caissier, P., Duret-Lutz, A., Pommellet, A.: Dissecting `ltlsynt`. Formal Methods Syst. Des. (2023). https://doi.org/10.1007/s10703-022-00407-6
66. Schewe, S.: Beyond hyper-minimisation—minimising DBAs and DPAs is NP-complete. In: Lodaya, K., Mahajan, M. (eds.) Proceedings of the IARCS Annual Conference on Foundations of Software Technology and Theoretical Computer Science (FSTTCS 2010). Leibniz International Proceedings in Informatics, vol. 8, pp. 400–411. Schloss Dagstuhl LZI, Dagstuhl, Germany (2010). https://doi.org/10.4230/LIPIcs.FSTTCS.2010.400
67. Somenzi, F., Bloem, R.: Efficient Büchi automata from LTL formulae. In: Emerson, E.A., Sistla, A.P. (eds.) CAV 2000. LNCS, vol. 1855, pp. 248–263. Springer, Heidelberg (2000). https://doi.org/10.1007/10722167_21
68. Tabakov, D., Vardi, M.Y.: Optimized temporal monitors for SystemC. In: Barringer, H., Falcone, Y., Finkbeiner, B., Havelund, K., Lee, I., Pace, G., Roşu, G., Sokolsky, O., Tillmann, N. (eds.) RV 2010. LNCS, vol. 6418, pp. 436–451. Springer, Heidelberg (2010). https://doi.org/10.1007/978-3-642-16612-9_33
69. Vardi, M.Y.: Automatic verification of probabilistic concurrent finite state programs. In: Proceedings of the 26th Annual Symposium on Foundations of Computer Science (SFCS 1985), pp. 327–338. IEEE (1985). https://doi.org/10.1109/SFCS.1985.12
70. Zhu, S., Tabajara, L.M., Li, J., Pu, G., Vardi, M.Y.: Symbolic LTLf synthesis. In: Proceedings of the 26th International Joint Conference on Artificial Intelligence (IJCAI 2017), pp. 1362–1369 (2017). https://doi.org/10.24963/ijcai.2017/189

sweap: Reactive Synthesis for Infinite-State Integer Problems

Shaun Azzopardi[1(✉)], Luca Di Stefano[2], and Nir Piterman[3]

[1] Dedaub, San Gwann, Malta
shaun.a@dedaub.com
[2] TU Wien, Institute of Computer Engineering, Treitlstraße 3, 1040 Vienna, Austria
[3] University of Gothenburg and Chalmers, University of Technology, Gothenburg, Sweden

Abstract. Recent years have seen a significant increase in the interest in reactive synthesis from specifications that relate to infinite state spaces. We present sweap, a tool for synthesis of infinite-state Linear Integer Arithmetic reactive systems. sweap implements a CEGAR approach, relying on state-of-the-art finite-state synthesis tools as black boxes to solve abstract synthesis problems. sweap supports most common input formalisms for infinite-state reactive-synthesis problems: Temporal Stream Logic Modulo Theories, Reactive Program Games, the bespoke input of the Issy tool, and our own bespoke input. We present a mature version of sweap with novel features: a dual abstraction approach that improves its capabilities in proving unrealisability, support for nondeterministic and unbounded updates, more general initialization of variables, and equirealisable reductions for optimisation. Experimental evaluation shows that sweap outperforms its only competitor in this domain.

Keywords: Reactive Synthesis · CEGAR · Infinite-State Systems

1 Introduction

Reactive synthesis aims at generating correct-by-construction programs from high-level temporal specifications. This problem is framed as a two-player game between a *controller* and an adversarial *environment* [18]. A program, then, is a winning strategy for the controller (if any exists). The traditional setting is that of synthesis over propositions. Given the success of state-of-the-art techniques in this finite domain, many in the community have started moving beyond, to infinite-state domains. Several tools and techniques have been developed, showing surprising effectiveness for an undecidable problem.

First attempts to tackle this problem relied on a counter-example guided abstraction refinement (CEGAR) approach—a finite abstraction of the infinite-state problem is computed and fed to an LTL synthesis tool, and the strategy received is used to refine the abstraction or conclude un/realisability. Approaches

E. Darulova et al. (Eds.): CAV 2026, LNCS 16682, pp. 340–353, 2026.
https://doi.org/10.1007/978-3-032-32519-8_18

that originally tackled problems defined in Temporal Stream Logic (TSL) [7], LTL modulo theories [14], and others [20], are of this kind. By design, these focus on learning new safety properties of the underlying theory, relative to the predicates and updates in the objective. Since the cost of finite LTL synthesis is high, these approaches start with essentially no abstraction and build it through refinement. In any case, the basic CEGAR setup proves insufficient for infinite-state problems where liveness is important: in this context, one may never learn enough properties to conclude that, e.g., incrementing an integer repeatedly will eventually make it greater than an arbitrary value.

Later approaches targeting Reactive Program Games (RPG) and ISSY improved using symbolic analysis of game graphs, with quantifier elimination computing winning regions of (symbolically represented infinite) graphs; using *acceleration* to bypass infinite refinement that CEGAR-based approaches had [9,10].

This paper concerns sweap, a CEGAR-based tool for synthesising strategies for LTL games over infinite-state arenas. Our approach [3] goes beyond previous CEGAR-based work, by starting with a full predicate abstraction and automatically learning relevant liveness properties of the game. The abstraction and the LTL objective are fed to an LTL synthesis tool in each CEGAR round. We rely on a novel binary encoding of predicates that reduces the size and computation time of predicate abstraction to polynomial rather than exponential. Thanks to this efficient encoding, the size of the LTL formula is no longer exponential in the number of predicates, reducing the cost of synthesis. This binary encoding enables sweap to eagerly add relevant LTL formulas, to the abstraction, that describe the effect of state updates (inc/decrementing) on the predicate state.

In this paper, we present a mature version of sweap supporting higher-level problem that include numeric inputs, uninitialised variables, and unbounded controller updates. Furthermore, we address sweap's previous limitations with solving unrealisable problems: we describe how sweap can dualise the problem by under-approximating control of the arena, rather than the standard over-approximating. We also describe how we implemented automatic translations of other languages into the sweap, allowing better comparison between different approaches, along with several equirealisable reductions. On benchmarks from literature, we show how these new features increase the capacity of sweap and that sweap outperforms the main tool in this domain on literature benchmarks.

2 The sweap Approach

Problem Formulation. sweap solves infinite-state reactive synthesis problems given as LTL games. The game arena is a symbolic automaton with a finitely many control states. Transitions relate to input, output, and state variables. The objective is an LTL formula over control states and first-order predicates over all state variables, inputs, and outputs. Inputs and state variables may have infinite domains, while outputs are Boolean. Unlike inputs and outputs, state variables, unless updated explicitly (w.r.t. previous values), preserve their value. Arena transitions describe conditions on the next value of state variables, with nondeterministic updates, including infinite-branching, resolved by the controller.

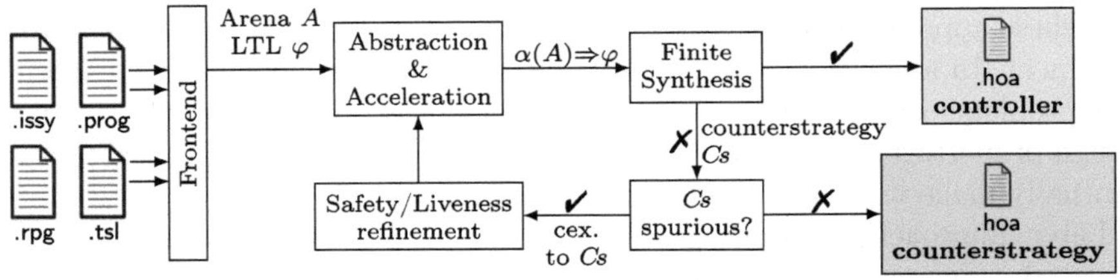

Fig. 1. Overview of sweap's workflow.

CEGAR Approach. sweap takes a standard CEGAR approach [5] (see Fig. 1). Given arena A and objective φ, sweap creates the abstract arena $\alpha(A)$ via predicate abstraction [8], and synthesises for $\alpha(A) \Rightarrow \varphi$ with a finite synthesis engine (Strix [16] or SemML [13,19]). By abstraction soundness, if a controller is found it is also valid for the concrete problem. Spurious counterstrategies (determined through invariant checking), are used to refine the abstraction for a new attempt.

sweap innovates on the CEGAR approach for synthesis [12,14] by using *liveness* refinement, only resorting to safety refinement when the former is unsuccessful. This refinement relies on termination checking of the concrete behaviour induced by spurious lassos in abstract counterstrategies; and then refining the abstract problem with the learned terminating behaviour.

Listing 1. sweap example.

```
INPUTS { i : natural }
OUTPUTS {}
STATE VARIABLES { x, y: natural }
CONTROL STATES { q: init }
OBJECTIVE { F y == 0 }
TRANSITIONS
 {q -> q [x > 0 & y > 0
          # x' >= x - 1 &
            y' = y],
  q -> q [x = 0 & y > 0
          # y' >= y - 1 &
            x' = i]   }
```

To manage the complexity of predicate abstraction (exponential) and synthesis (doubly exponential), sweap uses a unique and natural binary encoding of predicates. Intuitively, LIA predicates are normalised into the form $t \leq c$, where t is a term over variables, and c a term over constant values. For each term, predicates can be used to define mutually exclusive intervals that cover the number line. For example, given predicates $x \leq 0$, $x \leq 4$, and $x \leq 10$, we can define formulas over these predicates to state that $x \in (-\infty, 0)$, $x \in [0, 4)$, $x \in [4, 10)$, and $x \in [10, \infty)$. As these four statements are mutually exclusive, and their disjunction is a tautology, we can represent them using two Boolean variables. By following these in the abstraction, rather that the single predicates, computing the abstraction becomes polynomial rather than exponential. Other CEGAR approaches create a fresh Boolean variable per predicate [7,14,20], making the Boolean LTL synthesis problem doubly exponential in the number of predicates. In our case, given the binary encoding, the complexity of the abstract synthesis problem is only exponential in the number of predicates. Importantly, sweap further adds acceleration assumptions purely based on these intervals, encoding that incrementing a term infinitely often, without similar decrements, must lead to reaching higher intervals (and, similarly, decrementing leads to lower intervals) [3].

Example 1. Listing 1 is an example of a sweap problem. Transitions are guarded by two conditions, separated by #, respectively over the current state (a guard) and the state change (an update). A transition is triggered when its guard holds, and consequently we require determinism over these guards. A primed variable x' denotes the next value of variable x. The game has an LTL reachability goal stating that variable y eventually has value 0, to be achieved within the constraints of the arena. The arena has two transitions: the first is triggered when both x and y are greater than 0, and lets the controller choose the next value of x within the given constraints. Similarly, the second transition can only be taken when x is 0 and y is greater than 0, and allows some choice in the next value of y, but forces the next value of x to match the current value of input variable i. Transitions describe how the state is allowed to evolve under certain conditions; if no state change is allowed, e.g., when $x = y = 0$, the entire arena just stutters. sweap determines this problem realisable, and returns a controller that simply chooses the smallest allowed value of x and y in each turn.

Other Features. sweap also supports one-shot finite synthesis over its input language, when all the types are finite (Boolean, or bounded intervals). Moreover, it provides arguments to verify returned controllers against the arena and objective through composing these in a nuXmv model. The user can also use this model to simulate the execution of the program against the strategy.

3 Beyond Bounded Inputs and Updates (and More)

The theory behind the prototype version of sweap required fixed initial values of state variables, Boolean inputs, and a finite set of assignments for variable updates. This setting can encode specifications equirealisable to any LIA specification in TSL, RPG, and ISSY (up to addition of extra variables), with excellent comparative performance and success rate [3], but required manual translation of specification and the arena, which is error-prone [4]. We have since extended the syntax of sweap's own input language to enable higher-level specifications (see Listing 1). Here we describe the novel features. Throughout we refer to predicates that refer only to state variables as *state predicates* and those that also refer to inputs as *input predicates.*

Uninitialized State Variables. With unintialised state variables, sweap attempts to find a strategy that works for all possible initial values. When constructing the abstraction, sweap determines all possible satisfiable combinations of state predicates. These options become an initial assumption in the abstraction formula, limiting the abstract environment to a legal initial choice of state predicates.

Unbounded Inputs. Numeric inputs are now a first-class feature and the predicate abstraction now also follows input predicates.

Input predicates may relate inputs with state variables: in a naïve approach, where the environment is unconstrained in its choice of input predicates, it would be allowed to choose illegal predicate combinations. To maintain soundness, we construct the set of all legal input states as follows. First, we collect all satisfiable combinations of input predicates; then, for each combination, we perform quantifier elimination (QE), asking for a necessary condition on state variables for its satisfiability. We restrict the environment to this set of combinations and their conditions, enforcing local legality [20].

Given local legality, during spuriousness checking we can assume that inputs are always set in a way compatible with the input predicates chosen by the environment. Thus spuriousness is always due a wrong state predicate guess. However, such a wrong guess may be due to too coarse input predicates. Consider $x' = i$, where x and i are respectively state and input variables. The environment may wish $x = 7$ to be true in the next step, however it only knows $i \geq 0$. It sets this predicate in the current step and $x = 7$ in the next, as the transition is satisfiable. Spuriousness checking will find a mismatch, since not all models of $i \geq 0$ imply $x = 7$. Then we require refining of input predicates.

For safety refinement, given a counterexample, we previously relied solely on sequence interpolation [15]. This constructs a sequence of formulas corresponding to the counterexample: the initial concrete counterexample state, formulas corresponding to the arena transitions and predicate choices in each time step, and a final formula representing the wrong guesses of the counterstrategy. Note that we do not include the concrete values of input variables in the counterexample, and ground all Boolean variables on their concrete values, giving a purely numeric formula. Variables appearing in these formulas are time-step indexed, giving a sequence of formulas $F_0, ..., F_n, M$, where M is the conjunction of the wrong predicate guesses in the last counterexample state. Interpolants are computed for each time-step i, as formulas over the common alphabets of F_i and F_{i+1}. However, input variables are set freshly in each time-step and are never in the common alphabet: thus, interpolation can never discover input predicates.

When interpolation fails, we search for additional input predicates that would allow the abstract environment to reach the predicate state (M) exposed by the counterexample. This resembles how QE is used in other work [20]. We re-use the formulas constructed for interpolation: $f_{ce} = (F_0 \wedge ... \wedge F_n) \implies M$. As a quick first attempt, sweap proceeds by performing QE over $\forall S_0, ..., S_n . f_{ce}$, where S_i is the set of state variables indexed by i. This gives us a formula over pure input predicates. If no fresh predicates are found, we search for predicates that relate inputs with state variables at each time-step, i.e. to relate the inputs and state variables at step i, we apply QE on the formula $\forall S_{\neq i}, I_{\neq i} . f_{ce}$, where $S_{\neq i}$ is the set of state variables not indexed by i, and similarly $I_{\neq i}$ for inputs. This gives us n formulas. From each we extract a set of fresh input predicates, and choose the smallest non-empty such set to use in the next refinement step.

Unbounded Updates. sweap now supports underspecified updates to state variables, with the non-determinism resolved by the controller (see Listing 1). Canonical sweap arenas are still as in the prototype: transitions with guards and a list of assignments for every state variable ($s := f(V)$ is an assignement, where s is a state variable, and $f(V)$ a formula over all arena variables). The new high-level syntax is translated to this canonical form through a realisability-preserving transformation of the arena, that is essentially the same as we have previously described to encode numeric inputs in the arena state [3]. For every transition that requires unbounded controller choice over variables, we redirect it to a fresh state that allows the controller to increment or decrement the variables, allowing it to continue to the original target only when the update condition holds. A modification of the LTL objective is also required, to ensure the evaluation of the formula stutters when the arena is in the introduced states, and a guarantee is added to ensure the controller eventually leaves such states.

4 Flipping Control of the Arena Abstraction

By default the environment controls the state predicates. However, there are unrealisable problems which do not admit finite counterstrategies with this abstraction choice, leading to non-termination for our approach. We introduce a dual approach, that flips control of state variables to the controller, allowing for termination in these cases. We consider a simple illustrative example.

Example 2. Consider the problem in Listing 2, where $c1$ and $c2$ are controller propositions, i an integer input, and x an integer state variable. In q0 the controller can force any value of x, or move to q1 (if x is non-negative). At q1 the environment chooses an i to increment x with. The controller objective states that eventually the arena moves to q1 and that x is always bounded above by 10.

Listing 2. Dualisation example.

```
...
OBJECTIVE { (F q1) & (G x < 10) }
TRANSITIONS
 { q0 -> q0 [!c1 & !c2 # x' = x + 1]
   q0 -> q0 [!c1 & c2 # x' = x - 1]
   q0 -> q0 [c1 & x < 0 # x' = x]
   q0 -> q1 [c1 & x >= 0 # x' = x]
   q1 -> q1 [true # x' = x + i] }
```

This example is clearly unrealisable: if q1 is reached, there is always an integer i the environment can choose to make x larger than 10 (in fact, $i = 10$ always suffices). However, in our standard flow, where the environment must accurately emit the current predicate state in each turn, the winning counterstrategy is infinite. Consider $x = 0$ initially, and the controller decrements x, leading the environment to respond correctly with $x < 0$. At this point, if the controller chooses to increment x, the predicate abstraction offers two choices for the environment response: $x < 0$ or $x = 0$, i.e. precision is lost. In fact, responding precisely to any possible sequence of inc/decrements requires counting, and thus an infinite amount of state predicates.

Our solution is to provide a setting that switches control of state predicates to the controller. Essentially, in this dual approach, where the controller controls

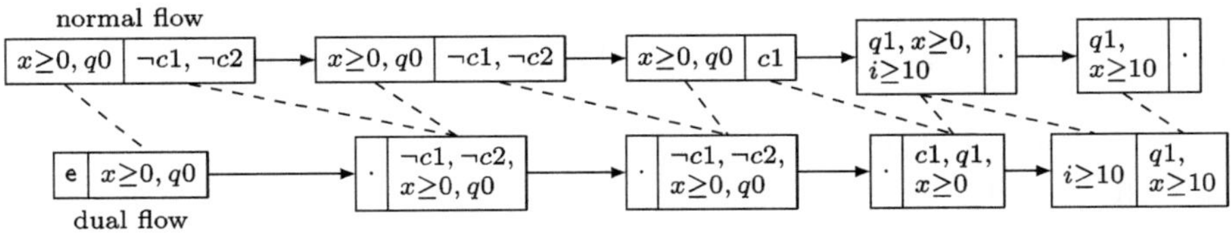

Fig. 2. A trace from the abstraction of Listing 2 and its dualised counterpart.

the state predicates (but the environment remains in control of input predicates) there is a finite counterstrategy: the environment can simply win by setting $i \geq 10$ when q1 is reached, regardless of the controller choice for state predicates.

To support the dual setting, we change the interaction between the controller and the environment. Normally, initially, the environment chooses initial values of state predicates. Then it chooses inputs followed by the controller choosing outputs. Then, in every step, the environment chooses predicates (based on the previously taken transition) followed by inputs, and the controller replies with outputs. Conceptually, a dual interaction instead includes a choice by the controller for values of state predicates, a choice by the environment of inputs, and another choice by the controller for outputs and predicates (repeatedly in every step). We support this by moving the choice of state predicates to the previous time step. Thus, initially, the controller chooses values for state predicates. Then, in every step, the environment chooses inputs (including input predicates), the controller chooses outputs and updates the state predicates based on the transition. It follows that arena transitions must be executed across time steps.

To enable this in the abstract problem, we change the produced LTL formulas by adding one next operator (X) before any occurrence of input or output variables, and input predicates. Namely, if the original formula is φ and the description of the arena is $\alpha(A)$, the new formula for finite synthesis becomes $\alpha^{dual}(A) \wedge \varphi^{dual}$, with the modifications described. Notice that, in this new problem, it is the responsibility of the controller to obey the constraints of the arena. Furthermore, the initial choices of inputs and outputs (at time 0) do not play a role in the evaluation of such formulas. In the case of undetermined initial values, we include an additional interaction between the environment and the controller at time 0. We check which initial predicate states are feasible and add enough Boolean inputs to the environment so that it can force one such state. We then allow the controller, as explained, to choose the actual predicates. We enforce that the controller copies correctly these values by adding a conjunct φ_{init}. Finally, input predicates, which are determined only by the environment, are also moved to the correct time step (i.e., scoped by X).

We force the environment to choose only legal combinations of input predicates, after the controller acts, by the formula $G(\varphi_{inputs})$, where φ_{inputs} is a disjunction over all legal input predicate combinations, and obtain the final specification $G(\varphi_{inputs}) \implies \varphi_{init} \wedge \alpha^{dual}(A) \wedge \varphi^{dual}$.

Figure 2 shows how an abstract trace for Example 2 changes between the normal and the dual flow, when following the predicates: $x \geq 0$, $x \geq 10$, and $i \geq 10$. For simplicity, we write $x \geq 0$ sfor $x \geq 0 \wedge \neg(x \geq 10)$, and ignore $i \geq 10$ until q1 is reached. Each trace step contains two boxes for the environment and controller's choices in each timestep, respectively. When certain choices do not affect the objective or abstraction, we simply write $\cdot$ in their place. For the dual flow, we introduce fresh propositions to let the environment choose the initial arena state: here we introduce the environment proposition e which when set forces the controller to choose $x \geq 0$ and q0. Note that state predicates (e.g., $x \geq 0$) stay at the same time step, but in the dual flow are chosen by controller. Controller outputs $(c1, c2)$ and original environment inputs (i) are instead pushed to the next state. Hence, if the LTL objective had an assumption $G(q1 \rightarrow (i \leq 0))$, then for the dual problem this would be transformed into $G(q1 \rightarrow X(i \geq 0))$, to maintain the semantics and preserve (un)realisablity.

5 Equirealisable Translations and Reductions

sweap now handles other input languages used by the community, specifically Temporal Stream Logic (TSL), Reactive Program Games (RPGs), and the Issy input format. Problems in each format can be translated to equirealisable problems in the other formats, but they differ in style. In this section, we detail how sweap transforms these into its format, while maintaining equirealisability. We also present equirealisable reductions sweap performs to reduce game size.

Reactive Program Games (RPG). A problem described in RPG is a deterministic symbolic arena with an explicit objective over arena control states (safety, reachability, Büchi, or parity). It includes numeric inputs with a finite set of assignments. The translation of the arena defined to sweap's arena format is thus simply a parsing and compilation problem. The RPG objectives are transformed into equivalent LTL objectives over arena states in the expected manner.

Temporal Stream Logic (TSL). TSL problems are LTL formulas, without any arena, over predicates and a finite set of assignments. To support assignments, we create an arena that allows the controller to choose among them. To keep the predicate abstraction small, rather than considering all the possible assignment combinations, we partition assignments based on a cone-of-influence analysis. Assignments depending on inputs are placed in the first partition. Each arena control state corresponds to a partition, and transitions from it to choosing a combination of assignments in the partition. The controller's non-deterministic choice is resolved with minimal fresh outputs. The TSL formula is modified to serve as the objective, by replacing explicit references to each assignment $u =$ v := expr, with where v is updated at state s by a statement $\neg s\, U\, (s \wedge f_u)$, where f_u is a formula over the fresh outputs that trigger u in the state s (s corresponds to the partition u is in). Predicates are handled similarly, so that they are only evaluated in the initial state of the arena, preserving equi-realisability.

Issy Input Format. An ISSY problem is a list of formula objectives and games, with transitions guarded by update formulas. Formula objectives cannot talk about game arena states, but range over input and state variables, and also over primed state variables, representing their next-state value. These formulas and games each express their own objectives, and are interpreted conjunctively.

We apply some optimisations: (i) Boolean state variables appearing only primed are transformed into (unprimed) controller propositions; and (ii) numeric state variables that are never related with other variables have their predicates given a binary encoding, and the fresh controller propositions are used instead.

ISSY problems do not require an explicit game arena. We check formula-only problems with Spot [6], to identify whether an arena can be extracted directly from an objective, or whether an arena, such as that described for TSL, can be constructed. When these are not possible, we construct a dummy arena that allows the controller to choose any next value of any state variable.

When arenas are explicitly defined, we transform these into one sweap arena. For each arena, we normalise transition conditions into DNF form. Unsatisfiable disjuncts are removed, while the update conditions and guards are separated. Then, for each state, we get a set of guard and update-condition pairs. By Issy semantics, the disjunction of the guards here must be a tautology. Given our optimisations (see (i) above), this may no longer be the case: we resolve this by a transition to a fresh losing state for the uncovered part of the domain. In the presence of multiple games, we compute their cross-product. Then, we resolve any non-determinism in the transition guards with fresh controller propositions, at which point we get a sweap arena. Game arena objectives are expressed equivalently in LTL and conjuncted to the formula objectives. Objectives need to be massaged, replacing any predicate that references primed variables into their next-state representation (e.g., $x > x'$ becomes $X(x_{prev} > x)$).

Equirealisable Reductions. sweap performs several reductions to simplify games into equirealisabile ones, resulting in smaller synthesis problems.

When there is a non-deterministic choice of next variable value, sweap analyses whether the choice is relevant to the game. It is relevant if the objective predicates over the variable, or if a data-flow analysis from the relevant state determines that it is accessed before being assigned a fresh value. Irrelevant variables from a state are stuttered, or, initially, given a default value.

sweap also employs a reachability analysis, removing any unreachable arena control states. Furthermore, it computes the arena's strongly-connected components (SCCs), using these to optimise acceleration formulas. SCCs are also used during the translation of ISSY and RPG problems to detect further losing states (e.g., states from which a Büchi objective is not reachable). Once a losing state is reached, the game stops and the arena state stutters.

6 Experimental Evaluation

In this section, we evaluate the presented version of sweap[1], and how it compares to the state-of-the-art tool Issy [10]. Issy is the only other available infinite-state synthesis tool that handles problems unsolvable by safety refinements alone, and supports the same formalisms as sweap.

sweap refers to a virtual portfolio approach: we attempt to solve the same problem as-is and dualised, always using SemML as the finite synthesis engine, and then take the fastest time among the two. When both configurations reach a verdict, these are consistent across all experiments. All experiments described in this section were run on a GNU/Linux computing cluster equipped with AMD EPYC 9355 processors. Each task was given 4 CPU cores, a time limit of 10 min, and a memory limit of 64 GiB. We run Issy by using a container image obtained from its official Github repository.[2]

Table 1. Results of comparative evaluations of sweap against sweap-strix and Issy. Columns report the number of **S**olved problems, **F**astest, and **U**nique solutions.

(a) All problems in sweap's input format.

Tool	S	F	U
sweap-strix	65	41	0
sweap	**84**	**42**	**19**

Breakdown of problems solved by sweap:

	PROG	ISSY	RPG	TSL
total:	84	91	77	55
only **base**:	52	61	51	36
only **dual**:	12	5	8	11
base faster than **dual**:	8	8	4	2
dual faster than **base**:	12	17	14	6

(b) Problems in ISSY, TSL, and RPG.

		Realisable			Unrealisable		
Format	Tool	S	F	U	S	F	U
ISSY	Issy	42	18	2	20	**14**	3
	sweap	**70**	**53**	**40**	**21**	5	**4**
RPG	Issy	52	**34**	2	16	**14**	0
	sweap	**57**	25	**7**	**20**	6	**4**
TSL	Issy	32	17	2	14	**10**	0
	sweap	**38**	**21**	**8**	**17**	7	**3**

Evaluation of Novel Features. First, we consider the new version of sweap alongside a configuration sweap-strix that uses Strix as the finite synthesis engine and does not use dualisation. This configuration roughly corresponds to the capabilities that the tool had in its prototype stage, but includes optimisations mentioned in this paper. We perform our comparison over a collection of 95 benchmarks written in sweap's input language (PROG) [3]. 72 of these are realisable. The results are summarised in Table 1a. The new version of sweap solves 84 problems, 19 more than sweap-strix, and is faster on 42 of them. sweap-strix manages to be faster on 41 problems, but there are no problems that it can solve and sweap cannot. We note that the prototype version of sweap required at least 20 min to solve a similar amount of these benchmarks as sweap-strix [3]. Specifically, we are able to solve 7 more problems than sweap-strix just by using SemML; the other 12 extra problems are solved through dualisation, which is also faster on 8 of the 20 problems solved by both workflows. Note that this represents 52% of all 23 unrealisable benchmarks in this set.

[1] The development repository for sweap is: https://github.com/shaunazzopardi/sweap.

[2] https://github.com/phheim/issy/, revision 423bd1a, as instructed by its developers.

The scatter plot in Fig. 3a compares the runtimes of sweap-strix and sweap. It shows that sweap's superiority over sweap-strix comes from solving unrealisable problems, which are hard without the novel dualisation feature, and from finding faster solutions to mildly complex problems, most of them with Büchi objectives. sweap-strix remains faster on small problems, where the overhead of SemML may be overkill, possibly a sign that sweap may benefit from optimising startup time.

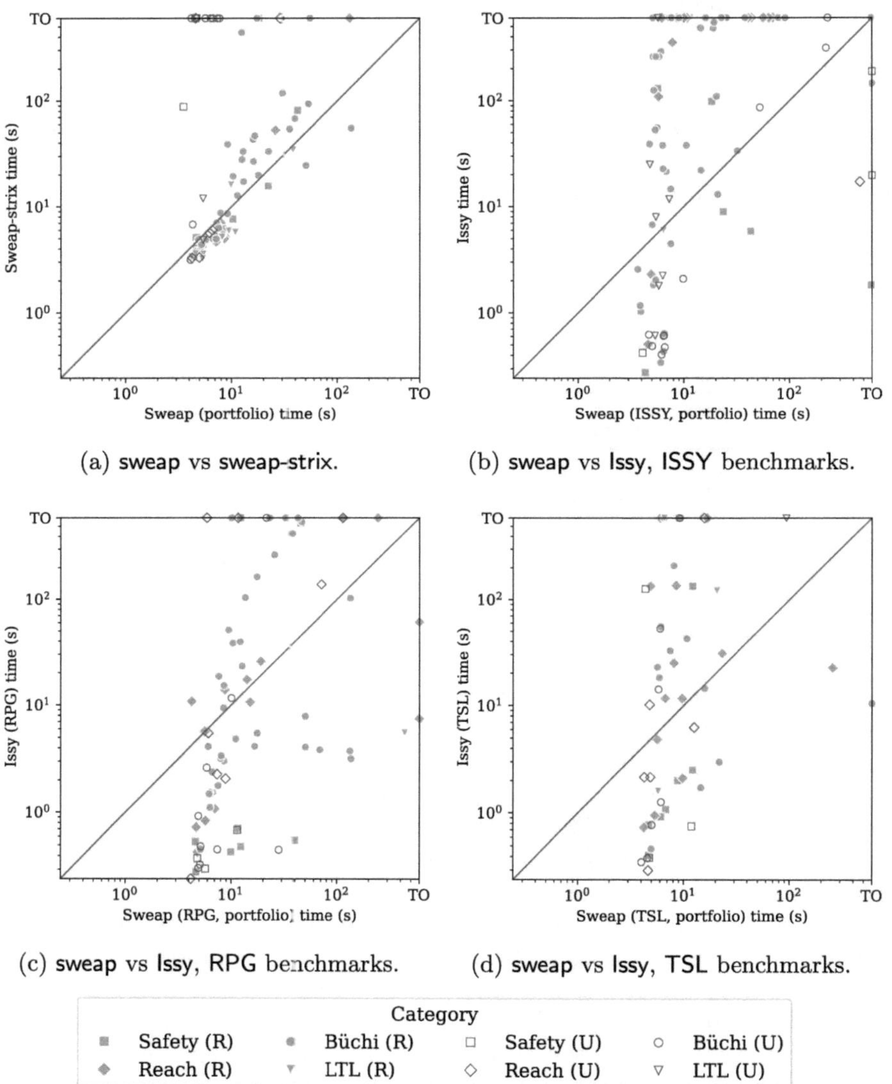

(a) sweap vs sweap-strix.

(b) sweap vs Issy, ISSY benchmarks.

(c) sweap vs Issy, RPG benchmarks.

(d) sweap vs Issy, TSL benchmarks.

Fig. 3. Each marker corresponds to a synthesis task that both tools carried out without runtime errors. Execution times for our new tool are always mapped to the hoizontal axis. Filled-out and outlined markers correspond to **R**ealisable and **U**nrealisable problems, respectively. Timeout (TO) is 10 min. Further details are provided in [2].

Comparative Evaluation with Issy. We collect a total of 266 reactive synthesis problems over Linear Integer Arithmetic from the literature [3,9–11,17,21] and try to synthesise for them using sweap and Issy. We wish to compare how they perform on the *synthesis problem*, rather than simply returning a verdict without a strategy. However, Issy does not produce counterstrategies, and thus we can only compare on realisable problems. For completeness, we also compare performance on unrealisable problems separately, but we stress that in this case Issy is solving a simpler problem, by only returning a verdict.

Out of 266 problems, 115 are expressed in ISSY (89 realisable), 86 in RPG (66 realisable), and 65 in TSL (45 realisable). Table 1b summarise the results for the two experiments. For realisability, sweap is able to solve more problems than Issy across all formats and find more unique solutions. Issy performs comparatively well, and is faster on more realisable RPG problems. Dualisation does not contribute significantly on realisable problems. For unrealisability, sweap performs relatively well, even though it is solving a harder problem. Dualisation is helpful here, uniquely solving 5 ISSY, 8 RPG, and 11 TSL problems, and is faster on average than the default configuration. Note that whenever both tools manage to solve a problem, their verdicts are always consistent.

Figure 3b–3d compare execution times for the two tools. Though describing conceptually different comparisons, we show the results for both realisable and unrealisable problems together, due to space constraints. In general, sweap incurs a certain overhead at startup, always requiring at least a few seconds to reach a verdict, but does better on larger problems.

We note that the Issy approach is less memory intensive than ours, due to our reliance on finite-synthesis tools. This is shown in Heim and Dimitrova's evaluation of Issy against the prototype version of sweap [10,11], where only 4 GiB/6 GiB of memory were allocated. sweap's default reliance on SemML further increases sweap memory requirements to at least 40 GiB of memory.

7 Conclusion

We presented a mature version of our reactive synthesis tool sweap. The tool supports all the major input formats that recently emerged from infinite-state synthesis research, and its bespoke format has been extended to support high-level specifications. With its novel features and optimisations, the new version of sweap significantly outperforms its earlier prototype [3] and compares positively against the state-of-the-art tool Issy [10].

We believe we can optimise our CEGAR loop by manipulating the abstract game structures directly, instead of formulating them through fresh LTL formulas at every iteration. In [3] we argued that our technique may generalise to linear real arithmetic (LRA), and we are investigating a practical implementation.

Acknowledgments. LDS is supported by the European Union (under grant agreement ID 101212818) and NP is supported by Swedish research council (VR) project (No. 2020-04963) and the Wallenberg AI, Autonomous Systems and Software Program (WASP) funded by the Knut and Alice Wallenberg Foundation.

Data Availibility Statement. Code and benchmark data are archived on Zenodo [1].

Disclosure of Interests. The authors have no competing interests to declare that are relevant to the content of this article.

References

1. Azzopardi, S., Di Stefano, L., Piterman, N.: Code and benchmark data for "sweap: reactive synthesis for infinite-state integer problems" (2026). https://doi.org/10.5281/zenodo.19684663
2. Azzopardi, S., Di Stefano, L., Piterman, N.: Sweap: reactive synthesis for infinite-state integer problems (extended version) (2026). https://doi.org/10.48550/arXiv.2605.11992
3. Azzopardi, S., Di Stefano, L., Piterman, N., Schneider, G.: Full LTL synthesis over infinite-state arenas. In: Piskac, R., Rakamaric, Z. (eds.) 37th International Conference on Computer Aided Verification (CAV). LNCS, vol. 15934, pp. 274–297. Springer, Cham (2025). https://doi.org/10.1007/978-3-031-98685-7_13
4. Azzopardi, S., Piterman, N., Schneider, G., Stefano, L.D.: LTL synthesis on infinite-state arenas defined by programs (2023). https://doi.org/10.48550/ARXIV.2307.09776, https://doi.org/10.48550/arXiv.2307.09776
5. Clarke, E.M., Grumberg, O., Jha, S., Lu, Y., Veith, H.: Counterexample-guided abstraction refinement for symbolic model checking. J. ACM **50**(5), 752–794 (2003). https://doi.org/10.1145/876638.876643
6. Duret-Lutz, A., et al.: From spot 2.0 to spot 2.10: what's new? CoRR **abs/2206.11366** (2022). https://doi.org/10.48550/ARXIV.2206.11366, https://doi.org/10.48550/arXiv.2206.11366
7. Finkbeiner, B., Klein, F., Piskac, R., Santolucito, M.: Temporal stream logic: synthesis beyond the bools. In: Dillig, I., Tasiran, S. (eds.) CAV 2019. LNCS, vol. 11561, pp. 609–629. Springer, Cham (2019). https://doi.org/10.1007/978-3-030-25540-4_35
8. Graf, S., Saidi, H.: Construction of abstract state graphs with PVS. In: Grumberg, O. (ed.) CAV 1997. LNCS, vol. 1254, pp. 72–83. Springer, Heidelberg (1997). https://doi.org/10.1007/3-540-63166-6_10
9. Heim, P., Dimitrova, R.: Solving infinite-state games via acceleration. Proc. ACM Program. Lang. **8**(POPL) (2024). https://doi.org/10.1145/3632899
10. Heim, P., Dimitrova, R.: Issy: a comprehensive tool for specification and synthesis of infinite-state reactive systems. In: Piskac, R., Rakamaric, Z. (eds.) 37th International Conference on Computer Aided Verification (CAV). LNCS, vol. 15934, pp. 298–312. Springer, Cham (2025). https://doi.org/10.1007/978-3-031-98685-7_14
11. Heim, P., Dimitrova, R.: Modular attractor acceleration in infinite-state games. In: Junges, S., Katz, G. (eds.) Tools and Algorithms for the Construction and Analysis of Systems - 32nd International Conference, TACAS. LNCS, vol. 16505, pp. 398–418. Springer, Cham (2026). https://doi.org/10.1007/978-3-032-22752-2_21
12. Henzinger, T.A., Jhala, R., Majumdar, R.: Counterexample-guided control. In: Baeten, J.C.M., Lenstra, J.K., Parrow, J., Woeginger, G.J. (eds.) Automata, Languages and Programming, 30th International Colloquium, ICALP 2003, Eindhoven, The Netherlands, June 30 - July 4, 2003. Proceedings, pp. 886–902. LNCS, Springer, Cham (2003). https://doi.org/10.1007/3-540-45061-0_69

13. Kretínský, J., Meggendorfer, T., Prokop, M., Zarkhah, A.: SemML: enhancing automata-theoretic LTL synthesis with machine learning. In: Gurfinkel, A., Heule, M. (eds.) 31st International Conference on Tools and Algorithms for the Construction and Analysis of Systems (TACAS). LNCS, vol. 15696, pp. 233–253. Springer, Cham (2025). https://doi.org/10.1007/978-3-031-90643-5_12
14. Maderbacher, B., Bloem, R.: Reactive synthesis modulo theories using abstraction refinement. In: 22nd Conference on Formal Methods in Computer-Aided Design, FMCAD 2022, pp. 315–324. TU Wien Academic Press (2022). https://doi.org/10.34727/2022/isbn.978-3-85448-053-2_38
15. McMillan, K.L.: Lazy abstraction with interpolants. In: Ball, T., Jones, R.B. (eds.) CAV 2006. LNCS, vol. 4144, pp. 123–136. Springer, Heidelberg (2006). https://doi.org/10.1007/11817963_14
16. Meyer, P.J., Sickert, S., Luttenberger, M.: Strix: explicit reactive synthesis strikes back! In: Chockler, H., Weissenbacher, G. (eds.) CAV 2018. LNCS, vol. 10981, pp. 578–586. Springer, Cham (2018). https://doi.org/10.1007/978-3-319-96145-3_31
17. Neider, D., Topcu, U.: An automaton learning approach to solving safety games over infinite graphs. In: Chechik, M., Raskin, J.-F. (eds.) TACAS 2016. LNCS, vol. 9636, pp. 204–221. Springer, Heidelberg (2016). https://doi.org/10.1007/978-3-662-49674-9_12
18. Pnueli, A., Rosner, R.: On the synthesis of a reactive module. In: Conference Record of the Sixteenth Annual ACM Symposium on Principles of Programming Languages, Austin, Texas, USA, 11–13 January 1989, pp. 179–190. ACM Press (1989). https://doi.org/10.1145/75277.75293
19. Prokop, M., Meggendorfer, T., Kretínský, J.: Semml 2.0: synthesizing controllers from LTL. In: 38th International Conference on Computer Aided Verification, CAV (2026)
20. Rodríguez, A., Gorostiaga, F., Sánchez, C.: Counter example guided reactive synthesis for LTL modulo theories. In: Proc. of the 37th Int'l Conference on Computer Aided Verification (CAV'25), Part IV. LNCS, vol. 15934, pp. 224–248. Springer, Cham (2025). https://doi.org/10.1007/978-3-031-98685-7_11, https://link.springer.com/chapter/10.1007/978-3-031-98685-7_11
21. Schmuck, A.K., Heim, P., Dimitrova, R., Nayak, S.P.: Localized attractor computations for infinite-state games. In: Gurfinkel, A., Ganesh, V. (eds.) 36th International Conference on Computer Aided Verification (CAV). LNCS, vol. 14683, pp. 135–158. Springer, Cham (2024). https://doi.org/10.1007/978-3-031-65633-0_7

Hardware Verification

$\mathcal{A}$-IC3: Learning-Guided Adaptive Inductive Generalization for Hardware Model Checking

Xiaofeng Zhou[1], Guangyu Hu[1], Hongce Zhang[2], and Wei Zhang[1(✉)]

[1] The Hong Kong University of Science and Technology, Sai Kung, China
{xzhoubu,ghuae}@connect.ust.hk, wei.zhang@ust.hk

[2] The Hong Kong University of Science and Technology (Guangzhou), Guangzhou, China
hongcezh@hkust-gz.edu.cn

Abstract. The IC3 algorithm represents the state-of-the-art (SOTA) hardware model checking technique, owing to its robust performance and scalability. A significant body of research has focused on enhancing the solving efficiency of the IC3 algorithm, with particular attention to the inductive generalization process—a critical phase wherein the algorithm seeks to generalize a counterexample to inductiveness (CTI), which typically is a state leading to a bad state, into a broader set of states. This inductive generalization is a primary source of clauses in IC3 and thus plays a pivotal role in determining the overall effectiveness of the algorithm.

Despite its importance, existing approaches often rely on fixed inductive generalization strategies, overlooking the dynamic and context-sensitive nature of the verification environment in which spurious counterexamples arise. This rigidity can limit the quality of generated clauses and, consequently, the performance of IC3.

To address this limitation, we propose a lightweight machine-learning-based framework that dynamically selects appropriate inductive generalization strategies in response to the evolving verification context. Specifically, we employ a multi-armed bandit (MAB) algorithm to adaptively choose inductive generalization strategies based on real-time feedback from the verification process. The agent is updated by evaluating the quality of generalization outcomes, thereby refining its strategy selection over time.

Empirical evaluation on a benchmark suite comprising 914 instances, primarily drawn from the latest HWMCC collection, demonstrates the efficacy of our approach. When implemented on the state-of-the-art model checker rIC3, our method solves 26 to 50 more cases than the baselines and improves the PAR-2 score by 194.72 to 389.29.

Keywords: Hardware Formal Verification · Model Checking · Inductive Generalization · Machine Learning

X. Zhou and G. Hu—Both authors contributed equally to this work.

E. Darulova et al. (Eds.): CAV 2026, LNCS 16682, pp. 357–379, 2026.
https://doi.org/10.1007/978-3-032-32519-8_19

1 Introduction

As the scale and complexity of modern *RTL (register transfer level)* designs continue to increase, simulation-based verification alone has become insufficient for uncovering subtle design bugs. Hardware model checking provides a formal and exhaustive means of verifying safety properties by exploring all reachable states. Among SAT-based techniques such as *BMC (bounded model checking)* [1], k-induction [18], and IC3/PDR [4,6], IC3 has emerged as a state-of-the-art algorithm due to its robustness and its ability to incrementally construct inductive invariants without explicit unrolling.

A key determinant of IC3's efficiency is the *inductive generalization* step, in which a CTI *counterexample to induction* is generalized into a clause that blocks a larger set of unreachable states. Techniques such as CtgDown [7] and its extensions (e.g., stronger ICP/IC3 generalization [23] and EXCTG [20]) significantly improve generalization by performing more powerful reasoning about *CTGs (counterexamples to generalization)*. These works show that better generalization, in terms of the width and depth of blocked state space, can substantially accelerate IC3. However, they still depend on fixed or manually tuned strategies: the trade-off between generalization strength and computational overhead is decided once and for all, or adjusted only by handcrafted rules. For example, EXCTG further proposes DynAMic [20], which dynamically switches between several predefined strategies based on the difficulty of blocking states, but the switching policy itself is static and hard-coded.

In practice, CTIs are generated under highly diverse circumstances: frame levels, clause densities, and the number of pending block tasks all evolve throughout the run of IC3. Overly aggressive generalization may produce clauses that cannot be propagated, while overly conservative generalization may fail to block meaningful regions of the state space, leading to slow convergence. The effectiveness of a generalization strategy is therefore highly context-dependent. Moreover, each generalization affects future CTIs, frame saturation, and clause propagation. From this perspective, inductive generalization is not an isolated subroutine, but part of a sequential, non-stationary decision process that unfolds over the entire proof.

Recent learning-based verification approaches operate at different points in this design space. NeuroPDR [9] integrates neural networks into PDR to guide the proof search, and DeepIC3 [8] uses a graph neural network to predict promising clauses for IC3. These methods demonstrate that machine learning can improve SAT/SMT-based model checking, but they rely on offline training, heavy models, and non-trivial inference cost. They are therefore not well-suited to be invoked millions of times inside IC3's inner inductive generalization loop. What is missing is a *lightweight, online* mechanism that can adaptively select generalization strategies based on the evolving proof state, without requiring pre-collected datasets or expensive training.

Our Approach. In this work, we introduce $\mathcal{A}$-IC3, a lightweight, learning-guided framework that adaptively selects inductive generalization strategies inside IC3. Rather than relying on a global fixed strategy or manually designed switching rules, $\mathcal{A}$-IC3 models generalization as a contextual multi-armed bandit problem. Before each generalization, the framework extracts a proof-aware context vector from IC3's internal state, including CTI characteristics (e.g., cube size, depth, activity) and global proof information (e.g., frame level, frame saturation, proof-obligation queue growth). A Proof-Aware LinUCB (PA-LinUCB) agent then selects among several predefined generalization strategies of varying aggressiveness. After generalization and intermediate clause propagation, the agent receives a reward that reflects the usefulness of the resulting clause, combining size reduction and push success, and updates its parameters online. Over time, $\mathcal{A}$-IC3 learns which strategies work best in which proof contexts, without any offline training.

Why Contextual Bandits and LinUCB? Strategy selection in IC3 is inherently discrete, must incur negligible overhead, and must cope with non-stationary proof dynamics. Contextual bandits provide exactly this combination of (i) online learning without pre-collected training data, (ii) low computational cost, and (iii) the ability to condition decisions on rich context. We adopt the LinUCB algorithm [12] as our decision agent: its linear value model matches the low-dimensional, structured features available in IC3, and its updates are simple enough to be integrated into industrial-scale model checking runs. The novelty of this work, therefore, does not lie in modifying LinUCB itself, but in identifying a proof-aware context and reward design, and an integration architecture that allows a contextual bandit to operate effectively inside the recursive IC3 generalization loop.

This work makes the following contributions:

- We formulate inductive generalization in IC3 as a contextual decision-making problem and propose $\mathcal{A}$-IC3[1], the first learning-based adaptive controller for generalization strategy selection in IC3.
- We design a proof-aware context representation and a push-aware reward function that jointly capture the local difficulty of generalizing a CTI and the global progress of the proof, enabling a standard LinUCB agent to provide meaningful guidance with negligible overhead.
- We integrate our method into rIC3 [19], a state-of-the-art IC3 implementation, and evaluate it on 914 HWMCC benchmark instances. The results show consistent improvements in solved instances and PAR-2 scores over multiple baselines, demonstrating the practical benefit of learning-guided, context-aware generalization.

By elevating inductive generalization from a static heuristic to an adaptive, learning-guided process, $\mathcal{A}$-IC3 complements existing generalization techniques such as CTG/EXCTG and opens a new direction for integrating lightweight machine learning techniques into symbolic model checking.

The remainder of this paper is organized as follows. Section 2 introduces the background of IC3 and the multi-armed bandit method. Section 3 presents

[1] Implementation available on Zenodo https://zenodo.org/records/19811923.

the proposed $\mathcal{A}$-IC3 framework and the proof-aware contextual bandit formulation. Section 4 reports our experimental results on rIC3 over the HWMCC'20, HWMCC'24 and HWMCC'25 benchmark suite. Section 5 discusses related work, and Sect. 6 concludes the paper.

2 Preliminaries

2.1 Transition Systems and IC3/PDR

We model a hardware system as a Boolean transition system $\langle V, T(V,V'), I(V)\rangle$, where V is a finite set of state variables, V' denotes the corresponding next-state variables, $I(V)$ characterizes the initial states, and $T(V,V')$ is the transition relation. A *literal* l is a variable $v \in V$ or its negation $\neg v$. A *clause* c is a disjunction of literals, and its negation is a *cube* s, representing a conjunction of literals. We write $P(V)$ for the safety property to be verified; states violating P are called *unsafe*.

Algorithm 1. The IC3 Algorithm (A simplified version with details omitted)

```
Input: Transition function T, initial states I, property P
Output: The proving result of P
Initialize frames F_i for i ≥ 0 such that F_0 = I, k ← 1
a ← GENERALIZATION_STRATEGY
while True do
    while SAT(F_k ∧ ¬P) do
        s ← GetModel()
        if ¬ Block(s, k, a) then
            return UNSAFE
    for 1 ≤ i < k do
        if Propagate(F_i, F_{i+1}) = CONVERGED then
            return SAFE
    k ← k + 1
procedure Block(s, k, a)
    if k = 0 then
        return False                          ▷ Find a trace to unsafe
    while SAT(F_k ∧ ¬s ∧ T ∧ s') do
        s_p ← GetModel()
        if ¬ Block(s_p, k − 1, a) then
            return False                      ▷ Failed to block on frame k
    c ← Generalize(s, a)
    F_i ← F_i ∧ c for 1 ≤ i ≤ k
    return True
```

IC3/PDR [4,6] decides whether unsafe states are reachable by constructing an inductive invariant $INV(V)$ that satisfies:

$$
\begin{aligned}
&I(V) \rightarrow INV(V),\\
&INV(V) \wedge T(V,V') \rightarrow INV(V'),\\
&INV(V) \rightarrow P(V).
\end{aligned}
\tag{1}
$$

If such an *INV* exists, it over-approximates the set of reachable states while excluding all unsafe states, thereby proving safety.

IC3 maintains a sequence of frames $F_0, F_1, \ldots, F_N$, where each frame F_i is represented as a conjunction of clauses:

$$F_i = c_1 \wedge c_2 \wedge \cdots \wedge c_{n_i}.$$

F_0 is initialized to $I(V)$, and the frames satisfy:

$$\begin{aligned}
&F_0(V) \rightarrow I(V),\\
&F_i(V) \rightarrow F_{i+1}(V) \quad \text{for all } i < N,\\
&F_i(V) \wedge T(V, V') \rightarrow F_{i+1}(V') \quad \text{for all } i < N,\\
&F_i(V) \rightarrow P(V) \quad \text{for all } i.
\end{aligned} \tag{2}$$

Intuitively, F_i over-approximates the set of states reachable from I in at most i steps, and the sequence becomes progressively less restrictive, i.e., $F_0 \Rightarrow F_1 \Rightarrow \cdots \Rightarrow F_N$. When two adjacent frames coincide, $F_k \equiv F_{k+1}$, the conjunction F_k is an inductive invariant that satisfies (1), and the property is proved.

Algorithm 1 presents the pseudocode of the IC3 procedure. At a high level, IC3 iteratively searches for counterexamples and refines the frames by learning clauses. **Block**: given a candidate bad predecessor, IC3 derives a generalized clause to exclude it and adds the clause to the corresponding frame(s). **Propagate**: IC3 then pushes learned clauses to higher frames whenever possible, which accelerates convergence. If a SAT query discovers a state s that reaches an unsafe state within i steps while $s \models F_i$, s is a CTI at frame F_i. IC3 then tries to *block* s by finding a clause c such that c excludes s, is inductive relative to F_{i-1}, and can be pushed forward to higher frames. We call a pair (s, i), where cube s must be blocked at frame F_i, a proof obligation (PO). The PO queue stores pending blocking tasks generated during recursive blocking. This blocking step is performed recursively on predecessor states and generates POs that must be blocked at lower frames. Figure 2 illustrates the IC3 frame structure together with the local (CTI-related) and global (frame-related) quantities introduced above. These quantities will later serve as the building blocks of our proof-aware context vector in Sect. 3.

2.2 Inductive Generalization and CTG-Based Methods

The clause used to block a CTI is typically obtained by *generalizing* the CTI cube s with respect to the current frame. Generalization seeks to drop literals from s while preserving inductiveness relative to F_{i-1}. The resulting clause determines how many states are blocked and how easily it can be propagated to higher frames. Two failure modes are well known in the IC3 literature [7]:

- **Over-generalization**: dropping too many literals yields a strong clause that is not valid at higher frames and therefore cannot be pushed, inflating the queue of proof obligations that must be blocked.

– **Under-generalization**: keeping too many literals yields a very weak clause that blocks only a tiny neighbourhood of the CTI, resulting in many similar CTIs and slow convergence.

CtgDown [7] improves generalization by introducing CTGs: when a literal dropping attempt fails, the model returned by the SAT solver is treated as a CTG whose predecessors are explored to search for more general clauses. EXCTG [20] further strengthens this idea by exploring CTGs recursively and carefully tuning the recursion depth, the number of CTGs considered, and the number of literal-dropping attempts. These methods demonstrate that better generalization—in terms of both width (states blocked) and depth (frames reached)—can substantially accelerate IC3, but they still rely on fixed or manually tuned settings for these parameters.

In this work, we build upon CTG-based generalization and treat the configuration of these parameters (e.g., recursion depth, CTG budget, literal-dropping effort) as a strategy whose strength varies from conservative to aggressive. Our goal is to adaptively select such strategies according to the current proof context, rather than use a single fixed configuration throughout the run.

2.3 Multi-Armed Bandits and LinUCB

The *multi-armed bandit* (MAB) problem models an agent that repeatedly chooses an arm a from a finite set $\mathcal{A}$ and receives a stochastic reward r. The objective is to maximize the cumulative reward (or equivalently, to minimize regret) by balancing exploration of different arms and exploitation of arms known to perform well. In contextual bandits, the agent additionally observes a feature vector x_t at each round t, representing the current context, and selects an arm based on both the context and past observations.

Among many contextual bandit algorithms, *LinUCB (Linear Upper Confidence Bound)* [12] assumes that the expected reward of each arm is a linear function of the context. For each arm $a \in \mathcal{A}$, LinUCB maintains a parameter vector and a (regularized) covariance matrix, and selects arms using an upper-confidence-bound rule that trades off estimated reward and uncertainty. Its per-round update cost is low and depends only on the dimension of the context vector, making it attractive for settings such as IC3, where decisions are made extremely frequently, and overhead must be tightly controlled.

In $\mathcal{A}$-IC3, we instantiate the contextual bandit with LinUCB and view each generalization configuration as an arm. The formal bandit formulation, the design of the proof-aware context vector, and the LinUCB integration into IC3's blocking loop are given in Sect. 3.

3 Method

3.1 A-IC3 Overview

Current IC3 implementations face a fundamental limitation in generalization strategy selection: fixed strategies cannot adapt to the highly dynamic

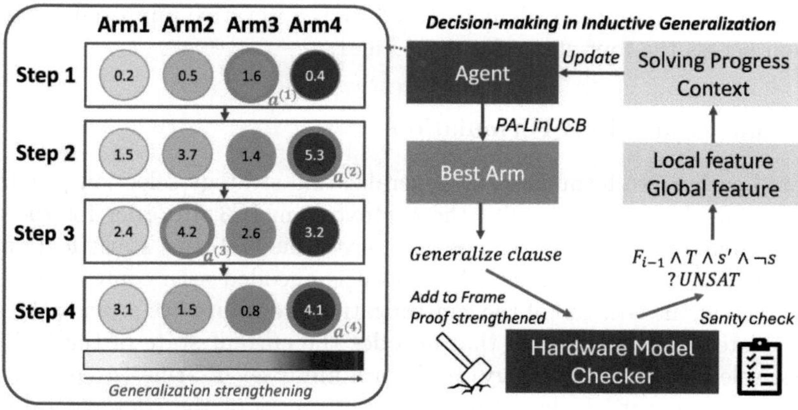

Fig. 1. Overview of $\mathcal{A}$-IC3.

nature of proof contexts. This rigidity leads to systematic inefficiencies—over-generalization wastes computational resources on hard-to-push clauses, while under-generalization fails to discover sufficiently broad blocking clauses, severely hindering proof convergence.

$\mathcal{A}$-IC3 overcomes this limitation by treating generalization strategy selection as a contextual multi-armed bandit problem, as illustrated in Fig. 1. The left side of the figure demonstrates the multi-armed bandit framework in action: at each step, our PA-LinUCB agent, which is inspired by LinUCB [12] and tailored for the environment of the IC3 algorithm observes the current proof context and selects among different generalization strategies (represented as arms with varying reward values). The agent continuously learns from the outcomes—for instance, in Step 1, Arm3 with the best score 1.6 is selected and marked with $a^{(1)}$, the corresponding strategy will be used in the next generalization in the IC3-based hardware model checker. In the next step, similarly, after the agent is updated, we observe that Arm4 achieves the highest score of 5.3, indicating that it will be better to use a more aggressive generalization. The Arm4 is then selected and marked with $a^{(2)}$. The agent will progressively refine selections that select different arms in subsequent steps according to the solving progress.

The right side of Fig. 1 shows our decision-making pipeline for inductive generalization. The agent leverages both local and global features from the solving progress context to make informed strategy selections. Each generalization strategy is encoded as a bandit arm, collectively orchestrated by our PA-LinUCB agent that adapts its choices based on real-time verification context inside the hardware model checker.

Following each generalization-and-propagation iteration, the agent evaluates the quality of the generated clause through internal metrics of IC3 and computes a reward based on this evaluation. This feedback enables adaptive learning over time, allowing the agent to refine its strategy selection policy in response to evolving proof dynamics, as demonstrated by the iterative improvement in arm selection across the four steps shown in Fig. 1.

3.2 Contextual MAB Formulation

As stated earlier, we formulate the generalization strategy selection problem as a contextual MAB problem with the context from IC3. In order for the agent to make informed selections, we need to convey the real-time statistical proving information to the agent. This information is encoded as a context vector. In this setting, at the t-th call of the generalization procedure, we provide the agent with a context vector $\mathbf{x}_t \in \mathbb{R}^d$ that encodes the current state of the IC3 proof process, selects an arm (strategy) a_t from a finite set of arms $\{a_1, a_2, \ldots, a_K\}$, and receives a reward r_t based on the effectiveness of the chosen strategy on generalization.

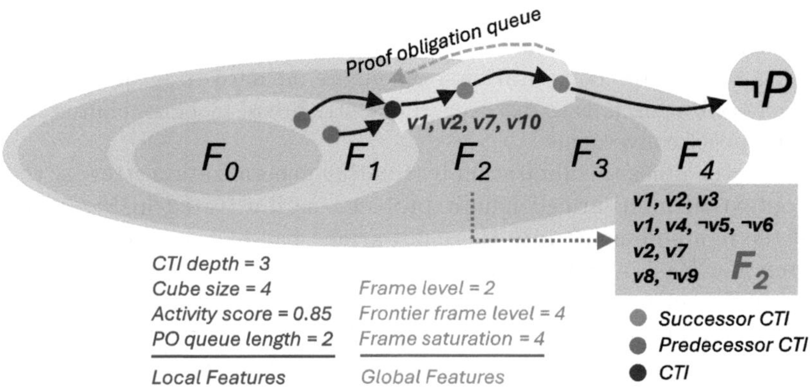

Fig. 2. Context vector extraction from IC3 proof state. The figure illustrates IC3's frame structure where each frame F_i contains clauses (e.g., "$v1, v2, v3$" represents one clause) that over-approximate reachable states at step i. The purple circle represents a CTI at frame F_2 with cube content v_1, v_2, v_7, v_{10}. The arrows show predecessor-successor relationships. The context vector combines local features (CTI depth, cube size, activity score) with global features (frame levels, frame saturation, proof obligation queue length) to guide MAB strategy selection.

Context Vector Design. The context vector $\mathbf{x}_t \in \mathbb{R}^d$ encodes the current proof state through carefully selected features. Figure 2 shows how $\mathcal{A}$-IC3 extracts context before the generalization procedure. This context design balances *local proof characteristics* with *global progression indicators* (indicated by "local features" and "global features" in Fig. 2), incorporating both absolute metrics (for global positioning) and relative metrics (for adaptive scaling).

The *local context component* captures information that is directly tied to the current CTI and its immediate blocking workload, including the **depth**, **cube**

size, **activity score**, and the **PO-queue length** when the CTI is encountered. The activity score, defined in [20], is a normalized measure of how frequently the CTI under generalization is encountered during proof search; we denote it as $\hat{x}_a$. The cube size is the number of literals in the cube to be generalized. The depth is the recursion depth of the BLOCK call stack (Algorithm 1) at which the CTI is discovered. The PO-queue length indicates how many proof obligations are pending alongside the current CTI, reflecting the *local blocking pressure* at the moment of generalization. Together, these features characterize the difficulty of handling the current CTI. For example, a shallow CTI with a high activity score often suggests a complex and still-uncovered predecessor region, where a strategy with more generalization effort may be beneficial. In Fig. 2, when blocking the purple CTI on frame F_2 (cube size $= 4$), the proof-obligation queue already contains two successor obligations from higher frames F_3 and F_4, indicating a PO-queue length of 2. Moreover, the current CTI is three transitions away from the bad states $\neg P$, so the BLOCK call-stack depth is 3. For normalization, we scale the depth by the relative frame index with respect to the frame where the PO queue is established, denoted as $\hat{x}_d$, normalize the cube size by the running average cube size observed so far, denoted as $\hat{x}_c$, and normalize the PO-queue length by its maximum observed value, denoted as $\hat{x}_q$.

The *global context component* summarizes the overall proof progress, including the current frame level, the frontier frame level, the **frame saturation**, and the **growth rate** of the PO queue. Frame saturation is quantified as the number of clauses in the current frame, followed by normalization for learning. The PO-queue growth rate is defined as the normalized difference between the current PO-queue length and that recorded at the previous generalization call. In Fig. 2, we generalize a CTI at frame F_2, the frontier is F_4, and frame F_2 contains 4 clauses; thus the corresponding global features are: current frame level $= 2$, frontier level $= 4$, and (raw) frame saturation $= 4$. The growth rate of the PO queue reflects the recent global trend of the search: whether proof obligations are being discharged effectively (queue shrinking) or accumulating (queue growing). For normalization, we represent the current frame level as a ratio to the frontier, denoted as $\hat{x}_{cf}$, normalize frame saturation by dividing it by 100, denoted as $\hat{x}_s$, and normalize the PO-queue growth rate by its maximum observed value, denoted as $\hat{x}_{qr}$.

In summary, we define the context vector $\mathbf{x}_t \in \mathbb{R}^8$ of $\mathcal{A}$-IC3 at time t as $\mathbf{x}_t = [\hat{x}_d, \hat{x}_c, \hat{x}_q, \hat{x}_{cf}, \hat{x}_s, \hat{x}_{qr}, \hat{x}_a, b]$, we set $b = 1.0$.

Such a multi-faceted representation enables the MAB agent to distinguish between scenarios favoring aggressive versus conservative generalization. The level-related information can inform the agent about the rough progress of the proof, while frame saturation indicates whether there are too many clauses in the current frame, which may slow down the blocking and generalization procedures. A long proof obligation queue or a rapid increase in its length may suggest adopting a more aggressive generalization strategy, which can help reduce the generation of new CTIs and CTGs. A higher saturation level means that the frame is highly restricted, possibly requiring the agent to pick up a strategy with less effort to prevent computational effort. It should be noted that, to better fuse the IC3 context information into the MAB agent, we perform normalization before loading the components into the context vector, and a bias term b for flexibility is attached at the end.

Strategic Arm Configuration. Our framework employs a spectrum of generalization strategies that differ in the aggressiveness of searching for clauses, including **Basic**, **Conservative**, **Balanced**, and **Aggressive**. These strategies are built upon the CtgDown generalization approach [7]. Each strategy controls the intensity of the generalization process through different configurations of CTG attempt counts, recursion depths, and literal-dropping constraints.

The four strategic arms employ progressively more aggressive parameter configurations:

- **Basic** is selected for low-activity proof obligations at constrained frames where minimal generalization is preferred. It disables CTG exploration entirely (setting attempt count and recursion depth to 0) while allowing extensive literal dropping trials to avoid wasting computation on simple cases.
- **Conservative** applies cautious exploration suitable for early proof stages. It uses limited CTG attempts (1–3 attempts) with shallow recursion depths (1–2 levels) while permitting substantial literal dropping trials to balance exploration with efficiency.
- **Balanced** represents standard generalization for typical verification scenarios. It employs moderate CTG attempts (1–5 attempts) with expanded recursion depths (1–4 levels) and generous literal dropping allowances for comprehensive but controlled exploration.
- **Aggressive** enables extensive exploration for high-activity proof obligations at advanced frames, utilizing substantial CTG attempts (2–4 attempts) with deep recursion levels (up to 8 levels), while maintaining flexible literal dropping policies to maximize generalization potential.

These tiered configurations enable adaptive generalization across diverse verification contexts, allowing the framework to dynamically find the strategy of appropriate exploration depth and width based on the proof obligation and the global environment of IC3 proving. Note that the ranges above describe the overall strategy design space; in $\mathcal{A}$-IC3, we discretize this space into a finite set of arms by instantiating each conservative/balanced/aggressive family with concrete settings.

Algorithm 2. MAB-based IC3 generalization

Global: MAB agent $\mathcal{A}$, Frames $\{F_i\}$, Time stamp t.
Initialize: $\mathcal{A}.A_{a_i} = \mathbf{I}, \mathcal{A}.b_{a_i} = \mathbf{0}$ for $1 \leq i \leq K$, $t = 1$.
procedure BLOCK(s, k)
  if $k = 0$ **then**
    return False ▷ Find a trace to unsafe
  while SAT($F_k \wedge \neg s \wedge \mathcal{T} \wedge s'$) **do**
    $s_p \leftarrow$GetModel()
    if $\neg$ Block(s_p, $k-1$) **then**
      return False ▷ Failed to block on frame k
  $\mathbf{x}_t \leftarrow$ ExtractContext($s, \{F_i\}$) ▷ Context extraction
  $a_t \leftarrow \mathcal{A}$.SelectArm($\mathbf{x}_t$) ▷ PA-LinUCB selection
  $c \leftarrow$ Generalize(s, a_t)
  pushed_frame $\leftarrow$ PushClause(c, k) ▷ Intermediate push
  $r_t \leftarrow$ ComputeReward(c, pushed_frame, $\{F_i\}$)
  $\mathcal{A}$.UpdateArm($a_t, \mathbf{x}_t, r_t$) ▷ LinUCB update
  return True

3.3 PA-LinUCB Algorithm for Strategy Selection

As discussed in Sect. 3.1, we develop PA-LinUCB (Proof-Aware LinUCB) as our decision agent, specifically tailored for IC3's generalization context. PA-LinUCB deeply integrates with IC3's proof structure, leveraging proof-specific contextual information to guide generalization strategy selection. This integration provides more information to the agent about the dynamic proof environment and adapt its decisions based on the current proof state, frame structure, and clause characteristics.

PA-LinUCB maintains a linear model for each generalization strategy, assuming that the expected reward can be expressed as a linear combination of proof-aware features. This assumption aligns well with IC3's structured proof process, where generalization effectiveness often correlates linearly with specific proof characteristics such as clause size, frame depth, and propagation potential according to our observations.

At each generalization step, PA-LinUCB computes the upper confidence bound for each strategy a:

$$\text{PA-LinUCB}_a(\mathbf{x}_t) = \boldsymbol{\theta}_a^T \mathbf{x}_t + \alpha \sqrt{\mathbf{x}_t^T \mathbf{A}_a^{-1} \mathbf{x}_t} \tag{3}$$

where $\mathbf{x}_t$ represents the proof-aware context vector extracted from the current IC3 state, $\boldsymbol{\theta}_a$ captures the strategy's learned parameters, $\mathbf{A}_a$ denotes the regularized covariance matrix associated with strategy a, and α controls the exploration level. The strategy with the highest score is selected as:

$$a_t = \arg\max_{a \in \mathcal{A}} \text{PA-LinUCB}_a(\mathbf{x}_t) \tag{4}$$

After observing the generalization result, PA-LinUCB updates the selected strategy's parameters to incorporate the proof-specific feedback:

$$\mathbf{A}_{a_t} \leftarrow \mathbf{A}_{a_t} + \mathbf{x}_t \mathbf{x}_t^T \tag{5}$$

$$\mathbf{b}_{a_t} \leftarrow \mathbf{b}_{a_t} + r_t \mathbf{x}_t \tag{6}$$

$$\boldsymbol{\theta}_{a_t} \leftarrow \mathbf{A}_{a_t}^{-1} \mathbf{b}_{a_t} \tag{7}$$

The reward r_t captures both immediate generalization effects and long-term proof progress, enabling PA-LinUCB to learn from IC3's complex feedback signals. The design of the reward r_t will be discussed in detail in Sect. 3.4. b_{a_t} is the weighted reward vector after performing the action a_t, and is derived via scaling r_t by their corresponding context vectors.

Algorithm 2 presents the deep integration of PA-LinUCB with IC3's blocking procedure. The key innovation is around lines 10–15, where proof-aware context extraction (Line 10), strategy selection (Line 11), and parameter updates (Line 15) are seamlessly embedded within IC3's core block and generalization process. An intermediate push is conducted via the function PushClause, pushing the generalized clause into higher frames during the block of the current frame, in order to derive the effect of the generalized clause (Line 13). This tight integration ensures that PA-LinUCB operates with full awareness of IC3's proof state and can adapt its strategy selection based on the evolving proof context.

3.4 Reward Function Design

The reward function serves as the critical feedback mechanism that guides our MAB agent toward effective generalization strategies. As introduced in earlier sections, fixed-strategy generalization often results in over-generalization and under-generalization. Our design explicitly addresses this generalization strength balancing problem in the reward calculation part. $\mathcal{A}$-IC3 uses a multi-component reward structure. We decompose the reward into the following complementary components that capture different aspects of generalization quality.

- **Size reduction quality** R_s directly reflects the clause simplification effectiveness, indicating the ability of state refinement of the generalized clause. It is calculated as the proportion of clause size reduction relative to the original size. If the size increases after generalization, we pose a penalty factor $\beta > 1$.
- **Push quality** R_p evaluates the propagation success of clause. It is calculated in two conditions: if the clause is pushed to higher frames successfully, R_p equals the ratio of the push distance and the maximum possible push distance (the distance between the frame of proof obligation and the frontier frame); If the clause cannot be pushed to another frame at all, we set a constant penalty to $R_p = p_p$.
- **Bonus** R_b highlights extreme outcomes of a generalization step in a reward signal (e.g., a clause reaches the frontier or exhibits over-generalization). The bonus helps the agent react quickly by discouraging consistently unproductive arms and reinforcing promising ones. Each event has a polarity $s_i \in \{+1, -1\}$

Table 1. Events used in the bonus term R_b.

Tag	Event	s_i	$\ell(i)$
E_{front}	Frontier push: Clause is pushed to frame F_k.	+1	High
E_{size1}	Complete generalization: clause size is 1 (one literal).	+1	Medium
E_{high}	High-level push: the clause is pushed to a frame $k' > 0.7k$ (where k is the frontier frame).	+1	Low
E_{ideal}	Ideal generalization: $R_s > 0.5$ and $R_p > 0.3$.	+1	Medium
E_{over}	Over-generalization: $R_s > 0.7$ and $R_p < 0.1$.	−1	Medium

(bonus/penalty) and an importance level $\ell(i) \in \{\text{H}, \text{M}, \text{L}\}$. We use qualitative magnitudes satisfying $\gamma_{\text{H}} > \gamma_{\text{M}} > \gamma_{\text{L}} > 0$ and define

$$R_b = \sum_i s_i \, \gamma_{\ell(i)} \, \mathbb{I}[E_i], \tag{8}$$

where $\mathbb{I}[E_i] \in \{0, 1\}$ indicates whether event E_i is triggered. The events are summarized in Table 1. When multiple events are triggered, their contributions are accumulated.

We set E_{front} to High because pushing a clause to the current frontier is a decisive success signal: such a clause does not hinder subsequent clause propagation toward the proof frontier, and it can effectively constrain the state space by strengthening the reachable frames. We set E_{size1} to Medium since a size-1 clause is often very strong, yet aggressive size reduction may occasionally introduce over-generalization and lead to adverse effects, so we avoid over-rewarding this signal. We treat E_{high} as a weaker variant of E_{front}: pushing to a relatively high frame indicates progress but is less conclusive and occurs more frequently than reaching the frontier, hence it receives a **Low** importance. We set E_{ideal} to Medium because it captures a well-balanced outcome: the generalization produces a clause that is both strong and sufficiently pushable, even if it is not the most extreme along either dimension. Empirically, repeatedly triggering E_{ideal} indicates that the selected arm constitutes a consistently feasible and effective strategy under the current proving context, and thus deserves a moderate importance weight. E_{over} captures over-generalization: although the derived clause is strong, it is barely pushable to higher frames. This outcome suggests that the current strategy is mismatched to the present proving context.

Finally, we can derive the overall reward, where w_s and w_p are weights for balancing the size reduction and push quality:

$$r_t = w_s R_s + w_p R_p + R_b. \tag{9}$$

4 Evaluation

4.1 Experimental Setup

All experiments were conducted on a high-performance computing cluster consisting of twenty nodes. Each node is equipped with 64 CPU cores, specifically Intel Xeon Gold 6338 CPUs operating at 2.00GHz. The system runs Red Hat Enterprise Linux Server version 7.9 and provides 1007GB of memory per node. Each invocation of the model checker was executed with one dedicated CPU and memory resources allocated by the scheduler to ensure consistency and reproducibility. The model checker is executed in a single thread, and no portfolio is included. The weights w_s and w_p in Eq. 9 are set to 0.65 and 0.35, respectively. We emphasize more on the size reduction term here because bonuses in Table 1 consider more on push quality. The qualitative magnitudes used in the bonus term are set to: $\gamma_H = 0.4$, $\gamma_M = 0.2$, and $\gamma_L = 0.1$. The exploration level $\alpha = 1.0$. The penalty factor in size reduction is $\beta = 1.5$. The penalty in push quality $p_p = 0.1$. All reward- and bandit-related hyperparameters are fixed globally across the entire benchmark suite to keep a consistent reward scale.

The benchmark suite comprises a total of 914 model checking problems from HWMCC'20, HWMCC'24, and HWMCC'25 [2,16,17]. To demonstrate the generality of the proposed method, experiments were conducted using rIC3 [19] (v1.3.6). rIC3 is the champion of both bit-level track and word-level track: bit-vectors in HWMCC'24 and HWMCC'25 [3,17].

The baselines in our experiments are the default rIC3 setting (denoted as rIC3-Standard), the rIC3 implementation of CtgDown [7] (denoted as rIC3-CtgDown), and the rIC3 DynAMic setting [20] (denoted as rIC3-DynAMic). The PA-LinUCB implementation utilizes the Rust crate `nalgebra` for linear algebra operations, ensuring efficient matrix computations across both platforms. The timeout limit for each model checking problem is 3600 s in wall-clock time.

4.2 MAB Configuration

The configuration of the $\mathcal{A}$-`IC3` is derived from extensions of the rIC3-DynAMic strategy.

Arm Design. An arm instantiates a concrete setting of three CTG-related parameters: ctgMax, ctgDepth, and exctgBudget. They denote the maximum number of CTG attempts, the CTG recursion depth, and the number of EXCTG block operations, respectively. We use one basic static arm, three static arms with fixed settings, and three activity-aware *dynamic* arms. Our dynamic arms are extended from the activity-based parameterization in DynAMic [20]: We keep the same piecewise structure, use the original mapping as the balanced dynamic arm, and add two variants. (aggressive/conservative) by lowering/raising the activity thresholds and adjusting the scaling factors. Table 2 summarizes all arms used in our experiments.

Table 2. Arms configurations for $\mathcal{A}$-IC3 and baselines.

Configuration	Arm	Type	ctgMax	ctgDepth	exctgBudget
$\mathcal{A}$-IC3 (Ours)	Basic	static	0	0	0
	Conservative	static	1	3	1
	Balanced	static	2	5	1
	Aggressive	static	8	4	1
	Conservative	dynamic	$f_{\text{cons}}(a)$ (Eq. 12)		
	Balanced	dynamic	$f_{\text{bala}}(a)$ (Eq. 10)		
	Aggressive	dynamic	$f_{\text{aggr}}(a)$ (Eq. 11)		
rIC3-Standard	—	static	0	0	0
rIC3-CtgDown	—	static	1	3	0
rIC3-DynAMic	—	dynamic	$f_{\text{bala}}(a)$ (Eq. 10)		

Dynamic Arms. Following DynAMic [20], an activity score a is used to characterize the difficulty of blocking the current CTI (higher a indicates that stronger generalization is needed). Based on a, DynAMic [20] defines an activity-aware mapping to produce (ctgMax, ctgDepth, exctgBudget); we adopt this mapping as our balanced dynamic arm. In addition, we introduce aggressive and conservative variants that keep the same three-regime (low/medium/high activity) form, but use lower/higher thresholds and scaling to encourage/discourage stronger generalization, respectively:

$$f_{\text{bala}}(a) = \begin{cases} (0,0,0), & a < 10, \\ (\lfloor (a-10)/10 \rfloor + 2,\ 1,\ 1), & 10 \le a < 40, \\ (5,\ 1,\ \text{round}((a-40)^{0.3} \cdot 2 + 5)), & a \ge 40, \end{cases} \tag{10}$$

$$f_{\text{aggr}}(a) = \begin{cases} (1,1,1), & a < 5, \\ (\lfloor (a-5)/8 \rfloor + 3,\ 1,\ 2), & 5 \le a < 25, \\ (6,\ 1,\ \text{round}((a-25)^{0.3} \cdot 2.5 + 6)), & a \ge 25, \end{cases} \tag{11}$$

$$f_{\text{cons}}(a) = \begin{cases} (0,0,0), & a < 15, \\ (\min(\lfloor (a-15)/12 \rfloor + 1, 3),\ 0,\ 1), & 15 \le a < 50, \\ (3,\ 1,\ \min(\text{round}((a-50)^{0.3} \cdot 1.5 + 4), 6)), & a \ge 50. \end{cases} \tag{12}$$

4.3 Results

The evaluation is organized around three questions. First, we compare $\mathcal{A}$-IC3 implementation on rIC3 with the baseline rIC3 configurations in terms of solved instances and runtime. Second, we inspect the arm-selection behavior of $\mathcal{A}$-IC3 to understand whether the learned controller reduces to a single fixed configuration or adapts across different proof phases. Third, we analyze the termination frame level to examine whether the performance improvement is accompanied by faster proof convergence.

Table 3. Summary of results.

Configuration	#Solved	Safe	Unsafe	Δ	Δ_s	Δ_u	PAR-2	PAR-2†	Average†
rIC3-Standard	603	464	139	0	0	0	2541.05	5214.20	2953.17
rIC3-CtgDown	629	478	151	+26	+14	+12	2336.71	4794.40	2848.64
rIC3-DynAMic	627	479	148	+24	+15	+9	2346.48	4815.32	2783.76
$\mathcal{A}$-IC3 (Ours)	653	499	154	+50	+35	+15	2151.76	4413.68	2755.06

† Calculated for non-trivial cases (cases unsolvable within 100 s).

Table 4. Per-benchmark PAR-2 breakdown.

Configuration	HWMCC'20	HWMCC'24	HWMCC'25
rIC3-Standard	1872.02	3210.70	2586.63
rIC3-CtgDown	1719.38	3015.54	2309.31
rIC3-DynAMic	1617.83	3061.78	2376.00
$\mathcal{A}$-IC3	1479.82	2821.75	2200.99

Overall Performance. Table 3 summarizes the experimental results on rIC3 model checker under four generalization configurations: rIC3-Standard, rIC3-CtgDown [7], rIC3-DynAMic [20], and our $\mathcal{A}$-IC3. The table reports the number of solved instances (#Solved), broken down into Safe and Unsafe, as well as the improvement over the baseline (Δ, Δ_s, Δ_u) for the whole benchmark suite. We also report PAR-2, and for non-trivial cases (instances not solvable within 100 s), the corresponding PAR-2† and average runtime†. The PAR-2 score is a commonly used metric in competitions. It is calculated as the average time taken to solve the instances, with the timeout cases counted as twice the time limit. A lower PAR-2 score indicates better performance. Overall, $\mathcal{A}$-IC3 achieves the best performance: it solves 653 instances in total (+50 over Standard, with +35 Safe and +15 Unsafe), and it also yields the lowest PAR-2 and PAR-2† scores together with the lowest average runtime on non-trivial cases, outperforming both rIC3-CtgDown and rIC3-DynAMic across all reported metrics. Table 4 further reports the PAR-2 breakdown on HWMCC'20 [2], HWMCC'24 [16], and HWMCC'25 [17] after duplicate removal. $\mathcal{A}$-IC3 obtains the best PAR-2 on all three benchmark families.

Notably, $\mathcal{A}$-IC3 yields a more pronounced improvement on Safe instances than the other two IC3 variants, suggesting that our method can better incorporate the proving context to guide generalization and thus accelerate convergence on safety proofs. In particular, considering that rIC3 was the champion of the latest HWMCC [3, 17], the fact that our method can deliver further improvements is especially noteworthy.

Figure 3 illustrates the performance comparison on the benchmark suite when running rIC3 with and without MAB. We observe a cluster of instances in the green region. These cases are effectively intractable for the baseline configurations within the time limit, yet become solvable once MAB is enabled. This indicates that adaptively selecting a context-appropriate generalization strategy can unlock substantial speedups, sometimes by orders of magnitude, on originally hard instances. Meanwhile, on moderately hard cases where multiple strategies are already viable, $\mathcal{A}$-IC3 closely tracks the baseline runtime, suggesting that the additional exploration introduced by MAB incurs little overhead in practice.

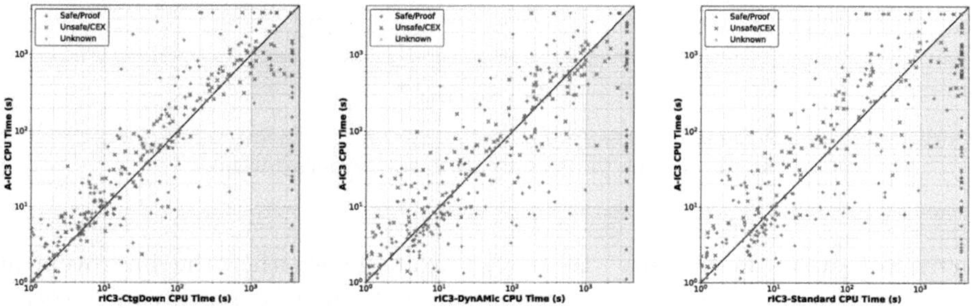

(a) (b) (c)

Fig. 3. Performance comparison of rIC3 with and without MAB: $\mathcal{A}$-IC3 (with MAB) vs. non-MAB baselines. (a) $\mathcal{A}$-IC3 vs. rIC3-CtgDown; (b) $\mathcal{A}$-IC3 vs. rIC3-DynAMic; (c) $\mathcal{A}$-IC3 vs. rIC3-Standard. Green regions indicate hard instances where the baseline struggled, but $\mathcal{A}$-IC3 achieved better results. (Color figure online)

Figure 4 shows the number of cases solved over time. The MAB-enhanced method consistently dominates the other configurations across the entire time range. Beyond the final number of solved instances, the cactus curves also highlight how MAB improves the efficiency of proof construction. The MAB curve rises faster in the early and middle time budgets, indicating that it reduces time spent on unpromising generalization choices and reaches effective proof trajectories sooner. As the timeout threshold increases, the gap remains and even expands for harder instances, suggesting that adaptive strategy selection continues to pay off when the proof search becomes more sensitive to generalization quality. At the same time, the curve does not exhibit a noticeable slowdown on easier and moderately hard cases, which supports our claim that the exploration overhead is well controlled and does not negate the gains from selecting better strategies.

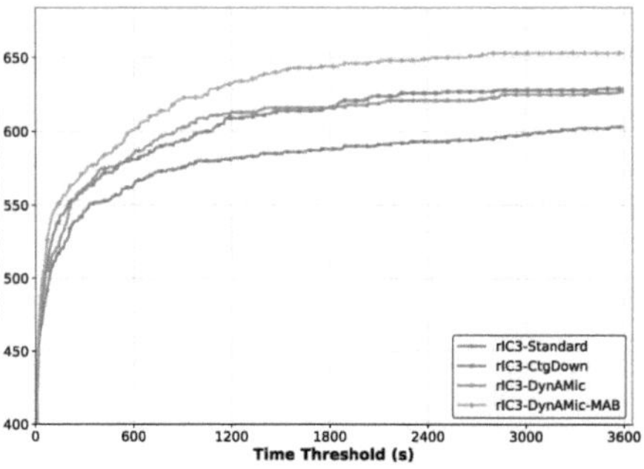

Fig. 4. Cactus plots comparing solver performance.

Arm Selection Behavior. To further examine whether the improvement comes from adaptive strategy selection rather than from repeatedly favoring one fixed configuration, we analyze the arm choices made by $\mathcal{A}$-IC3 during the solving process. Figure 5 reports the arm-selection distribution on three representative non-trivial instances where $\mathcal{A}$-IC3 obtains clear improvements over the baseline configurations. For each run, we divide the sequence of generalization calls into five equal phases according to normalized solving progress, and report the percentage of calls in which each arm is selected. These cases are used only for mechanism-level illustration; the aggregate performance claims are based on the full benchmark suite.

The results show that the dominant arms vary across both instances and solving phases. For example, on `xepic_a17-p02`, the selection gradually shifts from a mixed use of conservative and balanced arms toward a larger fraction of basic and conservative arms in the last phase. On `yosyshq_appnote_123_cv32e40x-p142`, conservative static generalization dominates most phases, but the early and middle phases still involve non-negligible selections of other static and dynamic arms. On `zipcpu-zipmmu-p00`, the first four phases use a more diverse mixture of arms, whereas the last phase is dominated by conservative generalization. Overall, these observations suggest that $\mathcal{A}$-IC3 re-ranks the arm space throughout the run according to the current proof context and accumulated reward feedback, rather than following a manually predefined switching schedule with better performance. In these successful non-trivial cases, the learned controller often allocates more effort to broader or deeper CTG exploration in the early and middle phases, and then shifts toward shallower choices near the end of solving to reduce frame saturation and over-generalization.

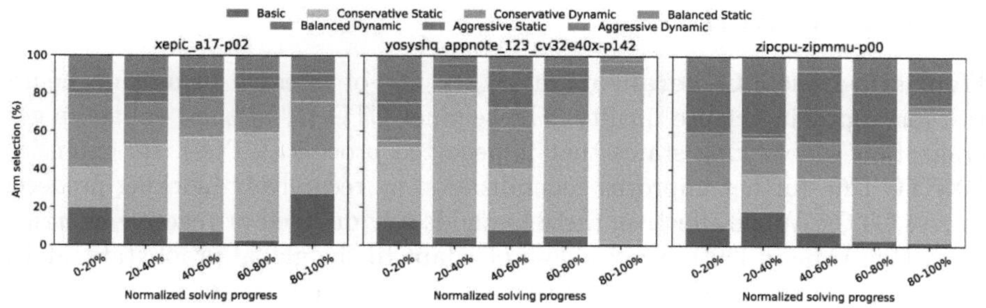

Fig. 5. Arm selection distribution over proof phases on case studies.

Effect on Proof Convergence. Figure 6 compares the termination level count (the index/number of frames when the solver terminates, either by reaching an inductive invariant or by finding a counterexample) of $\mathcal{A}$-IC3 against the baselines. Marker $\times$ denotes instances where the MAB-enhanced solver performs worse than the baseline, while + denotes instances where it performs better. It can be observed that a higher termination level generally indicates poorer performance. Across all three comparisons in Fig. 6, the overwhelming majority of points lie on or below the diagonal, and the level-count ratios are mostly below 1, indicating that MAB typically terminates at a lower level than the baselines, rather than improving only a small set of outliers. Since a lower convergence level in IC3 usually means fewer frames are needed to make the proof inductive or to expose a counterexample, this trend suggests that MAB accelerates solving by improving the proof trajectory itself. This observation also echoes our earlier claim that no single generalization heuristic is uniformly optimal: by adapting the strategy to the current proving context, MAB tends to derive clauses that are more "pushable" and better aligned with the proof frontier, which helps close the inductive gap earlier. Cases where MAB increases the termination level do exist, but they are relatively sparse and often close to the diagonal.

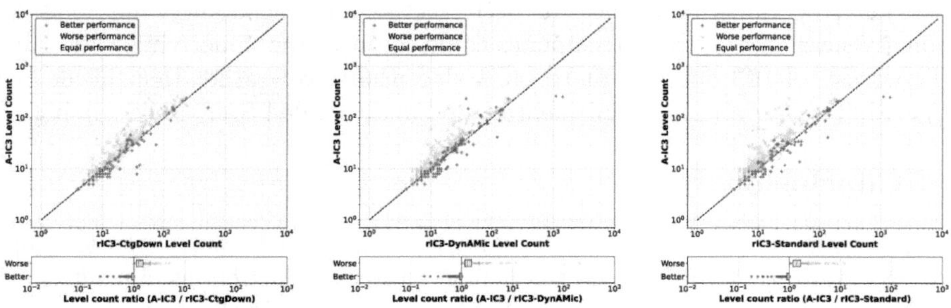

(a) (b) (c)

Fig. 6. Comparison of the termination level count. (a) $\mathcal{A}$-IC3 vs. rIC3-CtgDown; (b) $\mathcal{A}$-IC3 vs. rIC3-DynAMic; (c) $\mathcal{A}$-IC3 vs. rIC3-Standard.

5 Related Work

Heuristic-Based Generalization. A key line of research focuses on heuristics for improving clause quality. The seminal CTG [7] method enhances generalization by blocking states that impede the process (CTGs). Its extension, EXCTG [20], further improves generalization by recursively blocking predecessors of CTGs. While effective, these methods rely on fixed or reactive heuristics (e.g., DynAMic in [20]), which may not adapt to the global proof state. $\mathcal{A}$-`IC3` instead uses a richer context to anticipate the optimal strategy.

Global Guidance in Model Checking. Another direction complements local generalization with global guidance. GSPACER [21] uses theory-agnostic rules (Subsume, Concretize, Conjecture) to steer the search based on the global set of lemmas, mitigating issues like myopic generalization. GSPACER-BV [22] extends this to bit-vectors, using global guidance as a substitute for unavailable interpolation methods. These works focus on *what* to generalize. In contrast, $\mathcal{A}$-`IC3` is orthogonal and focuses on *how* to generalize by adaptively selecting the best procedure.

Data-Driven and Learning-Based Approaches. Machine learning has also been applied to guide generalization. ROPEY [11] uses a recurrent network to predict which literals to keep, while NeuroPDR [9] and DeepIC3 [8] employ Graph Neural Networks (GNNs) to predict effective clauses from the circuit structure. Although powerful, these supervised methods require extensive offline training and can introduce significant runtime overhead. $\mathcal{A}$-`IC3` sidesteps these issues with an MAB formulation that learns online with minimal overhead and no pre-existing data. It acts as a lightweight, adaptive control layer, making it more dynamic than fixed heuristics and more practical for hardware model checking than heavyweight deep learning approaches.

RL-Guided SAT/SMT Solving. Bandit and RL techniques have been explored for guiding SAT/SMT solving, including MAB-style branching heuristics such as CHB [13] and LRB [14], MAB-based switching of SAT branching heuristics [5], and MAB-guided SMT solver [15] or quantifier-instantiation selection [10]. Since IC3 relies on SAT queries for reachability and relative-inductiveness checks, these techniques could improve the underlying SAT calls. In contrast, $\mathcal{A}$-`IC3` operates at the IC3 algorithm layer rather than inside the SAT/SMT solver and is complementary to bandit-guided SAT/SMT solving.

6 Conclusion

In this work, we presented a lightweight, learning-guided framework for adaptive generalization in IC3. By modeling strategy selection as a contextual multi-armed bandit problem, our method dynamically adjusts generalization to the proof context, overcoming static heuristic limitations. Experiments demonstrated improvements over baseline strategies on extensive benchmarks. These results highlight the potential of integrating machine learning into formal verification for more efficient model checking. Future work includes deeper integration with other verification phases and advanced reinforcement learning methods.

Acknowledgments. This work is supported by the Guangdong S&T Program (No. 2025A0505000022) and the Hong Kong Research Grants Council General Research Fund (GRF) (No. 16218324). We thank Yuheng Su for his helpful discussions and support for this work. Hongce Zhang and Wei Zhang are co-corresponding authors.

Data Availibility Statement. Our implementation is available at: https://zenodo.org/records/19811923.

Disclosure of Interests. The authors have no competing interests to declare that are relevant to the content of this article.

References

1. Biere, A., Cimatti, A., Clarke, E., Fujita, M., Zhu, Y.: Symbolic model checking using SAT procedures instead of BDDs. In: Proceedings 1999 Design Automation Conference (Cat. No. 99CH36361), pp. 317–320 (1999). https://doi.org/10.1109/DAC.1999.781333
2. Biere, A., Froleyks, N., Preiner, M.: HWMCC'20 Benchmarks (2020). https://fmv.jku.at/hwmcc20/hwmcc20benchmarks.tar.xz, benchmark archive for the Hardware Model Checking Competition 2020 (BTOR2 and bit-blasted AIGER formats)
3. Biere, A., Froleyks, N., Preiner, M.: Hardware model checking competition 2024. In: 2024 Formal Methods in Computer-Aided Design (FMCAD), p. 1 (2024). https://doi.org/10.34727/2024/isbn.978-3-85448-065-5_6
4. Bradley, A.R.: SAT-based model checking without unrolling. In: Jhala, R., Schmidt, D. (eds.) Verification, Model Checking, and Abstract Interpretation. VMCAI 2011. LNCS, vol. 6538, pp. 70–87. Springer, Berlin, Heidelberg (2011). https://doi.org/10.1007/978-3-642-18275-4_7
5. Cherif, M.S., Habet, D., Terrioux, C.: Combining VSIDS and CHB using restarts in SAT. In: Michel, L.D. (ed.) 27th International Conference on Principles and Practice of Constraint Programming (CP 2021). Leibniz International Proceedings in Informatics (LIPIcs), vol. 210, pp. 20:1–20:19. Schloss Dagstuhl – Leibniz-Zentrum für Informatik, Dagstuhl, Germany (2021). https://doi.org/10.4230/LIPIcs.CP.2021.20
6. Een, N., Mishchenko, A., Brayton, R.: Efficient implementation of property directed reachability. In: 2011 Formal Methods in Computer-Aided Design (FMCAD), pp. 125–134 (2011). https://dl.acm.org/doi/10.5555/2157654.2157675
7. Hassan, Z., Bradley, A.R., Somenzi, F.: Better generalization in ic3. In: 2013 Formal Methods in Computer-Aided Design, pp. 157–164 (2013). https://doi.org/10.1109/FMCAD.2013.6679405
8. Hu, G., Tang, J., Yu, C., Zhang, W., Zhang, H.: DeepIC3: guiding IC3 algorithms by graph neural network clause prediction. In: 2024 29th Asia and South Pacific Design Automation Conference (ASP-DAC), pp. 262–268 (2024). https://doi.org/10.1109/ASP-DAC58780.2024.10473807
9. Hu, G., Zhang, W., Zhang, H.: NeuroPDR: integrating neural networks in the pdr algorithm for hardware model checking. In: 2023 ACM/IEEE 5th Workshop on Machine Learning for CAD (MLCAD), pp. 1–6 (2023). https://doi.org/10.1109/MLCAD58807.2023.10299875
10. Jakubův, J., Janota, M., Piotrowski, B., Piepenbrock, J., Reynolds, A.: Selecting quantifiers for instantiation in SMT. In: Proceedings of the 21st International

Workshop on Satisfiability Modulo Theories (SMT 2023). CEUR Workshop Proceedings, vol. 3429, pp. 71–77. CEUR-WS.org (2023). https://ceur-ws.org/Vol-3429/short10.pdf
11. Le, N., Si, X., Gurfinkel, A.: Data-driven optimization of inductive generalization. In: FMCAD, pp. 86–95 (2021). https://doi.org/10.34727/2021/isbn.978-3-85448-046-4_17
12. Li, L., Chu, W., Langford, J., Schapire, R.E.: A contextual-bandit approach to personalized news article recommendation. In: Proceedings of the 19th International Conference on World Wide Web, pp. 661–670. ACM (2010). https://doi.org/10.1145/1772690.1772758
13. Liang, J.H., Ganesh, V., Poupart, P., Czarnecki, K.: Exponential recency weighted average branching heuristic for SAT solvers. In: Proceedings of the Thirtieth AAAI Conference on Artificial Intelligence, pp. 3434–3440 (2016). https://doi.org/10.1609/aaai.v30i1.10439
14. Liang, J.H., Ganesh, V., Poupart, P., Czarnecki, K.: Learning rate based branching heuristic for SAT solvers. In: Creignou, N., Le Berre, D. (eds.) SAT 2016. LNCS, vol. 9710, pp. 123–140. Springer, Cham (2016). https://doi.org/10.1007/978-3-319-40970-2_9
15. Pimpalkhare, N., Mora, F., Polgreen, E., Seshia, S.A.: MedleySolver: Online SMT Algorithm Selection. In: Li, C.-M., Manyà, F. (eds.) SAT 2021. LNCS, vol. 12831, pp. 453–470. Springer, Cham (2021). https://doi.org/10.1007/978-3-030-80223-3_31
16. Preiner, M., Froleyks, N., Biere, A.: HWMCC'24 Benchmarks and Results. https://doi.org/10.5281/zenodo.14156844, https://zenodo.org/records/14156844
17. Preiner, M., Froleyks, N., Biere, A.: HWMCC'25 Benchmarks and Results (2025).https://doi.org/10.5281/zenodo.17428464, https://zenodo.org/records/17428464, dataset, version v1, published 2025-10-23
18. Sheeran, M., Singh, S., Stålmarck, G.: Checking safety properties using induction and a SAT-solver. In: Hunt, W.A., Johnson, S.D. (eds.) FMCAD 2000. LNCS, vol. 1954, pp. 127–144. Springer, Heidelberg (2000). https://doi.org/10.1007/3-540-40922-X_8
19. Su, Y., Yang, Q., Ci, Y., Bu, T., Huang, Z.: The rIC3 hardware model checker (2025). https://arxiv.org/abs/2502.13605
20. Su, Y., Yang, Q., Ci, Y., Huang, Z.: Extended ctg generalization and dynamic adjustment of generalization strategies in ic3 (2025). https://arxiv.org/abs/2501.02480
21. Vediramana Krishnan, H.G., Chen, Y., Shoham, S., Gurfinkel, A.: Global guidance for local generalization in model checking. Form. Methods Syst. Des. **63**(1), 81–109 (2024). https://doi.org/10.1007/s10703-023-00412-3
22. VK, H.G., Fedyukovich, G., Gurfinkel, A.: Word level property directed reachability. In: 2020 IEEE/ACM International Conference On Computer Aided Design (ICCAD), pp. 1–9. IEEE (2020). https://doi.org/10.1145/3400302.3415708
23. Winterer, F., Seufert, T., Scheibler, K., Teige, T., Scholl, C., Becker, B.: ICP and IC3 with stronger generalization. In: MBMV 2021; 24th Workshop, pp. 1–12. VDE (2021). https://abs.informatik.uni-freiburg.de/papers/2021/WSS+_2021.pdf

A Multi-width Parametric Bitvector Equivalence Solver

Luigi Rinaldi[1](✉), John Wickerson[2], and Samuel Coward[1]

[1] Department of Computer Science, University College London, London, UK
{luigi.rinaldi,sam.coward}@ucl.ac.uk

[2] Department of Electrical and Electronic Engineering, Imperial College London, London, UK
j.wickerson@imperial.ac.uk

Abstract. At the core of modern electronic design automation (EDA) tools is *rewriting*: a mechanism by which local transformations are iteratively applied to circuits to make them faster and more efficient. These rewrites are crucial for producing high-quality hardware, and they often depend on extremely delicate conditions, relating, for example, to the widths of the various bitvectors involved. As such, it is both *desirable* and *difficult* to prove them correct. Prior work has studied the correctness of parametric-bitwidth rewrites in the context of software compilers and SMT solvers, but those approaches struggle to handle rewrites that have *multiple* bitwidth parameters, as are commonplace in EDA. We propose a language for expressing these multi-width parametric rewrites and provide a translation into equivalences in modular arithmetic. We then show how these equivalences can be automatically and efficiently proved using equality saturation over a set of carefully chosen axioms, and finally reconstructed automatically as theorems in Isabelle. This process is implemented in our solver, ParaBit. Using benchmarks from prior compilers work and from industrial EDA tools, we demonstrate that ParaBit can solve a class of problems that are intractable using existing techniques.

Keywords: Bitvector · Modular Arithmetic · Equality Saturation

1 Introduction

The core purpose of logic synthesis tools is to optimise a user's hardware design [26]. A key mechanism for achieving this is *rewriting*: repeatedly transforming parts of the design into behaviourally equivalent parts, in the hope of improving the overall design's performance and resource usage. Real-world synthesis tools such as Cadence Genus [8], Synopsys Design Compiler [40,47], and Yosys [45] have hundreds of rewrites; some are simple like turning `x-x` into `0`, while some are remarkably complicated and only work under delicately crafted conditions.

It is *crucial* that these rewrites are correct. Logic synthesis occurs late in the hardware design process, after most verification activities have concluded,

E. Darulova et al. (Eds.): CAV 2026, LNCS 16682, pp. 380–402, 2026.
https://doi.org/10.1007/978-3-032-32519-8_20

```
input  wire[p-1:0] a, b, c;
       wire[q-1:0] tmp;
output wire[r-1:0] res;

// BEFORE REWRITING:              // AFTER REWRITING:
assign tmp = b + c;               assign tmp = a + b;
assign res = a + tmp;             assign res = tmp + c;
```

Fig. 1. An example of a rewrite, expressed as a transformation in Verilog

so unsound rewrites risk introducing circuit bugs that may only be fixed by patches to the synthesis tool itself. Since synthesis users and developers often reside in different companies, such bugs may cause costly delays in the chip development process.

Yet, at the same time, it is *difficult* to ensure that these rewrites are correct. One reason is that many rewrites are over expressions that involve bitvectors whose widths are parametric, and we need the rewrites to be correct for all values of those parameters.

Consider a parametric Verilog example (Fig. 1), adapted from Coward et al. [12]. Following the semantics of Verilog [19,43] and using e_u to abbreviate $e \bmod 2^u$, the rewrite shown is sound if the following equivalence holds:

$$(a_p + (b_p + c_p)_q)_r \equiv ((a_p + b_p)_q + c_p)_r. \tag{1}$$

What are the conditions on p, q, and r under which that equivalence holds? Coward et al. gave, without proof, a condition which they claim is sufficient:

$$(q > p \wedge r > q) \vee (q \geq r). \tag{2}$$

Accordingly, a synthesis tool can safely apply this transformation upon matching a concrete instance as long as the integer values for p, q, and r satisfy (2).

We would like to prove – foundationally and automatically – that (2)⇒(1), but existing tools cannot handle examples like this. For instance, although standard satisfiability modulo theories (SMT) solvers such as Bitwuzla [33] and CVC5 [2] are able to reason automatically about bitvector equivalences like (1), they can only handle cases where the bitwidths are constants. Proprietary verification tools, such as Cadence Jasper [7] and Synopsys VCFormal [20], are similarly unable to reason about parametric bitvector problems – they focus instead on proving properties of *specific* circuit designs.

The work that comes closest is by Berger et al. [4], who proposed an extension to SMT-LIB that allows bitvectors to have parametric widths. However, their solution does not quite work in our situation, because they attach the width parameters to *operators*. For instance, they define a $+_u$ operator for parametric u that adds two u-bit inputs and produces a u-bit output. This is suitable for the software compiler setting that they considered, but we need an operator that takes inputs and produces outputs of *different* widths. To express our $(a_p + b_p)_q$ using Berger et al.'s approach, we must pad or truncate depending on the sizes:

$$\textbf{if } p < q \textbf{ then } \texttt{zero\_extend}(a, q) +_q \texttt{zero\_extend}(b, q)$$
$$\textbf{else } \texttt{truncate}((a +_p b), q)$$

The ensuing proliferation of case-splits can ruin the performance of an automatic solver (as we shall see in Sect. 6).

Thus, in this paper we propose a representation in which bitwidth parameters are attached to *operands*, thus allowing equivalences like (1) to be encoded directly. We call this representation `BWLang` (Sect. 4), and we provide a set of `BWLang` axioms (Sect. 5.1), which are proven in the Isabelle proof assistant [36].

Unfortunately, naïve greedy rewriting over these axioms is insufficient for constructing proofs, so we turn to equality saturation [42,44]. Equality saturation has become a popular approach for implementing transformations in the context of compilers [42] and, more recently, logic synthesis tools [12]. In our work, we employ it "the other way round": we provide a candidate equivalence between `BWLang` expressions, and use equality saturation to seek a derivation of it using our set of axioms (Sect. 5.2).

If a derivation *is* found, we are able to recover the specific axioms that were used and how they were composed, and thus produce an Isabelle script that gives a foundational proof that the candidate equivalence is correct (Sect. 5.3), and hence that the original rewrite is sound. We implement the equality saturation-based solver and the proof certificate generation in a tool called ParaBit.

In summary, our contributions are:

- a concise representation for multi-width parametric bitvector transformations, inspired by modular arithmetic (Sect. 4),
- an equality saturation-based solver (ParaBit) that automatically constructs a chain of reasoning from a set of conditional modular arithmetic axioms (Sect. 5),
- a formalised certificate checker in Isabelle for the proposed theory (Sect. 5.3), and
- a comprehensive evaluation and comparison with the state-of-the-art parametric bitvector solver (Sect. 6).

2 Motivational Example

To demonstrate the general approach of composing a set of modular arithmetic axioms, we will now prove (2) $\Rightarrow$ (1), which we repeat here.

$$\begin{array}{lll} \text{(precondition)} & \forall p, q, r \in \mathbb{N}^+ & (q > p \land r > q) \lor (q \geq r) \Rightarrow \\ \text{(transformation)} & \forall a, b, c \in \mathbb{Z} & \underbrace{(a_p + (b_p + c_p)_q)_r}_{\text{lhs}} \equiv \underbrace{((a_p + b_p)_q + c_p)_r}_{\text{rhs}} \end{array}$$

Throughout we will use $a, b, c, \ldots$ to denote integer variables representing bitvectors and $p, q, r, \ldots$ to denote natural numbers representing bitwidth variables.

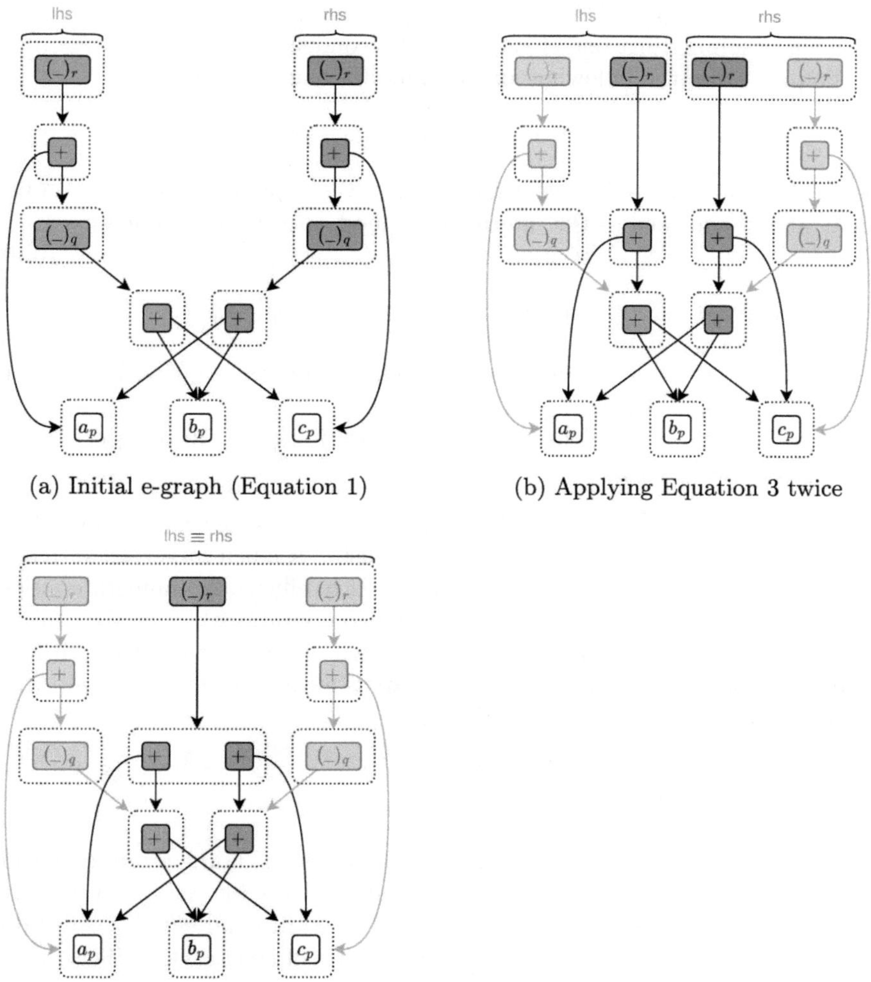

(a) Initial e-graph (Equation 1)

(b) Applying Equation 3 twice

(c) By associativity and congruence

Fig. 2. E-graph rewriting steps encoding the motivational example (Sect. 2) $q \geq r \Rightarrow$ lhs $\equiv$ rhs. Applying Eq. 3 twice to (a) adds new terms to the two root e-classes in (b). Applying associativity to (b) proves equivalence of an orange add and blue add, merging them into the same e-class. Congruence closure then merges the two root e-classes, removing a node due to congruence and proving the goal. We gray out unchanged nodes to highlight changes. (Color figure online)

In this example the inputs are integers $(a, b, c \in \mathbb{Z})$, which are constrained to be p-bit bitvectors (a_p, b_p, c_p). The intermediate results are stored in q-bit bitvectors and the final summations are stored in r-bit bitvectors. Note that the precondition is a function only of the bitwidth parameters and is expressed in disjunctive normal form (DNF). To simplify the presentation, we shall prove the statement assuming just one clause of the precondition ($q \geq r$).

The proof uses the following axiom of modular arithmetic:

$$u \geq v \Rightarrow (x + (y \bmod 2^u)) \bmod 2^v \equiv (x + y) \bmod 2^v. \tag{3}$$

The required sequence of transformations involves applying that axiom on both the *lhs* and *rhs* to remove the intermediate mod operation, as follows:

$$\begin{array}{ll} (a_p + (b_p + c_p)_q)_r & \\ \quad \equiv & \{ \text{ using (3) with condition } q \geq r \} \\ (a_p + (b_p + c_p))_r & \\ \quad \equiv & \{ \text{ using associativity of integer addition } \} \\ ((a_p + b_p) + c_p)_r & \\ \quad \equiv & \{ \text{ using (3) with condition } q \geq r \text{, in reverse } \} \\ ((a_p + b_p)_q + c_p)_r & \end{array} \tag{4}$$

Here we manually constructed the correct sequence of axiom applications. To automatically discover correct sequences using a much larger set of axioms (Sect. 5.1) we use equality saturation (Sect. 5.2) to efficiently enumerate all possible sequences of axiom applications, up to a computational limit. We can visualise (Fig. 2) the steps of equality saturation that construct this proof within an e-graph. If a proof is found, a proof certificate is automatically generated, which can be verified using Isabelle (Sect. 5.3).

3 Background

We provide a brief introduction to bitvector theories, including recent extensions to support bitvectors of parametric width, and solvers for these bitvector theories. We will then describe the e-graph data structure and equality saturation rewriting technique, which we use to automate proof construction (Sect. 5).

3.1 Bitvector Theories

SMT-LIB defines a theory of constant-width bitvectors T_{BV} [3]. For all constants $n \in \mathbb{N}^+$, SMT-LIB defines $\mathtt{BV}_n$ as the type of bitvectors of width n. In T_{BV}, all arithmetic and logical binary operators (excluding concatenation) satisfy the following signature,

$$\mathtt{BV}_n \times \mathtt{BV}_n \to \mathtt{BV}_n. \tag{5}$$

That is, the operands and result all have the same width – essentially specifying the bitwidth at the operation level. The T_{BV} theory has been used extensively to phrase hardware and software verification challenges [15,24,46]. The most effective automated solvers for T_{BV} combine bitvector-level rewriting with eager bit-blasting to a SAT solver [33].

In 2025, Berger et al. defined T_{PBV}, which extends T_{BV} to support bitvectors of parametric width [4]. The new theory provides a single type PBV for bitvectors of parametric size and defines new operators that take PBV inputs and produce PBV outputs. Unlike T_{BV}, which enforces width equality in the sort system, T_{PBV} instead generates additional proof obligations that ensure operand widths match. These proof obligations can, and often do, involve parametric width variables. The T_{PBV} solver also incorporates a set of rewrites, which are carefully selected from the existing rewrites for T_{BV}, then made parametric. The solver defines a translation from T_{PBV} to integer arithmetic plus a small set of uninterpreted function symbols and adds admissibility constraints [4,34]. Once translated to integer arithmetic they then combine existing integer solvers with a procedure to iteratively refine over-approximations of the uninterpreted function symbols [4]. We will similarly consider parametric bitvector problems as integer arithmetic problems, but will define a new representation that yields more concise integer arithmetic encodings in the multi-width case (Sect. 4).

3.2 E-Graphs and Equality Saturation

The e-graph is a data structure used to represent a set of terms and an equivalence relation over that set of terms, closed under congruence [21,32]. Nodes in the graph represent either function symbols of non-zero arity or constants or variables which are zero-arity symbols. To provide a compact representation, equivalent terms are grouped into equivalence classes, known as e-classes, by their root function symbol. Edges in the e-graph connect nodes to e-classes and represent operator inputs (Fig. 2). To enable efficient congruence closure, each e-class is represented using a union-find data structure [41].

Equality saturation is a program rewriting technique that applies rewrites directly to the e-graph [42,44]. Traditional term rewriting finds a term matching a rewrite's left-hand side (lhs) pattern and replaces it with the rewrite's right-hand side (rhs), making the appropriate substitutions [1]. In contrast, equality saturation adds the rhs to the matched e-class, monotonically growing the set of terms represented by the e-graph. The introduction of e-classes complicates the pattern matching procedure as each e-class may contain several matching terms, leading to the development of the e-matching procedure [28]. As new terms are added to the e-graph the congruence invariant needs to be restored. This can be deferred to improve efficiency by batching rewrites and applying them in iterations that alternate between adding terms and congruence closure [44].

Given a set of rewrite rules, equality saturation terminates when further rewrite rule applications no longer add new terms to the e-graph. We say that the e-graph has saturated. In practice, and as we do in this work, it is common to terminate equality saturation early, after achieving the desired goal or after some computational limit is reached. We can encode the motivational example (Sect. 2) in an e-graph and use equality saturation to prove the goal with the given axioms and congruence closure (Fig. 2).

E-graphs can be found at the heart of modern SMT solvers [2,29], although without typically using equality saturation to directly rewrite the e-graph. Equality saturation has gained popularity since the release of the egg library that

$$
\begin{array}{llll}
\mathbb{Z} & \ni n & & \\
\mathbb{N}^+ & \ni w & & \\
\mathsf{Var} & \ni a, p & & \\
\mathsf{BVExpr} & \ni B & ::= a \mid n \mid (B)_W \mid \mathtt{signed}(W, B) & \\
 & & \mid B \ll B \mid B \gg B \mid B \boxtimes B & \boxtimes \in \{+, -, \div, \times, \&, \oplus, |\} \\
 & & \mid (ite\, B, B, B) \mid \boxminus B & \boxminus \in \{-, \sim\} \\
\mathsf{WidthExpr} & \ni W & ::= W \boxplus W \mid \mathrm{pow}_2(W) \mid p \mid w & \boxplus \in \{+, -, \times\} \\
\mathsf{Precond} & \ni P & ::= P \wedge P \mid W \diamond W & \diamond \in \{>, \geq, <, \leq\}
\end{array}
$$

Fig. 3. BWLang grammar. P describes the representable preconditions.

introduced a number of innovations to improve performance and limit the computational overhead of equality saturation [44]. The egg library later gained the ability to produce a proof, essentially a sequence of rewrite applications, to justify why two terms were merged into the same e-class [16]. Researchers have developed numerous applications using egg, including tools to improve the numerical stability of programs [37], hardware design automation [9], and lemma discovery [22]. We build a solver using egg (Sect. 5.2) and use its proof production capabilities to generate a certificate that we formalise in Isabelle (Sect. 5.3).

4 BWLang

We introduce a new language, BWLang (Fig. 3), to express bitvector equivalences containing *multiple* bitwidth variables. In this language operators can be applied to bitvectors of different widths, and the result of the operation can itself assume a different width. To achieve this we introduce the $(\_)_{\_} : \mathbb{N}^+ \to \mathbb{Z} \to \mathbb{N}$ operator, which, given a positive non-zero natural number representing a width and an integer, returns the least positive residue of the integer modulo two to the power of the width. The result is an arbitrary bitvector if the width is non-positive. Bitvector operations are performed by interpreting the bitvectors as natural numbers (akin to SMT-LIB bv2nat), performing the integer operation and then recasting the result as a bitvector (akin to SMT-LIB nat2bv). Currently, BWLang only supports a subset of the operations defined in SMT-LIB's bitvector theory [3]. In BWLang, division by zero and logical shifts by negative integers are interpreted arbitrarily.

ParaBit is capable of solving a subset of the language admitted by the BWLang grammar, which we call well-formed.

Definition 1 (Well-Formed BVExpr). *A given $B \in$ BVExpr is well-formed if every constant, variable and operation result in B is cast to a bitvector, meaning it is wrapped in a $(\_)_p$ operation for some $p \in$ WidthExpr.*

For example, $(a_p+1_1)_q$ is well-formed but (a_p+1) is not. Intuitively, this restricts ParaBit to the domain where every intermediate result has a specified, although potentially parametric, width. ParaBit will reject input BVExprs that are not well-formed. We do not enforce this restriction in the BWLang grammar, as the axioms (Sect. 5.1) will remove bitvector casts when provably sound according to BWLang semantics (Sect. 4.1).

The restricted BWLang subset is able to capture bitvector expressions such as those defined in T_{PBV} [4], by encoding the widths of each operand and destination to be identical. Further, we are able to reason about parametric bitvector problems similar to those expressible in Verilog, where each operand can take on a different width and it is truncated or zero-extended accordingly. Indeed, zero-extension and truncation amount to the same operation in BWLang, i.e., changing the width of some expression to a new width, by nesting bitvector casts $((\_)_p)_q$. The difference lies in the fact that a truncation assumes the outer width is smaller than the inner, whereas extension assumes the opposite. Therefore, based on the provided conditions, the operator will be interpreted as either of the operations, but if no condition is provided it captures both.

4.1 Semantics

The semantics of BWLang are defined by the following denotation functions:

$$\begin{array}{ll} \mathcal{B}[\![\_]\!]_{\pi,\rho} : \mathsf{BVExpr} & \rightarrow ((\mathsf{WEnv} \times \mathsf{Env}) \rightarrow \mathbb{Z}) \\ \mathcal{W}[\![\_]\!]_{\pi} : \mathsf{WidthExpr} & \rightarrow (\mathsf{WEnv} \rightarrow \mathbb{Z}) \\ \mathcal{P}[\![\_]\!]_{\pi} : \mathsf{Precond} & \rightarrow (\mathsf{WEnv} \rightarrow \mathsf{Bool}) \end{array}$$

where the width environment $\pi : \mathsf{WEnv} \equiv \mathsf{Var} \rightarrow \mathbb{N}^+$ captures the mapping of width parameters to positive non-zero integers and the environment $\rho : \mathsf{Env} \equiv \mathsf{Var} \rightarrow \mathbb{Z}$ captures the mapping of the remaining variables in the BVExpr to integers. Preconditions are interpreted ($\mathcal{P}$) following the standard rules of Boolean algebra and integer comparisons.

The interpretation of a WidthExpr ($\mathcal{W}$) is standard integer arithmetic:

$$\begin{array}{ll} \mathcal{W}[\![p]\!]_{\pi} & = \pi(p) \\ \mathcal{W}[\![w]\!]_{\pi} & = w \\ \mathcal{W}[\![\mathrm{pow}_2(w)]\!]_{\pi} & = \mathrm{pow}_2(\mathcal{W}[\![w]\!]_{\pi}) \\ \mathcal{W}[\![a \boxplus b]\!]_{\pi} & = \mathcal{W}[\![a]\!]_{\pi} \boxplus \mathcal{W}[\![b]\!]_{\pi}. \end{array}$$

The interpretation of a BVExpr ($\mathcal{B}$) is defined via modular arithmetic.

$$\begin{array}{ll} \mathcal{B}[\![a]\!]_{\pi,\rho} & = \rho(a) \\ \mathcal{B}[\![n]\!]_{\pi,\rho} & = n \\ \mathcal{B}[\![(B)_W]\!]_{\pi,\rho} & = \mathcal{B}[\![B]\!]_{\pi,\rho} \bmod \mathrm{pow}_2(\mathcal{W}[\![W]\!]_{\pi}) \\ \mathcal{B}[\![\mathtt{signed}(W,B)]\!]_{\pi,\rho} & = 2 \times \mathcal{B}[\![(B)_{\mathcal{W}[\![W-1]\!]_{\pi}}]\!]_{\pi,\rho} - \mathcal{B}[\![(B)_{\mathcal{W}[\![W]\!]_{\pi}}]\!]_{\pi,\rho} \\ \mathcal{B}[\![B \gg C]\!]_{\pi,\rho} & = \mathcal{B}[\![B]\!]_{\pi,\rho} \div \mathrm{pow}_2(\mathcal{B}[\![C]\!]_{\pi,\rho}) \\ \mathcal{B}[\![B \ll C]\!]_{\pi,\rho} & = \mathcal{B}[\![B]\!]_{\pi,\rho} \times \mathrm{pow}_2(\mathcal{B}[\![C]\!]_{\pi,\rho}) \\ \mathcal{B}[\![B \boxtimes C]\!]_{\pi,\rho} & = \mathcal{B}[\![B]\!]_{\pi,\rho} \boxtimes \mathcal{B}[\![C]\!]_{\pi,\rho} \\ \mathcal{B}[\![(ite\, B, C, D)]\!]_{\pi,\rho} & = \mathcal{B}[\![(B)_1]\!]_{\pi,\rho} \times \mathcal{B}[\![C]\!]_{\pi,\rho} + \mathcal{B}[\![(\sim (B)_1)_1]\!]_{\pi,\rho} \times \mathcal{B}[\![D]\!]_{\pi,\rho} \\ \mathcal{B}[\![\boxminus B]\!]_{\pi,\rho} & = \boxminus \mathcal{B}[\![B]\!]_{\pi,\rho} \end{array}$$

The $\texttt{signed}(W, B)$ operation treats B as a two's complement encoded bitvector of length W. Its interpretation is the two's complement conversion to an integer. Letting $a = \mathcal{B}[\![a']\!]_{\pi,\rho}$, $p = \mathcal{W}[\![p']\!]_{\pi}$, we can rearrange the natural definition to recover the interpretation given, where $(a \gg (p-1))_1$ extracts the sign-bit.

$$\begin{aligned}\mathcal{B}[\![\texttt{signed}(p', a')]\!]_{\pi,\rho} &= a_{p-1} - \left(2^{p-1} \times (a \gg (p-1))_1\right)\\ &= 2 \times a_{p-1} - a_{p-1} - \left(2^{p-1} \times (a \gg (p-1))_1\right)\\ &= 2 \times a_{p-1} - a_p\end{aligned}$$

Bitwise operations are defined recursively over the integers following the Isabelle `Bit_Operation` definitions [17]. For example, & is defined as:

$$a \,\&\, b = \mathit{isodd}(a) \wedge \mathit{isodd}(b) + 2 \times ((a \div 2) \,\&\, (b \div 2)).$$

4.2 Problem Definition

We now define a BW problem that can be solved by ParaBit, as a tuple of type ($\mathsf{Precond} \times \mathsf{BVExpr} \times \mathsf{BVExpr}$), containing a precondition and two well-formed BVExpr terms. Given an instance of a BW problem, (P, B, C) ParaBit attempts to prove $P \Rightarrow B \equiv C$ which is shorthand for:

$$\forall \pi \in \mathsf{WEnv}.\, \mathcal{P}[\![P]\!]_{\pi} \implies \forall \rho \in \mathsf{Env}.\, \mathcal{B}[\![B]\!]_{\pi,\rho} = \mathcal{B}[\![C]\!]_{\pi,\rho} \tag{6}$$

The formulation of Eq. 6 means that if the statement is found to be true, this is equivalent to finding the UNSAT result for $\neg(6)$, where $\neg(6)$ is the conventional SMT formulation for proving bitvector rewrite rules [4]. The parametric case differs from bitvector problems with concrete widths (i.e., T_{BV}) in the further existential quantification of the width variables ($\exists \pi$).

$$\neg(6) = \exists \pi.\, \mathcal{P}[\![P]\!]_{\pi} \wedge \left(\exists \rho.\, \mathcal{B}[\![B]\!]_{\pi,\rho} \neq \mathcal{B}[\![C]\!]_{\pi,\rho}\right) \tag{7}$$

Our solver, ParaBit, can only prove unsatisfiability of Eq. 7. ParaBit cannot derive a satisfiable assignment, which would correspond to a set of inputs that disprove the equivalence. Existing work [4] already solves the satisfiability problem efficiently, but we could extend ParaBit to add satisfiability checking.

5 A Solver for BWLang

Having defined the `BWLang` representation, we now describe how our ParaBit solver automatically finds a proof for BW problems. We generate proofs by combining `BWLang` axioms (Sect. 5.1) using equality saturation to efficiently explore all possible paths (Sect. 5.2). To reduce the trusted computing base, we formalise the axioms in Isabelle and generate machine-checkable proof certificates (Sect. 5.3).

Table 1. The first half are axioms converting bitvector operations to arithmetic, whilst the second half are axioms removing or simplifying bitvector casts $(\_)_p$. The $\leftrightarrow$ indicates that the rule is applied in both directions.

Name	Precondition	Pattern Replacement
lshift.def	True	$a_p \ll b_q \rightarrow a_p * 2^{b_q}$
rshift.def	True	$a_p \gg b_q \rightarrow a_p \div 2^{b_q}$
ite.def	True	$(ite\ c_1\ a_p\ b_p) \rightarrow c_1 * a_p + (\sim c_1)_1 * b_p$
xor.def	True	$a_p \oplus b_p \leftrightarrow (a_p \| b_p) - (a_p \& b_p)$
signed.def	True	$\mathtt{signed}(p, a) \rightarrow 2 * a_{p-1} - a_p$
bw.1	True	$1_p \rightarrow 1$
bw.0	True	$0_p \rightarrow 0$
add.rm.l.prec	$q \geq p$	$(a_q + b)_p \rightarrow (a + b)_p$
add.rm.r.prec	$q \geq p$	$(a + b_q)_p \rightarrow (a + b)_p$
add.full.prec	$(q < p) \wedge (r < p)$	$(a_q + b_r)_p \rightarrow a_q + b_r$
diff.rm.l.prec	$q \geq p$	$(a_q - b)_p \rightarrow (a - b)_p$
diff.rm.r.prec	$q \geq p$	$(a - b_q)_p \rightarrow (a - b)_p$
mul.full.prec	$r \geq (p + q)$	$(a_q * b_p)_r \rightarrow a_q * b_p$
mul.rm.prec	$p \geq q$	$(a_p * b)_q \rightarrow (a * b)_q$
mul.bit	$q \geq p$	$(a_p * b_1)_q \rightarrow a_p * b_1$
div.gte	$p \geq q$	$(a_q \div b)_p \rightarrow a_q \div b$
div.floor	$b \geq 2^p$	$a_p \div b \rightarrow 0$
mod.inner	$q \geq p$	$(a_p)_q \rightarrow a_p$
mod.outer	$p \geq q$	$(a_p)_q \rightarrow a_q$
mul.pow2	$r \geq p + 2^q - 1$	$(a_p * 2^{b_q})_r \rightarrow a_p * 2^{b_q}$
rshift.mod	$p - q \geq b$	$(a_p \gg b)_q \rightarrow (a \gg b)_q$
rshift.pos	$b > 0$	$(a \gg b) \rightarrow (a \div 2^b)$
rm.signed	True	$\mathtt{signed}(p, a_p)_p \rightarrow a_p$
zext.signed	$q > p$	$\mathtt{signed}(q, a_p) \rightarrow a_p$
neg.signed	$q > p$	$\mathtt{signed}(q, (-a_p)_q) \rightarrow -a_p$
diff.signed	$r > p \wedge r > q$	$\mathtt{signed}(r, (a_p - b_q)_r) \rightarrow a_p - b_q$

5.1 Axioms

The BW problems admitted by ParaBit are restricted to the well-formed subset of `BWLang` (Sect. 4.2). By contrast, ParaBit's axioms are triples of type (Precond $\times$ BVExpr $\times$ BVExpr), comprised of a precondition and two (not necessarily well-formed) BVExpr terms, along with a direction of application. For each axiom we define, $(P, pat, repl)$ and prove that:

$$\forall \pi \in \mathsf{WEnv}.\, \mathcal{P}[\![P]\!]_\pi \implies \forall \rho \in \mathsf{Env}.\, \mathcal{B}[\![pat]\!]_{\pi,\rho} = \mathcal{B}[\![repl]\!]_{\pi,\rho}. \tag{8}$$

```
input  wire[p  :0] a;
       wire[p  :0] tmp;
output wire[p-1:0] res;

// OPTION 1:                          // OPTION 2:
                                      assign tmp = a + 1'b1;
assign res = a[p:1] + a[0];           assign res = tmp[p:1];
```

Fig. 4. Unsigned round-to-nearest implementations in Verilog.

Whilst essentially the same as Eq. 6, the axioms we define are far simpler to prove than the general class of BW problems.

In total ParaBit uses 99 axioms, of which a subset are presented here (Table 1). We omit axioms arising from standard properties of Boolean arithmetic, integer arithmetic (associativity, commutativity, distributivity etc.) and simplifications involving constants. The first set of axioms presented convert certain bitvector operations to integer arithmetic (Table 1 - top), following the previously defined semantics (Sect. 4.1). The second set of axioms presented are applied conditionally and describe all the axioms that essentially simplify `BWLang` expressions involving $(\_)_p$ operations (Table 1 - bottom). Specifically, these are all the axioms where the "Replacement" has fewer occurrences of bitwidth parameters than the "Pattern". It is these axioms that depend heavily upon the preconditions that accompany each BW problem. Namely, given a particular axiom, say "add.rm.l.prec", when we find a match we get an expression corresponding to each of the pattern variables (p, q, a, b) in the "Pattern". After replacing each variable by its matched expression, we then check whether the "Precondition" is implied by the preconditions given in the BW problem. Although we convert certain bitvector operations (e.g., $\gg$) to arithmetic, thanks to equality saturation we are still able to reason about these operations (e.g., "rshift.mod") as they are not removed from the e-graph.

One particularly unconventional axiom, "half.adder", does not fit within any axiom category described so far as it unrolls the definition of addition.

$$a_p + b_q \rightarrow (a_p \oplus b_q) + 2 * (a_p \,\&\, b_q) \tag{9}$$

The rule applies a half-adder then sums the results, but can be recursively applied to the "Replacement" creating a source of exponential e-graph growth (Sect. 5.2). Whilst costly, "half.adder" proves extremely helpful in proving BW problems that mix Boolean and arithmetic operations, as is common in circuit optimisation. Consider two equivalent unsigned round-to-nearest implementations (Fig. 4). Applying "half.adder" to `OPTION 2` we can then prove it equivalent to `OPTION 1` by simplifying Boolean operations with a constant argument (`1'b1`) and applying standard arithmetic axioms.

5.2 Equality Saturation

We define BWLang using an S-expression syntax (not presented here), allowing us to develop ParaBit using the egg equality saturation library. Given a BW problem, (P, lhs, rhs), we initialise the e-graph with the *lhs* and *rhs* BVExprs. ParaBit's goal is to unify the root e-classes of each expression, L and R, respectively. We then create a *special* e-class $C_{\texttt{True}}$ and add each P_i expression to it, where $P = \bigwedge_i P_i$, converting the precondition P to an assumption. We will use this e-graph to encode a contextual relation. Namely, given an e-class c, if $x, y \in c$ then $P \Rightarrow x \equiv y$. Recent work in contextual equality saturation has identified the challenge of handling multiple contexts within a single e-graph [11,18,38]. For example, if $P_1 \Rightarrow x \equiv y$ and $P_2 \Rightarrow x \equiv z$, $P_1 \vee P_2 \not\Rightarrow y \equiv z$, yet a standard e-graph only encodes a single equivalence relation, so reasoning under such a disjunction of preconditions can lead to incorrect derivations. Instead of turning to complex solutions for encoding multiple equivalence relations in an e-graph [38], we resolve this by restricting BW problem preconditions to conjunctions of preconditions (Precond). This means that the original motivational problem (Sect. 2) corresponds to two BW problems, with a separate e-graph for each clause of the DNF. Whilst this means that we must rediscover common equalities, e.g. those for which $P_1 \vee P_2 \Rightarrow y \equiv z$, in practice we did not encounter sufficient scalability or runtime issues to motivate a more complex solution.

Having initialised the e-graph, we now run iterations of equality saturation applying all the axioms (Sect. 5.1) at every iteration. Each time a conditional axiom is matched via e-matching, ParaBit performs the substitutions to generate a Precond comprised of variables declared in the input BW problem. ParaBit then checks whether that expression is contained within the $C_{\texttt{True}}$ e-class. If it is, the "Replacement" expression is then added to the matched e-class. We also implement a basic constant folding to handle trivial comparisons, such as $2 > 0$.

After each iteration of axiom application, ParaBit terminates immediately if L and R have been merged, and continues applying axioms until saturation otherwise (Sect. 3.2). If the e-graph saturates, it means that the two expressions cannot be shown to be equivalent using the current set of axioms.

5.3 Isabelle Formalisation

If ParaBit terminates having proven equivalence, we leverage egg's proof-producing capabilities [16] to obtain an equational explanation proving the equivalence of BVExprs *lhs* and *rhs*. The explanation is a sequence of equivalent expressions, where consecutive expressions differ by the application of a single axiom. Returning to the motivational example (Sect. 2), we present the egg-generated equational explanation which has been simplified to improve readability (Fig. 5a). During our evaluation we observed that some egg-generated explanations contained unproductive cycles, where the explanation repeatedly revisited identical proof terms. Therefore, before proceeding to proof certificate generation, the equational explanation is automatically reduced by removing these unproductive cycles.

```
(bw r (+ (bw p a) (bw q (+ (bw p b) (bw p c)))))
(Rewrite=> add_rm_r_prec (bw r (+ (bw p a) (+ (bw p b) (bw p c)))))
(bw r (Rewrite=> isabelle-add.assoc (+ (+ (bw p a) (bw p b)) (bw p c))))
(Rewrite<= add_rm_l_prec (bw r (+ (bw q (+ (bw p a) (bw p b))) (bw p c))))
```

(a) Simplified egg-generated explanation. Note, the addition is presented using prefix notation. The rewrite rule application direction is denoted by => and <=, representing top-to-bottom and bottom-to-top respectively.

```
theorem motivational_example:
  fixes p q r :: nat
  fixes a b c :: int
  assumes "p > 0" and "r > 0" and "q > 0"
  assumes "q >= r"
  shows "(bw r ((bw p a) + (bw q ((bw p b) + (bw p c)))))
        = (bw r ((bw q ((bw p a) + (bw p b))) + (bw p c)))"
        (is "?lhs = ?rhs")
proof -
  have "?lhs = (bw r ((bw p a) + ((bw p b) + (bw p c))))"
    using add_rm_r_prec assms
    by (simp; fail | simp only: add_rm_r_prec; fail
      | simp add: add_rm_r_prec; fail | blast; fail | metis)
  moreover have "... = (bw r (((bw p a) + (bw p b)) + (bw p c)))"
    using add.assoc assms by (simp; fail ...)
  moreover have "... = (bw r ((bw q ((bw p a) + (bw p b))) + (bw p c)))"
    using add_rm_l_prec assms by (simp; fail ...)
  ultimately show ?thesis by argo
qed
```

(b) ParaBit generated Isabelle script. We omit the full tactic application for brevity.

Fig. 5. Egg proof-production output and corresponding Isabelle script for proving the motivational example (Sect. 2). In both (bw p a) is used to denote the bitvector cast operation a_p.

Given a reduced equational explanation, ParaBit generates an Isabelle proof script that transforms *lhs* into *rhs* through a chain of justified equational steps, encoding the preconditions as assumptions in the theorem statement. The proof script generation proceeds by introducing intermediate subgoals, one for each step in the explanation, where each subgoal asserts the equality between consecutive expressions. The transformation is then justified by applying the specific axiom (ax) responsible for that rewriting step. To discharge these subgoals, we employ a sequence of tactics in the following order: `simp`, `simp only: ax`, `simp add: ax`, `blast` and finally `metis`. Each tactic application is chained by a `; fail |` term, so that if a tactic does not fully discharge the goal, a more powerful one is attempted. This goal resolution technique is robust and enabled verification of all certificates generated by ParaBit (Sect. 6.4). We include the Isabelle script generated by ParaBit for the motivational example (Fig. 5b), which depends

```
lemma add_rm_l_prec:
  "(bw p ((bw q a) + b)) = (bw p (a + b))"
  if "q >= p"
by (metis bw_def le_imp_power_dvd mod_add_cong mod_mod_cancel that)

lemma add_rm_r_prec:
  "(bw p (a + (bw q b))) = (bw p (a + b))"
  if "q >= p"
using add_rm_l_prec by (simp add: add.commute that)
```

Fig. 6. Isabelle scripts proving the `add.rm.l.prec` and `add.rm.r.prec` axioms.

on proofs for two of the axioms that are also shown (Fig. 6). Note that the `add.assoc` and `add.commute` axioms are native to Isabelle.

6 Evaluation

We have implemented ParaBit in approximately 2000 lines of Rust code, building on the `egg` library to perform equality saturation and using a total of 99 axioms, which are all mechanised in Isabelle.

We also developed an automatic translator between `BWLang` and PBV to allow for comparison against prior work [4]. As noted earlier (Sect. 1), each multi-width `BWLang` problem corresponds to potentially many PBV problems due to the ensuing proliferation of case-splits. We enumerate all valid case-splits and generate a separate PBV problem for each branch. We consider one BW problem solved if all the corresponding PBV problems can be solved.

6.1 Benchmarks

We evaluate ParaBit using benchmark sets arising from both hardware and software domains. Given ParaBit's focus on multi-width problems, we separate each benchmark set into those containing multiple parametric widths (i.e., p, q) and those containing a single-width (i.e., just p). Note, this differs from the definition used by Berger et al. [4], which counts the use of extension or extraction as multi-width, even if only a single bitwidth variable is used.

Alive consists of peephole optimisations used by LLVM-based compilers that were verified via enumeration by Alive [25]. The evaluation of Berger et al. [4] included 200 such peephole optimisations. 62 can be represented using `BWLang`, which we generate by converting from the PBV representation.

Hydra consists of software compiler peephole optimisations that were automatically generalised to support parametric width expressions using program synthesis techniques [30]. From a total set of 198 peephole optimisations, `BWLang` can express 70 whilst PBV can express 149. We generate `BWLang` and PBV directly from the Souper representation used by Hydra.

Rover consists of circuit design optimisations used by the Rover optimisation tool [10,12], which targeted arithmetic designs written in Verilog. Only the 2022 work contains both the transformations and the necessary preconditions [10]. `BWLang` can express 21 out of 27 transformations described. Encoding in `BWLang` produces 28 BW problems, and only 27 of these can be converted to PBV, due to the presence of a power of two in the precondition. We convert the Rover rules directly to `BWLang`, from which we automatically generate 3283 PBV problems.

Industry consists of representative circuit design optimisations employed by Cadence's Genus logic synthesis tool. Cadence was willing to share 7 such optimisations, of which both PBV and `BWLang` can express 5. As for Rover, we convert the Cadence representation directly to `BWLang` and use it to generate 49 PBV problems.

Although not fundamentally difficult, at present `BWLang` is able to encode fewer problems than PBV due to unsupported operators (bitvector comparisons) and an inability to encode data constraints. By data constraints we refer to conditions on the values of the bitvector variables as opposed to constraints on the width parameters. Consider for example the classic compiler optimisation: `a * c` $\rightarrow$ `a << i`. This is only valid if `c == 1 << i`, i.e., if c is a power of two. At present, `BWLang` cannot encode such conditions, or any conditions on the bitvector variables. Separately and more fundamentally, an equality saturation-based solver makes it challenging to encode existential quantifiers.

We only include the Alive set from the evaluation of Berger et al. [4] as the remaining sets either include existential quantifiers or did not contain any problems with multiple parametric widths, which is the focus of this work.

6.2 Experimental Setup

We compared ParaBit against the state-of-the-art parametric bitvector solver from Berger et al. [4], which we call PBV when reporting results. Since PBV can represent a larger class of problems, we present results for PBV on both the full set of benchmarks that can be represented by their language and results running PBV on the restricted subset that both solvers admit.

We ran the experiments single-threaded on an AMD EPYC-Milan family CPU running at 2.0 GHz. For each solver and benchmark instance we set a 60-second CPU time limit and a memory limit of 8 GB. Whilst PBV never breached the memory limit of the system, the memory demands of equality saturation meant that ParaBit did breach the memory limit for 11 benchmarks. We also ran the experiments with proof generation separately, with a 10-minute CPU time limit, since proof generation introduces additional overhead not present in the PBV solver.

Note, when evaluating the Rover and Industry benchmarks, where each `BWLang` problems is mapped to multiple SMT queries, we consider a problem solved only if all the corresponding queries were found to be UNSAT. In practice, we observed that the PBV solver either solved all queries or none, with a notable

Table 2. Number of solved benchmarks for each configuration. VBS represents the virtual best solver over PBV and ParaBit. The unique rows indicate how many benchmarks are *only* solved by that solver on the respective subset. We bold the best results on the restricted subset representable in **BWLang**.

Width	Benchmark Set	PBV [4]		ParaBit	VBS
		Full	Restricted	(our work)	
Single	Alive	104/196	31/61	**56/61**	130/196
	Hydra	55/74	**26/30**	24/30	56/74
	Rover	3/3	**3/3**	2/3	3/3
	Industry	2/4	2/4	**3/4**	4/4
	unique	108	6	29	-
	solved (%)	59%	63%	87%	70%
Multiple	Alive	3/4	0/1	**1/1**	4/4
	Hydra	33/75	9/40	**32/40**	56/75
	Rover	7/24	7/24	**25/25**	25/25
	Industry	0/1	0/1	**1/1**	1/1
	unique	27	0	43	-
	solved (%)	41%	24%	88%	82%

exception in the case of the associativity of multiplication, where it can solve 67% of the total (1254).

6.3 Results

We summarise the results (Table 2) for the different benchmark sets (Sect. 6.1), splitting them into their single- and multiple-width subsets. We also include the virtual best solver (VBS) across both ParaBit and PBV.

From these results we can see that on the subset of the benchmarks that ParaBit supports, we are able to solve a much higher proportion than PBV. Most noticeably, for benchmarks involving multiple parametric widths we see that ParaBit dramatically outperforms PBV. Whilst not surprising given the benchmarks used to evaluate PBV contained fewer instances involving multiple parametric widths, these results show that our approach works particularly well for the kind of problems commonly found in EDA (e.g., Rover, Industry). The Alive benchmarks provide the most meaningful comparison point, as they were part of the original PBV evaluation. In the single-width case we again see that ParaBit solves a much larger proportion of the problems it can support, suggesting that the equality saturation-based approach offers a major advantage.

PBV does outperform ParaBit on both the Hydra and Rover single-width subsets. Interestingly, the Rover benchmark that is uniquely solved by PBV is the relatively simple transformation, $(ite\, b_1, a_p, a_p)_p \rightarrow a_p$. This proves challenging for ParaBit due to the way in which *ite* is encoded in arithmetic, creating a

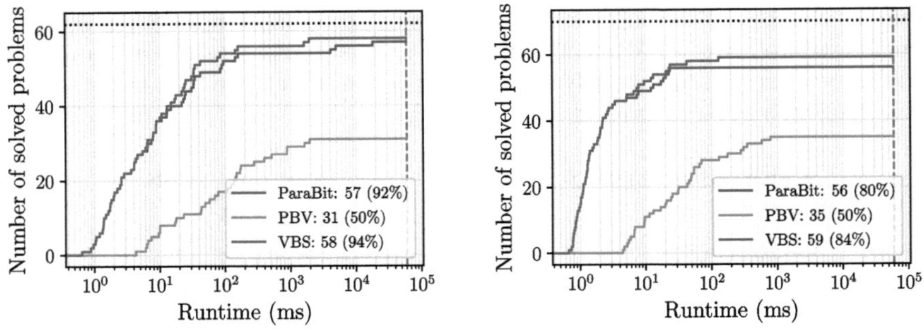

(a) Alive, 62 total problems.

(b) Hydra, 70 total problems

Fig. 7. Survival plots comparing ParaBit, PBV and the virtual best solver (VBS) on the Alive and Hydra benchmarks, with a 60-second timeout. The comparison is on the restricted subset representable in `BWLang`.

non-trivial algebraic rewriting challenge. For two Industry benchmarks, it was necessary to add trivial-to-prove preconditions to the BW problem, e.g., $(w+1)-w \geq 1$, to overcome limitations in ParaBit's syntactic precondition reasoning.

For benchmarks in the Hydra [30], Rover [10] and Industry sets, these results provide the first automated correctness proofs quantified over all possible bitwidths. Prior to ParaBit, each of these transformations had only been verified by proving the correctness for different combinations of concrete widths.

Out of the 165 benchmarks, ParaBit is unable to solve 21. These failures are due to the process timing out (7 benchmarks), the process running out of memory (11 benchmarks) and a crash due to an overflow bug in the constant folding code (1 benchmark). The last two benchmarks fail because the e-graph saturates without finding a proof, meaning that the set of axioms is insufficient to prove the underlying equivalence.

We present survival plots comparing the performance of our work with PBV for Hydra and Alive (Fig. 7), where we consider only the subset representable in `BWLang`. We omit the Industry benchmark due to its small size, and the Rover benchmarks since each problem corresponds to multiple PBV instances, making direct comparison less meaningful. In both benchmarks we observe ParaBit outperforms PBV, both in terms of the number of problems solved and the speed at which they are solved. However, in the Alive case (Fig. 7a), it is interesting to note how the problems last solved by ParaBit *do not* contribute to the virtual best solution, meaning they have already been solved by PBV.

6.4 Proof Production

Unlike PBV, each ParaBit proof is accompanied by a proof certificate (Sect. 5.3), which can be checked by Isabelle to increase confidence in the generated proof. Of the 144 problems ParaBit solved, 142 generated certificates which were successfully verified in Isabelle. For two problems in the Alive benchmark, certifi-

Table 3. Average (mean) statistics for solved ParaBit benchmarks.

Benchmark Set	ParaBit			PBV
	E-Nodes	Proof Steps	Time (ms)	Time (ms)
Alive	3872	320	485.84	508.53
Hydra	443	23	4.05	81.86
Rover	1101	22	23.58	58.05
Industry	11556	174	229.82	1004.95

cates could not be generated as the built-in egg proof generation step ran out of memory.

We provide solver statistics (Table 3) averaged across benchmarks that the solvers were able to solve. Comparing PBV's and ParaBit's average times to solution, it is difficult to draw strong conclusions, but we see that both typically find a proof in under a second. We can see that across the benchmark sets the size of e-graphs varied significantly and was reasonably correlated with average solve time. The average number of steps in the proof was less variable, with the exception of the Alive benchmarks. We attribute this to the conversion from PBV to `BWLang`, which produces a more verbose encoding of the problem.

7 Related Work

SMT. Across a series of works, the CVC5 SMT solver [2] has developed theory engines for parametric bitvector theories. In their 2021 work on the subject [35], Niemetz et al. propose a translation from parametric bitvector formulas to nonlinear integer arithmetic with uninterpreted functions. In 2025, they proposed the `PBV` theory which we introduced earlier (Sect. 3.1) and developed a solver which we compared against (Sect. 6). Unlike `BWLang`, their representation attached bitvector widths to operations rather than operands. Additionally, their solver relied on SMT theory solvers combined with a set of simplification rewrites, whilst we turned to equality saturation.

Rewrite Verification. Given their central role in compilers, solvers and many other applications, there has been plenty of research into the verification of rewrite rules. In the compilers domain, the Alive series of works [24,25] provided SMT-LIB semantics for the LLVM intermediate representation and a domain-specific language for expressing rewrites over concrete bitwidths. An SMT backend verifies the correctness of the proposed transformation. The interactive theorem prover community has also developed several automated decision procedures for proving compiler peephole rewrites [5,31], one of which they later extended to support parametric bitvectors with a single parametric width [6]. In the SMT community, the IsaRare work [23] formalised rewrites used during proof certificate checking in Isabelle. Whilst we also employ Isabelle for formalization, we aim to provide push-button verification of the rewrites, for a different class of multi-width parametric bitvector problems arising from the hardware domain.

Equality Saturation. One of the earliest applications of equality saturation performed translation validation for Java compilers [39, 42]. In the hardware domain, researchers extended the Rover work's foundations [10] to develop a basic equivalence checker that used equality saturation to construct an equivalence proof for specific circuits [13]. Whilst the Rover representation is visually similar to `BWLang`, it actually encodes operand and output widths in the operator definition, something `BWLang` specifically avoids. These works target concrete program instances, but if combined with the approach we presented here, they could, for example, prove the equivalence of bitwidth-parameterised circuit components.

8 Conclusion

In this paper, we have developed automatic techniques to prove the correctness of parametric bitvector equivalences, particularly focusing on the circuit transformations at the heart of EDA tools. We introduced the new `BWLang` representation which, unlike previous work on this problem, attaches width parameters to *operands* rather than *operators*. This allows for concise representation of multi-width bitvector problems, which are common in the hardware domain. We constructed a set of axioms, mechanised in Isabelle, that we combined to construct proofs using equality saturation. The techniques were implemented in an automated solver, ParaBit, that also produces proof certificates that can be checked using Isabelle. Evaluation on a diverse set of benchmarks demonstrated ParaBit's advantage over existing methods, solving 87% of the problems that could be encoded in `BWLang`.

Future work will explore the use of symbolic interval analyses to provide a more general reasoning engine that can capture data constraints as well as constraints on width parameters. More practically, we will explore whether the recently introduced grind tactic in Lean can provide a more integrated solver, as grind also conducts an e-graph-based search [27]. We will also extend `BWLang` to cover more operators and plan to integrate ParaBit with the CIRCT framework [14] to allow for Alive-style verification of circuit design transformations.

Acknowledgments. We are grateful for the early discussions with Yann Herklotz that helped to guide the initial ideation of the work. The work was generously supported by a Science and Engineering Research Fellowship from the Royal Commission for the Exhibition of 1851 and the Autoprobe ERC grant (no. 101002697).

Data Availibility Statement. The data and code that support the findings of this study are available on Zenodo at https://doi.org/10.5281/zenodo.19825890. The repository contains the implementation of ParaBit, the benchmark suite used for evaluation, and scripts to reproduce the experiments reported in Sect. 6.

Disclosure of Interests. The authors have no competing interests to declare that are relevant to the content of this article.

References

1. Baader, F., Nipkow, T.: Term Rewriting and All That. Cambridge University Press (1998). https://doi.org/10.1017/CBO9781139172752
2. Barbosa, H., et al.: cvc5: a versatile and industrial-strength SMT solver. In: Fisman, D., Rosu, G. (eds.) TACAS 2022. LNCS, vol. 13243, pp. 415–442. Springer, Cham (2022). https://doi.org/10.1007/978-3-030-99524-9_24
3. Barrett, C., Fontaine, P., Tinelli, C.: The satisfiability modulo theories library (SMT-LIB) (2016). https://smt-lib.org/
4. Berger, Z., et al.: Bit-precise reasoning with parametric bit-vectors. In: Berg, J., Nordström, J. (eds.) 28th International Conference on Theory and Applications of Satisfiability Testing (SAT 2025). Leibniz International Proceedings in Informatics (LIPIcs), vol. 341, pp. 4:1–4:24. Schloss Dagstuhl – Leibniz-Zentrum für Informatik, Dagstuhl, Germany (2025). https://doi.org/10.4230/LIPIcs.SAT.2025.4. https://drops.dagstuhl.de/entities/document/10.4230/LIPIcs.SAT.2025.4
5. Bhat, S., Keizer, A., Hughes, C., Goens, A., Grosser, T.: Verifying peephole rewriting in SSA compiler IRs. In: Bertot, Y., Kutsia, T., Norrish, M. (eds.) 15th International Conference on Interactive Theorem Proving (ITP 2024). Leibniz International Proceedings in Informatics (LIPIcs), vol. 309, pp. 9:1–9:20. Schloss Dagstuhl – Leibniz-Zentrum für Informatik, Dagstuhl, Germany (2024). https://doi.org/10.4230/LIPIcs.ITP.2024.9. https://drops.dagstuhl.de/entities/document/10.4230/LIPIcs.ITP.2024.9
6. Bhat, S., Stefanesco, L., Hughes, C., Grosser, T.: Certified decision procedures for width-independent bitvector predicates. Proc. ACM Program. Lang. **9**(OOPSLA2) (2025). https://doi.org/10.1145/3763148
7. Cadence Design Systems: Jasper formal verification platform (2024). https://www.cadence.com/en_US/home/tools/system-design-and-verification/formal-and-static-verification.html
8. Cadence Design Systems: Genus synthesis solution (2026). https://www.cadence.com/en_US/home/tools/digital-design-and-signoff/synthesis/genus-synthesis-solution.html
9. Cheng, J., Coward, S., Chelini, L., Barbalho, R., Drane, T.: SEER: super-optimization explorer for HLS using e-graph rewriting with MLIR. In: Proceedings of the 29th ACM International Conference on Architectural Support for Programming Languages and Operating Systems, pp. 1029–1044. Association for Computing Machinery (2024). https://doi.org/10.1145/3620665.3640392
10. Coward, S., Constantinides, G.A., Drane, T.: Automatic datapath optimization using e-graphs. In: 2022 IEEE 29th Symposium on Computer Arithmetic (ARITH), pp. 43–50 (2022). https://doi.org/10.1109/ARITH54963.2022.00016
11. Coward, S., Drane, T., Constantinides, G.A.: Constraint-aware e-graph rewriting for hardware performance optimization. IEEE Trans. Comput.-Aided Des. Integr. Circ. Syst. 1–14 (2024). https://doi.org/10.1109/TCAD.2024.3483096
12. Coward, S., Drane, T., Constantinides, G.A.: ROVER: RTL optimization via verified e-graph rewriting. IEEE Trans. Comput.-Aided Des. Integr. Circ. Syst. **43**, 4687–4700 (2024). https://doi.org/10.1109/TCAD.2024.3410154
13. Coward, S., Morini, E., Tan, B., Drane, T., Constantinides, G.: Datapath verification via word-level e-graph rewriting. In: Formal Methods in Computer-Aided Design (FMCAD) (2023). https://doi.org/10.34727/2023/isbn.978-3-85448-060-0_17

14. Eldridge, S., et al.: MLIR as hardware compiler infrastructure. In: WOSET 2021: Workshop on Open Source EDA Technology (2021)
15. Emmer, M., Khasidashvili, Z., Korovin, K., Voronkov, A.: Encoding industrial hardware verification problems into effectively propositional logic. In: Formal Methods in Computer Aided Design, pp. 137–144 (2010)
16. Flatt, O., Coward, S., Willsey, M., Tatlock, Z., Panchekha, P.: Small proofs from congruence closure. In: Proceedings of the 22nd Conference on Formal Methods in Computer-Aided Design, FMCAD 2022, p. 9. TU Wien Academic Press (2022). https://doi.org/10.34727/2022/isbn.978-3-85448-053-2-13
17. Haftmann, F.: Theory bit operations (2025). https://isabelle.in.tum.de/library/HOL/HOL/Bit_Operations.html#Bit_Operations.semiring_bit_operations_class
18. Hou, T., Laddad, S., Hellerstein, J.M.: Towards relational contextual equality saturation (2025). https://doi.org/10.48550/arXiv.2507.11897
19. IEEE: IEEE Standard for SystemVerilog–Unified Hardware Design, Specification, and Verification Language. Technical report, IEEE Std 1800-2023, IEEE (2023). https://doi.org/10.1109/IEEESTD.2024.10458102
20. Koelbl, A., Jacoby, R., Jain, H., Pixley, C.: Solver technology for system-level to RTL equivalence checking. In: Proceedings of the Conference on Design, Automation and Test in Europe, pp. 196–201. European Design and Automation Association (2009). https://doi.org/10.1109/DATE.2009.5090657
21. Kozen, D.: Complexity of finitely presented algebras. In: Proceedings of the Ninth Annual ACM Symposium on Theory of Computing, STOC 1977, pp. 164–177. Association for Computing Machinery, New York, NY, USA (1977). https://doi.org/10.1145/800105.803406
22. Kurashige, C., et al.: CCLemma: E-graph guided lemma discovery for inductive equational proofs. Proc. ACM Program. Lang. **8**, 818–844 (2024). https://doi.org/10.1145/3674653
23. Lachnitt, H., et al.: IsaRare: automatic verification of SMT rewrites in Isabelle/HOL. In: Tools and Algorithms for the Construction and Analysis of Systems: 30th International Conference, TACAS 2024, Held as Part of the European Joint Conferences on Theory and Practice of Software, ETAPS 2024, Luxembourg City, Luxembourg, 6–11 April 2024, Proceedings, Part I, pp. 311–330. Springer, Heidelberg (2024). https://doi.org/10.1007/978-3-031-57246-3_17
24. Lopes, N.P., Lee, J., Hur, C.K., Liu, Z., Regehr, J.: Alive2: bounded translation validation for LLVM. In: Proceedings of the 42nd ACM SIGPLAN International Conference on Programming Language Design and Implementation, PLDI 2021, pp. 65–79. Association for Computing Machinery, New York, NY, USA (2021). https://doi.org/10.1145/3453483.3454030
25. Lopes, N.P., Menendez, D., Nagarakatte, S., Regehr, J.: Provably correct peephole optimizations with Alive. SIGPLAN Not. **50**(6), 22–32 (2015). https://doi.org/10.1145/2813885.2737965
26. Micheli, G.D.: Synthesis and Optimization of Digital Circuits, 1st edn. McGraw-Hill Higher Education (1994)
27. de Moura, L.: Lean grind tactic (2025). https://lean-lang.org/doc/reference/latest/The--grind--tactic/
28. de Moura, L., Bjørner, N.: Efficient E-matching for SMT solvers. In: Pfenning, F. (ed.) CADE 2007. LNCS (LNAI), vol. 4603, pp. 183–198. Springer, Heidelberg (2007). https://doi.org/10.1007/978-3-540-73595-3_13

29. de Moura, L., Bjørner, N.: Z3: an efficient SMT solver. In: Ramakrishnan, C.R., Rehof, J. (eds.) TACAS 2008. LNCS, vol. 4963, pp. 337–340. Springer, Heidelberg (2008). https://doi.org/10.1007/978-3-540-78800-3_24
30. Mukherjee, M., Regehr, J.: Hydra: generalizing peephole optimizations with program synthesis. Proc. ACM Program. Lang. **8**(OOPSLA1) (2024). https://doi.org/10.1145/3649837
31. Mullen, E., Zuniga, D., Tatlock, Z., Grossman, D.: Verified peephole optimizations for compcert. SIGPLAN Not. **51**(6), 448–461 (2016). https://doi.org/10.1145/2980983.2908109
32. Nelson, C.G.: Techniques for program verification. Ph.D. thesis, Stanford University, Stanford, CA, USA (1980)
33. Niemetz, A., Preiner, M.: Bitwuzla. In: Enea, C., Lal, A. (eds.) Computer Aided Verification - 35th International Conference, CAV 2023, Paris, France, 17–22 July 2023, Proceedings, Part II, pp. 3–17. Lecture Notes in Computer Science. Springer (2023). https://doi.org/10.1007/978-3-031-37703-7_1
34. Niemetz, A., Preiner, M., Reynolds, A., Zohar, Y., Barrett, C., Tinelli, C.: Towards bit-width-independent proofs in SMT solvers. In: Fontaine, P. (ed.) CADE 2019. LNCS (LNAI), vol. 11716, pp. 366–384. Springer, Cham (2019). https://doi.org/10.1007/978-3-030-29436-6_22
35. Niemetz, A., Preiner, M., Reynolds, A., Zohar, Y., Barrett, C., Tinelli, C.: Towards satisfiability modulo parametric bit-vectors. J. Autom. Reason. **65**(7), 1001–1025 (2021). https://doi.org/10.1007/s10817-021-09598-9
36. Nipkow, T., Wenzel, M., Paulson, L.C.: Isabelle/HOL: A Proof Assistant for Higher-Order Logic. Springer, Heidelberg (2002). https://doi.org/10.1007/3-540-45949-9
37. Panchekha, P., Sanchez-Stern, A., Wilcox, J.R., Tatlock, Z.: Automatically improving accuracy for floating point expressions. In: Proceedings of the 36th ACM SIGPLAN Conference on Programming Language Design and Implementation, PLDI 2015, pp. 1–11. Association for Computing Machinery, New York, NY, USA (2015). https://doi.org/10.1145/2737924.2737959
38. Singher, E., Shachar, I.: Easter egg: equality reasoning based on e-graphs with multiple assumptions. In: Narodytska, N., Rümmer, P. (eds.) Proceedings of the 24th Conference on Formal Methods in Computer-Aided Design – FMCAD 2024. Conference Series: Formal Methods in Computer-Aided Design, vol. 5, pp. 70–83. TU Wien Academic Press (2024). https://doi.org/10.34727/2024/isbn.978-3-85448-065-5_13
39. Stepp, M., Tate, R., Lerner, S.: Equality-based translation validator for LLVM. In: Gopalakrishnan, G., Qadeer, S. (eds.) CAV 2011. LNCS, vol. 6806, pp. 737–742. Springer, Heidelberg (2011). https://doi.org/10.1007/978-3-642-22110-1_59
40. Synopsys: Design compiler (2026). https://www.synopsys.com/implementation-and-signoff/rtl-synthesis-test/design-compiler.html
41. Tarjan, R.E.: Efficiency of a good but not linear set union algorithm. J. ACM (JACM) **22** (1975). https://doi.org/10.1145/321879.321884
42. Tate, R., Stepp, M., Tatlock, Z., Lerner, S.: Equality saturation: a new approach to optimization. In: Proceedings of the 36th Annual ACM SIGPLAN-SIGACT Symposium on Principles of Programming Languages, vol. 44, pp. 264–276. Association for Computing Machinery (2009). https://doi.org/10.1145/1480881.1480915
43. Thomas, D.E., Moorby, P.R.: The Verilog Hardware Description Language, 5 edn. Springer, New York (2002). https://doi.org/10.1007/b116662

44. Willsey, M., Nandi, C., Wang, Y.R., Flatt, O., Tatlock, Z., Panchekha, P.: Egg: fast and extensible equality saturation. In: Proceedings of the ACM on Principles of Programming Languages, vol. 5. Association for Computing Machinery (2021). https://doi.org/10.1145/3434304
45. Wolf, C.: Yosys open synthesis suite. https://yosyshq.net/yosys/
46. Wolf, C.: SymbiYosys (sby) – front-end for Yosys-based formal verification flows (2017)
47. Zimmermann, R.: Datapath synthesis for standard-cell design. In: 19th IEEE Symposium on Computer Arithmetic, pp. 207–211 (2009). https://doi.org/10.1109/ARITH.2009.28

Massively Parallel Mining of Specifications for Hardware Designs

Leiqi Ye(✉), Guy Frankel, Jianyi Cheng, and Elizabeth Polgreen

University of Edinburgh, Edinburgh, UK
{leiqi.ye,G.Frankel-1,jianyi.cheng, elizabeth.polgreen}@ed.ac.uk

Abstract. Formal hardware verification ensures that a design satisfies its specifications, but writing these specifications requires substantial manual effort. Specification mining automates this process, and existing work has their own merits. The classic approaches rely on pre-defined templates, which have limited expressiveness and lack formal correctness guarantees. However, recent years have seen the emergence of using formal program synthesis for specification mining, which provides general and correct specifications but struggles to scale to complex designs.

In this work, we present MAPminer, a parallel framework for synthesis-based hardware specification mining. MAPminer exploits its novel algorithm based on the Maximal Universal Subset and partitions the synthesis problem into efficient sub-problems. These sub-problems are automatically scheduled across multiple threads for parallel synthesis. Experimental results show that MAPminer produces more effective assertions, improving verification coverage while reducing assertion size.

1 Introduction

Hardware verification ensures that a hardware design meets its functional specifications before fabrication. While writing these specifications is a laborious and time-consuming process, there has been growing interest in automatically generating them, also known as hardware specification mining [14]. Automatically mined specifications can be used to detect bugs, validate correctness, and guide formal verification, improving verification coverage and reducing human effort.

A recent theme in specification mining research exploits oracle-guided synthesis [33], which generates correct and meaningful specifications for arbitrary hardware designs compared to existing approaches such as machine learning [24,27,31,32] and template-guided [12,20] techniques. Still, it remains the case that synthesis-based techniques cannot be directly applied to verification tasks for realistic hardware designs due to two main challenges, *large problem size* and *limited parallelism*. First, synthesis scales exponentially with the number of variables,

L. Ye and G. Frankel—Equal contribution.

E. Darulova et al. (Eds.): CAV 2026, LNCS 16682, pp. 403–425, 2026.
https://doi.org/10.1007/978-3-032-32519-8_21

while real-world hardware designs often contain thousands of signals and state variables. Second, specification mining approaches typically compute sequentially and can take an impractically long time to achieve meaningful results.

Existing solutions for automated specification mining are limited and still face these challenges. In order to reduce the problem size, existing approaches typically rely on heuristics that fail to ensure that mined specifications reason about distinct and meaningful subsets of variables. GoldMine [14] exploits static analysis of the hardware source but only accepts Boolean circuits. HARM [12] and ARTmine [20] rely on template-based pattern matching and have limited variable reasoning for arbitrary hardware designs. SMART [33] relies on random choices of problem partitioning and may lead to sub-optimal specification results. Additionally, most related works follow sequential execution. While naive parallelism is possible, this could lead to substantial unnecessary duplication of computation for the same work.

In order to address these challenges, we seek an efficient solution that achieves the following design goals:

1) **Efficient problem partitioning:** Not all variables are equally relevant for specification mining, and they should be partitioned into smaller sets to reduce the problem size while preserving the quality of the mined specifications.
2) **Redundancy-free parallelism:** Only the mining work should be parallelized across threads, and shared components should be effectively shared by these threads to save computing costs.
3) **Efficient assertion size:** The generated assertions should be concise and readable, helping further reasoning and debugging in practice and friendly to the model checker.

In this work, we present MAPminer, a MAssively Parallel specification miner that determines an efficient set of synthesis problems, schedules them into efficient parallel computation, and generates a set of efficient and meaningful assertions. MAPminer exploits a technique from the domain of satisfiability solving named Maximal Universal Subsets (mUS) to identify under-specified variables in the hardware design, and efficiently partitions the mining problem while minimizing duplicate work between threads. MAPminer generates SystemVerilog Assertions (SVA) for Verilog, a hardware description language. MAPminer supports both structural Verilog (low-level, reflecting underlying circuit topology) and behavioral Verilog (describing high-level functionality).

This paper makes the following contributions: 1) a fully automated synthesis framework for massively parallel hardware specification mining; 2) a partition technique that exploits mUS to partition the synthesis problem into efficient sets of independent sub-problems for acceleration; 3) a scheduling technique that maps partitioned problems into efficient parallel tasks; and 4) experimental results and case studies show that MAPminer can produce specifications with both significant speedup and improved assertion quality, contributing to the verification of realistic hardware designs.

2 Motivating Example

We consider the **s344** benchmark from the ISCAS'89 benchmark suite [2] as a motivating example and show how existing specification mining work produces inefficient assertions. This benchmark is a 4-bit multiplier using the add-shift algorithm, as shown in Fig. 1a, but it has been widely used in common hardware designs. We choose this small design for simplicity, but it already shows the limitations of existing work, as further verified in Sect. 5.

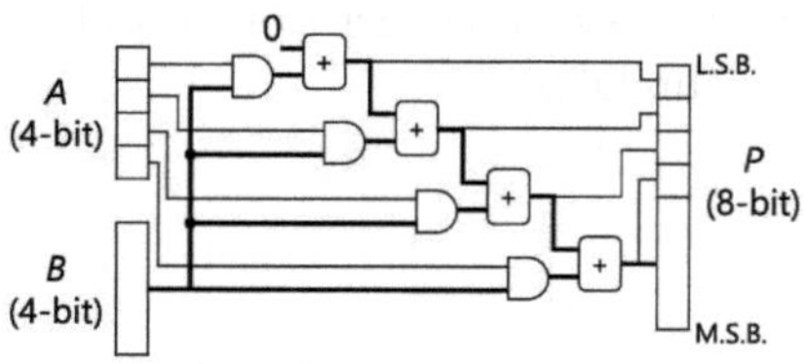

(a) A schematic of the hardware design to be verified ($P = A \times B$).

```
1 assert property
2   (ADDVG3VCNVOR1NF == S3);
3 assert property (CNTVCON1 == S3);
4 assert property
5   (ADDVG3VCNVOR1NF == CNTVCON1);
6 assert property
7   (ADDVG3VCNVOR1NF == CNTVCON1);
```

(b) Redundant assertions (lines 6 and 7) generated by SMART[33].

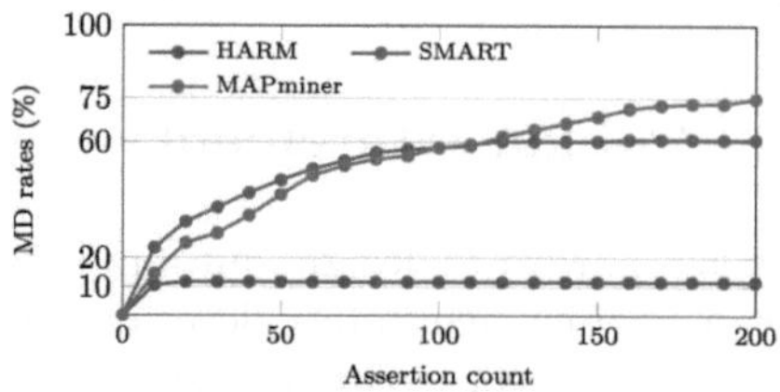

(c) A higher MD-rate means better verification coverage. HARM [12] relies on limited templates and stops improving after generating 20 assertions. SMART [33] relies on random partitioning and stops improving after generating 110 assertions. Our work continues improving while maintaining an efficient set of assertions.

Fig. 1. An example of mining specifications for a 4x4 Add-Shift Multiplier (s344).

When mining the specifications of the multiplier, the template-based approach Harm [12] enumerates its pre-defined templates and generates unverified and redundant assertions. The state-of-the-art method SMART [33] ensures the correctness of the generated assertions using formal synthesis. However, since synthesis techniques do not scale well with large sets of variables, SMART relies on random partitioning of the variable set to effectively capture specifications, which leads to redundancy in generated assertions.

Figure 1b shows four assertions generated by SMART for the multiplier. There are two types of redundancy in assertions, both logical and syntactic. The first two assertions capture the equivalence among three signals, `ADDVG3VCNVOR1NF`, `S3`, and `CNTVCON1`. The third assertion is syntactically different from the first two assertions but is logically redundant, because it describes a known relation between `ADDVG3VCNVOR1NF` and `CNTVCON1`. The fourth assertion is syntactically redundant, as it is the same as the third assertion.

We show how these mined assertions affect the verification coverage in Fig. 1c. We use a metric named mutation detection (MD) rate to evaluate the quality of specifications, which, inspired by mutation testing, calculates the proportion of mutations applied to the design that can be detected by the specification. A higher mutation detection rate means better specifications. In the figure, the template-based Harm stops improving after enumerating all the templates. SMART achieves a higher mutation detection rate, but the random variable selection limits the mutation detection rate to around 60%, after which it fails to identify any additional meaningful assertions.

In order to address this, our work MAPminer exploits mUS for efficient problem partitioning and generates assertions with reduced redundancy. This leads to a continuously increasing MD rate in the figure, with a significant improvement compared to other approaches. In the rest of the paper, we will describe our mUS-based partitioning algorithm and show how these partitioned problems can be effectively parallelized across multiple threads.

3 Problem Statement

Given a hardware design, our aim is to efficiently find a *meaningful* set of specifications, which accurately describe the behavior of the hardware (i.e., the specifications are never violated) and are sufficiently detailed that they can differentiate between the original hardware design and other designs, including those that are very similar but include small semantic bugs.
Formally, let:

- Σ be a set of observable design variables.
- $\mathcal{T} = \{\tau_1, \ldots, \tau_n\}$ be a set of executing traces, where each trace $\tau_1 : \mathbb{N} \to Val(\Sigma)$ maps time to signal/variable valuations.
- $\mathcal{L}$ be a specification language, i.e., System Verilog Assertions
- $\mathcal{C} \subseteq \mathcal{L}$ be a constrained hypothesis space. In this instance a grammar expressing a subset of the language $\mathcal{L}$.

Specification mining is the problem of automatically inferring a set of formal (possibly temporal) properties $\Phi = \{\varphi_1, \ldots \varphi_k\} \subseteq \mathcal{C}$ such that:

- Φ is *trace consistent* with $\mathcal{D}$, i.e., $\forall \varphi \in \Phi, \forall \tau \in \mathcal{T} : \tau \models \varphi$
- The design under test satisfies Φ, i.e., $\forall \Sigma . \mathcal{D} \models \varphi_1 \wedge \varphi_2 \wedge \ldots$, as checked by a formal verification tool.
- Φ captures a non-trivial and meaningful relationship among signals in Σ, and is thus able to differentiate between semantic mutations of $\mathcal{D}$.

The first requirement (trace consistency) is implied by the second (formally verifiable), but we present the requirements separately as many specification mining tools satisfy only the first requirement.

3.1 Specification Mining as Oracle-Guided Inductive Synthesis

Oracle-Guided Inductive Synthesis. Our specification mining approach is based around formal synthesis techniques. Formal synthesis aims to synthesize a function f such that it satisfies a formal constraint for all possible inputs. That is, it

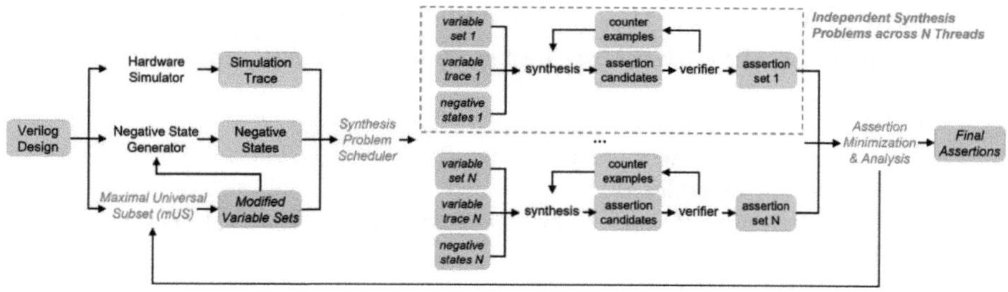

Fig. 2. An overview of the MAPminer flow. Our contributions are *highlighted*. The synthesis algorithm is taken from [33], the verifier is EBMC [1].

aims to solve the formula $\exists f.\forall x.\sigma$, where σ is a first-order formula which contains one or more invocations of f, and the free variables x.

These problems are solved by Oracle-Guided Inductive Synthesis (OGIS) [23], whereby an algorithm alternates between a synthesis phase which guesses candidate solutions, and an oracle which validates whether the solutions are correct or not, and may provide further guidance. The synthesis phase is typically implemented as an enumerative search through the space of a context-free grammar.

Specification Mining as a Synthesis Problem. Prior work [33] demonstrates that the specification mining problem outlined above can be formulated as an oracle-guided synthesis problem. This approach requires a set of traces $\mathcal{T}$ and an additional set of negative states $\mathcal{N}$, defined as states that are unreachable in the hardware design. Instead of attempting to synthesize a specification by directly requiring the synthesizer to reason about $\mathcal{D}$, this approach generates a specification that approximates this requirement.

Namely, it generates specifications Φ that satisfy the following constraint: $\forall \tau \in \mathcal{T}.(\forall s \in \tau.s \models \Phi) \wedge \forall n \in \mathcal{N}.n \not\models \Phi$, where s is a single state in the trace τ. This constraint can then be further refined by adding more traces or more negative states. We note that negative states are used to guide the synthesis away from generating vacuously true specifications, but it is not necessary that the specifications evaluate to false in *every* unreachable state in the hardware design.

A key limitation of this approach is the scalability of the oracle guided inductive synthesizer when the number of variables in the hardware design becomes large. Given a specification problem, we aim to efficiently parallelize it into multiple tractable smaller synthesis problems.

4 Our Approach

An overview of the architecture of MAPminer is shown in Fig. 2 and Algorithm 1. We build on existing synthesis-based specification mining techniques in the literature that use oracle-guided synthesis to generate specifications [33], captured by the *synthesis* block in the diagram. Specifically, we provide a means to run this

Algorithm 1. MAPminer: Massively Parallel Specification Mining

procedure MapMiner(Hardware design D, testbench TB, number of threads k, timeout T)
  $\Phi \leftarrow \emptyset$
  Collect simulation traces from $\mathcal{D}$ using TB
  Extract design variables V
  Randomly partition V into k variable sets: $\mathcal{V} = \{V_1, V_2, \ldots, V_k\}$
  while time $< T$ **do**
    for all $V_i \in \mathcal{V}$ **do**
      Generate negative states N_i for variables in V_i
      Generate grammar G_i for variables in V_i
    end for
    in parallel for $i = 1$ to k:
      $\Phi_i \leftarrow$ Synthesize($\mathcal{D}, V_i, N_i, G_i$)
    Collect assertions: $\Phi \leftarrow \Phi \cup \bigcup_{i=1}^{k} \Phi_i$
    if no new assertions were added to Φ **then**
      break
    end if
    $M \leftarrow$ ComputeMUS(Φ)
    if |M| is stable **then**
      break
    end if
    Derive new variable sets $\mathcal{V}$ from M
  end while
  Minimize Φ using equivalence checking
  return Φ
end procedure

method in parallel while maintaining high specification specificity and limiting the amount of redundant work carried out across threads.

The key components of our approach are as follows:

Synthesis Problem Decomposition via Variable Selection. A key problem in enumerative search over grammars is the size of the search space. This is exacerbated when dealing with traces that contain a large number of variables. Prior work solves this by sequentially solving many simple problems through selecting random sets of variables to be fed to the synthesizer. In MAPminer, we run multiple synthesizers in parallel, each solving a smaller problem over a subset of the variables.

This is enabled by our novel approach to iteratively identify *meaningful* sets of variables for synthesis, based on identifying variables in the hardware design that are not yet constrained by the specification. We refer to these variables as "under-specified" variables, and we identify them by calculating the mUS of the specification obtained so far.

Once the under-specified variables have been identified, we partition this into multiple variable sets, and construct synthesis queries to be run in parallel to mine assertions over each variable set. Along with providing guidance to the search, these meaningful variable sets also ensure minimal duplicate work between threads.

Parallel Synthesis Problem Construction. As described in Sect. 3.1, the synthesis tool requires three inputs: a set of traces $\mathcal{T}$ and a set of negative states $\mathcal{N}$ and a grammar G from which to construct assertions. Given a variable set generated by the previous step, we generate $\mathcal{N}$ by randomly generating states and selecting for those that are deemed unreachable using a hardware model checker. Importantly, each negative state is defined only over the variables in the current synthesis query, not over the full RTL state space, so the corresponding reachability check is small; in practice, EBMC verifies each negative state within a second. Furthermore, negative states are shared across parallel synthesis tasks, so this step is not a runtime bottleneck. We assume we are provided with a hardware testbench for $\mathcal{D}$, and we use this simulation environment with a standard Verilog simulator to generate simulation traces from the design under verification.
The grammar we provide, given a variable set V, is shown below and allows for a broad class of predicates over bitvectors and booleans.

$$
\begin{aligned}
Expr ::=& Atom \mid Atom \implies Atom \\
Atom ::=& Bool \simeq Bool \mid \neg Bool \mid Bool \wedge Bool \mid Bool \vee Bool \mid Bv \simeq Bv \mid \\
& Bv \geq Bv \mid Bv \leq Bv \mid Bv < Bv \mid Bv > Bv \mid Bv \geq_u Bv \mid \\
& Bv \leq_u Bv \mid Bv <_u Bv \mid Bv >_u Bv \mid \text{any boolean } v \text{ in } V \\
Bv ::=& - Bv \mid\sim Bv \mid Bv \ \&\ Bv \mid Bv \mid Bv \mid Bv + Bv \mid Bv - Bv \mid \\
& Bv * Bv \mid \text{any bitvector } v \text{ in } V
\end{aligned}
$$

Specification Verification and Refinement. When a synthesis job generates an assertion, it is verified using a hardware model checking tool. If the hardware model checking tool says that the assertion does not hold on the design under test, the counterexample is fed back to the synthesizer as an additional trace, refining the synthesis conjecture. This process repeats until either we reach a timeout, or we have found an assertion that passes verification.
We use the tool EBMC in k-induction mode to verify each assertion. k-induction is a standard technique for proving safety properties of transition systems, and generalizes mathematical induction to hardware models by checking two conditions: a base case and an inductive step. In the base case, the model checker verifies that the specification holds for all states reachable within the first k steps from the initial states. In the inductive step, it assumes that the specification holds for k consecutive states and proves that it also holds for the $(k+1)^{th}$ state under the system's transition relation. If both conditions succeed, the specification is guaranteed to hold for all reachable states.

Specification Minimization. Once all parallel synthesis jobs are terminated, we have a set of verified assertions. Given this set, a minimization procedure is implemented, making use of an iterative search through a lattice of assertions to reduce the amount of redundancy in the specifications. The minimized assertions are returned to the variable-selection step, the set of under-specified variables is updated, and the process repeats. The minimizer not only improves the readability of the specifications for the user, but also reduces the size of the problem that the variable selection must reason about.

MAPminer continues in this loop until either: 1) a timeout is reached; 2) no new assertions are generated; or 3) the number of under-specified variables is stable between the last blocks. We now describe the variable selection and minimization in detail.

4.1 Variable Selection via Maximal Universal Subsets

During assertion generation, MAPminer uses subsets of the variable set in order to ensure computation feasibility and parallelism of the generation process. This requires a 'smart' method of selecting which variables are provided to each block. We hypothesize that a variable that has not yet been constrained by the specification is likely to be a variable of interest that should be considered in future specification mining attempts.

We use the concept of Minimal Satisfying Assignments (mSA) [8,19] and their dual, mUS, from satisfiability solving to identify variables of interest. Intuitively, an mSA is the minimal cost partial assignment of values to variables in the formula that guarantees the formula is true, and the corresponding mUS includes every variable not included in the mSA.

Given a formula f and a domain D, an assignment σ is a function mapping the free variables in f (denoted $free(f)$) to elements of D. An assignment is full if it maps all variables in $free(f)$ to the domain and partial otherwise. The formula is satisfiable if there exists an assignment under which the formula evaluates to true (a *satisfying assignment*). We use $vars(\sigma)$ to indicate the set of variables that σ has assigned to. For example, the formula $x + y = 7$ is satisfiable and the assignment $\sigma = [x \mapsto 1, y \mapsto 6]$ is a satisfying assignment, and $vars(\sigma) = \{x, y\}$. We use the notation $f[\sigma]$ to indicate the result of substituting $vars(\sigma)$ in f for their corresponding assignments, so $f[\sigma]$ would be $1 + 6 = 7$.

Definition 1. *Given a formula f, a partial satisfying assignment σ is a satisfying assignment, such that $vars(\sigma) \subseteq free(f)$ and for every assignment ρ to the variables in $free(f) \setminus vars(\sigma)$, $f[\sigma \cup \rho] = true$. The satisfying assignment is a minimal satisfying assignment (mSA) if it minimizes $|vars(\sigma)|$.*

Given a design under verification $\mathcal{D}$ and a specification Φ, we know that Φ is satisfiable as, by construction, the specification is true for the design under verification. We define the mSA to be the minimal set of design variables in Σ which must be assigned to in order to determine that a single state is a state which satisfies the specification Φ.

Definition 2. *Given a specification Φ, a minimal satisfying assignment (mSA) is an assignment σ such that $vars(\sigma) \subseteq free(\Phi)$ and for every assignment ρ to the variables in $free(\Phi) \setminus vars(\sigma)$, $\Phi[\sigma \cup \rho] = true$, and which minimizes $|vars(\sigma)|$.*

Intuitively, the variables in the mSA are the variables that *are* currently constrained by the specification. In order to identify the variables that we should send to the next iteration of MAPminer, we are interested in finding the dual of the mSA: the mUS, or the *under-specified variables.*

Definition 3. *Given a specification Φ, a universal set is the set of variables $X \subseteq free(\Phi)$ such that $\forall X.\Phi$ is satisfiable. A Maximal Universal Subset is the universal set $X \subseteq free(\Phi)$ maximizing $|X|$. Given an mSA σ for a specification Φ, as defined in Definition 2, the mUS can be calculated as $mUS = free(\Phi) \setminus vars(\sigma)$.*

There are many possible mSAs and mUSs, and so we carry out a greedy search to find an mUS. We first note that our specification Φ is always of the form $\bigwedge_i \varphi_i$, i.e., a conjunction of predicates. As a consequence of this, we know that the mSA must include at least one variable from every $\varphi_i \in \Phi$. We thus begin by searching for the minimal set of variables for which this is true. This is known as a Minimal Hitting Set (mHS).

Definition 4. *Given a specification Φ, a hitting set is a set of variables $\mathcal{H} \subseteq free(\Phi)$ such that for all $\varphi \in \Phi$, $free(\varphi) \cap \mathcal{H} \neq \emptyset$. A mHS is a hitting set such that for all $h \in \mathcal{H}$, $\mathcal{H} \setminus \{h\}$ is not a hitting set.*

We use minimal hitting sets to search for an mUS using the following steps:

1. **Find an mHS.** To generate an initial mHS, we first order the variables in $free(\Phi)$ by the number of predicates in ϕ in which they appear. Formally, let

$$\mathcal{O}(free(\Phi)) = \{x_{(1)}, x_{(2)}, \ldots, x_{(n)}\}$$

be an ordering of the variables $free(\Phi)$ such that $\mathrm{occ}_\Phi(x_{(1)}) \geq \mathrm{occ}_\Phi(x_{(2)}) \geq \cdots \geq \mathrm{occ}_\Phi(x_{(n)})$, where $\mathrm{occ}_\Phi(x) = \big|\{\, i \mid x \in \mathrm{free}(\varphi_i) \,\}\big|$.
We traverse the variables in the order $x_{(1)}, \ldots, x_{(n)}$, adding $x_{(k)}$ to the selected set iff it appears in some predicate whose free variables are not yet covered by the previously selected variables.
Formally, define the coverage of a variable set S as $\mathrm{cov}_\Phi(S) := \{\, i \mid \mathrm{free}(\varphi_i) \cap S \neq \varnothing \,\}$. The minimal Hitting Set of Φ is then defined as follows:

$$\mathcal{H}(\Phi) := \big\{\, x_{(k)} \;\big|\; \exists i \notin \mathrm{cov}_\Phi(\{x_{(1)}, \ldots, x_{(k-1)}\}) \text{ such that } x_{(k)} \in \mathrm{free}(\varphi_i) \,\big\}.$$

2. **Guess an mUS.** We know that any mSA must also be an mHS. So, suppose that a minimal satisfying assignment σ exists, and $vars(\sigma) = \mathcal{H}(\Phi)$. The corresponding mUS is given by $X = free(\Phi) \setminus \mathcal{H}(\Phi)$.

3. **Check the mUS.** We then check if X is a valid mUS by checking whether the formula $\forall X.\Phi$ is satisfiable. If it is satisfiable, X is a valid mUS, and we know that a corresponding mSA σ exists and $vars(\sigma) = free(\Phi) \setminus X$, and we are done. If it is unsatisfiable, we aim to find a minimal set of predicates $\varphi \in \Phi$ that are sufficient to determine that this formula is unsatisfiable. To do this, we use the fact that universal quantification distributes over conjunction.

$$\forall X.\Phi \iff \forall X. \bigwedge_{\varphi \in \Phi} \varphi \iff \bigwedge_{\varphi \in \Phi} \forall X.\varphi$$

   We query an oracle with the distributed conjunction, and extract the unsat core, $\mathcal{C}$, i.e., the subset of clauses whose conjunction is still unsatisfiable.
4. **Correct the mUS.** We use the unsat core $\mathcal{C}$ to determine a possible fix for the invalid mUS. Given $\mathcal{C}$ is a set of clauses $c_1, \ldots, c_n$, we use the same process as before to find an mHS of $\mathcal{C}$, except that we exclude any variables already present in $\mathcal{H}$. That is, we find:

$$\{\, x_{(k)} \mid \exists i \notin \mathrm{cov}_{\mathcal{C}}(\{x_{(1)}, \ldots, x_{(k-1)}\}) \text{ such that } x_{(k)} \in \mathrm{free}(c_i) \setminus \mathcal{H}(\Phi) \,\}.$$

   where $\mathrm{cov}_{\mathcal{C}}(S) := \{\, i \mid \mathrm{free}(c_i) \cap S \neq \varnothing \,\}$. By abuse of notation, we refer to this as $\mathcal{H}(\mathcal{C} \setminus \mathcal{H}(\Phi))$.
   We add the variables in $\mathcal{H}(\mathcal{C} \setminus \mathcal{H}(\Phi))$ to $\mathcal{H}(\Phi)$ and return to step 2.

This is an over-approximation of the required addition to X, however, in practice often $|\mathcal{C}| = 1$ and thus we only add a single variable at a time.

Using the mUS within MAPminer. We use the mUS to select the variables that should be considered for specification mining at the beginning of each iteration. Note that in the first iteration, the mUS is equal to Σ, the full set of variables in the hardware design. We then randomly select subsets of variables from the mUS X for the next iteration of MAPminer. The size of the variable sets is determined by the number of variables available and is calculated as $\mathrm{round}(2.7 + 1.6 \log_{10} |X|)$. We avoid subsets which contain the same variable twice, and subsets that we have chosen before.

Additional Positive and Negative States. On finding an mUS, X, the SMT solver provides the mSA in the form of a satisfying assignment σ for the query $\forall X.\Phi$. We use this assignment to generate additional negative states: given a target variable set V, we take the assignments from σ for the variables in V. We then randomly assign values to any remaining variables in V and check whether the state corresponding to this assignment is reachable in the original hardware model using k-induction. If the state is unreachable, we add this assignment to the list of negative states used to guide the synthesis based assertion mining.

4.2 Specification Minimization

Variables are present in multiple variable sets, which is necessary in order to consider relationships between multiple different variables, but this means that

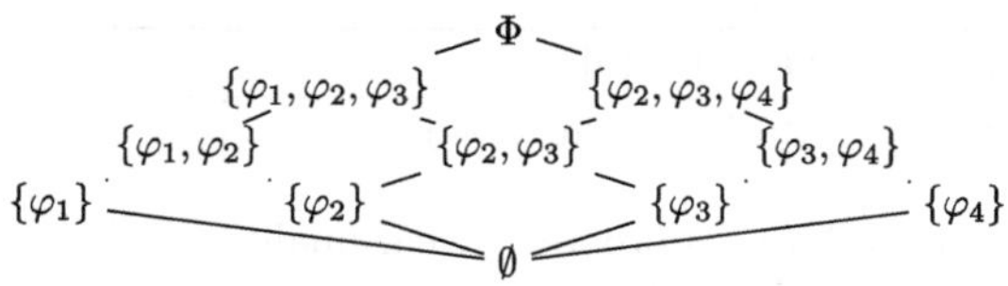

Fig. 3. Subset lattice of an assertion set illustrating greedy redundancy reduction. Starting from the full set, the search descends to smaller subsets that are implied by the original assertion set (green nodes), stopping when no further valid descendant exists.

Algorithm 2. Maximal Universal Subset

procedure MAXIMAL UNIVERSAL SUBSET(Assertion set Φ)
  $H \leftarrow$ MINIMALHITTINGSET(Φ)
  while 1 **do**
    $X \leftarrow \text{free}(\Phi) \setminus H$
    $q \leftarrow \forall X.\Phi$
    if ISSAT(q) **then**
      return X
    end if
    $\mathcal{C} \leftarrow$ UNSATCORE($\forall X.\Phi$)
    $H \leftarrow H \cup$ MINIMALHITTINGSET($\mathcal{C} \setminus H$)
  end while
end procedure

we may create redundant assertions. Take $\Sigma = \{x_1, x_2, x_3, x_4\}$ to be our set of design variables. Say we split Σ into $V_1 = \{x_2, x_3\}$ and $V_2 = \{x_2, x_4\}$ and generate the following assertions $\Phi = \varphi_1 \wedge \varphi_2$, where $\varphi_1 = x_2 \vee x_3$ and $\varphi_2 = x_4$. We then split Σ into $V_3 = \{x_1, x_3\}$ and $V_4 = \{x_2, x_4\}$ and generate $\varphi_3 = x_1 \vee x_3$ and $\varphi_4 = x_2$. Assertion φ_1 is redundant in $\Phi' = \varphi_1 \wedge \varphi_2 \wedge \varphi_3 \wedge \varphi_4$ since we have φ_4.

To ensure our final solution contains little redundancy and to reduce the size of the assertion set given to the mSA calculation we carry out assertion minimization at the end of each iteration of MAPminer and before returning the solutions to the user.

Given a specification Φ containing redundancy, the minimal set of assertions Π is a subset of Φ such that $\Pi \equiv \Phi$ and $\forall \varphi \in \Pi, (\Pi \setminus \varphi) \not\equiv \Phi$. Computing a perfectly minimal set is too computationally expensive to integrate into MAPminer, and so we implement a greedy search to find the best minimization we can in a practical amount of time. We take advantage of the partial order $(\mathcal{P}(\Phi), \subseteq)$ over subsets of the assertion set Φ, ordered by cardinality. Starting with the conjunction over the whole assertion set, Φ, we greedily search for a subset, $\Pi \subseteq \Phi$, such that Π is logically equivalent to Φ.

The search proceeds by traversing the subset lattice level by level, removing predicates from Π. Whenever a candidate subset Π is found to be valid, we descend in the lattice and test its descendants. Either we find another $\Pi' \subset \Pi$

Algorithm 3. Assertion Set Minimization

```
procedure Minimization(Assertion set Φ)
    Π ← Φ
    Construct lattice (𝒫(Φ), ⊆) ordered by cardinality
    for k = |Φ| − 1 down to 1 do
        for all Π′ ⊂ Π such that |Π′| = k do
            if Π′ ≡ Φ then
                Π ← Π′
                break
            end if
        end for
    end for
    return Π
end procedure
```

such that $\Pi' \implies \Phi$ from which we continue descending, or we find no such Π' and return Π. This search is illustrated in Fig. 3, where we see the search space and the target Π, in this case $\{\varphi_2, \varphi_3\}$. The pseudocode for minimization is shown in Algorithm 3.

5 Evaluation

Evaluating the Utility of Specifications. Evaluating the utility of a specification is challenging. We use the standard metric from the literature, namely Mutation Detection. Mutation Detection, inspired by Mutation Testing [18], assesses how good a specification or test is by mutating the design under verification/test. A good specification should be able to differentiate between the original design and the mutated design. Thus, given a design under test $\mathcal{D}$ and a set of n mutated designs, $\mathcal{M} = \{D_1^*, D_2^*, \ldots, D_n^*\}$, we report the Mutation Detection Rate (MD-Rate) as the proportion of mutants for which the specification does not hold, calculated as MD-rate $= \frac{1}{|\mathcal{M}|}|\{D^* \in \mathcal{M} \mid D^* \not\models \phi\}|$.

Generating the Mutants. We use a set of mutation rules from the literature [18, 33] to generate mutants. We identify the rules that could be applied to the design under verification. For each mutant, we randomly select one rule and apply it to one location in the file. These rules can generate mutations that do not meaningfully change the semantics of the design under verification, and so it should be noted that, while a higher mutation detection rate is clearly better, it might be impossible to achieve a mutation detection rate of 100%.

Formal Verification of Specifications. All specifications generated by MAPminer are formally verified against the hardware design and are therefore guaranteed to be correct to the design. However, not all specification mining tools provide this guarantee. In particular, we compare to HARM [12], which does not guarantee that all assertions hold on the design. We verify assertions generated by

HARM post-hoc, using EBMC, and report the proportion of assertions generated that pass verification as the Verification Correctness (VC)-rate. In addition, HARM produces unverified assertions, so we evaluate the MD-rates only on the assertions that pass the verification, taking the best case of their work.

5.1 Benchmarks and Experimental Setup

We implement MAPminer, using cvc5-1.2.0 from [5] and use the same core miner as the related work SMART [33]. We use Z3-4.15.4.0 from [25] as the underlying solver for calculating the mUS and simplifying the assertions. We use Cocotb-1.8.0 [29] and ebmc-5.6 [1] as the hardware simulator and formal assertion verifier, respectively.

All experiments are conducted on a dual-socket server equipped with two Intel Xeon Gold 6438Y+ processors, providing 128 logical CPUs (2 sockets × 32 cores × 2 threads). The machine has 125 GiB of main memory and runs a 64-bit Linux operating system on x86_64 architecture. In each experiment, we limit execution to 32 threads to ensure consistent and fair comparison across different configurations. Each tool is run with a 12-hour (43,200 s) timeout; if a tool does not terminate within this budget, its runtime is recorded as 43,200 s.

We compare MAPminer to SMART [33] and HARM [12]. HARM is a template-based miner that matches patterns on simulation traces. All three tools are evaluated using the same simulation testbench for each benchmark. We run HARM using 10,000-cycle random input traces with a larger random step depth than MAPminer and SMART, which in practice gives HARM a more favorable setup in the comparison. HARM is parallelized across 32 threads. Within MAPminer, we conduct an ablation study under different configurations to analyze the contribution of each component, in particular the use of mUS and the minimizer. We consider four variants: mUS+Minimizer (default: uses mUS and the minimizer after every iteration of the loop), mUS only (uses mUS to select variables but no minimization), Random+mUS (mixes mUS selected variables with randomly selected variables), and Full Random (does not use mUS at all).

To evaluate MAPminer, we employ benchmarks from prior work alongside two widely used hardware benchmark suites. From GoldMine [14], we select behavioral Verilog designs derived from the Ibex RISC-V CPU [28]—including `arb2`, `controller`, `decoder`, and `multdiv_slow`—which model representative microarchitectural components featuring non-trivial control logic and stateful behavior. Additionally, we incorporate the ISCAS'85 and ISCAS'89 benchmark suites [2], comprising purely combinational and sequential circuits, respectively. ISCAS'85 includes circuits ranging from simple logic (e.g., `c17` with 6 gates) to complex arithmetic units (e.g., `c6288`, a 16×16 multiplier with over 2,400 gates). ISCAS'89 provides sequential benchmarks of varying complexity, from small finite state machines such as `s27` (3 flip-flops) to large-scale industrial designs such as `s38584` and `s35932`, which contain over 20,000 gates and more than 1,700 flip-flops. Together, these benchmarks provide comprehensive coverage of both behavioral and gate-level hardware designs across a wide range of circuit scales (Fig. 4).

Table 1. Summary of results comparing MAPminer and related work. We report the average size of the generated assertion set $|\Phi|$, VC-rate, MD-rate, and average runtime over the 38 benchmarks common to all three tools. Each tool is run with a 12-hour timeout.

Category (#)	Metric	MAPminer	SMART	HARM
Structural (34)	avg. $\|\Phi\|$	3,957	1,319	60,887
	avg. VC (%)	100.0	100.0	15.28
	avg. MD (%)	76.94	59.57	17.77
	avg. Time (s)	12,089	2,076	303
Behavioral (4)	avg. $\|\Phi\|$	21	13	3,114
	avg. VC (%)	100.0	100.0	18.13
	avg. MD (%)	21.96	19.31	29.70
	avg. Time (s)	126	51	1,994
All (38)	avg. $\|\Phi\|$	3,543	1,181	54,806
	avg. VC (%)	100.0	100.0	15.58
	avg. MD (%)	71.16	55.33	19.03
	avg. Time (s)	10,830	1,863	481

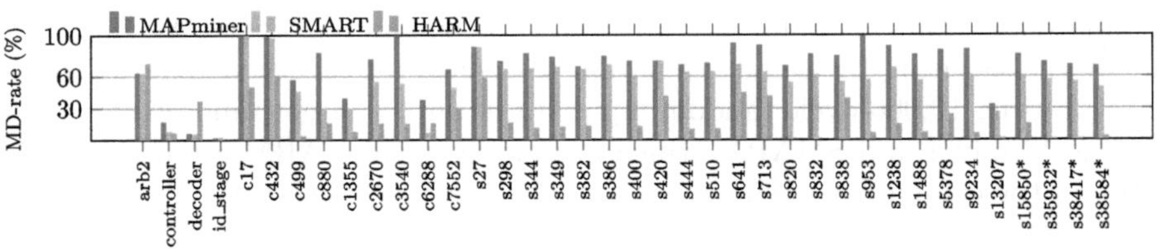

Fig. 4. Comparison of MD-rates between MAPminer, SMART [33], and HARM [12] on the benchmarks.

5.2 Results

VC-rate. All assertions generated by MAPminer and SMART are further validated using formal verification, and so both achieve a 100% VC-rate. HARM frequently fails to produce verified assertions.

MD-rate. The mutation detection results are summarized in Table 1. Compared with the state-of-the-art tool SMART, MAPminer achieves higher MD-rates on most benchmarks. Overall, MAPminer improves the average MD-rate from 55.33% to 71.16%, corresponding to an absolute gain of 15.83% points.

Assertion Size. Table 1 reports the average number of generated assertions $|\Phi|$ across the common benchmark set. Overall, MAPminer generates a moderate number of assertions compared with existing approaches. On average, MAPminer produces 3,543 assertions, which is larger than SMART (1,181) but more than an order of magnitude smaller than HARM (54,806). Although it generates more assertions than SMART, MAPminer achieves substantially higher

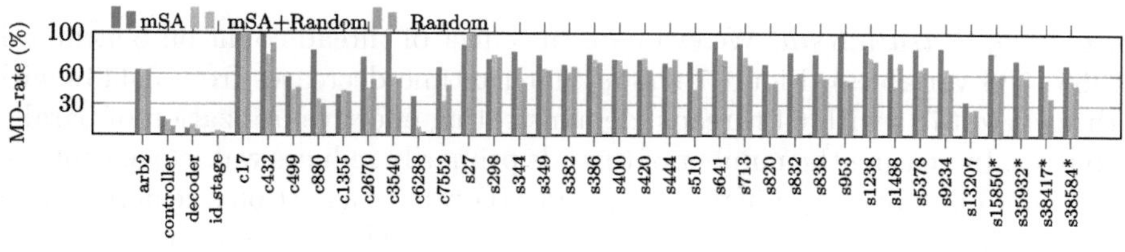

Fig. 5. Comparison of MD-rates between mUS, mUS+Random, and Random.

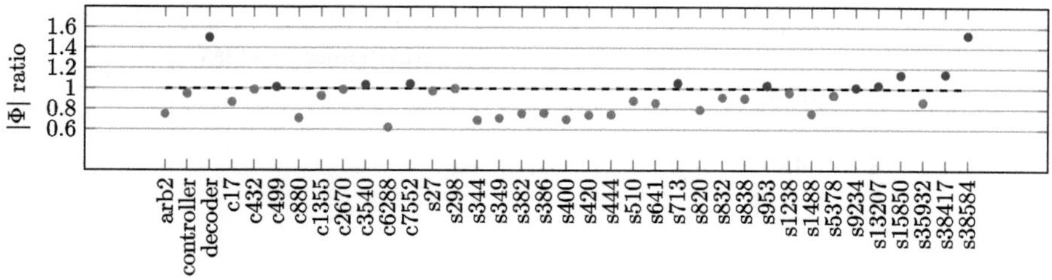

Fig. 6. Ratio of assertion set size between mUS+Minimizer and mUS $(\frac{|\Phi_{mUS+Minimizer}|}{|\Phi_{mUS}|})$. Green points are benchmarks where the $|\Phi|$ is reduced by the minimizer. *We omit the outlier benchmark **ibex_id_stage** (ratio = 8.25)

MD-rates, indicating that the additional assertions contribute to improved verification coverage rather than redundancy.

Impact of Variable Selection. Figure 5 compares MAPminer with different variable selection strategies. Overall, mUS-based selection improves mutation detection rates across the benchmark set. The benefit becomes increasingly pronounced on larger benchmarks, where random or partially random selection fails to scale, leading to substantially higher MD-rates. On smaller benchmarks, fully random selection can occasionally achieve comparable results due to the limited variable space.

Impact of Minimization. We evaluate the impact of assertion minimization. Figure 6 reports the ratio between the final number of assertions generated with minimization enabled (mUS+Min) and without minimization (mUS).

For most benchmarks, this ratio is below one, indicating that enabling minimization leads to a smaller final assertion set. This shows that a substantial fraction of mined assertions are redundant and can be effectively eliminated by the minimizer. For some larger benchmarks and timeout-prone cases, the ratio exceeds one. In these cases, minimization removes redundancy earlier during the mining process, which allows the miner to make further progress within the same time budget. As a result, more non-redundant assertions can be discovered overall, leading to a larger final assertion set compared to disabling minimization.

Overall, this ratio-based comparison shows that minimization is effective in most cases, either by reducing the final assertion size or by enabling additional useful assertions to be mined within the same resource constraints.

Impact of Parallelism. We evaluate the effect of thread count on benchmark `c1355` (588 variables). Figure 7 shows that runtime decreases from 3,443 s with 2 threads to 678 s with 64 threads, demonstrating effective utilization of parallel resources. Increasing the number of threads primarily reduces wall-clock runtime; we did not observe a meaningful change in MD-rate or assertion size across these configurations. This confirms that the parallelism in MAPminer provides a direct speedup without affecting the quality of the mined specifications.

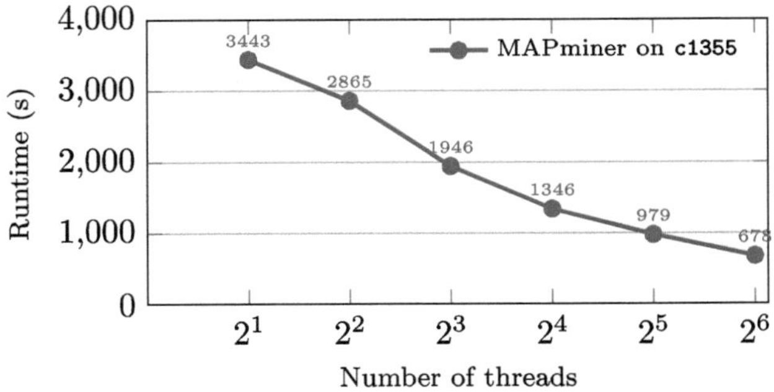

Fig. 7. Impact of thread count on runtime for benchmark `c1355`. Runtime decreases steadily as the number of threads increases.

Runtime Analysis. Table 1 reports the average runtime across the common benchmark set. HARM is the fastest tool on average (481 s), as its template-based pattern matching avoids expensive synthesis queries, but it produces the lowest-quality assertions. SMART averages 1,863 s and MAPminer averages 10,830 s. Both SMART and MAPminer reach the 12-hour timeout on some of the largest benchmarks. Runtime differences are strongly benchmark-dependent: on `c6288`, MAPminer finishes in 2,288 s while SMART takes 23,670 s, whereas on `s641`, SMART finishes in 66 s while MAPminer takes 2,097 s. MAPminer can take longer because it continues to discover new meaningful assertions via mUS-guided variable selection, whereas SMART and HARM may terminate earlier once their search spaces are exhausted. The ablation study (Fig. 5) confirms that the MD-rate improvement of MAPminer over SMART is attributable to mUS-based variable selection rather than longer runtime alone, since the Full Random variant, which is run under the same time budget, achieves substantially lower MD-rates.

6 Case Studies

In this section, we show how the proposed work can be applied to verification tasks for realistic hardware designs. Here we take the artifact published by [13] as two case studies for evaluation. The artifact contains two hardware implementations of cache components for improved memory isolation, which use

```
assume(|attacker_hitmap);
if (choice == 2'b00) begin
  assume(hitmap1 ==
      attacker_hitmap
  && hitmap2 ==
      attacker_hitmap);
  ...
end
```

(a) User-defined assumptions for a cache design with the Not Recently Used (NRU) eviction policy [13].

```
assert(
  ... &&
  (!(hitmap2 <= c2_metadata
      ) || c1_rst) &&
  (!(-((-attacker_hitmap) |
        (!attacker_hitmap))
       || attacker_hitmap) &&
  ...);
```

(b) Verified invariants of `hitmap1` and `attacker_hitmap` generated by MAPminer under assumptions in Figure 8a.

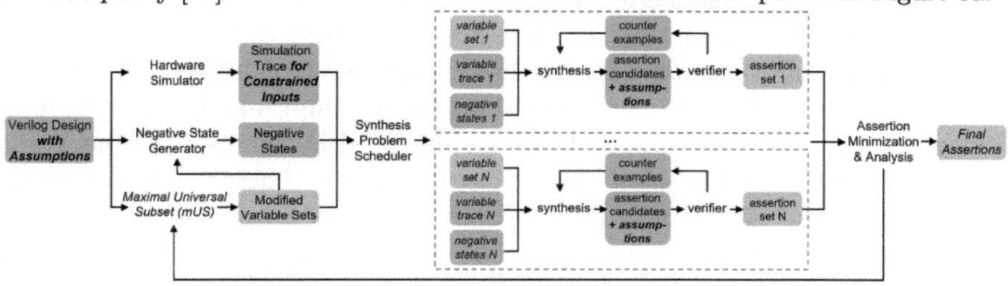

(c) Assumptions handled by MAPminer without needing to change the toolflow. The components encoded with assumptions are ***highlighted***.

Fig. 8. External environment-guided synthesis for producing specifications with constrained inputs.

replacement policies of Not Recently Used (NRU) and Pseudo-Least Recently Used (PLRU), respectively. Verifying the properties of such hardware components is crucial, especially since they are designed for memory protection, where any design flaws could lead to serious system vulnerabilities.

In the rest of this section, we compare the assertions automatically generated by MAPminer with the manually implemented assertions [13] for evaluation. We first show how MAPminer handles external environment constraints in assumptions for producing more precise assertions, as human experts do in practice. Second, we show how MAPminer could help identify steps towards verifying an end-to-end property of a realistic hardware design.

6.1 Handling Assumptions

In the previous sections, MAPminer checks whether a property always holds for a hardware design under all the possible states of its input signals. However, not all possible input states occur in practice because most hardware designs do not operate independently. A hardware component interacts with its external environment only under restricted input conditions. Missing such external environment constraints could lead to false negative verification results and state-space explosion during model checking.

In practice, these external environments for the hardware designs are described in the form of assumptions, which constrain the behaviors of input signals, such as timing constraints and value ranges. Here we provide an example of how MAPminer handles assumptions for generating more precise specifications.

Figure 8a shows part of the assumptions used for describing the external inputs to a cache to perform the NRU policy. The assumptions describe the scenario in which the attacker starts to work on two different machines. Figure 8b shows an assertion automatically generated by MAPminer that describes the behavior of these two signal components. We observed that these hardware states always hold under the assumption in Fig. 8a but cannot be verified for any input states. This indicates that MAPminer could produce more precise specifications when input constraints for the hardware design are provided.

Supporting these assumptions in MAPminer is straightforward. Figure 8c highlights the refined components based on the assumptions in the MAPminer toolflow. In the figure, the assumptions are provided by the users in the Verilog design, restricting the states of their external inputs. These input constraints are applied to the test inputs for hardware simulation and ensure that they always hold in the simulation traces. The assumptions are also encoded into the synthesis conjecture given to the synthesis-based assertion miner, so that it generates assertions under the given assumptions. The toolflow of MAPminer does not need any changes and naturally supports the integration of assumptions. The assumptions are integrated as metadata in the components.

6.2 Generating Auxiliary Invariants for Verification

While Sect. 5 shows that MAPminer produces meaningful assertions, here we evaluate the utility of MAPminer for realistic verification tasks. In practice, the designer inputs end-to-end properties of the design that describe systematic hardware states. These properties often have complex data and timing dependencies, and cannot be directly verified by the SMT solver. As a result, verifying these properties requires significant manual effort by human experts to write and verify complex intermediate properties, which can then be used as auxiliary invariants to ensure the verification query for the end-to-end property is provable [13].

In this case study, we show that MAPminer can produce assertions comparable to manually written auxiliary invariants, enabling automated verification of the given end-to-end properties. Specifically, although MAPminer generates a different set of assertions from the manually implemented ones, both sets enable verification of the same end-to-end property.

Table 2 evaluates various approaches to verifying the end-to-end properties for both cache designs. We compare MAPminer with three baselines: manual k-induction as used in the prior work [13], Bounded Model Checking (BMC) [7] and Property-Directed Reachability (PDR) [16]. To ensure fairness, we use the same k-induction depth as the prior work. We show run-time for both specification mining and verification, and whether the proofs are bounded.

Table 2. Comparison of different approaches in run-time breakdown and proof boundness. MAPminer achieves the best results in both the end-to-end time and unbounded proof. k-Ind = k-induction. BMC = Bounded Model Checking. PDR = Property-Directed Reachability.

Benchmark	Approach	Mining (s)	Proof (s)	End-to-end (s)	Unbounded
PLRU	k-Ind (MAPminer)	139	2	141	✓
	k-Ind (manual)	days	5	days	✓
	BMC ($d = 20$)	-	8743	8743	✗
	PDR	-	1450	1450	✓
NRU	k-Ind (MAPminer)	129	2	131	✓
	k-Ind (manual)	days	3	days	✓
	BMC ($d = 20$)	-	10756	10756	✗
	PDR	-	Timeout	-	✗

In the table, MAPminer completes the same unbounded security proof as the manual efforts, accelerating development time from days to seconds. BMC requires significantly longer runtimes and only establishes bounded guarantees, and PDR leads to a timeout of one day when proving the property for the NRU policy. This indicates that MAPminer can produce helpful invariants, automating certain verification efforts in verifying end-to-end properties for realistic hardware designs.

7 Related Work

Partitioning of search to allow parallelization is indispensable for many search tasks whose search is exorbitantly large. There are a number of related fields that have explored such methods and ideas. The work most closely related to MAPminer is HARM [12], which also parallelizes specification mining. Unlike MAPminer, HARM assigns different combinations of pattern matching and user hints to different cores. However, its pattern-matching approach limits the invariants that can be generated, leading to lower mutation detection rates compared to MAPminer. Other mining approaches applied to software, such as DAIKON [10], are broadly statistical. Although such approaches can be parallelized, ensuring that each thread performs meaningful work remains challenging. Many existing specification mining tools are sequential and rely on pattern matching or static analysis, as in GoldMine [14] and ARTMine [20]. Parallel methods have also been explored in invariant synthesis. H-HOUDINI [9] makes use of Machine-Learning-Inspired Synthesis to decompose inductiveness checks into many small parallelizable checks whose results can soundly compose into a global invariant. Prior work in invariant synthesis has also leveraged invalidating candidates to improve sampling [11].

There are a number of methods used in SAT solving to partition the search space. Many tools make use of *divide-and-conquer*, whereby the space is split a-priori. There are a number of techniques to overcome the difficulty of determining these splits; propagation-rate [26], partition-trees [17], symbolic partitioning of execution traces [21] and variable-level partitioning [34], all utilizing data from preprocessing formulas. *Cube-and-conquer* is a specific type of divide-and-conquer; formulas are broken down into *cubes*, with each cube fixing a subset of the variables. A separate solver for each cube is then tasked with trying to fill the free variables [6,15]. This same idea has also been used in program synthesis [22].

Lazy clause exchange [3] in portfolio solving allows clauses to be passed between partitions when they are required; similarly selective clause sharing shares 'good-looking' clauses between solvers [4,30]. Both are methods to better harness parallelism in SAT solving by sharing useful information.

8 Conclusions

We presented MAPminer, a parallel synthesis-based framework for automated specification mining in hardware designs. By combining mUS-guided variable selection with assertion minimization, MAPminer scales synthesis-based mining to realistic Verilog designs while preserving formal correctness guarantees. Compared with prior work, MAPminer achieves higher verification coverage with a moderate number of assertions, balancing assertion quality and quantity. Case studies on security-oriented cache designs demonstrate that MAPminer can automatically generate auxiliary invariants enabling unbounded verification of realistic end-to-end properties. These results highlight the practical value of MAPminer in reducing manual effort for formal hardware verification. Future work includes extending MAPminer to richer temporal specifications and tighter integration with industrial verification flows.

Acknowledgments. This work is supported by a Royal Academy of Engineering Research Fellowship RF2223-22-262 and the EPSRC Centre for Doctoral Training in Machine Learning Systems (EP/Y03516X/1). It is partially based upon work supported by the Defense Advanced Research Projects Agency (DARPA) under Agreement No. HR00112590131.

Data Availibility Statement. The artifact supporting this paper, including source code, benchmarks, and instructions for reproducing the experimental results, is available on Zenodo at https://doi.org/10.5281/zenodo.20393223.

Disclosure of Interests. The authors have no competing interests to declare that are relevant to the content of this article.

References

1. EBMC. https://github.com/diffblue/hw-cbmc/
2. Circuit netlist benchmarks (2025). https://sportlab.usc.edu/~msabrishami/benchmarks.html
3. Audemard, G., Simon, L.: Lazy clause exchange policy for parallel SAT solvers. In: Sinz, C., Egly, U. (eds.) SAT 2014. LNCS, vol. 8561, pp. 197–205. Springer, Cham (2014). https://doi.org/10.1007/978-3-319-09284-3_15
4. Balyo, T., Sanders, P., Sinz, C.: HordeSat: a massively parallel portfolio SAT solver. In: Heule, M., Weaver, S. (eds.) SAT 2015. LNCS, vol. 9340, pp. 156–172. Springer, Cham (2015). https://doi.org/10.1007/978-3-319-24318-4_12
5. Barbosa, H., et al.: cvc5: a versatile and industrial-strength SMT solver. In: TACAS 2022. LNCS, vol. 13243, pp. 415–442. Springer, Cham (2022). https://doi.org/10.1007/978-3-030-99524-9_24
6. Biere, A., et al.: Lingeling, Plingeling and Treengeling entering the SAT competition 2013. Proc. SAT Compet. **2013**, 1 (2013)
7. Clarke, E., Biere, A., Raimi, R., Zhu, Y.: Bounded model checking using satisfiability solving. Formal Methods Syst. Des. **19**(1), 7–34 (2001). https://doi.org/10.1023/A:1011276507260
8. Dillig, I., Dillig, T., McMillan, K.L., Aiken, A.: Minimum satisfying assignments for SMT. In: Madhusudan, P., Seshia, S.A. (eds.) CAV 2012. LNCS, vol. 7358, pp. 394–409. Springer, Heidelberg (2012). https://doi.org/10.1007/978-3-642-31424-7_30
9. Dinesh, S., Zhu, Y., Fletcher, C.W.: H-Houdini: scalable invariant learning. In: Proceedings of the 30th ACM International Conference on Architectural Support for Programming Languages and Operating Systems, Volume 1, pp. 603–618 (2025). https://doi.org/10.1145/3669940.3707263
10. Ernst, M.D., et al.: The Daikon system for dynamic detection of likely invariants. Sci. Comput. Program. **69**(1–3), 35–45 (2007). https://doi.org/10.1016/j.scico.2007.01.015
11. Fedyukovich, G., Bodík, R.: Accelerating syntax-guided invariant synthesis. In: Beyer, D., Huisman, M. (eds.) TACAS 2018. LNCS, vol. 10805, pp. 251–269. Springer, Cham (2018). https://doi.org/10.1007/978-3-319-89960-2_14
12. Germiniani, S., Pravadelli, G.: Harm: a hint-based assertion miner. IEEE Trans. Comput. Aided Des. Integr. Circuits Syst. **41**(11), 4277–4288 (2022). https://doi.org/10.1109/TCAD.2022.3197525
13. Godbole, A., Ye, L., Manerkar, Y.A., Seshia, S.A.: Modelling and verification of security-oriented resource partitioning schemes. In: FMCAD, pp. 268–273 (2023). https://doi.org/10.34727/2023/isbn.978-3-85448-060-0_35
14. Hertz, S., Sheridan, D., Vasudevan, S.: Mining hardware assertions with guidance from static analysis. IEEE Trans. Comput. Aided Des. Integr. Circuits Syst. **32**(6), 952–965 (2013). https://doi.org/10.1109/TCAD.2013.2241176
15. Heule, M.J.H., Kullmann, O., Wieringa, S., Biere, A.: Cube and conquer: guiding CDCL SAT solvers by lookaheads. In: Eder, K., Lourenço, J., Shehory, O. (eds.) HVC 2011. LNCS, vol. 7261, pp. 50–65. Springer, Heidelberg (2012). https://doi.org/10.1007/978-3-642-34188-5_8
16. Hoder, K., Bjørner, N.: Generalized property directed reachability. In: Cimatti, A., Sebastiani, R. (eds.) SAT 2012. LNCS, vol. 7317, pp. 157–171. Springer, Heidelberg (2012). https://doi.org/10.1007/978-3-642-31612-8_13

17. Hyvärinen, A.E.J., Junttila, T., Niemelä, I.: Partitioning SAT instances for distributed solving. In: Fermüller, C.G., Voronkov, A. (eds.) LPAR 2010. LNCS, vol. 6397, pp. 372–386. Springer, Heidelberg (2010). https://doi.org/10.1007/978-3-642-16242-8_27
18. IEEE: Combining dynamic slicing and mutation operators for ESL correction (2012). https://doi.org/10.1109/ETS.2012.6233020
19. Ignatiev, A., Previti, A., Marques-Silva, J.: On finding minimum satisfying assignments. In: Rueher, M. (ed.) CP 2016. LNCS, vol. 9892, pp. 287–297. Springer, Cham (2016). https://doi.org/10.1007/978-3-319-44953-1_19
20. Iman, M.R.H., Jervan, G., Ghasempouri, T.: Artmine: automatic association rule mining with temporal behavior for hardware verification. In: 2024 Design, Automation & Test in Europe Conference & Exhibition (DATE), pp. 1–6. IEEE (2024). https://doi.org/10.23919/DATE58400.2024.10546742
21. Inverso, O., Trubiani, C.: Parallel and distributed bounded model checking of multi-threaded programs. In: Proceedings of the 25th ACM SIGPLAN Symposium on Principles and Practice of Parallel Programming, pp. 202–216 (2020). https://doi.org/10.1145/3332466.3374529
22. Jeon, J., Qiu, X., Solar-Lezama, A., Foster, J.S.: Adaptive concretization for parallel program synthesis. In: Kroening, D., Păsăreanu, C.S. (eds.) CAV 2015. LNCS, vol. 9207, pp. 377–394. Springer, Cham (2015). https://doi.org/10.1007/978-3-319-21668-3_22
23. Jha, S., Seshia, S.A.: A theory of formal synthesis via inductive learning. Acta Inf. **54**(7), 693–726 (2017). https://doi.org/10.1007/s00236-017-0294-5
24. Kande, R., et al.: LLM-assisted generation of hardware assertions. arXiv preprint arXiv:2306.14027 (2023). https://doi.org/10.48550/arXiv.2306.14027
25. de Moura, L., Bjørner, N.: Z3: an efficient SMT solver. In: Ramakrishnan, C.R., Rehof, J. (eds.) TACAS 2008. LNCS, vol. 4963, pp. 337–340. Springer, Heidelberg (2008). https://doi.org/10.1007/978-3-540-78800-3_24
26. Nejati, S., et al.: A propagation rate based splitting heuristic for divide-and-conquer solvers. In: Gaspers, S., Walsh, T. (eds.) SAT 2017. LNCS, vol. 10491, pp. 251–260. Springer, Cham (2017). https://doi.org/10.1007/978-3-319-66263-3_16
27. Orenes-Vera, M., Martonosi, M., Wentzlaff, D.: Using LLMs to facilitate formal verification of RTL. arXiv preprint arXiv:2309.09437 (2023). https://doi.org/10.48550/arXiv.2309.09437
28. Raveendran, R., Bhuinya, S.: Customization of ibex RISC-V processor core. Customization of Ibex RISC-V Processor Core (2021)
29. Rosser, B.J.: Cocotb: a python-based digital logic verification framework. In: Micro-Electronics Section Seminar. CERN, Geneva, Switzerland (2018)
30. Schreiber, D., Sanders, P.: MallobSat: scalable SAT solving by clause sharing. J. Artif. Intell. Res. **80**, 1437–1495 (2024). https://doi.org/10.1613/jair.1.15827
31. Sun, C., Hahn, C., Trippel, C.: Towards improving verification productivity with circuit-aware translation of natural language to systemverilog assertions. In: First International Workshop on Deep Learning-aided Verification (2023)
32. Yan, Z., et al.: AssertLLM: generating hardware verification assertions from design specifications via multi-LLMs. In: Proceedings of the 30th Asia and South Pacific Design Automation Conference, ASPDAC 2025, pp. 614–621. Association for Computing Machinery, New York, NY, USA (2025). https://doi.org/10.1145/3658617.3697756

33. Ye, L., Li, Y., Frankel, G., Cheng, J., Polgreen, E.: Unlocking hardware verification with oracle guided synthesis. In: Proceedings of the 25th Conference on Formal Methods in Computer-Aided Design, pp. 235–245. TU Wien Academic Press (2025). https://doi.org/10.34727/2025/isbn.978-3-85448-084-6_30
34. Zhao, M., Cai, S., Qian, Y.: Distributed SMT solving based on dynamic variable-level partitioning. In: Computer Aided Verification – 36th International Conference, CAV 2024, Montreal, QC, Canada, 24–27 July 2024, Proceedings, Part I, pp. 68–88. Springer (2024). https://doi.org/10.1007/978-3-031-65627-9_4

A Mechanised, Bidirectional Type System for Bit-Width Determination in SystemVerilog

Gabriel Desfrene[1,2], Quentin Corradi[2], Michalis Pardalos[2], and John Wickerson[2](✉)

[1] École normale supérieure – PSL, Paris, France
gabriel.desfrene@ens.psl.eu
[2] Imperial College London, London, UK
{q.corradi22,michail.pardalos17,j.wickerson}@imperial.ac.uk

Abstract. SystemVerilog remains one of the most widely used languages for designing and verifying digital circuits. Despite its importance, the SystemVerilog standard suffers from ambiguities, which can lead to inconsistent implementations and portability challenges. Formal methods can provide precise semantics to address these issues.

We focus on SystemVerilog's mechanism for determining the bit-width of each expression that appears in a design. This is surprisingly subtle because an expression's bit-width can depend on both its children *and* its parents. First, we develop a Rocq formalization of the existing IEEE standard for SystemVerilog. We then construct a bidirectional type system that captures the context-dependent nature of SystemVerilog expressions and prove it equivalent to our formalization of the standard using Rocq. We provide a reference implementation that determines bit-widths in linear time and prove its correspondence to our system, also in Rocq. Based on these results, we propose revisions to the text of the standard that reduce redundancy and improve precision.

Keywords: Bidirectional typing · Type inference · Hardware description languages · Formal semantics · Context-dependent typing · Machine-checked proofs · Language standardization · SystemVerilog

1 Introduction

Verilog and its successor SystemVerilog have been foundational to digital design since 1984 [9], enabling the design, verification, and synthesis of everything from simple logic gates to complex system-on-chip designs. But important aspects of the language remain poorly understood and inconsistently implemented [3], thanks to its large and cumbersome prose specification, the IEEE 1800-2023 SystemVerilog Language Reference Manual (LRM) [11].

For instance: because SystemVerilog designs map to physical hardware, the width in bits of every operation in every expression must be determined precisely. Too narrow, and arithmetic precision is lost; too wide, and the circuit

E. Darulova et al. (Eds.): CAV 2026, LNCS 16682, pp. 426–445, 2026.
https://doi.org/10.1007/978-3-032-32519-8_22

will consume area unnecessarily. Some widths are provided by the designer via constants and variable declarations; others are determined during compilation following rules set out in the standard.

However, these rules are complex and widely misunderstood. Consider the following example, in which `a` is declared as a 4-bit variable, `3'b110` is the 3-bit binary constant `110`, and `>>` is a right-shift operation:

```
logic [3:0] a;
assign a = (3'b110 + 3'b110 + 3'b110 + 3'b110) >> 2;
```

What value is assigned to `a`?

- One option is that the additions are performed at whatever width is necessary for no bits to be lost to overflow. In this case, the intermediate sum would be `5'b11000`, so after the right-shift, `a` would become `4'b0110`.
- A second option is to perform the additions at the width of their operands, which is 3 bits. In this case, the intermediate sum would be `3'b000`, so after the right-shift, `a` would become `4'b0000`.

In fact, SystemVerilog opts for a *third* option: the addition is performed at the width determined by the assignment's left-hand side (`a`), which is 4 bits. So, the intermediate sum is `4'b1000`, and hence after the right shift, `a` becomes `4'b0010`.

Further complexities arise when other operations are involved; for instance, although we see here widths propagating down through addition and shift operations, there are other operations, such as concatenation, that they do *not* propagate through.

While there are no documented cases of rockets having fallen to earth as a direct result of SystemVerilog's bit-width rules being misunderstood, there is plenty of anecdotal evidence of confusion surrounding them. For instance, an established online Verilog tutorial, after warning its readers that bit-width rules are 'subtle', wrongly states that operations have their widths determined by their operands (i.e., our 'second option' mentioned above) [19]. There have also been cases where companies have been so concerned about bugs relating to bit-widths that they have required their designers to make even benign zero-extensions explicit [15]. And there are known quirks in how commercial tools handle bit-widths: for instance, SystemVerilog forbids unsized constants appearing in concatenations, and Cadence tools duly reject expressions like `{1'b0, 16}`—yet, according to the developer of the Icarus Verilog simulator [21], they happily accept `{1'b0, 15+1}`!

In short, bit-width determination in SystemVerilog is complicated; partly because of the wide variety of rules for the different operations and partly because of the unusual context-dependent manner in which they are applied. Because of this, and because of the importance of correct hardware compilation, our position is that bit-width determination in SystemVerilog is an ideal candidate for formalisation.

Prior Work. SystemVerilog has been the focus of several recent formalisation efforts, but none have addressed bit-width determination with sufficient rigour. Featherweight Verilog introduces a minimal core calculus for the synthesizable subset of Verilog [10], but relies on generic types and omits bit-width determination entirely. Choi et al.'s denotational semantics assumes bit-widths are fixed *a priori* [4], thereby sidestepping bit-width determination, while Lööw's analysis of inconsistencies in the SystemVerilog LRM focuses on simulation semantics rather than formalizing bit-width determination rules [13]. Other efforts aim to define executable or reference semantics for large fragments of SystemVerilog, but do not provide an efficient, mechanically verified procedure for computing bit-width information. Chen et al. propose a tractable operational semantics that computes bit-widths algorithmically [2], but their approach lacks formal judgments suitable for mechanized correctness proofs. Meredith et al.'s rewriting-based executable semantics covers a substantial portion of SystemVerilog [14], but does not support sized integers and fails to yield a clear or efficient decision procedure for bit-width determination.

Our Work. This paper addresses this gap by developing the first verified system for determining SystemVerilog bit-widths. As mentioned above, what complicates matters is that in SystemVerilog, the bit-width of an expression cannot be determined in isolation; it depends on contextual information that may itself rely on bit-widths computed earlier. This circular dependency leads the LRM to specify a complex two-phase algorithm for bit-width determination, in which bit-width information first flows from the operands up to the root of the expression (the 'determine' phase), and then flows back down, fixing the final size of each sub-expression (the 'propagate' phase). Our approach resolves this interdependency in a principled way by setting up a bidirectional typing system [8,18], in which bidirectional typing's *synthesis* mode maps to the 'determine' phase, its *checking* mode maps to the 'propagate' phase, and a bit-vector of width s is defined to be a subtype of a bit-vector of width t whenever $s \leq t$. This typing system is proven equivalent to a formalisation of the LRM, but it is easier to use in a context of a proof assistant because it is fully compositional. It is also designed to be easily integrated (in future work) with existing formally verified Verilog-consuming tools, such as the Vera verified equivalence checker [17] and the Lustig verified synthesis tool [12], potentially enhancing the formal guarantees they provide.

Contributions. We claim the following contributions:

1. We formalize an important subset of the IEEE 1800-2023 specification for bit-width determination in the Rocq theorem prover [20], providing a precise mathematical interpretation of the standard's prose descriptions (Sect. 2).
2. We develop a bidirectional type system that captures the context-dependent nature of SystemVerilog expression bit-widths, introducing formal rules and proving key properties (Sect. 3).
3. We provide machine-checked proofs that our rule system is equivalent to our formalization of the LRM (Sect. 4).

4. We derive a reference implementation that computes bit-widths in linear time and provide a Rocq-checked proof of its correctness with respect to our rule system (Sect. 5).

2 Formalizing the LRM

In this section, we explain how SystemVerilog's expression bit-width mechanisms work. After presenting examples and a note on our expression grammar, we detail our approach to formalising it in Rocq.

2.1 How Sizing Works in SystemVerilog

The *self-determined width* of an expression is the bit-width determined solely by the expression itself, independent of its context. This constitutes an intrinsic property of the expression, corresponding to what the LRM refers to in its latest version[11, §I.11.6] as a *self-determined* expression. Practically, this property ensures that the widths of such expressions can be computed through local analysis alone. For instance, the self-determined width of an 8-bit bus is 8, as is the self-determined width of the literal `8'd128`.

The computation of self-determined width follows a recursive, bottom-up traversal strategy that we will call Determine. This process begins with leaf nodes (operands) whose bit-widths are explicitly known, then propagates upward through the abstract syntax tree according to operator-specific rules. Figure 1a illustrates this phase using the following example code (which is similar to the example from Sect. 1 but involves fewer additions and includes a concatenation operation).

```
logic [3:0] a;
assign a = (3'b110 + {2'b11, 1'b0}) >> 2;
```

Each node of the AST is annotated with the kind of operation being performed (`BinOp` for +, and so on), and also its self-determined width. The bold orange arrows show how the self-determined widths are propagated *up* the AST: the width of the concatenation is the sum of the widths of its operands; the width of the binary operation is the maximum of the widths of its operands; the shift's width is determined by its left-hand operand (the value being shifted); and the width of the result of the assignment is determined by the width of its left-hand side (`a` in this case). Thus, the Determine phase computes the self-determined width of the top-level expression and all sub-expressions.

The self-determined width of the top-level expression also becomes its final width. Then the final widths of all the sub-expressions are calculated during a subsequent Propagate phase. This is illustrated in Fig. 1b. Here, nodes of the AST are annotated with two widths, $w \to v$: the self-determined width w and the final width v. The bold orange arrows show how the widths are propagated *down*

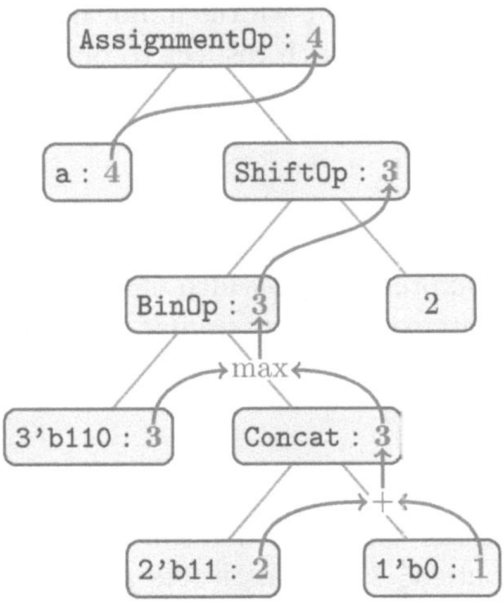

(a) The Determine phase

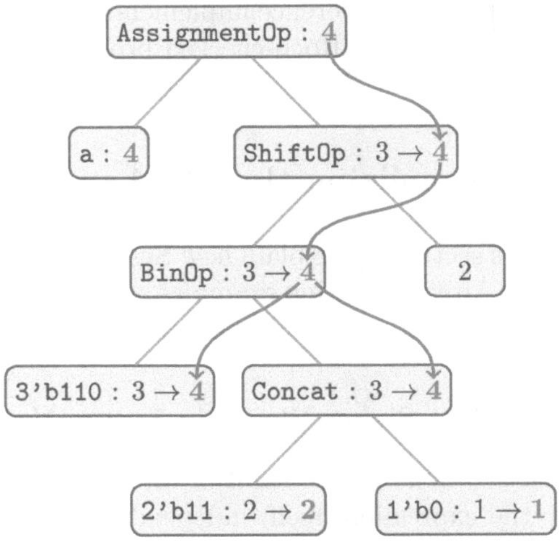

(b) The Propagate phase

Fig. 1. An example of the two phases of bitwidth calculation

the AST: the final width of the shift is determined by the width of its parent; as is the width of the binary operation and both of its operands. However, the width information does *not* flow down to the operands of the `Concat` operation: these belong to a separate 'context', so their final widths remain as their self-determined widths.

In summary, the complete sizing mechanism operates through a two-phase process. The first phase, Determine, synthesizes self-determined bit-widths throughout the expression hierarchy, plus the final width of the top-level expression. The second phase, Propagate, computes the final width for all sub-expressions by propagating bit-width information downward through the AST.

2.2 Formal Expression Model

For our Rocq formalization of the LRM mechanism, we present a simplified formalization of SystemVerilog expressions that captures all the behaviours relevant to bit-width determination.

We begin with operands, which are the atomic parts of SystemVerilog expressions: literals, variables, structure members, union members, function calls, and other primitive constructs such as bit selects and bit-slicing [11, §I.11.2]. For our formalization, we require operands to satisfy the following property:

Property 1. The self-determined width of an operand is always well-defined and determined by its declaration, literal specification, or result type.

We assume a normalization preprocessing step that ensures no operand contains nested expressions. This transformation introduces fresh variables for

```
e ::= o                              operands
    | BinaryOp(e1, e2)               binary and bitwise operations (+, *, &, |, ...)
    | UnaryOp(e)                     unary operations (+, -, ~, ++, --)
    | ComparisonOp(e1, e2)           comparison operations (==, !=, >, >=, ...)
    | LogicOp(e1, e2)                logical operations (&&, ||, ->, <->)
    | ReductionOp(e)                 reduction operations (!, &, |, ^, ...)
    | ShiftOp(e1, e2)                shift operations and power (>>, <<, **, ...)
    | AssignmentOp(l, e)             assignment
    | Conditional Op(e1, e2, e3)     conditional expression
    | Concat(e1, ..., ek)            concatenation
    | Replication(n, e)              replication
```

Fig. 2. SystemVerilog expressions, categorized by bit-width determination behaviour

expressions composing operands, particularly targeting function calls. Since function calls are classified as operands, their self-determined widths are defined by the function's return type. For bit-width generic functions such as type casts, the output width can be determined from the function signature and the self-determined widths from its arguments (which themselves require bit-width analysis). This normalization guarantees that all operands possess well-defined self-determined widths while simplifying subsequent operations.

We categorize SystemVerilog operations by their sizing behaviors, yielding the expression grammar shown in Fig. 2. In this grammar, o denotes a SystemVerilog operand, l represents a left-hand side expression during assignment, and n is an integer. We assume that all constant expressions have been pre-evaluated.

A few Verilog-specific features are worth explaining. Reduction operations apply a bitwise operator across all bits of one operand (e.g., `\& x` is true if all bits of `x` are 1). Concatenation builds a wider bitvector by joining operands side by side (e.g., `{a, b}` places `a`'s bits above `b`'s). Replication repeats an expression a fixed number of times to form a larger vector (e.g., `{3{a}}` concatenates three copies of `a`).

We remark on a few simplications in our grammar. First, compound assignment operators (`+=`, etc.) are treated as syntactic sugar (e.g. `a += b` is interpreted as `a = a + b`) as specified in the LRM [11, §I.11.4.1]. Second, the LRM constrains the `Replication` operator to operate solely on `Concat` expressions, but we adopt a more permissive approach by allowing replication of *any* expression, because it simplifies our inference rules. Third, we do not formalize the `Inside` operator since it can be derived from a sequence of `Or` operations during normalization; this aligns with the semantics prescribed in the LRM [11, §I.11.4.13]. Fourth, we exclude streaming operators from our formalization as they behave identically to concatenation with respect to bit-width determination. Finally, we exclude the `dist` operator since Annex A of the LRM restricts its usage to constraint blocks, which fall outside the scope of general expression evaluation.

$$
\begin{aligned}
&\mathsf{det}(o) &&= \Gamma(o) \quad (\text{where } o \in \mathcal{O})\\
&\mathsf{det}(\texttt{BinaryOp}(e_1, e_2)) &&= \max(\mathsf{det}(e_1), \mathsf{det}(e_2))\\
&\mathsf{det}(\texttt{UnaryOp}(e)) &&= \mathsf{det}(e)\\
&\mathsf{det}(\texttt{ComparisonOp}(e_1, e_2)) &&= 1\\
&\mathsf{det}(\texttt{LogicOp}(e_1, e_2)) &&= 1\\
&\mathsf{det}(\texttt{ReductionOp}(e)) &&= 1\\
&\mathsf{det}(\texttt{ShiftOp}(e_1, e_2)) &&= \mathsf{det}(e_1)\\
&\mathsf{det}(\texttt{AssignmentOp}(l, e)) &&= \phi(l)\\
&\mathsf{det}(\texttt{ConditionalOp}(e_1, e_2, e_3) &&= \max(\mathsf{det}(e_2), \mathsf{det}(e_3))\\
&\mathsf{det}(\texttt{Replication}(n, e)) &&= n \times \mathsf{det}(e)\\
&\mathsf{det}(\texttt{Concat}(e_1, \ldots, e_k)) &&= \textstyle\sum_{i=1}^{k} \mathsf{det}(e_i)
\end{aligned}
$$

Fig. 3. Our det function, inspired by Table 11–21 in the LRM [11, §I.11.6.1]

2.3 Formalizing the LRM

The LRM does not present a unified system for bit-width determination. Instead, it provides fragments of an algorithm distributed across multiple sections. This algorithm consists of two primary phases: Determine and Propagate, as described in §I.11.8.2:

> **Determine** the expression size based upon the standard rules of expression size determination [...]. **Propagate** the type and size of the expression (or *self-determined* subexpression) back down to the *context-determined* operands of the expression. [11, §I.11.8.2]

The LRM defines a *context-determined* expression as one whose bit length

> [...] is determined by the bit length of the expression and by the fact that it is part of another expression. [11, §I.11.6.1]

The Determine Phase. The first phase is well-defined by Table 11–21 in the LRM [11, §I.11.6.1]. This phase computes the self-determined width for each expression in a bottom-up fashion, as seen in Fig. 1. We formalize this as a recursive function $\mathsf{det} : \text{Expr} \to \mathbb{N}$, defined in Fig. 3.

This formalization relies on two auxiliary functions, Γ and ϕ. The function Γ maps each operand in $\mathcal{O}$ (the set of all operands) to its declared bit-width, providing the foundation for all bit-width computations. This function is a direct consequence of property 1 that we established for operands. The function ϕ determines the bit-width of left-hand sides in assignments. This function exists because assignment targets have a simpler syntactic structure than general expressions [11, §A.8.5]. They consist of operands, concatenations of assignment targets, or streaming concatenations of assignment targets. This restricted structure allows us to construct a simple recursive function to compute their width.

$$\begin{aligned}
& & \mathsf{prop}_e([]) &= \mathsf{det}(e) & (1)\\
&\text{For } e|_p = \texttt{ReductionOp}(e') : & \mathsf{prop}_e(p \cdot 0) &= \mathsf{det}(e') & (2)\\
&\text{For } e|_p = \texttt{LogicOp}(e_0, e_1) : & \mathsf{prop}_e(p \cdot 0) &= \mathsf{det}(e_0) & (3)\\
& & \mathsf{prop}_e(p \cdot 1) &= \mathsf{det}(e_1) & (4)\\
&\text{For } e|_p = \texttt{Concat}(e_0, \ldots, e_k), 0 \leq i \leq k : & \mathsf{prop}_e(p \cdot i) &= \mathsf{det}(e_i) & (5)\\
&\text{For } e|_p = \texttt{Replication}(n, e') : & \mathsf{prop}_e(p \cdot 0) &= \mathsf{det}(e') & (6)\\
&\text{For } e|_p = \texttt{ComparisonOp}(e_0, e_1) : & \mathsf{prop}_e(p \cdot 0) &= \max(\mathsf{det}(e_0), \mathsf{det}(e_1)) & (7)\\
& & \mathsf{prop}_e(p \cdot 1) &= \max(\mathsf{det}(e_0), \mathsf{det}(e_1)) & (8)\\
&\text{For } e|_p = \texttt{BinaryOp}(e_0, e_1) : & \mathsf{prop}_e(p \cdot 0) &= \mathsf{prop}_e(p) & (9)\\
& & \mathsf{prop}_e(p \cdot 1) &= \mathsf{prop}_e(p) & (10)\\
&\text{For } e|_p = \texttt{UnaryOp}(e') : & \mathsf{prop}_e(p \cdot 0) &= \mathsf{prop}_e(p) & (11)\\
&\text{For } e|_p = \texttt{ShiftOp}(e_0, e_1) : & \mathsf{prop}_e(p \cdot 0) &= \mathsf{prop}_e(p) & (12)\\
& & \mathsf{prop}_e(p \cdot 1) &= \mathsf{det}(e_1) & (13)\\
&\text{For } e|_p = \texttt{ConditionalOp}(e_0, e_1, e_2) : & \mathsf{prop}_e(p \cdot 0) &= \mathsf{det}(e_0) & (14)\\
& & \mathsf{prop}_e(p \cdot 1) &= \mathsf{prop}_e(p) & (15)\\
& & \mathsf{prop}_e(p \cdot 2) &= \mathsf{prop}_e(p) & (16)\\
&\text{For } e|_p = \texttt{AssignmentOp}(l, e') : & \mathsf{prop}_e(p \cdot 0) &= \max(\mathsf{det}(e'), \phi(l)) & (17)
\end{aligned}$$

Fig. 4. LRM-derived constraints defining our prop_e function.

The Propagate Phase. The Propagate phase operates top-down, as described earlier and illustrated in Fig. 1b. Starting from the result of the Determine phase, it flows bit-width information back into the expression tree to compute the final width of each sub-expression. While not explicitly defined in the LRM, this phase is implied by various requirements scattered throughout the specification (in §I.10.7, and from §I.11.6 to §I.11.8).

Let e be an expression. We model this phase as a function $\mathsf{prop}_e : \mathrm{Path}(e) \to \mathbb{N}$ that maps each valid path in e to the final width of the corresponding sub-expression. A path is represented as a list of natural numbers encoding navigation through the abstract syntax tree: starting from the root, each number indicates which child to visit next (0 denotes the first child, 1 the second, and so on). For example, the path $[1, 0]$ refers to the first child of the second child of the root expression. The empty path $[]$ refers to the root expression itself. We use the notation $p \cdot k$ to denote extending path p with index k. We denote by $e|_p$ the sub-expression of e reached by following the path p. Figure 4 shows all constraints mandated by the LRM for prop_e.

Section §I.11.8.2 of the LRM states that this phase should:

> Propagate the type and size of the expression (or *self-determined* subexpression) back down [...] the expression. [11, §I.11.8.2]

From this statement, we derive our first constraint, Eq. (1), which applies to the top-level expression. Furthermore, when a sub-expression at position p within an expression e is *self-determined*, the following constraint applies:

$$\mathsf{prop}_e(p) = \mathsf{det}\,(e|_p) \tag{1}$$

This principle serves as the basis for the constraints presented in Eqs. (2) to (6), since Table 11–21 identifies these child expressions as self-determined. In particular, Eq. (2) is a specific instance of Eq. (18) for the child of a reduction operator. In this case, the reduction operator itself is located at position p, its child expression e' at position $p \cdot 0$, and we have $e|_{p\cdot 0} = e'$.

Comparison operations require special treatment. Table 11–21 specifies that 'Operands are sized to $\max(L(\mathtt{i}), L(\mathtt{j}))$', where i and j denote the operands and L represents the det function. This yields the constraints in Eqs. (7)and (8).

We assume that operands not marked as *self-determined* in Table 11–21 are *context-determined.* For operations with such operands, the LRM states that:

> In general, any *context-determined* operand of an operator shall be the same type and size as the result of the operator. [11, §I.11.8.2]

This constraint applies to binary and unary operations (Eqs. (9) to (11))and extends naturally to operators with mixed operand types, such as shifts and conditionals (Eqs. 12) to (16).

Assignment expressions require careful treatment. The LRM specifies that:

> When the right-hand side evaluates to fewer bits than the left-hand side, the right-hand side value is padded to the size of the left-hand side. [...] If the width of the right-hand expression is larger than the width of the left-hand side in an assignment, the MSBs of the right-hand expression shall be discarded to match the size of the left-hand side. [11, §I.10.7]

These requirements imply that the maximum of the left-hand side's bit-width and the right-hand side's self-determined width propagates downward. When truncation occurs, it happens at the top level ('the MSBs of the right-hand expression shall be discarded'), treating the expression as self-determined. These properties yield the constraint formalized in Eq. (17).

From the constraints of Fig. 4, we verified in Rocq that prop_e is uniquely defined for every sub-expression of any expression.

3 Bidirectional Typing Framework

We now present our bidirectional type system [8,18], which is designed to capture the bit-width computation of SystemVerilog expressions. Bidirectional typing combines two modes: type *checking*, which checks that a program e in a context Γ has type τ (written $\Gamma \vdash e \Leftarrow \tau$), and type *synthesis*, which determines

$$\text{Unary}(f, t) ::= \begin{cases} [] & \mapsto t \\ 0 \cdot p \mapsto f(p) \end{cases} \qquad \text{Binary}(t, f, g) ::= \begin{cases} [] & \mapsto t \\ 0 \cdot p \mapsto f(p) \\ 1 \cdot p \mapsto g(p) \end{cases}$$

$$\text{Ternary}(t, f, g, h) ::= \begin{cases} [] & \mapsto t \\ 0 \cdot p \mapsto f(p) \\ 1 \cdot p \mapsto g(p) \\ 2 \cdot p \mapsto h(p) \end{cases} \quad \text{Nary}(t, f_1, \ldots, f_k) ::= \begin{cases} [] & \mapsto t \\ i \cdot p \mapsto f_i(p) \end{cases}$$

Fig. 5. Sizing function combinators

a type τ from the program e in a context Γ (written $\Gamma \vdash e \Rightarrow \tau$). Using checking enables bidirectional typing to support features for which determination is undecidable; using synthesis enables bidirectional typing to avoid the large annotation burden of explicitly typed languages [7]. This technique has been used for dependent types [5], subtyping [18], polymorphism [16], and object-oriented languages including C# [1]. The computation of bit-widths in SystemVerilog presents a particularly suitable application domain for bidirectional typing due to the natural subtyping relation on bit-widths. We introduce two complementary judgments:

- The *synthesis* judgment, written $e \Rightarrow n \dashv f$, states that expression e has a *self-determined width* n, where f maps each sub-expression of e to its *final width.*
- The *checking* judgment, written $e \Leftarrow n \dashv f$, states that expression e *may be resized* to bit-width n, where f maps each sub-expression of e to its *final width.*

In both judgments, the sizing function f serves as a record of the decisions made for all sub-expressions, including the root one. Formally, $f : \text{Path}(e) \to \mathbb{N}$ maps each valid path in expression e to the final width of the corresponding sub-expression. This path-based representation allows us to precisely track the final width of every sub-expression within an expression tree. This capability is essential for proving the equivalence between our type system and the current LRM specification.

To construct these functions during the inference process, we define the combinators shown in Fig. 5. These combinators construct sizing functions from a bit-width t (representing the final width of the current expression e) and one or more functions $\text{Path}(i) \to \mathbb{N}$ (representing the sizing history of child expressions). The result is a complete sizing function $\text{Path}(e) \to \mathbb{N}$ for the entire expression.

We present the rules by first explaining how expressions are resized in SystemVerilog. In the following section, we discuss how the self-determined width of an expression is computed.

3.1 Context-Dependent Resizing Rules

This section explains how expressions are resized when their context requires it. We focus on implicit resizing, not explicit resize casts. This operation preserves all information: expressions are never truncated, only extended when resized.

In SystemVerilog, resizing occurs at the deepest possible nodes in the AST, meaning resize operations propagate downward through the tree. We organize expressions into two categories based on their resizing behavior.

Atomically Resizable Expressions. They may be resized without affecting their internal operand widths. These include operands, comparisons, logical expressions, reductions, assignments, concatenations and replications. We denote the set of atomically resizable expressions as $\mathcal{R}$. When an atomically resizable expression is resized to its final width, only the expression's result is extended; its operands remain unchanged. The corresponding rule is $\textsf{Resize}{\Leftarrow}$, shown in Fig. 6. To resize expression e to the bit-width t, we verify that its self-determined width s is no larger than t. This rule parallels bidirectional typing in subtyping systems [8], where a bit-vector of width s acts as a subtype of a bit-vector of width t when $s \leqslant t$. The bit-width mapping f is updated to reflect the new width, but since resizing atomically resizable expressions leaves their operands unchanged, only the empty path requires updating.

Propagating Resize Operations. Certain expressions propagate their target width to some or all of their operands. These operations correspond to expressions with *context-determined* arguments. The formal judgments for the propagating statements are presented in Fig. 6. We distinguish four cases:

- binary operations propagate the target width to both operands, as shown by the $\textsf{BinOp}{\Leftarrow}$rule;
- unary operations propagate the target width to their single operand, as shown by the $\textsf{UnOp}{\Leftarrow}$rule;
- shift operations propagate the target width only to the left operand, while the right operand is fixed to its self-determined width, as shown by the $\textsf{Shift}{\Leftarrow}$rule; and
- conditional operations propagate the target width to both branches, while the condition is fixed to its self-determined width, as shown by the $\textsf{Cond}{\Leftarrow}$rule.

These four cases encompass all non-atomically resizable expressions in SystemVerilog's expression bit-width determination system.

3.2 Computing *Self-determined* Width

This subsection presents the rules for computing the self-determined width of expressions, which represents the natural bit-width an expression would have without any external contextual constraints. The complete set of synthesis rules is presented in Fig. 7.

$$\frac{e \Rightarrow s \dashv f \quad s \leqslant t \quad e \in \mathcal{R}}{e \Leftarrow t \dashv f[[] \mapsto t]}\ \textsf{Resize}\Leftarrow$$

$$\frac{e \Leftarrow t \dashv f}{\oplus e \Leftarrow t \dashv \text{Unary}(t, f)}\ \textsf{UnOp}\Leftarrow \qquad \frac{e \Rightarrow t_e \dashv f_e \quad a \Leftarrow t \dashv f_a \quad b \Leftarrow t \dashv f_b}{e?a\!:\!b \Leftarrow t \dashv \text{Ternary}(t, f_e, f_a, f_b)}\ \textsf{Cond}\Leftarrow$$

$$\frac{a \Leftarrow t \dashv f_a \quad b \Leftarrow t \dashv f_b}{a \oplus b \Leftarrow t \dashv \text{Binary}(t, f_a, f_b)}\ \textsf{BinOp}\Leftarrow \qquad \frac{a \Leftarrow t \dashv f_a \quad b \Rightarrow t_b \dashv f_b}{a \oplus b \Leftarrow t \dashv \text{Binary}(t, f_a, f_b)}\ \textsf{Shift}\Leftarrow$$

Fig. 6. *Resizing* rules

$$\frac{\Gamma(e) = s \quad e \in \mathcal{O}}{e \Rightarrow s \dashv \{[] \mapsto s\}}\ \textsf{Operand}\Rightarrow$$

$$\frac{e \Rightarrow t \dashv f}{\oplus e \Rightarrow t \dashv \text{Unary}(t, f)}\ \textsf{UnOp}\Rightarrow \qquad \frac{e \Rightarrow t \dashv f}{\oplus e \Rightarrow 1 \dashv \text{Unary}(1, f)}\ \textsf{Red}\Rightarrow$$

$$\frac{a \Rightarrow t \dashv f_a \quad b \Rightarrow t_b \dashv f_b}{a \oplus b \Rightarrow t \dashv \text{Binary}(t, f_a, f_b)}\ \textsf{Shift}\Rightarrow \qquad \frac{a \Rightarrow t_a \dashv f_a \quad b \Rightarrow t_b \dashv f_b}{a \oplus b \Rightarrow 1 \dashv \text{Binary}(1, f_a, f_b)}\ \textsf{Logic}\Rightarrow$$

$$\frac{a \Rightarrow t \dashv f_a \quad b \Leftarrow t \dashv f_b}{a \oplus b \Rightarrow t \dashv \text{Binary}(t, f_a, f_b)}\ \textsf{LBinOp}\Rightarrow \qquad \frac{a \Leftarrow t \dashv f_a \quad b \Rightarrow t \dashv f_b}{a \oplus b \Rightarrow t \dashv \text{Binary}(t, f_a, f_b)}\ \textsf{RBinOp}\Rightarrow$$

$$\frac{a \Rightarrow t \dashv f_a \quad b \Leftarrow t \dashv f_b}{a \oplus b \Rightarrow 1 \dashv \text{Binary}(1, f_a, f_b)}\ \textsf{LCmp}\Rightarrow \qquad \frac{a \Leftarrow t \dashv f_a \quad b \Rightarrow t \dashv f_b}{a \oplus b \Rightarrow 1 \dashv \text{Binary}(1, f_a, f_b)}\ \textsf{RCmp}\Rightarrow$$

$$\frac{\phi(l) = t \quad e \Leftarrow t \dashv f}{(l = e) \Rightarrow t \dashv \text{Unary}(t, f)}\ \textsf{LAssign}\Rightarrow \qquad \frac{\phi(l) = t \quad e \Rightarrow t_e \dashv f \quad t < t_e}{(l = e) \Rightarrow t \dashv \text{Unary}(t, f)}\ \textsf{RAssign}\Rightarrow$$

$$\frac{e \Rightarrow t_e \dashv f_e \quad a \Rightarrow t \dashv f_a \quad b \Leftarrow t \dashv f_b}{e?a\!:\!b \Rightarrow t \dashv \text{Ternary}(t, f_e, f_a, f_b)}\ \textsf{LCond}\Rightarrow$$

$$\frac{e \Rightarrow t_e \dashv f_e \quad a \Leftarrow t \dashv f_a \quad b \Rightarrow t \dashv f_b}{e?a\!:\!b \Rightarrow t \dashv \text{Ternary}(t, f_e, f_a, f_b)}\ \textsf{RCond}\Rightarrow$$

$$\frac{i \in \mathbb{N} \quad e \Rightarrow t_e \dashv f \quad t = i \times t_e}{\{i\ e\} \Rightarrow t \dashv \text{Unary}(t, f)}\ \textsf{Repl}\Rightarrow$$

$$\frac{e_1 \Rightarrow t_1 \dashv f_i \quad \ldots \quad e_k \Rightarrow t_k \dashv f_k \quad t = t_1 + \cdots + t_k}{\{e_1, \ldots, e_k\} \Rightarrow t \dashv \text{Nary}(t, f_1, \ldots, f_k)}\ \textsf{Concat}\Rightarrow$$

Fig. 7. *Self-determined width* rules

The most critical aspect of self-determined width computation involves operations that require multiple judgments. Binary operations, comparisons, assignments, and conditionals each require two rules because one of their operands may be resized to match the other's self-determined width.

Consider binary operations, which must ensure both operands have the same width for evaluation. Since operands can only grow, the result width must be the maximum of both operand bit-width. When the left-hand side is larger, we apply the LBinOp⇒rule, which synthesizes the self-determined width of the left operand t and requires that the right operand may be resized to t. Conversely, when the right-hand side is larger, we apply the RBinOp⇒rule, which synthesizes the self-determined width of the right operand and requires that the left operand may be resized accordingly. The same pattern applies to comparisons and conditionals, though with different result widths. Comparisons always produce 1-bit results despite requiring operand width matching, while conditionals must ensure both branches have compatible widths.

Assignment operations demonstrate additional complexity. The RAssign⇒rule applies when the right-hand side is strictly larger than the left-hand side of the assignment. In this case, the upper bits of the right-hand side are discarded to match the left-hand side's smaller width. The alternative rule, LAssign⇒, applies when the right-hand side may be resized to the left-hand side width. In both cases, the self-determined width of an assignment is determined by the left-hand side width.

Operations with asymmetric semantics, such as shifts and logical operations, have simpler synthesis rules. Shift operations inherit their width from the left operand only (Shift⇒), while logical operations always produce 1-bit results regardless of operand widths (Logic⇒). Structural operations such as replication and concatenation have straightforward width computations: replication multiplies the operand size by the replication count (Repl⇒), while concatenation sums all operand widths (Concat⇒).

3.3 Soundness and Completeness Properties

Our system satisfies several fundamental properties that establish its soundness and completeness. All properties presented here have been mechanically verified in the Rocq theorem prover [20] with the functional extensionality axiom.

Totality. Every SystemVerilog expression can be used in both synthesis and checking modes. This property ensures our type system is complete: it can assign bit-widths to any syntactically valid SystemVerilog expression.

Lemma 1. *For every expression e, (1) there exist t and f such that $e \Rightarrow t \dashv f$, and (2) there exist t and f such that $e \Leftarrow t \dashv f$.*

Determinism. The type system produces unique results for each expression. That is, the synthesis mode uniquely determines both the self-determined width and the complete sizing function, and the checking mode, given a target width, uniquely determines how sub-expressions are sized.

Lemma 2. *For any expression e: (1) if* $e \Rightarrow t_1 \dashv f_1$ *and* $e \Rightarrow t_2 \dashv f_2$*, then* $t_1 = t_2$ *and* $f_1 = f_2$*, and (2) if* $e \Leftarrow t \dashv f_1$ *and* $e \Leftarrow t \dashv f_2$*, then* $f_1 = f_2$*.*

Synthesis-Checking Correspondence. An expression may be resized to s if and only if s is at least as large as its self-determined width. This captures the fundamental principle that expressions in SystemVerilog can only grow, never shrink.

Lemma 3. *If* $e \Rightarrow t \dashv f$*, then for any width s, we have* $t \leq s$ *if and only if* $\exists g.\, e \Leftarrow s \dashv g$*.*

Minimality. The following theorem, which follows from Lemma 1and 3, states that the self-determined width represents the minimal width at which an expression may be resized without losing information.

Theorem 1. *For any expression e: if s is the minimal width such that there exists g where* $e \Leftarrow s \dashv g$*, then there exists f such that* $e \Rightarrow s \dashv f$*.*

4 Formal Verification of LRM Compliance

Establishing backward compatibility with the current LRM specification is essential for the adoption of our formal framework. To achieve this, we prove that our bidirectional type system is equivalent to the algorithmic description scattered throughout the LRM. To demonstrate this correspondence, we prove that for any expression e, the function f produced by our synthesis judgment $e \Rightarrow t \dashv f$ coincides with the prop_e function derived from the LRM specification. The complete mechanized proofs can be interactively browsed online [6].

Sub-expression Correspondence. The following lemmas establish that sizing functions compose properly: the sizing function for a sub-expression can be extracted from the parent's sizing function by shifting paths appropriately. This compositional property is essential for relating our type system to the LRM's recursive structure.

Lemma 4. *If* $e \Rightarrow t \dashv f$ *and* $e|_p = e'$ *for some path p, then there exist* t' *and* f' *such that either* $e' \Rightarrow t' \dashv f'$ *or* $e' \Leftarrow t' \dashv f'$*, and for all paths k:* $f(p \cdot k) = f'(k)$*.*

Lemma 5. *If* $e \Leftarrow t \dashv f$ *and* $e|_p = e'$ *for some path p, then there exist* t' *and* f' *such that either* $e' \Rightarrow t' \dashv f'$ *or* $e' \Leftarrow t' \dashv f'$*, and for all paths k:* $f(p \cdot k) = f'(k)$*.*

The following lemma ensures that our synthesis judgment correctly computes what the LRM defines as the *self-determined width*, establishing the foundation for our equivalence proof.

Lemma 6. *For every expression e, there exists a sizing function f such that* $e \Rightarrow \mathsf{det}(e) \dashv f$*.*

From Specification to a Rule System. We first prove that the function satisfying the LRM's propagation constraints correspond to a valid derivation:

Lemma 7. *For any expression* e *and function* $f : \mathrm{Path}(e) \to \mathbb{N}$, *if* f *satisfies all LRM propagate constraints, then* $e \Rightarrow \mathsf{det}(e) \dashv f$.

From Rule System to Specification. The converse direction establishes that our type system generates the function that satisfy all LRM constraints:

Lemma 8. *For any expression* e, *sizing function* f, *and width* t, *if* $e \Rightarrow t \dashv f$ *holds, then* f *satisfies all LRM propagate constraints.*

Main Equivalence Result. Combining Lemma 7 and Lemma 8, we obtain our main equivalence result: that our bidirectional type system provides a precise mathematical characterization of the LRM's bit-width determination algorithm.

Theorem 2. *For any expression* e *and function* $f : \mathrm{Path}(e) \to \mathbb{N}$, *the following two statements are equivalent: (1)* f *satisfies all LRM propagation constraints for expression* e, *and (2)* $e \Rightarrow \mathsf{det}(e) \dashv f$.

5 Implementation

Building upon our bidirectional type system, we derive a concrete algorithm for computing expression bit-widths that closely follows the LRM's two-phase approach. Algorithm 1 computes the *self-determined width* bottom-up and Algorithm 2 propagates width information top-down to determine the *final width* of each sub-expression. Computing the width of a top-level expression e is done with the expression PROPAGATE(e, DETERMINE(e)).

Our implementation has been mechanically verified in Rocq and can be extracted from our formalization to produce executable code. The complete source code for our formalization and extracted algorithms is publicly available [6].

In a sense, we have almost come full circle: DETERMINE and PROPAGATE closely resemble det and prop from our original formalisation of the LRM (Sect. 2). But the type system of Sect. 3 remains a valuable intermediate step for proving the LRM and this implementation (as well as other possible future implementations) equivalent. This is partly because the type system is compositional—it does not need to carry around the top-level expression e like prop does—and partly because typing rules are very natural to work with in Rocq.

Correctness. The following theorem establishes that our two-phase algorithm correctly implements the synthesis judgement at the root expression with all sub-expressions properly typed according to our formal system.

Theorem 3 (Algorithm Correctness). *For any expression* e, *the sizing function* f *resulting from the call to* PROPAGATE(e, DETERMINE(e)) *is such that* $e \Rightarrow \mathsf{det}(e) \dashv f$.

Algorithm 1: Determine

Input: A SystemVerilog expression expr
Output: The self-determined width of expr

```
switch expr do
    when expr is an operand do
        return Γ(expr)
    when expr is lhs ⊕ rhs do                 // ⊕ can be +, *, &, |, ...
        lhs_w ← DETERMINE(lhs)
        rhs_w ← DETERMINE(rhs)
        return max(lhs_w, rhs_w)
    when expr is ⊕arg do                      // ⊕ can be +, -, ~, ++, --
        arg_w ← DETERMINE(arg)
        return arg_w
    when expr is lhs ⊕ rhs do                 // ⊕ can be ==, !=, >, >=, ...
        return 1
    when expr is lhs ⊕ rhs do                 // ⊕ can be &&, ||, ->, <->
        return 1
    when expr is ⊕arg do                      // ⊕ can be !, &, |, ^, ...
        return 1
    when expr is lhs ⊕ rhs do                 // ⊕ can be >>, <<, **, ...
        lhs_w ← DETERMINE(lhs)
        return lhs_w
    when expr is lval = rhs do
        lval_w ← φ(lval)
        return lval_w
    when expr is cond ? lhs : rhs do
        lhs_w ← DETERMINE(lhs)
        rhs_w ← DETERMINE(rhs)
        return max(lhs_w, rhs_w)
    when expr is {expr_1, ... , expr_N} do
        for i ∈ {1, ..., N} do
            width_i ← DETERMINE(expr_i)
        return Σ_{i=0}^{N} width_i
    when expr is {n arg} do
        arg_w ← DETERMINE(arg)
        return n × arg_w
```

Algorithm 2: Propagate

Input: A SystemVerilog expression expr, A targetWidth to resize expr to.
Result: All sub-expressions of expr are annotated with their final width

```
switch expr do
    when expr is an operand do
        Annotate expr with targetWidth
    when expr is lhs ⊕ rhs do                        // ⊕ can be +, *, &, |, ...
        PROPAGATE(lhs, targetWidth)
        PROPAGATE(rhs, targetWidth)
        Annotate expr with targetWidth
    when expr is ⊕arg do                             // ⊕ can be +, -, ~, ++, --
        PROPAGATE(arg, targetWidth)
        Annotate expr with targetWidth
    when expr is lhs ⊕ rhs do                        // ⊕ can be ==, !=, >, >=, ...
        arg_w ← max (DETERMINE(lhs), DETERMINE(rhs))
        PROPAGATE(lhs, arg_w)
        PROPAGATE(rhs, arg_w)
        Annotate expr with targetWidth
    when expr is lhs ⊕ rhs do                        // ⊕ can be &&, ||, ->, <->
        PROPAGATE(lhs, DETERMINE(lhs))
        PROPAGATE(rhs, DETERMINE(rhs))
        Annotate expr with targetWidth
    when expr is ⊕arg do                             // ⊕ can be !, &, |, ^, ...
        PROPAGATE(arg, DETERMINE(arg))
        Annotate expr with targetWidth
    when expr is lhs ⊕ rhs do                        // ⊕ can be >>, <<, **, ...
        PROPAGATE(lhs, targetWidth)
        PROPAGATE(rhs, DETERMINE(rhs))
        Annotate expr with targetWidth
    when expr is lval = rhs do
        PROPAGATE(rhs, max (ϕ(lval), DETERMINE(rhs)))
        Annotate expr with targetWidth
    when expr is cond ? lhs : rhs do
        PROPAGATE(cond, DETERMINE(cond))
        PROPAGATE(lhs, targetWidth)
        PROPAGATE(rhs, targetWidth)
        Annotate expr with targetWidth
    when expr is {expr_1, ... , expr_N} do
        for i ∈ {1, ..., N} do
            PROPAGATE(expr_i, DETERMINE(expr_i))
        Annotate expr with targetWidth
    when expr is {n arg} do
        PROPAGATE(arg, DETERMINE(arg))
        Annotate expr with targetWidth
```

Complexity Analysis. The algorithm achieves linear time complexity in the size of the expression tree when DETERMINE calls are memoized. Without memoization, repeated calls to DETERMINE during PROPAGATE lead to quadratic behavior, for instance, on deeply nested concatenations where each level requires recomputing widths of all inner expressions. With memoization, each expression node is visited exactly twice: once during the bottom-up DETERMINE phase and once during the top-down PROPAGATE phase.

6 Conclusion and Future Directions

We have presented a formal framework for SystemVerilog expression bit-width determination based on bidirectional typing. We have demonstrated that the informal prose specifications scattered throughout 25 pages of the 1,354-page LRM can be captured by a clean mathematical framework, while maintaining full backward compatibility with the IEEE 1800-2023 standard. Our bidirectional type system naturally expresses the context-dependent nature of SystemVerilog expression sizing through the interplay of synthesis and checking judgments. Our mechanized proofs in Rocq establish both the internal consistency of our system and its equivalence to the LRM specification.

Based on this formal framework, we have developed some proposed text [6] that clarifies how expression bit-widths are determined, while preserving backward compatibility. We intend to submit our proposal for consideration by the IEEE SystemVerilog Working Group when it starts up again.

We hope that our system will be integrated into existing formally verified Verilog-consuming tools, such as the Vera verified equivalence checker [17] and the Lustig verified synthesis tool [12]. Both Vera and Lustig currently assume that their inputs are already 'elaborated', i.e. all intermediate expressions are explicitly annotated with their bitwidths. By enabling those tools to drop that assumption, our work could enhance the formal guarantees they provide.

Looking forward, we intend to expand the coverage and flexibility of this framework. While the current system requires concrete variable widths, we aim to introduce *parametric typing* to handle symbolic widths (e.g., determining a result width as $\max(4, N)$ with a size parameter N). Additionally, we plan to extend support to the full spectrum of SystemVerilog types, specifically incorporating floating-point and integer variables, as well as handling signedness.

Finally, we are exploring an alternative typing system that formalizes the notion of "context" informally introduced in Sect. 2. A system in which AST nodes are first mapped to contexts, and then contexts are subsequently assigned bit-widths, may offer a more generic and intuitive formulation. This explicit definition of context could better align the formal semantics with the conceptual model used by hardware engineers.

Ultimately, by bridging the gap between informal language specifications and formal methods, we hope to enable more reliable hardware design tools and more trustworthy digital systems.

Acknowledgments. We're grateful to George A. Constantinides and Alastair F. Donaldson for their support. We also acknowledge financial support from the UK EPSRC via a PhD scholarship.

Data Availibility Statement. Our online appendix [6] contains all implementations and Rocq proofs. It also presents our draft proposal to improve the treatment of bit-width determination in the IEEE 1800-2023 standard.

Disclosure of Interests. The authors have no competing interests to declare that are relevant to the content of this article.

References

1. Bierman, G.M., Meijer, E., Torgersen, M.: Lost in translation: formalizing proposed extensions to C#. In: Gabriel, R.P., Bacon, D.F., Lopes, C.V., Steele Jr., G.L. (eds.) Proceedings of the 22nd Annual ACM SIGPLAN Conference on Object-Oriented Programming, Systems, Languages, and Applications, OOPSLA 2007, 21–25 October 2007, Montreal, Quebec, Canada, pp. 479–498. ACM (2007). https://doi.org/10.1145/1297027.1297063
2. Chen, Q., et al.: The essence of verilog: a tractable and tested operational semantics for verilog. Proc. ACM Program. Lang. **7**(OOPSLA2) (2023). https://doi.org/10.1145/3622805
3. ChipsAlliance: SV-tests: test suite designed to check compliance with the SystemVerilog standard. GitHub repository. https://github.com/chipsalliance/sv-tests
4. Choi, J., Kim, J., Kang, J.: Revamping Verilog semantics for foundational verification. Proc. ACM Program. Lang. **9**(OOPSLA2) (2025). https://doi.org/10.1145/3763084
5. Coquand, T.: An algorithm for type-checking dependent types. Sci. Comput. Program. **26**(1), 167–177 (1996). https://doi.org/10.1016/0167-6423(95)00021-6
6. Desfrene, G., Corradi, Q., Pardalos, M., Wickerson, J.: Rocq formalization of SystemVerilog expression bit-width determination (2026)
7. Dunfield, J., Krishnaswami, N.: Bidirectional typing. ACM Comput. Surv. **54**(5) (2021). https://doi.org/10.1145/3450952
8. Dunfield, J., Krishnaswami, N.R.: Complete and easy bidirectional typechecking for higher-rank polymorphism. SIGPLAN Not. **48**(9), 429–442 (2013). https://doi.org/10.1145/2544174.2500582
9. Flake, P., Moorby, P., Golson, S., Salz, A., Davidmann, S.: Verilog HDL and its ancestors and descendants. Proc. ACM Program. Lang. **4**(HOPL) (2020). https://doi.org/10.1145/3386337
10. Gillenwater, J., et al.: Synthesizable high level hardware descriptions: using statically typed two-level languages to guarantee verilog synthesizability. In: Proceedings of the 2008 ACM SIGPLAN Symposium on Partial Evaluation and Semantics-Based Program Manipulation, PEPM 2008, pp. 41–50. Association for Computing Machinery, New York (2008). https://doi.org/10.1145/1328408.1328416
11. IEEE: Standard for SystemVerilog–Unified Hardware Design, Specification, and Verification Language. IEEE Std 1800-2023 (2024). https://doi.org/10.1109/IEEESTD.2024.10458102

12. Lööw, A.: Lutsig: a verified Verilog compiler for verified circuit development. In: Proceedings of the 10th ACM SIGPLAN International Conference on Certified Programs and Proofs, CPP 2021, pp. 46–60. Association for Computing Machinery, New York (2021). https://doi.org/10.1145/3437992.3439916
13. Lööw, A.: The simulation semantics of synthesisable Verilog. Proc. ACM Program. Lang. **9**(OOPSLA1) (2025). https://doi.org/10.1145/3720484
14. Meredith, P., Katelman, M., Meseguer, J., Rosu, G.: A formal executable semantics of Verilog. In: Eighth ACM/IEEE International Conference on Formal Methods and Models for Codesign (MEMOCODE 2010), pp. 179–188 (2010). https://doi.org/10.1109/MEMCOD.2010.5558634
15. nebuchadnezzar_II: Lint tool is throwing an error about bit width when adding two 10-bit unsigned numbers and assigning to a 11-bit net. Electrical Engineering Stack Exchange (2023). https://electronics.stackexchange.com/q/665616
16. Odersky, M., Zenger, C., Zenger, M.: Colored local type inference. In: Hankin, C., Schmidt, D. (eds.) Conference Record of POPL 2001: The 28th ACM SIGPLAN-SIGACT Symposium on Principles of Programming Languages, London, UK, 17–19 January 2001, pp. 41–53. ACM (2001). https://doi.org/10.1145/360204.360207
17. Pardalos, M., Pozzi, L., Wickerson, J.: Towards mechanized verification of Verilog equivalence checking. In: Workshop on Languages, Tools, and Techniques for Accelerator Design (LATTE) (2025). https://capra.cs.cornell.edu/latte25/paper/9.pdf
18. Pierce, B.C., Turner, D.N.: Local type inference. ACM Trans. Program. Lang. Syst. **22**(1), 1–44 (2000). https://doi.org/10.1145/345099.345100
19. r/Verilog: Tutorial is wrong about truncation rules? (2026). https://www.reddit.com/r/Verilog/comments/1t0nb27/tutorial_is_wrong_about_truncation_rules/
20. The Rocq Development Team: The Rocq Prover (2025). https://rocq-prover.org/, version 9.0.0
21. Williams, S.: Icarus Verilog quirks: unsized expressions as arguments to concatenation (2024). https://steveicarus.github.io/iverilog/usage/icarus_verilog_quirks.html#unsized-expressions-as-arguments-to-concatenation

Security, Privacy and Hyperproperties

Differentially Private Runtime Monitoring

Bernd Finkbeiner and Frederik Scheerer(✉)

CISPA Helmholtz Center for Information Security, Saarbrücken, Germany
{finkbeiner,frederik.scheerer}@cispa.de

Abstract. Modern stream-based monitors collect detailed statistics of the runtime behavior of the system under observation. If the system runs in a privacy-sensitive context, this poses the risk of disclosing sensitive information. Differential privacy is the state-of-the-art approach for protecting sensitive information, however, integrating it into runtime monitoring is challenging: temporal operators can cause individual input values to influence multiple outputs over time, leading to repeated disclosure of private information. We propose an approach that automatically enforces differential privacy in stream-based monitoring specifications by analyzing temporal dependencies and injecting carefully calibrated noise into the specification. To preserve the utility of the outputs, we identify strategically chosen positions in the specification for noise injection and leverage tree-based mechanisms to mitigate the accuracy loss caused by noise injected into aggregation operators. We demonstrate the practicality and effectiveness of our approach in a case study on monitoring public transportation usage.

Keywords: Runtime Verification · Stream-Based Monitoring · Privacy

1 Introduction

Runtime monitoring is a powerful technique for ensuring a system's correctness during operation, especially in complex, real-world applications where static verification is difficult to obtain. In many cases, a binary yes/no verdict is insufficient, and instead, stream-based languages output values that summarize and aggregate the system's current state over time. At the same time, runtime monitoring is increasingly deployed in privacy-sensitive domains, where richer monitor outputs increase the risk of revealing private information.

For example, consider a car-rental company that continuously monitors the distance driven by each vehicle in order to schedule maintenance, detect abnormal wear, or ensure contractual conditions. Even if the monitor reports only aggregated values, such as average daily distance driven, these outputs may still reveal sensitive information about the renter's behavior, including typical usage patterns and inferred routines when observed over time. Similar concerns arise when monitoring commercial vehicle fleets, where runtime monitors are used to

E. Darulova et al. (Eds.): CAV 2026, LNCS 16682, pp. 449–472, 2026.
https://doi.org/10.1007/978-3-032-32519-8_23

assess efficiency, safety, or regulatory compliance but inadvertently expose routes or operating schedules of drivers. While runtime monitoring is essential for ensuring safety, performance, and compliance in such systems, it is crucial to ensure that the monitoring process does not become a source of privacy violations.

Differential privacy (DP) [20] is widely regarded as the gold standard for providing formal privacy guarantees. Informally, it ensures that the presence or absence of a single individual in the dataset has minimal impact on the output of a query. This is typically achieved by adding carefully calibrated noise to the output and thereby producing a mechanism with provable privacy guarantees.

Integrating differential privacy into stream-based monitoring, however, introduces unique challenges due to the temporal nature of streams and the temporal operators describing them. In contrast to static queries, monitors repeatedly release information over time, often derived from overlapping portions of the input data. Releasing information derived from a single data point multiple times increases the overall privacy loss, as each release leaks additional information. With temporal operators such as sliding-window aggregations, we observe exactly this behavior, and to reason about privacy in this setting, it is necessary to understand how individual inputs propagate through the temporal operators.

This observation introduces two key challenges. First, we must be able to precisely characterize and compute the impact of individual inputs on the outputs, accounting for the effects of asynchronous streams and temporal operators, such as sliding-window aggregations. Second, beyond providing formal privacy guarantees, we must ensure that the resulting private monitors remain accurate. In particular, temporal operators amplify the influence of individual inputs, and the required amount of noise may degrade the quality of monitoring outputs.

In this paper, we present a runtime monitoring framework that enables users without privacy expertise to deploy monitors that prevent the leakage of sensitive information. Our framework integrates differential privacy by analyzing the specification and automatically injecting appropriate amounts of noise. It strategically selects positions in the specification that are beneficial to the accuracy of the output, and leverages tree-based constructs to further improve monitoring accuracy. We demonstrate our approach using the stream-based specification language RTLola [5], which has already been applied in several real-world, privacy-sensitive areas [7,9,24,28]. In a case study on public transportation usage, we show that our approach enables private monitoring with high accuracy.

The remainder of this paper is organized as follows. Section 2 gives an intuition of our approach using a motivating example, and Sect. 3 introduces our formalization of differential privacy for stream-based monitors. In Sect. 4, we detail the sensitivity calculations for stream-based specifications, while Sect. 5 discusses our strategies for improving the accuracy of the private monitors. Finally, Sect. 6 explores extensions of our approach to stricter privacy guarantees, and Sect. 7 reports on experimental results.

1.1 Related Work

Closest to our work is the approach of Henzinger et al. [33], which studies private runtime monitoring based on private function evaluation while maintaining an internal state. Further, prior work has explored alternative notions of privacy in LTL monitoring [1,2]. However, these approaches do not rely on differential privacy and do not support the rich output provided by stream-based languages.

We are the first to integrate DP directly into runtime verification frameworks. Previous work has focused on enforcing DP on database-style queries, especially SQL-like languages [10,34,38–41,43]. Some related work also considers queries on data streams [37]. All these approaches, however, are designed for database-style queries and emphasize operators such as joins, rather than the temporal operators used in runtime verification.

An algorithmic idea adopted in our work is tree-based mechanisms for continual queries under DP. Dwork et al. [21] introduced tree-based mechanisms for continual counting queries and Chan et al. [14] independently proposed a similar approach for infinite streams. Tree-based mechanisms were later extended to other aggregations such as sums [13,42,44,48]. In addition to tree-based approaches, matrix-based mechanisms have been proposed for streaming data [19,31,32,37], offering alternative trade-offs between accuracy and efficiency. Some approaches also enforce DP for sliding window aggregations [11,15,47], a temporal operator commonly used in stream-based monitoring. Most streaming DP works assume event-level privacy and independent data; however, some approaches support user-level privacy [12,16,18,26] or correlated data [23,46].

We demonstrate our approach using the stream-based specification language RTLola [5], an extension of Lola [17] that incorporates asynchronous streams and real-time functionality. RTLola has been applied in multiple domains, including several privacy-sensitive domains such as monitoring sensor data from private vehicles [9], analyzing network traffic [24], monitoring automatic decision and prediction systems [7], and processing medical health data [28]. Although our approach is presented in the context of RTLola, the underlying ideas extend to other stream-based specification languages such as TeSSLa [35] and Striver [30].

2 Motivating Example

We begin with a motivating example that illustrates the key ideas of our approach. The methods will be detailed in the following sections. We work in the setting of stream-based monitoring, where specifications define sets of streams, representing infinite sequences of values. Input streams represent incoming data from the monitored system, while output streams are defined through stream equations and compute new streams by transforming and aggregating the inputs.

Consider Fig. 1, which shows an example for the stream-based specification language RTLola [5]. It models a monitoring scenario in which user feedback is continually collected and evaluated over time. Each user's feedback consists of new values added to the two input streams: a `score`, ranging from 1 (best) to 6

```
input score : Int64 // ∈ {1,2,3,4,5,6}
input conf : Int64 // ∈ {−1,0,1}
output adj := (6-score)*3 + conf + 1
output davg @1d :=
    adj.aggregate(over: 3d, using: avg).defaults(to: 0.0)
output low @1d := min(low.offset(by: -1).defaults(to: 15.0), davg)
output high @1d := max(high.offset(by: -1).defaults(to: 0.0), davg)
#[public]
output range @1d := (low, high)
```

Fig. 1. An example RTLola specification calculating statistics of user feedback.

(worst), and a `conf` value indicating positive (1), neutral (0), or negative (-1) confidence. The specification combines these inputs into a single adjusted rating between 0 and 17, and emits the result as a new value of the output stream `adj`. Using a sliding window aggregation, the stream `davg` computes the average rating over the last three days. Finally, the streams `low` and `high` track the minimum and maximum daily averages observed so far. The `range` stream, consisting of both statistics, is marked as public using RTLola's annotation mechanism [6], indicating that its values are output by the monitor to the public.

Individual user feedback is privacy-sensitive. While we assume the monitor itself is trusted, its public outputs go into an untrusted world. Therefore, the monitor must ensure that no private information is leaked by observing the publicly emitted values of `range` over time. To incorporate differential privacy into a stream-based specification, we must understand how a change to a single input influences observable outputs. Offset accesses propagate information across time, as seen in the recursive definitions of `low` and `high`, where a single rating influences arbitrarily many future outputs. Similarly, in sliding-window aggregations, each input contributes to multiple overlapping windows, so a single change affects multiple results.

Dependencies are made explicit in the *dependency graph* [5] of the specification. Each stream in the specification corresponds to a node, and stream accesses are represented by directed edges in the graph, annotated with the access kind. The dependency graph for the example is shown in Fig. 2. In the graph, the private input streams are marked with a red outline, but streams that (indirectly) depend on private inputs also contain private information. The extent to which private information influences a stream is quantified by the *sensitivity*. Intuitively, the sensitivity of a stream bounds how much its values can change when a single user's feedback is modified. In a temporal setting, this captures both how strongly values change and how often this change reappears over time. Sensitivity

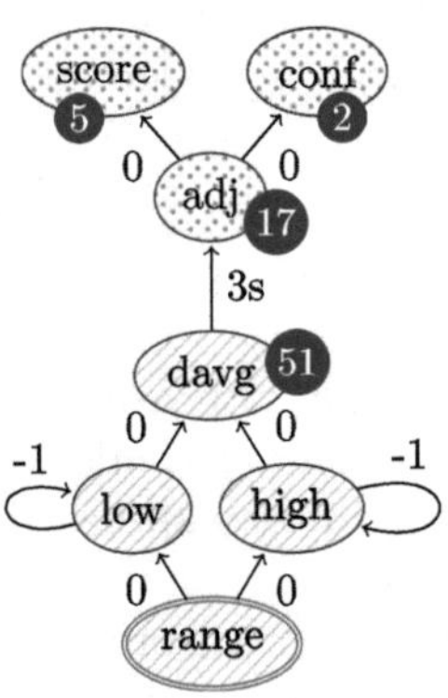

Fig. 2. The dependency graph for the specification in Fig. 1.

propagates through the dependency graph, accumulating at arithmetic operations and amplifying across temporal operators.

For instance, the sensitivity of the `score` stream is 5, reflecting its input range. The `adj` stream combines multiple pieces of private information and therefore has higher sensitivity. The sliding window further amplifies this: A single value contributes to three overlapping windows, resulting in a sensitivity of 51 for `davg`. This sensitivity information allows us to track how private information flows through the specification. Based on this information, we select a subset of nodes at which the monitor adds noise to each value. Adding noise to a node renders the corresponding information in the stream privacy-preserving, which in turn makes all downstream computations safe to publish. This yields a placement problem: where should noise be added so that all public outputs are protected, while keeping the loss of accuracy as small as possible?

In the example, we select the `davg` stream and add noise calibrated to its sensitivity. This choice ensures that all values flowing into the recursive definitions of `low` and `high` are already privacy-preserving. Applying noise earlier, for example at the inputs, would reduce accuracy because each aggregated value would be noisy by itself. After the aggregation, a single rating can be hidden among multiple others, making its individual contribution smaller and requiring less perturbation relative to the result. Now, as this node is privacy-preserving, it and all downstream nodes are marked as green. As all public outputs are among these green nodes, the overall specification satisfies the desired privacy guarantees.

In this example, the sliding window amplifies the sensitivity linearly with the window size. Later in the paper, we show how tree-based aggregation methods can substantially increase accuracy for longer windows.

3 Differential Privacy of Stream-Based Monitors

This section formalizes differential privacy for stream-based runtime monitoring. We first summarize the standard definitions and mechanisms of differential privacy, stated with respect to a general adjacency relation. We then present the evaluation model used to represent monitor executions and define an event-level adjacency notion capturing the privacy requirements for stream-based monitors.

3.1 Differential Privacy Background

Differential privacy [20] is the de facto standard for ensuring privacy, grounded in a rigorous mathematical definition. Originally introduced in the context of databases, it provides a strong guarantee: the presence or absence of any individual in the dataset has only a minimal impact on the output of a query on the database. Intuitively, a randomized mechanism is differentially private if an observer cannot distinguish whether a particular record was part of the database based on the output of the mechanism.

Definition 1 (Differential Privacy [22]**).** *Let $\mathcal{D}$ be a domain and $\sim\, \subseteq \mathcal{D} \times \mathcal{D}$ a symmetric adjacency relation. A randomized mechanism $\mathcal{K} : \mathcal{D} \to \mathcal{R}$ is ε-differentially private w.r.t. $\sim$ if for all $D, D' \in \mathcal{D}$ with $D \sim D'$ and for all $S \subseteq \mathcal{R}$,*

$$\Pr[\mathcal{K}(D) \in S] \leq \exp(\varepsilon) \cdot \Pr[\mathcal{K}(D') \in S],$$

where the probability is over the randomness of $\mathcal{K}$.

We state the definition in its general form with respect to an arbitrary adjacency relation. The *adjacency relation* $\sim$ specifies which pairs of inputs should be considered indistinguishable by an observer. In the classical database setting, the relation captures neighboring databases that differ by a single row. The Probability $\Pr[\mathcal{K}(D) \in S]$ captures the chance that the mechanism $\mathcal{K}$ produces an output in the set S. Differential privacy bounds how much this probability can change between adjacent inputs. The *privacy parameter* ε quantifies the strength of the privacy guarantee. Smaller values of ε correspond to stronger privacy. Choosing ε involves balancing the level of privacy with the output utility, depending on the privacy requirements of the data and the intended application.

To design differentially private mechanisms, we must understand how much the output of a query can change between two adjacent inputs. This quantity is called the sensitivity of the query.

Definition 2 (Sensitivity [22]**).** *For $f : \mathcal{D} \to \mathbf{R}^d$, the L_1 sensitivity of f w.r.t. $\sim$ is $\Delta_{\sim} f = \max_{\substack{D,D' \\ D \sim D'}} \|f(D) - f(D')\|_1$.*

Intuitively, the sensitivity measures the maximum possible change in the output between two adjacent inputs. For instance, a query that counts the number of rows satisfying a certain predicate has sensitivity 1, since modifying or removing a single row can change the count by at most one. In contrast, a query that sums numerical values can have a much larger sensitivity, depending on the possible ranges of those values.

Once the sensitivity of a query is known, differential privacy can be achieved by adding Laplace noise calibrated to that sensitivity.

Theorem 1 (Laplace Mechanism [22]**).** *For $f : \mathcal{D} \to \mathbf{R}^d$, the mechanism $\mathcal{K}(\mathcal{D}) = f(\mathcal{D}) + \eta$ that adds independently generated noise η with distribution $\eta_i \sim Lap(\Delta_{\sim} f/\varepsilon)$ to each of the d output terms satisfies ε-differential privacy w.r.t. $\sim$.*

While the Laplace mechanism establishes privacy guarantees for individual mechanisms, composition theorems describe how these guarantees change when multiple mechanisms are combined. Under *sequential composition* [22], publishing the outputs of multiple mechanisms results in an additive privacy loss: combining mechanisms with privacy parameters ε_1 and ε_2 gives an overall privacy guarantee of $(\varepsilon_1 + \varepsilon_2)$ with respect to the same adjacency relation. As a result, repeatedly releasing noisy versions of the same query gradually weakens privacy, so individual mechanisms must use smaller privacy parameters to stay within a fixed overall budget. *Post-processing* [22] ensures that any transformation applied to the output of a differentially private mechanism preserves its privacy guarantee. Once a mechanism has produced a privacy-preserving output, it can be safely transformed without adding any extra privacy loss. Together, these properties let us reason modularly about privacy in stream-based monitors.

3.2 Evaluation Models for Runtime Monitoring

To formalize differential privacy in the context of runtime monitoring, we need a model allowing us to compare different monitor executions. For this purpose, we introduce the notion of an evaluation model. Let Time $= \mathbb{N}$ be the set of discrete timestamps, $\mathbb{V}_\perp = \mathbb{R} \cup \{\perp\}$ the set of optional stream values, and $\mathbb{R}^+$ the set of non-negative real numbers.

Definition 3 (Evaluation Model [5,7]). *An* evaluation model $\omega \in \mathbb{W}$ *consists of timed data streams over a set of input stream references* $\mathtt{ID}^\uparrow$ *and output stream references* $\mathtt{ID}^\downarrow$*. It is represented as the combination of a stream map and a timing map:*

$$\begin{aligned} \mathit{Stream} &:= \mathit{Time} \rightarrow \mathbb{V}_\perp \\ \mathit{StreamMap} &:= \left(\mathtt{ID}^\uparrow \uplus \mathtt{ID}^\downarrow\right) \rightarrow \mathit{Stream} \\ \mathit{TimeMap} &:= \mathit{Time} \rightarrow \mathbb{R}^+ \\ \mathbb{W} &:= \mathit{StreamMap} \times \mathit{TimeMap}. \end{aligned}$$

Intuitively, an evaluation model captures all values produced by the monitor during one execution. The stream mapping assigns each input and output stream reference to a stream of values indexed by discrete timestamps. Because the monitor operates asynchronously, a stream may have no new value at a given timestamp. This absence is represented by the symbol $\perp$. The time mapping associates each discrete timestamp with its corresponding real-time timestamp.

For convenience, given an evaluation model $\omega = (\mathit{streams}, \mathit{times})$, we define $\omega(t) := \mathit{times}(t)$ to denote the real-time timestamp of $t \in$ Time, and $\omega(s) := \mathit{streams}(s)$ to denote the stream assigned to reference $s \in \mathtt{ID}^\uparrow \uplus \mathtt{ID}^\downarrow$.

3.3 Adjacency of Evaluation Models

To reason about differential privacy in the context of monitor executions, we define a suitable adjacency relation between evaluation models. Different choices of adjacency correspond to different privacy guarantees and reflect what aspect of the monitored behavior is intended to be protected. In this work, we adopt an *event-level* [21] notion of privacy: Two evaluation models are adjacent if their input streams differ by exactly one event occurring at a single timestamp. Moreover, we assume that only the content of an event is sensitive, not its timing. Consequently, adjacent evaluation models share the same timing map, ensuring that temporal information remains unchanged:

Definition 4 (Event-Level Adjacency). *Two evaluation models* $\omega, \omega' \in \mathbb{W}$ *are considered* event-level adjacent, *if*

1. *For all* $t \in Time$, *it holds that* $\omega(t) = \omega'(t)$,
2. *For all* $t \in Time$ *and* $i \in \mathtt{ID}^{\uparrow}$, *it holds that* $\omega(i)(t) = \bot \Leftrightarrow \omega'(i)(t) = \bot$,
3. *There exists at most one* $t \in Time$, *such that* $\exists i \in \mathtt{ID}^{\uparrow}.\omega(i)(t) \neq \omega'(i)(t)$.

*Further, we consider them s-*distant *if* $\forall t \in Time. \forall i \in \mathtt{ID}^{\uparrow}. |\omega(i)(t) - \omega'(i)(t)| \leq s$.

The notion of s-distance restricts how much two adjacent evaluation models may differ in their input values: each input can change by at most s. This assumption reflects many realistic scenarios, where input domains are naturally bounded, for instance, sensor readings limited by the hardware, or demographic data such as age constrained within feasible ranges.

Our notion of privacy protects individual datapoints. For example, it can hide a single detour when tracking a person's car, but it cannot hide the daily commute to work. This choice is motivated by our approach using static analysis, and stronger notions of adjacency would require significant amounts of noise, making it difficult to produce accurate monitors. In Sect. 6, we nevertheless explore strategies for supporting stronger notions of privacy within our framework.

4 Sensitivity Calculations for Stream-Based Languages

The sensitivity of a function measures how much its output can change for two adjacent inputs. For stream-based monitors, we analyze how much output streams may differ between two adjacent and valid evaluation models. We introduce a formal framework for the sensitivity of streams, discuss practical challenges in stream-based computations, and establish static bounds that enable differentially private monitoring.

4.1 Specifications

A *specification* φ consists of a set of stream equations $\{x := \varphi_x \mid x \in \mathtt{ID}^{\downarrow}\}$, where each φ_x is a stream expression over $\mathtt{ID}^{\uparrow} \uplus \mathtt{ID}^{\downarrow}$. Each output stream is additionally annotated with a *pacing type* that determines when it is evaluated relative to the input streams. An evaluation model $\omega \in \mathbb{W}$ is *valid* for φ if every output stream value $\omega(x)(t)$ is computed according to the defining equation φ_x for all $t \in$ Time.

4.2 Stream Expressions

Sensitivities are defined recursively over stream expressions. Expressions may reference a stream y, a constant c, an offset $o \in \mathbb{N}$, or be combined using a binary operator $\circ \in \{+, -, \cdot\}$:

$$\begin{aligned} exp \;=\; & \mathsf{sync}(y) \mid \mathsf{offset}(y, o) \mid \mathsf{hold}(y) \mid \mathsf{aggr}(y, W, f) \\ & \mid \mathsf{default}(exp, exp) \mid \mathsf{ite}(exp, exp, exp) \mid exp \circ exp \mid c \end{aligned}$$

We distinguish between *synchronous accesses*, namely sync and offset, which access the value of y at the current (resp. offset) discrete timepoint, and *asynchronous accesses*, such as hold, which returns the most recent available value, and aggr, which applies the aggregation function $f \in \{\Sigma, \mathit{last}, \mathit{count}\}$ over a window W of values of y. As asynchronous accesses may be undefined at certain time points, we provide the default operator, which supplies a fallback value whenever an access fails. For a formal definition of the semantics of stream expressions, we refer to the full version of this paper [29].

4.3 Timing Abstraction

Since the sensitivity analysis should be independent of the specific stream values but may depend on the timing of events, we separate the timing information of an evaluation model. For this purpose, we introduce a *pacing model*, which captures only the temporal structure of stream evaluations.

Definition 5 (Pacing Model). *A* pacing model $p \in \mathbb{P}$ *captures the timing of stream evaluations independent of stream values. It consists of a pacing and timing map, where* $\mathbb{B} = \{\bot, \top\}$ *denotes the set of boolean values:*

$$\begin{aligned} \mathit{PacingMap} &:= \left(\mathtt{ID}^{\uparrow} \uplus \mathtt{ID}^{\downarrow}\right) \to \mathit{Time} \to \mathbb{B} \\ \mathit{TimeMap} &:= \mathit{Time} \to \mathbb{R}^{+} \\ \mathbb{P} &:= \mathit{PacingMap} \times \mathit{TimeMap} \end{aligned}$$

Analogously to the evaluation model, we introduce shorthand notation. For a pacing model $p = (\mathit{pacings}, \mathit{times})$, we define $p(t) := \mathit{times}(t)$ for a time $t \in \text{Time}$, and $p(s) := \mathit{pacings}(s)$ for a stream $s \in \mathtt{ID}^{\uparrow} \uplus \mathtt{ID}^{\downarrow}$. Further, we say an evaluation model *behaves according to* a pacing model if all real-time timestamps are equal and a stream has a value exactly if the corresponding pacing is true.

To enable an automatic analysis of specifications, we impose assumptions on the pacing of stream evaluations. Among other checks, such as dependency and value type analysis, each specification is statically verified to satisfy these pacing constraints before execution. These constraints guarantee that the monitoring algorithm produces only valid evaluation models and that the resulting monitor operates within bounded memory requirements.

Definition 6 (Correctly Typed Pacing Model). *For a pacing model* $p \in \mathbb{P}$ *to be considered correctly typed according to a specification* φ*, it must hold that*

1. *For each synchronous access* sync *and* offset *from output stream* $x \in \mathtt{ID}^{\downarrow}$ *to stream* $y \in \mathtt{ID}^{\uparrow} \uplus \mathtt{ID}^{\downarrow}$*, it must hold that whenever* x *evaluates,* y *evaluates as well:* $\forall t \in \mathit{Time}. p(x)(t) \Rightarrow p(y)(t)$.
2. *For each sliding window aggregation* aggr *from output stream* $x \in \mathtt{ID}^{\downarrow}$ *over a stream* $y \in \mathtt{ID}^{\uparrow} \uplus \mathtt{ID}^{\downarrow}$*, it must hold that* x *is periodic with some period* δ_x*, i.e.* $\forall t \in \mathit{Time}. p(x)(t) \Rightarrow \exists k \in \mathbb{N}. p(t) = k \cdot \delta_x$.

A specification φ is *well-typed* if it statically satisfies the pacing constraints above. For every valid evaluation model $\omega \in \mathbb{W}$ of a well-typed specification, there exists a correctly-typed pacing model $p \in \mathbb{P}$ that ω behaves according to.

4.4 Per-event Sensitivity

To measure how much the values of an output stream can differ between two adjacent evaluation models, we introduce *per-event sensitivity*, which captures the maximum impact a single changed input has on a stream value at a given timestamp, taking into account the timing constraints imposed by a pacing model.

Definition 7 (Per-Event Sensitivity). *Given a specification φ, a pacing model $p \in \mathbb{P}$, and two timestamps $t, t' \in Time$, the per-event sensitivity defines how much the value of a stream $x \in \mathtt{ID}^{\uparrow} \uplus \mathtt{ID}^{\downarrow}$ at timestamp t' can change, if the inputs at timestamp t are changed by at most s.*

$$\Delta_{t,p,s}^{t'} : \mathtt{ID}^{\uparrow} \uplus \mathtt{ID}^{\downarrow} \rightarrow \mathbb{R}^{+}$$

$$\Delta_{t,p,s}^{t'}(x) = \begin{cases} s & \text{if } x \in \mathtt{ID}^{\uparrow} \wedge t' = t \\ 0 & \text{if } x \in \mathtt{ID}^{\uparrow} \wedge t' \neq t \\ \Delta_{t,p,s}^{t'}(\varphi_x) & \text{if } x \in \mathtt{ID}^{\downarrow} \end{cases}$$

where $\Delta_{t,p,s}^{t'}(\varphi_x)$ computes the sensitivity for the stream expression φ_x of x. Given stream expressions e, e_1 and e_2, the constant c, and the stream reference y, we define

$$\begin{aligned} \Delta_{t,p,s}^{t'}(e_1 + e_2) &= \Delta_{t,p,s}^{t'}(e_1) + \Delta_{t,p,s}^{t'}(e_2) \\ \Delta_{t,p,s}^{t'}(c \cdot e) &= |c| \cdot \Delta_{t,p,s}^{t'}(e) \\ \Delta_{t,p,s}^{t'}(\mathsf{sync}(y)) &= \Delta_{t,p,s}^{t'}(y) \\ \Delta_{t,p,s}^{t'}(\mathsf{offset}(y, o)) &= \Delta_{t,p,s}^{last(y,t',p,o)}(y) \\ \Delta_{t,p,s}^{t'}(\mathsf{aggr}(y, W, \Sigma)) &= \sum_{t'' \in wtimes(y,t',p,W)} \Delta_{t,p,s}^{t''}(y) \end{aligned}$$

where $last(y, t, p, o)$ returns the timestamp of the o-th most recent value of y, and $wtimes(y, t, p, W)$ returns timestamps of y from the W sized window behind t. Consider the full version of this paper [29] for the full definition with all operators.

For an input stream, the sensitivity depends on the timestamp t' being considered. If $t' = t$, the sensitivity is exactly s, reflecting the allowed change at that time. For all other timestamps, the input sensitivity is zero, since only a single input value may be modified. For an output stream x, the sensitivity is determined by its defining stream expression φ_x in the specification. Most operations compute values at the current timestamp, so recursion does not shift the timestamp. An exception is the *offset*-operator: The sensitivity at timestamp t' depends on the sensitivity of the value retrieved from the past. As this is determined by the pacing model, the function *last* identifies the timestamp of the accessed value. In the case of summation over sliding windows, the sensitivity at time t' accumulates contributions from all aggregated values within the window.

Our intuition of the per-event sensitivity function is captured by this theorem:

Theorem 2. *Let $\omega, \omega' \in \mathbb{W}$ be valid evaluation models for an acyclic specification φ which are s-distant, event-level adjacent, and differ at timestamp t. Then, for each stream $x \in \mathtt{ID}^{\uparrow} \uplus \mathtt{ID}^{\downarrow}$ and each timestamp $t' \in Time$,*

$$|\omega(x)(t') - \omega'(x)(t')| \leq \Delta^{t'}_{t,p,s}(x),$$

where both evaluation models define a unique and common pacing model $p \in \mathbb{P}$.

The proof is by structural induction over the defining stream expressions and can be found Note that throughout this chapter, the dependency graph is assumed acyclic. Dependency cycles are handled in Sect. 5.1.

4.5 Value-Dependent Operators

So far, we have assumed that an expression's sensitivity depends only on the sensitivities of the accessed streams. For some operators, such as multiplication and conditionals, the sensitivity also depends on the actual values. For instance, in a conditional $\mathsf{ite}(c, e_1, e_2)$, the output may switch between e_1 and e_2 for neighboring executions, and the resulting sensitivity depends on the maximum difference between the two branches. Similarly, for a multiplication, the output sensitivity scales with the operand values. To handle such operators, we extend the analysis to propagate *value ranges* alongside sensitivities. Each expression is associated with an interval that over-approximates the values it may produce at runtime. Using this range information, the per-event sensitivity function $\Delta^{t'}_{t,p,s}$ can be extended as follows:

Definition 8 (Extended Per-Event Sensitivity). *Let $\Delta^{t'}_{t,p,s}(x)$ be defined as in Definition 7 for all standard operators. For operators whose sensitivity depends on the input values, we extend it by*

$$\Delta^{t'}_{t,p,s}(x) := \begin{cases} ub(x) - lb(x) & \text{if } t \rightsquigarrow^{x}_{p} t' \\ 0 & \text{otherwise,} \end{cases}$$

where $t \rightsquigarrow^{x}_{p} t'$ indicates that a change of inputs at time t can influence the value of stream x at time t' under the pacing model p, and $ub(\cdot)$ and $lb(\cdot)$ are the propagated value bounds. Find the definitions in the full version of this paper [29].

Note that sliding-window aggregations do not preserve bounded value ranges, as their output range grows unboundedly even when the output sensitivity is bounded. As a consequence, we impose an additional typing constraint: value-dependent operators are only permitted on expressions for which a finite value range can be statically derived. Note that bounded value ranges can always be re-established explicitly using the clamp operator, which enforces fixed lower and upper bounds on the produced values.

4.6 Asynchronous Accesses

Stream-based specifications allow asynchronous stream evaluations, so a single input value may be accessed multiple times by dependent streams. For some asynchronous operators, such as sliding-window aggregations, well-typed pacing restrictions ensure that the number of contributions of a single input is bounded. However, the *hold access* operator retrieves the most recent value of another stream, allowing a single input to influence an unbounded number of timestamps.

Consider a stream c that accesses the latest value of a whenever b occurs:

```
output c @b := a.hold().defaults(to: 0)
```

Because the timing of a and b need not be known in advance, it is impossible to determine how often a single value of a is accessed, and thus how much it may contribute to c.

In general, unrestricted hold accesses prevent bounding the total effect of a single input across all timestamps. However, in practice, these accesses can often be constrained either by bounding the time span during which a value is relevant or by limiting the number of accesses. For instance, a bounded hold can be expressed as a sliding-window aggregation, e.g., $\mathsf{aggr}(a, 5s, \mathit{last})$ or by explicitly restricting the number of accesses, e.g., $\mathsf{hold}_5(a)$ with a newly introduced hold variant. Once such bounds are made explicit, the contribution of a single input value becomes finite, and a static global sensitivity bound can be derived.

4.7 Static Bounds

While the per-event sensitivity Δ provides a way to quantify the sensitivity at a specific timestamp, it depends on a concrete pacing model and assumes knowledge of the timestamp at which the inputs differ, which is both unavailable at runtime. To address this, we overapproximate the total L_1-sensitivity of Δ accumulated across all timestamps, by deriving a static upper bound for each stream. The only assumption we make is that the pacing model is well-typed, a property statically verified on the specification. Under this assumption, the following result establishes the existence of a finite bound for every stream.

Theorem 3 (Sensitivity Bound). *Given a well-typed specification φ with an acyclic dependency graph without unbounded hold operators and a distance value s, it holds that*

$$\forall x \in \left(\mathtt{ID}^{\uparrow} \uplus \mathtt{ID}^{\downarrow}\right).\exists b_{\varphi,x,s}.\forall p \in \mathbb{P}_{\varphi}.\forall t \in \mathit{Time}.\left(\sum_{t' \in T_{p,x}} \Delta^{t'}_{t,p,s}(x)\right) \leq b_{\varphi,x,s}.$$

where $\mathbb{P}_{\varphi}$ denotes all correctly-typed pacing models according to φ and $T_{p,x} = \{t' \in \mathit{Time} \mid p(x)(t')\}$ denotes the timestamps at which stream x is evaluated.

Intuitively, this theorem ensures that each stream x has a finite, statically derivable upper bound $b_{\varphi,x,s}$ on its total L_1-sensitivity given an s-bounded change to the inputs. This upper bound can be computed recursively along the dependency graph. For example, the bound for an input stream is given by s, the bound for an addition is the sum of the bounds of its operands, and the bound for a synchronous access coincides with the bound of the accessed stream. Precise bounds for each operator and the full proof can be found

With this static bound available, differential privacy can be achieved by injecting appropriately scaled noise into each value of an output stream.

Theorem 4. *Let φ be a well-typed specification with an acyclic dependency graph without unbounded hold operators. Let s be a distance value, and $\omega \in \mathbb{W}$ a valid evaluation model for φ. Further, let $\mathcal{K}$ be a randomized mechanism $\mathcal{K}_x : \mathbb{W} \to$ Stream which produces a noisy version of the output stream x by adding independent Laplace noise to each value:*

$$\mathcal{K}_x(\omega) := \lambda t.\omega(x)(t) + \eta_t,$$

where each term η_t is drawn independently from the Laplace distribution with

$$\eta_t \sim Lap\left(\frac{b_{\varphi,x,s}}{\varepsilon}\right).$$

Then, $\mathcal{K}_s$ satisfies ε-private s-distant event-level differential privacy.

The result shows that by calibrating Laplace noise to the global sensitivity bound $b_{\varphi,x,s}$, we can guarantee ε-differential privacy for all s-distant, event-level adjacent executions. The proof follows immediately from the combination of Theorem 2 and Theorem 3 with Theorem 1 and can be found While the randomized mechanism described above releases only a single output stream, standard composition theorems of differential privacy ensure that multiple output streams can also be released with appropriately adjusted privacy parameters.

5 Accurate Monitoring Under Differential Privacy

Differential privacy of individual streams can be ensured by appropriately adding noise to their values. Simply adding noise to all inputs would guarantee privacy, but it can lead to poor utility of the results. In this section, we present strategies to maintain accurate monitoring while preserving privacy.

5.1 Ensuring Privacy for Unbounded Specifications

Certain language features, such as unbounded hold operators or circular definitions, can cause a single input event to influence an unbounded number of outputs. This makes it impossible to compute a finite global sensitivity for the entire specification directly. However, every specification can still be made differentially private by controlling where in the specification noise is injected. The key idea is to partition the dependency graph of the specification into two segments:

(a) Different segments of the example specification.

(b) Possible placement options for privacy barriers in the private segment.

Fig. 3. Dependency Graph examples for the RTLola specification in Fig. 1.

- An upper *private segment*, which is acyclic and contains only computations for which the sensitivity can be statically bounded, and
- A lower *post-processed segment*, which may include features that induce unbounded sensitivity.

The segments are illustrated in Fig. 3a for the specification from Fig. 1. Noise can be safely injected at the boundaries between the segments, ensuring that all values entering the post-processed segment already satisfy differential privacy. Downstream computations, no matter how complex or unbounded, can then be treated as post-processing, which cannot weaken the privacy guarantees.

5.2 Privacy Barriers

Adding noise at the transition between private and post-processed segments ensures differential privacy for any specification. However, it is not always optimal: injecting noise earlier in the specification can significantly improve the utility of the outputs. To formalize where noise can be injected into the specification, we introduce the notion of *privacy barriers*, which separate private inputs from the public outputs in the dependency graph:

Definition 9 (Privacy Barriers). *Let* $\mathtt{ID}^{\uparrow}$ *be the set of input streams and* $\mathtt{ID}^{\downarrow}_{pub} \subseteq \mathtt{ID}^{\downarrow}$ *the set of public output streams. A set* $\mathcal{C} \subseteq \mathtt{ID}^{\uparrow} \uplus \mathtt{ID}^{\downarrow}$ *is a valid set of* privacy barriers *if every path in the dependency graph from any* $i \in \mathtt{ID}^{\uparrow}$ *to any* $o \in \mathtt{ID}^{\downarrow}_{pub}$ *passes through exactly one* $c \in \mathcal{C}$*.*

Any valid set of privacy barriers is a valid option for adding noise. At each barrier, noise is injected, and all downstream computations are treated as post-processing. Figure 3b shows all valid options for the example specification.

A natural goal is to choose a barrier placement that maximizes the utility of the monitored outputs. However, such an optimal placement does not exist: different choices can favor short-term vs. long-term accuracy, or prioritize the accuracy of different output streams against others. A placement that is locally optimal for one output stream may be suboptimal for another, leading to

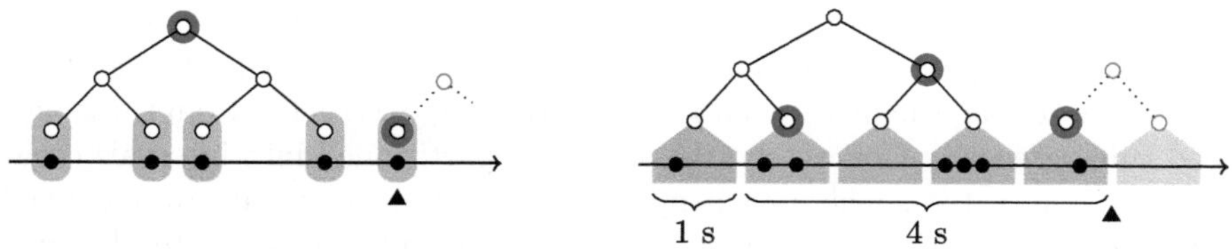

(a) Discrete aggregation over all values.

(b) Sliding window aggregation over 4 seconds. A new value is produced every second.

Fig. 4. Tree-Based Aggregation Examples.

inherent trade-offs between streams. We therefore do not prescribe a single optimal strategy, but instead suggest several heuristics for selecting privacy barriers whose trade-offs can be predicted and reasoned about.

The *input-only* heuristic injects noise at input streams, ensuring that all computations operate on perturbed data. The *deep* heuristic targets the transition from private to post-processed segments. This preserves the accuracy of intermediate computations as much as possible, but may require a lot of barriers and, therefore, more noise due to the composition theorem. The *post-aggregation* heuristic places barriers immediately after the first aggregation. Compared to adding noise before aggregations, this often reduces the overall noise required since the private input is combined with multiple others before being perturbed. The *minimal barriers* heuristic selects the smallest set of valid barriers to reduce the number of noise injections. Fewer injection points reduce runtime cost but may lead to a higher variance compared to more fine-grained barrier placements. Importantly, all placement strategies preserve the same differential privacy guarantees.

Beyond these, other heuristics are conceivable, for example, tracking the propagated error symbolically through the specification, similar to approaches in monitoring under uncertainty [27].

5.3 Tree-Based Aggregations

In Sect. 5.1, we showed that we exclude cycles in the dependency graph from the privacy segment as they introduce unbounded sensitivity. In practice, however, circular definitions are most commonly used to aggregate all values of a stream over time. Beyond sliding-window aggregations, many stream-based languages support discrete all-aggregations, which aggregate all stream values since the start of the monitor. The most common loops in specifications can therefore automatically be rewritten as all-aggregations.

To introduce a barrier at an all-aggregation, noise must be added to each released aggregate in order to preserve differential privacy. However, independently perturbing each aggregated result leads to unbounded privacy loss, since each private value contributes to all future aggregations. A standard solution to this problem is provided by tree-based mechanisms for differential privacy under continual observation [13,14,21,42,44,48]. In these approaches, noisy intermediate aggregates are precomputed and reused across multiple releases. Rather than repeatedly accessing the private data, aggregates are constructed from these perturbed subaggregates. Concretely, the stream is partitioned into intervals organized in a binary tree, where each node represents an aggregate over a fixed interval and is perturbed only once. Aggregates at any time step are obtained by combining the noisy values of a small number of nodes in the tree whose intervals form a partition of the required range. Several approaches have been proposed to handle unbounded time with these tree-based mechanisms [14,48]. In this work, we adopt a construction based on a geometric series that distributes the privacy budget across the infinite height of the tree.

Particular to our setting is that aggregations are not restricted to input streams, where only a single event must be hidden. Aggregations may also be applied to output streams, where temporal operators have already propagated a single change to multiple stream values. Our tree-based construction accommodates this, as it only reasons about the total L_1-sensitivity of the aggregated stream. Formal details and proofs are provided

Figure 4a illustrates this construction for a discrete all-aggregation. Each leaf of the tree corresponds to a value of the aggregated stream. At the position marked with the black triangle, the aggregation over all values is computed by combining the precomputed noisy aggregate over the first four values (the blue node at the top of the tree) with the noisy aggregate of the fifth value at the current position.

In contrast to all-aggregations, whose aggregation is done over a growing prefix of the stream, sliding-window aggregations operate over a time window that shifts with the current evaluation point. The pacing type requirement in Definition 6 ensures that aggregation results are released at a fixed frequency. This restriction was originally introduced to guarantee that monitoring can be performed using finite memory. To this end, values are first aggregated into buckets, where the bucket size is determined by the aggregating stream's frequency and the length of the window [45]. We can improve the utility of sliding window aggregations by adopting the tree-based approach, where the buckets form the leaves of the tree, as illustrated in Fig. 4b. To compute, for example, the aggregation over the last four seconds, one sums the noisy values in the blue-marked nodes of the tree. Using this tree-based construction, in the example, each private value is only released three times, compared to four times without the tree-based approach when each aggregated result is perturbed independently.

6 Stricter Privacy Guarantees

Our approach assumes that the values at the individual input stream positions are independent, but this assumption does not hold in all applications. For example, consecutive sensor readings, such as GPS coordinates, are often correlated. In such cases, standard event-level differential privacy underestimates the required amount of noise. One way to address this is to adopt w-consecutive differential privacy (w-DP) [36], which hides the effect of up to w consecutive input

Table 1. Analysis runtime comparison for different specifications.

Specification	no-priv	priv
Fraud Detection	3 ms	7 ms
Geofence Small [4]	118 ms	278 ms
Geofence Large [4]	594 ms	1368 ms
Peak Detection [8]	3 ms	8 ms
Public Transport	5 ms	12 ms
Driving Emissions [9]	123 ms	247 ms
Sensor Validation [8]	2 ms	7 ms

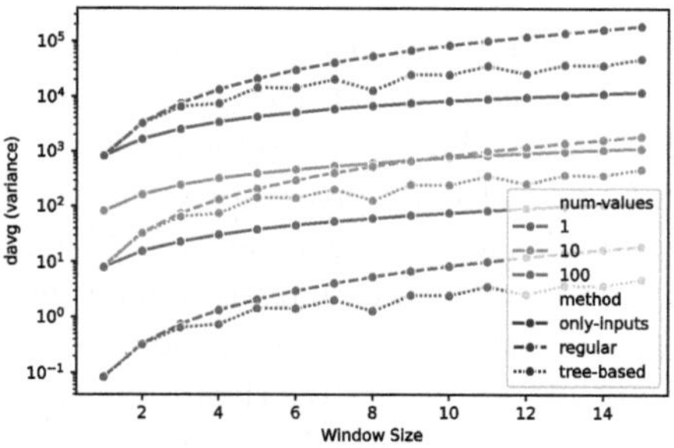

Fig. 5. Output variances for different sliding window aggregations.

values. If correlations are limited to w consecutive values, w-DP provides meaningful privacy guarantees. Extending our approach to w-DP is straightforward, since our mechanisms already handle correlated outputs: we can apply the same techniques to w-sized groups of input values.

Another complementary strategy is to use a preprocessing monitor. In this approach, a first monitor transforms correlated inputs into independent values or aggregated summaries. These independent streams are then fed into a second, privacy-preserving monitor that ensures differential privacy. For example, the first monitor could extract individual trips from raw GPS data. The second monitor then computes the private outputs over these independent summaries. This strategy of using a preprocessing monitor can even ensure user-level privacy [21] by ensuring the second privacy-preserving monitor receives a single event per user.

7 Implementation and Evaluation

This section evaluates the practical applicability of our approach. We first describe the implementation of the privacy analysis within the RTLola framework and then assess the impact of different design choices using synthetic examples and a case study on monitoring public transportation data.

7.1 Implementation

Our implementation extends the RTLola frontend [5] with a privacy analysis that is executed after the dependency analysis. This analysis identifies all valid privacy barriers in the dependency graph and applies the heuristics described in Sect. 5.2 to select the barriers at which noise is injected. Using propagated sensitivity and range information, noise expressions are inserted into the intermediate representation of the specification, and tree-based aggregation is translated into corresponding RTLola constructs. This way, no modifications to the existing backend implementations [3,25] are required for private monitoring.

We evaluate the runtime of the privacy analysis. The results are summarized in Table 1, where the *priv* column reports the maximum runtime across all heuristics. The measurements were obtained on a system with a 13th Gen Intel Core i7-1355U processor over 50 runs. We observe that the runtime more than doubles for all specifications. This increase is primarily due to the fact that, following the privacy analysis, which introduces new expressions and streams in the specification, we rerun earlier stages such as dependency analysis and type checking. Despite this overhead, all runtimes remain well below a few seconds, rendering the additional cost negligible for an analysis performed once prior to monitor deployment.

7.2 Impact of Tree-Based Aggregations

Next, we assess the impact of the tree-based aggregation on the accuracy of the output using the example shown in Fig. 1. Accuracy is quantified by computing, for each timestamp, the variance across 100 runs of the private monitor ($\varepsilon = 1$) on the same input trace and then averaging this variance across all timestamps. Lower variance indicates higher accuracy of the output.

We compare how accuracy is influenced by the structure of the aggregation window. First, we vary the number of buckets in the window. Increasing the number of buckets causes individual values to contribute to multiple aggregates, which in turn requires more perturbation to ensure privacy. Second, we vary the number of values per bucket. More values per bucket allow individual values to be more effectively obscured by others, thereby reducing the variance.

We compare three perturbation strategies. As a baseline, we add noise directly to each input before aggregation. We then consider the basic sensitivity-based perturbation described in Sect. 4 and the tree-based aggregation approach from Sect. 5.3. Figure 5 shows that for small windows, all three methods achieve similar utility. As the window size grows, the differences become more pronounced, with the tree-based approach yielding significantly lower variance than the sensitivity-based method. When each bucket contains only a single value, directly perturbing the inputs yields the highest accuracy. However, this approach rapidly degrades in utility as the number of values per bucket increases.

7.3 Case Study

To demonstrate the applicability of our approach in a realistic setting, we present a case study from the public transportation domain. We implemented a system that crowdsources information about public transportation usage by allowing users to report trips on specific bus lines. The reported events are processed by an RTLola monitor, which aggregates the data and displays anonymized usage statistics to users. The aggregated results provide insights into temporal usage patterns, such as the expected level of crowding on a bus line at different times of day. Since the collected data reflects individual movement behavior, it is inherently privacy-sensitive. By relying on our privacy-preserving framework, all

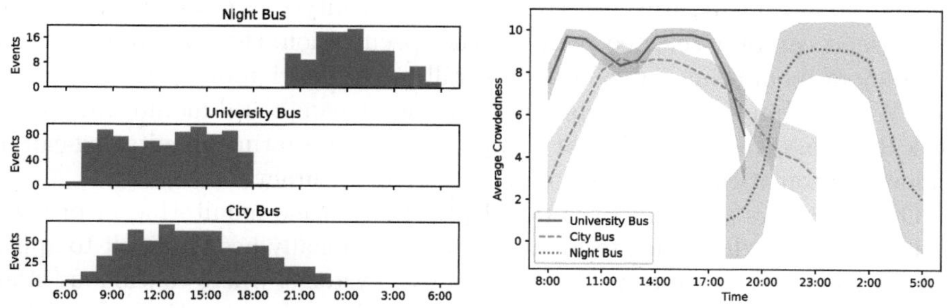

(a) Histogram of the number of events per hour per bus line.

(b) The average crowdedness per hour output by the differentially private monitor.

Fig. 6. Results from monitoring synthetic public transportation data.

privacy guarantees are enforced automatically by the frontend analysis, allowing the application to be implemented without manual reasoning about privacy concerns. The corresponding RTLola specification is provided in the full version of this paper [29].

We evaluate our case study using synthetic data. Specifically, we consider three bus lines and generate a varying number of users depending on the time of day, as shown in Fig. 6a. The first is a university bus, highly frequented but only during a shorter period of the day. The second is a city bus, which is frequently used throughout daytime hours. The third is a night bus, which also exhibits high usage per bus, but with significantly fewer buses and users overall.

In Fig. 6b, we show the average crowdedness per time of day as reported by the private monitor ($\varepsilon = 1$, deep heuristic), with the standard deviation (SD) shown as error bars. The SD indicates that the confidence of the monitor output depends on the number of users. To estimate the SD introduced by differential privacy, we execute the monitor 1500 times and calculate statistics over these runs. During high-traffic daytime hours, the differentially private estimates closely match the true crowdedness. At night, the smaller number of participants leads to a higher SD. But even during nighttime hours with fewer participants, the monitor output closely approximates the actual crowdedness.

8 Conclusion

In this paper, we have presented a method for integrating differential privacy into runtime monitoring to ensure system correctness while preserving the privacy of sensitive system data. Our approach analyzes the specifications and automatically enforces privacy guarantees without requiring any user interaction. As a result, users without privacy expertise can benefit from differential privacy without having to reason about sensitivities, noise calibration, or privacy budgets, which is particularly challenging given temporal dependencies in stream-based specifications. Finally, privacy is enforced in a utility-aware manner by injecting noise at carefully selected points in the specification, thereby preserving the accuracy of monitoring outcomes while still providing rigorous privacy guarantees. We have implemented our approach in the stream-based monitoring framework RTLola, demonstrating that privacy-preserving runtime monitoring can be achieved automatically and with minimal loss of accuracy.

Our work lays the foundation for deploying runtime monitoring in privacy-critical domains where such techniques have traditionally been difficult to apply. This includes areas such as medical or financial systems, where continuous monitoring is essential, but the underlying data is highly privacy-critical. We believe that making privacy guarantees an integral part of runtime monitoring is a step toward making runtime verification applicable in a broader range of real-world, safety-critical and privacy-sensitive systems.

Acknowledgments. This work was partially supported by the German Research Foundation (DFG) as part of TRR 248 (No. 389792660) and PreCePT (No. 521273327), and by the European Research Council (ERC) Grant HYPER (No. 101055412).

Data Availibility Statement. The artifacts and resources associated with this article are accessible via https://doi.org/10.5281/zenodo.19694096.

Disclosure of Interests. The authors have no competing interests to declare that are relevant to the content of this article.

References

1. Abbas, H.: Private runtime verification: work-in-progress. In: Proceedings of the International Conference on Embedded Software Companion, New York, NY, USA, 13–18 October 2019, p. 11. ACM (2019). https://doi.org/10.1145/3349568.3351552
2. Banno, R., Matsuoka, K., Matsumoto, N., Bian, S., Waga, M., Suenaga, K.: Oblivious online monitoring for safety LTL specification via fully homomorphic encryption. In: Shoham, S., Vizel, Y. (eds.) CAV 2022. LNCS, vol. 13371, pp. 447–468. Springer, Cham (2022). https://doi.org/10.1007/978-3-031-13185-1_22
3. Baumeister, J., Correnson, A., Finkbeiner, B., Scheerer, F.: An intermediate program representation for optimizing stream-based languages. In: Piskac, R., Rakamaric, Z. (eds.) CAV 2025, Part III. LNCS, vol. 15933, pp. 393–407. Springer, Cham (2025). https://doi.org/10.1007/978-3-031-98682-6_20
4. Baumeister, J., et al.: Monitoring unmanned aircraft: specification, integration, and lessons-learned. In: Gurfinkel, A., Ganesh, V. (eds.) CAV 2024, Part II. LNCS, vol. 14682, pp. 207–218. Springer, Cham (2024). https://doi.org/10.1007/978-3-031-65630-9_10
5. Baumeister, J., Finkbeiner, B., Kohn, F., Scheerer, F.: A tutorial on stream-based monitoring. In: Platzer, A., Rozier, K.Y., Pradella, M., Rossi, M. (eds.) FM 2024, Part II. LNCS, vol. 14934, pp. 624–648. Springer, Cham (2024). https://doi.org/10.1007/978-3-031-71177-0_33
6. Baumeister, J., Finkbeiner, B., Scheerer, F.: Active monitoring with RTLola: a specification-guided scheduling approach. In: Könighofer, B., Torfah, H. (eds.) RV

2025. LNCS, vol. 16087, pp. 181–201. Springer, Cham (2025). https://doi.org/10.1007/978-3-032-05435-7_11
7. Baumeister, J., Finkbeiner, B., Scheerer, F., Siber, J., Wagenpfeil, T.: Stream-based monitoring of algorithmic fairness. In: Gurfinkel, A., Heule, M. (eds.) ETAPS 2025, Part I. LNCS, vol. 15696, pp. 60–81. Springer, Cham (2025). https://doi.org/10.1007/978-3-031-90643-5_4
8. Baumeister, J., Finkbeiner, B., Schirmer, S., Schwenger, M., Torens, C.: RTLola cleared for take-off: monitoring autonomous aircraft. In: Lahiri, S.K., Wang, C. (eds.) CAV 2020, Part II. LNCS, vol. 12225, pp. 28–39. Springer, Cham (2020). https://doi.org/10.1007/978-3-030-53291-8_3
9. Biewer, S., Finkbeiner, B., Hermanns, H., Köhl, M.A., Schnitzer, Y., Schwenger, M.: RTLola on board: testing real driving emissions on your phone. In: TACAS 2021, Part II. LNCS, vol. 12652, pp. 365–372. Springer, Cham (2021). https://doi.org/10.1007/978-3-030-72013-1_20
10. Blocki, J., Blum, A., Datta, A., Sheffet, O.: Differentially private data analysis of social networks via restricted sensitivity. In: Kleinberg, R.D. (ed.) Innovations in Theoretical Computer Science, ITCS 2013, Berkeley, CA, USA, 9–12 January 2013, pp. 87–96. ACM (2013). https://doi.org/10.1145/2422436.2422449
11. Cao, J., Xiao, Q., Ghinita, G., Li, N., Bertino, E., Tan, K.: Efficient and accurate strategies for differentially-private sliding window queries. In: Guerrini, G., Paton, N.W. (eds.) Joint 2013 EDBT/ICDT Conferences, EDBT 2013 Proceedings, Genoa, Italy, 18–22 March 2013, pp. 191–202. ACM (2013). https://doi.org/10.1145/2452376.2452400
12. Cao, Y., Yoshikawa, M., Xiao, Y., Xiong, L.: Quantifying differential privacy under temporal correlations. In: 33rd IEEE International Conference on Data Engineering, ICDE 2017, San Diego, CA, USA, April 19-22, 2017. pp. 821–832. IEEE Computer Society (2017). https://doi.org/10.1109/ICDE.2017.132
13. Cardoso, A.R., Rogers, R.: Differentially private histograms under continual observation: streaming selection into the unknown. In: Camps-Valls, G., Ruiz, F.J.R., Valera, I. (eds.) International Conference on Artificial Intelligence and Statistics, AISTATS 2022, 28–30 March 2022, Virtual Event. Proceedings of Machine Learning Research, vol. 151, pp. 2397–2419. PMLR (2022). https://proceedings.mlr.press/v151/rivera-cardoso22a.html
14. Chan, T.H., Shi, E., Song, D.: Private and continual release of statistics. ACM Trans. Inf. Syst. Secur. **14**(3), 26:1–26:24 (2011). https://doi.org/10.1145/2043621.2043626
15. Chen, Q., Ni, Z., Zhu, X., Xia, P.: Differential privacy histogram publishing method based on dynamic sliding window. Frontiers Comput. Sci. **17**(4), 174809 (2023). https://doi.org/10.1007/S11704-022-1651-2
16. Chen, Y., Machanavajjhala, A., Hay, M., Miklau, G.: Pegasus: data-adaptive differentially private stream processing. In: Thuraisingham, B., Evans, D., Malkin, T., Xu, D. (eds.) Proceedings of the 2017 ACM SIGSAC Conference on Computer and Communications Security, CCS 2017, Dallas, TX, USA, 30 October–03 November 2017, pp. 1375–1388. ACM (2017). https://doi.org/10.1145/3133956.3134102
17. D'Angelo, B., et al.: LOLA: runtime monitoring of synchronous systems. In: 12th International Symposium on Temporal Representation and Reasoning (TIME 2005), 23–25 June 2005, Burlington, Vermont, USA, pp. 166–174. IEEE Computer Society (2005). https://doi.org/10.1109/TIME.2005.26
18. Dong, W., Luo, Q., Yi, K.: Continual observation under user-level differential privacy. In: 44th IEEE Symposium on Security and Privacy, SP 2023, San Francisco,

CA, USA, 21–25 May 2023, pp. 2190–2207. IEEE (2023). https://doi.org/10.1109/SP46215.2023.10179466
19. Dvijotham, K.D., McMahan, H.B., Pillutla, K., Steinke, T., Thakurta, A.: Efficient and near-optimal noise generation for streaming differential privacy. In: 65th IEEE Annual Symposium on Foundations of Computer Science, FOCS 2024, Chicago, IL, USA, 27–30 October 2024, pp. 2306–2317. IEEE (2024). https://doi.org/10.1109/FOCS61266.2024.00135
20. Dwork, C., McSherry, F., Nissim, K., Smith, A.: Calibrating noise to sensitivity in private data analysis. In: Halevi, S., Rabin, T. (eds.) TCC 2006. LNCS, vol. 3876, pp. 265–284. Springer, Heidelberg (2006). https://doi.org/10.1007/11681878_14
21. Dwork, C., Naor, M., Pitassi, T., Rothblum, G.N.: Differential privacy under continual observation. In: Schulman, L.J. (ed.) Proceedings of the 42nd ACM Symposium on Theory of Computing, STOC 2010, Cambridge, Massachusetts, USA, 5–8 June 2010, pp. 715–724. ACM (2010). https://doi.org/10.1145/1806689.1806787
22. Dwork, C., Roth, A.: The algorithmic foundations of differential privacy. Found. Trends Theor. Comput. Sci. **9**(3–4), 211–407 (2014). https://doi.org/10.1561/0400000042
23. Fan, L., Xiong, L.: Real-time aggregate monitoring with differential privacy. In: Chen, X., Lebanon, G., Wang, H., Zaki, M.J. (eds.) 21st ACM International Conference on Information and Knowledge Management, CIKM 2012, Maui, HI, USA, 29 October–02 November 2012, pp. 2169–2173. ACM (2012). https://doi.org/10.1145/2396761.2398595
24. Faymonville, P., Finkbeiner, B., Schirmer, S., Torfah, H.: A stream-based specification language for network monitoring. In: Falcone, Y., Sánchez, C. (eds.) RV 2016. LNCS, vol. 10012, pp. 152–168. Springer, Cham (2016). https://doi.org/10.1007/978-3-319-46982-9_10
25. Faymonville, P., Finkbeiner, B., Schledjewski, M., Schwenger, M., Stenger, M., Tentrup, L., Torfah, H.: StreamLAB: stream-based monitoring of cyber-physical systems. In: Dillig, I., Tasiran, S. (eds.) CAV 2019, Part I. LNCS, vol. 11561, pp. 421–431. Springer, Cham (2019). https://doi.org/10.1007/978-3-030-25540-4_24
26. Feng, S., Mohammady, M., Wang, H., Li, X., Qin, Z., Hong, Y.: DPI: ensuring strict differential privacy for infinite data streaming. In: IEEE Symposium on Security and Privacy, SP 2024, San Francisco, CA, USA, 19–23 May 2024, pp. 1009–1027. IEEE (2024). https://doi.org/10.1109/SP54263.2024.00124
27. Finkbeiner, B., Fränzle, M., Kohn, F., Kröger, P.: Stream-based monitoring under measurement noise. In: Ábrahám, E., Abbas, H. (eds.) RV 2024. LNCS, vol. 15191, pp. 22–39. Springer, Cham (2024). https://doi.org/10.1007/978-3-031-74234-7_2
28. Finkbeiner, B., Keller, A., Schmidt, J., Schwenger, M.: Robust monitoring for medical cyber-physical systems. In: Proceedings of the Workshop on Medical Cyber Physical Systems and Internet of Medical Things, pp. 17–22 (2021)
29. Finkbeiner, B., Scheerer, F.: Differentially private runtime monitoring (2026). https://doi.org/10.48550/arXiv.2605.02391
30. Gorostiaga, F., Sánchez, C.: Striver: stream runtime verification for real-time event-streams. In: Colombo, C., Leucker, M. (eds.) RV 2018. LNCS, vol. 11237, pp. 282–298. Springer, Cham (2018). https://doi.org/10.1007/978-3-030-03769-7_16
31. Henzinger, M., Upadhyay, J., Upadhyay, S.: Almost tight error bounds on differentially private continual counting. In: Bansal, N., Nagarajan, V. (eds.) Proceedings of the 2023 ACM-SIAM Symposium on Discrete Algorithms, SODA 2023, Florence, Italy, 22–25 January 2023, pp. 5003–5039. SIAM (2023). https://doi.org/10.1137/1.9781611977554.CH183

32. Henzinger, M., Upadhyay, J., Upadhyay, S.: A unifying framework for differentially private sums under continual observation. In: Woodruff, D.P. (ed.) Proceedings of the 2024 ACM-SIAM Symposium on Discrete Algorithms, SODA 2024, Alexandria, VA, USA, 7–10 January 2024, pp. 995–1018. SIAM (2024). https://doi.org/10.1137/1.9781611977912.38
33. Henzinger, T.A., Karimi, M., Thejaswini, K.S.: Privacy-preserving runtime verification. In: Huang, C., Chen, J., Shieh, S., Lie, D., Cortier, V. (eds.) Proceedings of the 2025 ACM SIGSAC Conference on Computer and Communications Security, CCS 2025, Taipei, Taiwan, 13–17 October 2025, pp. 2774–2787. ACM (2025). https://doi.org/10.1145/3719027.3765137
34. Johnson, N.M., Near, J.P., Song, D.: Towards practical differential privacy for SQL queries. Proc. VLDB Endow. **11**(5), 526–539 (2018)
35. Kallwies, H., Leucker, M., Schmitz, M., Schulz, A., Thoma, D., Weiss, A.: Tessla-an ecosystem for runtime verification. In: Dang, T., Stolz, V. (eds.) RV 2022. LNCS, vol 13498, pp. 314–324. Springer, Cham (2022). https://doi.org/10.1007/978-3-031-17196-3_20
36. Kellaris, G., Papadopoulos, S., Xiao, X., Papadias, D.: Differentially private event sequences over infinite streams. Proc. VLDB Endow. **7**(12), 1155–1166 (2014). https://doi.org/10.14778/2732977.2732989, http://www.vldb.org/pvldb/vol7/p1155-kellaris.pdf
37. Li, S., Wen, Y., Wang, Z., Wang, W., Zhang, L., Meng, D.: StreamDP: continual observation of real-world data streams with differential privacy. In: IEEE International Performance, Computing, and Communications Conference, IPCCC 2024, Orlando, FL, USA, 22–24 November 2024, pp. 1–10. IEEE (2024). https://doi.org/10.1109/IPCCC59868.2024.10850443
38. McSherry, F.: Privacy integrated queries: an extensible platform for privacy-preserving data analysis. Commun. ACM **53**(9), 89–97 (2010). https://doi.org/10.1145/1810891.1810916
39. Mohan, P., Thakurta, A., Shi, E., Song, D., Culler, D.E.: GUPT: privacy preserving data analysis made easy. In: Candan, K.S., Chen, Y., Snodgrass, R.T., Gravano, L., Fuxman, A. (eds.) Proceedings of the ACM SIGMOD International Conference on Management of Data, SIGMOD 2012, Scottsdale, AZ, USA, 20–24 May 2012, pp. 349–360. ACM (2012). https://doi.org/10.1145/2213836.2213876
40. Narayan, A., Haeberlen, A.: Djoin: differentially private join queries over distributed databases. In: Thekkath, C., Vahdat, A. (eds.) 10th USENIX Symposium on Operating Systems Design and Implementation, OSDI 2012, Hollywood, CA, USA, 8–10 October 2012, pp. 149–162. USENIX Association (2012). https://www.usenix.org/conference/osdi12/technical-sessions/presentation/narayan
41. Nissim, K., Raskhodnikova, S., Smith, A.D.: Smooth sensitivity and sampling in private data analysis. In: Johnson, D.S., Feige, U. (eds.) Proceedings of the 39th Annual ACM Symposium on Theory of Computing, San Diego, California, USA, 11–13 June 2007, pp. 75–84. ACM (2007). https://doi.org/10.1145/1250790.1250803
42. Perrier, V., Asghar, H.J., Kaafar, D.: Private continual release of real-valued data streams. In: 26th Annual Network and Distributed System Security Symposium, NDSS 2019, San Diego, California, USA, 24–27 February 2019. The Internet Society (2019). https://www.ndss-symposium.org/ndss-paper/private-continual-release-of-real-valued-data-streams/
43. Proserpio, D., Goldberg, S., McSherry, F.: Calibrating data to sensitivity in private data analysis. Proc. VLDB Endow. **7**(8), 637–648 (2014). https://doi.org/10.14778/2732296.2732300, http://www.vldb.org/pvldb/vol7/p637-proserpio.pdf

44. Qardaji, W.H., Yang, W., Li, N.: Understanding hierarchical methods for differentially private histograms. Proc. VLDB Endow. **6**(14), 1954–1965 (2013). https://doi.org/10.14778/2556549.2556576, http://www.vldb.org/pvldb/vol6/p1954-qardaji.pdf
45. Schwenger, M.: Statically-analyzed stream monitoring for cyber-physical Systems. Ph.D. thesis, Saarland University, Saarbrücken, Germany (2022). https://publikationen.sulb.uni-saarland.de/handle/20.500.11880/33890
46. Song, S., Wang, Y., Chaudhuri, K.: Pufferfish privacy mechanisms for correlated data. In: Salihoglu, S., Zhou, W., Chirkova, R., Yang, J., Suciu, D. (eds.) Proceedings of the 2017 ACM International Conference on Management of Data, SIGMOD Conference 2017, Chicago, IL, USA, 14–19 May 2017, pp. 1291–1306. ACM (2017). https://doi.org/10.1145/3035918.3064025
47. Upadhyay, J.: Sublinear space private algorithms under the sliding window model. In: Chaudhuri, K., Salakhutdinov, R. (eds.) Proceedings of the 36th International Conference on Machine Learning, ICML 2019, 9–15 June 2019, Long Beach, California, USA. Proceedings of Machine Learning Research, vol. 97, pp. 6363–6372. PMLR (2019). http://proceedings.mlr.press/v97/upadhyay19a.html
48. Wang, T., et al.: Continuous release of data streams under both centralized and local differential privacy. In: Kim, Y., Kim, J., Vigna, G., Shi, E. (eds.) CCS 2021: 2021 ACM SIGSAC Conference on Computer and Communications Security, Virtual Event, Republic of Korea, 15–19 November 2021, pp. 1237–1253. ACM (2021). https://doi.org/10.1145/3460120.3484750

HyperLasso: Bounded Model Checking of $\forall^+\exists^+$-Liveness Hyperproperties

Alcino Cunha, Hugo Pacheco(✉), and Nuno Macedo

University of Minho and INESC TEC, Minho, Portugal
{alcino,hpacheco,nmacedo}@di.uminho.pt

Abstract. This paper presents the first symbolic bounded model checking technique capable of verifying $\forall^+\exists^+$-liveness hyperproperties (expressed in HyperLTL) over arbitrary (non-terminating) reactive systems. Previous bounded procedures for HyperLTL handled only safety hyperproperties or arbitrary properties over terminating systems. We implement our technique as HyperLasso. Our evaluation results show that it consistently outperforms the explicit-state complete model checker AutoHyper (the only existing tool capable of automatically verifying this class of problems) at several complex bug-finding and synthesis problems.

Keywords: Hyperproperties · Bounded Model Checking · Liveness

1 Introduction

Hyperproperties [16] are specifications that relate multiple traces of execution. They can be used to specify properties that are not possible to express with standard temporal logics that only consider one execution trace at a time, namely security properties such as non-interference or observational determinism. HyperLTL [15] extends the standard *Linear Temporal Logic* (LTL) with explicit quantifiers over traces, thus allowing the specification of general hyperproperties. There has been considerable research addressing the automatic verification of restricted classes of hyperproperties expressed in HyperLTL. However, as far as we are aware, the complete model checker AutoHyper [6] is the only tool capable of verifying arbitrary HyperLTL properties over arbitrary reactive systems. Unfortunately, due to its explicit-state nature, AutoHyper does not cope well with the state explosion problem that characterizes most realistic system models. To overcome this problem, symbolic model checking techniques can be used, namely *Bounded Model Checking* (BMC) [10] procedures that rely on SAT or SMT solving to find bugs in a system, by analyzing all traces up to a given length bound. HyperQB [26,27] is such a symbolic BMC tool for HyperLTL. Currently, it can be used to find bugs of arbitrary hyperproperties on terminating systems, or of safety properties (with any quantifier alternations) on any reactive (possibly non-terminating) system. Other existing symbolic model checking techniques for hyperproperties suffer from similar restrictions.

E. Darulova et al. (Eds.): CAV 2026, LNCS 16682, pp. 473–496, 2026.
https://doi.org/10.1007/978-3-032-32519-8_24

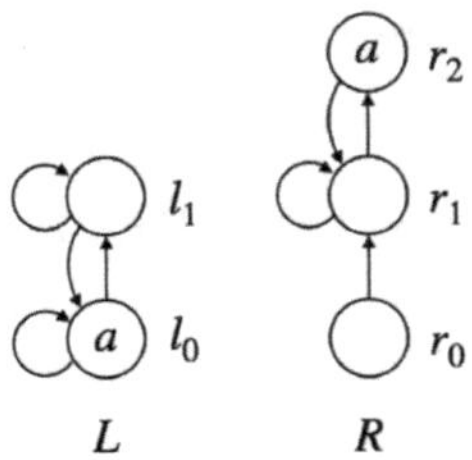

Fig. 1. Example models

This paper presents the first symbolic BMC technique that can be used to find bugs of $\forall^+\exists^+$-liveness properties[1], [2] on reactive systems. In this class of hyperproperties there is a sequence of universal trace quantifiers, followed by a sequence of existential trace quantifiers, followed by an LTL liveness property. Likewise for safety hyperproperties, a single quantifier alternation suffices to express most properties of interest in practice. An example of such a liveness hyperproperty is the following, stating that: for any trace π_1, there exists another trace π_2 where a will eventually be true in both traces at the same time.

$$\forall\pi_1.\exists\pi_2.\Diamond(a_{\pi_1} \wedge a_{\pi_2})$$

Our BMC technique allows quantified trace variables to range over different models. In this example, π_1 and π_2 range, respectively, over traces of models L and R depicted in Fig. 1. Both these models are reactive systems that do not terminate. This hyperproperty is false because, for example, the trace corresponding to path $l_0(l_1)^\omega$ of model L does not have a counterpart trace of model R, since a only holds in the first state of that trace, and any trace of R needs 3 steps to reach a. The challenge of refuting such a hyperproperty is twofold: the $\Diamond$ in the LTL body requires reasoning about infinite paths, while the $\exists$ hyper quantification requires the exploration of all traces even in a BMC setting.

An LTL liveness requirement states that something "good" must happen, so a counter-example must be a full (infinite) path where that "good" thing never happens. With BMC, the verification is performed up to a given state k – a bound limiting the size of the analyzed paths. Bounded infinite paths are *lasso* shaped, meaning that we have a prefix of size l followed by a loop of size $k - l + 1$ that repeats forever; such paths are denoted (k, l)-loops or just a k-loops if the concrete value of l is irrelevant. The counter-example to our property, path $l_0(l_1)^\omega$, is a $(1, 1)$-loop of model L. Not all infinite paths are lasso shaped, but a classic result from temporal logic is that any property that is false in a model can be falsified by a lasso-shaped path. This result is also valid for HyperLTL [28]. However, since different paths can have loops of

[1] Our technique is motivated by properties with quantifier alternations; without alternation, one could simply apply self-composition and a standard LTL model checker.

[2] This is not to be confused with the notion of *hyperliveness* [16], which refers to hyperproperties with existentially quantified traces.

different sizes, the BMC procedure must align the traces resulting from each quantification, which might require exploring the composed models up to depth k^n for n quantified traces.

Given a formula φ, $\models \varphi$ means it is valid considering all possible paths, while the bounded version $\models^k \varphi$ means φ is valid considering only paths of size k. BMC for standard LTL is particularly useful for bug finding because if $\not\models^k \varphi$ then $\not\models \varphi$, i.e., any found counter-example is a bug of the full system (in contrast, the absence of counter-examples for bound k does not guarantee φ is valid for higher k values). However, such infinite inference is not valid in a direct application of classical BMC to HyperLTL when liveness properties are involved: such a procedure might report $\not\models^k \varphi$ but it could actually be the case that $\models \varphi$, meaning that a counter-example might be a false positive and not a true bug in the system. Consider again our example property. To refute it with BMC with bound k we must find a witness for its negation $\exists\pi_1.\forall\pi_2.\Box(\neg a_{\pi_1} \vee \neg a_{\pi_2})$, i.e., a k-loop π_1 of L such that for all k-loops π_2 of R we have $\Box(\neg a_{\pi_1} \vee \neg a_{\pi_2})$. For $k = 0$ the only 0-loop of model L is $(l_0)^\omega$ and there are no 0-loops of model R, so instantiating π_1 as $(l_0)^\omega$ trivially satisfies the negated property for $k = 0$. Unfortunately, this path cannot be used to show that $\not\models \forall\pi_1.\exists\pi_2.\Diamond(a_{\pi_1} \wedge a_{\pi_2})$ with unbounded semantics, because the $(2,1)$-loop $r_0(r_1r_2)^\omega$ is a valid counter-part in R. For $k = 1$ we have additional 1-loops that satisfy the negated property but are spurious counter-examples, namely the $(1,0)$-loop $(l_0l_1)^\omega$. However, we also have the 1-loop $l_0(l_1)^\omega$ that is indeed a valid bug. Thus, classical BMC reasoning is not applicable in the HyperLTL context when we have liveness properties, because one would have to constantly question the validity of counter-examples, completely defeating the premise of BMC. Existing BMC techniques for hyperproperties circumvent these issues by supporting only terminating systems (that stop in k or less steps) or safety hyperproperties.

Our technique solves this issue by pairing a HyperLTL BMC procedure, that will be used as a candidate *synthesizer*, with a *checker* that verifies if candidates are real bugs of the full system. The key insight is that, if we only have a single quantifier alternation, a standard complete model checker for LTL can be used to implement the *checker* using the self-composition technique [2]. When the *checker* flags a candidate as spurious, the *synthesizer* is asked to generate a new one, and the process is iterated until a valid counter-example is found or all possible candidates of size k are exhausted. We implement the technique as the HyperLasso model checker, which we compare against the only existing tool that can automatically verify this class of properties, AutoHyper. To this end, we created a new benchmark consisting of example systems of parameterized complexity, together with hyperproperties with liveness constraints, obtained by analyzing prior work. Our evaluation shows that our BMC procedure implemented with a reduction to *Quantified Boolean Formulas* (QBF) formulas is already efficient enough to handle the complexity for multiple traces with different loops. Moreover, it shows that for large systems, as expected, the symbolic technique implemented in HyperLasso clearly outperforms the explicit-state technique implemented in AutoHyper at bug-finding or synthesis problems.

In summary, we make the following contributions to the state-of-art in order to achieve the first usable symbolic BMC for $\forall^+\exists^+$-liveness hyperproperties:

- We propose the first BMC procedure for HyperLTL that handles lasso-shaped paths, by encoding properties to QBF.
- We propose to iterate this BMC procedure and pairing it with a checking step to ensure that the produced counter-examples are true bugs of the system.
- We create, and make publicly available, a benchmark of liveness hyperproperties over systems of parametrized complexity.
- We implement the procedure as HyperLasso, which consumes models and properties in standard formats, and evaluate it against the state-of-the-art.

The remainder of this paper is structured as follows: the next section briefly presents HyperLTL and Sect. 3 reviews the related work; Sect. 4 presents our symbolic BMC procedure to implement a counter-example *synthesizer* and how an off-the-shelf model checker can be used to implement the *checker*; Sect. 5 presents the research questions, benchmark, and results of our evaluation; and, finally, Sect. 6 concludes the paper, including some ideas for future work.

2 HyperLTL in a Nutshell

The syntax of HyperLTL is defined by the following grammar, where $a \in \mathsf{AP}$ is an atomic proposition and $\pi \in \mathcal{V}$ is a path variable.

$$\psi ::= \mathsf{true} \mid a_\pi \mid \neg\psi \mid \psi \wedge \psi \mid \bigcirc\psi \mid \psi\, \mathcal{U}\, \psi$$
$$\varphi ::= \exists\pi.\varphi \mid \forall\pi.\varphi \mid \psi$$

As usual, we also have the derived logical (false, $\vee$, $\rightarrow$) and temporal operators (such as $\Diamond\psi := \mathsf{true}\, \mathcal{U}\, \psi$ and $\Box\psi := \neg(\Diamond\neg\psi)$).

The semantics of HyperLTL is defined over Kripke structures. A Kripke structure is a tuple $K = \langle S, S_0, \delta, L\rangle$, where S is a finite set of states, $S_0 \subseteq S$ is a set of initial states, $\delta \subseteq S \times S$ is a transition relation, and $L : S \rightarrow \Sigma$ is a labelling function, where $\Sigma ::= 2^{\mathsf{AP}}$. A path in a Kripke structure is an infinite sequence of states $s_0 s_1 s_2 \ldots \in S^\omega$ such that $s_0 \in S_0$ and $(s_i, s_{i+1}) \in \delta$ for all i. Each path corresponds to a trace $L(s_0)L(S_1)L(S_2) \ldots \in \Sigma^\omega$, and $\mathit{Traces}(K) \subseteq \Sigma^\omega$ denotes the set of all traces of K.

The semantics of a closed HyperLTL formula is given in Fig. 2, with respect to a trace assignment $\Pi : \mathcal{V} \hookrightarrow \Sigma^\omega$ and a mapping $\mathbb{T} : \mathcal{V} \hookrightarrow 2^{\Sigma^\omega}$ associating each quantified trace variable with the set of traces over which it ranges.

We say a formula is valid, denoted $\models \varphi$ iff $\mathbb{T}, \emptyset \models \varphi$ with $\mathbb{T}$ being the mapping that associates each quantified trace variable π with the set $\mathit{Traces}(K_\pi)$ of the respective Kripke structure K_π.

$$
\begin{array}{lll}
\Pi, i \models \mathsf{true} & & \\
\Pi, i \models a_\pi & \text{iff} & a \in \Pi(\pi)(i) \\
\Pi, i \models \neg\psi & \text{iff} & \Pi, i \not\models \psi \\
\Pi, i \models \psi_1 \wedge \psi_2 & \text{iff} & \Pi, i \models \psi_1 \text{ and } \Pi, i \models \psi_2 \\
\Pi, i \models \bigcirc\psi & \text{iff} & \Pi, i+1 \models \psi \\
\Pi, i \models \psi_1 \,\mathcal{U}\, \psi_2 & \text{iff} & \exists j \geq i. \Pi, j \models \psi_2 \text{ and } \forall i \leq n < j. \Pi, n \models \psi_1 \\
 & & \\
\mathbb{T}, \Pi \models \psi & \text{iff} & \Pi, 0 \models \psi \\
\mathbb{T}, \Pi \models \exists\pi.\varphi & \text{iff} & \exists t \in \mathbb{T}(\pi). \mathbb{T}, \Pi[\pi \mapsto t] \models \varphi \\
\mathbb{T}, \Pi \models \forall\pi.\varphi & \text{iff} & \forall t \in \mathbb{T}(\pi). \mathbb{T}, \Pi[\pi \mapsto t] \models \varphi
\end{array}
$$

Fig. 2. HyperLTL semantics.

Lasso-shaped Paths for HyperLTL. The bounded semantics $\models^k \varphi$ is defined in the same way as the unbounded one, except that $\mathbb{T}$ will only consider the subset of traces of each Kripke structure corresponding to k-loops (again, lasso-shaped paths that loopback in state k). Lasso-shaped traces capture all relevant infinite paths for HyperLTL, as shown in [28] that: any falsifiable formula admits a counter-example whose constituent traces are lasso-shaped. This is what makes a bounded encoding meaningful in the presence of liveness constraints.

Full BMC for HyperLTL generally accounts for non-lasso-shaped paths of length k – those where only a finite prefix is known. For these paths, a "pessimistic" bounded semantics is typically employed, where any formula evaluation beyond the known states is assumed to be false [10]. Consequently, non-lasso paths cannot identify counterexamples to liveness properties, as they cannot guarantee that a "good" event will not occur in the future. Since this work focuses specifically on the verification of liveness properties, we restrict our analysis to infinite (lasso-shaped) paths and omit the pessimistic semantics for finite prefixes. However, our technique could be naturally adapted to finite paths to provide a more comprehensive BMC framework for HyperLTL.

3 Related Work

In recent years, considerable work has addressed the problem of verifying hyperproperties encoded in general hyperlogics, in particular HyperLTL. In this section, we focus on model checking approaches, although considerable work has also been dedicated to verification of hyperproperties over programs [4,18,20,29].

Symbolic Approaches. HyperQB [27] is the state-of-the-art symbolic bounded model checker for HyperLTL. It addresses the verification of arbitrary HyperLTL properties for acyclic Kripke structures through an encoding into QBF. The absence of cycles in the Kripke structure (apart from self-looping states) severely limits its application to reactive systems. HyperQB also implements finite path semantics, which could in principle be used to verify safety hyperproperties for arbitrary Krikpe structures, but not liveness hyperproperties for the reasons presented in Sect. 1. In subsequent work [28], members of the HyperQB team addressed the model checking of lasso-shaped paths for $\forall\exists\Box\psi$ and $\exists\forall\Box\psi$ properties. Unfortunately, the technique requires the enumeration of all states of the Kripke structure, and does not scale for complex systems. To support the verification of asynchronous systems (i.e., that allow stuttering), the authors also proposed a BMC technique [25] for A-HLTL [3], a hyperlogic that allows the quantification of different *trajectories* of a trace. However, A-HLTL model checking is undecidable, and the BMC approach is restricted to acyclic, terminating systems. All these advancements have recently been integrated into a new version of HyperQB [26], as well as an alternative encoding into SMT. None of these BMC approaches support liveness hyperproperties over non-terminanting systems.

Explicit-State Approaches. Extensive work has focused on explicit-state complete model checking approaches for HyperLTL, since the seminal work by Clarkson et al. showed HyperLTL model checking is decidable and developed a prototype model checker [15]. MCHyper [23] is the first explicit-state model checker for HyperLTL to support models of some complexity. It is an automata-based model checker, but requires user input to solve existential quantifications. AutoHyper [6] is the state-of-the-art automata-based model checker, which fully supports HyperLTL through automata complementations. Subsequent work [7] has extended AutoHyper to support a version of HyperLTL with propositional quantifications. Although explicit-state model checking approaches allow for the complete verification of arbitrary hyperproperties over non-terminating systems, they suffer from state-explosion which severely hinders scalability. Game-based approaches have also been proposed to automatically derive strategies to instantiate existential quantifiers, both for HyperLTL [5,17] and asynchronous extensions such as OHyperLTL [8] and A-HLTL [9]. The evaluation of [6] suggests that AutoHyper can outperform such strategies for HyperLTL.

Input Formats. Most of the tools described above support models at low levels of abstraction or subsets of the SMV language, the input language for the NuSMV [13] and nuXmv [12] symbolic model checkers for LTL. Recent work has provided a higher-level abstraction for state-of-the-art symbolic and explicit-state model checkers [34].

4 BMC for Liveness Hyperproperties

We reduce the problem of bounded model checking $\forall^+\exists^+$ hyperproperties with a bound k, i.e., $\models_k \forall^+\exists^+\psi$, to the problem of checking its negation, i.e., $\models_k \exists^+\forall^+\neg\psi$. If this (negated) property is valid, the BMC procedure will yield a counter-example for the original formula. This counter-example is an instantiation for the existentially quantified traces for which $\forall^+\neg\psi$ holds, and since ψ may be a liveness property, refuting it requires lasso-shaped paths.

Algorithm 1 presents an overview of the proposed procedure. As mentioned in the introduction, it searches for k-loop candidates using a *synthesizer* that

Input: Formula $\exists\pi_1 \ldots \exists\pi_n.\forall\pi_{n+1} \ldots \forall\pi_m.\psi$, models $K_{\pi_1}, \ldots, K_{\pi_m}$, length k.
Output: Traces $t_1, \ldots, t_n : \mathcal{V} \hookrightarrow \Sigma^\omega$ or UNSAT

```
for i ∈ [1, ..., m] do  k_i ← k ;
result ← ⊥ ;
while result = ⊥ do
    [t_1, ..., t_n] ← synthesizer(k_1, ..., k_m, K_π1, ..., K_πm, ∃π_1 ... ∀π_m.ψ) ;
    if [t_1, ..., t_n] = UNSAT then
        result ← UNSAT ;
    else
        K'_πm, ..., K'_πn ← K_π1 ⊕ t_1, ..., K_πn ⊕ t_n ;
        [c_1, ..., c_m] ← checker(K'_π1, ..., K'_πn, K_πn+1, ..., K_πm, ∀π_1 ... ∀π_m.ψ) ;
        if [c_1, ..., c_m] = UNSAT then
            result ← [t_1, ..., t_n] ;
        else
            for i ∈ [n + 1, ..., m] do  k_i ← |c_i| ;
return result;
```

Algorithm 1: Overview of the *synthesis*/*checker* verification loop

implements a BMC procedure by reduction to QBF solving, extending the one implemented in HyperQB [27] with support for lasso-shaped paths. Candidates are then verified by a *checker*, to see if they are true paths of the full system or spurious candidates. Given that the input formula has a single quantifier alternation, once a candidate is found for the outermost existential quantifiers, its validation amounts to checking $\forall^+\psi$ with the existential quantifiers instantiated with the candidate. If the formula contains more than one universal quantifier, although still a hyperproperty, it can be analyzed using a standard model checker using self-composition [2]. Thus, this *checker* can be implemented using an off-the-self model checker for LTL. If a candidate is found to be spurious, the *synthesizer* is asked to generate a new one, and the process is iterated until a valid candidate is found or all possible candidate k-loops are exhausted, in which case $\not\models_k \exists^+\forall^+\neg\psi$.

To avoid iterating too many candidates, information from the *checker* when a candidate is identified as spurious is integrated into the next iteration of the *synthesizer*, implementing something similar to a CEGAR verification loop [14]. A candidate (an instantiation of the existentially quantified traces) is flagged as spurious by the *checker* when the LTL model checker finds a counter-part instantiation for the universally quantified traces that breaks the property. Rather than just negating the spurious candidate in the *synthesizer* and asking for another candidate, we instead expand the search space of the universally quantified traces. For the candidate to be spurious the counter-part instantiation must contain at least a k'-loop with $k' > k$, otherwise it would have already been found by the *synthesizer*. The k values for the universal quantifications are incremented to this higher k' for the next iteration of the *synthesizer* (bound k is always used for the existentially quantified traces). This excludes the previously found spurious candidate (since the counter-part will be found within the k' length), but also any other potential candidates that have counter-parts of similar length.[3]

Theorem 1 (Infinite Inference). *All k-loops returned by Algorithm 1 are witnesses of both $\models_k \exists^+\forall^+\psi$ and $\models \exists^+\forall^+\psi$.*

Proof. $\models_k \exists^+\forall^+\psi$ is guaranteed because the *synthesizer* directly implements the BMC semantics described in Sect. 2. The returned k-loops are also witnesses of $\models \exists^+\forall^+\psi$ because, to become invalid for any $k' > k$, it would need to become an invalid instantiation of the existential quantifiers (not possible for lasso-shaped paths because they can be unrolled for any $k' > k$) or for the universal quantification to find longer counter-parts, but this is already discarded by the complete *checker.*

Lemma 1 (Bounded Inference). *If Algorithm 1 does not return a witness, then $\not\models_k \exists^+\forall^+\psi$.*

Proof. If no witness is returned, then the procedure found some $k' \geq k$ such that every k-loop instantiation of the existentially quantified traces is rendered invalid by some k'-loop instantiation for the universally quantified traces. Increasing the k' bound for the universally quantified traces does not remove traces from the search-space, so k-loop candidates cannot become valid.

Note that the proposed approach fixes an outer k and terminates when no spurious counterexamples are found for some inner $k' \geq k$. Identifying whether the given k allows infinite inference for invalid results–which would require identifying a completeness threshold for HyperLTL problems – remains an orthogonal and often infeasible challenge at scale [28]. Bounded inference provides a partial completeness result, offering users a monotonic increase in confidence as k grows.[4]

In the remainder of this section we detail the *synthesizer* and the *checker.*

4.1 The Synthesizer

The *synthesizer* implements a standard BMC procedure. Likewise the procedure implemented by HyperQB [27], trace quantifiers are handled by reduction to QBF which can then be checked by an off-the-shelf solver. There are, however, two main differences when compared to HyperQB: 1) we consider lasso-shaped paths – and hence no special bounded semantics – in order to enable the verification of liveness properties over arbitrary reactive systems; and 2) we support

[3] In a sense, this process tries to iteratively approximate the completeness threshold for the instantiated inner problem, the value of k for which an invalid outcome applies to any trace. Note that this is now a regular LTL problem, for which classical results exist [30]. Nonetheless, statically determining a tight threshold is very difficult in practice or it would be too large for the analysis to be feasible.

[4] This contrasts with BMC for LTL, for which such results exist, and k can be iteratively increased up to that threshold (although this is often infeasible in practice).

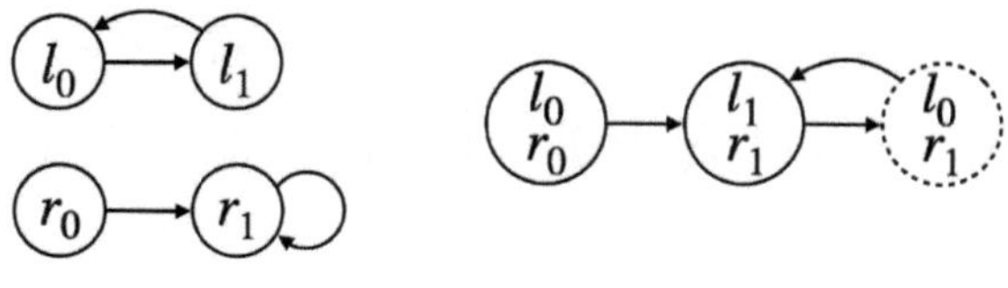

Fig. 3. Lasso synchronization.

different bounds for the quantified traces in order to implement the synthesis loop described in Algorithm 1.

The second generalization is more direct, and to simplify the presentation we will explain the procedure using the same bound k for all traces. The first generalization follows an observation already made in [28], in that loops arising from different traces may have different lengths, so any sound procedure must align them across the least common multiple (LCM) of their periods. But the primary technical insight underpinning our synthesizer is precisely that, for a hyperproperty over two models analysed up to bound k, the symbolic encoding need not unroll each model to depth $k \cdot k$ – the worst case suggested by the LCM alignment. We unroll each model only to depth k, and the hyperformula – which may logically require analysis up to depth $k \cdot k$ – refers back to the variables of the depth-k unrolling.

Overview. Going back to our running example hyperproperty, to generate a candidate with BMC we must show that $\models^k \exists\pi_1.\forall\pi_2.\Box(\neg a_{\pi_1} \vee \neg a_{\pi_2})$ holds, that is, find a k-loop π_1 of model L such that, for all k-loops π_2 of model, R the negation of the original inner LTL formula holds. For $k = 1$, one such candidate is the path $(l_0 l_1)^\omega$ depicted in the left-upper corner of Fig. 3. To show that this is a valid instantiation for π_1 with the bounded semantics we must explore all 1-loops of model R, for example the path $r_0(r_1)^\omega$ depicted in the left-lower corner of Fig. 3. For each such pair of k-loops π_1 and π_2 we must show that $\Box(\neg a_{\pi_1} \vee \neg a_{\pi_2})$ holds. This requires exploring all pairs of states reachable when executing both models synchronously, which in turn requires aligning different k-loops to fully explore the combined paths. When aligning a (k, i)-loop and a (k, j)-loop we end-up with a combined lasso-shaped path of size $\max(i, j) + \text{lcm}(k+1-i, k+1-j)$, where the last state loops back to state $\max(i, j)$ [28]. For the $(1, 0)$- and $(1, 1)$-loops in the left side of Fig. 3, the combined path is the $(2, 1)$-loop on the right side. The length of the combined path can thus be $(k + 1) \times k$ in the worst case. This was one of the reasons why HyperQB chose to adopt a bounded semantics considering only finite paths of size k (with the consequent limitation to safety properties or terminating systems). However, as we will show in the evaluation, with proper encodings it is efficient enough to enable BMC of $\forall^+\exists^+$-liveness properties in many complex reactive systems.

BMC Procedure. The reduction of BMC to QBF is presented in Fig. 4 (the direct encoding of derived operators $\Box$ and $\Diamond$ is also included to ease the understanding). To simplify the presentation, we assume that each quantified trace variables π is

$$[\![\exists\pi_1 \ldots \exists\pi_n.\forall\pi_{n+1} \ldots \forall\pi_m.\psi]\!]_k := \exists\overline{x_{\pi_1}}.\exists l_1 \ldots \exists\overline{x_{\pi_n}}.\exists l_n.\forall\overline{x_{\pi_{n+1}}}.\forall l_{n+1} \ldots \forall\overline{x_{\pi_m}}.\forall l_m.$$
$$\bigvee_{\substack{0\leq i_1\leq k\\ \ldots \\ 0\leq i_m\leq k}} \left(\bigwedge_{1\leq j\leq m} l_j = i_j \wedge \bigwedge_{1\leq j\leq n} [\![\pi_j]\!]_k^{i_j} \wedge \left(\bigwedge_{n<j\leq m} [\![\pi_j]\!]_k^{i_j} \rightarrow {}_0[\![\psi]\!]_k^{\pi_1\mapsto i_1,\ldots,\pi_m\mapsto i_m} \right)\right)$$

$$[\![\pi]\!]_k^i := I_\pi(x_\pi^0) \wedge R_\pi(x_\pi^0, x_\pi^1) \wedge \ldots \wedge R_\pi(x_\pi^{k-1}, x_\pi^k) \wedge R_\pi(x_\pi^k, x_\pi^i)$$

$$\begin{aligned}
{}_i[\![a_\pi]\!]_k^\Lambda &:= \begin{cases} a_\pi^i \text{ if } i < \Lambda(\pi) \\ a_\pi^{\underline{i}} \text{ otherwise} \end{cases}\\
{}_i[\![\neg\psi]\!]_k^\Lambda &:= \neg_i[\![\psi]\!]_k^\Lambda\\
{}_i[\![\psi_1 \wedge \psi_2]\!]_k^\Lambda &:= {}_i[\![\psi_1]\!]_k^\Lambda \wedge {}_i[\![\psi_2]\!]_k^\Lambda\\
{}_i[\![\bigcirc\psi]\!]_k^\Lambda &:= \begin{cases} {}_{i+1}[\![\psi]\!]_k^\Lambda \text{ if } i < \underline{k} \\ {}_{\underline{l}}[\![\psi]\!]_k^\Lambda \quad \text{otherwise} \end{cases}\\
{}_i[\![\Box\psi]\!]_k^\Lambda &:= \textstyle\bigwedge_{\min(i,\underline{l})\leq j\leq \underline{k}}\, {}_j[\![\psi]\!]_k^\Lambda\\
{}_i[\![\Diamond\psi]\!]_k^\Lambda &:= \textstyle\bigvee_{\min(i,\underline{l})\leq j\leq \underline{k}}\, {}_j[\![\psi]\!]_k^\Lambda\\
{}_i[\![\psi_1\, \mathcal{U}\, \psi_2]\!]_k^\Lambda &:= \textstyle\bigvee_{i\leq j\leq \underline{k}} \left({}_j[\![\psi_2]\!]_k^\Lambda \wedge \bigwedge_{i\leq n<j}\, {}_n[\![\psi_1]\!]_k^\Lambda \right) \vee\\
&\quad\ \textstyle\bigvee_{\underline{l}\leq j<i} \left({}_j[\![\psi_2]\!]_k^\Lambda \wedge \bigwedge_{i\leq n\leq \underline{k}}\, {}_n[\![\psi_1]\!]_k^\Lambda \wedge \bigwedge_{\underline{l}\leq n<j}\, {}_n[\![\psi_1]\!]_k^\Lambda \right)
\end{aligned}$$

$$\text{where } \begin{aligned} \underline{i} &:= \Lambda(\pi) + ((i - \Lambda(\pi)) \bmod (k + 1 - \Lambda(\pi)))\\ \underline{l} &:= \max(\{l \mid \pi \mapsto l \in \Lambda\})\\ \underline{k} &:= \underline{l} + \operatorname{lcm}(\{k + 1 - l \mid \pi \mapsto l \in \Lambda\}) - 1 \end{aligned}$$

Fig. 4. Reducing BMC to QBF solving

implicitly associated with the respective Kripke structures K_π. Moreover, $\overline{x_\pi}$ is a vector of Boolean variables with k copies of the state variables of K_π, x_π^i retrieves the variables from that vector relating to state i, and a_π^i refers to the Boolean variable for the atomic proposition a at state i. The encoding $[\![\exists\pi_1 \ldots \forall\pi_m.\psi]\!]_k$ of a HyperLTL formula with m quantifications is parametrized by the bound k. For each quantified trace π_j, the encoding starts with a similar quantification over k copies of the respective state variables, plus one quantified variable l_j that will range over all possible loopback indexes. These quantifications ensure that all possible k-loops are analyzed. The rest of the translation depends on the concrete values of the loopback indexes, so an outermost disjunction blasts those for all possible combinations. Then, for each quantified trace variable π, we ensure that the k copies of $\overline{x_\pi}$ and the respective loopback index i behave according to the respective Kripke structure using the formula $[\![\pi]\!]_k^i$, where I_π denotes the initial state predicate of the Kripke structure associated with π, and R_π the respective transition predicate. These (symbolic) predicates can be easily derived from high-level descriptions of Kripke structures. The last conjunct of $[\![\pi]\!]_k^i$ ensures that there is a loop back from the last state k to state i.

Finally, formula ${}_i[\![\psi]\!]_k^\Lambda$ encodes the standard bounded semantics of the inner LTL formula over k-loops [10], extended with model variable projections to express the combined execution of multiple paths. This encoding is parametrized by the bound k, a mapping Λ from trace variables to the respective loopback indexes being considered, and the state index i over which the formula should be evaluated (initially 0). To determine the value of an atomic proposition a_π at state i we need to reason about the position of i relative to the respective loopback index $\Lambda(\pi)$: if i is in the prefix before the loop, the i-th copy of the variable is accessed; otherwise, we need to determine which index $\underline{i}$ in the loop corresponds to the combined path index i, by performing modular arithmetic over the loop size, which for variable π is $k + 1 - \Lambda(\pi)$. Note that, for efficiency reasons, only the first k states of the individual paths are represented in the encoding. The states of the combined path with indexes $i > k$ are "virtual", and put together on-the-fly by combining states with possibly different indexes in the individual paths. That is the case of the (dashed) state at index 2 in the combined path on the right side of Fig. 3. To encode the standard semantics of the next operator $\bigcirc\phi$ over the combined lasso path, we need to determine both its last state index $\underline{k}$ and loopback index $\underline{l}$ using the maximum and LCM functions as described before: if i happens to be the last state $\underline{k}$ then ϕ is evaluated in the loopback state $\underline{l}$. For the remainder temporal operators, standard bounded semantics over lasso-shaped paths is used [10].

Comparison to [28]. The exponential growth in the bound necessary to perform BMC induced by the LCM was considered to be too inefficient by the authors of [28], who proposed an alternative BMC procedure – implemented in [26] – specifically for safety ($\forall\exists\Box\psi$) and co-safety ($\exists\forall\Box\psi$) properties. However, this method does not support the liveness properties addressed in our work. Unlike our approach, their technique relies on simulation relations, and the fundamental distinction lies in the fact that, while [28] exhaustively explores the state space for universal quantifiers, our synthesizer remains strictly bounded for all quantifiers. This leads to a significant disparity in scalability; for instance, the procedure in [28] unrolls one model to bound k but requires the other to reach its full state-space cardinality $|S|$, resulting in $|S| \cdot k$ variables for the simulation relation. In contrast, our encoding keeps the variable count independent of the explicit state count, scaling only with the unrolling depth.

4.2 The Checker

Given a HyperLTL formula $\exists\pi_1 \dots \forall\pi_m.\psi$, the *checker* can be implemented largely using off-the-shelf components. A candidate is an instantiation $\{\pi_1 \mapsto t_1, \dots, \pi_n \mapsto t_n\}$ to the existentially quantified trace variables. To check that it is a valid candidate we essentially need to verify that $\forall\pi_{n+1} \dots \forall\pi_m.\psi[t_1/\pi_1, \dots, t_n/\pi_n]$ holds, that is, that there are no possible counterpart traces that could possibly satisfy the original formula, regardless of the k value. In general this is still a HyperLTL formula, but since it contains only universally quantified trace variables it can be verified by a standard LTL model checker after applying self-composition [2].

Since performing the substitution $\psi[t_1/\pi_1, \dots, t_n/\pi_n]$ is not trivial, as one needs to encode also the loop behavior for each instantiated trace t_i, we instead verify formula $\forall\pi_1 \ldots \forall\pi_n.\forall\pi_{n+1} \ldots \forall\pi_m.\psi$ using self-composition, adjusting models K_{π_j} for $1 \leq j \leq n$ to only admit the single trace t_i. This can be done by adding an extra variable s_{π_i} to each model π_i ranging over possible state indexes 0 to k, constraining this variable to encode the correct evolution of the indexes in the k-loop t_i, and adding invariants ensuring the state variables of model π_i have the concrete values at each state in t_i; we denote this procedure by $K_{\pi_j} \oplus t_j$. When checking if the candidate $\pi_1 = (l_0 l_1)^\omega$ of model L satisfies $\forall\pi_2.\Box(\neg a_{\pi_1} \vee \neg a_{\pi_2})$, the complete model checker will return a counter-example because the candidate is spurious. As mentioned above, this counter-example is inspected by the *checker* to determine the value $k' > k$ to be used in the next iteration of the *synthesizer* to bound the existentially quantified traces.

4.3 HyperLasso

We implement the technique described above as the HyperLasso bounded model checker for HyperLTL[5]. HyperLasso receives a HyperLTL formula (in AutoHyper or HyperQB syntax), a bound k, and a model for each quantified trace (defined in the SMV syntax, from which the Kripke structures can be extracted). For our running example, the input formula to be checked and the respective SMV models are presented in Fig. 5. Each model from Fig. 1 contains a single integer enumeration variable whose value ranges over possible state indexes (for example, in the left model, $l = k$ iff the system is in state l_k).

HyperLasso then checks if there exist k-loop counter-examples for the outermost $\forall$ quantifiers that refute the formula. If no such counter-examples are found, the formula is reported as "maybe valid", as counter-examples might still exist for higher values of k. HyperLasso relies on off-the-shelf tools that follow standard formats, and can easily be replaced given advances in the state of the art. The overall technique and implementation are evaluated in the next section.

Synthesizer. To solve QBF we employ Z3 [21], using a subset of the SMT-LIB language [1] consisting of quantifiers over bit-vector variables. In comparison to the encoding described in Fig. 4, the most significant remark is that we do not need to blast all loop combinations eagerly at the start. Instead, we lazily blast loop combinations only when temporal operators appear in a formula, and only for the traces that are mentioned in the respective sub-formula. Our preliminary experiments revealed that this strategy yields smaller formulas that are also easier to solve. As Z3 revealed to be sensitive to the total count of quantified variables, we implemented optimizations to reduce the number of encoded QBF variables while preserving the original semantics. We include a constant-folding-like pass that identifies assignment expressions (e.g., $x = 5$ or $x = y$), allowing us to eliminate quantifiers for variables whose values are already determined. Additionally, during the conversion of SMV Boolean and integer variables to bit-vectors, we pack all k-expanded temporal instances of a model variable into a single bit-vector.

[5] The tool is publicly available at https://github.com/haslab/HyperLasso.

```
forall L. exists R. F (a[L] & a[R])
```

```
MODULE main
VAR l : 0..1;
ASSIGN
    init(l) := 0;
    next(l) := case
        l = 0 : {0,1};
        TRUE : {0,1};
    esac;
DEFINE a := (l = 0);
```

```
MODULE main
VAR r : 0..2;
ASSIGN
    init(r) := 0;
    next(r) := case
        r = 0 : 1;
        r = 1 : {1,2};
        TRUE : 1;
    esac;
DEFINE a := (r = 2);
```

Fig. 5. Input hyperproperty and SMV models L and R.

Checker. For the LTL model checker, we rely on NUXMV [12]. We first compose the models corresponding to the innermost universally quantified traces into a single SMV model[6]. We then extend the composed model with dedicated variables and assignments that fix the outermost existential traces, as described above. The negation of the LTL body of the original HyperLTL formula is specified as the property to be checked. For example, the SMV model in Fig. 6 represents the checking problem when L is fixed to the candidate $(l_0, l_1)^\omega$ (which, as we have seen, is spurious).

5 Evaluation

Our evaluation aimed at answering the following research questions:

RQ1 How does the efficiency of HYPERLASSO compare with that of state-of-the-art explicit model checking tools?
RQ2 How prevalent is the issue of spurious counter-example candidates?

Recall from Sect. 3 that the explicit-state AUTOHYPER is the only model checker for HyperLTL that supports liveness hyperproperties over non-terminating systems, so it is the focus of our comparison with the state-of-the-art.

5.1 Benchmark Suite

To answer these questions we defined a new benchmark suite[7], since existing benchmarks consisted mostly of safety properties or trivial toy examples. Although HYPERLASSO supports SMV models written in a declarative style, the models in our benchmarks are all described with explicit (possibly non-deterministic) assigns because this is the only style accepted by AUTOHYPER.

[6] Future work could consider experimental NUXMV support for self-composition [11].
[7] The benchmark suite is publicly available in HYPERLASSO's repository.

Our benchmark suite contains 5 verification and 2 synthesis problems. We consider synthesis problems those with $\exists^+\forall^+$ hyperproperties, whose validity verification entails finding appropriate instantiations for the existentially quantified variables. In the benchmarks, we consider $\exists^+\forall^+$ properties with safety requirements, which are the dual problem of $\forall^+\exists^+$ properties with liveness requirements and can be verified with the same technique. All our examples are parameterized by some sort of scope that dictates their size, and several instantiations of those scopes were verified to assess the tools' scalability. Our benchmarks contains both valid and invalid properties in verification problems, and both satisfiable and unsatisfiable properties in synthesis problems. BMC is particularly useful for invalid/satisfiable properties, where the found counter-examples/instances constitute a proof that applies to the full system, but we also compared the performance in valid/unsatisfiable properties for reasonable bounds k. Table 1 summarizes the information for each **Property**, showing the sequence of trace quantifiers ($\mathbb{Q}^\star$), the **Models** over which the quantifiers range (if a single model is listed, all quantifers range over it), and a restriction on the **Scope** (– means the result holds regardless of scope) to guarantee the expected outcome (**Res**, ✓ for valid/satisfiable verification/synthesis, ✗ for invalid/unsatisfiable verification/synthesis) according to (non-bounded) HyperLTL semantics. The 5 verification problems (and the paper's running toy example) appear at the top, and the 2 synthesis ones at the bottom. We now describe these problems in more detail.

```
MODULE main
VAR
    L_l : 0..1;
    R_r : 0..2;
    L_s : 0..1;
ASSIGN
    init(L_l) := 0;
    next(L_l) := case L_l = 0 : {0,1}; TRUE : {0,1}; esac;
    init(R_r) := 0;
    next(R_r) := case R_r = 0 : 1; R_r = 1 : {1,2}; TRUE : 1; esac;
    init(L_s) := 0;
    next(L_s) := case L_s < 1 : L_s+1; TRUE : 0; esac;
INVAR
    (L_s = 0 & L_l = 0) | (L_s = 1 & L_l = 1);
DEFINE
    L_a := (L_l = 0);
    R_a := (R_r = 2);
LTLSPEC
    G (!L_a | !R_a)
```

Fig. 6. SMV model for checking a candidate.

Table 1. Benchmark summary

Property	$\mathbb{Q}^\star$	Model(s)	Scope	Res
toy	$\forall\exists$	left right	–	✗
gni_any_rxa	$\forall\forall\exists$	cms_any_rxa	$r \geq 2 \wedge a \geq 2$	✗
gni_ndet_rxa	$\forall\forall\exists$	cms_ndet_rxa	–	✓
gni_max_rxa	$\forall\forall\exists$	cms_max_rxa	–	✓
rc_ser_txv	$\forall\exists$	rc_txv ser_txv	$t \geq 3 \wedge v \geq 2$	✗
ser_rc_txv	$\forall\exists$	ser_txv rc_txv	–	✓
cni_any_n	$\forall\exists$	mask_any_n	–	✗
cni_lte_n	$\forall\exists$	mask_lte_n	$n \geq 3$	✓
selfstab_gf_n	$\forall\exists$	herman_n	$n \geq 2$	✗
selfstab_lf_n	$\forall\exists$	herman_n	–	✓
robust_crit_n	$\forall\exists$	bakery_n	$n \geq 2$	✗
robust_ncrit_n	$\forall\exists$	bakery_n	–	✓
spec1_sxt	$\exists\forall$	controller_sxt system_s	$s \geq 4$	✓
spec2_sxt	$\exists\forall$	controller_sxt system_s	$t \geq 2$	✓
plan_nxe	$\exists\forall^e$	robot_n	$n > e$	✓

Generalized Non-interference in a Conference Management System. This verification problem is slightly adapted from one of the examples used in the evaluation of [34]. It describes a conference management system where a papers are rated by r reviewers, before an acceptance decision is made for each paper. The goal is to verify that the system satisfies *Generalized Non-Interference* (GNI), namely that individual ratings are not leaked to reviewers to which papers are not assigned. The system is non-terminating because reviewers are allowed to change their ratings while no final decision is made on an assigned paper. Unlike traditional GNI, which is just a safety property, this variant also entails liveness because it requires all papers to eventually have final decisions. The property is also conditional on the alignment of traces: the system model allows stuttering, and as shown in [32], public events must be aligned to happen at the same time in different traces to ensure that counter-examples make sense. This example contains three variants of the system, two where GNI holds and one where it does not: cms_max_rxa where the final decision for each paper is its highest rating; cms_ndet_rxa where the final decision for each paper is any of its ratings; and cms_any_rxa where the final decision for each paper is any rating of any paper.

Isolation Level Equivalence. For efficiency reasons, distributed transactional databases can be run with different *isolation levels*. The strongest one is *Serializability* (SER), where the results of trying to commit a set of transactions are the same as if the database was not distributed. Among the weaker isolation levels we have *Read Committed* (RC), where one transaction is not allowed to read data modified but not yet committed by another transaction. Several formalisms have been proposed to specify such isolation levels, for example the one by Crooks et al. [19] that we use in this problem. It is not trivial to reason about isolation levels, for example to check their equivalence, because they are basically defined as hyperproperties: given a transactional workload, a database satisfies an isolation level if there exists some execution where all transactions can be committed respecting some rules about what values can be read or written. The verified hyperproperty checks if a database running a given isolation level also satisfies another isolation level, assuming a workload of t transactions and v keys each holding one of v possible values. It is a property with liveness because the latter database must eventually commit all transactions. Two different models of databases are encoded: `ser_`t`x`v encodes a database ensuring SER and `rc_`t`x`v a database ensuring RC. Obviously, SER implies RC (`ser_rc_`t`x`v), while RC does not imply SER (`rc_ser_`t`x`v), with the counter-example being the well-known *dirty read* anomaly of RC.

Information Flow in Multi-threaded Programs. This problem considers a ∀∃ variant of non-interference (NI) proposed in [35] to check whether high-security information can flow to low-security variables. The model encodes a multi-threaded imperative program that applies a mask to a secret PIN, with a parameter n denoting the length of the bitvectors. Although a variant of this problem is present in previous benchmarks [27], it is a synchronous and terminating version. The version in our benchmark is asynchronous, with each thread acting interleaved according to a non-deterministic scheduler (essentially, a freely evolving variable whose possible values are process ids), as originally defined. This makes the system non-terminating since the scheduler may choose threads that are blocked. The property to be verified includes liveness because it states that, if a fair scheduler is considered (i.e., each process is allowed to act infinitely often), for whatever trace there is another with a different secret that eventually reaches the same public output. This property is invalid if the mask is chosen arbitrarily (`cni_any_`n) but valid if the mask is less than half the PIN (`cni_lte_`n).

We employ a classical strategy where in each state a "scheduler" decides which process is to act (essentially a freely evolving "turn" variable whose possible values are process ids). Then, in the hyperproperty, we restrict the verification of the desirable outcome to traces with a "fair scheduler", i.e., traces where each process is allowed to act infinitely often (GF turn = id).

Self-stabilization Algorithm for Ring of Processes. This problem encodes Herman's self-stabilization algorithm [24] for a ring of n identical processes, following the formulation for an asynchronous scheduler as presented in [33]. The goal is to guarantee that any ring circulating an arbitrary number of tokens eventually stabilizes in a single circulating token. The system is non-terminating because the scheduler chooses the process to act arbitrarily, and the acting process can choose to act or not depending on a coin flip. Self-stabilization is a hyperproperty with liveness because it states that whatever execution, there is an execution with the same initial token configuration and scheduler choices that can stabilize. This property is invalid even if assuming a global notion of fairness where some process will always eventually act (`selfstab_gf_`n), but valid for a local notion of fairness where all processes will always eventually act (`selfstab_lf_`n). [33] constructed a proof for an arbitrary n with additional linear assumptions due to the inability to model fairness constraints.

Robustness of the Bakery Protocol. This problem verifies a robustness hyperproperty [17] on Lamport's Bakery Protocol [31], a classic mutual exclusion algorithm where n processes take tickets to enter a critical section. In this context, robustness defines the system's fault tolerance: specifically, its ability to maintain liveness despite a process failure. This is a non-terminating model since the processes continuously attempt to access the critical section. We verify that if a process halts in the non-critical section, it does not block others from progressing, or more precisely, for every trace in which a process halts outside the critical section, there exists a trace in which that process behaves the same and the remaining processes still succeed in entering the critical section (`robust_ncrit_`n). In general, if a process halts while holding a ticket or inside the critical section, it can permanently starve other processes (`robust_crit_`n).

Controller Synthesis. The goal in this problem is to synthesize a controller for two semaphores at an intersection. This is essentially an LTL synthesis problem [22], expressed as an hyperproperty. A controller is a Mealy machine that for each input (requests for the semaphores) decides what is the output (which semaphores are green). The machine can have some sort of memory by having s different states, and can have t transitions, each mapping a source state and input to a destination state and an output. Each state also has a default transition with no input that applies when no other transition can be executed. A controller `controller_`s`x`t can run on a `system_`s with a state variable ranging over the s possible states. We have two variant specifications. In both, we assume that button presses are pressed infinitely often and wish to ensure that all possible executions satisfy the safety requirement that the two semaphores are not green simultaneously and the (liveness) requirement that all requests are eventually attended: `spec1_`s`x`t additionally requires that when a semaphore turns green it stays green for at least two states in a row, while `spec2_`s`x`t relaxes the requirements by assuming that two semaphore requests cannot appear consecutively. To encode this synthesis problem as a hyperproperty, an outer existential quantifier ranges over possible controllers modeled just by frozen variables (variables that once assigned in the initial state cannot change value), and the system properties are defined over an inner universal quantifier. This pattern, where one only wishes to find an appropriate system configuration, is rather common in synthesis problems [22].

Path Planning. In this problem, the goal is to synthesize a path for a robot moving in an $n \times n$ board that is guaranteed to avoid e enemies. It is inspired by other robot path planning problems from the hyperproperty literature [27]. The robot starts in position $(0, 0)$ while each enemy $0 \leq i < e$ starts in position $(n-1, i)$ and is only allowed to move in row i. This is a non-terminating system because the robots keep running indefinitely. If $e < n$ it is possible to find such a path – the robot moves down to row $n-1$ and then keeps moving right and left, meaning that it requires a lasso trace to be satisfiable. If seen from a verification perspective, `plan_`n`x`e is a liveness property because no such path exists if any of the enemies eventually catches the robot. Both the robot and the enemies are described with the same generic model `robot_`n, with the start positions and movement restrictions encoded in the property.

5.2 Results

Table 2 presents the evaluation results. Each **Property** is paired with its expected outcome (**Res**) and the general order of **Magnitude** of the sizes of

Table 2. Evaluation results

			AutoHyper		HyperLasso					
Property	**Res**	**Magnitude**	**Solver**	**Total**	k	k'	**Cands**	**Synth**	**Check**	**Total**
toy	✗	$10^0 \times 10^0$	spot	0.5	1	–	1	0.2	0.1	0.3
gni_any_1x1	✓	$(10^2)^3$	spot	12.1	8	–	0	137.9	0.0	137.9
gni_any_2x2	✗	$(10^5)^3$	spot	TO	4	–	1	1.3	0.1	1.4
gni_any_3x3	✗	$(10^9)^3$	spot	TO	6	–	1	3.7	0.1	3.8
gni_ndet_1x1	✓	$(10^2)^3$	spot	19.1	8	–	0	194.4	0.0	194.4
gni_ndet_2x2	✓	$(10^5)^3$	spot	TO	5	–	0	165.0	0.0	165.0
gni_ndet_3x3	✓	$(10^8)^3$	spot	TO	5	–	0	2.5	0.0	2.5
gni_max_1x1	✓	$(10^2)^3$	spot	19.6	8	–	0	209.8	0.0	209.8
gni_max_2x2	✓	$(10^4)^3$	spot	TO	5	–	0	96.2	0.0	96.2
gni_max_3x3	✓	$(10^8)^3$	spot	TO	5	–	0	2.5	0.0	2.5
rc_ser_2x1	✓	$10^2 \times 10^2$	forklift	0.6	109	–	0	287.7	0.0	287.7
rc_ser_3x2	✗	$10^6 \times 10^6$	forklift	TO	3	–	1	0.3	0.1	0.4
rc_ser_4x3	✗	–	forklift	TO	4	–	1	1.5	0.1	1.6
ser_rc_2x1	✓	$10^2 \times 10^2$	forklift	0.6	99	–	0	295.4	0.0	295.4
ser_rc_3x2	✓	$10^6 \times 10^6$	forklift	TO	17	–	0	228.1	0.0	228.1
ser_rc_4x3	✓	–	forklift	TO	3	–	0	1.2	0.0	1.2
cni_any_1	✗	$(10^2)^2$	roll	1.0	12	–	1	7.9	1.2	9.1
cni_any_2	✗	$(10^3)^2$	roll	TO	22	–	1	64.8	0.7	65.5
cni_any_3	✗	$(10^4)^2$	roll	TO	22	–	1	156.1	0.2	156.3
cni_any_4	✗	$(10^4)^2$	roll	TO	22	–	1	222.2	0.3	222.5
cni_lte_1	✗	$(10^0)^2$	roll	1.0	2	–	1	0.3	0.1	0.4
cni_lte_2	✗	$(10^2)^2$	roll	8.3	23	–	1	65.7	0.2	65.9
cni_lte_3	✓	$(10^3)^2$	roll	TO	24	–	0	267.2	0.0	267.2
cni_lte_4	✓	$(10^4)^2$	roll	TO	22	–	0	240.6	0.0	240.6

(continued)

Table 2. (*continued*)

			AutoHyper		HyperLasso					
Property	**Res**	**Magnitude**	**Solver**	**Total**	k	k'	**Cands**	**Synth**	**Check**	**Total**
selfstab_gf_3	✗	$(10^1)^2$	forklift	0.9	1	5	2	0.3	0.3	0.6
selfstab_gf_5	✗	$(10^2)^2$	forklift	39.6	1	1	1	0.4	0.2	0.6
selfstab_gf_7	✗	$(10^3)^2$	forklift	TO	1	1	1	0.5	0.2	0.7
selfstab_lf_3	✓	$(10^1)^2$	forklift	0.8	5	12	2	117.3	0.5	117.8
selfstab_lf_5	✓	$(10^2)^2$	forklift	TO	4	17	3	86.9	0.1	87.0
selfstab_lf_7	✓	$(10^3)^2$	forklift	TO	5	–	0	0.8	0.0	0.8
robust_crit_1	✓	$(10^1)^2$	roll	0.8	2	–	1	0.2	1.0	1.2
robust_crit_2	✗	$(10^2)^2$	roll	TO	2	6	2	0.4	0.3	0.7
robust_crit_3	✗	$(10^3)^2$	roll	TO	2	23	2	7.5	1.2	8.7
robust_ncrit_1	✓	$(10^1)^2$	roll	0.9	26	–	1	95.6	0	95.6
robust_ncrit_2	✓	$(10^2)^2$	roll	TO	21	27	1	217.1	0.2	217.3
robust_ncrit_3	✓	$(10^3)^2$	roll	TO	12	42	1	264.9	0.2	265.1
spec1_2x0	✗	$10^2 \times 10^1$	roll	5.0	27	–	0	220.1	0.0	220.1
spec1_4x0	✓	$10^5 \times 10^2$	roll	TO	0	4	1	4.1	0.2	4.3
spec1_4x2	✓	$10^9 \times 10^2$	roll	TO	0	4	1	101.3	2.0	103.3
spec2_1x1	✗	$10^2 \times 10^1$	roll	8.3	24	–	0	192.5	0.0	192.5
spec2_1x2	✓	$10^3 \times 10^1$	roll	TO	0	3	1	0.1	0.1	0.2
spec2_4x4	✓	$10^{14} \times 10^3$	roll	TO	0	3	1	0.5	2.1	2.6
plan_3x1	✓	$(10^1)^2$	forklift	2.7	2	–	1	0.3	1.0	1.3
plan_3x2	✓	$(10^1)^3$	forklift	TO	3	–	1	0.4	0.1	0.5
plan_3x3	✗	$(10^1)^4$	forklift	TO	21	–	0	231.8	0.0	231.8
plan_4x1	✓	$(10^2)^2$	forklift	TO	2	–	1	0.3	0.2	0.5
plan_4x2	✓	$(10^2)^3$	forklift	TO	3	–	1	0.6	0.1	0.7
plan_4x3	✓	$(10^2)^4$	forklift	TO	4	–	1	1.3	0.4	1.7
plan_4x4	✗	$(10^2)^5$	forklift	TO	18	–	0	246.4	0.0	246.4

the individual state machines (as number of states of the Krikpe structure).[8] We then show the underlying automaton **Solver** and the **Total** time taken by AutoHyper to verify the property, and report several metrics for HyperLasso, namely: the considered BMC bound k, the bound k' for the inner universally quantified traces by the end of the verification loop, the number of **Cand**idates tried (for invalid/satisfiable problems, this includes the valid candidate), the time spent in (possibly multiple iterations) of the **Synth**esizer and of the **Check**er, as well as the **Total** verification time. We run AutoHyper with witness mode enabled and for a fair comparison, we selected the best performing underlying automata solver (as supported in [34]) for each class of examples. All properties

[8] A – indicates that the state machine was too large to compute its size with `nuXmv`.

were checked in a MacBook Pro M1 machine with 16GB RAM, with a time-out of 300 s (marked TO in the table). While AutoHyper performs complete model checking, exploring all paths regardless of length, HyperLasso performs bounded model checking, and thus a k bound must be chosen for each problem. For invalid/satisfiable problems, since k-loops returned by HyperLasso are guaranteed to be paths of the full model, we select the minimal value that produces a witness; for valid/unsatisfiable problems, the output of HyperLasso is inconclusive, and we select the largest k value (which can be read as the maximum level of confidence), for which HyperLasso responds within the timeout.

Regarding **RQ1**, the results show that HyperLasso consistently outperforms AutoHyper for any problem beyond minimal scopes. When such minimal scope is below the restrictions stated in Table 1, changing the property's expected outcome, it is marked as red. The exception is problem `selfstab_lf_3` where AutoHyper considerably outperforms HyperLasso; for `selfstab_lf_5` AutoHyper already times out while HyperLasso still reports withing the timeout. It should again be remarked that AutoHyper is solving a much harder problem than HyperLasso. However, AutoHyper's feedback is all-or-nothing, while HyperLasso guarantees that all k-loop bugs are found, providing a more incremental level of confidence. However, it should be noted that for some valid problems, HyperLasso can provide a false sense of confidence, since small values k also make certain problems vacuous. This is evidenced, for instance, by the sudden decrease of solving time in `selfstab_lf_7`: this problem's fairness constraint forces the token to at least go around the ring once in all traces, which is not possible with $k = 5$. A similar phenomenon occurs, for instance, for `gni_ndet_3x3`, `gni_max_3x3`, or `ser_rc_4x3`.

Focusing on **RQ2**, results show that, although not prevalent, spurious candidates occurred for both invalid/satisfiable cases, namely `selfstab_gf`, `robust_crit`, `spec1` or `spec2`, where spurious counter-examples are discarded before a valid one is found; and in valid/unsatisfiable problems, namely `selfstab_lf` and `robust_ncrit`, where spurious candidates must be discarded before concluding the formula is valid. This means that the *checker* was effectively needed to guarantee sound results. There are also other problems for which we know spurious candidates exist (such as the satisfiable path planning problems), but the first candidate returned by the *synthesizer* happened to be valid. Another concern was whether the number of iterations would encumber the whole process. For our problems, the number of spurious candidates generated was quite low, never going beyond 2. Results also show that the time spent on the *checker* was negligible compared with that spent on the *synthesizer*, so this extra step does not seem to be a bottleneck. In order to further reason about the impact of the iteration, we look at the final bound $k' > k$ for the inner universally quantified traces. Interestingly, for several problems the process jumped in a single iteration to a k' that ensured termination in the next iteration. That was the case, for example, of `selfstab_lf_5` that jumped from bound 4 to bound 17 in a single iteration, allowing HyperLasso to conclude that the formula was valid for bound k in the next iteration. Notice that this bound k' is not necessarily minimal, since counter-examples generated by nuXmv (in complete mode) are not guaranteed to have minimal length. Nonetheless, this over-approximation did not seem to affect the performance of the procedure.

6 Conclusion

This paper proposed the first symbolic technique for the bounded model checking of arbitrary HyperLTL properties over reactive systems, including the scarcely addressed class of $\forall^+\exists^+$-liveness hyperproperties. The technique consists of a verification loop where candidate witnesses are synthesized by a bounded procedure, and subsequently checked for validity with a complete model checker for plain LTL. We created a benchmark suite specially tailored for this class of properties, and used it to evaluate our implementation of the technique, HyperLasso. Results show that HyperLasso consistently outperforms AutoHyper, the only other state-of-the-art tool that is able to support our benchmarks.

For future work, we intend to generalize this technique for multiple quantifier alternations. This is expected to have a toll on performance, so we may need to implement further optimizations to guarantee scalability, such as more refined strategies to handle the BMC bound or the support for more solving procedures, such as dedicated QBF solvers.

Acknowledgments. The work of Alcino Cunha is financed by National Funds through the FCT - Fundação para a Ciência e a Tecnologia, I.P. (Portuguese Foundation for Science and Technology) within the CMU Portugal Visiting Faculty and Researchers Program. The work of Hugo Pacheco is funded by national funds through FCT – Fundação para a Ciência e a Tecnologia, I.P., under the support UID/50014/2025 (https://doi.org/10.54499/UID/50014/2025). The work of Nuno Macedo is financed by National Funds through the FCT - Fundação para a Ciência e a Tecnologia, I.P. (Portuguese Foundation for Science and Technology) within the project POISE, with reference 2024.15783.PEX (https://doi.org/10.54499/2024.15783.PEX).

Data Availibility Statement. The source code, benchmarks, and experimental framework used in this study are publicly available on GitHub at https://github.com/haslab/HyperLasso. A persistent artifact snapshot, including reproduction instructions, is archived on Zenodo at https://doi.org/10.5281/zenodo.19850821.

Disclosure of Interests. The authors have no competing interests to declare that are relevant to the content of this article.

References

1. Barrett, C., Stump, A., Tinelli, C., et al.: The SMT-LIB standard: version 2.0. In: Proceedings of the 8th International Workshop on Satisfiability Modulo Theories. Edinburgh, UK. vol. 13, p. 14 (2010). https://smt-lib.org/papers/smt-lib-reference-v2.7-r2025-07-07.pdf
2. Barthe, G., D'argenio, P.R., Rezk, T.: Secure information flow by self-composition. Math. Struct. Comput. Sci. **21**(6), 1207–1252 (2011). https://doi.org/10.1109/CSFW.2004.1310735

3. Baumeister, J., Coenen, N., Bonakdarpour, B., Finkbeiner, B., Sánchez, C.: A temporal logic for asynchronous hyperproperties. In: Silva, A., Leino, K.R.M. (eds.) CAV 2021. LNCS, vol. 12759, pp. 694–717. Springer, Cham (2021). https://doi.org/10.1007/978-3-030-81685-8_33
4. Beutner, R.: Automated software verification of hyperliveness. In: TACAS (2). LNCS, vol. 14571, pp. 196–216. Springer (2024). https://doi.org/10.1007/978-3-031-57249-4_10
5. Beutner, R., Finkbeiner, B.: Prophecy variables for hyperproperty verification. In: CSF, pp. 471–485. IEEE (2022). https://doi.org/10.1109/CSF54842.2022.9919658
6. Beutner, R., Finkbeiner, B.: AutoHyper: explicit-state model checking for HyperLTL. In: International Conference on Tools and Algorithms for the Construction and Analysis of Systems, pp. 145–163. Springer (2023). https://doi.org/10.1007/978-3-031-30823-9_8
7. Beutner, R., Finkbeiner, B.: Model checking omega-regular hyperproperties with AutoHyperQ. In: LPAR. EPiC Series in Computing, vol. 94, pp. 23–35. EasyChair (2023).https://doi.org/10.29007/1xjt
8. Beutner, R., Finkbeiner, B.: Predicate abstraction for hyperliveness verification. Formal Methods Syst. Des. **66**(2), 238–277 (2025). https://doi.org/10.1007/s10703-025-00482-5
9. Beutner, R., Finkbeiner, B.: Verifying asynchronous hyperproperties in reactive systems. Proc. ACM Program. Lang. **9**(OOPSLA2) (2025). https://doi.org/10.1145/3763130
10. Biere, A., Cimatti, A., Clarke, E., Zhu, Y.: Symbolic model checking without BDDs. In: Cleaveland, W.R. (ed.) TACAS 1999. LNCS, vol. 1579, pp. 193–207. Springer, Heidelberg (1999). https://doi.org/10.1007/3-540-49059-0_14
11. Bombardelli, A., Bozzelli, L., Sanchez, C., Tonetta, S.: (Asynchronous) temporal logics for hyperproperties on finite traces. In: International Symposium on Model Checking Software, pp. 25–43. Springer (2025). https://doi.org/10.1007/978-3-032-06847-7_2
12. Cavada, R., et al.: The NUXMV symbolic model checker. In: International Conference on Computer Aided Verification, pp. 334–342. Springer (2014). https://doi.org/10.1007/978-3-319-08867-9_22
13. Cavada, R., et al.: NuSMV 2.6 user manual. FBK-IRST (2010). http://nusmv.fbk.eu/NuSMV/userman/v26/nusmv.pdf
14. Clarke, E., Grumberg, O., Jha, S., Lu, Y., Veith, H.: Counterexample-guided abstraction refinement for symbolic model checking. J. ACM (JACM) **50**(5), 752–794 (2003). https://doi.org/10.1145/876638.876643
15. Clarkson, M.R., Finkbeiner, B., Koleini, M., Micinski, K.K., Rabe, M.N., Sánchez, C.: Temporal logics for hyperproperties. In: International Conference on Principles of Security and Trust, pp. 265–284. Springer (2014). https://doi.org/10.1007/978-3-642-54792-8_15
16. Clarkson, M.R., Schneider, F.B.: Hyperproperties. J. Comput. Secur. **18**(6), 1157–1210 (2010). https://doi.org/10.3233/JCS-2009-0393
17. Coenen, N., Finkbeiner, B., Sánchez, C., Tentrup, L.: Verifying hyperliveness. In: International Conference on Computer Aided Verification, pp. 121–139. Springer (2019). https://doi.org/10.1007/978-3-030-25540-4_7
18. Correnson, A., Nießen, T., Finkbeiner, B., Weissenbacher, G.: Finding ∀∃ hyperbugs using symbolic execution. Proc. ACM Program. Lang. **8**(OOPSLA2), 1420–1445 (2024). https://doi.org/10.1145/3689761

19. Crooks, N., Pu, Y., Alvisi, L., Clement, A.: Seeing is believing: a client-centric specification of database isolation. In: Proceedings of the ACM Symposium on Principles of Distributed Computing, pp. 73–82 (2017). https://doi.org/10.1145/3087801.3087802
20. Dardinier, T., Li, A., Müller, P.: Hypra: a deductive program verifier for hyper Hoare logic. Proc. ACM Program. Lang. **8**(OOPSLA2), 1279–1308 (2024). https://doi.org/10.1145/3689756
21. de Moura, L., Bjørner, N.: Z3: an efficient SMT solver. In: Ramakrishnan, C.R., Rehof, J. (eds.) TACAS 2008. LNCS, vol. 4963, pp. 337–340. Springer, Heidelberg (2008). https://doi.org/10.1007/978-3-540-78800-3_24
22. Faymonville, P., Finkbeiner, B., Tentrup, L.: Bosy: an experimentation framework for bounded synthesis. In: Majumdar, R., Kunčak, V. (eds.) Computer Aided Verification, pp. 325–332. Springer International Publishing, Cham (2017). https://doi.org/10.1007/978-3-319-63390-9_17
23. Finkbeiner, B., Rabe, M.N., Sánchez, C.: Algorithms for model checking HyperLTL and HyperCTL*. In: CAV (1). LNCS, vol. 9206, pp. 30–48. Springer (2015). https://doi.org/10.1007/978-3-319-21690-4_3
24. Herman, T.: Probabilistic self-stabilization. Inf. Process. Lett. **35**(2), 63–67 (1990). https://doi.org/10.1016/0020-0190(90)90107-9
25. Hsu, T., Bonakdarpour, B., Finkbeiner, B., Sánchez, C.: Bounded model checking for asynchronous hyperproperties. In: TACAS (1). LNCS, vol. 13993, pp. 29–46. Springer (2023). https://doi.org/10.1007/978-3-031-30823-9_2
26. Hsu, T.H., Rabizadeh, M., Rogale, K., Filippov, F., de Oliveira Batista, M.A., Bonakdarpour, B.: HyperQB 2.0: a bounded model checker for hyperproperties. In: International Conference on Computer Aided Verification. to appear (2026). https://arxiv.org/abs/2109.12989
27. Hsu, T.H., Sánchez, C., Bonakdarpour, B.: Bounded model checking for hyperproperties. In: International Conference on Tools and Algorithms for the Construction and Analysis of Systems, pp. 94–112. Springer (2021). https://doi.org/10.1007/978-3-030-72016-2_6
28. Hsu, T.H., Sánchez, C., Sheinvald, S., Bonakdarpour, B.: Efficient loop conditions for bounded model checking hyperproperties. In: International Conference on Tools and Algorithms for the Construction and Analysis of Systems, pp. 66–84. Springer (2023). https://doi.org/10.1007/978-3-031-30823-9_4
29. Itzhaky, S., Shoham, S., Vizel, Y.: Hyperproperty verification as CHC satisfiability. In: ESOP (2). LNCS, vol. 14577, pp. 212–241. Springer (2024). https://doi.org/10.1007/978-3-031-57267-8_9
30. Kroening, D., Ouaknine, J., Strichman, O., Wahl, T., Worrell, J.: Linear completeness thresholds for bounded model checking. In: CAV. LNCS, vol. 6806, pp. 557–572. Springer (2011). https://doi.org/10.1007/978-3-642-22110-1_44
31. Lamport, L.: A new solution of Dijkstra's concurrent programming problem, pp. 171–178. Association for Computing Machinery, New York, NY, USA (2019). https://doi.org/10.1145/3335772.3335782
32. Lamport, L., Schneider, F.B.: Verifying hyperproperties with TLA. In: 2021 IEEE 34th Computer Security Foundations Symposium (CSF), pp. 1–16. IEEE (2021). https://doi.org/10.1109/CSF51468.2021.00012
33. Lin, A.W., Rümmer, P.: Liveness of randomised parameterised systems under arbitrary schedulers. In: Chaudhuri, S., Farzan, A. (eds.) CAV 2016. LNCS, vol. 9780, pp. 112–133. Springer, Cham (2016). https://doi.org/10.1007/978-3-319-41540-6_7

34. Macedo, N., Pacheco, H.: Model checking of hyperproperties for high-level relational models (2026). https://arxiv.org/abs/2512.12024
35. Smith, G., Volpano, D.M.: Secure information flow in a multi-threaded imperative language. In: POPL, pp. 355–364. ACM (1998). https://doi.org/10.1145/268946.268975

The Simulator's Blueprint: Automata Learning from Cybersecurity Logs

Tudor Braicu[1](✉), Benjamin Ylvisaker[1], Nicolas Espinosa Dice[1], Yiding Chen[1], Yiyi Zhang[1], Nate Foster[2,3], and Hossein Hojjat[4]

[1] Cornell University, Ithaca, USA
tb574@cornell.edu
[2] EPFL, Lausanne, Switzerland
[3] Jane Street, New York City, USA
[4] Tehran Institute for Advanced Studies, Tehran, Iran

Abstract. We show how to use passive automata learning to infer models of attacker-defender interactions in cybersecurity. By treating system event logs as words in a formal language, we can apply algorithms such as RPNI to infer compact deterministic finite automata from observed traces. We evaluate this approach through a case study on the Cyber Operations Research Gymnasium (CybORG), a widely-used simulation framework for training defensive agents using machine learning. We analyze the structural properties of the inferred automata and assess their empirical fidelity with respect to the semantics of CybORG. Our results show that accurate formal models can be learned from a relatively small number of traces, suggesting a promising path toward more automated and data-driven approaches to cybersecurity.

1 Introduction

Reinforcement learning (RL) [19] is a promising approach to cybersecurity, enabling defensive agents to be trained simply by interacting with an environment, without requiring explicit models of system dynamics or attacker behavior. However, RL is notoriously data hungry [6] and typically requires millions of interactions during training, far beyond what is feasible using live systems or emulated environments. As a result, most RL-based approaches to cybersecurity rely on simulators that approximate the state space and transition behavior of the underlying system using more efficient representations. Building simulators is itself a major challenge, requiring domain expertise and significant engineering.

This state of affairs motivates a natural question: *can simulators be constructed automatically from data?* That is, rather than having to design and build complex simulators by hand, one might hope to infer formal representations from system traces automatically. Automata learning offers a principled foundation, including techniques for synthesizing finite-state models that are guaranteed to be consistent with the provided system traces. Even when a

E. Darulova et al. (Eds.): CAV 2026, LNCS 16682, pp. 497–510, 2026.
https://doi.org/10.1007/978-3-032-32519-8_25

learned model does not capture all aspects of a system's behavior, it can provide high-fidelity approximations that are sufficient for downstream tasks such as RL training.

This paper presents a case study of using automata learning to infer formal models of networked systems. We show how to interpret system event logs as words in a formal language and apply the Regular Positive and Negative Inference (RPNI) algorithm to obtain compact deterministic finite-state automata (DFA) consistent with the observed traces. We measure the impact of the length of traces on the size and accuracy of the learned automata and we compare the use of random and heuristic agents for exploring the state space of the system. We evaluate our approach on the Cyber Operations Research Gymnasium (CybORG) [18], a widely-used Python simulator for RL-based cybersecurity.

Our results show that it is possible to infer high-fidelity models that closely match the behavior of the original system, but run much faster in practice. We also highlight several empirical lessons. First, preprocessing the raw system event logs is a key step as it both simplifies the task and provides a way to mitigate complications, such as limited forms of non-determinism. Second, shorter traces are often effective for learning bounded models—an intuitive finding that we see in the data. Finally, heuristic exploration strategies are useful for effectively exploring the state space.

Overall, this paper makes the following contributions:

- We show how to model system event logs as words in a formal language, enabling the use of passive learning for inferring formal models of behavior.
- We develop heuristic techniques to help scale learning up to realistic systems.
- We conduct a case study using CybORG and analyze the size and accuracy of the inferred models.

2 Related Work

Automata learning is a branch of machine learning dedicated to inferring formal grammars or automata from observational data [7]. In the case of regular languages, the objective is typically to learn a deterministic finite automaton (DFA) that accurately models a target language over a given alphabet. Due to its theoretical significance and practical applications in formal verification, synthesis, and system analysis, automata learning has drawn substantial and growing interest from the verification community [5,8,22]. The survey article by Vaandrager provides a good overview [20].

In the literature, automata learning techniques are commonly distinguished by the nature of the information available to the learner. The first paradigm, active learning, involves an interactive process where the learner dynamically queries a "teacher" or "oracle" (e.g., as in Angluin's L^* algorithm [2]). In contrast, the second paradigm, passive learning, does not involve such an interaction. Here, the learner is presented with a static, fixed dataset of labeled examples from which it must infer the underlying language. Examples of passive learning algorithms include RPNI [16], which builds a prefix tree acceptor from the positive examples and then merges states while respecting the negative examples; EDSM [10], which improves on RPNI using advanced heuristics for merging states; and Alergia [3], which uses the state-merging approach to probabilistic automata. Standard benchmarks for comparing different approaches to automata learning have also been developed [15].

Automata learning has been applied in many fields, including RL, where the automaton might model policy or reward structure, and in networking, where it might model protocols or device behavior. For instance, JIRP [23] jointly learns a reward machine and a policy by iteratively refining candidates using counterexamples produced by the environment. Shehab et al. [17] develop an extension of inverse RL that uses automata learning and SAT solvers to infer formal models of reward structure. Alembic [13] infers models of stateful network functions such as NATs and firewalls, yielding artifacts that can be analyzed by downstream tools. Prognosis [4] learns models of protocol implementations in a closed-box setting and uses differential testing to find differences between TCP and QUIC stacks. Moeller et al. [12] develop an Angluin-style algorithm that infers a model of the network fabric, represented as symbolic NetKAT automata. This paper focuses on applications of automata learning in cybersecurity, using system logs of events initiated by offensive (red) or defensive (blue) agents, to infer a DFA that models the behavior of the underlying system.

3 Background

Cybersecurity is often framed as a competition between defenders and attackers: attackers exploit a vulnerability, defenders respond, and the cycle repeats. However, a growing community of researchers is exploring how data-driven approaches based on machine learning can be used to put an end to the cat-and-mouse game, making defense continuous and automated rather than reactive and manual.

3.1 RL-Based Cybersecurity

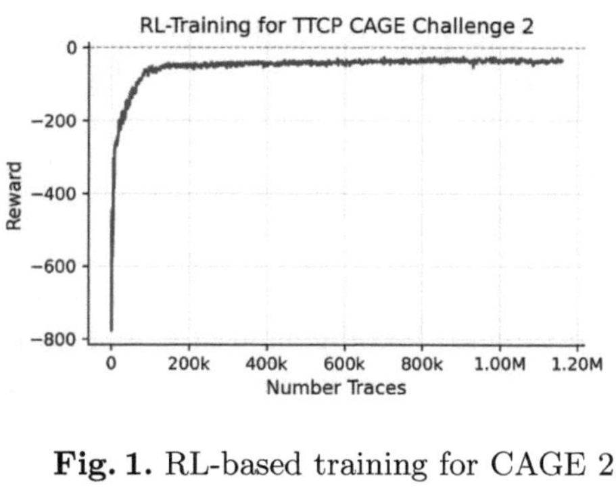

Fig. 1. RL-based training for CAGE 2.

DARPA's CASTLE program is developing technologies for training defensive agents based on RL. However, while RL is general, requiring only notions of observations, actions, and rewards, it is also notoriously data hungry. Figure 1 shows the number of steps required to train a competitive agent for the TTCP CAGE Challenge 2 (CAGE 2) [9] using RL. It is not practical to execute millions of steps in a live or emulated system—doing so requires executing shell commands,

```
Episode 1:
  Step 1:
    {action:DecoyTomcat, hostname:Subnet_Op_DB, ip_address:10.0.151.89, success:FALSE}
    {action:DiscoverSystems, subnet:10.0.128.112/28, success:TRUE}
  Step 2:
    {action:Restore, hostname:Subnet_1_Host_1, ip_address:10.0.46.185, success:TRUE}
    {action:DiscoverServices, ip_address:10.0.128.113, hostname:Subnet1, success:FALSE}
  Step 3:
...
Episode 2:
  Step 1:
    {action:DecoySmss, hostname:Subnet_1_Host_1, ip_address:10.0.175.124, success:FALSE}
    {action:DiscoverSystems, subnet:10.0.230.32/28, success:TRUE}
...
```

Fig. 2. An example event log, grouped into steps and episodes.

communicating over the network, synchronizing with other nodes, etc. One way to deal with this problem could be to shift to a purely data-driven formulation of RL, also known as offline RL [11]. However, many RL practitioners still rely on simulators like CybORG, a Python-based simulation framework. Of course, building accurate simulators is not easy, requiring domain knowledge and significant engineering effort.

3.2 Passive Automata Learning

Passive learning is defined in terms of two disjoint sets: a set of positive examples $S^+ \subseteq L$ (valid sequences) and a set of negative examples $S^- \subseteq (\Sigma^* \setminus L)$ (invalid sequences). The learner seeks a DFA M such that $S^+ \subseteq L(M)$ and $S^- \cap L(M) = \emptyset$. The Regular Positive and Negative Inference (RPNI) algorithm is the foundational state-merging method for passive learning of regular languages in polynomial time [16]. It starts from a Prefix Tree Acceptor (PTA) built from positive examples S^+. It then generalizes this structure by deterministically traversing the PTA's states in a fixed order, attempting to merge each candidate state with an earlier state. A merge is accepted only if the resulting DFA remains consistent with the negative examples S^-; otherwise, the merge is undone. This process yields a DFA consistent with the examples.

We use RPNI as our primary algorithm because it is the classic and canonical algorithm in the field, serving as a strong representative of passive learning approaches. It is guaranteed, in the limit of infinite data, to identify the target language correctly, providing a solid theoretical foundation. As a point of comparison, we consider one of its well-known extensions: Evidence-Driven State Merging (EDSM) [10]. EDSM replaces RPNI's fixed merge order with an evidence-based scoring heuristic: it evaluates all compatible candidate merges and greedily selects the highest-scoring one.

4 System Event Logs as Language Inclusion Problem

Figure 2 depicts an event log from CAGE 2, which captures a sequential interaction between offensive (red) and defensive (blue) agents. At a high level, it records an adversarial cycle of reconnaissance and remediation: the red agent gathers information about accessible hosts (`DiscoverSystems`), while the blue agent alternates between failed attempts at deception (`DecoyTomcat` and `DecoySmss`) and operations to restore a possibly-infected host back to a known good state (`Restore`). We treat these logs as a continuous execution trace, where the alternating actions of both agents generate a cumulative history.

Table 1. Agent Actions for CAGE 2

Agent	Action	Description
Blue	Analyze Host	Detect malicious vs. benign activity on a host
	Remove	Eliminate red agent sessions on a host
	Restore	Revert a host to clean backup
	Create Decoy	Deploy decoy services (causes red exploits to fail)
Red	Discover Systems	Gather information about accessible hosts
	Discover Services	Scan for open ports and available services on a host
	Exploit	Gain access to a host via vulnerable service
	Privilege Escalate	Gain root access on compromised host
	Impact	Disrupt the critical Operational Server service
	Lateral Movement	Move from compromised host to other hosts

This section formalizes a preprocessing transformation that maps raw event logs into strings in a formal language L, where the validity of a trace is determined by the success of the final action. Consider two disjoint sets of actions (Table 1). $\mathcal{A}_B = \{\texttt{DecoyTomcat}, \texttt{Restore}, \cdots\}$ represents the set of actions for blue and $\mathcal{A}_R = \{\texttt{DiscoverSystems}, \texttt{DiscoverServices}, \cdots\}$ represents the set of actions for red. The space of all actions is the union of these sets: $\mathcal{A} = \mathcal{A}_B \cup \mathcal{A}_R$.

We define the location of an event in the log using its spatiotemporal index. The Episode Index $k \in \{1, 2, \ldots, K\}$ represents a single cycle of interaction between the agents and the simulation environment. The Step Index (or Timestep) $t \in \{1, 2, \ldots, T_k\}$ represents the turn within that specific episode.

Definition 1. *An event at the spatiotemporal coordinates* (k, t) *is a tuple* $e_{i,k,t} = \langle i, \alpha_i, P, \omega \rangle$ *containing: player* $i \in \mathcal{I} = \{B, R\}$*, action* $\alpha_i \in \mathcal{A}_B$ *if* $i = B$*, and* $\alpha_i \in \mathcal{A}_R$ *if* $i = R$*, key-value pairs* $P = \{(attr_1, val_1), (attr_2, val_2), \ldots\}$ *representing hostnames, IPs, and subnets, and outcome* $\omega \in \mathbb{B} = \{True, False\}$.

Definition 2. *A log* $\mathcal{L}$ *is the union of all episodes, where each episode is an ordered sequence of steps, and each step is an ordered pair of agent events:*

$$\mathcal{L} = \bigcup_{k=1}^{K} \left(\prod_{t=1}^{T_k} (e_{B,k,t}, e_{R,k,t}) \right)$$

4.1 Trace Semantics

Next we show how to transform a log ($\mathcal{L}$) into a formal language (L) over an alphabet of actions and parameters.

Alphabet (Σ). Let $\mathcal{V}$ be the set of all parameter values. Define $\Sigma = \mathcal{A} \cup \mathcal{V}$.

Tokenization Function (ϕ). Define a tokenization function $\phi : \mathcal{E} \to \Sigma^*$, which maps from an event space $\mathcal{E}$ to a string in Σ^*. For an event $e = \langle i, \alpha, P, \omega \rangle$, where parameters P yield values $v_1, v_2, \ldots, v_m$, we have $\phi(e) = \alpha \cdot v_1 \cdot v_2 \cdot \cdots \cdot v_m$, where $(\cdot)$ denotes string concatenation, as usual. For example, if

$$e = \langle \texttt{B}, \texttt{DecoyTomcat}, \{\texttt{ip:10.0.151.89}\}, \{\texttt{hostname:Host\_1}\}, \texttt{TRUE} \rangle$$

then $\phi(e) = \texttt{DecoyTomcat}\cdot\texttt{10.0.151.89}\cdot\texttt{Host\_1}$. This results in a single string of length 3. Note that the individual symbols (e.g., `DecoyTomcat`) are not tokenized (e.g., `D`, `e`, ...), as individual characters will not be relevant in our analysis.

To treat the log as a formal language over Σ^*, we linearize the triple-indexed events $e_{i,k,t}$ into a single chronological sequence $e_1, e_2, \cdots, e_N$. This linearization follows the natural order of the log: events are ordered by increasing episode index, then by step index within each episode, and finally by the fixed agent order (Blue then Red) within each step, yielding a total order that preserves the temporal progression of the interaction.

Total Order ($\prec$). Define a total order on events $\prec$ by:

$$e_{i,k,t} \prec e_{i',k',t'} \iff (k < k') \vee (k = k' \wedge t < t') \vee (k = k' \wedge t = t' \wedge i = B \wedge i' = R)$$

Let $f : \mathcal{E} \to \{1, 2, \ldots, N\}$ be a bijection preserving $\prec$, and define $e_n = f^{-1}(n)$.

Definition 3 (Cumulative History Function). *We define the history H at any point n as the concatenation of all tokenized events from the beginning of the log up to the current event, that is, $H(n) = \prod_{m=1}^{n} \phi(e_m)$.*

Note that this model assumes a non-resetting environment, where system state persists across episodes. Consequently, vulnerabilities remain and agent knowledge accumulates over time, enabling the study of long-term behaviors.

Definition 4 (Formal Language). *The Language L is defined over the prefix closure of this global trace. A string w is in the language L if it corresponds to a global history ending in a successful event:*

$$L = \{H(n) \mid 1 \leq n \leq N \text{ and } \omega_n = \mathit{True}\}$$

Definition 5 (Passive Learning). *Let $S^+ = \{H(n) \mid \omega_n = \mathit{True}\}$ and $S^- = \{H(n) \mid \omega_n = \mathit{False}\}$ be the positive/negative samples derived from histories $H(n) = \prod_{m=1}^{n} \phi(e_m)$. The passive DFA learning problem seeks a DFA M over $\Sigma = \mathcal{A} \cup \mathcal{V}$ that satisfies $S^+ \subseteq L(M)$ and $S^- \cap L(M) = \emptyset$.*

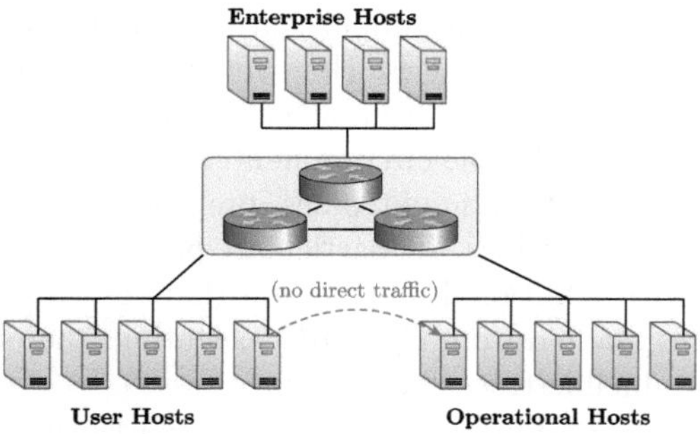

Fig. 3. Network topology for CAGE 2.

5 Case Study: Learning Models of CAGE Challenge 2

We now report on our experiences using passive learning to infer a state-machine model of CAGE 2 [9], using the RPNI implementation from AALpy [14]. In CAGE 2, agents interact in a small enterprise network modeled using CybORG, with red and blue performing actions like the ones discussed in the preceding section. The network topology has three subnets with user hosts, enterprise servers, and operational hosts, as shown in Fig. 3. The red agent starts with a presence on one of the hosts in the user subnet and seeks to impact a designated server in the operational subnet; the blue agent starts with a presence on a host in the enterprise subnet and seeks to prevent red from achieving its goal. Additionally, green agents may generate non-malicious traffic from user hosts, making it harder for blue to detect red.

Each of the hosts in the topology can be in one of five high-level states: unknown, services unknown, discovered, exploited, fully compromised. However, note that the state observation vector in the Python implementation is more complicated: each state maintains 2 bits to indicate whether it is being scanned by the attacker, and 4 bits to indicate whether it has been compromised. Further, the semantics of the transitions depends on a detailed model of hosts, including OS type and patching level, users and groups, a file system, processes, network interfaces and sessions, etc. So the actual state space of the simulator is huge.

We augmented CybORG to extract simulator traces. The trace data includes the actions chosen by agents, the observations about the state provided to agents, as well as information about the true state of the simulation (e.g., whether red has a session, blue has a decoy, etc.) that cannot be perfectly known by either agent. We then collected traces over a long training run for a blue agent. Traces collected early in the run reflect the logic of a naive agent, with many invalid steps, while traces collected later reflect the logic of a more refined agent. For red, we used two standard agents: B-line, which attempts to move directly toward the target host, and Meander, which follows a random path.

Although many simulators exhibit non-determinism, CAGE 2 is nearly deterministic in practice, and the remaining sources of variability can be systematically eliminated through preprocessing. CybORG models interactions between agents and the environment in discrete execution rounds, and the agents themselves may employ stochastic policies. However, it is possible to separate non-deterministic decisions originating from agent behavior from the corresponding system responses generated by the environment. In cases where the environment itself introduces non-deterministic outcomes, preprocessing is used to normalize and augment the generated logs. In particular, preprocessing enriches exploit-related log entries with additional information that resolves ambiguous or non-deterministic choices made during CybORG execution, thereby enabling highly consistent and reproducible traces across runs.

Accordingly, to prepare CAGE 2 traces for RPNI learning, we apply several preprocessing steps. First, we map raw subnet identifiers expressed in CIDR notation (e.g., `10.0.128.112/28`) to semantic names such as *User*, *Enterprise*, and *Operational*, reducing the alphabet size and improving generalization across network configurations. Second, we translate IP addresses to hostnames to ensure consistent host naming across traces. Third, we augment action symbols with an exploit class (e.g., `SSHBruteForce`, `EternalBlue`) to eliminate residual non-determinism and guarantee that identical inputs produce identical outcomes.

After preprocessing, we converted 5000 raw CAGE 2 traces into our format. The first set of experiments investigates how trace length affects DFA learning quality. We shuffled all 5000 traces exactly once, then partitioned them into five non-overlapping sets of 1000 traces each. Trial 1 uses the first 1000 shuffled indices, Trial 2 uses the next 1000, and so on. Within each trial, we use the first 900 traces for learning and the remaining 100 traces for evaluation. We measure the accuracy of a learned DFA on a held-out set by removing each trace's success labels, feeding the trace's actions to the DFA one at a time, recording the accept/reject prediction at every step, and computing the fraction of predictions that match the recorded outcomes. The critical design choice in this experiment is that we created three versions of each trial by truncating the traces to different lengths: 100 steps, 50 steps, and 30 steps, corresponding to the trace lengths used to evaluate agents in the actual CAGE 2 competition. Thus, the same source traces are used across all three step lengths for a given trial. For each configuration, we ran incremental learning starting at 50 traces and adding 50 more traces at each checkpoint until reaching 900 traces, resulting in 18 checkpoints per trial.

5.1 CAGE 2 Experiments

Size of Inferred DFA. Figure 4 shows how the complexity of the learned model grows, averaged across all five trials with standard deviation shown as shaded regions. For the 100-step configuration, the state space grows continuously, reaching 899 ± 50 states with 900 traces and showing no sign of converging. In contrast, the other configurations exhibit slower growth: 50-step traces yield 362 ± 19 states, while 30-step traces yield only 161 ± 11 states. This demonstrates that scalability is a fundamental challenge—longer traces lead to models that quickly become unwieldy—but bounded learning offers a practical path forward.

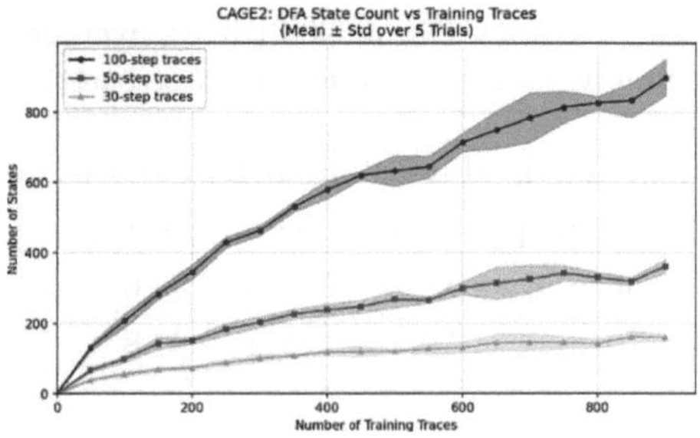

Fig. 4. DFA state count vs. trace count. Shaded regions indicate standard deviation over 5 trials. Bounded traces (30/50 steps) reduce state explosion vs. 100-step traces.

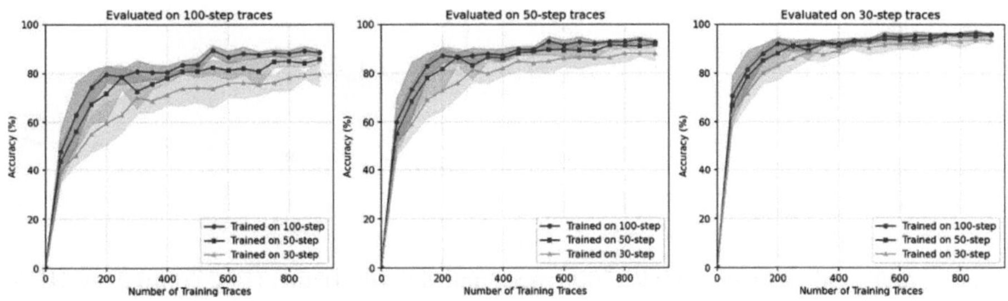

Fig. 5. Cross-evaluation fidelity. Each plot shows accuracy and standard deviation for 5 trials, with models learned using different lengths and evaluated on a specific length.

Accuracy of Inferred DFA. Figure 5 examines how models learned from traces of varying length generalize when evaluated on traces also of varying length. For this cross-evaluation, we first inferred DFAs using traces of length 30, 50, and 100, and then evaluated them against a held-out set, truncated to the same three lengths. We report averages across five trials. Table 2 shows the cross-evaluation accuracy after 900 traces. All three configurations achieve comparable accuracy when evaluated on the same test length: on 100-step evaluation, 100-step trained models achieve 88.5%, followed by 50-step (85.7%) and 30-step (79.7%). On 50-step evaluation, the pattern is similar with 100-step trained at 92.8%, 50-step at 91.9%, and 30-step at 88.2%. As expected, all models perform best on shorter traces, which provide fewer opportunities for error. These results suggest that for RPNI-based learning, shorter traces can achieve accuracy comparable to longer traces while producing significantly simpler automata (161 states for 30-step vs. 362 for 50-step vs. 899 for 100-step), offering a favorable trade-off between model complexity and predictive performance. Further, we hypothesize that shorter traces may sometimes yield models that generalize better, as the resulting automata are simpler and less prone to overfitting to specific sequences.

Accuracy in the Limit. To further study the accuracy of the inferred DFAs, we performed an evaluation using all 5000 traces in our collected trace set. We perform three trials, shuffling the traces separately for each trial; within

Table 2. Cross-evaluation accuracy (%) at 900 traces, averaged across 5 trials. Rows indicate trace length, columns indicate evaluation trace length.

Train\Eval	100-step	50-step	30-step
100-step	88.5	92.8	96.1
50-step	85.7	91.9	95.6
30-step	79.7	88.2	93.8

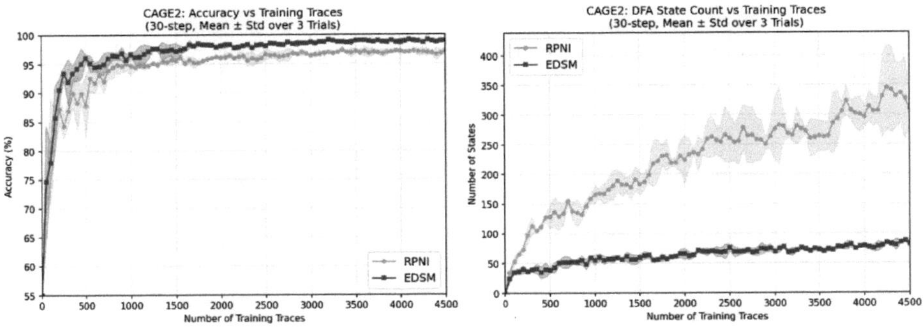

Fig. 6. Large-scale learning with 4500 traces and 30-step truncation, comparing RPNI and EDSM. Left: accuracy vs. traces. Right: state count vs. traces. Shaded regions show standard deviation across 3 trials.

each trial, the first 4500 traces are used for learning and the remaining 500 for evaluation. Based on observations from the previous experiment, where 30-step traces achieved good generalization while maintaining manageable state counts, all traces are truncated to 30 steps. Incremental learning starts at 50 traces and proceeds in steps of 50 until reaching 4500 traces, yielding 90 checkpoints per trial. To also assess the impact of the merging strategy, we ran the same experiment with EDSM (using the FlexFringe implementation [21]) under identical splits, shuffles, and truncations so that all reported numbers are directly comparable.

Figure 6 shows accuracy (left) and state count (right) as functions of data set size, averaged across the three trials, for both algorithms. RPNI achieves $97.3\% \pm 0.1\%$ accuracy with 310 ± 25 states at 4500 traces; EDSM achieves $99.0\% \pm 0.04\%$ accuracy with only 82 ± 5 states—roughly $4\times$ smaller and more accurate. For both algorithms, accuracy improves rapidly in the early stages and increases gradually with more data, while state counts grow sub-linearly, suggesting that the models are effectively generalizing. We attribute the gap to EDSM's evidence-driven merges, which are less likely to introduce spurious states from rare or noisy prefixes, producing a more compact recovered automaton that generalizes better to unseen traces.

5.2 Impact of Heuristic Agents

To investigate how learning can be improved using better data, we developed a CybORG-like simulator called BabyCyborg, which offers two key benefits. First, the resulting state space is smaller than that of the original system, as BabyCyborg is a simplified variant of CybORG with four hosts, a reduced action set for red and blue: `DiscoverRemoteSystems`, `DiscoverNetworkServices`, `ExploitRemoteService`, `PrivilegeEscalate`, `Impact`, `Remove`, and `NoOp`. Second, because we built the framework, we gain access to the underlying state machine, allowing us to evaluate correctness with precision. Because BabyCyborg's transition function is defined by an explicit set of deterministic rules with known ground truth, it enables us to cleanly attribute differences in learning performance to specific design choices rather than to CybORG's more complicated dynamics. We discuss only the RPNI results for this experiment; we verified that the same qualitative trend holds for EDSM. For the experiments below, both agents act on a single host of BabyCyborg.

Table 3. Number of traces required for 100% accuracy (mean ± std over three trials).

Agent	Trace Length	Mean	Std Dev
Random	200-step	130	36
	100-step	427	302
	50-step	510	249
	15-step	3,203	128
Heuristic	200-step	613	19
	100-step	613	19
	50-step	613	19
	15-step	667	21

We developed two red agents for data collection: one that selects actions uniformly at random, and another that biases exploration according to the attack kill chain (`DiscoverRemoteSystems` and `DiscoverNetworkServices` → `ExploitRemoteService` → `PrivilegeEscalate` → `Impact`), while retaining a 30% probability of random action selection to maintain trace diversity. The heuristic-guided exploration of this second agent is intended to capture salient behavioral patterns within shorter interaction traces while mitigating excessive automaton growth. The blue agent follows a random policy, selecting between `Remove` and `NoOp`. Motivated by prior work [1] demonstrating that structured exploration can improve automata learning efficiency relative to purely random sampling, we conducted three independent trials comparing models learned from random-generated and heuristic-generated traces. In each trial, we generated 200-step traces, produced shorter variants (100, 50, and 15 steps) via truncation, and measured the number of traces required during learning to reach 100% accuracy on a held-out set of 500 50-step traces. Table 3 reports the results.

A clear pattern can be seen in the data. For heuristic traces, convergence occurs after a nearly constant number of traces across all lengths (approximately 600–670 traces), indicating that the heuristic agent consistently captures the core attack structure even in short traces. In contrast, convergence under random exploration is highly sensitive to trace length, ranging from 130 traces for 200-step traces to 3,203 traces for 15-step traces, as shorter random traces are unlikely to contain complete attack sequences. This pattern reveals that the heuristic agent provides significant benefits for shorter traces. For 15-step traces, convergence is 4.8× faster on average (667 vs. 3,203 traces). However, this benefit diminishes with longer traces: for 200-step traces, the random agent converges 4.7× faster on average (130 vs. 613 traces). This suggests that the heuristic agent's focused exploration is beneficial when traces are too short for random exploration to cover all transitions, but becomes counterproductive for longer traces where the random agent can achieve good coverage through sampling. Overall, while scalability remains a challenge for passive learning, bounded learning is a promising approach, achieving good accuracy and manageable model complexity.

6 Conclusions

This paper presented a framework for modeling cybersecurity agent interactions as a language inclusion problem, using CybORG and CAGE 2 as a case study. By transforming raw CybORG logs into formal languages where strings represent event histories ending in successful actions, we demonstrated how passive automata learning techniques, specifically RPNI, can extract interpretable behavioral models from observed traces. The learned deterministic finite automata capture the implicit rules governing attacker-defender dynamics, providing both a mechanism for strategy analysis and a foundation for anomaly detection. Our results show that even limited observational data can yield meaningful automata models, creating a pathway for automated inference of simulators as well as applications of formal methods in the future.

Of course, although our work shows promise, it is not without limitations. Applying automata learning to problems in other domains could require new strategies for preprocessing event logs and new heuristics for exploring the state space. In settings where simulators are highly non-deterministic, more complicated models could be required, such as probabilistic automata. Developing techniques for addressing these limitations is an excellent topic for future work.

Acknowledgments. The authors wish to thank the CAV '26 reviewers for helpful feedback and suggestions. This work was supported by the Defense Advanced Research Projects Agency (DARPA) under contract number W912CG23C0032 and a gift from the VMware University Research Fund.

Data Availibility Statement. All data and code supporting the findings of this study are available on Zenodo at https://doi.org/10.5281/zenodo.19828945.

Disclosure of Interests. Foster is a visiting researcher at Jane Street. The authors have no other competing interests to declare that are relevant to this article.

References

1. Aichernig, B.K., Muskardin, E., Pferscher, A.: Active vs. passive: a comparison of automata learning paradigms for network protocols. In: International Workshop on Formal Methods for Autonomous Systems (FMAS) and International Workshop on Automated and verifiable Software System Development (ASYDE). EPTCS, vol. 371, pp. 1–19 (2022). https://doi.org/10.4204/EPTCS.371.1
2. Angluin, D.: Learning regular sets from queries and counterexamples. Inf. Comput. **75**(2), 87–106 (1987). https://doi.org/10.1016/0890-5401(87)90052-6
3. Carrasco, R.C., Oncina, J.: Learning stochastic regular grammars by means of a state merging method. In: International Colloquium on Grammatical Inference and Applications (ICGI). LNCS, vol. 862, pp. 139–152. Springer (1994). https://doi.org/10.1007/3-540-58473-0_144
4. Ferreira, T., Brewton, H., D'Antoni, L., Silva, A.: Prognosis: closed-box analysis of network protocol implementations. In: ACM SIGCOMM Conference, pp. 762–774 (2021). https://doi.org/10.1145/3452296.3472938
5. Frohme, M., Howar, F., Steffen, B.: LearnLib: 10 years later. In: Computer Aided Verification (CAV). LNCS, vol. 15934, pp. 141–160. Springer (2025). https://doi.org/10.1007/978-3-031-98685-7_7
6. Henderson, P., Islam, R., Bachman, P., Pineau, J., Precup, D., Meger, D.: Deep reinforcement learning that matters. In: AAAI Conference on Artificial Intelligence, vol. 32, pp. 3207–3214 (2018). https://doi.org/10.1609/AAAI.V32I1.11694
7. de la Higuera, C.: Grammatical Inference: Learning Automata and Grammars. Cambridge University Press (2010). https://doi.org/10.1017/CBO9781139194655
8. Hsiung, E., Biswas, J., Chaudhuri, S.: Automata learning from preference and equivalence queries. In: Computer Aided Verification (CAV). LNCS, vol. 15934, pp. 104–126. Springer (2025). https://doi.org/10.1007/978-3-031-98685-7_5
9. Kiely, M., Bowman, D., Standen, M., Moir, C.: On autonomous agents in a cyber defence environment (2023). https://doi.org/10.48550/arXiv.2309.07388
10. Lang, K.J., Pearlmutter, B.A., Price, R.A.: Results of the Abbadingo one DFA learning competition and a new evidence-driven state merging algorithm. In: International Colloquium on Grammatical Inference (ICGI). LNCS, pp. 1–12. Springer (1998). https://doi.org/10.1007/BFB0054059
11. Levine, S., Kumar, A., Tucker, G., Fu, J.: Offline reinforcement learning: tutorial, review, and perspectives on open problems (2020). https://doi.org/10.48550/arXiv.2005.01643
12. Moeller, M., Ferreira, T., Lu, T., Foster, N., Silva, A.: Active learning of symbolic NetKAT automata. In: Proceedings of the ACM on Programming Languages (PACMPL) 9(PLDI), pp. 1119–1142 (2025). https://doi.org/10.1145/3729295
13. Moon, S., et al.: Alembic: automated model inference for stateful network functions. In: Symposium on Networked Systems Design and Implementation (NSDI), pp. 699–718. USENIX (2019). https://www.usenix.org/conference/nsdi19/presentation/moon
14. Muskardin, E., Aichernig, B.K., Pill, I., Pferscher, A., Tappler, M.: AALpy: an active automata learning library. Innov. Syst. Softw. Eng. **18**(3), 417–426 (2022). https://doi.org/10.1007/S11334-022-00449-3

15. Neider, D., Smetsers, R., Vaandrager, F., Kuppens, H.: Benchmarks for automata learning and conformance testing. In: Models, Mindsets, Meta: The What, the How, and the Why Not? Essays Dedicated to Bernhard Steffen on the Occasion of His 60th Birthday, LNCS, vol. 11200, pp. 390–416. Springer (2019). https://doi.org/10.1007/978-3-030-22348-9_23
16. Oncina, J., Garcia, P., et al.: Inferring regular languages in polynomial update time. Patt. Recogn. Image Anal. **1**(49–61), 10–1142 (1992). https://doi.org/10.1142/9789812797902_0004
17. Shehab, M.L., Aspeel, A., Ozay, N.: Learning reward machines from partially observed policies. Trans. Mach. Learn. Res. (TMLR) (2025). https://doi.org/10.48550/arXiv.2502.03762
18. Standen, M., Lucas, M., Bowman, D., Richer, T.J., Kim, J., Marriott, D.: Cyborg: a gym for the development of autonomous cyber agents (2021). https://doi.org/10.48550/arXiv.2108.09118
19. Sutton, R.S., Barto, A.G.: Reinforcement Learning: An Introduction, 2nd edn. MIT Press (2018). http://www.incompleteideas.net/book/the-book-2nd.html
20. Vaandrager, F.: Model learning. Commun. ACM (CACM) **60**(2), 86–95 (2017). https://doi.org/10.1145/2967606
21. Verwer, S., Hammerschmidt, C.A.: Flexfringe: a passive automaton learning package. In: International Conference on Software Maintenance and Evolution (ICSME), pp. 638–642. IEEE (2017). https://doi.org/10.1109/ICSME.2017.58
22. Waga, M.: Active learning of deterministic timed automata with Myhill-Nerode style characterization. In: Enea, C., Lal, A. (eds.) Computer Aided Verification (CAV). LNCS, vol. 13964, pp. 3–26. Springer (2023). https://doi.org/10.1007/978-3-031-37706-8_1
23. Xu, Z., et al.: Joint inference of reward machines and policies for reinforcement learning. In: International Conference on Automated Planning and Scheduling (ICAPS), pp. 590–598. AAAI Press (2020). https://doi.org/10.1609/icaps.v30i1.6756

HyperQB 2.0: A Bounded Model Checker for Hyperproperties

Tzu-Han Hsu, Milad Rabizadeh, Kenneth Rogale, Fedor Filippov, Marco A. de Oliveira Batista, and Borzoo Bonakdarpour(✉)

Michigan State University, East Lansing, MI, USA
{tzuhan,milad,rogaleke,filippo2,demarc39, borzoo}@msu.edu

Abstract. We introduce the tool HyperQB$^{2.0}$, the first highly efficient push-button bounded model checker (BMC) for hyperproperties. HyperQB takes as input a model in NuSMV or Verilog and a formula expressed in the temporal logics HyperLTL or A-HLTL. The core decision procedures to implement BMC are SMT and QBF solvers, enabling verification of finite- and infinite-state programs. HyperQB offers command-line, standalone graphical, and web-based interfaces. Based on the selection of either bug-hunting or synthesis, instances of counterexamples or path witnesses are returned. The tool is entirely implemented in Rust and we report on successful and effective model checking results for a rich set of experiments on a variety of case studies with rigorous performance comparison and contrast with similar tools.

1 Introduction

Hyperproperties [9] are *system-wide* properties (rather than the property of individual execution traces). They can express important information-flow security policies (e.g., non-interference [15]), consistency models in concurrent computing [4] (e.g., linearizability [16]), robustness conditions in cyber-physical systems [27], and path planning in multi-agent systems. The temporal logics HyperLTL [8] and A-HLTL [2] extend LTL with explicit and simultaneous quantification over execution traces, describing relational properties of multiple synchronous and asynchronous traces, respectively. For example, generalized non-interference (GNI) can be expressed by the following HyperLTL formula:

$$\varphi_{\mathsf{GNI}} = \forall \pi_A . \forall \pi_B . \exists \pi_C .\ X(high_{\pi_A} \leftrightarrow high_{\pi_C}) \ \wedge \ G(low_{\pi_B} \leftrightarrow low_{\pi_C}),$$

It stipulates that for all traces π_A and π_B, there must exists a π_C, such that π_C agrees on *high* (i.e., *high-security* secret) with π_A, and agrees on *low* (i.e., *low-security* observation) with π_B. Satisfying φ_{GNI} implies that an attacker cannot infer the high-security value by speculating the observable parts of a program.

E. Darulova et al. (Eds.): CAV 2026, LNCS 16682, pp. 511–525, 2026.
https://doi.org/10.1007/978-3-032-32519-8_26

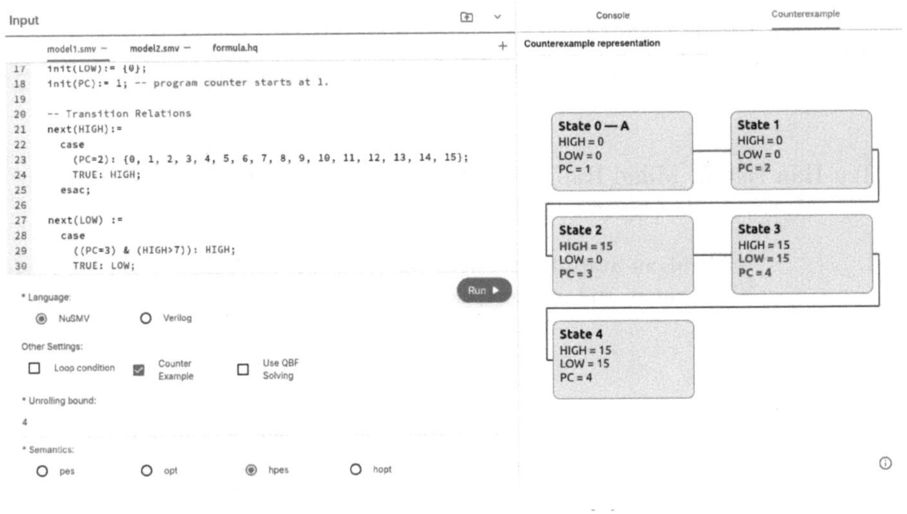

Fig. 1. The standalone and web-based GUI of HyperQB$^{2.0}$ showing a counterexample.

Main Challenge

We currently lack serious tool support for the verification of hyperproperties. Our objective is to develop an expressive, robust, user-friendly, downloadable, efficient, and accessible model checking tool accompanied by a rich set of benchmarks and case studies.

This paper presents HyperQB$^{2.0}$, a *bounded model checker* for hyperproperties with techniques introduced in [17–19][1]. The key features are:

- It provides three user interfaces: (1) command line, (2) desktop standalone GUI, and (3) web-based playground for remote access (see Fig. 1).
- The tool inputs are: (1) a set of models (up to one per trace quantifier) in either NuSMV [6] or Verilog [21], (2) a specification in HyperLTL or A-HLTL, (3) the choice of bounded semantics, and (4) the unrolling bound $k \geq 1$.
- The possible tool outputs are: `sat`, `unsat`, or `unknown`. If the model does not satisfy the formula, a counterexample (either textual for command-line or visualized in the GUI) is generated (see Fig. 1).

[1] A comprehensive tool website with an interactive online playground, as shown in Fig. 1, is available at: https://hyperqb.github.io/index.html.

Overall Architecture. Figure 2 shows the overall architecture of HyperQB$^{2.0}$ implemented in Rust. As the first step, we developed parsers for HyperLTL, A-HLTL, and NuSMV. Verilog programs are parsed using Yosys [14], where the C → LLVM path is currently under development. These parsers translate NuSMV and Verilog models to a unified abstract intermediate representation as a *program graph* [1] (i.e., a transition relation with data).

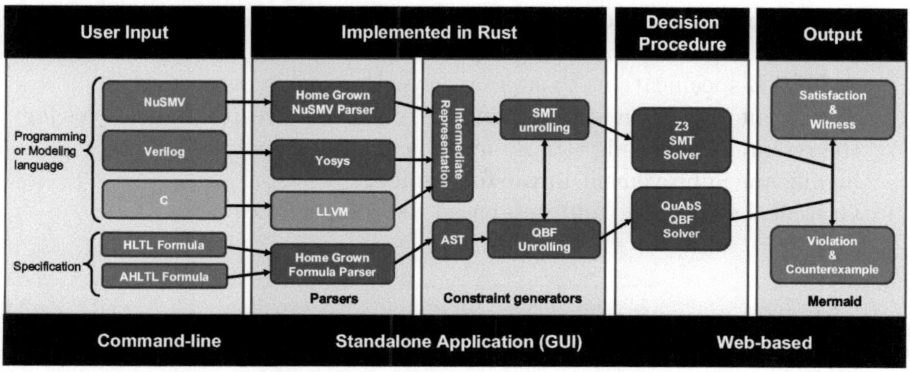

Fig. 2. Overall architecture of HyperQB$^{2.0}$.

Next, the program graph of models and the abstract syntax tree of the specification are handed to another home-grown component for BMC unrolling and constraint generation. HyperQB$^{2.0}$ supports both SMT and QBF constraint generation, enabling verification of finite- and infinite-state programs. Finally, we run the SMT-solver Z3 [24] or the QBF-solver QuAbS [26] to check the satisfiability of the unrolled instance and interpret the output. HyperQB$^{2.0}$ also incorporates the loop conditions identified in [18] to ensure completeness of model checking for certain fragments of HyperLTL. We note that besides verification, HyperQB can also be used for synthesis through returning witnesses to existential quantifiers in the input HyperLTL and A-HLTL formulas.

Comparison to HyperQB 1.0

An earlier prototype version of HyperQB was developed to support the experimental evaluation in [19]. In this paper, we present $\text{HyperQB}^{2.0}$, whose development required massive theoretical and engineering effort, and has the following unique and new features:

- End-to-end implementation in **Rust.**
- **SMT-based** decision procedure (in addition to the original QBF-based), enabling verification of *infinite-state* programs.
- Implementation of **loop conditions** to support BMC completeness.
- **Verilog** as an additional language for hardware security applications.
- **A-HLTL** specifications to support asynchronous hyperproperties.
- Significant expansion of **benchmarks**, creating a wealth of examples for the research community (those in Table 2, 4, 3 are all new).
- Significant improvement in **performance.**
- Graphical standalone and web-based **user interfaces.**

We also present a rigorous experimental evaluation and compare $\text{HyperQB}^{2.0}$ to our preliminary findings in [17–19] as well as the state-of-the-art tool AutoHyper [3]. Our experimental evaluation includes a wide range of case studies, such as information-flow security, linearizability in concurrent data structures, path planning for robots, co-termination, deniability, intransitivity of non-interference, and secrecy-preserving mapping synthesis. Our evaluation shows that our technique is effective and efficient in identifying bugs in several prominent examples.

```
MODULE main
VAR
  low, high:  boolean;
  halt: boolean; PC: 1..3;
ASSIGN
  -- Initial Conditions
  init(low)   := FALSE;
  init(high)  := FALSE;
  init(halt)  := FALSE;
  init(PC)    := 1;

  -- Transition Relations
  next(high) :=
    case
     (PC=1): {TRUE, FALSE
     };
     TRUE: high;
    esac;

next(low) :=
 case
  (PC=2 & high): TRUE;
  TRUE: low;
 esac;
next(halt) :=
 case
  (PC=3): TRUE;
  TRUE: halt;
 esac;
next(PC) :=
 case
  (PC<3): PC+1;
  -- (PC=3):1;//if loop
  TRUE: PC;
esac;
```

Fig. 3. A NuSMV model with implicit leak from Boolean variables `high` to `low`.

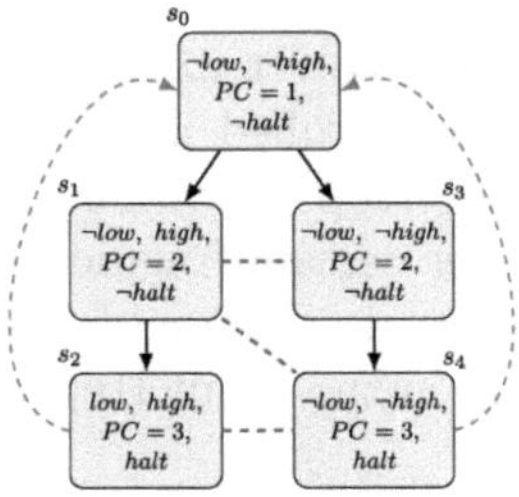

Fig. 4. Transition relation of Fig. 3.

2 Input/Output Features of HyperQB

HyperQB accepts input models in NuSMV [6] and the HDL Verilog [21]. For NuSMV, we have built a parser to extract transition relations. For example, the NuSMV model in Fig. 3 encodes a system where the low-security variable *low* is updated under conditions depending on the high-security variable *high*. Although no explicit flow from *high* to *low* exists, the model induces an implicit leak and violates formula φ_{GNI} introduced in Sect. 1. The corresponding transition relation in Fig. 4 shows two possible executions, branching on the value of *high*, showing that an attacker observing *low* as true at $PC = 3$ can immediately infer that the secret input *high* must be true. For Verilog, the top-level module must be provided, where the open-source tool Yosys [14] translate the HDL into its SMT-LIB representation. Through Yosys, we inherit support for a substantial fragment of the 2005 Verilog standard [21].

2.1 Input Specification and Semantics

Specification Language. HyperQB supports input specification in two temporal logics: (1) HyperLTL [8] for *synchronous*, and (2) A-HLTL [2] for *asynchronous* hyperproperties. To motivate these two variations, consider Fig. 4 and traces $t_1 = s_0s_1s_2$ and $t_2 = s_0s_3s_4$. One way to evaluate the security policy is to pair s_1 with s_3 and then s_2 with s_4 (i.e., lock-step synchronous evaluation of traces t_1 an t_2). This is how HyperLTL would evaluate t_1 and t_2. Alternatively, one may need to evaluate t_1 and t_2, where t_1 stutters at s_1 (illustrated here by the red dashed alignment). This is how A-HLTL evaluates t_1 and t_2 asynchronously. More specifically, traces t_1 and t_2 satisfy formula $\varphi_{eq} = \mathbf{G}(PC_{\pi_A} = PC_{\pi_B})$ in HyperLTL but violate the same formula in A-HLTL for the red alignment.

Formula Grammars. Grammars within HyperQB are shown in Fig. 5. The grammar for each logic has two rules `path_formula`, which quantifies over traces, and `traj_formula`, which quantifies over trajectories (asynchronous alignments). When the input logic is `AHLTL_rec`, the grammar temporal core is `inner_AHLTL` (otherwise, `inner_HLTL`) followed by rules `hform` and `aform` for paths and trajectories. Expressions are inductively generated by Boolean connectives, arithmetic comparisons, and temporal operations (see `binary_op` and `unary_op`).

Bounded Semantics. HyperQB incorporates all the bounded semantics introduced in [19]. These bounded variations guarantee sound inference with respect to the unbounded semantics, ensuring that no incorrect conclusions are drawn from finite exploration. This enables verification within a fixed bound $k \geq 0$ or until program termination (denoted as `halt`). For instance, to verify whether the model in Fig. 4 satisfies φ_{GNI}, we first negate the property and apply the pessimistic semantics (`-pes`) for bug hunting. In this setting, φ_{GNI} is reported as violated because a counterexample is found within the unrolling bound k. The choice of semantics depends on the verification objective: pessimistic (`-pes`) for bug-hunting (detecting violations), optimistic (`-opt`) for witness finding (establishing that a property holds along a finite prefix), halting-pessimistic (`-hpes`), or halting-optimistic (`-hopt`) semantics for terminating programs (ensuring conclusions remain valid even under larger bounds).

```
path_formula ::=  ("forall" | "exists") pid . form_rec
traj_formula ::= ("A" | "E" ) tid . AHLTL_rec

form_rec     ::= path_formula | traj_formula | inner_HLTL
AHLTL_rec    ::= traj_formula | inner_AHLTL
inner_HLTL   ::= hform               inner_AHLTL  ::= aform

hform ::= hform binary_op hform | unary_op hform | h_atom
aform ::= aform binary_op aform | unary_op aform | a_atom
h_atom ::= id[pid] | constant | number | "(" hform ")"
a_atom ::= id[pid][tid] | constant | number | "(" aform ")"

binary_op ::= "U" | "R" | "=" | "->" | "&" | "|"
unary_op  ::= "G" | "F" | "X" | "~"
constant ::= "TRUE" | "FALSE"
number ::= [0-9]+ | "#b" (0|1)+
```

Fig. 5. HyperLTL/A-HLTL input formula grammar (see [20] for details).

```
Synopsis
hyperqb (-n|-v) <models> -f <formula> -k <int> -s <sem> [options]

Arguments
(Required)
-n <files> | -v <files>  List of model files (NuSMV/Verilog).
-f <file>                Formula file (.hq).
-t <name>                Top module (required for Verilog only).
-k <int> | -l            Unrolling bound (with k steps) or if loop
                         condition is used.
-s <pes|opt|hpes|hopt>   Choice of the bounded semantics.
(Optional)
-m <int>                 Trajectory bound.
-c                       Emit counterexample for unsat outcome.
-q                       Use QuAbS QBF solver (default: Z3).

Example Usage
hyperqb -n snark_conc.smv snark_seq.smv -f lin.hq -k 18 -s hpes -c
```

Fig. 6. HyperQB$^{2.0}$ command-line interface usage and arguments.

Loop Conditions. Similar to the classic BMC approach [7], HyperQB$^{2.0}$ implements loop conditions to ensure completeness. The encoding relies on two simulation relations: one for $\forall\exists$ formulas, which requires successor states in the two models to correspond, and one for $\exists\forall$ formulas, which capture a lasso in the first model that simulates all behaviors of the second [18]. This construction supports all alternations of the form $\forall/\exists$ over small and large models. For example, in Fig. 3, if we extend the NuSMV model with an additional line, where in state $PC = 3$ the counter is reset to $PC = 1$ (Line 32 in Fig. 3), then the extracted transition system will contain cycles (shown as the gray dashed transitions in Fig. 4). In this setting, verifying $\forall\pi_A.\ \exists\pi_B.\ \mathbf{G}(PC_{\pi_A} = PC_{\pi_B})$ requires checking the satisfiability of $\mathsf{SIM}_{\forall\exists}$, where the corresponding models are of equal size (see [18] for details).

2.2 User Interface, Tool Usage, and Output

Tool Interface and Output. The output of HyperQB consists of the verification result (i.e., either `sat`, `unsat`, or `unknown`) produced by the selected backend solver (i.e., Z3 [24] or QuAbS [26]), accompanied by a counterexample when requested. The `unknown` outcome indicates that the solver was not able to decide the satisfiability of the instance. When the counterexample option (`-c`) is enabled and the result is unsatisfiable, HyperQB generates a counterexample textual trace.

Command-Line Usage Example. An overview of HyperQB's CLI usage, arguments, and an example usage is given in Fig. 6. In the example, the given linearizability formula (`-f lin.hq`) is of the form $\forall\exists$, so one model per quantifier is required: `-n snark_conc.smv snark_seq.smv`. The unrolling bound is: `-k 18`, and the semantics chosen are halting-pessimistic (`-s hpes`). The flag `-c` requests HyperQB to return the verdict accompanied by a counterexample.

Graphical User Interface (GUI). HyperQB also offers a GUI (see Fig. 1), available as both *standalone desktop* and *web-based* (playground at https://hyperqb.egr.msu.edu/) applications. In the GUI, inputs are organized into tabs, enabling users to manage multiple model files and the formula within a single session. Languages NuSMV or Verilog can be selected, and configuration parameters are fully accessible. The solver output is shown in a dedicated pane. When counterexample generation is enabled, the violating trace is shown as a graphical sequence of states, each annotated with the color-coded values of the relevant variables using the Mermaid [23] diagramming tool format (see Fig. 1).

3 Algorithmic Backbone and Implementation

This section outlines the technical details of our Rust implementation. The core is a streamlined intermediate representation (IR) that is both precise and flexible. Both NuSMV and Verilog models are parsed into this IR, which is then compiled into SMT/QBF encodings. The IR also supports the construction of simulation-based loop conditions. Details of the IR are in [20].

SMT vs. QBF Encodings

We only describe the SMT encoding in this section. Every SMT encoding can be systematically transformed into an equivalent QBF encoding via standard *bit-blasting*, where each bounded integer variable i is represented using $\lfloor \log(i) \rfloor + 1$ Boolean variables.

Intermediate Representation (IR) of Input Models. We use program graphs as the unified IR of input languages after parsing. A program graph provides an abstract yet precise representation of program behavior: control locations correspond to program points, edges represent conditional checks, and the effect function specifies how variables evolve. Models in NuSMV and Verilog are parsed and compiled into a program-graph IR, which is then materialized as a SMT-LIB–equivalent *abstract syntax trees* (AST), enabling *infinite state spaces* arising from unbounded integers, arrays, or data domains[2]. This represents a significant improvement over the prototype in [19], where the QBF-based IR required bit-blasted bounded integers.

From IR to Bounded Model Checking Encoding. The final stage bridges our IR with the SAT/QBF-based BMC unrolling, introduced in [17,19]. From the Z3 AST–based IR in Sect. 3, we systematically derive the BMC encoding in either SMT or QBF, which the resulting SAT/UNSAT outcome is interpreted according to the chosen bounded semantics to determine the model checking result (see Sect. 2.1). For A-HLTL, we adopt the encoding proposed in [17], which involves additional quantifiers over *trajectory variables* $\tau_a, \tau_b, \ldots, \tau_z$ for parameterizing the *position encoding* φ_{pos}. This encoding introduces quantified sets of position variables $\overline{t_a}, \overline{t_b}, \ldots, \overline{t_z}$, together with auxiliary variables $\overline{pos}$ and

[2] When the encoding requires a finite-state representation, the resulting IR is likewise finite-state; this reflects the encoding rather than a limitation of the IR itself.

$\overline{\mathit{off}}$ (for encoding trace positions while avoiding any trace to "fall off" from its bound), enabling the formalization of asynchronous alignments between traces (see [17] for details). This mechanism allows different traces to advance at different speeds, thereby capturing asynchronous alignments that are not possible under the standard synchronous semantics. The full encoding is given as follows:

$$\llbracket \mathbb{P}, \varphi \rrbracket_{k,m} = \mathbb{Q}_A \overline{x_A}.\mathbb{Q}_B \overline{x_B}.\cdots \mathbb{Q}_Z \overline{x_Z}.\ \mathbb{Q}_a \overline{t_a}.\mathbb{Q}_b \overline{t_b}.\cdots \mathbb{Q}_z \overline{t_z}.\ \exists \overline{pos}.\ \exists \overline{\mathit{off}}.$$
$$\left(\llbracket \mathcal{P} \rrbracket_k \circ A \cdots \llbracket \mathcal{P} \rrbracket_k \circ Z \ (\varphi_{pos} \wedge enc(\psi)) \right).$$

From IR to Loop Conditions. The encoding in [18] requires *explicit states* in order to establish simulation relation over traces of programs with loops. To this end, we enumerate the Z3 AST IR to extract all reachable states along with the transition relation. While our IR in principle accommodates infinite state spaces, the simulation-based encoding assumes the state space is finite.

4 Empirical Evaluation

We extensively evaluated HyperQB on a comprehensive suite of benchmarks spanning all major dimensions: (1) different logics (HyperLTL and A-HLTL), (2) input languages (NuSMV and Verilog), and (3) direct comparisons with the model checker AutoHyper [3] and the earlier prototype of HyperQB, where applicable. We are also significantly expanding our benchmark suite and case studies, creating a wealth of examples for the research community[3].

For clarity, in this section, we write HQ2.0$_{SMT}$ to denote the model checking time for HyperQB with Z3 as the backend solver, and HQ2.0$_{QBF}$ to denote the configuration using QuAbS. All experiments are run on a MacBook Pro with Apple M4 Max chip and 48 GB of memory running Docker.

4.1 HyperLTL Benchmarks (Table 1)

We begin our evaluation with the benchmark suite that originally appeared in [19] (see Table 1), including hyperproperties expressing symmetry, linearizability, non-interference, fairness, and robotic path planning. The optimizations in the new version (most notably, the adoption of Z3 ASTs and the Rust implementation) yield significant performance gains when compared to the original prototype across the entire benchmark suite.

For comparison with AutoHyper, since the same benchmarks were used in [3] (which the authors compared with our earlier prototype), we re-ran all experiments and observe that HyperQB$^{2.0}$ significantly outperforms AutoHyper in the vast majority of cases, demonstrating clear advantages in both expressiveness and efficiency. Several numbers differ from those originally reported in [3]. We communicated this to the authors and they confirmed that this discrepancy is

[3] The detailed descriptions, models, and formulas of all benchmarks can be found at: https://hyperqb.github.io/case-studies.

Table 1. Summary of results for HyperLTL benchmarks from [19]. $\mathbb{Q}$ is the form of quantifiers in the formula, **Enc.** is the time to construct the unrolled IR; 'AH' refers to AutoHyper [3]; **verification** reports only SAT/UNSAT result, while **Witness** generation can be triggered for cases with either verified (✓) with a leading ∃, or falsified (✗) for a leading ∀ (all other non-applicable cases are specified with dash '-'). For colored cells: **yellow** is the best overall performance, **green** is the best performance among results that provide a witness, and **both yellow and green** indicate results that are both the best overall and provide a witness.

				Verification Only				Verification + Witness							
				$HQ2.0_{SMT}$			AH	$HQ2.0_{SMT}$			$HQ2.0_{QBF}$			AH	
	Benchmark	$\mathbb{Q}$	|S|	Enc.	Solve	Total	Total	Enc.	Solve	Total	Enc.	Solve	Total	Total	
Benchmarks from [19]	Bakery3	∀∃	167	0.02	0.04	0.06	0.25	0.01	0.01	**0.03**	0.01	0.17	0.17	0.21	✗
	Bakery7	∀∃	996	0.02	0.04	0.06	2.51	0.02	0.02	**0.04**	0.01	0.81	0.82	1.10	✗
	Bakery9	∀∃	8464	4.07	0.06	4.13	4.57	3.85	0.03	3.88	0.01	MO	MO	**3.73**	✗
	Bakery11	∀∃	12,544	25.46	0.08	25.54	25.83	23.34	0.03	**23.39**	0.01	MO	MO	24.14	✗
	SNARK1	∀∃	4914/548	0.05	0.86	0.91	3.51	0.04	0.49	0.54	0.02	0.36	**0.37**	2.82	✗
	$NI_{Correct}$	∀∃	4761	0.04	0.37	0.41	**0.23**	-	-	-	0.01	0.26	0.27	-	✓
	$NI_{Inorrect}$	∀∃	4761	0.04	0.09	**0.12**	0.19	0.04	0.08	**0.12**	0.01	0.27	0.27	0.19	✗
	$NRP_{Correct}$	∃∀	69	0.01	0.03	**0.04**	0.20	0.01	0.03	0.04	0.00	0.02	**0.02**	0.20	✓
	$NRP_{Incorrect}$	∃∀	69	0.01	0.05	0.06	0.40	-	-	-	0.00	0.02	**0.02**	-	✗
	Robust 10^2	∀∃	266	0.02	0.11	**0.13**	ERR	-	-	-	0.01	0.19	0.20	-	✓
	Robust 20^2	∀∃	572	0.08	1.70	1.78	ERR	-	-	-	0.02	1.40	**1.41**	-	✓
	Robust 40^2	∀∃	1212	0.32	4.41	**4.73**	ERR	-	-	-	0.03	5.88	5.91	-	✓
	Robust 60^2	∀∃	1852	2.14	865.84	867.98	**364.19**	-	-	-	0.04	MO	MO	-	✓
	SP 10^2	∃∀	49	0.04	4.74	4.78	2.49	0.04	2.04	2.08	0.01	0.69	**0.70**	2.01	✓
	SP 20^2	∃∀	126	0.37	TO	TO	2.18	0.35	TO	TO	0.01	75.24	75.25	**0.74**	✓
	SP 40^2	∃∀	248	18.93	1251.66	1270.59	51.01	19.05	1433.99	1453.33	0.02	MO	MO	**13.04**	✓
	SP 60^2	∃∀	357	0.52	560.82	561.34	TO	0.53	758.02	758.77	0.03	95.88	**95.91**	MO	✓
	Mutation	∃∀	32	0.00	0.01	**0.01**	0.20	0.01	0.02	0.02	0.00	0.01	**0.01**	0.21	✓
New Benchmarks	Co-term	∀∀	9	0.01	0.00	**0.01**	0.19	-	-	-	0.00	1.06	1.07	-	✓
	Deniability	∀∃∃	13	0.01	0.06	**0.07**	8.22	-	-	-	0.01	1.02	1.03	-	✓
	$Buffer_{OD^c}$	∀∀	42	0.01	0.00	**0.01**	0.32	0.01	0.01	0.02	0.00	0.01	**0.01**	0.56	✓
	$Buffer_{OD^i}$	∀∀	42	0.01	0.03	**0.04**	0.40	-	-	-	0.01	0.02	0.03	-	✓
	$Buffer_{GMNI^i}$	∀∃	42	0.01	0.11	**0.12**	1.61	-	-	-	0.01	0.03	0.03	-	✓
	$Buffer_{OD^c}$	∀∀	16	0.01	0.01	0.03	0.33	0.01	0.00	**0.01**	0.00	0.01	0.01	5.80	✓
	$Nodet_{TINI}$	∀∃	16	0.01	0.02	**0.02**	0.57	-	-	-	0.00	0.08	0.08	-	✓
	$Nodet_{TSNI}$	∀∃	16	0.01	0.02	**0.03**	0.58	-	-	-	0.00	0.08	0.08	-	✓
	K-Safety	∀∀	35	0.01	0.51	**0.52**	1.43	-	-	-	0.01	MO	MO	-	✓
	MapSynth1	$\exists\forall^2\exists^2$	9	0.01	0.02	0.04	0.21	0.01	0.01	**0.02**	0.01	0.01	0.02	0.19	✓
	MapSynth2	$\exists\forall^2\exists^2$	10	0.01	2.78	**2.79**	TO	0.01	2.94	2.95	0.01	0.18	**0.19**	TO	✓
	$TeamLTL_{v1}$	∃∃∀	65	0.01	0.17	0.18	0.20	-	-	-	0.01	0.03	**0.03**	-	✓
	$TeamLTL_{v2}$	∃∃∀	257	0.01	0.94	0.95	0.36	-	-	-	0.01	0.12	**0.13**	-	✓
	$NDET_{v1}$	∀∃	4	0.00	0.01	**0.01**	0.18	0.00	0.01	**0.01**	0.00	0.00	0.01	0.17	✓
	$NDET_{v2}$	∀∃	17	0.00	0.02	0.03	0.18	0.00	0.02	**0.02**	0.00	0.01	0.02	14.58	✓
	$NDET_{v3}$	∀∃	8	0.00	0.01	**0.01**	40.61	0.00	0.01	**0.01**	0.00	0.01	0.02	TO	✓
	$Bank_{v1}$	$\forall^2\exists$	20	0.01	0.06	0.07	0.31	0.01	0.02	**0.03**	0.01	0.02	0.03	8.10	✓
	$Bank_{v2}$	$\forall^2\exists$	15	0.01	0.05	0.05	0.20	0.01	0.01	**0.02**	0.01	0.02	0.02	.51	✓
	$Bank_{v3}$	$\forall^2\exists$	14	0.01	0.04	0.04	0.21	0.01	0.01	**0.02**	0.01	0.02	0.02	0.50	✓
	Constructor	∀∃	26	0.01	0.04	0.05	0.21	0.01	0.04	0.05	0.01	0.03	**0.04**	0.20	✓
	$Bidding_{v1}$	∀∀	17	0.01	0.00	**0.01**	0.18	-	-	-	0.00	0.05	0.05	-	✓
	$Bidding_{v2}$	∀∀	12	0.00	0.00	**0.01**	0.19	-	-	-	0.00	0.03	0.03	-	✓
	$Bidding_{v3}$	∀∀	16	0.01	0.00	**0.01**	0.46	-	-	-	0.00	0.06	0.06	-	✓
	$Bidding_{v4}$	∀∀	15	0.01	0.01	0.02	0.21	0.00	0.01	**0.01**	0.00	0.05	0.05	2.10	✓
	IQueue	∀∃	89	0.02	0.30	**0.32**	ERR	0.02	0.21	0.23	0.01	0.20	**0.21**	TO	✓
	Keypad	∃∃	6	0.00	0.01	**0.01**	10.39	0.00	0.01	**0.01**	0.00	0.17	0.17	6.72	✓
	SimpleQueue	∀∀	49	0.01	0.01	**0.01**	0.19	0.01	0.01	**0.01**	0.01	0.06	0.06	0.18	✓
	EMM ABA	∀∃	56	0.01	0.04	0.06	ERR	0.01	0.04	0.06	0.01	0.04	**0.05**	TO	✓
	Lazy List	∀∃	34	0.02	0.17	0.19	460.12	0.02	0.06	**0.08**	0.01	0.12	0.12	TO	✓

TO = 1800 seconds MO = Out of Memory ERR (AH) = SPOT solver error due to version updates made after publication. For fairness, we report results using the most up-to-date version of AutoHyper as of September 1, 2025.

In addition to the original benchmark suite from [19], we extend our evaluation with 29 new case studies to further assess the efficiency and effectiveness of HyperQB. These new benchmarks primarily focus on two aspects: (1) formulas with more than two quantifiers, which increase the computational complexity of verification, and (2) models exhibiting strong non-determinism, which challenge the scalability and robustness of the underlying encodings.

The results demonstrate that HyperQB significantly outperforms AutoHyper across the vast majority of the new benchmarks. In particular, for formulas with more than two quantifiers (e.g., MapSynth 2 with five quantifiers $\exists\forall\forall\exists\exists$), AutoHyper incurs heavy overhead to constructing automata complementation, which is its core technique to handle quantifier alternation. Likewise, in cases with substantial input or transition non-determinism, AutoHyper's reliance on language inclusion checking leads to significant performance overhead (e.g., NDET v2, NDET v3, and IQueue).

By contrast, these factors have little impact on HyperQB, highlighting the robustness of our SMT-based approach. This illustrates not only the scalability of HyperQB to complex quantifier structures and nondeterministic models, but also its versatility as a general framework for hyperproperty verification.

4.2 A-HLTL Benchmarks from [17] (Table 2)

Here, we experiment with challenging information-flow problems in concurrent programs, speculative execution, compiler optimizations, and cache-based timing attacks (details in [17]). We emphasize that AutoHyper cannot deal with A-HLTL properties, so no comparison is included in Table 2. HyperQB constitutes a breakthrough: to the best of our knowledge, it is the *first and only* tool to offer automated model checking for A-HLTL.

4.3 Benchmarks of Programs with Loops from [18] (Table 3)

Our results show that HyperQB$^{2.0}$ consistently outperforms the hard-coded implementation in [17], regardless of the chosen backend solver (SMT/QBF). Notably, in several benchmarks, the QBF backend exhibits an advantage: because the A-HLTL originally proposed position encoding [17] is fully Booleanized and thus, it naturally aligns with QBF solvers. By contrast, using an SMT backend on such encodings may introduce unnecessary overhead due to the additional reasoning over theories. Nevertheless, across the benchmark, HyperQB$^{2.0}$ has a significantly reduced solving time compared to [17], demonstrating the efficiency of our solver-based design.

Recall that the benchmarks in Sect. 4.1 are all loop-free. Reasoning about infinite semantics in BMC, however, has long been a major challenge, leaving a significant gap in prior approaches. HyperQB$^{2.0}$ closes this gap by implementing the loop conditions identified in [18] and it can seamlessly and efficiently verify global properties in the presence of loops.

Table 2. Summary of results for A-HLTL benchmarks from [17], where $\mathbb{Q}$ denotes the form of quantifiers in the given A-HLTL formula, where $\{\mathsf{A}, \mathsf{E}\}$ are trajectory quantifiers from path and $\{\forall, \exists\}$ are path quantifiers. k and M are unrolling and trajectory bounds, respectively, and **Enc.** is the time to construct the BMC encoding.

					HQ2.0$_{\text{SMT}}$				**HQ2.0$_{\text{QBF}}$**			
Benchmark	$\mathbb{Q}$	|S|	k	M	**Enc.**	**Solve**	**Total**	[17]	**Enc.**	**Solve**	**Total**	
ACDB	∀∃E	109	11	22	0.04	0.08	**0.13**	3.35	0.01	1.44	1.46	✗
ACDB$_{nd}$	∀∃E	696	8	16	0.02	0.05	**0.08**	14.01	0.01	0.53	0.53	✗
ConcLeak	∀∃E	597	11	22	0.03	0.10	**0.13**	30.24	0.01	1.73	1.76	✗
ConcLeak$_{nd}$	∀∃E	2988	18	36	0.08	1.07	**1.17**	911.72	0.01	MO	MO	✗
SpecExcu$_{V1}$	∀∃E	132 / 340	6	12	0.03	0.19	**0.24**	12.24	0.01	0.86	0.88	✗
SpecExcu$_{V2}$	∀∃E	144 / 168	6	12	0.03	0.12	**0.15**	9.33	0.01	0.93	0.96	✓
SpecExcu$_{V3}$	∀∃E	87 / 340	6	12	0.03	0.23	**0.26**	11.95	0.01	0.87	0.89	✗
SpecExcu$_{V4}$	∀∃E	93 / 340	6	12	0.03	0.23	**0.26**	13.58	0.01	0.87	0.89	✗
SpecExcu$_{V5}$	∀∃E	132 / 168	6	12	0.03	0.13	**0.16**	10.94	0.01	0.90	0.93	✓
SpecExcu$_{V6}$	∀∃E	132 / 340	6	12	0.03	0.20	**0.24**	12.55	0.01	0.86	0.88	✗
SpecExcu$_{V7}$	∀∃E	144 / 168	6	12	0.03	0.12	**0.15**	9.69	0.01	0.90	0.93	✓
DBE	∀∀E	8 / 6	4	8	0.02	0.01	0.02	0.98	0.00	0.02	**0.02**	✓
DBE$_{ndet}$	∀∀E	82 / 72	13	26	0.02	0.23	**0.26**	11.77	0.00	1.21	1.23	✓
DBE$^{bugs}_{ndet}$	∀∀E	82 / 72	13	26	0.03	0.39	**0.42**	3.90	0.00	1.33	1.35	✗
LP	∀∀E	80 / 76	22	44	0.06	1024.87	1024.93	3.90	0.01	1.95	**1.98**	✓
LP$_{ndet}$	∀∀E	558 / 811	17	34	0.04	TO	TO	59.38	0.01	3.85	**3.90**	✓
LP$^{loops}_{ndet}$	∀∀E	757 / 1591	35	70	0.17	TO*	TO*	**4231.05**	0.01	MO	MO	✓
LP$^{bugs}_{ndet}$	∀∀E	558 / 661	17	34	0.04	1343.25	1343.28	30.86	0.01	3.64	**3.68**	✗
EFLP	∀∀E	80 / 248	32	64	0.19	44.47	44.72	**22.58**	0.01	MO	MO	✓
EFLP$_{ndet}$	∀∀E	582 / 1729	22	44	0.07	TO	TO	**160.30**	0.01	MO	MO	✓
CacheTA	∀∀AE	48	13	26	0.06	TO	TO	2.40	0.01	0.56	**0.58**	✗

TO = 1800 seconds TO* = 5000 seconds MO = Out of Memory

Table 3. Results on loop cases.

Type	Cases	Enc.	Solving	HyperQB$^{2.0}$	[18]
SIM$_{\forall\exists}$	ABP	0.11	0.003	**0.11**	9.37
	ABP$_{bug}$	0.09	0.002	**0.10**	9.46
	MM	0.19	0.006	**0.20**	67.74
	MM$_{bug}$	0.18	0.003	**0.19**	66.85
	CBF	0.08	0.002	**0.08**	3.49
	CBF$_{bug}$	0.07	0.002	**0.08**	3.51
SIM$_{\exists\forall}$	RP	0.11	0.12	**0.23**	1.09
	RP$_{no\ sol.}$	0.10	0.11	**0.21**	1.02
	GCW	0.06	0.11	**0.17**	3.36
	GCW$_{no\ sol.}$	0.06	0.11	**0.18**	2.27

Table 4. Results on Verilog benchmarks. Since state counts are not straightforward to derive from Verilog modules, we instead report the number of IR transitions.

Cases	Trans.	Encode	Solving	HyperQB$^{2.0}$
LED EA	44	0.34	0.23	0.57
LED AE	35	0.25	0.01	0.26
LED EE$_F$	9	0.26	0.09	0.35
LED EE$_T$	9	0.25	0.02	0.27
SPI	60	0.72	0.02	0.74
FPU	311	0.61	0.42	1.03

We construct the loop conditions encoding directly from the IR by using performance-tuned strategies. For the $\forall\exists$ case, we explicitly enumerate states and build a transition matrix. Since the $\forall\exists$ encoding of [18] relies on pairwise simulation, having concrete state values makes constraint checking substantially easier for the solver. By contrast, for the $\exists\forall$ case, we use an implicit-state formulation that lets the solver assign state values subject to the initial constraints and transition relation. This encoding searches for a lasso in the first model that simulates all paths of the second. Explicit-state encodings would require exhaustive path exploration and lead to heavy formulas, whereas implicit states allow the solver to construct the lasso on the fly. Table 3 shows that our new implementation in HyperQB$^{2.0}$ significantly outperforms [18] on all benchmarks.

4.4 Hardware Security Benchmarks in Verilog (Table 4)

A subset of our evaluation focuses on hardware-oriented designs written in Verilog. These case studies are drawn from the benchmarks used in [2,13]. These cases cover constant-time execution and observational determinism, as hardware-level implementations often expose subtle timing and information-flow vulnerabilities. Descriptions of these case studies can be found in [20].

5 Related Work

There has been a recent surge of model checking techniques for hyperproperties [8,10–12]. To our knowledge, there are only two existing model checkers for hyperproperties: MCHyper [8] and AutoHyper [3]. MCHyper computes the self-composition of models and reducing the problem to LTL model checking via ABC [5]. However, it does not provide a general push-button approach for bug finding under arbitrary quantifier alternation. Unlike HyperQB, MCHyper requires external intervention to eliminate trace quantifier alternations. AutoHyper [3], as an *explicit-state* tool, implements an automata-based verification approach based on language complementation and inclusion, and supports HyperLTL with arbitrary quantifier alternations, However, as shown in Sect. 4, HyperQB significantly outperforms AutoHyper, but the two tools are complementary: AutoHyper targets full verification, whereas HyperQB is more effective for rapid bug finding and uniquely supports A-HLTL specifications

Finally, bounded model checkers, such as EBMC [22], accept both Verilog and SystemVerilog inputs for the verification of LTL properties. Specialized tools exist to check for specific categories of information-flow properties such as IODINE [13] verify constant-time execution on Verilog designs. Similarly, SYLVIA [25], a symbolic execution engine, is used to identify security vulnerabilities, a subset of which includes observational determinism properties.

6 Conclusion and Future Work

We introduced HyperQB$^{2.0}$, a QBF/SMT-based bounded model checker for HLTL and A-HLTL that supports NuSMV and Verilog models. HyperQB implements bounded semantics to ensure soundness of verification, provides both CLI and GUI interfaces. Through a rich set of case studies, we demonstrated the effectiveness and efficiency of HyperQB in the verification of information-flow properties, linearizability in concurrent data structures, path planning in robotics, and fairness in non-repudiation protocols.

For future work, we are extending HyperQB to support C programs and developing an API to expose its core functionality to other developers. In addition, there remains significant room for optimization, particularly in improving QBF/SMT encodings and designing more scalable modeling strategies for NuSMV, Verilog, and future C support.

Acknowledgments. This project is partially sponsored by the United State NSF award CCF 2525050 and SaTC award 2245114. We thank César Sánchez for his contributions to the original research paper, the development of the initial version of HyperQB, and valuable discussions. We also thank Alisha Brenholt, Tess Murphy, and Lilly Yanke for contributing to the intermediate prototypes.

Data Availibility Statement. The data, benchmarks, source code, and experimental artifacts supporting the results presented in this paper are publicly available through our Zenodo archive: https://zenodo.org/records/20085800. The artifact includes the implementation of HyperQB$^{2.0}$, benchmark instances, scripts for reproducing the experimental results, and documentation for installation and usage. All experiments reported in the paper can be reproduced using the provided artifact under the documented software and hardware environment. The artifact may be updated in future releases to incorporate bug fixes and usability improvements while preserving reproducibility of the reported results. In addition, an interactive web interface and online playground for HyperQB$^{2.0}$ is publicly available at the following URL: https://hyperqb.github.io/index.html. We welcome the reader to visit the website and explore our tool.

Disclosure of Interests. The authors have no competing interests to declare that are relevant to the content of this article.

References

1. Baier, C., Katoen, J.P.: Principles of model checking. The MIT Press (2008). https://doi.org/10.1093/comjnl/bxp025
2. Baumeister, J., Coenen, N., Bonakdarpour, B., Finkbeiner, B., Sánchez, C.: A temporal logic for asynchronous hyperproperties. In: The 33rd International Conference on Computer Aided Verification (CAV), pp. 694–717 (2021). https://doi.org/10.1007/978-3-030-81685-8_33
3. Beutner, R., Finkbeiner, B.: AutoHyper: explicit-state model checking for HyperLTL. In: Proceedings of the 29th International Conference on Tools and Algorithms for the Construction and Analysis of Systems(TACAS), pp. 145–163 (2023). https://doi.org/10.1007/978-3-031-30823-9_8
4. Bonakdarpour, B., Sánchez, C., Schneider, G.: Monitoring hyperproperties by combining static analysis and runtime verification. In: Proceedings of the 8th Leveraging Applications of Formal Methods, Verification and Validation (ISoLA), pp. 8–27 (2018). https://doi.org/10.1007/978-3-030-03421-4_2

5. Brayton, R.K., Mishchenko, A.: ABC: an academic industrial-strength verification tool. In: Computer Aided Verification (CAV). LNCS, vol. 6174, pp. 24–40. Springer (2010). https://doi.org/10.1007/978-3-642-14295-6_5
6. Cimatti, A., Clarke, E., Giunchiglia, F., Roveri, M.: Nusmv: A new symbolic model verifier. In: International conference on computer aided verification, pp. 495–499. Springer (1999). https://doi.org/10.1007/3-540-48683-6_44
7. Clarke, E.M., Biere, A., Raimi, R., Zhu, Y.: Bounded model checking using satisfiability solving. Formal Methods Syst. Design **19**(1), 7–34 (2001). https://doi.org/10.1023/A:1011276507260
8. Clarkson, M.R., Finkbeiner, B., Koleini, M., Micinski, K.K., Rabe, M.N., Sánchez, C.: Temporal logics for hyperproperties. In: Proceedings of the 3rd Conference on Principles of Security and Trust POST, pp. 265–284 (2014). https://doi.org/10.1007/978-3-642-54792-8_15
9. Clarkson, M.R., Schneider, F.B.: Hyperproperties. J. Comput. Secur. **18**(6), 1157–1210 (2010). https://doi.org/10.3233/JCS-2009-0393
10. Coenen, N., Finkbeiner, B., Sánchez, C., Tentrup, L.: Verifying hyperliveness. In: Dillig, I., Tasiran, S. (eds.) CAV 2019. LNCS, vol. 11561, pp. 121–139. Springer, Cham (2019). https://doi.org/10.1007/978-3-030-25540-4_7
11. Finkbeiner, B., Hahn, C., Torfah, H.: Model checking quantitative hyperproperties. In: Proceedings of the 30th International Conference on Computer Aided Verification, pp. 144–163 (2018). https://doi.org/10.1007/978-3-319-96145-3_8
12. Finkbeiner, B., Rabe, M.N., Sánchez, C.: Algorithms for model checking HyperLTL and HyperCTL*. In: Proceedings of the 27th International Conference on Computer Aided Verification (CAV), pp. 30–48 (2015). https://doi.org/10.1007/978-3-319-21690-4_3
13. Gleissenthall, K.V., Kici, R.G., Stefan, D., Jhala, R.: Iodine: verifying constant-time execution of hardware. In: Proceedings of the 28th USENIX Conference on Security Symposium, pp. 1411–1428. SEC'2019, USENIX Association (2019)
14. GmbH, Y.: Yosys open synthesis suite. https://yosyshq.net/yosys/
15. Goguen, J.A., Meseguer, J.: Security policies and security models. In: IEEE Symp. on Security and Privacy, pp. 11–20 (1982). https://doi.org/10.1109/SP.1982.10014
16. Herlihy, M., Wing, J.M.: Linearizability: a correctness condition for concurrent objects. ACM Trans. Program. Lang. Syst. **12**(3), 463–492 (1990). https://doi.org/10.1145/78969.78972
17. Hsu, T.H., Bonakdarpour, B., Finkbeiner, B., Sánchez, C.: Bounded model checking for asynchronous hyperproperties. In: Proceedings of the 29th International Conference on Tools and Algorithms for Construction and Analysis of Systems (TACAS), pp. 29–46 (2023). https://doi.org/10.1007/978-3-031-30823-9_2
18. Hsu, T.H., Sánchez, C., , Sheinvald, S., Bonakdarpour, B.: Efficient loop conditions for bounded model checking hyperproperties. In: Proceedings of the 29th International Conference on Tools and Algorithms for Construction and Analysis of Systems (TACAS), pp. 66 – 84 (2023). https://doi.org/10.1007/978-3-031-30823-9_4
19. Hsu, T.H., Sánchez, C., Bonakdarpour, B.: Bounded model checking for hyperproperties. In: Proceedings of the 27th International Conference on Tools and Algorithms for the Construction and Analysis of Systems (TACAS), pp. 94–112 (2021). https://doi.org/10.1007/978-3-030-72016-2_6
20. Hsu, T.H., Rabizadeh, M., Rogale, K., Filippov, F., Batista, M.A., Bonakdarpour, B.: Hyperqb: A bounded model checker for hyperproperties. arXiv preprint arXiv:2109.12989 (2021). https://doi.org/10.48550/arXiv.2109.12989

21. IEEE: IEEE Standard for Verilog Hardware Description Language (2005). IEEE Std 1364-2005
22. Kroening, D.: Ebmc. https://www.cprover.org/ebmc/
23. Mermaid Contributors: Mermaid (2025). https://mermaid.js.org
24. de Moura, L.M., Bjørner, N.: Z3: An efficient SMT solver. In: Tools and Algorithms for the Construction and Analysis of Systems (TACAS), pp. 337–340 (2008). https://doi.org/10.1007/978-3-540-78800-3_24
25. Ryan, K., Sturton, C.: Sylvia: Countering the path explosion problem in the symbolic execution of hardware designs. In: Proceedings of the 23rd Conference on Formal Methods in Computer-Aided Design (FMCAD), pp. 110–121. FMCAD (2023). https://doi.org/10.34727/2023/isbn.978-3-85448-060-0_19
26. Tentrup, L.: CAQE and quabs: Abstraction based QBF solvers. J. Satisfiability Boolean Model. Comput. **11**(1), 155–210 (2019). https://doi.org/10.3233/SAT190121
27. Wang, Y., Zarei, M., Bonakdarpour, B., Pajic, M.: Statistical verification of hyperproperties for cyber-physical systems. ACM Trans. Embedded Comput. Syst. **18**(5s), 92:1–92:23 (2019). https://doi.org/10.1145/3358232

Author Index

E. Darulova et al. (Eds.): CAV 2026, LNCS 16682, pp. 527–528, 2026.
https://doi.org/10.1007/978-3-032-32519-8

MIX
Papier aus verantwortungsvollen Quellen
Paper from responsible sources
FSC® C105338
FSC
www.fsc.org

If you have any concerns about our products,
you can contact us on
ProductSafety@springernature.com

In case Publisher is established outside the EU,
the EU authorized representative is:
Springer Nature Customer Service Center GmbH
Europaplatz 3, 69115 Heidelberg, Germany

Printed by Libri Plureos GmbH
in Hamburg, Germany